Embedded Systems Design and Applications with the 68HC12 and HCS12

Embedded Systems Design and Applications with the 68HC12 and HCS12

Steven F. Barrett
University of Wyoming

Daniel J. Pack
United States Air Force Academy

PEARSON
Prentice
Hall

Upper Saddle River, New Jersey 07458

Library of Congress Cataloging-in-Publication Data

Barrett, Steven F. (Steven Frank), 1957-
   Embedded systems design and applications with the 68HC12 and HCS12 / Steven F. Barrett, Daniel J. Pack.
      p. cm.
   Includes bibliographical references and index.
   ISBN 0-13-140141-6
      1. Embedded computer systems. 2. Motorola 68HC11 (Microprocessor) I. Pack, Daniel J. II. Title.

TK7895.E42B376 2004
004.2′56–dc22

2004054924

Vice President and Editorial Director, ECS: *Marcia J. Horton*
Vice President and Director of Production and Manufacturing, ESM: *David W. Riccardi*
Executive Managing Editor: *Vince O'Brien*
Managing Editor: *David A. George*
Production Editor: *Kevin Bradley*
Director of Creative Services: *Paul Belfanti*
Art Director: *Jayne Conte*
Cover Designer: *Bruce Kenselaar*
Art Editor: *Greg Dulles*
Manufacturing Manager: *Trudy Pisciotti*
Manufacturing Buyer: *Lynda Castillo*
Senior Marketing Manager: *Holly Stark*

© 2005 by Pearson Education, Inc.
Pearson Prentice Hall
Pearson Education, Inc.
Upper Saddle River, NJ 07458

Pearson Prentice Hall® is a trademark of Pearson Education, Inc.

Printed in the United States of America

10 9 8 7 6 5 4 3 2

ISBN 0-13-140141-6

Pearson Education Ltd., *London*
Pearson Education Australia Pty. Ltd., *Sydney*
Pearson Education Singapore, Pte. Ltd.
Pearson Education North Asia Ltd., *Hong Kong*
Pearson Education Canada, Inc., *Toronto*
Pearson Educación de Mexico, S.A. de C.V.
Pearson Education–Japan, *Tokyo*
Pearson Education Malaysia, Pte. Ltd.
Pearson Education, *Upper Saddle River, New Jersey*

Contents

Preface

Early in 2002 our first book *The 68HC12 Microcontroller: Theory and Application* was published by Prentice Hall. Our objectives for this text were threefold: (1) to present fundamental assembly-language programming skills, (2) to illustrate the functional hardware components of a microcontroller, and (3) to present the skills needed to interface a variety of external devices with microcontrollers. We used an autonomous mobile robot as the target system to illustrate how the subsystems of an embedded controller work together to perform a variety of tasks and meet system requirements.

Our second book on embedded controller systems, *Embedded Systems Design and Applications with the 68HC12 and the HCS12*, picks up where the first left off. Our overall approach on this project has been to develop a tutorial, stand-alone text on embedded system design. We guide the reader from the basics of system-level programming through the advanced topics of real-time operating systems to distributed processing. Rather than jump into the "deep end of the pool," we begin with a tutorial on systems design concepts and programming in C. We then move on to specific discussions on the hardware subsystems aboard the 68HC12/HCS12 microcontroller. In these early chapters we are providing a walk-before-run philosophy. We have assumed that the reader has a fundamental but basic background in microprocessor hardware and software concepts. We feel this is an appropriate assumption since the target audience of the book is a college student enrolled in a second course on embedded system design. The tutorial topics in the beginning chapters can be skipped by practicing engineers; however, we have met many engineers who insist on having books that contain such tutorial topics.

With this stage complete, we then transition into multiple examples of embedded controller systems. The examples have been chosen to expose the reader to a wide variety of input and output devices in a system setting. The last portion of the book deals with the advanced concepts of embedded systems programming—real-time operating systems (RTOS) and multiple processors. We tackle these more difficult concepts only after we have developed a sound background in systems design and microprocessor systems.

We have several objectives for writing this book. We want the reader to learn (1) fundamental programming skills using both the C programming language and assembly language for microcontroller-based embedded systems, (2) methodical procedures for designing embedded controller based systems, (3) functional hardware components of a microcontroller, (4) skills to interface a variety of external devices with microcontrollers to construct embedded systems, and (5) skills and procedures to tackle the toughest embedded controller system issues—real-time operating systems and multiprocessor systems. The entire book is designed with these objectives in mind. Our motivation to write this book stems from the reality that there is no comprehensive 68HC12/HCS12 microcontroller textbook that teaches students how to design and program the embedded systems using microcontrollers.

We take a very hands-on approach with extensive tutorial information and numerous examples. Based on real-world applications, these examples address concerns such as microcontroller top-down/bottom-up implementation system design skills, noise and timing considerations, and troubleshooting techniques. The book provides a thorough review of C, structured programming techniques, the 68HC12/HCS12 microprocessor, detailed discussions of RTOS issues, multiprocessor systems, and many cases that illustrate embedded system design concepts.

Early in the book we introduce the reader to structured systems design concepts. Using this top-down, functional decomposition design approach, the students should be able to tackle any design problems associated with complex embedded controller systems. We review some of the basic tenets of this systematic design approach described by Meilir Page-Jones in his classic book *The Practical Guide to Structured Systems Design*. These techniques work equally well for software, hardware, or software/hardware designs often encountered in embedded systems. Once these concepts are presented, we use them extensively throughout the remainder of the book.

FLOW OF THE BOOK

In organizing each chapter, we gave a great deal of consideration to the order and the means of subject presentations. Each chapter starts with a list of chapter objectives to give the reader a clear purpose for reading the entire chapter. A brief introduction follows, which describes the contents of the chapter. After the main concepts of a chapter are presented, a particular application will be chosen to illustrate the key points in the chapter.

In Chapter 1 we introduce the concept of an embedded system and the special challenges involved in designing and implementing embedded controller-based systems. Chapter 2 introduces the advantages of programming in a high-level language (HLL). We provide a balanced trade-off discussion of programming with an HLL versus an assembly language. We then demonstrate that embedded system programs may contain a mixture of both. We discuss the key concepts of structured programming that allow large projects to be subdivided into more manageable "bite-size" pieces. We then apply these concepts to system design, implementation, and testing. We get comfortable with these concepts and practices on simple systems before applying them to more complex ones.

In Chapter 3 we discuss the software compilation/assembly process accompanied by a thorough review of C programming concepts. We finish the chapter with a review of programming and debugging tools. In our software discussions we purposely steer clear of any compiler specific details. There are many good compilers available for the 68HC12/HCS12. In Chapter 4 we review the hardware for the 68HC12/HCS12 microcontroller and its associated subsystems. We then apply these subsystem descriptions to real-world applications.

In Chapter 5 we explore the fundamentals of interfacing different hardware components to the controller. We begin with fundamental interfaces to switches and indicators and finish the chapter with some advanced applications involving liquid crystal displays (LCDs). Chapter 6 extends these interface concepts to real-world implementation issues. This chapter contains topics that separate a theoretical embedded controller design from one that works in the real world. Each topic is first defined and then followed by methods to alleviate corresponding problems, in a practical design.

In Chapter 7 we tie the 68HC12/HCS12 systems together to create real-world systems. In each detailed example, we provide a thorough project description, a project structure chart, and the code required to implement the system. We have carefully chosen the applications to exercise all systems aboard the 68HC12/HCS12 processor. In Chapter 8 we investigate the advanced concept of real-time operating systems. We begin with the basic definitions associated with an RTOS and then proceed to discuss how to design such a system. We then review issues associated with implementing an RTOS. We assume the reader has no experience or background with these potentially complex systems.

Chapter 9 investigates distributed processing systems. These include systems containing more than one microprocessor. We investigate techniques and methods to link processors into a cohesive system using the built-in CAN controller of the 68HC12/HCS12 microprocessor.

In addition to the contents of the book, we have prepared and maintain an accompanying textbook Web site at www.prenhall.com/pack. This Web site contains the current errata sheet and appendices for the book covering 68HC12/HCS12 instruction sets, 68HC12/HCS12 register sets, header files for example C programs, information on a variety of variants of the 68HC12 and the HCS12 microcontrollers, and 68HC12/HCS12 hardware and software support resources. For instructors, the Web site also contains additional instructional materials including sample syllabi, PowerPoint© lecture slides, and directions on how to order the solutions manual that provides detailed solutions to all chapter homework problems.

THE TARGET SYSTEMS: THE M68EVB912B32 EVB AND THE MC9S12DP256B PROCESSOR-BASED EVB

To illuminate system concepts discussed in Chapters 1–9 we have provided multiple examples. The examples have been written for two sample systems, or targets: the M68EVB912B32 Evaluation Board (B32 EVB) and the MC9S12DP256 or DP256. We have chosen to use the B32 EVB for its widespread availability, moderate price, and—most importantly—its many useful features. The EVB is equipped with an RS-232C interface, single power supply operation, easy access to controller pins via four header pin groups, and a prototype area for application-specific hardware. The EVB is also equipped with extensive memory features, including a 32 Kbyte flash electrically erasable programmable read-only memory (EEPROM) for program memory, 1 Kbyte of static random access memory (RAM), and 768 bytes of byte-erasable EEPROM for storing system data. Resident within flash memory is the D-Bug12 monitor/debugger program. We discuss these features in great detail in Chapter 4. The B32 is an excellent teaching tool but it can also be used to rapidly prototype an embedded controller system product.

Readers who choose *not* to use the B32 EVB, should realize that most of the concepts presented throughout the book also apply to other variants of the 68HC12 and the HCS12. Since the underlying concepts and functional components of different types of microcontrollers are very similar to each other, the acquired knowledge of the 68HC12/HCS12 can naturally be applied to other microprocessors and microcontrollers. In Chapters 7 and 9 we use the

MC9S12DP256 processor. This HCS12 configuration has a 256 Kbyte flash memory and several msCAN controller area network channels. It is also equipped with a large RAM complement. There are several evaluation boards based on the DP256 processor.

INTENDED AUDIENCE

The main audience of this book is university students enrolled in electrical/computer engineering microcontroller courses. Since all ABET (Accreditation Board for Engineering and Technology, Inc.) accredited electrical/computer engineering programs require such courses, we expect this book will be received enthusiastically by instructors who teach such courses. We expect students to have taken an introductory logic course and a first-year programming language course. Having taken a computer language course will help students to understand program examples. We expect students with a minimal exposure to computer programming will follow the text subjects without too much trouble. Ideally, students will have completed an introductory microprocessor course. However, due to the tutorial nature of the text, students should be able to fill in knowledge gaps where necessary.

Specifically, this book is targeted for a second semester microprocessor/ microcontroller course in an electrical and computer engineering curriculum. Different schools offer their microprocessor course in different stages of student development. Our students take a basic digital-design course during their sophomore year. They then take the first microprocessor course as a junior or senior. The second microprocessor course would then be taken during the senior year or as a graduate student. We believe that the book will continue where a typical first microprocessor course would leave off.

We wrote this book for use as the textbook for college microprocessor courses. However, we believe the tutorial nature of our presentation will allow practicing engineers to learn the subject on their own. We believe that knowledge of embedded systems should be required for all electrical and computer engineering students as we live in a society where more and more engineering problems are solved by embedded systems. We foresee the scope of applications for embedded systems expanding as products require increasingly sophisticated local intelligence.

ACKNOWLEDGMENTS

This book is the culmination of the efforts of many individuals. Of course, no good book can appear without a great publisher and their people. We are grateful to Tom Robbins and Alice Dworkin at Prentice Hall for their faith in this project. It was a pleasure to work with Kevin Bradley and his staff at Sunflower Publishing Services. We thank them for their excellent editorial support. We benefited greatly by the initial, detailed feedback provided by Barry Mullins of the Air Force Institute of Technology. As a result, the quality of this book improved significantly. We also appreciate the detailed comments and feedback we received on the final draft from Jerry Hamann of the University of Wyoming; John Reece of Mercer College in Macon, Georgia; and William Stapleton of the University of Alabama. We would also like to thank Karen Bosco of Motorola for her assistance in obtaining Motorola's gracious permission to use their figures throughout this book.

We would also like to acknowledge our department heads for their support. Colonel Alan Klayton (USAF Academy) strongly supported our work and enthusiastically embraced the project. John Steadman (formerly with the University of Wyoming, now Dean of Engineering at the University of Southern Alabama) displayed tremendous encouragement for pursuing this project. We would also like to thank numerous students who were enrolled in microcontroller courses at both institutions and provided us with useful feedback and comments. Abbie Wells, Scott Lewis, Joel Perlin, Carrie Hernandez, Ted Dibble, Tom Schei, Charles Straley, Pamela Beavis, and Austin Griffith wrote some of the software examples in this book and helped immeasurably to transition from the 68HC11 to the 68HC12 at the University of Wyoming. In addition, we wish to acknowledge many colleagues at both the Air Force Academy and the University of Wyoming.

Some of the examples we have presented in this book were based on problems developed by the past and present instructors in the Department of Electrical Engineering at our two universities. Although we have made every effort to avoid errors in this book, some may still be found and we cannot assume any liability for damage they may cause.

I (sb) would first like to acknowledge Clarence Zarn, a very dear family friend who is the reason I became an engineer. When I was a child, my family spent many holidays with the Zarns. I would hang out in Clarence's office, which was filled with the books, manuals, construction plans, and slide rules that introduced me to the fascinating world of engineering. Clarence served as an engineer and vice president for the Pentzien Corporation in Omaha, Nebraska, for many decades. He recently gave me his slide rule (circa 1940) that he used daily on the job. I will treasure it always. The field of engineering is everything he said and everything I hoped it would be. We acknowledge our parents. Thank you moms, Eleanore and Jackie, and thank you dad, Frank, for always believing in me (sb). Thank you moms, Young Shin and Rana, and thank you dads, Sung Bock and Chong Kon, for your encouragement and unfailing support (dp). I (dp) want to especially acknowledge my father's inspirational display of courage as he bouts with cancer during my writing of this book. Finally, our work could not have been possible without the sacrifices of our family members: Cindy, Heidi, Heather, Jon R., Christine, Jon B., Andrew, and Graham. We thank you!

STEVEN F. BARRETT
DANIEL J. PACK

1

Introduction to Embedded Systems

Objectives: After reading this chapter, you should be able to

- Define embedded systems, microcontrollers, and general purpose computers.
- List unique challenges involved in designing embedded systems.
- Illustrate the use of embedded systems.
- Describe the key functional units of the 68HC12 and the HCS12 microcontrollers.

In this chapter, we introduce critical issues to consider when designing, implementing, and testing embedded systems. We begin our discussion in a general manner, but starting with Section 1.3 we present embedded system issues using the 68HC12 and HCS12 microcontrollers.

1.1 WHAT IS AN EMBEDDED SYSTEM?

Any mechanical or electrical system that is controlled by a computer working as part of an overall system is called an *embedded system*. Before continuing, we must first define the term *computer*. All computers must have the following four

1

subparts: (1) a central processing unit (CPU), (2) a memory unit, (3) input/output (I/O) devices, and (4) a bus system. The CPU contains an arithmetic and logic unit (ALU) and a control unit. The ALU is responsible for performing arithmetic operations such as addition, subtraction, multiplication, and division. It also performs logic operations such as logical AND, OR, XOR, and NOT.

A computer that uses the microprocessor as its CPU is called a *microcomputer*. A personal computer is a good example of a microcomputer. In contrast, microcontrollers are created by packaging all computer components, the CPU, the memory, the I/O parts, and buses in a single very large scale integrated (VLSI) chip.

The memory unit holds both the instructions and the data necessary for a computer to execute instructions. A memory system is typically based on either a von Neumann architecture or a Harvard architecture (although there are many hybrids of these). In the von Neumann system, each memory location can store either data or an instruction. In the Harvard system, there are separate locations for data and instructions. The Harvard architecture is often found in the design of cache (pronounced same as "cash"), a memory unit used by a CPU for fast memory access. In general, we encounter combinations of the two memory architectures in most computers today.

I/O devices provide a computer with the means to interact with the external world. Typically, input devices retrieve desired data or sensor values from outside the computer, while output devices generate and display results of an operation, the state of some computation, the status of the CPU, or signals to control external devices. The fourth component of a computer, a bus system, consists of sophisticated connections between the CPU, the memory, and the I/O devices, providing pathways to carry data, instructions, and control signals. The bus system is subdivided into three categories: (1) the data bus, (2) the address bus, and (3) the control bus. As the names indicate, these buses carry data, addresses of memory or I/O devices, and control signals.

An embedded system thus simply refers to a system that is controlled by a computer that resides within the system. We need to stop here and make a clear distinction between general purpose computers and embedded computers. A general purpose computer is made to perform a variety of functions. A good example of a general purpose computer is a desktop or laptop computer: it must run programs ranging from a simple word processor/editor to complex scientific programs. An embedded computer, which may contain a high performance CPU as in general purpose computers, has a set of specific tasks for which the system is made. Therefore, an embedded computer must meet system specific constraints that are different from general purpose computers.

You may be surprised to know that far more computers made for embedded systems are sold each year than general purpose computers. For example, in

2000, some 150 million general purpose computers were sold, while more than 8 billion embedded computers were purchased during the same year.[1] Embedded systems typically use a type of computer called a *microcontroller*—a computer whose functional modules are contained within a single integrated circuit (IC) chip. Two prominent examples of these microcontrollers are the subject of this book: the Motorola 68HC12 and HCS12 microcontrollers. Major companies such as Intel, Microchip Hitachi, NEC, Hewlett-Packard, and Atmel produce microcontrollers. For complex embedded systems, such as an on-board airplane control system and military and communication systems, sophisticated microcontrollers and processors are employed.

Embedded systems with microcontrollers can easily be found around you. In fact, you would have a hard time living without embedded systems. For example, your digital alarm clock, cellular phone, and palm computer are embedded systems with built-in microcontrollers. Your home has a wide array of embedded systems: your coffeemaker, remote control, oven, range, dishwasher, clothes washer, dryer, stereo, heating/cooling system, home security system, automatic sprinkler system, automatic garage door opener, VCR, DVD player, CD player, and even the subsystems in your general purpose home computer. Your car is an embedded system with 10 to 50 microcontrollers. These controllers work in concert to make your car fuel efficient and give you a comfortable ride. Embedded controllers are responsible for controlling the antilock brake system, the antiskid control system, the fuel-injection system, the suspension control, and the front panel display. They are also responsible for communicating with satellites using a global positioning system (GPS) to update directional maps, controlling the inside temperature of your vehicle, and operating a multimedia system. These controllers warm (or cool) your seats and control power windows, mirrors, and doors. In some cars, these controllers are even used to sense tire pressure, record the mileage from the last car service, and measure various fluid levels. Surely, your life would not be the same without these embedded systems.

Let's consider some areas of industry where these embedded systems play critical roles, as shown in Figure 1.1. Today's consumer electronics and multimedia industry cannot exist without embedded controllers. Our military and government rely heavily on the use of embedded systems to accomplish their missions. The computer industry constantly develops and creates microcontrollers/microprocessors for embedded systems. The automotive and transportation industries make improvements with the help of embedded systems design technologies. Aerospace and space electronics count on embedded systems. Embedded systems are the business of the electronic instruments and test equipment industry. And finally, most electronic medical devices contain embedded systems.

---

[1] "Proactive Computing," David Tennenhouse, *Communications of the ACM*, Vol. 43, No. 5, May 2000.

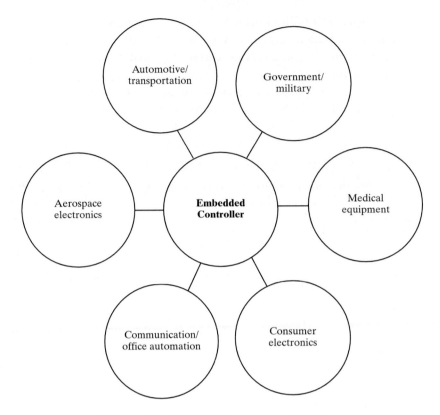

Figure 1.1   Embedded systems applications.

1.2 SPECIAL CHALLENGES WITH EMBEDDED SYSTEMS

Because of the varied applications of embedded systems, a separate set of issues that typically do not exist for general purpose computers must be considered. These issues include real-time execution, physical size, development environment, testing performance, power consumption, user interface, multirate operation, and memory usage.

1.2.1 Real-Time Execution

When we say that a system must perform a task in real time, we mean that the results of the task must be available for use at the end of a designated time interval. In general, we use terms such as *real-time computation* and *real-time execution* when the designated time interval is relatively short. For example, an automatic antilock brake system must sense the positions of all four wheels (whether or not a wheel is slipping) and use the results to generate appropriate control signals within milliseconds. We say that the task must be performed in real time. For another example, consider a GPS-based map displaying system. The system must update its map on the order of seconds. We say that the display system performs successfully if it meets the deadline. We do not say, however, that computation of optimal filter coefficients, which might take three hours to compute, is an example of real-time execution.

Now that we understand the terms, we will consider how an embedded system must deal with the real-time execution issues. First, an embedded system must be designed to meet a time deadline, if possible. This means fast computational hardware, smart software design, and hardware design for minimum latency techniques must be employed. Second, the embedded system must have a mechanism to deal with external data. Suppose that the system depends on some external data to generate a desired result at the end of a deadline. In a wireless Internet device, the system will not produce the desired result if the communication system cannot provide necessary information in time. In such cases, the embedded system must still perform the task in real time at a degraded level, providing users with some useful information versus no information.

In contrast, general purpose computers do not have deadlines to complete a task even if this may frustrate users during the time it takes to generate results. If real-time tasks are not completed by the end of a designated deadline, it can be dangerous or fatal to users, as in the case of embedded systems employed in medical devices. This makes the design of real-time embedded systems particularly challenging.

1.2.2 Physical Size, Development Environment, Testing Performance

The design of an embedded system is often dictated by the design of the product in which the embedded system will reside. The designer of an embedded system must thus meet the physical product requirements by carefully selecting and designing each component. The development environment can also be challenging since most embedded systems are designed by a small group of people. This limits the exchange of creative ideas that would typically occur in a larger group. Any testing of the system should therefore be done by a team of people who were not involved in the development of the system. System testing is further complicated when all of the subcomponents must be assembled together before the entire product can be tested.

1.2.3 Power Consumption

Unlike general purpose computers, embedded systems must run on a limited amount of power. We typically find an embedded system running on a battery—as is the case with a cellular phone, palm personal organizer, or portable CD player, to name a few. In the past, the designers of general purpose computers typically did not pay much attention to the amount of power the system used. Today, embedded system designers must consider these issues to make the system perform satisfactorily while conserving the limited amount of available power.

In general, to maximize the use of limited, available energy, designers attempt to run a system on the slowest clock speed allowed by the specific application. But running a system on a slower clock can have adverse effects (e.g., real-time execution) on system performance. The alternative, used in industry, is to design a system in which submodules that are not active can be turned off (i.e., placed in a sleep mode). This forces the system designers to carefully engineer the systems so that they may be selectively powered down without affecting other systems (orthogonal systems).

1.2.4 User Interface: Interaction with Environment

Embedded systems must interact with users or the environment to function properly. For example, a navigational robot, such as the one shown in Figure 1.2, must interact with its environment via infrared sensors to avoid running into walls. A microwave oven must accept user inputs via push buttons on the front panel. A telephone answering machine must follow user commands, and a home security system must interact with sensors and user commands to function properly. The user interface then introduces a set of new issues that general purpose computers typically do not have. A designer must rigorously consider the interface specifications and list germane constraints and requirements in order to make the system successfully meet the objectives. We discuss how to do this in Chapter 2.

1.2.5 Multirate Operation

A multirate operation must carry out several different tasks at the same time, with certain tasks demanding notably different time scales for computation. We encounter such systems in products that must perform relatively complex tasks. Multirate systems are implemented by using multiple single-task microprocessors or by sharing the resources of a single, more powerful microprocessor. The responsibility of the system designer is to weigh the advantages and disadvantages of the two approaches and design the system to perform the multirate tasks.

1.2.6 Manufacturing Cost

For low-end, less-expensive embedded systems—from microwave ovens and cellular phones to palm organizers—it is critical to make the system as affordable as possible to attract a large number of consumers. This means that the system

Figure 1.2   A navigational robot.

designer must carefully consider, compare, and evaluate the hardware costs—using field-programmable gate arrays (FPGAs), logic gates, or a microcontroller-based system—and software development costs—using software code generation and tests. A successful designer must perform extensive analysis to determine the best strategy to implement required system features at the lowest possible cost.

1.2.7 Limited Memory

If you have been around the computer industry for any length of time, you know how inexpensive memory has become over the past two decades. In an embedded system, however, we are still governed by the limited space for memory, not necessarily the cost. Yes, we can make a cellular phone with gigabytes of memory, but the bulky phone will not appeal to many people. This means that memory utilization must be optimal: a succinct code that uses minimum memory space.

1.2.8 Hardware-Software Trade-offs

In many applications, designers have options to implement solutions in the form of hardware or software. For example, an embedded system that utilizes neural networks can be implemented on a VLSI chip or within a software program. The main concern is the cost and the speed of the resulting system. In general, the start-up costs for an embedded system that uses additional hardware are higher than the same system implemented using software. As for the speed, the system based on hardware tends to have superior performance.

1.3 INTRODUCTION TO THE 68HC12 AND HCS12 MICROCONTROLLERS

In the previous sections we have discussed issues related to embedded systems in general without a particular embedded computer in mind. Since this book is about embedded systems using the Motorola 68HC12/HCS12 microcontroller, we now shift gears and introduce this controller. Our discussion here will be brief, leaving details of the controller systems for the rest of the book.

The Motorola 68HC12/HCS12 microcontroller families are 16-bit CPU-based controllers whose predecessor is the 68HC11, the 8-bit microcontroller that was the workhorse of many embedded systems after the controller was introduced in the mid-1980s. In 1996, Motorola started the 68HC12 controller family featuring two different variants: the 68HC12A4 series and the 68HC912B32 series. Many other types of 68HC12 microcontrollers have been introduced since then. The 68HC12A4 series were made to run in an expanded mode (resources such as external memory to run the computer lie outside the controller chip), while the B32 series were intended to run in a single-chip mode. In 2002, Motorola introduced the HCS12 product line, a direct upgrade of the 68HC12 line of controllers. (The information provided in this book is applicable to this upgraded line of controllers; Section 1.4 fully discusses the variants of this product line.) We focus on the 68HC12B32 series of controllers—low-cost processors readily available to educators and practicing engineers alike. Most of the discussions presented in this book, however, also apply to other processors in the 68HC12 and HCS12 lines.

Motorola currently offers four 68HC12 B32 series controllers: (1) the MC68HC912B32, (2) the MC68HC12BE32, (3) the MC68HC912BC32, and (4) the MC68HC12BC32. The primary differences between these systems are related to the size of on-chip flash electrically erasable programmable read-only memory (EEPROM) and byte-erasable EEPROM, or the inclusion of a controller area network (CAN) module.

Figures 1.3 and 1.4 show the block diagram of the 68HC912B32/68HC12-BE32 controller and its pin configuration, respectively. Figures 1.5 and 1.6 show the block diagram and the pin configuration of the BC32 and the BE32, respectively. Figure 1.7 summarizes the differences between the four controllers.

The 68HC12 controller is a 16-bit controller, which means that the data bus is 16 bits wide. The controller is also equipped with a 16-bit address bus, which means there are 2^{16} addressable memory locations. It uses a queue-instruction

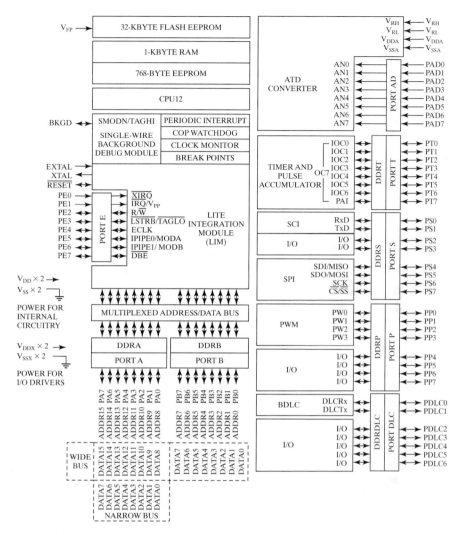

Figure 1.3   A block diagram of the MC68HC912B32 and MC68HC12BE32 controller and its pin configuration. (Copyright of Motorola, used by permission.)

mechanism, similar to pipeline hardware found in sophisticated microprocessors, to execute up to one instruction per clock cycle. The 68HC12 controller uses an 8 MHz clock that conducts program execution at a much faster speed than its predecessor, the 68HC11. The controller's instruction set is a superset of the one used for the 68HC11, making the software written for the older controller upward compatible. The controller uses a 20-bit arithmetic and logical unit (ALU), expanded mathematical functions, a fuzzy logic related instruction

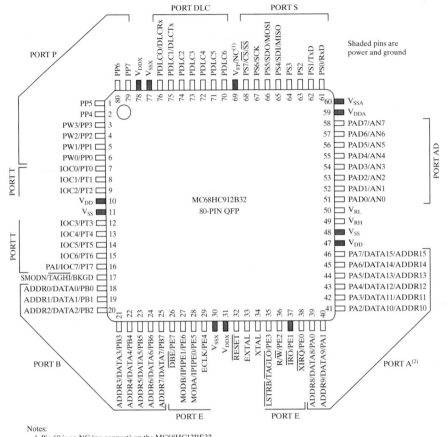

Figure 1.4 Pin assignments for the MC68HC912B32 and MC68HC12BE32. (Copyright of Motorola, used by permission.)

set, and a powerful set of indexed addressing modes.[2] The controller also provides users with an option to connect the controller to a 16-bit or an 8-bit based external system using either the 16-bit wide external data bus or the 8-bit narrow data bus.

The controller also has an on-chip analog-to-digital (ATD) converter, one 16-bit pulse accumulator to count external events or to measure gated events, 32 K-bytes of Flash EEPROM or ROM, 768 bytes of EEPROM, 1 K-byte RAM, and a single wire background debug mode, which allows a programmer to monitor and debug programs in real time without sacrificing any clock cycles. In addition, the controller has a sophisticated timer module that is used to capture the times of

---

[2]An addressing mode is a method used by an instruction to obtain necessary data for the instruction. The 68HC12 contains seven addressing modes.

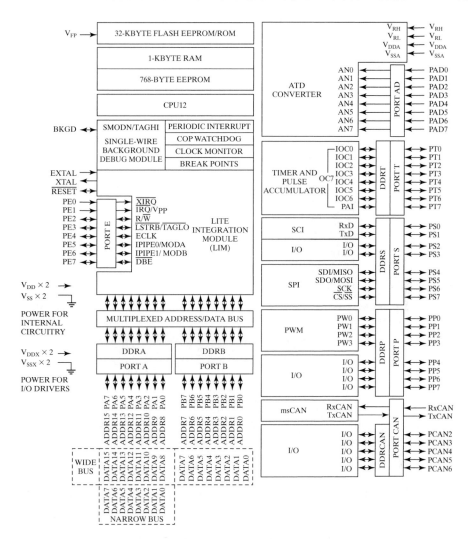

Figure 1.5 A block diagram of the MC68HC912BC32. (Copyright of Motorola, used by permission.)

external events (Input Capture), generate external events (Output Compare), and to help govern time-related internal tasks. The controller also has seven external ports that can be programmed as general input or output ports. For external device control, the controller contains a pulse width modulator (PWM) that can be easily programmed to produce a variety of pulses with varying duty cycles. For serial communications, the controller has both an asynchronous serial communication interface (SCI) and a synchronous peripheral interface (SPI) module. For a summary of the functional components of the controller, see again Figure 1.7.

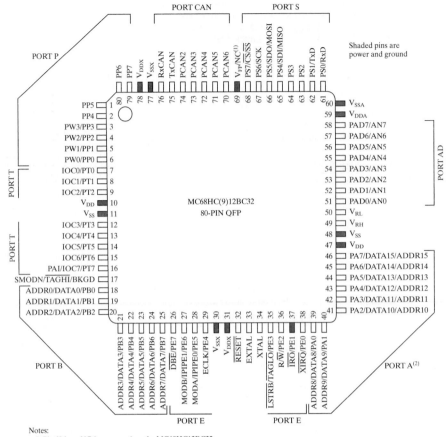

Figure 1.6 Pin assignments for the MC68HC912BC32. (Copyright of Motorola, used by permission.)

1.4 HCS12 MICROCONTROLLER

Like the 68HC12 family, the HCS12 family consists of a line of products with different features and systems, including a large memory complement (up to 12K RAM and 256K Flash) and a 5 VDC operating voltage. Operating with up to a 25 MHz clock speed, all variants in the HCS12 family are equipped with the following:

- Memory system consisting of ROM, RAM, EEPROM, and Flash components
- Timer system equipped with an 8 channel, 16 bit timer

Features	MC68HC912B32	MC68HC12BE32	MC68HC912BC32	MC68HC12BC32
CPU12	X	X	X	X
Multiplexed bus	X	X	X	X
32-Kbyte FLASH electrically erasable programmable read-only memory (EEPROM)	X		X	
32-Kbyte read-only memory (ROM)		X		X
768-byte EEPROM	X	X	X	X
1-Kbyte random access memory (RAM)	X	X	X	X
Analog-to-digital (ATD) converter	X	X	X	X
Standard timer module (TIM)	X		X	X
Enhanced capture timer (ECT)		X		
Pulse width modulator (PWM)	X	X	X	X
Asynchronous serial communications interface (SCII)	X	X	X	X
Synchronous serial peripheral interface (SPI)	X	X	X	X
J1850 byte data link communication (BDLC)	X	X		
Controller area network (CAN) module			X	X
Computer operating properly (COP) watchdog timer	X	X	X	X
Slow mode clock divider	X	X	X	X
80-pin quad flat pack (QFP)	X	X	X	X
Single-wire background debug mode (BDM)	X	X	X	X

Figure 1.7   A comparison of the features offered by controllers in the M68HC12B series. (Copyright of Motorola, used by permission.)

- Multiple digital input/output pins
- Serial communications capability
- Analog-to-digital (ATD) system
- Pulse width modulation system

A block diagram of the MC9S12DP256B processor is provided in Figure 1.8. Note that this HCS12 variant has systems similar to the 68HC12. As you can see in the diagram, this variant is equipped with two 8-channel analog-to-digital systems, five CAN channels, an enhanced capture timer (ECT) system, and a memory paging system that allows more than 64 Kbytes of memory to be addressed. The most noticeable feature of the DP256 is the 256 Kbytes of Flash

EEPROM. Additional information on the HCS12 series of microcontrollers is provided throughout this book.

1.4.1 HCS12 Family

The HCS12 family is available in a wide range of variants. We want to emphasize that the concepts covered throughout this text apply to both the 68HC12 and HCS12 families. We will begin by investigating the numbering system used by Motorola to describe these different variants. We will then briefly review the HCS12 family line of products.

1.4.2 Product Numbering System

The numbering system used by Motorola for both the 68HC12 and the HCS12 is actually a compact code providing insight into the features aboard the specific variant. The numbering system is illustrated in Figure 1.9. As you can see, each part of the product number describes different aspects of the product.

1.4.3 HCS12 Variants

The HCS12 is available in a wide range of variants. A summary of some of these variants is provided in Figure 1.10. We only provide features in the figure that are different for each variant.

1.5 SUMMARY

In this chapter we have defined and described embedded systems with examples we encounter daily. We have also presented unique issues facing embedded system designers who must deal with a new design paradigm. The challenges include real-time execution, physical size constraints, power usage, multirate operation, and user interface, to name a few. Finally, we have briefly introduced the 68HC12 microcontroller and the HCS12 microcontroller, the platforms we will use throughout this book.

1.6 PROBLEMS

Fundamental

1. List the four components of a computer.
2. What is the main function of the central processing unit of a computer?

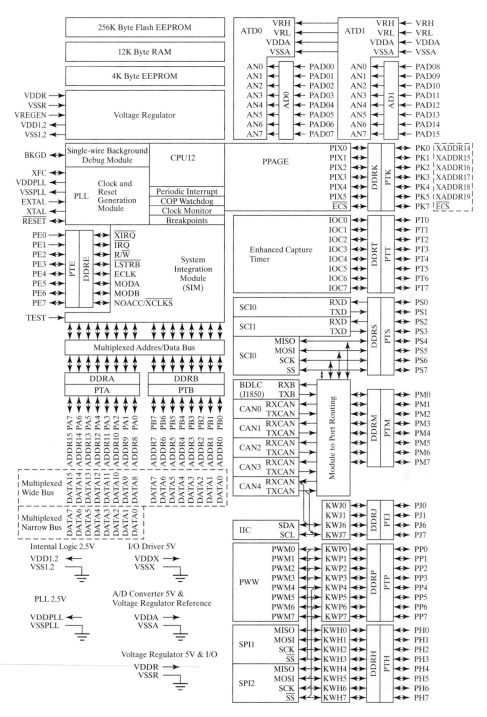

Figure 1.8 A block diagram of the MC9S12DP256B processor. (Copyright of Motorola, used by permission.)

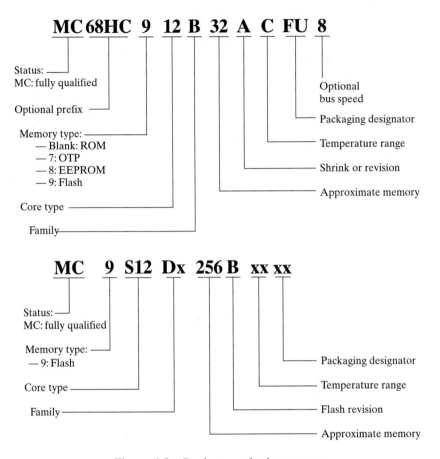

Figure 1.9 Product numbering system.

3. What is the name for the path used to send control signals between a CPU and memory?

4. What is a microcontroller?

5. What is a microprocessor?

6. What is a microcomputer?

7. List three embedded systems you can find around your home that were not mentioned in the chapter text.

8. What is the purpose of the PWM module in the 68HC12 microcontroller?

Advanced

1. Describe the difference between a microcontroller and a general purpose computer.

HCS12 Variants

	Memory Configuration (bytes)				Serial Comm	PWM
	ROM	RAM	EEPROM	Flash		
MC9S12D64	---	4K	1K	64K	SCI, SPI, CAN	8 ch 8 bit or 4 ch 16 bit
MC9S12DG128B	---	8K	2K	128K	SCI, SPI, CAN	8 ch 8 bit or 4 ch 16 bit
MC9S12DP256B	---	12K	4K	256K	SCI, SPI, CAN	8 ch 8 bit or 4 ch 16 bit
MC9S12DP512	---	14K	4K	512K	SCI, SPI, CAN	8 ch 8 bit or 4 ch 16 bit

Figure 1.10   HCS12 variants.

2. The text states that a general purpose computer designer does not need to pay too much attention to the power usage and the physical size of the memory for the computer. Why so? Is this issue changing?

3. List two examples of real-time operations.

4. Why would you want to run a microcontroller designed to run in a single-chip mode in an expanded mode?

5. The text states that testing an embedded system is a challenging task. Why?

Challenging

1. What are some factors that a designer must consider to implement a solution using software or hardware (software-hardware trade-offs)?

2. Today, embedded systems are ubiquitous. In fact, some researchers in the computer systems field predict that a large number of embedded systems will be connected together, similar to the Internet, to accomplish a variety of tasks in the near future. This means that users will not be in a tight loop with an individual embedded system. Rather, they will interact with the embedded system at a higher abstract level. What are some challenges to create such a network? What are the implications of such a network to our society?

2

Microcontroller Programming and Structured Design

Objectives: After reading this chapter, you should be able to

- Describe the trade-offs of using an assembly language versus a higher-level language, such as C, to program an embedded controller system.
- Summarize the origins of the C language.
- Define and apply the key tenets of the structured programming approach to an embedded system design.
- Value the importance of employing good documentation techniques.
- Describe in detail how to maintain a well-documented laboratory notebook.
- Apply the key concepts of the Unified Modeling Language (UML) to an embedded system design.

This may be the most important chapter in this book, providing you with the big picture of embedded system design. We will describe here why the C language has become the high-level language (HLL) of choice for programming embedded controller systems. There are inherent disadvantages and advantages to the target language chosen for a microcontroller application. On one hand, we have the hardware control features and compact code of assembly language. On the other hand, we have the readability, portability, and coding efficiency of C. We will explain here that the optimal answer is a combination of both—that is, a C program that has assembly language instructions within it. We will also investigate the importance of applying structured design techniques to embedded system design. We cover the basic tenets of this technique followed by modern modeling tools that help the system designer apply these techniques. The results are readable, reliable, and maintainable systems. We apply these techniques to several examples of progressive difficulty.

2.1 WHY PROGRAM IN A HIGH LEVEL LANGUAGE?

In this book we program primarily in C for our applications. We chose C as the target language for many reasons that should become readily apparent as we progress through the chapter. As we described in the preface, this book is intended for readers who have completed a first course in microprocessors. Therefore, we expect the reader to be thoroughly grounded in basic digital logic design techniques, the fundamentals of some microprocessor hardware architecture, and assembly language programming techniques.

If you find yourself lacking in these areas, do not be alarmed. We have intentionally written the text to be very tutorial in nature. For a review of digital logic fundamentals we recommend *Digital Design Principles and Practices* by John Wakerly. To review a microprocessor architecture and assembly language specifically for the 68HC12, we recommend our own book, *68HC12: Theory and Applications*.

To get started, in the next several sections we identify the advantages and disadvantages of using C versus assembly language. We also explain why C has become an industry standard in embedded controller design.

2.2 ADVANTAGES OF PROGRAMMING IN ASSEMBLY LANGUAGE

Many microcontroller system designers program only in assembly language. There are many good reasons for doing this. In general, well-written assembly language programs run faster and are more compact (require less memory for storage) than their high-level language counterparts. The additional memory requirement is due in part to an HLL program's requisite memory overhead. The features of faster, smaller programs in assembly language are extremely important in embedded systems where clock speeds are relatively slow and memory resources are precious.

In one of the undergraduate microprocessor courses we teach, we have students complete a laboratory exercise where they write the same program in both assembly language and C for an embedded controller. Specifically, they are required to write a program that searches a buffer (memory area) of 16-bit unsigned integers and count the numbers that exceed a given constant.

Since the C compiler converts the program first to assembly language and then to machine language, the students can compare their assembly language program with the one generated by the compiler. The students are amazed that their assembly language program is more compact and better written than that rendered by the compiler. Upon investigation, they realize the compiler does an overall good job in handling the conversion from C to assembly for many general cases; however, the students learn that they can do a much better job of programming a specific case using assembly language directly.

In addition to smaller, faster code, the assembly language programmer typically has absolute control over the embedded controller hardware. Some level of hardware control is also available in C but not at the same level as that for assembly language. These assembly language advantages come at a price. For programmers to become efficient in assembly language, they must thoroughly understand the intimate details of both the assembly language and also the target controller's hardware.

2.3 ADVANTAGES OF PROGRAMMING IN HLL

If you have programmed in assembly language, you can appreciate the learning curve involved in becoming proficient with the language. You must become thoroughly acquainted not only with the details of a specific processor but also with the specific details of its associated assembly language. Although different microprocessors may be similar in architecture, programs written in assembly language for one processor may not be easily used on another. That is, the code is not portable.

Recently, one of the authors worked on two projects where the customer requested the use of an Atmel microcontroller. He had not used the Atmel line of 8-bit reduced instruction set computing (RISC) microcontrollers before, but he was willing to learn. He purposely decided to program both projects in C. This allowed him to more quickly complete the project. Had he chosen to use assembly as the target language, he would have spent considerably more time learning not only the hardware details of the Atmel controller but also the details of the assembly language. (It should be mentioned that the hardware architecture and assembly language of the Atmel controller was significantly different from that of the Motorola processors although it possesses similar subsystems.) The project schedules simply did not provide time for learning these details. Furthermore, in both cases he was not concerned about program execution speed or insufficient memory resources. Therefore, an HLL was a natural choice for these projects.

In general, high-level languages are known for portability, programmer efficiency, code readability, complex math capability, and ease of application to structured design techniques. We discuss these concepts in turn in the next several paragraphs. A seasoned, experienced assembly language programmer may refute our general concepts; however, these concepts are based on the experience of a generic, average programmer.

Portability allows code written for a specific platform or embedded controller to be readily ported to another platform. This allows a program written on an American National Standards Institute (ANSI) compiler to be easily reused (to have reusability) for other applications on a different platform than that for which it was originally written. The overall idea is to spend time writing good reusable functions up front and then reusing the functions multiple times in many different programs. The first author's older son Jon, although not an embedded system designer, was a major proponent of this concept. His philosophy was "you pay for good tools only once." This is consistent with some of the basic tenets of structured design we discuss in this chapter.

Because an HLL program is written at a higher level of abstraction, programmer efficiency is generally higher. That is, average programmers can complete projects in less time than they would need to program in assembly language. Also, if the concept of code reusability is heavily employed, programmer efficiency is that much better.

HLLs also lend themselves to code readability. If a program is "well-written," someone not familiar with the code should be able to read over it and readily describe the overall structure of the code and have a general idea of how it executes. We purposely do not define what we mean by "well-written" code just yet. We defer this most important concept until Section 2.5, which discusses structured design.

An HLL typically handles higher level math functions better than assembly language. For example, floating point multiplication and division is very difficult to program in assembly language. There are libraries available, callable from assembly language, which provide these computations. However, multiple arithmetic steps are handled nicely by HLLs. For example, in Chapter 4 we introduce the following equation to calculate elapsed time using the standard timer module (TIM):

$$\text{Elapsed clock ticks} = (n \times 2^{16}) + (\text{Stop count} - \text{Start count}) \text{ [Clock ticks]}$$

This equation would be difficult to program in assembly language. However, in HLL programming the equation is quite straightforward. Realize that this ease of use comes at a price. We must include the math libraries as part of our overall program. This requires additional memory resources.

With this brief comparison of assembly language and higher-level language complete, we investigate available HLLs for embedded systems.

2.3.1 Choosing the Best HLL Available for Embedded Systems

A quick search on the Internet reveals many HLL compilers available for embedded controller programming. You will find compilers for Forth, C, C++, Java, Ada, and FORTRAN. Each HLL has its inherent advantages and disadvantages. Often, the choice of a compiler may be driven by the specifics of the project or the desires of the customer. Space does not permit a thorough treatment of the pros and cons of each HLL compiler.

We have chosen to use C as the target HLL for this book because of its wide use throughout industry and its inherent hardware-associated features. Most notably, C is known as an intermediate language. That is, it provides the convenience of an HLL while at the same time allowing close contact and control of the target hardware. Ritchie, one of the original developers of C, refers to it as a "portable assembly language [Ritchie 1993]."

Over the years, C has evolved from its origin in the late 1960s. However, it remains a simple and terse language. Originally designed as a tool to program the Unix operating system, it has retained its fundamental premise as "a tool to build larger tools." It covers the basic needs of programmers without bloating itself with seldom-used features. Furthermore, a programmer can learn how to generate code that comes close to being as fast and space efficient as assembly language. Finally, the fundamental constructs of C lend themselves to many of the basic tenets of structured design [Ritchie 1993].

2.3.2 A Brief History of C

A discussion of C would not be complete without a brief review of the origins of this powerful language. For a full treatment of this topic, the interested reader is referred to "The Development of the C Language" by Dennis Ritchie. The following paragraphs provide a brief summary of this paper.

Originating in the late 1960s, C was developed for the Unix operating system at Bell Laboratories. One of the early developers of the system, Ken Thompson, decided a system programming language was needed. He created such a language and called it B. During the development of the language, Thompson continually struggled with limited memory resources (much like an embedded system designer). Dennis Ritchie decided to extend the B language with the goal of creating a compiler capable of producing small and fast programs to rival assembly language. By 1973, the essential features of modern C were completely developed.

The growth of C's popularity was tied to its portability. As it was extended to more platforms, its popularity grew. C enjoyed rapid growth during the 1980s. In particular, it became the main programming tool for personal computers. The

American National Standards Institute (ANSI) established the X3J11 committee in 1982 with the goal of producing a C standard. The committee's report of 1989 was issued by the International Organization for Standardization (ISO) and the International Electrotechnical Commission as ISO/IEC 9899-1990. Several more steps in standardization have taken place, with the most current update completed in 1999 (ISO/IEC 9899). It has become the language most commonly used throughout the computer industry.

2.4 OPTIMAL APPROACH: MIXED C AND ASSEMBLY LANGUAGE

Hopefully, we have not caused total confusion here: First we build a case for why to choose assembly language and then we build an equally convincing case to use an HLL—specifically C. The real answer exists somewhere between the two options. It is a common and easily employed technique to write an embedded control application in C and then write the time-sensitive portions of the application in assembly language. Also, you can easily trade off between the two such that those actions requiring close hardware control may be rendered using assembly language from within a C program. We provide examples of mixed assembly and C programming in Chapter 7 when employing the interrupt system and the fuzzy logic features of the 68HC12. As mentioned earlier, C lends itself nicely to the tenets of structured design. We will now investigate these features in some detail.

2.5 STRUCTURED PROGRAMMING AND DESIGN

In the next several sections we carefully describe the important concepts of structured programming. Our discussion is a synthesis of the techniques described by Page-Jones [1988], Dale and Lilly [1995], and our own experience. After this introduction to structured design concepts, we cover a modern modeling approach to these concepts using the Unified Modeling Language (UML).

First, an aside. Even if you have never written a book, you can appreciate how much work is involved. Quite frankly, at times it's a bit overwhelming. We start with a brainstorming session on what the contents of the book should be and then assemble these ideas into a rough outline. We then fill in the details of the outline. Only after the outline is complete do we begin working on the actual writing. Once we begin writing, we tackle only a chapter at a time. Even a chapter is too big to tackle at once, so we concentrate on a single section within the chapter. The section is divided into paragraphs. The book is written one paragraph at a time, sentence by sentence, word by word. This may seem obvious but this "divide-and-conquer" technique breaks the overwhelming task of writing a lengthy book into doable "bite-size" pieces. Also, a detailed well-constructed outline provides an overall structure for the book and clearly shows how different book sections relate to one another.

The same process should be followed when writing a large software/hardware project. The basic concept behind a structured design approach is to use a "divide-and-conquer" technique to take a large design project and break it into understandable, doable pieces. These techniques are referred to by various names, including top-down design, bottom-up implementation, functional decomposition, structured design, structured programming, and step-wise refinement. There is much more to these techniques than merely breaking a big project into small pieces. They provide a logical, methodical design approach to convert system requirements into a plan to implement these requirements. The plan precedes the actual writing of the software.

You may be wondering why you should bother to read this section or take the time to learn these concepts. What's the payoff? What's in it for you? Structured design techniques will not guarantee a quality end product, but they will increase the likelihood of producing a good design. Good design is measured in terms of maintainable, reliable, and easily adaptable code and systems. It will also reduce the lifetime cost of the system.

We begin by reviewing the basic tenets of structured, documented, and testable designs. We then transition to an introduction of UML, which provides standardized modeling techniques to aid the design of complex software systems. In all cases, we have space only to cover the bare essentials. The reader is encouraged to explore these topics in greater detail. The recommended reading at the end of this chapter is a good starting place to learn more about these concepts.

2.5.1 The Basic Tenets of Structured Programming

Theory.   As previously mentioned, the overall goal of structured design is to provide tools to transform system requirements into a plan to implement the system. The first step is to clearly delineate system requirements. In most cases, the requirements are not implemented by those who developed them. Therefore, the requirements must be clearly communicated to the designer. It is the designer's responsibility to ensure that they clearly understand the requirements of the desired system. Imagine the tragedy of designing a system that works correctly but matches incorrect requirements! No amount of maintenance will fix this situation. The bottom line: structured design uses the definition of the problem to guide the definition of the solution.

Application.   Throughout this section, we illustrate the presented concepts with a running example—the design of a controller for a stereo amplifier. This controller was designed for Dr. Parris Neal of the U.S. Air Force (USAF)

Academy in Colorado Springs, Colorado. A consummate engineer, Parris designs world-class, low-noise stereo amplifiers. Each of his stereo projects is a labor of love. For this particular design, Parris had designed an amplifier that would accept inputs from six different audio sources. The user would select the audio source to be amplified by a front panel switch or via a remote control, as shown in Figure 2.1. As you can see in the illustration, the amplifier is a work of art. Parris asked the first author to design a controller for the amplifier using an 8-bit RISC Atmel processor. He was interested in investigating the Atmel line as a potential low-cost processor for senior design projects in the Department of Electrical Engineering at the USAF Academy.

From the first discussion of the project, a list of goals and requirements was developed, as shown below.

GOALS AND REQUIREMENTS

- Develop an embedded controller system to control a stereo amplifier.
- Design the controller to respond to six different inputs from either a front panel switch or from an infrared-based remote control.
- Use the Atmel line of controllers, as requested by the customer (Parris).

After drawing up this initial list of requirements, the following list of questions was created to further delineate the requirements and to aid in the development of detailed project specifications:

QUESTIONS ON REQUIREMENTS/SPECIFICATIONS

- What should the controller do in response to an input selection?
- Who is responsible for the interface between the amplifier and the controller?
- What are the characteristics of the incoming signals from the remote and the front panel switches?
- What are the characteristics of the outgoing control signals to the amplifier?

In response to the questions, Parris provided a detailed word description (four pages of single-spaced text) of the specifications of the desired controller. He also provided a rough flowchart of the desired control flow. From this description a detailed structure chart and flowchart were formalized. Over the next two months we e-mailed the charts back and forth until all of the finest project details were resolved. Please note we had not coded anything yet!

Theory. A careful, detailed analysis of the user's requirements must precede design. The requirements are then converted to a detailed specification. The project specifications include a complete definition of the project. This detailed

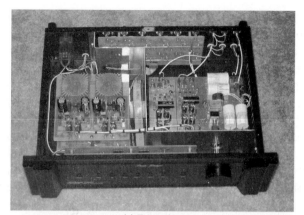

(a) Front view

(b) Close-up of microcontroller

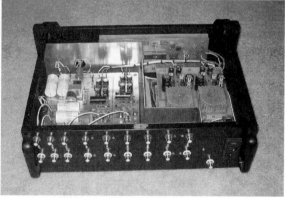

(c) Rear view

Figure 2.1   A stereo amplifier with infrared remote. (Courtesy of Parris Neal, Monument, CO.)

description includes expected output activities for a given input and also any additional processing and error-handling requirements. Any area of project ambiguity should also be resolved between the designer and the customer. When the design is complete, a detailed plan of implementing the user's requirements is available.

The second aspect of structured design is to use partitioning techniques to break a large, complex system into a hierarchical description of "black boxes." What does this all mean? Basically, we divide the system into individual small, definable pieces. Furthermore, we also define the relationships between the black boxes.

By now you are probably wondering, "What's a black box?" A black box is simply a well-defined piece of a system with a specific function. We know the input(s) to the function and its desired output(s); however, we do not know the details of the function. We continue to partition a system into black boxes so that each function is easy to understand. Furthermore, as we develop this hierarchical arrangement of black boxes, we should illustrate the connection between them.

The next aspect of structured design is to use graphical tools such as the structure chart and the activity diagram to readily understand the inter-relations of our black boxes.

Application.   As previously mentioned, we used a detailed structure chart and flowchart to communicate the amplifier control system description. It was essentially impossible to formulate the four pages of detailed requirements into an understandable, cohesive big picture of the project without these tools.

Theory.   The structure chart is the major tool of structured design used to illustrate the big picture of the system, consisting of a hierarchical, graphical depiction of the system modules (black boxes) and the relationship between them. An arrow is used to indicate that one module calls another. An open arrow (a circle with an attached arrow) indicates a module that communicates data to another module. A flowchart is a useful tool to show the overall flow of a program. However, its use is limited to small systems. In the Unified Modeling Language the flowchart has been replaced by an activities diagram. We will discuss this new tool shortly.

Application.   The structure chart of the stereo amplifier is shown in Figure 2.2 and the flowchart is provided in Figure 2.3. As you can see, the structure chart shows the overall hierarchical structure of the program while the flowchart provides a graphical depiction of the overall program flow. At this time you must be thinking, "Surely, coding is the next step." Sorry, we have several steps of the structured design approach to complete prior to beginning the actual coding.

Theory.   The next aspect of structured design is that it offers a set of tools and strategies for developing a design solution. Once we have a hierarchical

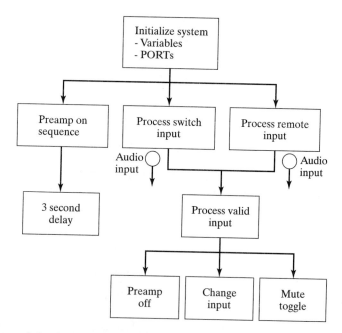

Figure 2.2   A structure chart for a stereo amplifier. This chart illustrates how the amplifier control system was partitioned into subsystems and each subsystem was partitioned into functions. The data flow is shown with an open arrow.

structure chart, we can begin working out the details of the contents of each black box. Here we develop the functional relationship between the box inputs and outputs. We now use a coding strategy called *pseudocode* (pseudo = fake) to describe the relation between inputs and outputs.

The use of pseudocode to define the modules allows us to defer the details of coding as long as possible until we have to tackle them. Our intent in this technique is not to avoid the details but to defer them until all higher level details have been resolved. When you complete this step, you will have a big structure tree with the general problem at the top and all the details branching out beneath it.

Application.   For the stereo amplifier design, the pseudocode is directly applied to the flowchart. The overall result is shown in Figure 2.4. As you can see, we now have a detailed road map of the program ready to be coded. We have used a top-down design approach to break a large project into small, doable, understandable bite-size pieces. However, it is still not time for coding.

Theory.   If we were to now code the pseudocode illustrated in Figure 2.4, our chances of having a working program would be slim. Note that in this figure we are using a hybrid of pseudocode embedded within a flowchart. This has

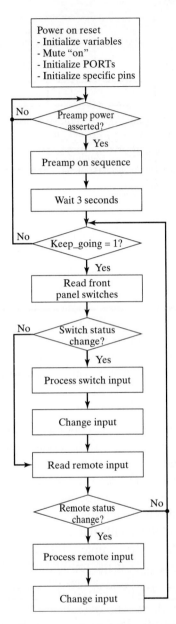

Figure 2.3   A flowchart for a stereo amplifier. The amplifier controller is first initialized and is then placed in a polling loop waiting for the user to select the preamp power selection. Once preamp power is selected, the controller is placed in another polling loop where it waits for an assertion on the front panel switches or from the remote. When a selection is made, the algorithm processes the correct control steps for the specific action selected.

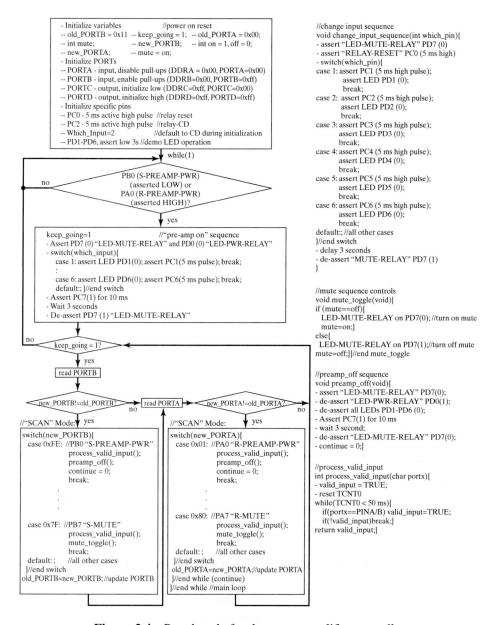

Figure 2.4   Pseudocode for the stereo amplifier controller.

proved to be a useful technique for translating pseudocode and program flow into finished code. We need to develop some implementation techniques that lend themselves to successful program implementation. There are three basic approaches that we cover in turn, all of them based on an incremental approach to implementation where a module is implemented (coded) and tested to ensure that it works according to requirements. Other modules are then tested and incrementally added to the first function. The overall system function evolves as additional modules are added. The elegance in this approach is that we can quickly identify and fix troublesome modules before they are added to others.

The first approach is top-down incremental implementation, in which the top module of the structure chart is implemented first. The lower-level modules are simulated by empty modules (stubs). Once the top-level module is operating correctly, the next lower level of modules are added one at a time. This process continues until the system is complete. This would be a useful technique in a software system that consisted of an overall "umbrella" function that called other functions (e.g., the stereo amplifier controller).

At the opposite extreme is the second approach—the bottom-up incremental implementation. This technique implements a module at the lowest level of the structure chart. The module is activated at a higher level by a stand-in piece of software called a *driver*. This technique allows us to slowly build up a program from the ground floor.

The third approach to implementation is a hybrid of the previous two, in which we work on implementation from the top and bottom simultaneously and meet in the middle. Once an implementation approach has been selected, coding can finally commence.

Up until now you would surmise that these techniques can only be applied to software design and implementation. Actually, these techniques work equally well for hardware projects. Most importantly, they work very well for an embedded controller system that involves software, hardware, and the interface between them.

Application.   The implementation of the controller for the stereo amplifier was quite complicated. Now wait a minute, didn't we spend a lot of time developing the software down to the pseudocode level to avoid this? Remember, the controller was developed to control a high-end, esoteric amplifier. Would you be willing to put a controller into an expensive amplifier without some level of assurance that it operated correctly? How do you initially test a system that will respond to hardware inputs and issue hardware activation signals?

For the amplifier control project, an amplifier hardware simulator was first developed. It consisted of a series of input switches and light-emitting diodes as outputs to simulate the amplifier hardware. With this simulator, we could exhaustively test the functions of the amplifier controller prior to inserting the embedded controller into the actual amplifier. Parris was also asked to exhaustively test the controller under every conceivable scenario prior to putting the controller into the amplifier. The amplifier hardware simulator is shown in Figure 2.5. We defer a detailed discussion of the simulator components until Chapter 5. Variations of this simulator have been used on several different projects with good success.

Theory.   The final aspect of structured design is that it offers a set of evaluation criteria to determine if a design meets its requirements. This implies some method of project verification, debugging, and testing. Program verification is so much more than testing. However, testing is a significant portion of verification. To properly test a system, a test plan is developed to thoroughly test all requirements and operations of the system. The overall goal is to identify and fix errors and most importantly to ensure that the project meets its intended requirements.

Errors come in a variety of flavors and can be described here in order of increasing severity. Compile-time errors are syntax errors. These errors are reported by the compiler. The compiler may report problems as "Warnings" or "Errors." A warning occurs when a compiler does not like something you are doing in code. Even though the code will compile, you should resolve these warnings. An error on the other hand, will not allow the code to successfully compile to completion. Realize that often a single syntax error might generate multiple compile-time error messages. As you gain more experience with C programming, you will get better at quickly identifying the source of syntax errors.

Run-time errors are those that occur during program execution. These are usually due to a faulty algorithm. For example, if you write a routine to delay for 3 seconds and incorrectly calculate the constants that provide the delay, the program will execute although incorrectly. Run-time errors are much more difficult to identify than compile-time errors. A thorough testing plan helps alleviate run-time errors.

The worst kind of error is one due to incorrect program specifications and requirements. In this case the program may meet requirements but the requirements are wrong! No amount of software maintenance fixes this type of error. That is why we spend so much time up front carefully understanding and developing project requirements.

A thorough test plan may use top-down testing techniques with software stubs, a bottom-up testing technique using a driver, or a mixed approach. The most appropriate technique depends on the project. A good test plan also tests the robustness of the software. In other words, what happens if the system is used outside the procedures established for its use? A robust system will not crash due to incorrect inputs but will instead continue to operate as designed.

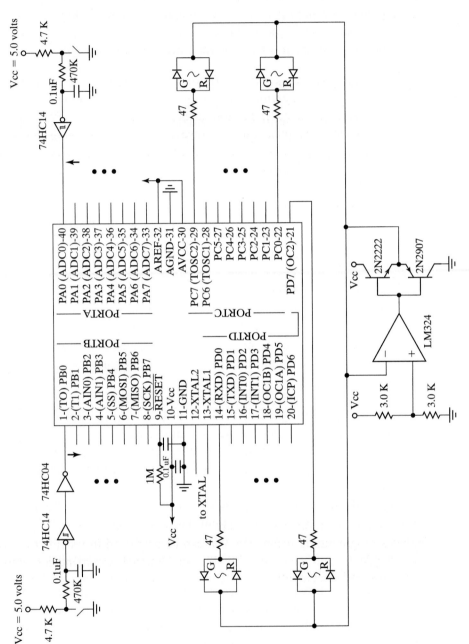

Figure 2.5   An amplifier hardware simulator.

Application.   During the testing of the amplifier controller, we identified certain scenarios that we had not considered during establishment of initial requirements. For example, any time an audio input was selected, the previous audio input was disconnected from the amplifier and the newly selected input would then be connected to the amplifier. What we had not considered was what would happen if the user selected the same audio input that was already connected to the amplifier. In this scenario our original algorithm would disconnect the audio input and then reconnect it. This caused a noticeable audio glitch. Only through thorough testing were we able to identify this run-time error. Once identified, it was easy to modify the code for this particular case.

It should be emphasized that testing is very iterative in nature. As errors are exposed, they are corrected, and testing resumes. When the code is modified, previously satisfied tests should be reexamined to confirm compliance.

Well, that completes our first look at structured design. In the next section we discuss important documentation techniques followed by cutting-edge methods of modeling using UML techniques.

2.5.2 Documentation

Theory.   Many new programmers believe that software documentation is simply the comments you add to your program once it is running. This could not be farther from the truth. Good software documentation is just as important (or more important) than the software itself. Good documentation consists of all the structured design tools we have discussed previously in this chapter. All these tools help us to implement the software but they also serve to document the operation of the system.

Complete documentation includes the comments, a written description of the code, the system specifications and requirements, the actual source code, the user's manual developed for the code, and a history of program development and modifications. This body of documentation can be subdivided into external documentation and internal documentation. External documentation consists of the written information outside the body of the source code. Internal documentation includes programming techniques that can be employed to provide for readable, understandable, and easily modifiable code. Internal documentation consists of comments, self-documenting code techniques, and source program formatting for readability.

Comments help the reader determine what the programmer is trying to do at various points in the program. In our amplifier controller, we had four pages of comments preceding the program, which carefully described the operation of the system. We also used comments to describe the algorithm within the body of the code and also detailed descriptions of each function written. Furthermore, we provided comments on just about every line of code. This may seem a bit excessive but more time spent in commenting significantly saves time in maintaining the code.

Self-documenting code uses meaningful names for variables, constants, and functions to convey their intended functions. For example, a function named "delay_3seconds" clearly identifies its function.

Program formatting for readability techniques (a.k.a. "pretty printing") uses blank spaces to help illustrate the control structure within a program. For example, the body of a loop is indented from the control line of the loop to illustrate the logical structure of a program at a glance.

Application.   Several months after completing the amplifier controller, Parris asked for several modifications to the control algorithm. The code was reviewed for about 20 minutes and then we quickly identified how and where to modify the code. It is important to note, we then took several extra minutes to update the documentation. Had we not carefully documented the code several months before, we would have spent considerable time reacquainting ourselves with the code prior to implementing any updates.

2.5.3 How C Lends Itself to Structured Design

The syntax of the C language lends itself nicely to the concepts of structured design. A C program consists of a main program at the top level. The main program calls functions to execute specific tasks. The functions may be viewed as the direct implementation of the black boxes we discussed earlier. These functions may call other functions in a hierarchical manner.

Information-hiding techniques can be readily implemented in C. The main program provides an overall view of the flow of the program. As you delve down deeper into lower-level functions, additional details of the program are exposed.

2.6 LABORATORY NOTEBOOKS

Closely related to the topic of proper documentation are laboratory notebooks. In this section we detail the whys and wherefores of lab notebooks. This information was condensed from an article written by a group of colleagues from over a decade ago [McCormack et. al. 1990]. Their article was based on the key literature available on laboratory notebooks over a period of many decades.

Lab notebooks are used to record the process of scientific discovery, project evolution, design rationale, steps in engineering analysis, procedures followed, and raw data collected. In engineering practice, one of the principle reasons for keeping a laboratory notebook is to create legally admissible evidence. It is for this reason that laboratory notebooks are frequently used in patent claims. Furthermore, a carefully maintained notebook allows for adequate reconstruction of original work years from the original entry and can be used to write a doctoral dissertation, produce a technical report, or present a patent claim.

2.6.1 Notebook Mechanics

Because of legal requirements, the format of a laboratory notebook is rigidly defined. The following guidelines should be followed in maintaining a good laboratory notebook:

1. Bind all notebooks so that individual pages cannot be removed. If a page is removed, evidence of its removal should be obvious.
2. Make all entries sequentially in indelible ink.
3. Number all pages sequentially.
4. Sign and date entries before a witness. Dates should be unambiguous (e.g. May 9, 2004 rather than 5/9/2004).
5. Sign and date any alterations or pasted in material.
6. Do not obliterate errors, cross them out with a single line.
7. Mark unused space with an "X" or "Z" to ensure that material is not added later.

2.6.2 Notebook Contents

When a patent lawyer was asked what should be included in a laboratory notebook, the reply was "everything." To effectively do this, answer the six questions asked by newspaper reporters regarding who, what, when, where, why, and how. When recording this information, use a readable writing style. The basic premise is to allow someone to easily follow a project's progress.

The Bottom Line.   Laboratory notebooks, when properly used and maintained, are an excellent tool to document work. In the next section we investigate modern techniques of structured design—the Unified Modeling Language.

2.7 UNIFIED MODELING LANGUAGE (UML)

Theory.   The Unified Modeling Language (UML) is a modern method to graphically illustrate and model complex software system operation. The motivation is to provide a standardized set of graphical tools to model a complex system prior to implementation. There are more than 100 book titles available on this topic. Our intent here is to provide only a brief overview of the UML techniques applicable to embedded controller system design. The interested reader is referred to the additional readings provided at the end of this chapter.

UML development has been primarily driven by the work of Grady Booch, Ivar Jacobson, and James Rumbaugh. Their goal has been to produce a standard means of expressing the best practices of industry software design techniques. UML helps in the process of visualizing and documenting the models, structure, and design of software systems. It has become the standard way to draw diagrams of object-oriented designs; however, UML techniques may be applied to non-object-oriented designs. It is important to note that UML went through a standardization process with the Object Management Group (OMG), and it is now a standard modeling method [Fowler 2000; Douglass 2000].

First and foremost, UML is a graphical modeling language with the fundamental purpose of communication. It uses a set of graphical tools, including UML cases, class diagrams, and interaction models, to describe object-oriented software designs. We will not be using object-oriented software in this book; however, some UML techniques still have a place in our designs. In particular we employ the UML activity diagram to illustrate program flow. The activity diagram describes the sequence of activities, or program flow. In fact, Fowler describes the activity diagram as "nothing more than a UML-compliant flowchart." However, he clearly indicates that a flowchart is normally limited to sequential processes; whereas, activity diagrams can handle parallel processes [Fowler 2000; Douglass 2000].

The syntax for the UML activity diagram is provided in Figure 2.6. Program flow is initiated with the *starting activity* and terminated with the *final pseudostate*. The various *action states* or activities are a state of doing an action. The flow from activity to activity is shown with *transfer of control* arrows. More complicated control flow can be diagrammed with *branch pseudostates* or branches. A branch has a single input transition and several *guarded* outgoing transitions. Only one of the multiple paths may be taken out of the branch. Therefore, the guards that specify the argument to take a path out of the branch should be mutually exclusive. A *merge* as its name implies terminates the branching activity initiated by a branch. For completeness we have included the syntax for a *fork* and a *join*. These are used to model parallel behavior [Fowler 2000; Douglass 2000]. Figure 2.7 summarizes the structured design process using UML activity diagram techniques. Figure 2.8 shows a UML activity diagram that provides additional details on the design, implementation, and testing steps of Figure 2.7. As you can see in these two examples, the UML activity diagram aids in the visualization of overall flow.

2.8 APPLICATION: RETINAL LASER SURGERY SYSTEM

One unifying concept throughout this chapter has been to take a large, complex design task and break it into small, doable pieces. We previously mentioned that this structured design technique worked equally well for a software system, a

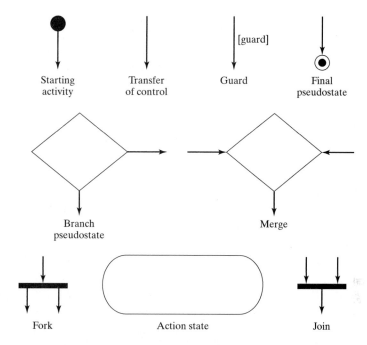

Figure 2.6   The syntax for a Unified Modeling Language activity diagram.

hardware system, or a combined system consisting of both hardware and software much like what you would find in an embedded controller system design. This technique may also be applied to nonhardware and software design issues within a system. As a graduate student, the first author was given the task of developing an automated laser system to treat retinal disorders. He spent six months finding out where the edge of technology existed in laser eye surgery. At the end of this extensive library search, he was overwhelmed with the sheer magnitude of the project. He developed a structure chart to help map out all of the pieces of the project and how they fit together. This procedure allowed him to concentrate on a single task at a time while keeping an eye on the larger overall task at hand. The structure chart for this project is provided in Figure 2.9. Note how the chart also helps to model nonsoftware and hardware aspects of a project.

2.9 SUMMARY

We began this chapter by exposing you to the trade-offs of using assembly language versus a high-level language (HLL) such as C to program an embedded controller system. We saw that each had their inherent advantages and

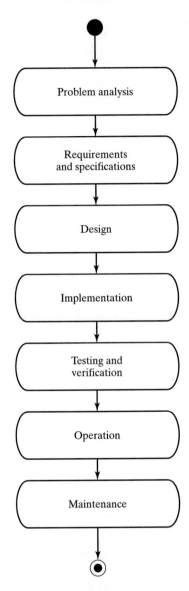

Figure 2.7   The structured design process.

disadvantages. We found that the real solution is to use a combination of both within the same program: a program rendered in C and containing inline assembly statements. We then provided a brief review of the interesting origins of the C language, which has become the language of choice for scientific embedded systems because it is an intermediate language, "a portable assembly language." We then investigated the key tenets of the structured programming approach to

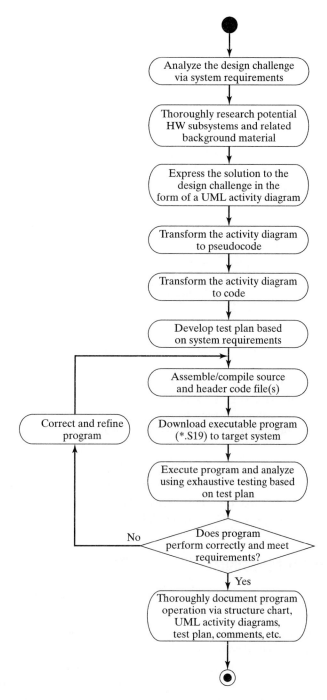

Figure 2.8   An expanded view of design, implementation, and testing.

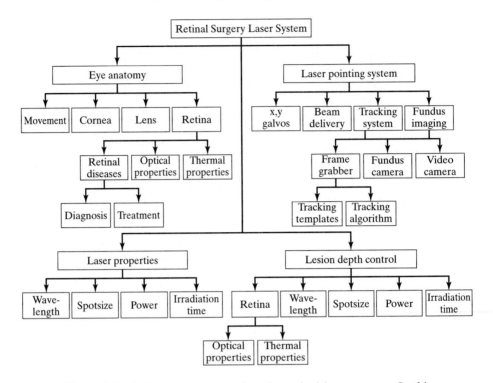

Figure 2.9 A System structure chart for retinal laser surgery. In this example a large system was partitioned into hardware, software, and even anatomical aspects. The project was continually partitioned to a level consisting of understandable, doable pieces.

an embedded system design. The key idea is to systematically apply structured design to guide the design of a robust, maintainable, and well-documented system. We concluded the chapter by briefly investigating modern techniques of structured design, the Unified Modeling Language (UML).

2.10 FURTHER READING

Dale, Nell, and Susan C. Lilly. *Pascal Plus Data Structures*. 4th ed. Englewood Cliffs, NJ: Jones and Bartlett, 1995.

Douglass, Bruce Powel. *Real-Time UML—Developing Efficient Objects for Embedded Systems*. 2nd ed. Boston: Addison-Wesley, 2000.

Fowler, Martin, with Kendall Scott. *"UML Distilled—A Brief Guide to the Standard Object Modeling Language*. 2nd ed. Boston: Addison-Wesley, 2000.

Kobryn, Chris. "UML 2001." *Communications of the ACM* 42, no. 10, (October 1999): 29–37.

McCormack, J. B., R. K. Morrow, H. F. Bare, R. J. Burns, and R. L. Rasmussen "The Complementary Roles of Laboratory Notebooks and Laboratory Reports." Paper presented at the annual meeting of the American Society for Engineering Educators Toronto, Canada, 1990.

Pack, Daniel, and Steven Barrett. *68HC12: Theory and Applications*. Upper Saddle River, NJ: Prentice Hall, 2002.

Page-Jones, Meilir. *The Practical Guide to Structured Systems Design*. 2nd ed. Upper Saddle River, NJ: Yourdon Press, 1988.

Ritchie, Dennis M. "The Development of the C Language." Paper presented at a meeting of the Association for Computing Machinery, Second History of Programming Languages Conference, Cambridge, MA, 1993.

Wakerly, John F. *Digital Design Principles and Practices*. 3rd ed. Upper Saddle River, NJ: Prentice Hall, 2000.

2.11 PROBLEMS

Fundamental

1. Summarize the pros and cons of using assembly language versus C to program an embedded control system.
2. Describe the following tenets of structured design: portability, reusability, readability.
3. What other HLL compilers are available for the 68HC12? Provide sources for these compilers.
4. What was the key factor that was responsible for the rapid acceptance of C?
5. What is a "black box"?
6. What is the difference between a structure chart and a flowchart?

Advanced

1. What is the difference between a structure chart and a UML activity diagram?
2. What is pseudocode?
3. Describe the difference between top-down and bottom-up incremental implementation. Which is the better choice?
4. What is the difference between compile-time and run-time errors?
5. What is a stub? A driver?
6. What is the difference between internal and external documentation?

Challenging

1. Convert the flowchart of Figure 2.3 to a UML activity diagram.

2. You have been asked by your employer (Remote Access Weather) to develop a portable weather station (see Figure 2.10). These remote weather stations will be placed throughout the region and report back to a central facility. The weather station is equipped with the following weather instruments:

- Anemometer: Provides information on wind velocity. The anemometer consists of four wind-catching cups attached to a rotating spindle, and it will provide a 5 volt pulse every time it completes a revolution.
- Barometer: Provides a signal that ranges from 0 to 5 volts depending on the sensed barometric pressure. The barometer will provide a 0 volt output for 640 mm of mercury and 5 volts for 810 mm of mercury. For values between these two extremes, there is a linear relationship between output voltage and barometric pressure.
- Hygrometer: Senses relative humidity and will provide a signal that ranges from 0 to 5 volts, depending on the sensed atmospheric humidity. It will provide a

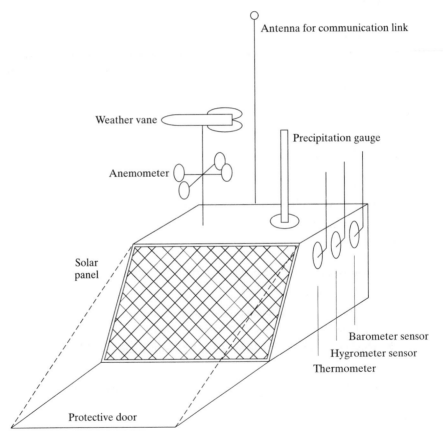

Figure 2.10   A remote weather station.

0 volt output for 0 percent relative humidity and 5 volts for 100 percent relative humidity. For values between these two extremes, there is a linear relationship between output voltage and relative humidity.

- Rain gauge: Measures the amount of precipitation present and provides 20 millivolts of output for each centimeter of accumulated precipitation.
- Thermometer: Senses temperature and provides a 0 volt output for −50 degrees centigrade and a 5 volt output for +120 degrees centigrade. For values between these two extremes, there is a linear relationship between output voltage and sensed temperature.
- Weather vane: Senses wind direction and provides a 0 volt output when it is pointing north. As the weather vane turns clockwise to the east, south, and west, the voltage increments linearly until it reaches a full scale value of 5 volts as soon as it completes its rotation back to north.

The system will also require the following:

- The remote weather station should forward weather data to the central facility at 15-minute intervals. Another engineer is designing the communication link between the remote station and the central facility. You are required to provide the weather parameters serially to the communication link at regular intervals.
- If wind speed exceeds a critical value (yet to be determined), motor-controlled doors on the remote station will close.
- The rain gauge must be periodically emptied.
- Aside from providing the weather data to the serial communication link, key weather parameters must be displayed on an LCD panel for troubleshooting purposes.

Provide a structure chart for the remote weather station.

3. Choose a household appliance that contains an embedded controller. Develop a structure chart for the appliance. Choose from the following list:

- Microwave oven
- Thermostat
- Boom box (combination AM/FM receiver, cassette player, compact disk stereo)

4. Develop a UML activity diagram for the problem above.

3

C Microcontrollers Programming Skills

Objectives: After reading this chapter, you should be able to

- Describe essential building blocks of the C programming language
- Write simple C programs for embedded systems applications
- Explain the process involved in generating an executable program for the 68HC12 and HCS12 microcontroller
- Illustrate the use of tools to edit, compile, assemble, link, and debug programs

This chapter presents software topics necessary to program, compile, debug, and execute C programs on 68HC12 and the HCS12 microcontrollers. We will refer to these two processors generically as the 68HC12 throughout this chapter. For topics related to programming, our main focus is to discuss skills required to write programs in C; however, we also present techniques to combine C programs with assembly language programs since an appropriate mixture of the two programming languages is essential in creating efficient software programs for embedded systems. We also show how to translate C programs into executable files for the controller by demonstrating the compile, assemble, link, and load procedures using Imagecraft ICC12 software, a typical platform for developing and testing programs for the 68HC12 microcontroller. The process we discuss here is readily transferrable to other similar software platforms with minor modifications. The last topic in the chapter is a general approach and discusses tools for debugging programs that are written in C. The approach involves matching C code with corresponding assembly language instructions generated as a result of compiling, assembling, and linking associated programs, and testing the assembly language instructions for one module at a time. The 68HC12 also provides system developers with a real-time debug module, called the background debug mode (BDM). We present the BDM in this chapter. An example process of generating an executable 68HC12 file for a sample program and an application section close this chapter.

3.1 INTRODUCTION

As mentioned in Chapter 2, the C programming language became one of the most used high-level programming languages in the engineering community due to its portability and flexibility, which allows programmers to control hardware components directly while retaining the desired abstract nature of other high-level languages. For example, a programmer has immediate access to contents of arbitrary memory locations, a feature more familiar to assembly programming languages. To understand how to program the 68HC12 in C, we must first learn the basic features of the C programming language, which we present in the next few sections. We hasten to add that our coverage of C is brief, dealing only with essential parts of the language. For complete coverage of the language, we refer readers to our short list of C programming books at the end of the chapter.

C is a structured language. Keywords, numbers, identifiers, and operators are used to create programs that follow prescribed rules. Identifiers are user-defined variable names, function names, labels, and objects. Before any programming can start, we first need a set of variables. These variables must be declared as one of the data types, and symbols must be used to declare those variables.

3.1.1 Global and Local Variables

A variable is a storage place in memory to hold values during the execution of a program. It is a memory location in RAM or in ROM (or even a processor register) for embedded systems. There are two types of variables: (1) global variables, which can be accessed by all functions (sets of instructions) and (2) local variables, which can only be accessed from a particular function where the local variables are declared. In embedded systems, these local variables usually appear as stack locations.[1] The subject of variable validity duration within a program belongs to the identifier scope declaration. A variable is valid and accessible according to how that variable is declared. The scope of declaration determines the area within a program that a particular variable is valid and accessible. The identifier scope covers not only variables but also functions, structure components, type tags, and preprocessor macros to name a few. Based on a declaration, these identifiers are "visible" in different parts of a program body. A detailed discussion of the identifier scope cannot be included in this book, but we refer interested readers to *C: A Reference Manual* by Harbison and Steele (2002) which is listed at the end of this chapter.

In the 68HC12 microcontroller, a variable is represented as a memory location in ROM or RAM. A variable that does not change during the execution of a program, called a *constant variable*, should reside in ROM while a *nonconstant variable* should be stored in RAM. Thus a variable is a convenient way to name a memory location to store a constant or a varying value. For example, suppose your controller is connected to a temperature sensor through an analog-to-digital converter, and you must frequently update the temperature within the controller. Storing the current temperature in a RAM location and naming it as `temp` will enhance the access of the memory location for the purpose of data manipulation or data display. The following code shows how the variable `temp` is accessed and displayed indefinitely.

```
1   while (1)
2   {
3       temp = *(unsigned char volatile *)(0x1000);
4       printf("The current temperature is %d\n", temp);
5   }
```

In the code above, we are assuming that variable `temp` is already declared and there exists a mechanism to update the `temp` variable, as in line 3 of the code. We use `0x1000` to represent hexadecimal number 1000 (decimal number 4096) in C. The `0x` that precedes a number indicates that the number that follows is in hexadecimal.[2] Do not be alarmed if you do not understand the syntax of the instructions in the example code. By the time you finish reading this chapter, you will find them straightforward. By the way, the numbers appearing in the left margin are not part of the program. They are code line numbers included for clarification and will allow us to refer to specific lines within our discussion of the code. In this example, the `temp` variable could be declared either as a global variable or a local variable.

The difference between a local variable and a global variable is the location within your program where it is declared. A global variable must be declared

---

[1] A stack location is a part of RAM.
[2] The dollar sign ($) is typically used to indicate a hexadecimal number in assembly programs.

Table 3.1   Types of Data Found in C for the 68HC12 Using ICC12 Software

Type	Description	Memory Size in 68HC12/ICC12	Range in 68HC12/ICC12
char	character	1 byte	−128 to 127
unsigned char	character	1 byte	0 to 255
short int	integer	2 bytes	−32768 to 32727
int	integer	2 bytes	−32768 to 32767
unsigned int	integer	2 bytes	0 to 65535
long int	integer	4 bytes	$-2,147,483,648$ to $2,147,483,647$
float	floating point	4 bytes	Not recommended for use
double	double	4 bytes	Not recommended for use

outside of all functions whereas a local variable must be declared inside of a particular function. We take on the issue of how to declare a variable after the discussion of the different C data types in the next section.

3.2 DATA TYPES IN C

The C programming language contains eight fundamental data types, listed in Table 3.1. Each type of data specifies the number of bytes allocated for each particular variable. A variety of data types can be used to specify integer variables. In the 68HC12, the integer and the short integer can be used interchangeably; in some systems, the short integer uses only a single byte to contain a short integer value. For the float and the double data types, we advise that you avoid using them as much as possible with the 68HC12. Manipulation of a float or double variable takes up a considerable number of instructions and impedes efficient program execution. Besides, most mathematical computations suitable for the 68HC12 can be performed using integer variables.

In addition to the above data types, the following five additional data types are available in C:

1. Array: a set of data elements with the same data type.
2. Pointer: a variable that contains the address of a data type.
3. Structure: a set of data elements where each element can be a different data type.

4. Union: a memory element that is shared by two different data types.

5. Function: a function being itself a data type can generate a data type and can return a data type.

These are sometimes referred to as derived data types since we use the fundamental data types to declare them. We discuss these data types in greater detail later in this chapter and also in Chapter 8.

In C, variables are declared and optionally initialized using the following format:

```
access (and-or) storage-type
 type-specifier identifier ([optional array element count]) value;
```

The first field, *access/storage-type*, is used to dictate the type of memory used to store the variable; the second field, type-specifier, should contain one of the data types specified in Table 3.1; the identifier is a user-defined variable name; and the equate operator along with a numerical value or a character string is used to define or initialize a variable.

For example, we declare an integer variable called change as

```
int     change;
```

where keyword int specifies the type of variable, and identifier change is the assigned variable name. The semicolon at the end of the expression terminates a C expression; you must have a semicolon at the end of each expression.

Any reserved words in C are called *keywords*. These words are set aside for special purposes and should not be used as identifiers. The following list shows the 32 keywords used in C; we encounter most of them in this chapter.

```
auto, break, case, char, const, continue, default, do, double,
else, enum, extern, float, for, goto, if, int, long, register,
return, short, signed, sizeof, static, struct, switch, typedef,
union, unsigned, void, volatile, while
```

The C language has six *access/storage-type* keywords available: extern, auto, static, register, const, and volatile.

The keyword extern specifies a variable that has been declared and defined in some other object code file. These variables are stored in appropriate memory locations and may be accessible by all functions. The keyword auto is a default storage type used when no storage type is specified. In the 68HC12, the stack is used to store variables declared with this storage type. Once a function (a small segment of a program, which we discuss in Section 3.4) completes its task, the variables declared with the auto storage type are removed from the stack and no longer available. In addition, only the function where a variable is declared with the `auto` storage type has an access to the variable. The `static` storage type is similar to the `auto` storage type except that the variable values declared with the `static` keyword are stored in RAM rather than in the stack, making the values available during the entire execution of a program. Finally, when the keyword `register` is used to declare a variable, you are asking the compiler to use, if possible, one of the CPU registers to store the particular variable. Storing a variable in a CPU register instead of a memory location facilitates the execution of the program by cutting down the bus time to access the memory. Thus, for a variable that will be used over and over again within your program, we recommend that you use this keyword to declare the variable.

The `const` access type keyword should be used when the value of a variable does not change during the execution of the program. These variables are usually stored in ROM. A `const` variable must be initialized by the programmer.[3] The `volatile` access type keyword is used to indicate that a variable can change its value without specific instructions within a program. This keyword should be used for variables whose values are modified by hardware input ports in the applications of the 68HC12. We will see examples of variables declared with `volatile` when we discuss 68HC12 interface applications.

We can also initialize a variable with a value. Suppose we want to initialize variable `change` with the value `23`. We can do so as shown in the following declaration.

```
const int change = 23;
```

Once we have variables that are declared, we are now ready to discuss how to manipulate these variables to obtain desired results. To support such manipulations, the C language makes a number of arithmetic and logical operations available. We discuss them next.

3.3 OPERATORS

The C programming language has a number of operators, as shown in Table 3.2. We categorize all operators into five different groups: general, arithmetic, logical, bit manipulative, and unary. Contrary to the name, general operators are used to perform special operations. The arithmetic operators are used to perform mathematical operations such as addition, subtraction, multiplication, and division. The logical operators are used to determine whether or not a statement is true. Bit operators are used to change one or more bits of a memory location and the unary operation requires only one variable to perform an assigned task. Referring to Table 3.2, the precedence number in the first column shows the overall operator

---

[3]In some cases, hardware-dependent methods can be used to initialize such variables.

precedence when multiple operators appear in an expression. We illustrate these operators using examples.

General Operators   A pair of parenthesis, ( ), is used to group an operation and assign a higher priority. Suppose we have the following expression:

```
2 * 23 + 15
```

The multiplication operator has precedence over the addition operator, and the result will be 61. What if we want to add 23 and 15 first before multiplying by 2? We use the regular parenthesis operator to overrule the precedence as shown.

```
2 * (23 + 15)
```

The resulting value now will be 76.

The curly bracket pair should be used to group a set of instructions together—for example, to group the instructions for a function and a loop. Example use of these operators are discussed in Section 3.4. We also postpone our discussion of the structure access, conditional, and assignment operators.

Arithmetic Operators   The addition operator, +, adds two numbers and returns their sum. Adding 2 with 3 is done by the simple statement

```
sum = 2 + 3;
```

where we use the addition operator and assignment operator together. As shown in Table 3.2, the addition operator has precedence over the assignment operator. Therefore, numbers 2 and 3 are added first, and the result is then assigned to variable sum, assuming that the variable sum has been declared ahead of time as an integer. What happens if the variable is declared as some other type than an integer? The result is converted to a data type of the assigned variable once the computation is completed. Of course, we can use variable names instead of actual numbers to perform the same task, as shown below.

```
num1 = 2;
num2 = 3;
sum = num1 + num2;
```

Once again, we must declare the type of all variables before we use them. The subtraction, multiplication, and division operators work similarly. Increment and decrement operators are used to conveniently add or subtract one from a variable. For example, the following three instructions have the same effect.

```
number = 1 + number;
number++;
++number;
```

Table 3.2 C Operators

Precedence	Name	Symbol
General		
1	Parenthesis	(), {}
1	Structure access	− >, .
11	Conditional	?:
12	Assignment	=, + =, * =, etc.
Arithmetic		
3	Multiply	★
3	Divide	/
3	Modulus	%
4	Add	+
4	Subtract	−
Logical		
6	Less than	<
6	Less than or equal	<=
6	Greater than	>
6	Greater than or equal	>=
7	Equal	==
7	Not equal	!=
9	Logical AND	&&
10	Logical OR	‖
Bit Manipulative		
5	Shift left	<<
5	Shift right	>>
8	Bitwise AND	&
8	Bitwise exclusive OR	∧
8	Bitwise OR		
Unary		
2	Unary negative	!
2	One's complement	∼

Table 3.2 *Continued*

Precedence	Name	Symbol
Unary		
2	Increment	++
2	Decrement	−−
2	Unary minus	−
2	Cast	(type)
2	Indirection	*
2	Address of	&
2	Size of	sizeof

The latter two instructions are unary operations to increment the value. Similarly, the three statements shown below perform the same task.

```
number = number - 1;
number--;
--number;
```

Again, the last two operations are done using unary operators.

The modulus operator % is used when we are interested in finding a remainder of an integer division. For example, 2%3 results in 2 since the solution to the division is 0 with remainder 2. As another example, 14%3 will also result in 2 since the division yields 4 with remainder 2.

Logical Operators Logical operators are used to determine whether a condition is true or false. The result is returned as 1 for true and 0 for false. Suppose we want to evaluate a variable against a threshold value. We can use the greater than ($>$), the less than ($<$), the greater than or equal to ($>=$), the less than or equal to ($<=$), the not equal to ($!=$), or the equal to ($==$) operator to perform the task. Consider the following instruction:

```
value = temperature > 82;
```

The instruction above will assign either 1 or 0 to variable `value`. Recall that the logical operation has a precedence above the assignment operator. Since a logical statement on the right results in either true (1) or false (0), the variable `value` will be assigned accordingly.

Bit Operators As mentioned, one of the advantages of using the C programming language over others is its ability to manipulate contents of memory locations using bit operators such as bit-by-bit AND, bit-by-bit OR, and bit-by-bit EXCLUSIVE OR. The most common use of shift operators is to multiply or divide a number with a 2's power number. Note that the division is strictly an integer division not a floating point division. Suppose we have the following statements:

```
number = 24;
new_number_one = number<<1;
new_number_two = number>>1;
```

The first shift left operator, $<<$, will move the bits in variable `number` (00000000 00011000 in binary) to the left by one bit (00000000 00110000) resulting in decimal 48; variable `new_number_one` will be assigned with 48. On the other hand, the next instruction will shift the original number to the right by a bit resulting in value decimal 12 (00000000 00001100). Variable `new_number_two` will contain 12 after the third instruction. Of course, we can shift to left or right more than once to obtain a result equivalent to multiplying and dividing the number by 2^n where n represents the number of shifts you perform.

Now we discuss two other bit manipulative operators. The following examples show the use of two logical operations: AND and OR.

```
Symbol      Action              Example
  &         Logical AND         *(0x0023) & 0x57
  |         Logical OR          *(0x0000) | 0x35
```

As mentioned, in C programming, a hexadecimal number is specified by preceding the number with 0x. Therefore, all the numbers in the example column are represented using the hexadecimal representation. The & operator performs a bit-by-bit AND operation for the two 8-bit values and returns the result. The * operator is an unary operator that extracts the contents of a memory location, which is the topic of our discussion for the next section. For example, a bit-by-bit AND operation with two binary numbers 01011100 and 11000111 results in the following number:

```
      0101 1100
 &    1100 0111
 ---------------
      0100 0100
```

With the same two numbers, a similar operation using the bit-by-bit OR operator produces

```
      0101 1100
 |    1100 0111
 ---------------
      1101 1111
```

So where do we use these operators? In embedded controller applications, we often encounter the need to manipulate the contents of memory locations. For example, in the 68HC12 controller, we take advantage of bit manipulation to change or test signals on input/output ports since physical ports are mapped to memory locations. To use port A (0x0000) as an input port, the data direction register for Port A, DDRA (0x0002), must be first programmed as shown:

```
*(unsigned char volatile *)(0x0002) = 0x00;
```

This statement programs all pins of port A as input port pins.

Example

> The bitwise operators may be used in "bit twiddling" or controlling individual bits [ImageCraft 2002]. For example, to turn on bit 7 of PORTA, the following statement may be used:
>
> ```
> PORTA |= 0x80;          //turn on PORTA[7]
> ```
>
> This is a shorthand method of writing
>
> ```
> PORTA = PORTA | 0x80; //turn on PORTA[7]
> ```

Here the current contents of PORTA are bitwise ORed with the 0x80. The most significant bit (PORTA[7]) is forced to a logic "1" while the remaining bits in PORTA are not changed.

> Similarly, a specific bit or bits can be turned off using the following statement:
>
> ```
> PORTA &= ~0x80;         //turn off PORTA[7]
> ```

The current contents of PORTA are bitwise ANDed with the one's complement of 0x80. The one's complement of 0x80 is 0x7F. The most significant bit position contains a logic 0. Therefore, this bit position will be forced to a logic 0 and the remaining bit positions will remain unchanged.

> The bitwise AND function may also be used to check if specific bits are set. For example in this code snapshot, the current contents of PORTA are bitwise ANDed with 0x81. If the result of this bitwise AND operation is zero (PORTA[7] and PORTA[0] are zeros), the code in the bracketed portion of the if statement is executed.
>
> ```
> if ((PORTA & 0x81) == 0)
>    {
>    :
>    :
>    }
> ```

Finally, a helpful method for complementing a bit is with the use of the bitwise EXCLUSIVE OR operator. For example, the code snapshot below complements or "flips" the value of PORTA bit 7.

```
PORTA ~= 0x80;          //complement PORTA[7]
```

Unary Operators   Since you have seen the increment and decrement unary operators in the arithmetic operators section, our focus in this subsection is to present two special operators of the C language. These operators play an important part in accessing and locating memory contents. The unary * operator is used to specify the contents of a memory location while the unary & operator placed in front of a variable extracts the address of the memory location for the variable. For example, suppose we have the following declaration for integer variables:

```
int num, address, new_num;
```

Also, suppose variable num is located at 0x2000 and we write the expression

```
address=&num;
```

This expression assigns the memory address of variable num to variable address: variable address now contains 0x2000. Now suppose we have the following expression:

```
new_num=*address;
```

This statement assigns the contents of a memory location pointed by the contents of variable address, which equals the value in variable num. The * operator, working in such a capacity, is called a *dereference*. Thus, in our example the & and the * operators interact together to assign either the address of a variable or the contents of a variable. Although the above illustration uses correct syntax, an ANSI C standard way to use the operator is shown below. We should declare variable address as

```
int *address;
```

The difference is that now the pointer variable address is ANSI C compliant and informs the compiler to allocate proper space for the variable. In this declaration the variable address is declared to contain the address of a memory location. For example, consider the following statement:

```
address=(int *)0x1000;
```

The expression assigns memory location 0x1000 as the pointer variable address. To extract the contents of memory location, one needs to place a * operator in front of variable address.

3.4 FUNCTIONS

In this section, we define the term *function* and describe its role in C programs. We also illustrate how to declare a function in a program and how to send and receive parameter values to and from a function.

3.4.1 What Is a Function?

A function is an independent body of code written to perform a specific task. Suppose you are working as a member of a large engineering team whose goal is to implement a complex control algorithm for an airplane. It is obvious that, at the initial stage of the design process, the team must go through steps similar to those presented in Chapter 2. At the end of that designing process, after the overarching goal has been divided into "bite-size" tasks, team members are assigned to tackle each subtask. Among these subtasks, those that can be resolved using software are usually assigned to functions.

The above scenario illustrates three key features that each function must have: (1) independence, (2) flexibility, and (3) portability. A function must be independent of other programming code since the function may be used by multiple users. Returning to our example, suppose you are assigned to write a function that removes noise from an incoming signal (filtering). Your program will be "called" (used) by a number of different programs to remove particular noise for a variety of signals; your function must be independent of any programs that use it, and it must also be flexible. Suppose your noise-removing function works only with noise in one predetermined frequency range and the range cannot be changed. The value of your function then is very limited, especially when compared with a function that allows the range of noise to be assigned by a user. Finally, your function must be portable. The C programming language revolutionized the engineering community by offering the capability to use the same code on multiple hardware platforms. Once a program is written, it can be ported to run on any hardware platforms provided it has software (compiler/assembler) that converts the original software into the corresponding machine code for each particular hardware platform. To make a function portable, you must make the code independent of other program segments, coming back to the first desired feature of a function.

3.4.2 Main Program

A main program is a type of function; the difference is that this function is executed when the program name is called. A properly written main program works as a high-level program execution manager. It contains the entire program structure but avoids details of individual tasks by calling various functions that perform detailed tasks. We can consider a main program to be like a manager who controls the execution order of instructions with the help of functions. For example, suppose we want to perform tasks 1 through n in that order, and functions 1 through n are written to carry out the tasks. Then, we write a main program as follows to complete the overall task.

```
1    void main(void)
2     {
3      function_one();
4      function_two();
5      function_three();
6        :
7        :
8        :
9      function_n();
10    }
```

As we explained earlier, for all program segments we present in this chapter, the numbers in the left margin are not part of the program segments. They simply help us to locate specific lines in the program. Line 1 contains identifier main to differentiate this function from the rest. The keyword void within the parentheses indicates that the program does not take an input argument. Lines 3 through 9 contain *n* function calls to call each function one at a time. That is, when function_one is completed, function_two is called, and when function_two is finished, function_three is called, etc.

3.4.3 Function Prototypes

Functions must be declared at the start of a program before they can be called. The declarations are called *prototypes.*

The proper format for a function prototype is as follows:

```
return-type function-name(variable-type-1 variable-name-1,
                          variable-type-2 variable-name-2,
                          ...... variable-type-n variable-name-n);
```

In this format variable names are optional but can be used for self-documenting purposes. Note the required semicolon in the last line. We illustrate function prototypes using three examples:

```
example 1]  int compute(int, int);
example 2]  float change(char name, float number, int a);
example 3]  double find(unsigned int, float, double);
```

In example 1, the function compute requires two input arguments. The arguments for the function, the initial conditions to start the function, are specified within the parentheses. Both arguments must be integers and the function should use the two integer values to compute a result and provide a return value that is also an integer value. The first int before function compute indicates the data type that will be returned by the function. In example 2, the function name is change, which needs three input parameters—a character, a floating-point number, and an integer—before the function can start. The return value is a floating-point value, as specified by the `float` keyword in front of the function name. In example 3, we see the function declaration for function `find`, which requires three input parameters: an unsigned integer, a floating-point value, and a double value.

You will also encounter the C programming keyword `extern` as the first word of a function declaration:

```
extern not_here(int a, int b, int c);
```

This keyword informs the compiler that the `not_here` function definition is not included in the current source file but it resides in an external program.

Once the functions are declared at the start of a source file, we must define them in the same source file or other source files (libraries) the current source file will be linked with. We discuss the topic of function definition in the next subsection. For all declared, and later defined, functions, a programmer can call them anywhere within his or her program. For example, the following three instructions call the three functions shown above, respectively.

```
compute(23, 12);
change('b', 7.825, 3);
find(25, 5.1524, 23.54721);
```

We discuss calling functions, passing parameters, and returning values further in Section 3.4.5.

3.4.4 Function Definition

Once a function is declared at the beginning of a source file, a programmer must then define the function either within the body of the source file or in one of the accompanying source files. A function can also be defined in an accompanying library. A function definition can appear anywhere in a program, but usually it appears after a main program segment. The definition starts with the same format statement as the corresponding function declaration, with one exception: the semicolon at the end of the statement is removed. For example, suppose that the `compute` function declared in the previous subsection computes the magnitude of a vector with the two parameter values specified and returns the result. The function definition begins with the following statement:

```
int compute(int a, int b)
```

The actual instructions that define a function reside within a curly bracket pair. The complete function definition for function `compute` is shown below:

```
/* This function computes the magnitude of a two element vector */
1    int compute(int a, int b)
2    {
3        int sum, result;
4        sum = a*a + b*b;
5        result =(int)(sqrt(sum));
6        return(result);
7    }
```

The statement in line 1 starts the function definition. It indicates that the function returns an integer and requires two integer parameters. We declare local variables on line 3. The instructions on lines 4 and 5 actually compute the magnitude of the vector using the Pythagorean equation. Note that on line 5, we used a math library function sqrt, which computes the square root of the value in variable sum. The function is defined in the math library, and we can include the library using a compiler directive command, which we discuss in Section 3.6. The (int) operator is an example of a cast operator that converts a value to an integer data type. We need the cast operator since the result of taking a square root of sum is not an integer. The return instruction on line 6 then sends the integer result to the portion of the program that originally called the function. The curly bracket pair in lines 2 and 7 indicates the start and the end of the function.

As shown in the above example, each function must be defined using the appropriate format: a statement to start the definition containing return type and necessary arguments, instructions to perform the function, and a return statement at the end of the function. If the return type is a void, the last return statement is not necessary; meticulous programmers who follow all the programming rules insist that one must include return() in such cases.

3.4.5 Calling Functions, Passing Parameters, and Returning Values

A function can be called anywhere within a program with the function name followed by the required arguments within parentheses. We continue with the example of finding the vector magnitude of two numbers. To call the function we use

```
magnitude = compute(12, 24);
```

Here, we assume the variable magnitude is already declared as an integer variable. After the function is called and completed, this variable contains value 26. The actual answer is 26.832816. Since the function casts the result to an integer value, the fractional part is eliminated. This brings us to the topic of passing parameters between callers and those being called. A caller, the one who invokes a function, can pass multiple parameters to a function. The compute function is called by passing two integer parameter values since the function is declared and defined to be called with two parameter values. On the other hand, the function can return only a single value. Can a function return (pass) multiple values back to a caller? The answer is yes if you are careful. We must talk about pointers and memory addresses before we can discuss this subject fully, which we discuss later in this chapter. A short answer is that we can return a set of data by returning the starting address of data. This assumes that the caller understands the structure of a data block in advance.

3.5 HEADER FILE

In this section, we expand our knowledge of the C programming language by introducing header files, preconstructed files created by you or others. In particular, the C programming language has several standard library functions specified in a variety of header files. For example, recall the `sqrt` function that computes a square root of a number. This function is declared in the `math.h` header file.

The inclusion of a header file usually appears at the top of a program. A header file contains constant variable definitions, macros, and function declarations, allowing a programmer to embed them within his or her programs. During a compile process, the constant variables defined in the header file replace variables that appear in the program. The most typical header file in the built-in library is the standard input/output header file called `stdio.h`. This header file contains function declarations for displaying messages and accepting keyboard inputs from a user. A commercial compiler comes with standard library header files that are commonly used by all programmers. Another well-used header file is the `math.h` file, which contains useful math functions such as sine, cosine, square root, and absolute value functions. In many occasions where system specific constant variables are used, a user should create his or her own header files to be included within a program.

To include a header file, you must use the compiler directive (discussed in the next section), `#include` in the beginning of your program:

```
#include <stdio.h>
#include <math.h>
#include "myheader.h"
```

The first two examples tell a compiler to include declarations in the standard input output library header files. The symbols < and > inform the compiler to look for these header files in a designated location. Typically, these files are located in an `include` subdirectory under the main C directory. For the third example to work, you must first create your own header file and name it `myheader.h`. The double quotation marks indicate that this header file can be found in the directory where the source code of the current file resides. We now turn to other compiler directives.

3.6 COMPILER DIRECTIVES

Compiler directives are instructions for compilers, sometimes also called preprocessor directives. There are eleven directives in the C programming language: #if, #ifdef, #ifndef, #else, #elif, #include, #define, #undef, #line, #error, and #pragma. We discuss each directive in this section. As can be seen from the list, all directives start with a # sign.

3.6.1 Conditional Compilation Directives

The #if, #ifdef, #ifndef, #else, #elif, and #endif are conditional compilation directives. These directives are used to conditionally compile a portion of code based on an expression. For example, we can compile a portion of a program only during a debugging stage of a program development using these directives.

Directives #if and #endif are used together to selectively compile a segment of code. An expression that is either true or false follows the #if directive. If the expression is true, all instructions between the #if directive and the #endif directive are compiled for execution. Otherwise, those expressions are skipped and do not become a part of the program. For example, suppose we want to debug the code at a certain location of the program by printing out a message. The following shows how the directives are used to do just that:

```
1       #include <stdio.h>
2       #define DEBUG 1
3       void main(void)
4       {
              :
              :
m       #if DEBUG

m+1     printf("The program reached this point in the program\n");

m+2     #endif
              :
              :
n    }
```

We define symbol DEBUG to be "1" (true) on line 2 using another preprocessor directive define, which we discuss shortly. Since the statement on line m is true, the printf instruction on line m+1 will be included in the compilation process and carried out during the program execution. The printf function is one of the functions declared in the stdio.h header file that prints the message enclosed within the parentheses onto the PC screen. Also, note that we do not put the semicolon at the end of the directive statements.

The #else and #elif directives are used to give added selectivity of compiling codes. These directives are again used with the #if and the #end directives. The following example illustrates the use of these directives:

```
1    #define M68HC11 0
2    #define M68HC12 1
3    #define M8051    2
4    #define Processor 1
5    void main(void)
6    {
7        #if Processor == M68HC11
8              Instruction(s) A
9        #elif Processor == M68HC12
10             Instruction(s) B
11       #elif Processor == M8051
12             Instruction(s) C
13       #else
14             Instruction(s) D
15       endif
16   }
```

In the above example, the code is written such that it can be executed on multiple controller platforms. The directives #if, #elif, and #else are used to select one of the three processors. The statement on line 4 is used to select one of the three processors. On line 7, symbol Processor is tested against the M68HC11 (Processor value 0). Since we have selected the Processor to be the 68HC12 on line 4, the instruction(s) on line 8 is ignored and not included in the compiled code. On line 9, the Processor is again tested against the 68HC12. This time since the condition is true, the instruction(s) on line 10 is included in the compiling process. Once a true condition is met, the rest of the code is skipped until the #end directive is reached. In cases where all conditions are false, the instructions that follow the #else directive are included as default. As can be seen from this example, the four directives are used to conveniently include and exclude a segment of code for compilation to make a program flexible.

In the same train of thought, suppose you want to write a program that can run on both the 68HC11 microcontroller and the 68HC12 microcontroller. These two controllers have different memory maps that govern the memory locations of the input and output ports. To accommodate both controllers, we can take advantage of the current directives as shown in the following example:

```
1 #if (Processor == 68HC11)
2   #define PORTA *(unsigned char volatile *)(0x1000)
3 #elseif (Processor == 68HC12)
4   #define PORTA *(unsigned char volatile *)(0x0000)
5 #endif
```

Lines 1 and 3 are used to test the current controller. Obviously, you must define symbol Processor using the define directive at the beginning of the program or in a separate header file that is included as in the previous example. Lines 2 and 4 contain definitions for PORTA for two different controllers. The #endif directive on line 5 ends the instruction segment.

Two more directives work similarly: #ifdef and #ifndef. The #ifdef directive is used with the #endif directive to group a set of instructions that are compiled if a symbol is defined. Consider the following example:

```
#ifdef   OUTPUT
     instructions A
#else
     instructions B
#endif
```

If symbol OUTPUT is defined before the compiler reaches the above code lines, instructions A will be included in the compilation process. Otherwise, instructions B will be included. In the same manner, the instructions that follow #ifndef directive become a part of a compiled program if the symbol that immediately follows the #ifndef directive has not been defined. Consider this example:

```
#ifndef   OUTPUT
     instructions A
#else
     instructions B
#endif
```

If symbol OUTPUT is not defined, instructions A will be compiled; instructions B are compiled if the symbol is defined. We discuss the #define directive next.

C Preprocessor Directives   In this subsection, we describe directives for a compiler to replace a part of a program with designated values or instructions. The most frequently used is the #define directive, which as the name indicates, defines a symbol as well as a macro function. A macro function is a set of instructions with a name. The instructions in the set are replaced each time the corresponding name appears in a program.

Suppose we want to define symbol HIGH with a constant value 98. We can do so in a header file using the #define directive:

```
#define HIGH    98
```

A macro function is also defined using the #define directive. Again suppose we want to define a macro that chooses a maximum of two values. We do so as follows:

```
#define max(a,b)    (a>b ? a : b)
```

The symbol `max`, the name of a macro, and the second item, `(a > b ? a : b)`, define the macro. The definition is a short way to assign the larger of `a` or `b` as the output of the function.

We can also undefine a symbol or a macro. We can do that using the `#undef` directive. When do we use this directive? This directive is for a conscientious programmer. Once we define a symbol and we no longer use it in the rest of the program, this directive is used as follows:

```
#define VALUE    10
int number[VALUE];
#undef   VALUE
```

Symbol `VALUE` is used to declare integer array `number` with 10 elements.[4] We discuss the topic of arrays in the Arrays and Strings section. Once symbol `VALUE` is used and we no longer need it, the `#undef` is used to undefine the symbol.

We next describe the `#include` directive. As you have seen in the Header File section, this directive is used to include other predefined files in your program for two purposes: (1) to use predeclared symbols in other header files and (2) to call functions defined in other header files.

The following example shows how a standard input and output header file is included using the directive:

```
#include <stdio.h>
```

As mentioned before, the angle bracket informs the compiler to look for the header file in a designated location (usually in an `include` directory).

The purpose of the `#error` directive is mainly for debugging. One can specify an error by following the directive with an error message:

```
#error   Program made a logic error
```

The `#error` directive should be inserted within your program during a debugging process. When your program reaches this directive, indicating you have made a misjudgement in your programming logic, the error message will print to the PC screen. The `#error` directive is a useful tool to inform programmers of programming errors.

Other C Directives   We now discuss two other C directives: `#line` and `#pragma`.

The `#line` directive is used for debugging purposes. The directive assigns a line number of the instruction that follows the directive. The directive is used to specify where in the original program a particular instruction of interest appeared. The `#pragma` directive is an implementation specific command for

---

[4]This is a rather convoluted example since we could simply declare the array as `number[10]`, instead of what we showed. We include this example only for a didactic purpose.

each individual compiler. For the ICC12 compiler, we use this directive to assign the locations of data and program segments. The directive is also used to declare interrupt routines, assign data and code addresses, and change the names of text and data sections. For a complete explanation, you should refer to the manual supporting your specific compiler. We show a couple of examples on how the `#pragma` directive is used in the context of the ICC12 compiler.

The following example shows how an interrupt service routine should be declared using the directive. This instruction informs the compiler to replace the last return instruction of an interrupt service routine from `rts` to `rti`.

```
#pragma interrupt_handler TOIISR()
void TOIISR(void);
```

The above code declares the times overflow interrupt service routine, called `TOI-ISR`. As with any other function, the corresponding interrupt service routine must be defined within the program. We show a complete example using the interrupt service routine in the Compiler/Assembler Specifics section, section 3.14.

The `#pragma` directive is also used to specify the starting address of a particular segment of a code. For example, in addition to the declaration of the interrupt service routine for the timer overflow, we must also specify the location of the interrupt service routine. In the 68HC12, using the ICC12 compiler, we do so as

```
#pragma abs_address:0x0B1E
void (*Timer_Overflow_interrupt_vector[])() = {TOIISR};
#pragma end_abs_address
```

We fully discuss the 68HC12 interrupt issues in Chapter 4. Briefly, the above statements designate the start location address of the service routine (`TOIISR`) at memory location `0x0B1E` with the help of a pointer operator.

3.7 C PROGRAMMING CONSTRUCTS

Three basic programming constructs exist in the C programming language: (1) sequence, (2) loop, and (3) if-then-else. A sequence is made up of a set of instructions that are executed one after the other in a sequence. A loop is a set of instructions that are repeatedly executed for a designated number of times before moving on to other parts of the program. The if-then-else programming construct allows programmers to design software in such a way to execute different sets of instructions based on specified conditions. There are other programming C constructs such as `goto`, `switch`, and `break`, which we discuss after the presentation of the if-then-else programming constructs.

3.8 LOOPS

Three different types of loops exist in the C programming language: the `for` loop, the `while` loop, and the `do-while` loop. We begin our discussion with the `for` loop.

3.8.1 The `for` Loop

The `for` loop starts with an initialization, a condition to conclude the loop, and an update statement. Following the update statement, a `for` loop contains a body of instructions that are executed so long as the concluding condition is not met. For example, we can write a `for` loop to repeat a process 10 times as shown below.[5]

```
1    for (i=0; i<10; i++)
2    {
3      inst 1;
4      inst 2;
5      :
6      :
7      inst n;
8    }
```

The first line starts with keyword `for`, which is followed by three separate expressions appearing within parentheses. The first expression initializes the index i to be zero, the second expression is the terminating condition that directs the `for` loop to continue as long as index i is less than 10, and the third expression specifies the updating procedure where index i is updated by one each time the `for` loop is executed. The instructions that must be executed within the `for` loop are enclosed within the curly brackets (line 2 and line 8). The instructions in lines 3 through 7 are executed sequentially during each iteration of the `for` loop.

When a `for` loop is encountered, the initial condition is established, the terminating condition is tested, and the instructions (lines 3 through 7) are executed, if the terminating condition is not met. Once the instructions are performed, the updating statement (i++) is executed. The update statement is equivalent to i = i+1. This updated index is then tested again against the terminating condition. The process continues until the terminating condition is satisfied—that is, until i is greater than or equal to 10. Notice that the semicolon separates the three statements within the parentheses on line 1.

In many applications the index of a `for` loop is used within the body of the loop. The following `for` loop is used to convert a set of Celsius temperature values from −10 degrees to 40 degrees to their corresponding Fahrenheit temperature values and to display the results:

---

[5]We assume that variable i is not modified within the `for` loop.

```
1 for (k=-10; k <= 40; k++)
2 {
  /*convert Celsius temp to Fahrenheit temp */
3      Temperature = k*9/5 + 32;
4      printf("Current temperature is \%f \n", Temperature);
5 }
```

Index k was used as a parameter to calculate values for the variable Temperature.

3.8.2 The while Loop

The second type of loop to repeat a set of instructions uses the reserved word while. The while loop is similar to the for loop in executing the instructions enclosed within a pair of curly brackets, but it contains only a loop-terminating condition in the first line of the loop program segment, as shown below. The following example illustrates a while loop that performs the identical task of the temperature conversion performed by the for loop:

```
1    k = -10;
2    while (k <= 40)
3    {
4      Temperature = k*9/5 + 32;
5      k++;
6      printf("Current temperature is \%f \n", Temperature);
7    }
```

If we use the while loop, we must first initialize index k with an initial number before we start the loop. On line 2, note that the parentheses that follows the keyword while contains only the terminating condition and that we must also have a statement, such as the instruction on line 5, to update the index within the while loop. In order to carry out the same function, the for loop code was more compact than the while loop code. That is, if we know ahead of time the number of iterations we must execute for a loop, the for loop is more suitable than the while loop, even if we can implement a task with either of the two loop methods. In many applications, however, we do not know in advance the number of iterations that must be executed before a terminating condition is met. In addition, we often need an infinite loop (a loop that executes a set of instructions indefinitely), which arises in many embedded system applications. To implement an infinite loop, we use the following instruction:

```
1    while (1)
2    {
3       instructions /* perform a task */
4    }
```

In the preceding example, the terminating condition is never false; the condition to execute instructions within the curly brackets is always true. Once the program reaches the `while` statement, the instructions of the loop will be executed over and over again until a reset is initiated.

3.8.3 The `do-while` Loop

The third type of loop construct in the C programming language is the `do-while` loop, which is almost identical to the `while` loop discussed in the previous subsection. The one difference is that the terminating condition is tested after the instructions within the loop have been executed. Returning to the temperature conversion example, if we use the `do-while` loop instead of the `while` loop, we have the following programming segment:

```
1    k = -10;
2    do
3    {
        /* Converting a Fahrenheit to Celsius temp */
4    Temperature = k*9/5 + 32;
5      k++;
6      printf("Current temperature is \%f \n", Temperature);
7    }
8    while (k <= 40)
```

Note that the instructions in lines 4 through 6 are executed first before the terminating condition is tested for the first time. Since the terminating condition is tested at the end, a programmer must be careful with the terminating condition to meet application requirements.

3.9 DECISION PROCESSING

In this section we describe the `if-then-else` programming construct. When we implement algorithms using the C programming language, we often encounter occasions when a set of instructions should be executed only if a specific condition is true. We present four different ways to make and execute such decisions in this section.

3.9.1 `if`

The reserved word `if` and the condition that follows determine whether a set of instructions should be executed. The following segment of code illustrates an example.

```
1   if (input == 0x00)
2   {
3     output = 0x0F;
4   }
```

In this example, a variable named `input` is tested against a constant value zero before the decision is made to execute the instruction on line 3. Notice that the C programming language uses a delimiter, a semicolon, to indicate the end of each instruction, and we can write the code as follows without the curly brackets:[6]

```
1   if (input == 0x00)
2       output = 0x0F;
```

The decision is made based on the value returned by the test condition. If a condition is true, a 1 is returned, and a 0 is returned otherwise. Thus, for a debugging purpose, we can write

```
1   if (1)
2       output = 0x0F;
```

From our discussion, it should be clear that the test statement within the parentheses must be a logical statement. Thus, any statement that is used as a test condition must evaluate to either true (1) or false (0).

3.9.2 `if-else`

In many applications, a decision is made to select one set of instructions versus another. Such cases require the use of the `if-else` programming construct. For example, suppose we want to turn an air conditioning system on or off based on the current temperature. We implement the task using the following instruction:

```
1   if (input > 78)          /* temperature in Fahrenheit */
2      air_condition = on;
3   else
4      air_condition = off;
```

We assume that the variable `input` contains the current temperature in Fahrenheit. Our decision is based on a comparison of the current temperature with a threshold value (78 degrees). Since this decision is based on a logical statement, we can rewrite the code using the opposite logic. That is, we end up with the same results using the following instructions:

```
1   if (input <= 78)
2      air_condition = off;
3   else
4      air_condition = on;
```

---

[6]This works only if the instruction list consists of just one instruction; otherwise, {} must be used.

3.9.3 `if-else if-else`

If we have more than one condition when selecting the code to be executed, we use the `if-else if-else` programming construct, as in the following example:

```
1    if (input > 78)
2        air_condition = on;   /* turn on the air condition if hot */
3    else if (input > 58)
4        fan = on; /* turn on the fan only if warm */
5    else
6        heater = on; /* turn on the heater if cold */
```

An extension of the temperature control example, this programming segment tests the current temperature against three different temperature ranges, again in Fahrenheit: above 78 degrees, between 78 degrees and 59 degrees, and below 59 degrees, assuming that the resolution of the temperature is in integer degrees. We can translate the programming statements into words as follows: If the current temperature is above 78 degrees, the air conditioner is turned on; if the current temperature is below 79 degrees but above 58 degrees, only the fan is turned on; and if the temperature is 58 degrees or below, the heater is turned on. Note that the above code is very different from the following programming segment, which uses only `if` statements:

```
1    if (input > 78)
2        air_condition = on;
3    if (input > 58)
4        fan = on;
5    else
6        heater = on;
```

Note that we are assuming that the temperature values are integers. The difference lies in line 3 of the two segments. Without the `else if` keywords in the current example, the first `if` statement and the second `if` statements become independent of each other: the current temperature is tested against the threshold value 78 degrees to make a decision to turn on the air conditioner and the current temperature is tested to turn on the fan independently. Thus if the current temperature is, say, 80 degrees, the second implementation turns on both the air conditioner and the fan while the first implementation turns on only the air conditioner. If we want the same function using only the `if` statement, we should write the following, which is not as convenient:

```
1    if (input > 78)
2        air_condition = on;
3    if ((58 < input) && (input < 79))
4        fan = on;
5    if (input < 59)
6        heater = on;
```

We can iterate the `else if` statement for a complex decision-making process where a multiple number of conditions must be tested:

```
1    if (condition 1)
2        {instruction set 1};
3    else if (condition 2)
4        {instruction set 2};
5    else if (condition 3)
6        {instruction set 3};
     :

     :
n-1 else if (condition k)
n        {instruction set k};
```

If the number of alternatives is greater than four or five, a more convenient programming tool, `switch`, exists in C, which we discuss in the next subsection.

3.9.4 The `switch` Programming Construct

As mentioned earlier, the `switch` programming construct should be used when there are multiple alternative instructions to be executed based on a given conditional test result. In ANSI C, we can use up to 257 different alternatives for each test condition. The switch expression has the following format:

```
1    switch (expression)
2    {
3      case a:
4          statements;
5          break;
6      case b:
7          statements;
8          break;
9      case c:
10         statements;
11         break;
12         :
13         :
14     case z:
15         statements;
16         break;
17     default:
18         statements;
19   }
```

The expression on line 1 must be an integer or character value. The keyword `case` precedes a value, which is matched against one of the case values. The statements that follow a matched case segment are then executed. Note that the keyword `break` concludes each case segment, which forces the program to skip the rest of the cases to the end of the switch segment. The default case contains instructions that are executed in situations where no match occurs. Consider the following example. Suppose the variable a has a user input value ranging from 1 to 10, and we need to display different messages depending on the value in variable a.

```
1    switch (a){
2      case 1:
3       printf("Correct value %d was chosen\n", a);
4       break;
5      case 2:
6       printf("Close but try again\n");
7       break;
8      case 3:
9       printf("Value %d is two away from the answer\n", a);
10      break;
11     default:
12      printf("Your chosen value is way off\n");
13     }
```

The current value in variable a is compared with three different values: 1, 2, or 3. The desired message is displayed only if variable a contains value 1. Otherwise, an error message is displayed. If variable a does not match any of the three possibilities, the default message on line 12 is displayed. Note that we did not include the break statement on line 13. In fact, you do not need to have the default case in a switch programming segment. If a default case is absent and no case is matched, none of the instructions are executed.

Suppose we omit the break statement on line 4. What would happen? After displaying the message on line 3, the program will continue to execute statements until a break statement or the end of the switch programming segment is reached. In our case, with line 4 omitted, the program will display messages in line 3 and line 6 before ending the segment. One may omit one or more break statements on purpose if the resulting program flow matches requirements.

3.10 ARRAYS AND STRINGS

An array is a set of elements that are of the same type. There are many different types of arrays—from floating-point number arrays, double number arrays, and character arrays to short integer arrays, long integer arrays, character arrays, unsigned integer arrays, and structure arrays, to name a few. Arrays are declared with a fixed size number of elements. For example, suppose we want to create an array of 10 integers, named list. We declare the array as

```
int  list[10];
```

Note that we use square brackets to enclose the number specifying the size of the array. Each element is designated by an index number. In the 68HC12, the declaration reserves 20 bytes of memory for 10 integer values. Note also that in C, the index starts with zero. Thus the first array element is `list[0]` and the last element is `list[9]`, not `list[10]`. As a matter of fact, if we try to access `list[10]`, we will get an error. We can also declare an array with initial values. An example is shown below.

```
int list[10] = {1,2,3,4,5,6,7,8,9,10};
```

When initializing an array with a character string, we enclose the message within double quotes:

```
char  message[6] = "Smile";
```

The first element `message[0]` contains the character `S` and the last element, `message[5]`, contains a null character, `\0`, to indicate the end of the character string.

A higher dimensional array can also be constructed. A two-dimensional array of numbers, a matrix, is often used in engineering applications. To declare a two-dimensional array of integers, we use the following format:

```
int  matrix[2][3];
```

The declaration creates a 2×3 matrix whose indices for the row and the column vectors again start with zeros. To assign initial values of the two-dimensional array, we use the following syntax:

```
int matrix[2][3] = {{1,2,3},{4,5,6}};
```

We can access each element using proper indices. For example, `matrix[1][2]` refers to the value 6. If the value stays the same throughout a program execution, it is preferable to declare the array as a constant integer array:

```
const  int  matrix[2][3] = {{1,2,3},{4,5,6}};
```

Arrays are useful since we can store and manipulate a group of data as a single unit using indices. Now suppose we want to add one to each element of an integer array, called `odd`, made up of 100 odd number elements, creating an array of even numbers. We can do so easily using a `for` loop with an index variable. The following segment of code shows how this is done:

```
for (i=0; i<100; i++)
    odd[i] = odd[i] + 1;
```

Careful readers may have noticed that the numerical array examples we used are all integer arrays. The reason for our emphasis on integer arrays in this section is that for 68HC12 microcontroller applications, use of floating-point and double-number manipulation is discouraged due to the complex and lengthy instructions involved in performing such tasks. We can also create an array of structures, which we discuss in Section 3.12.

3.11 POINTERS

Pointers are defined as variables that hold addresses of other variables. For example, a pointer for a character variable holds the address of the character variable. To declare a variable as a pointer, we use the exact same expression with the exception of appending an * operator in front of the variable as shown in the example below.

```
int *ptr;
```

The variable `ptr` is defined to hold the starting address of an integer variable. A pointer can hold the address of any variable such as a character, an array of characters, an integer, an array of integers, a floating number, or a double number. As a matter of fact, having the capability to point to different parts of arrays is one of the reasons for the popularity of the C programming language within the engineering community.

Since a pointer holds an address of a variable, we must be careful that a pointer indeed does contain a memory address. One of the common mistakes of C programming in the use of pointers is to assign a nonaddress to a pointer, which is not hard to do. Consider the following example:

```
1 void main(void)
2 {
3   char *ptr;
4   static char message[] = "What a wonderful day!";
5   ptr = message;
6   printf("%s\n", ptr);
7 }
```

The variable `ptr` was first declared as a pointer for a character, dictating variable `ptr` to hold a 16-bit address. In line 4, a character string message is defined using the static `char` declaration. In the example above, the message character string will take up 22 bytes: 21 bytes for the message and 1 byte for the null character indicating the end of the string. The expression in line 5 assigns the address of the first element of the string, `W`, to character pointer variable `ptr`. The last `printf` expression starts displaying characters at the address designated by the `ptr` variable and continues until a null character is reached.

We could also use the following expression in place of the `ptr` = `message`.

```
ptr = &message[0];
```

Note that the ampersand symbol indicates the address of the first element of the character array (`W`). We could also write the above example program as follows:

```
void main(void)
    {
    static char message[] = "What a wonderful day!";
```

```
  int i;
  for (i=0; i<21; i++)
    putchar(message[i]);
}
```

Note that the index i starts from 0 and ends at 20, totaling 21 characters as before. In this example, we are not using a pointer at all. We are simply displaying one character at a time. This type of implementation will work if we know the size of all the arrays in advance, which is usually not the case. We could also have written the program in the following way:

```
void main(void)
 {
  char *ptr;
  static char message[] = "What a wonderful day!";
  ptr = message;
  while (*ptr != '\0')
    {
     putchar(*ptr);
     ptr++;
    }
 }
```

The pointer ptr is used to print one character at a time while changing the pointer to the next character until a null character is reached.

A convenient use of the pointer comes when we need to deal with input and output ports of the 68HC12. Consider the following example:

```
#define PORTA *(volatile unsigned char *)0x1000
```

The symbol PORTA is declared to hold the contents of address 0x1000 by casting the memory location of PORTA as a pointer for a volatile unsigned character variable. Once the port is declared as shown, the following instructions configure PORTA for input using the DDRA register and then reads the logic values present at PORTA.

```
DDRA = 0x00;   /* Configure PORTA for input */
              /* Read a value from PORTA into variable new_value */
new_value = PORTA;
```

One of the important applications of pointers in C is found in dynamic memory allocation tasks. Dynamic allocation is different from other memory assignments we have seen so far in that memory locations are allocated during programming execution. Typically, the allocated memory comes from a RAM memory region not currently used called the heap. Dynamic memory allocations should be implemented for programs that want to make maximum use of RAM space when the size of the RAM is not known in advance. In embedded systems, engineers usually know the size of RAM when they design their programs; we complete our discussion by presenting this topic.

Two primary functions in dynamic memory allocation are `malloc()` and `free()`.[7] The `malloc()` function is used to allocate memory space while the `free()` function releases used memory space. The format used for the functions are

```
void *malloc(sizeof(variable));
void free(void *ptr);
```

The `malloc()` function returns a pointer that can be assigned to any type of pointer. If the requested memory is available, a pointer to the first memory location of the requested memory region is returned. If the request fails, the function returns a null. Remember to always check whether the return pointer is a null before using the pointer.

The following code segment shows how the pointer is used in the `malloc()` and the `free()` functions to allocate 100 bytes of memory, use the space, and release it.

```
        :
        :
i     char *ptr;
i+1   if(!(ptr = malloc(100*sizeof(char))))
i+2       {
              :
              :
j             free(ptr);
j+1       }
        :
        :
```

In line `i`, a character pointer is declared. We check whether the returned pointer of the `malloc()` function is null on line `i+1`. If it is safe to use the memory locations, the instructions within the parentheses (lines `i+2` and `j+1`) are executed. Notice that the last instruction within the parentheses is the `free()` function that releases the allocated memory space.

3.12 STRUCTURES

In C, we can combine multiple types of data and create an object called a structure. A structure can have a single element or many elements where each

---

[7]ANSI C has other dynamic allocation functions: `calloc()`, `mlalloc()`, `clalloc()`, `realloc()`, and `cfree()`. We limit our coverage to `malloc()` and `free()` since they perform the major functions of dynamic memory allocation tasks, while others provide additional flexibility.

element is defined by one type of C variable. For example, we can define a structure called a `car` with variables such as the number of `doors`, `color` of the car, `maker` of the car, the number of cylinders for the engine, and the `year` of the model. We define the structure car as

```
struct car{
    int doors;
    char color[10];
    char *maker;
    int  num_cyl;
    int  year;
    }
```

Once the structure is defined, we can use it to declare variables as we do with any other type of variables. In a sense, we are creating another type of variable that can have multiple subelements:

```
struct car your_car, my_car, his_car;
```

In the above declaration, `your_car`, `my_car`, and `his_car` all have the five different subelements. You can access each element of the structure by using the dot operator (.). For example, if we want to assign 4 as the number of doors for `your_car`, we do so by writing

```
your_car.doors = 4;
```

Similarly, we can assign `"yellow"` as the color of the car by writing

```
your_car.color = strcpy(your_car.color, "yellow");
```

where `strcpy` is a function declared in the `stdio.h file`. If a structure is passed on to a function, you must use the indirect component section (`"->"`) operator instead of the dot operator. Note that we are passing the pointer of the structure, not the structure itself. Suppose we have a function that takes `your_car` as its argument, and you assign the number of doors for `your_car` in the function as illustrated in the following description. Note that we now use the `"->"` operator instead of the dot operator.

```
void assign_doornumber(struct car *some_car);
:

:
assign_doornumber(&your_car);
:

:
void assign_doornumber(struct car *some_car)
{
  some_car->doors = 4;
  return 0;
}
```

We now discuss how to declare an array of structures. Suppose we have created the following structure called `circuit_board`:

```
struct  circuit_board{
        int transistor;    /* number of transistors on board */
        int bus;           /* number of bus lines on board */
        int serial_port;   /* number of serial ports on board */
        int parallel_port  /* number of parallel ports on board */
        }
```

We can create an array of theses structures as follows:

```
    struct  circuit_board   newboard[5];
```

Once we have declared the structure, we can access each element of a board by using the dot operator as in the following code statement:

```
    newboard[2].transistor = 100
```

The expression assigns `100` as the number of transistors for circuit board number 3 (recall the index starts with zero).

We thus complete our brief review of the C programming language. In the next section we discuss the procedure of starting with a C source file, compiling, downloading, and running the executable file on a target embedded controller.

3.13 PROGRAMMING AND DEBUGGING PROCEDURES

In this section we discuss the procedures and tools involved in programming and debugging. We first describe the process to program and generate an executable file.

3.13.1 Programming Procedure

Programming seems easy when a program needs to perform only a simple task. Most seasoned programmers know, however, the task quickly becomes complex in a moderate or large project that does not utilize the proper tools. For that reason, it is crucial that we start correctly even if the task at hand is simple. We are advocating that you use a systematic approach to writing programs. Once you acquire the skills of systematic programming, regardless of the language being used, they can be directly applied to any project you encounter. Since this is not a computer science text on programming, our coverage will be terse.

The first step in writing a program is to clearly understand the purpose of the program and to devise a process to fulfill the requirements. You can begin by going through the process described in Chapter 2. Creating a detailed activity diagram, structure chart, and equivalent pseudocode are a must. The table will allow you to see the task as a whole as well as the block level tasks that must be performed. Once an activity diagram flowchart is constructed, the next task is to break down the overall task into a set of subtasks. Each subtask should be completed in the form of a small program or a function. These submodules then should be integrated one at a time until the entire subtask modules are integrated together. Of course, each submodule, corresponding to a subtask, must be tested and debugged before it can be incorporated into an overall program. As you will quickly see, the programming, testing, and debugging processes are closely intertwined. You should never write an entire program and then start the debugging process. The correct approach is to write, test, and debug each submodule of the program before combining them together. The combining process should also follow the same approach: incorporate one module at a time in the overall program while testing and debugging, if necessary, the intermediate functionality of the program as a result of the insertion of a module.

Let's now look at the process involved in generating an executable file, given a C source file. Our illustration will use the software package ICC12 version 6.12B from ImageCraft. If you are using another software compiler, note that what we present in this section is not parochial but that the procedure and techniques discussed are readily transferable directly to other software packages.

Figure 3.1 shows a screen capture of the ICC12 software when the program is first opened. The top-left window is designated as an editor window—the place where you actually write C programs. The smaller window on the right is a project window where all files used to create a project are shown. The long window at the bottom of the screen informs a user about status and errors during the compilation as well as the assembly, linking, and downloading of a program. Any editor can be used to write C programs, but software packages such as the ICC12 help programmers to easily write, compile, assemble, link, and download programs for the 68HC12. All the steps shown in this subsection are executed simply by clicking designated menu buttons shown at the top of the programming environment. Figure 3.2 shows the same environment with actual code in the editor window and the corresponding compilation results in the status window.

Once your program is written, the program must first go through a C preprocessor, a part of the compiler that searches for expressions starting with the # sign. Recall these expressions include header files, conditional insert or omit instructions, and error-handling statements. The compiler then continues with a C parser and a code generator to create an equivalent assembly language program. As shown in Figure 3.3, given the original C program and necessary header files, the output of the compiler is an assembly language program with an s or an asm extension. Such a compiler is sometimes called a *cross compiler* due to its ability to generate assembly programs for a hardware platform that differs

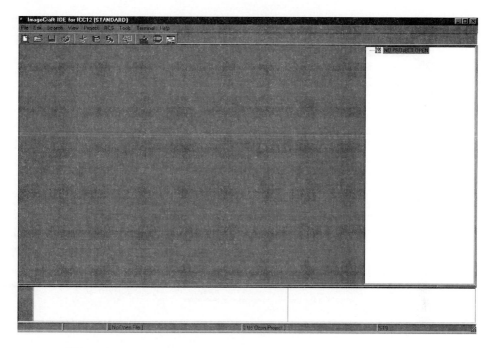

Figure 3.1 Screen capture of the ICC12 development environment opening page. (Courtesy of ImageCraft, Palo Alto, CA.)

from the hardware where the original C programs are generated. For example, your C programs are written on a PC while the converted assembly programs are for the 68HC12. Note that a source file can be written in either the assembly language or in the C language. A source file is the one you write to perform a desired task.

In many time critical applications, parts of the overall program are written in a particular assembly programming language. These language programs can then be combined with the one generated by the compiler to generate object code with an extension o, as shown in Figure 3.3.

In many applications, source files are made of multiple files. In other cases, some of the required source files have been compiled in advance and do not need to be compiled again. In such cases, we need to link object files—files that have been compiled already and are in the object code format—with files that are compiled and assembled. This job is done by a linker program. Thus the responsibility of the linker is to combine all object files generated, such as library functions and object files from other C programs, to create a single machine code. The output of the linker are files with the `map`, `lst`, and `s19` extensions. The `map` file specifies the locations of data and code in terms of the absolute memory address. The `lst` file includes all instructions and their corresponding locations in the

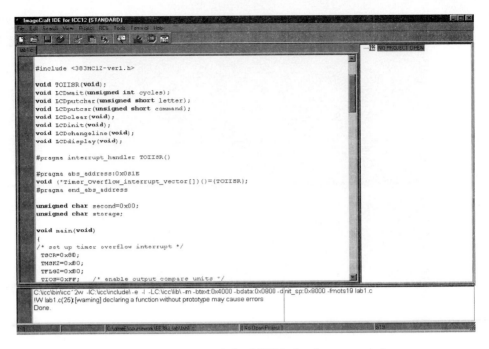

Figure 3.2 Screen capture of the ICC12 development environment. The upper-left window contains a program and the bottom window shows that the compilation process of the code was successful. (Courtesy of ImageCraft, Palo Alto, CA.)

memory. Finally, the s19 file is the Motorola 68HC12 machine code to be loaded to and executed on the controller. As a result, we have a single machine code file that is created by compiling/assembling a source file, or a set of source files, and linking it with files that have already been converted into object code format.

The process of building a small piece at a time is called *modular programming*. Due to number of files that are involved in creating a final executable machine code, a typical software package uses a project approach to combine the multiple files that are necessary. Putting all such files together is a tricky business that takes some time and experience. The project approach eases the difficulty of this task. Many software vendors now offer products such as the ICC12 that take care of the intricacy of combining multiple source files and object files.

The ICC12 software allows a programmer to easily create projects. Once a project is created with multiple source files (*C* and assembly), its project-builder software manages the relationships between all source files and their dependency on header files. To facilitate the construction of a project, the ICC12 software contains an aforementioned project window where a programmer can collect all

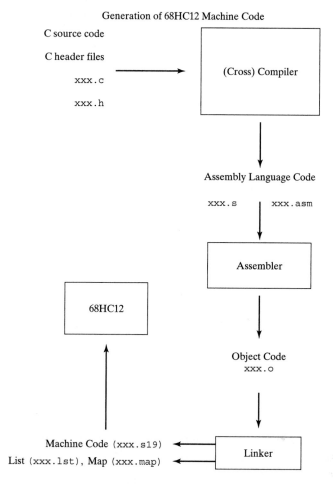

Figure 3.3   Flow of program generation.

source files and a set of menu commands to preprocess, compile, assemble, and link files to generate one resulting machine code. For details on the specific use of the ICC12 Project Builder, we refer the reader to the ICC12 software manual.

Finally, a loader is responsible for downloading the machine code into the memory of an embedded system. Typically, a commercial software system contains a cross-compiler, an assembler, and a loader in a single package. ICC12 from ImageCraft and CodeWarrior from Motorola are two such examples. We show a complete example starting from source code and ending with a machine program in Section 3.14, which discusses the compiler/assembler specifics. In summary, a proper programming procedure goes through a number of steps to generate a suitable machine program for the 68HC12, as shown in Figure 3.4.

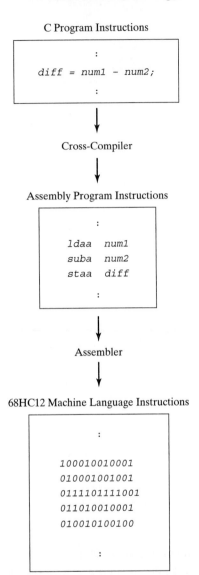

Figure 3.4 The process used to generate 68HC12 machine instructions.

3.13.2 Background Debug Mode

Unlike its predecessor, the 68HC11 microcontroller, the 68HC12 allows a programmer to debug a program while it is running. In the 68HC11, we monitored program execution with the help of a monitor program residing on the controller, such as the BUFFALO program. Using such a monitor program, we read the

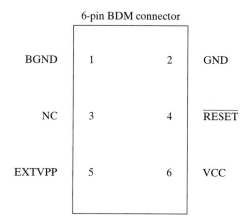

Figure 3.5   Hardware pin outs for the BDM port.

contents of memory locations and the CPU registers, but it was done using a software interrupt, which halted program execution each time we wanted to view the contents. Furthermore, it was impossible to trace a program, executing a program one instruction at a time, that involved hardware interrupts. The 68HC12 solved the problem by introducing the background debug mode (BDM), which either independently or in conjunction with the CPU performs instruction debug. Two separate sets of instructions, firmware and hardware BDM commands, exist in the 68HC12.

Motorola designed a 6-pin standard interface to the BDM in order to encourage commercial vendors to develop software and hardware to run on the BDM. The standard interface is shown in Figure 3.5.

The debug commands, either firmware or hardware, are delivered to the 68HC12 using a single connector, and the 68HC12 in return provides data using the same path. The hardware commands that can be performed as a program are executed by the 68HC12 CPU by the BDM. A list of available hardware commands is shown in Tables 3.3 and 3.4.

These commands can be executed without the CPU being placed in the background mode. This is done by using the free CPU clock cycles to perform each command. If the BDM cannot find a free CPU clock cycle within 128 clock cycles, the BDM goes ahead and steals a clock cycle from the CPU. These commands can only be sent every 150 clock cycles. As can be seen from Table 3.5, we can read and write 16-bit data using the hardware commands. Notice that we cannot read just 8-bit data. The firmware BDM commands are located in ROM. The list showing all firmware commands is shown in Table 3.5.

To use firmware commands, we must first enable the BDM by setting the ENBDM bit in the BDM status register (0xFF01) and activate the BDM by the

Table 3.3 BDM Commands Implemented in Hardware

	Command	Opcode(Hex)	Data
1	BACKGROUND	90	None
2	READ_BD_BYTE	E4	16-bit address, 16-bit data out
3	STATUS	E4	FF01, 0000 0000 (out)
4			FF01, 1000 0000 (out)
5			FF01, 1100 0000 (out)
6	READ_BD_WORD	EC	16-bit address, 16-bit data out
7	READ_BYTE	E0	16-bit address, 16-bit data out
8	READ_WORD	E8	16-bit address, 16-bit data out
9	WRITE_BD_BYTE	C4	16-bit address, 16-bit data in
10	ENABLE_FIRMWARE	C4	FF01, 1xxx xxxx(in)
11	WRITE_BD_WORD	CC	16-bit address, 16-bit data in
12	WRITE_BYTE	C0	16-bit address, 16-bit data in
13	WRITE_WORD	C8	16-bit address, 16-bit data in

Register: STATUS - BDM Status Register   Address: $FF01

7	6	5	4	3	2	1	0
ENBDM	BDMACT	ENTAG	SDV	TRACE	0	0	0
0	0	0	0	0	0	0	0

Reset:

Figure 3.6   BDM status register.

hardware BACKGROUND command. The BDM status register contents are shown in Figure 3.6.

The ENBDM bit must be written using the single wire interface (BKGD) pin using the ENABLE_FIRMWARE command, and the BDM is activated by sending the BACKGROUND hardware command using the same interface. Note that if the 68HC12B32 board is configured to run in a single-chip mode, the ENBDM bit is enabled at reset. To execute the firmware commands, the BDM temporarily controls the internal buses of the CPU. If possible, the execution of a firmware command does not affect the CPU by using only a single clock cycle; however, if multiple clock cycles are necessary, the CPU is halted until the firmware command is completed.

Table 3.4 BDM Commands Description

Num	Description
1	Enter background mode (if firmware enabled)
2	Read from memory with BDM in map (may steal cycles if external access) data for odd address on low byte, data for even address on high byte
3	RED_BD_BYTE 0xFF01 Running user code (BGND instruction is not allowed)
4	READ_BD_BYTE 0xFF01 BGND instruction is allowed
5	READ_BD_BYTE 0xFF01 Background mode active (waiting for single wire serial command)
6	Read from memory with BDM in map (may steal cycles if external access)must be aligned access
7	Read from memory with BDM out of map (may steal cycles if external excess) data for odd address on low byte, data for even address on high byte
8	Read from memory with BDM out of map (may steal cycles if external access) must be aligned access
9	Write to memory with BDM in map (may steal cycles if external access) data for odd address on low byte, data for even address on high byte
10	Write byte 0xFF01, set the ENBDM bit. This allows execution of commands that are implemented in firmware. Typically, read STATUS, OR in the MSB, write the result back to STATUS
11	Write to memory with BDM in map (may steal cycles if external access) must be aligned access
12	Write to memory with BDM out of map (may steal cycles if external access) data for odd address on low byte, data for even address on high byte
13	Write to memory with BDM out of map (may steal cycles if external access) must be aligned access

There are five registers allocated for the BDM operations, as shown in Table 3.6. The BDM instruction register contains the opcode of either hardware or firmware commands. The BDM status register shown in Figure 3.6 displays the BDM status with the BDM enable bit, the active flag, the tagging enable flag, shifter data valid flag, and the trace flag. The ENBDM flag shows whether or not the BDM is enabled, where logic 1 indicates that the system is enabled while logic 0 shows that system is disabled. The BDMACT bit represents whether the BDM is active (logic 1) or not active (logic 0), the ENTAG flag shows whether or not the instruction tagging is enabled (logic 1) or disabled (logic 0), the Shift Data Valid (SDV) bit is used by the firmware commands to indicate data is valid (logic 1) or not valid (logic 0), and the TRACE flag displays whether tracing instruction is enabled (logic 1) or disabled (logic 0).

Table 3.5 BDM Firmware Commands

Command	Opcode	Data	Description
GO	08	none	Resume normal processing
TRACE1	10	none	Execute one user instruction then return to BDM
TAGGO	18	none	Enable tagging then resume normal processing
WRITE_NEXT	42	16-bit data in	$X = X + 2$; Write next word at $0, X$
WRITE_PC	43	16-bit data in	Write program counter
WRITE_D	44	16-bit data in	Write D accumulator
WRITE_X	45	16-bit data in	Write X index register
WRITE_Y	46	16-bit data in	Write Y index register
WRITE_SP	47	16-data in	Write stack pointer
READ_NEXT	62	16-bit data out	$X = X + 2$; Read next word at $0, X$
READ_PC	63	16-bit data out	Read program counter
READ_D	64	16-bit data out	Read D accumulator
READ_X	65	16-bit data out	Read X index register
READ_Y	66	16-bit data out	Read Y index register
READ_SP	67	16-bit data out	Read stack pointer

Table 3.6 BDM Register Mapping

Address	Register
0xFF00	BDM instruction register
0xFF01	BDM status register
0xFF02-0xFF03	BDM shift register
0xFF04-0xFF05	BDM address register
0xFF06	BDM CCR register

The shift register is used to send and receive data between the BDM and a debugger, the address register stores the BDM commands before being executed, and the BDM condition code register (CCR) stores the contents of the CPU CCR during the BDM command execution.

The tagging mechanism of the BDM allows a programmer to tag an instruction such that when the tagged instruction reaches the head of the instruction queue, the CPU automatically activates the background debug mode. This mechanism provides an added tool to debug a segment of code that may contain a problem. The TAGGO firmware command is used to tag an instruction using both the $\overline{LSTRB}$ pin and the **BKGD** pin. Based on the logic shown on the two pins, instructions are tagged. We now discuss a commercial product (a software/hardware pair) that incorporates the commands discussed in this section for a user-friendly interface between a PC and the 68HC12.

3.13.3 P&E BDM Hardware and Software

In this section, we demonstrate one of the commercial hardware/software products developed to interface a PC with the 68HC12 controller via the BDM port. Other products work similarly. Our coverage of the product focuses on the debugging feature of the software package, called the WinIDE Development Environment. Within the environment, a user can invoke the in-circuit debugger (ICD12Z) to communicate with the 68HC12. By using a set of debugging commands, a user can detect and fix problems either while programs are running or as the user traces the execution of programs. The list of commands that users have at their disposal are shown in Tables 3.7 and 3.8.

The actual hardware setup for the use of the software along with the 68HC12 is shown in Figure 3.7. Figure 3.8 shows a screen capture of the P&E ICD12Z window interfacing with the 68HC12B32 board. As shown in this figure, a user has access to the CPU register contents (top left corner window), declared values (upper middle window), memory contents (upper right corner window), source code windows (middle windows), and a status window (bottom window).

You can also perform the same debugging task with two separate 68HC12B32 boards. We show how this can be done using the M68EVB912B32 boards. Figure 3.9 shows the hardware setup necessary for such implementation. At least one of the two boards must contain the Motorola D-Bug12 monitor program. You should connect your PC to the one with the D-Bug12 program and use this board as the pod. To do so, you must set the W3 and W4 jumpers (consult the M68EVB912B32 Evaluation Board User's Manual) to 0 and 1, respectively. Connect a BDM cable from the pod to the remaining M68EVB912B32 board, the target board shown in the figure. You must supply power to the target. Note that the pod receives its power from the same power supply via the BDM cable. Now you can send any D-Bug12 commands, including BDM commands, to the target board from your PC via the pod board.

3.13.4 Emulators

Another form of program development uses an emulator, a software package that mimics the hardware operations of a controller. Companies such as Noral and

Table 3.7   List 1 of P&E Debug Commands

Command	Description
A or ACC	Set accumulator A
B	Set accumulator B
BR	Set break point
CAPTURE	Open a capture file named `filename`
CCR	Set condition code register
CLEARSYMBOL	Clear `Away` symbols
CODE	Show disassembled code in the code window
COUNTER	Add or subtract a location from the internal counter table
DASM	Disassemble instructions
DUMP	Dump Memory to the status window
EXIT	Return to DOS
G or GO	Begin program execution
GONEXT	Go from the current PC until the next instruction is reached
GOTILROM	Execute fast single steps until the address is reached
HELP	Display help information
IX	Set X index register
LF or LOGFILE	Open/close log file
LOADALL	Execute a `LOAD` and a `LOADMAP` command
LOADV	Execute the `LOAD` and `VERIFY` commands
LOADV_BIN	Execute the `LOAD_BIN` command and verify
MACRO	Execute script file
MACROSTART	Start recording script file
MD or MDx	Display code in memory window `x`
N	Set/clear `N` bit
QUIET	Turn off (on) refresh of memory based windows
R	Start register disassembler
REG	Display CPU registers to status Window
RTVAR	Displays a specified address and its contents in the variable window
S	Set/clear `S` bit

Table 3.7 *Continued*

Command	Description
SERIAL	Set up parameters for serial port
SERIALON	Turn the communication window into a dumb terminal
SNAPSHOT	Take a snapshot (black and white) of the current screen
SS	Performs one step of source level code
STEP or ST or T	Single step (Trace)
STEPTIL	Repeatedly single step to a given address
T [n]	Same as ST
TRACE	Similar to the GO command in non-real-time
V	Set/clear V bit
VERIFY	Compare the contents of program memory with an S-record file
WHEREIS	Give the value for the given symbol
Z	Set/clear Z bit

Table 3.8 List 2 of P&E Debug Commands

Command	Description
ASM [add]	Assemble instructions to memory
BELL	Sound bell
BF	Block fill
C	Set/Clear C bit
CAPTUREOFF	Turn off capturing and close the current capture file
CLEARMAP	Clear away map file
COLORS	Change debugger colors
COUNT	Set breakpoint at second address
D	Set double accumulator D
DUMP_TRACE	Dump the current trace buffer to the debug window
EVAL	Evaluate a numerical term
FILL	Block bill (same as BF command)
GOEXIT	Similar to GO command and debugger is terminated

Table 3.8 *Continued*

Command	Description
GOUNTIL	Execute program until address
H	Set/clear H bit
I	Set/clear I bit
IY	Set Y index register
LOAD	Load s19 file
LOADMAP	Load debug map
LOAD_BIN	Load a binary file of bytes starting at address add
LPT1, LPT2, LPT3	Specify the PC compatible parallel port
MACROEND	Stop recording script file
MACS	Bring up a window with a list of macros
MM or MEM	Modify memory
NOBR	Clear all break points
QUIT	Exit the program
REM	Add comments to script file
RESET	Reset emulation MCU
RUN	Begin program execution
SCRIPT	Execute script file
SERIALOFF	Turn off serial port use during GO
SHOWTRACE	Allows the user to view trace buffer
SOURCEPATH	Specifies filename
STATUS	Display CPU registers to status window
STEPFOR	Step forever
SYMBOL	Add the given label to a temporary symbol table
TIME	Shows the amount of real execution time
UPLOAD_SREC	Uploads the memory locations
VAR	Displays a specified address and its contents in the variables window
VERSION	Display the version number of the ICD software
X	Set/clear X bit

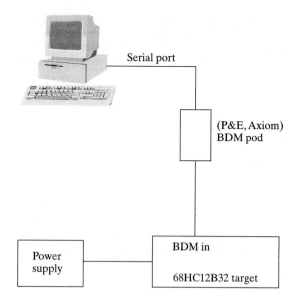

Figure 3.7   Hardware setup to use the BDM with a P&E pod and a cable.

Hitex Development Tools produce and sell 68HC12 emulators. Such emulators are valuable for users whose budgets may not allow them to purchase the actual hardware. Emulators, however, should not be used to test time-critical tasks since emulators run on a PC and its clock speed is generally different than the clock speed of the 68HC12 microcontroller.[8]

3.13.5 Logic Analyzers

A logic analyzer is a display tool that is used to capture the activities of digital systems, similar to an oscilloscope for analog system measurement. Figure 3.10 shows a typical logic analyzer made by Hewlett-Packard (now Agilent). It can measure the logic states of signals and capture time periods for events. A set of probes is used to connect the analyzer to hardware pins to monitor and measure logic states. Typically, a logic analyzer can display results in both a graphical form or a text form for convenience. It can also store the change of signals over a period of time, allowing a user to study the history of logic states for debugging purposes. Logic analyzers can help debug mistakes in program coding when the controller system is interacting with external devices. For example, when an external memory chip is added to a microcontroller, the data bus, address bus, and

---

[8]Recently, companies have been offering emulators that provide accurate accounting of clock speed.

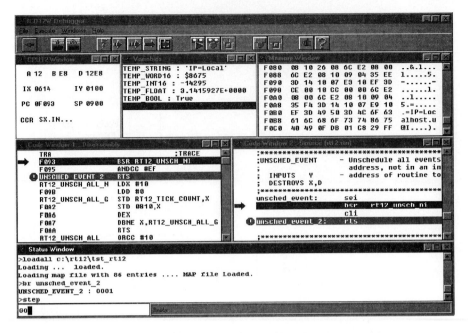

Figure 3.8   Screen capture of the P&E ICD12Z software. (Courtesy of P&E Microcomputer Systems).

control bus signals must all be monitored to test the correctness of the hardware and software setup. A logic analyzer is typically used in such situations.

3.14 COMPILER/ASSEMBLER SPECIFICS

In this section, we provide an example using the ICC12 software to illustrate the compile/assembly process described in Section 3.13.1. Our presentation of the software is not complete, and we point readers to the software manual for complete coverage. Our presentation focuses on generating executable code for the 68HC12 starting with a C program.

Our example program turns on and off a set of LED lights connected to port A of the 68HC12B32 board with the help of the timer overflow system of the 68HC12 microcontroller. The hardware setup for the task is shown in Figure 3.11.

```
/********************************************/
/*                                          */
/* Title: Sample.c                          */
/* Description: This program turns LED       */
/*   lights on and off every 1 sec           */
```

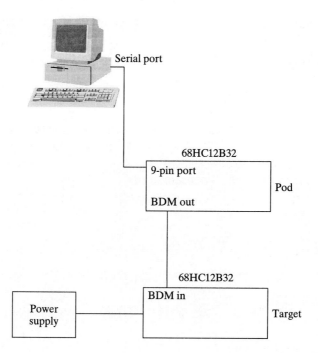

Figure 3.9   Hardware setup to use the BDM with two 68HC12B32 boards.

```
       /*   using the 68HC12B32 microcontroller. */
       /*   The header file contains definitions */
       /*   for all ports and special registers. */
       /*   The controller should be configured  */
       /*   to run in single chip mode.          */
       /*                                         */
       /* Date: May 15, 2004                      */
       /* Author: Daniel Pack and Steve Barrett   */
       /*                                         */
       /*****************************************/
1      #include <68HC12B32.h>
2      /*****************************************/
3      void TOIISR(void);
4      /*****************************************/
5      #pragma interrupt_handler TOIISR() /* declare the timer
6                           overflow interrupt service routine */
7      #pragma abs_address:0x0B1E        /* assigns the ISR
                                            starting  address */
8      void (* Timer_Overflow_interrupt_vector[])()={TOIISR}
9      #pragma end_abs_address
10     unsigned char second=0x00;
11     void main (void)
```

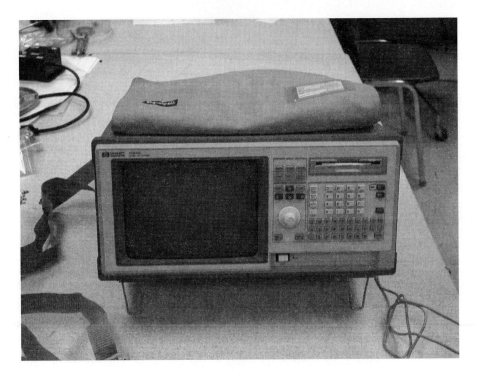

Figure 3.10   A Hewlett-Packard (Agilent) logic analyzer.

```
12  {
13     TSCR=0x80;           /* turn on the timer */
14     TMSK2=0x80;          /* enable the timer overflow
                                           interrupt  */
15     TFLG2=0x80;          /* clear TOIF flag */
16     DDRA=0xFF;           /* program port H to be output */
17     CLI();               /* turn on the interrupt system */
18     while(1){}           /* an infinite loop */
19     EXIT();
20  }
21
22  void TOIISR(void)       /* interrupt service routine */
23  {
24     TFLG2=0x80;          /* clears the TOIF flag */
25     second += 1;         /* increment the second counter */
26     if (second == 122)
27       {
28         PORTA = PORTA;   /* convert logic on portA and */
29         second = 0x00;   /* reset counter */
30       }
31  }
```

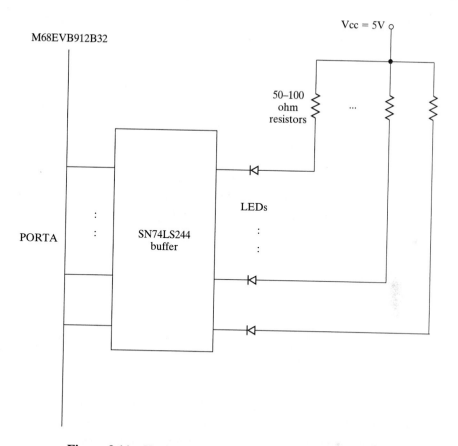

Figure 3.11   Hardware setup for the LED control example.

Note that the program has header information at the beginning, which includes the name of the program, description, date, and authors. The header file 68HC12B32.h contains register definitions and macro definitions using compiler preprocessor commands. The line numbers in the left margin are not part of the program. We provided them to facilitate our discussion of the program.

The preprocessor instruction on line 1 commands the compiler to include a header file, which we show after we explain the program. Line 3 contains the function prototype for the timer overflow interrupt service routine. The statements in lines 7 through 9 declare memory location 0x0B1E as a pointer to hold the starting address of the interrupt service routine. On line 10, we declare variable second, used as a counter, as a global variable. Lines 11 through 20 make up the main program where all the initializations are performed on lines 13 through 16 and the interrupt system is turned on using the macro function on line 17. Line 18 contains an infinite loop that waits for the interrupt service routine to turn on and off the LEDs connected to port A. The macro function on line 19, a software interrupt instruction, is also declared in the header file. On line 22, the timer overflow interrupt service routine starts. The timer overflow flag is cleared on line 24. Note that the counter on line 25 is incremented every 8.19 milliseconds: time for the 68HC12 TCNT counter to count from 0x0000 to 0xFFFF using the 8 MHz clock. We execute the two instructions on lines 28 and 29 only when the counter indicates that a second has passed. Notice that the instruction on line 28 complements the logic states of port A, and the instruction on line 29 resets the counter to be zero.

We now take a close look at the statements that are pertinent from the header file. We do not show the entire header file but rather a segment that contains appropriate register and macro function definitions used in the program.

```
1 #define _IO_BASE 0
2 #define _P(off) *(unsigned char volatile*)(_IO_BASE + off)
3 #define TSCR   _P(0x86)
4 #define TMSK2 _P(0x8D)
5 #define TFLG2 _P(0x8F)
6 #define DDRA   _P(0x02)
7 #define PORTA _P(0x00)
8 #define CLI() asm("cli\n")
9 #define EXIT() asm("swi\n")
```

The two instructions on lines 1 and 2 are used to declare a macro function _P with an argument off. Note that a pointer is used to cast a memory location as a pointer. The statements on lines 3 through 7 define control register symbols to hold the contents of the memory locations by type casting physical memory locations as pointers first then assigning the contents of the pointers as control register symbols. Lines 8 and 9 contain the macro definitions for CLI() and EXIT(). Note that the expressions on the right for both statements replace the macro with assembly language program instructions cli and swi, respectively. The symbol asm simply commands a compiler to place enclosed assembly instruction immediately into the compiled code.

The following assembly language program was created using the ICC12 software when the above LED program along with the header file was used as the source code.

```
1     .module interrupt.c
2     .area memory(abs)
3     .org 0xb1e
4_Timer_Overflow_interrupt_vector::
5     .word _TOIISR
6     .area data
7 _second::
8     .blkb 1
```

```
9     .area idata
10 .byte 0
11 .area data
12    .area text _main::
13 ; #include <383HC12-ver1.h>
14 ; void TOIISR(void);
15 ; #pragma interrupt_handler TOIISR() ;
16 ; #pragma abs_address:0x0B1E
17 ; void (*Timer_Overflow_interrupt_vector[])()={TOIISR};
18 ; #pragma end_abs_address ;
19 ; unsigned char second=0x00;
20 ;
21 ;void main(void)
22 ; {
23 ;   TSCR=0x80;
24     ldab #128
25     stab 0x86
26 ; TMSK2=0x80;
27     ldab #128
28     stab 0x8d
29 ; TFLG2=0x80;
30     ldab #128
31 stab 0x8f
32 ;   DDRA=0xFF;
33 ldab #255
34     stab 0x2
35 ; CLI();
36 cli
37 L3: L4:
38 bra L3
39 X0:
40 ; while(1){};
41 ; EXIT();
42 swi
43 ; }L2:
44 .dbline 0
45 ; func end
46 rts
47 _TOIISR::
48 ; void TOIISR(void)
49 ; {
50 ;   TFLG2=0x80;
51 ldab #128
52 stab 0x8f
53 ;   second += 1;
54 ldab _second
55 clra
56 addd #1
```

```
57 stab _second
58 ; if(second == 122)
59 ldab _second
60 cmpb #122
61    bne L7
62 ; {
63 ;    PORTA =~PORTA;
64 ; vol
65 ldab 0
66 clra
67 coma
68 comb
69 stab 0
70 ; second = 0X00;
71    clr _second
72 ; }
73 L7:
74 ; }
75 L6:
76 .dbline 0
77 ; func end
78 rti
```

The cross-compiler generates assembly instructions and assembly directives. Assembly directives are instructions for the assembler and do not cause the corresponding assembler to generate object code. In the ICC12 software, these directives start with a dot (.). The first line of the assembly code is a directive that indicates the program name. The directives .area and .org are generated to specify the timer overflow vector address and are generated as a result of the #pragma abs_address: 0x0B1E segment of the source program. The ICC12 compiler attaches an under-bar at the beginning of a variable declared in the source code as shown in the expressions on lines 4, 7, and 47. The two colons at the end of lines 4 and 7 indicate that the symbols can be accessed from all programs: the current functions and any external functions. The .word directive on line 5 is used to allocate word length memory (2 bytes) to store the starting address of the interrupt service routine (TOIISR). The expressions in lines 6 through 11 are used to allocate memory space for the global variable second.

Starting at line 12, the assembly instructions corresponding to the actual program start. Notice that all C program instructions are shown but have been commented out by the use of the semicolon on the first column of each C instruction (lines 13 through 23). The first assembly instruction starts on line 24 where the 68HC12 timer system is turned on by loading 0x80 to accumulator B and, on line 25, the contents of the accumulator is stored to the TSCR register (memory location 0x86). Note that the definition in the header file is used to identify the actual location of the TSCR register. The assembly instructions in lines 26 through 36 are the rest of the initialization process before an infinite loop with label L3 starts on line 37. The expressions on lines 37 through 40 make up the infinite loop while the expressions in lines 41 through 46 complete the main function. Again note that the macros CLI() and EXIT() in the original source code were replaced with the corresponding assembly code cli and swi in the current program with the help of the header file definitions.

Line 47 starts the timer overflow interrupt service routine. Note that each C instruction is converted to corresponding instructions in the assembly code. The service routine ends on line 78; note that the rti instruction ends the service routine to restore CPU registers and a return address from the stack.

The next step in the process of generating machine code is to assemble the above code and produce its corresponding object code (interrupt.o). The following object code is generated by the ICC12 software.

```
XH
H 4 areas 4 global symbols
M interrupt.c

A text size 3D flags 0

S _main Def0000
S _TOIISR Def001A
A memory size B20 flags C

S _Timer_Overflow_interrupt_vector Def0B1E
A data size 1 flags 0

S _second Def0000
A idata size 1 flags 0

T 0B 1E 00 1A
R 00 00 00 01 00 02 00 00
T 00 00 00
R 00 00 00 03

T 00 00 C6 80 7B 00 86 C6 80 7B 00 8D C6 80 7B
R 00 00 00 00

T 00 0D 00 8F C6 FF 7B 00 02 10 EF 20 FE 3F 3D C6
R 00 00 00 00

T 00 1B 80 7B 00 8F F6 00 00 87 C3 00 01 7B 00 00

R 00 00 00 00 00 07 00 02 00 0E 00 02

T 00 29 F6 00 00 C1 7A 26 0C F6 00 00 87 41 51 7B
```

```
R 00 00 00 00 00 03 00 02

T 00 37 00 00 79 00 00 0B

R 00 00 00 00 00 05 00 02
```

Note that the top half of the object file contains instructions for the linker while the bottom half of the file makes up the actual code in hex number representation. The final step is performed by the linker, and it produces three different files: interrupt.1st, interrupt.map, and interrupt.s19.

The interrupt.1st file is a list file that contains assembly language instructions, the corresponding machine instructions, and their physical locations in memory as shown in the following file:

```
                    .module interrupt.c
                     .area memory(abs)
                     .org 0xb1e
    0B1E            _Timer_Overflow_interrupt_vector::
    0B1E   8044      .word _TOIISR
                     .area data
    0800            _second::
    0800             .blkb 1
                     .area idata
--- 0000 00          .byte 0
                     .area data
                    .area text
    802A            _main::
                    ; #include <383HC12-ver1.h>
                    ; void TOIISR(void);
                    ; #pragma interrupt_handler TOIISR()
                    ;
                    ; #pragma abs_address:0x0B1E
                    ; void (*Timer_Overflow_interrupt_vector[]) ()={TOIISR};
                    ; #pragma end_abs_address
                    ;
                    ; unsigned char second=0x00;
                    ;
                    ; void main(void)
                    ; {
                    ; TSCR=0x80;
    802A   C680      ldab #128
    802C   7B0086   stab 0x86
                    ;   TMSK2=0x80;
    802F   C680      ldab #128
    8031   7B008D   stab 0x8d
                    ;   TFLG2=0x80;
    8034   C680      ldab #128
    8036   7B008F   stab 0x8f
                    ;   DDRA=0xFF;
    8039   C6FF      ldab #255
```

```
803B   7B0002       stab 0x2
                 ;  CLI();
803E   10EF          cli


8040                  L3:
8040                   L4:
8040   20FE             bra L3
8042                  X0:
                 ;  while(1){};
                 ;  EXIT();
8042   3F             swi


                 ;  }
8043                L2:
8043               .dbline 0 ; func end
8043   3D            rts
8044               _TOIISR::
                 ;
                 ;  void TOIISR(void)
                 ;  {
                 ;  TFLG2=0x80;
8044   C680          ldab #128
8046   7B008F        stab 0x8f
                 ;  second += 1;
8049   F60800        ldab _second
804C   87            clra
804D   C30001        addd #1
8050   7B0800        stab _second
                 ;  if(second == 122)
8053   F60800        ldab _second
8056   C17A          cmpb #122
8058   260C          bne L7
                 ;  {
                 ;    PORTA =~PORTA;
                 ; vol
805A   F60000        ldab 0
805D   87            clra
805E   41            coma
805F   51            comb
8060   7B0000        stab 0
                 ;    second = 0X00;
8063   790800        clr _second
                 ;  }
8066                L7:
                 ;  }
8066                L6:
8066               .dbline 0 ; func end
8066   0B            rti
```

The list file is extremely useful during the debugging process to identify any mismatching problems resulted from the programmer's intention and the actual program contents on the 68HC12 memory. The map file for the `sample.c` program is shown next.

```
Area                           Addr   Size   Decimal Bytes
(Attributes)
------------------------       ----   ----   ------- ----- ------
                     text      8000   006B =    107. bytes (rel,con)


        Addr   Global Symbol
        -----  ------------------------------
        8000   __start
        8028   _exit
        802A   _main
        8044   _TOIISR
        8067   __HC12Setup
        806B   __text_end

Area                           Addr   Size   Decimal Bytes
(Attributes)
------------------------       ----   ----   ------- ----- ---------
                     idata     806B   0001 =      1. bytes (rel,con)


        Addr   Global Symbol
        -----  ----------------------------
        806B   __idata_start
        806C   __idata_end

Area                           Addr   Size   Decimal Bytes
(Attributes)
------------------------       ----   ----   ------- ----- ---------
                     data      0800   0001 =      1. bytes (rel,con)


        Addr   Global Symbol
        -----  ----------------------------
        0800   _second
        0800   __data_start
        0801   __data_end

Area                           Addr   Size   Decimal Bytes
(Attributes)
------------------------       ----   ----   ------- ----- ---------
                     memory    0000   0B20 =   2848. bytes (abs,ovr)


        Addr   Global Symbol
        -----  ----------------------------
        0B1E   _Timer_Overflow_interrupt_vector

Files Linked       [ module(s) ]
```

```
C:\icc \lib \crt12.o  [  crt12.s ] interrupt.o        [ interrup ]
<library>                 [  setup.c ]

User Global Definitions

init_sp = 0xc00

User Base Address Definitions

text = 0x8000 data = 0x800
```

As the name indicates, the map file provides a programmer with an overview of the locations for the data, instructions, and text of a program. Finally, the actual program that is downloaded to the 68HC12 memory `interrupt.s19` code is shown below.

```
S10E8000CF0C0016806787CE08018EAD
S110800B080127056A000820F6CE806BCD21
S111801808008E806C2706180A307020F516BA
S1078026802A20FE8A
S1050B1E80440D
S104806B0010
S110802AC6807B0086C6807B008DC6807BEF
S1118037008FC6FF7B000210EF20FE3F3DC607
S1118045807B008FF6080087C300017B0800D3
S1118053F60800C17A260CF600008741517B26
S109806100007908000B89
S10780677900163D45
S90380007C
```

The file follows the Motorola s19 file format, which contains information on type, data length, address, data, and error checksum. For a full description of the Motorola s19 file format, readers are directed to the user's manual for the M68EVB912B32 Evaluation Board.

In summary, we described the entire process of generating a machine code file using a sample program in C. The process described follows the flow of progression shown in Figure 3.4.

3.15 SUMMARY

In this chapter, we presented a short version of essential C and related programming techniques. In particular, we introduced the process of writing C programs in the context of an embedded system using the 68HC812B32 board. In Chapter 4 we will present an in-depth coverage of 68HC12 programming techniques using functional parts of the controller. Our treatment of the C language is brief, and interested readers are referred to books dedicated entirely to the C language, such as the two books suggested below in the further reading section. We also discussed the procedure to convert a C code into an executable program through a compiling, assembling, and linking process. The off-line debugging process is accomplished using a source C code, its corresponding assembly program, and a list program that contains memory addresses and the memory contents. The D-BUG12 monitor program, provided by Motorola, residing on the ROM of the 68HC812B32 board, offers a set of useful tools to debug a program. The real-time program debugging is done using the background debug mode mechanism of the 68HC12.

3.16 FURTHER READING

Kernighan, B. W., and D. M. Ritchie. *The C Programming Language*, 2nd ed. Upper Saddle River, NJ: Prentice Hall, 1988.

Schildt, H. *C: The Complete Reference*. Osborne McGraw-Hill.

Harbison, Samuel P. III, and Guy Steele Jr. *C A Reference Manual*, 5th ed. Upper Saddle River, NJ: Prentice Hall, 2002.

ImageCraft C Compiler and Development Environment for Motorola HC12, ImageCraft Creations Inc., Palo Alto, CA, 2002.

3.17 PROBLEMS

Fundamental

1. What is the function of a semicolon in a C expression?
2. What is the number of bytes for an integer variable on the 68HC12?
3. What is the number of bytes allocated for an integer pointer variable on the 68HC12?
4. In what type of memory do static variables declared in a C program reside on the 68HC12B32?
5. What are two meanings of the symbol * in the C programming language?
6. Describe the steps required to process a C program to an executable program.

Advanced

1. A global variable is desirable, since all functions can access it. Then, why don't good programmers declare all variables as global variables, making the entire programming process simple?
2. Create a structure variable for customers of a telephone company. The structure must contain the name, customer number, street address, city address, state address, and zip code.

3. When a C source code and an assembly source program are combined together and viewed as one assembly language program using the ICC12 software, some variables start with an underbar and some do not, even if variables in both the C and the assembly programs do not start with any underbar. What is happening?

4. You have been given the declaration `static int array[10]`. What does `&array` represent?

5. Explain macros. Where do we use them in C?

Challenging

1. Given the hardware setup shown in Figure 3.12, write a C program that turns the LEDs on and off every 5 seconds.

2. Using pointers and structures, write a function that prints a telephone customer's information described in Advanced Problem 2.

3. Write a program to display integers from 0 to 9, one at a time, on a seven-segment display (common cathode) repeatedly. Each number should be displayed for 100 milliseconds each. The hardware setup is shown in Figure 3.12 where a 74ALS244 buffer is used to supply sufficient current to light up each LED (light-emitting diode).

   A seven-segment display is a common display unit used extensively in engineering applications. The display is made up of a set of eight LEDs (seven numerical segments, one decimal point) as shown in Figure 3.13. The particular seven-segment display has a common cathode.

   By applying 5 V to the anode end and connecting a ground to the cathode end, you can light up the corresponding LED. To control the current through each LED, a current limiting resistor should be connected in series with the LED as shown in Figure 3.12. Given the 50 to 100 ohm range resistor and the voltage drop across the diode, you can compute the current easily using Ohm's law. To turn each LED on or off on the seven-segment display, you must send appropriate logic states to

Table 3.9   Hex Values Needed to Light Up Hexadecimal Digits

Hex Digit	Hex Number	Hex Digit	Hex Number
0	0x3F	1	0x06
2	0x5B	3	0x4F
4	0x66	5	0x6D
6	0x7D	7	0x07
8	0x7F	9	0x6F
A	0x77	B	0x7F
C	0x39	D	0x3F
E	0x79	F	0x71

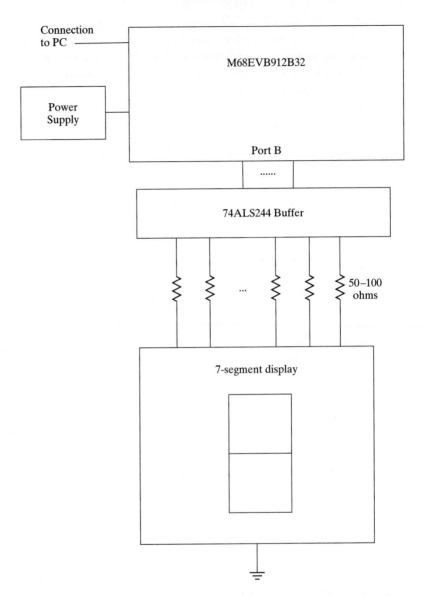

Figure 3.12 Hardware setup for the laboratory exercise using the M68HCEVB912B32 board.

port B. For example, to turn on the f LED only, shown in Figure 3.13, you must send 0x20 to port B. Table 3.9 shows the hex value representation of logic levels you must send to port B to display various numerical digits, assuming that pins 6, 5, 4, 3, 2, 1, 0 of the port are connected to LEDs g, f, e, d, c, b, and a, respectively.

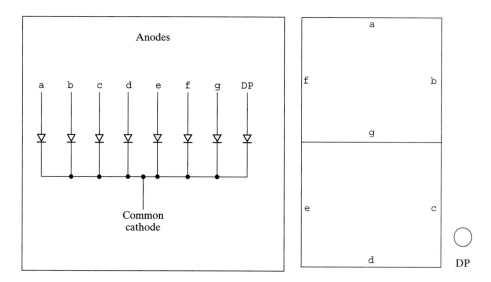

Figure 3.13   A common cathode seven-segment display.

Complete the following:

(a) Provide a structure chart, an activity diagram, and pseudocode for the program.

(b) Write a function that receives a number as a parameter and displays it on the seven-segment display using port B.

(c) Write a function that performs a 100 msec time delay.

(d) Write a main function that calls on the display function with numerical values and the time delay loop within an infinite loop.

4

68HC12/HCS12 System Description and Programming

Objectives: After reading this chapter, you should be able to

- Summarize and describe the hardware features of the 68HC12 microcontroller and its systems
- Describe the different operating modes of the 68HC12
- Describe the memory components and technologies employed within the 68HC12 "B32" variant
- Explain the need for a microcontroller interrupt system
- List the steps accomplished by the 68HC12 in servicing an interrupt
- Describe the operational procedures of the 68HC12 systems configured with interrupt and reset features
- Describe the operation of the 68HC12 Clock Module
- Illustrate the Standard Timer Module (TIM), Input Capture, Output Compare, Pulse Accumulator, and Real-Time Interrupt systems and how to program them
- Describe in detail the features of the Enhanced Capture Timer (MC68 HC12BE32, HCS12)

- Define terms related to serial communications
- Program and use the Serial Communication Interface (SCI) system of the 68HC12
- Program the Serial Communication Interface (SCI) system to meet a given specification
- Describe the Serial Peripheral Interface (SPI) system of the 68HC12
- Illustrate and apply key operations associated with an analog-to-digital (ATD) conversion process such as sampling frequency, quantizing, resolution, and encoding
- Calculate different ATD parameters for a given scenario
- Describe the ATD conversion system used aboard the 68HC12
- Program the 68HC12 to accomplish ATD conversions
- Describe the enhanced features of the HCS12 ATD system
- Program and design using the Pulse Width Modulation (PWM) features of the 68HC12 "B32" configuration

As you might have gathered from this long list of objectives, this is a particularly lengthy chapter. We will describe here in detail the hardware systems aboard the MC68HC912B32 or "B32" variant and the MC9S12DP256 or "DP256." The systems aboard the 68HC12 and HCS12 are quite similar and therefore will be discussed together. Certain systems specific to the HCS12 will be clearly identified. Our approach will be to provide the necessary fundamental knowledge to understand the hardware features of the system, the registers associated with the system, and then detailed programming examples. It is important that you fully understand how to use a specific system aboard the 68HC12 prior to combining the systems in different applications. What you should take away from this chapter is a fundamental understanding of the 68HC12 and HCS12 systems and how they may be employed in different applications. If you are already familiar with the 68HC12 functional hardware systems, you may want to skip this chapter. However, we want to point out that a thorough review of the 68HC12 systems will prove beneficial for the discussions in the remaining chapters of the book. This chapter will also include programming examples to help you get 68HC12 systems up and operating on the B32 evaluation board.

4.1 THE 68HC12 HARDWARE SYSTEM

Figure 4.1 provides a detailed block diagram of the Motorola MC68HC912B32 or "B32." (We provided this figure in Chapter 1; we provide it again for convenience.) As noted earlier, the 68HC12 is a 16-bit microcontroller. It is available in several different variants including the 68HC812A4 (or A4) and the

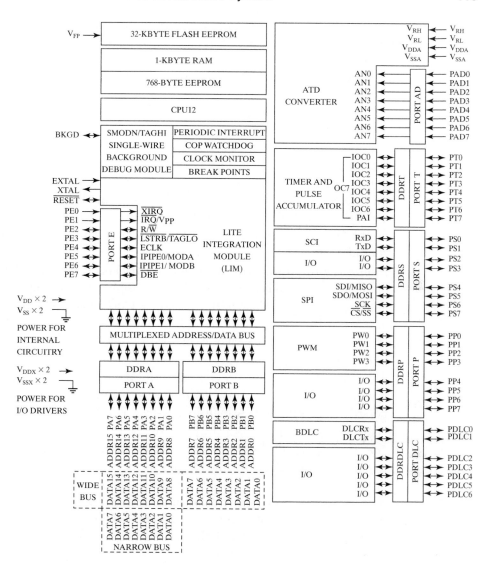

Figure 4.1 A block diagram of the MC68HC912B32. (Copyright of Motorola. Used by permission.)

68HC912B32 (or B32). All of these variants consist of a series of modules or systems connected by an intermodule bus called the lite integration module (LIM). The primary differences between the 68HC12 variants is the memory, port, and communication capability. Throughout this chapter we base our hardware discussion on the B32 variant, which we have chosen for its many and varied features. As you will see later in this chapter, it is also available in an easy-to-use evaluation board (EVB). We want to emphasize that our coverage of the B32 controller applies directly to other 68HC12 and HCS12 variants with minor differences.

The following features are available in the 68HC912B32:

- *Low power operation*: The 68HC12 is manufactured with complementary metal oxide semiconductor (CMOS) technology, which is known for its low power consumption characteristics. Therefore, the 68HC12 is ideal for remote, battery-operated applications. However, the power consumption of CMOS is directly related to the frequency of processor operations. Therefore, you should operate the processor at the lowest practical fre- quency for a specific application. We can also power-up different systems on the 68HC12 when needed and then power down to minimize power consumption.

- *High-speed 16-bit processing unit*: A 16-bit data path allows a wider range of allowable operands and 2-byte operation (op) codes as compared to an 8-bit microprocessor. The 68HC12 may be clocked at a frequency of up to 8 MHz. The time base for the B32 is normally provided by a 16 MHz crystal. The crystal frequency is divided by two to provide the 8 MHz time base.

- *1024-byte (1K) random access memory(RAM)*: RAM is a volatile mem- ory (no power, no memory) used during program execution to tem- porarily store variables. A built-in 1 K-byte RAM is adequate for many applications.

- *768-byte electrically erasable programmable read-only memory (EEP- ROM)*: This type of nonvolatile (retains memory under power loss) mem- ory is useful for storing constants for a program. For example, this would be a useful place to store combinations for an electronic security lock or to store fault counters for a system. EEPROM allows a value to be written to memory, updated during the course of program execution, and subsequently read from memory.

- *32-K byte flash EEPROM*: This type of nonvolatile memory is used to store complete, tested and debugged programs. Since the B32 is equipped with a 32 Kbyte flash memory, it has the capability to store fairly large programs. As we work through examples, you will get a good feel for how much program you can place within a memory of this size. Flash memory also allows for In System Programming (ISP) capability. The ISP feature allows a processor to be reprogrammed with a new or an updated program while it remains resident within its circuit. Normally the

D-Bug12 monitor program is resident within the flash memory. There-fore, prior to downloading your program into Flash memory, it must be erased, thereby losing the monitor program. In Section 7.8 we discuss how to accomplish these tasks using the P & E Microcomputer, Incor-porated CABLE12 Background Debug Mode (BDM) Interface cable for the CPU12.

- *Multiplexed address and data buses (B32)*: Microcontrollers have a limited number of external pins. In some microcontrollers a portion of the address bus and data bus are time division multiplexed for efficient use of the pins. What is time division multiplexing? Time division multiplexing uses the same set of pins for distinctly different functions during predesignated time slots. The pins alternate between providing address and data information. External latches are required to de-interleave the multiplexed information. The 68HC12 B32 provides multiplexed address and data lines that allow for expanded (external) memory configurations. Carefully examine PORT A and PORT B in Figure 4.1 and note the time-division multiplexed address and data pins.

- *8-channel, 16-bit timer with a programmable prescaler with each channel configurable as an input or output channel*: The timer system aboard the 68HC12 is equipped with eight different channels that can be configured to function as either an input signal analysis (input capture) channel or an output signal generation (output compare) channel. This timing system provides the 68HC12 with the capability to precisely measure the char-acteristics of an incoming signal or to generate precision digital output signals. These channels can all be configured as either output or input, or some combination of both output and input channels.

- *16-bit pulse accumulator*: The pulse accumulator is used to count exter-nal events. For example, in Chapter 7 we examine a motor speed control system. The motor is equipped with an optical encoder that outputs 60 pulses per motor revolution. If motor revolutions are counted for a spe-cific length of time, the motor's speed in revolutions per minute (RPM) is easily calculated.

- *Real-time interrupt circuit*: A real-time interrupt capability allows the mi-crocontroller to temporarily suspend normal operations at specified inter-vals to perform another operation. This feature can be used to "remind" the processor to perform a regular event such as checking the battery voltage level every 15 minutes. As we shall see in Chapter 8, this is a key feature of a real-time operating system.

- *Serial communication interface (SCI) and serial peripheral interface (SPI)*: The 68HC12 is equipped with a powerful and flexible serial communications system. This means the 68HC12 can communicate with other devices using a built-in communication channel. The primary difference between the SCI and SPI systems is the complexity of the communications interface and the speed of data transmission. In general, the SPI provides for faster data transmission at the expense of a slightly more complicated interface. Aside from communications, the SPI system may also be used to extend the features of the 68HC12. For example, the 68HC12 is *not* equipped with a digital-to-analog conversion (DAC) system. The 68HC12 can be easily equipped with a multichannel DAC system by connecting it to the SPI system. The SPI is labeled as a synchronous system since the processor provides a clock signal to the peripheral devices. On the other hand, the SCI system is an asynchronous system since it uses start and stop bits around each transmitted data byte to maintain synchronization with external components.

- *Eight-channel, 8-bit analog-to-digital converters (ATD)*: A microcontroller is used extensively to monitor and analyze the external environment. Naturally occurring phenomena are analog in nature. For example, pressure and temperature vary continuously. These analog phenomena need to be converted to a digital representation for processing by an embedded controller. The ATD system allows the 68HC12 to simultaneously monitor eight different analog signals and convert them to unsigned binary representations. The ATD system aboard the B32 EVB can be configured for either 8-bit or 10-bit operation. The extra two bits of resolution increases the sensitivity from approximately 19.53 mV to 4.88 mV.

- *Computer operating properly (COP) watchdog timer*: When an embedded microcontroller based system is fielded, it is essential that it continues to operate correctly. In the event of an error, the processor should have the capability to recover. The COP watchdog timer is one method that allows a processor to recover from being "stuck." This timer must be continually reset during normal program execution. Should the COP watchdog timer expire, a COP reset will be generated. To reset the timer on a regular basis the arm/reset COP timer register (COPRST) must sequentially receive a $55 followed by an $AA. Intervening instructions may be sent between the commands; however, they must be sent close enough together to prevent the COP watchdog timer timeout during normal program execution. Multiple reset sequences of $55 and $AA pairs may be strategically placed throughout key portions of a program. Should the program incorrectly get "stuck," the COPRST will not receive its required reset sequence of $55 and $AA. Hence, the controller will experience a COP reset. The reset might then clear the fault that originally caused the "stuck" condition. In Chapter 5 we discuss sources of noise that could cause an embedded control system to get "stuck" in an undesired location. In Chapter 6 we investigate additional defensive programming techniques to prevent a program from getting stuck.

* *Pulse width modulation (PWM)*: PWM is a method to output a digital signal of varying duty cycle. This technique is frequently used to control the speed of a direct current motor or to activate a servo motor. The B32 standard timer module (TIM) can be used to generate PWM signals. However, the B32 has a built-in PWM system. It can generate four independent 8-bit PWM waveforms, two independent 16-bit PWM waveforms, or a combination of both. For example, the servo motors that control the steering in a radio-controlled car require a PWM signal to render a turn. That is, the servo motor must receive a digital control signal at a constant frequency; however, the motor will cause a left or right turn if the duty cycle of the control signal is adjusted appropriately. The duty cycle is defined as the ratio of the "on time" of the signal to the total signal period. The B32 PWM system provides an easy-to-use, easy-to-update PWM system. Figure 4.2 illustrates the PWM concept.

* *Byte data link communication (BDLC)*: The BDLC module provides a SAE J1850 Class B Data Communications Network Interface for serial data communications within automobile applications.

* *Motorola Scalable Controller Area Network (msCAN12)*: This system implements the CAN 2.0 A/B communication protocol. This system is not available on the M68HC912B32 EVB. However, the CAN system is available in other HC12 and HCS12 variants. This system is discussed in detail in Chapter 9.

We conclude this section with an example application.

Example

A 68HC12-based motor speed control system is illustrated in Figure 4.3. The keypad is used to input the desired motor RPM. The 68HC12 converts this keypad input to a PWM modulated signal for the motor. The motor's speed is monitored via the optical encoder. Rather than employing constant monitoring, the motor's speed is checked on a periodic basis. The PWM signal is adjusted to maintain the motor at a constant speed. The motor's speed is displayed on the liquid crystal display.

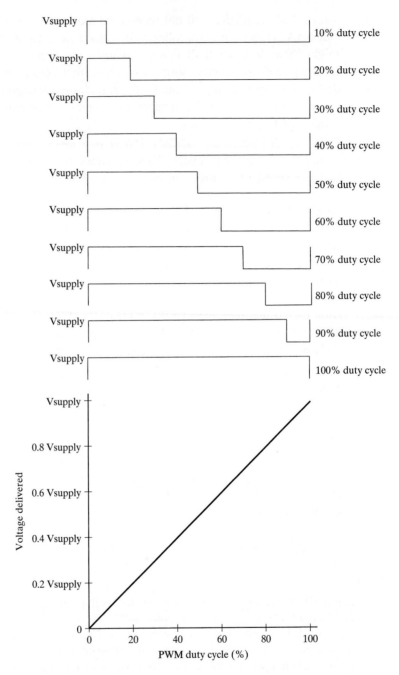

Figure 4.2   The pulse width modulation concept. PWM may be used to vary the average voltage to a load. As the PWM duty cycle is increased, the average voltage delivered to a load is also increased in a linear fashion.

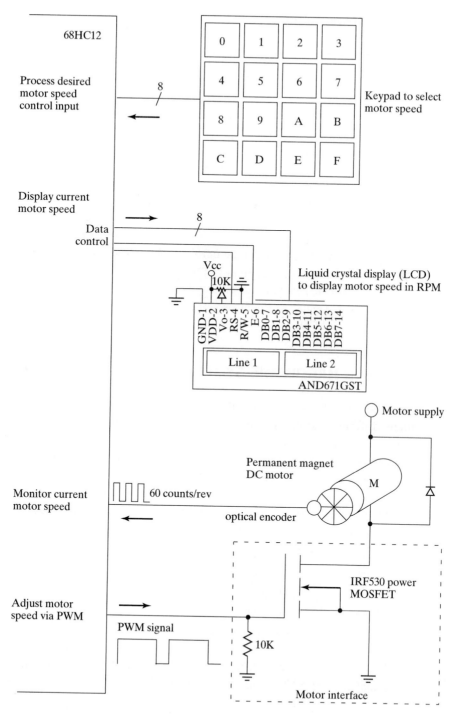

Figure 4.3 A 68HC12-based motor speed control system.

Practice Questions

1. **Question:** Based on what you have learned in this section, what 68HC12 systems are required to implement this application?

   Answer: The following 68HC12 systems are required to implement the system:

   - A parallel port is required to process inputs from the keypad.
   - The PWM system is required to generate PWM signals for the motor. If the 68HC12 variant you are using is not equipped with a PWM system (such as the A4), the PWM signal may be generated with the timer system output compare.
   - Some interface electronics as shown in Figure 4.3 are required between the 68HC12 processor and the motor.
   - The output from the optical encoder is provided to the pulse accumulator (PA) system aboard the 68HC12 for feedback control.
   - The real-time interrupt (RTI) system is used to periodically check the PA count. This information may be used to calculate motor speed.
   - A parallel port with several additional control signals is required to drive the LCD.

4.2 THE HCS12 HARDWARE SYSTEM

Like the 68HC12 family, the HCS12 family consists of a line of products with many different features and systems. The different variants have a 5 VDC operating voltage and operate with up to a 25 MHz clock speed. Notice the large memory (up to 12K RAM and 512K flash) complement on this family of products. All variants in the HCS12 family are equipped with the following:

- Memory system consisting of ROM, RAM, byte-addressable EEPROM, and flash memory components
- Timer system equipped with an 8 channel, 16 bit timer
- Multiple digital input/output pins
- Serial communications capability
- Analog-to-digital (ATD) system
- Pulse width modulation system

A block diagram of the MC9S12DP256B processor is provided in Figure 4.4. Note that this HCS12 variant has similar systems to the 68HC12. As you can see in the diagram, this variant is equipped with two eight-channel analog-to-digital systems, five CAN channels, an enhanced capture timer (ECT) system,

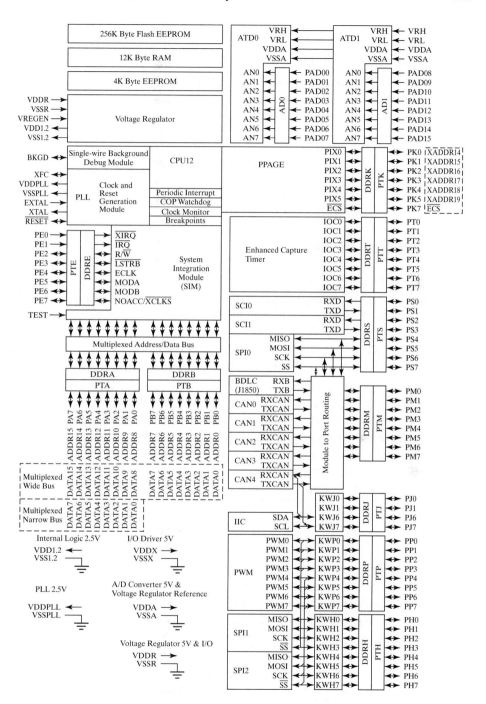

Figure 4.4   A block diagram of the MC9S12DP256B. (Copyright of Motorola. Used by permission.)

and a memory paging system that allows more than 64 Kbytes of memory to be addressed. The most noticeable feature of the DP256 is the 256 Kbytes of flash EEPROM. Additional information on the HCS12 specific systems (ECT and ATD) are provided later in this chapter.

With this brief overview of the 68HC12/HCS12 systems complete, we now delve into each system in much greater detail. We provide tutorial information where needed, followed by a hardware system description and a description of system registers. We provide programming examples using a single controller system in this chapter. Once we are comfortable with the operation of the individual systems, we combine them to solve a variety of application problems in Chapter 7, which discusses embedded controller systems.

4.3 MODES OF OPERATION

The 68HC12 has eight operating modes divided into normal operating modes and special operating modes. In normal operating modes some registers and bits are protected against accidental changes. Special operating modes are commonly used in factory testing and factory system development. Therefore, we do not operate the 68HC12 in a special operating mode.

Each normal mode of operation has an associated memory map and external bus configuration. A specific operating mode of the 68HC12 is determined by the logic states of the external BKGD, MODB, and MODA pins during a processor reset. After reset, the processor will examine the configuration of these pins to determine its operating mode. Figure 4.5 summarizes each operating mode and the corresponding logic states on those pins at reset. The Port A and Port B columns describe the function of each port in a specific configuration. G.P. I/O

BKGD MODB MODA	Mode	Port A	Port B
0 0 0	Special single chip mode	G.P. I/O	G.P. I/O
0 0 1	Special expanded narrow mode	ADDR[15:8] DATA[7:0]	ADDR[7:0]
0 1 0	Special peripheral	ADDR DATA	ADDR DATA
0 1 1	Special expanded wide	ADDR DATA	ADDR DATA
1 0 0	Normal single chip mode	G.P. I/O	G.P. I/O
1 0 1	Normal expanded narrow	ADDR[15:8] DATA[7:0]	ADDR[7:0]
1 1 0	Reserved (forced to peripheral)	—	—
1 1 1	Normal expanded wide	ADDR DATA	ADDR DATA

Figure 4.5   Mode selection.

indicates that the ports are used for general purpose digital input/output pins. In the expanded wide modes, Ports A and B contain the time division multiplexed 16-bit address and 16-bit data buses. During a specific time interval, the 16-bit bus contains address information while during a different time interval the 16-bit bus contains data information. The 68HC12 alternates between providing address and data on these ports. This concept provides for an efficient use of the limited number of external processor pins. In the narrow modes, the controller has a 16-bit address bus and an 8-bit data bus. Port A provides the time division multiplexed upper address lines (ADDR[15:8]) and the 8-bit data bus (DATA[7:0]). Port B in the narrow modes provide the lower address lines (ADDR[7:0]).

4.3.1 Normal Operating Modes

In most applications, you will use the 68HC12 in one of three normal operating modes available for use: (1) normal single chip mode, (2) normal expanded narrow mode, and (3) normal expanded wide mode. A description of each normal mode will follow shortly. In two of the normal modes, a 16-bit data bus and a 16-bit address bus are used to communicate with external devices. In these modes, Ports A and B normally used for input and output of signals must be sacrificed.

Normal Single-Chip Mode (BKGD: 1, MODB: 0, MODA: 0)
In normal single-chip mode, applications do not require any external address and data buses. The 68HC12 operates as a stand-alone, self-contained device. That is, all program and data resources are contained on-chip. External Ports A and B normally associated with address and data buses can be used for general-purpose input/output functions.

Normal Expanded Wide Mode (BKGD: 1, MODB: 1, MODA: 1)   In normal expanded wide mode of operation, the 16-bit expanded data bus is present. The 16-bit external address and data buses use Ports A and B. The high address bits (ADDR[15:8]) and the high data bits (DATA[15:8]) are multiplexed on Port A; whereas, the lower address byte (ADDR[7:0]) and the lower data bits (DATA[7:0]) are multiplexed on Port B.

Normal Expanded Narrow Mode (BKGD: 1, MODB: 0, MODA: 1)   Normal expanded narrow mode is the same as the normal expanded wide mode except the external data bus uses an 8-bit port instead of two 8-bit ports. The 16-bit external address bus uses Port A for the high byte and Port B for the low byte. The 8-bit external data bus uses Port A. Information ADDR[15:8] and DATA[7:0] are multiplexed on Port A. This operating mode is made available to allow the 68HC12 to interface with 8-bit data-based devices.

4.3.2 The B32 EVB Modes of Operation

In this section we focus on the operating modes of the M68EVB912B32 evaluation board (EVB). The EVB is factory configured for the normal single-chip mode. As previously noted, the B32 has multiplexed address and data ports that can be used to expand (external) memory capability.

Although configured within the normal single-chip mode, the EVB can begin operation in one of four jumper configurable modes:

- *EVB Mode*: In the EVB Mode, the EVB will execute the D-Bug12 monitor program if it is resident within the flash EEPROM. If the D-Bug12 has been replaced by a user program in flash EEPROM, it will begin executing the user program. D-Bug12 is the EVB's firmware resident monitor program. It provides a self-contained operating environment that allows a system developer to write, test, and debug user programs. It is extremely useful for its troubleshooting features during code development.
- *JUMP-EE Mode*: In this mode the EVB begins executing a user program located at $0D00 in byte-erasable EEPROM. This mode should be used after a system program has been tested, debugged, and loaded into EEPROM. Recall there are only 768 bytes of byte-addressable EEPROM memory. Therefore, only fairly short programs may be stored here.
- *POD Mode*: In this mode, the EVB uses the background debug mode (BDM) features to interrogate another processor (EVB). BDM is used for system development, in-circuit testing, field testing, and programming. BDM is implemented in on-chip hardware and provides a full set of debug options. The BDM communicates serially with an external host development system via the BKGD pins of the two boards.
- *BOOTLOAD Mode*: In this mode, the host EVB's byte-erasable or flash EEPROM may be programmed with user code.

4.4 HARDWARE PIN ASSIGNMENTS

As with any integrated circuit, the 68HC12 is available in different configurations. The 68HC12 B32 configuration is available in an 80-pin quad flat pack (QFP). The pin assignments for the QFP package are provided in Figure 4.6. The pins of the 68HC12 may be divided into three groups:

- *Voltage supply or voltage reference pins*: The designator for this group of pins begins with a "V." These pins are used to provide power supply voltages to the 68HC12 and reference voltages for different systems within the 68HC12.

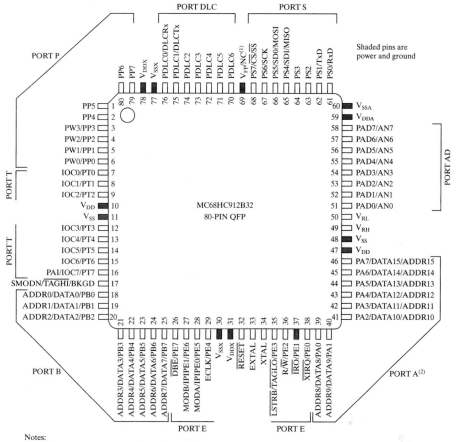

Figure 4.6 B32 pin assignments. Even with 80 pins, most pins will have two or more functions depending on the 68HC12 operating mode selected. The pins of the 68HC12 may be divided into three groups: voltage supply or voltage reference pins, port pins, and miscellaneous pins. (Copyright of Motorola. Used by permission.)

- *Port pins*: The designator for this group of pins begins with a "P." Following the P is the designator for the function of the port pin. For example, pin PT0 is the first pin of Port T. Pins for a given port are numbered 0 through 7.

- *Miscellaneous pins*: These pins are used to provide external signals to the 68HC12. For example, the EXTAL pin allows an external crystal time base to be connected to the 68HC12.

Even with 80 pins, most pins will have two or more functions, depending on the 68HC12 operating mode selected. We discuss the dual nature of these pins during our discussion in the rest of this chapter.

4.5 REGISTER BLOCK

Imagine the control room of a large industrial complex, as shown in Figure 4.7. Systems within the industrial complex can be turned "on" and "off" from the bank-upon-bank of switches within the control room. The operation of specific systems within the industrial complex can be tailored for a specific job. Also, assume that the current status of the industrial complex can be monitored from lights on the indicator panel within the control room. For a given job, only certain systems will be employed.

The 68HC12's register block is the "control room" for the processor. It consists of a 512-byte memory-mapped collection of registers. Visualize each register as a bank of toggle switches and/or indicator lights. The "switches" may be flipped "on" or "off." The indicator lights are register bits that may be set and reset to indicate system status. Each switch has its own specific function. It is through these registers that you configure the 68HC12. Normally systems

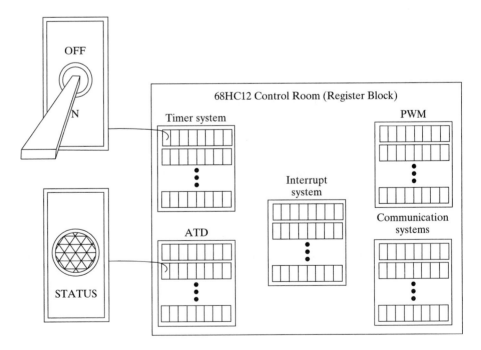

Figure 4.7   A control room for the 68HC12.

aboard the 68HC12 are turned off after processor reset to conserve power. As the system developer, you must turn the systems on prior to use and then turn them off when you are done using them. This is a good method of conserving power in a battery-based system.

"Memory mapped" registers mean that each 8-bit register has a specific memory address associated with it. This will allow us to access the registers with memory reference instructions. When the 68HC12 is reset, every register is configured to a known default setting. These reset settings will be provided as we discuss each register. To configure a specific register, the user must examine each and every bit of the register to determine its required setting. With the setting determined, an appropriate setting value is sent to the specific register using a memory store type instruction. The user must first define the memory addresses of each register that will be used in a given application.

In assembly language, the user configures the registers using memory load (e.g., load accumulator A, LDAA) and store type instructions (e.g., Store Accumulator A, STAA) or MOV instructions. To associate a specific register with a specific address, assembler directives are employed. For example, the P & E microsystems assembler uses an EQU directive to associate a register name label with its memory address. The ImageCraft ICC12 assembler/compiler uses the "=" directive to accomplish this task.

When programming a 68HC12 with C, you must still communicate each register location to the processor, usually using the C preprocessor directive `#define`. This is accomplished through the use of a header file containing register definitions, which must be provided to the compiler. As shown in Chapter 3, the header file must associate the register's name with a specific memory location. When you write a program, this header file must be included as part of the program. This will then allow you to refer to registers by name in your program. The header file provides the mechanism to hide information between you, the high-level user, and the microprocessor.

The header files define a memory location for each register, and in some cases, specific register bit descriptions. This will allow you to refer to the contents of a specific register or bit by using its name (a symbol) within a program. You must, however, use the same case sensitive name as it appears in the header file. For example, the header file defines the ATDCTL2 register with the following line of code:

```
#define ATDCTL2 *(unsigned char volatile *) (IO_BASE + 0x62)
```

What does all of this mean? As we discussed in Chapter 3, the `#define` is a preprocessing directive that is used to define constants in a program, or in this case the description of a specific register. The preprocessor will substitute the description following ATDCTL2 everywhere that it occurs within the program.

Clearly, it is much easier to define the cumbersome description of the ATDCTL2 register only once in the program and then use its name thereafter.

The ATDCTL2 register is defined as an unsigned `char` (character), an 8-bit value. It is further modified by the volatile keyword, which indicates that the variable may be modified by actions external to the program while the program is running. When a variable is declared as volatile, the compiler will not attempt to optimize the variable. Sixteen-bit registers are defined as unsigned `int` (integer) in the header file.

The `*` after the volatile keyword casts this as a pointer (address). Furthermore, the pointer is then assigned the address of IO_BASE + 0x62. The IO_BASE is the first address of the register block. It is defined for the B32 variant at 0x0000. The ATDCTL2 is memory-mapped 0x62 memory locations beyond the register base. Finally, the `*` after the ATDCTL2 designator is a dereference operator that refers to the contents of the specified memory location.

The Bottom Line.   The `#define` statement within the header file allows you to refer to the contents of the ATDCTL2 register within a C program by simply using its name. Note that every 68HC12 register is defined in a similar manner within the header files. This will allow you to refer to the contents of every register simply by referring to it by name in your program.

Example

The ATDCTL2 register is located at memory address 0x0062. This register is used to power up the analog-to-digital (ATD) conversion system. It is also used to control some of the flags and interrupts associated with the ATD system. Bit 7 of ATDCTL2 is the on/off switch for the ATD system. This bit, called an ATD Powerup Bit or ADPU, is reset to 0 after the processor is reset. To power up the ATD system, this bit must be set to "1." To configure the ATDCTL2 register to power up the ATD system using the 68HC12 assembly language program, the following code may be used:

```
;----------------------------------------
;MAIN PROGRAM ;
;----------------------------------------

ATDCTL2   EQU    $0062      ;addr of ATDCTL2
ATD_INI   EQU    $80        ;bit config to power up ATD

          LDAA   #ATD_INI   ;load ATD startup mask to accum A
          STAA   ATDCTL2    ;store ATD startup mask to ATDCTL2
          .
          .
          .
```

The first line of code is an assembler directive equating the register label ATD-CTL2 to hexadecimal number $0062. Likewise, the second line of code equates the register content label ATD_INI to hexadecimal number $80. This $80 value represents the individual bit settings (%1 0 0 0 0 0 0 0) for the ATDCTL2 register, where the symbol % represents a binary number. The LDAA step uses an immediate addressing mode technique to load accumulator A with the ATD register mask value. The STAA instruction stores the ATD register mask value to the ATDCTL2 register.

To accomplish the same action in C, the code shown below is employed. Note that we have defined the ATD_INI initialization mask as an unsigned character, an 8-bit value. Our single line of code assigns 0x80 as the contents of the ATDCTL2 register.

```
/*-----------------------------------------*/
/*MAIN PROGRAM                             */
/*-----------------------------------------*/
#include<912b32.h>

void main(void){

unsigned char  ATD_INI=0x80;     /*bit config to power up ATD*/


ATDCTL2 = ATD_INI;

}
```

As you can see, we do not need to tell the processor where to find the ATDCTL2 register. This is accomplished by the 912b32.h header file definitions.

4.5.1 Register Block Relocation

The register block normally begins at address $0000 and occupies the 512 byte space that follows; however, the register block can be mapped to any 2 Kbyte space within the standard 64 Kbyte address space by changing the bits in the INITRG register. The register block occupies the first 512 bytes of the 2 Kbyte block. If the register block is moved to a different location in memory, the relative location of a specific register within the block remains fixed. Why would you want to do this? In an expanded mode with additional external memory, the registers may not be located in a convenient location within the memory map. That is, the register block may be in the middle of a planned memory expansion location. The registers can then be moved to a more convenient location in the memory map. If you elect to relocate the register block, you must reassign the register block base address in the header file. This is accomplished by changing the base address entry in the header file.

4.6 PORT SYSTEM

A port is a predesignated location to load data on and off the microcontroller. The 68HC12 employs an extensive port system to exchange data and control signals with the external environment. A port includes an input register, an output register, or a configurable input/output register that has been assigned as a memory address. The port system also has complex hardware that connects a physical pin to a particular control register. The ports are accessed through port registers within the register block. Before they can be used, the 68HC12 port associated registers must be defined using a header file entry. Take a moment to look again at Figure 4.1 in detail. You can recognize at a glance whether a port is input, output, or configurable as either an input or output by examining the directional arrows connected to the port. For example, Port T can be configured as either a digital input or output port.

A bidirectional port, such as Port T, must be configured as either an input or an output port. To provide complete flexibility, each bit within the port is separately configured for input or output duty. This is accomplished by setting specific bits within the data direction register associated with a configurable port. A logic "0" sets a specific port bit as an input; whereas a 1 configures the specific port pin as an output. Upon reset, the DDRx registers, data directional registers, are set to $00. This configures the port pins as a high-impedance input.

Example

This example shows how to configure Port T as eight output pins and then sends out a $62 on Port T.

```
/*----------------------------------------*/
/*MAIN PROGRAM                            */
/*----------------------------------------*/
#include<912b32.h>

void main(void){

unsigned char  DDRT_INI=0xFF;     /*PORT T mask for output*/

DDRT = DDRT_INI;
PORTT = 0x62;


}
```

4.6.1 Port Descriptions

The 68HC12 B32 variant is well equipped with an extensive and flexible port system. We provide here a brief explanation of each port. Note that most ports have different functions depending upon the operating mode of the 68HC12. We cover the ports in a clockwise direction as shown in Figure 4.1, beginning with Port A.

- *Port A*: Port A is a general-purpose input/output port when the 68HC12 is operating in the normal single-chip mode. It is equipped with an associated data direction register (DDRA) to independently set the input/output configuration of each pin. It provides the high-order external multiplexed address/data byte lines ADDR[15:8]/DATA[15:8] in the normal expanded wide modes. Port A only provides the data bits in expanded narrow mode.

- *Port B*: Port B is a general-purpose input/output port when the 68HC12 is operating in the normal single-chip mode. It too is equipped with an associated data direction register (DDRB) to independently set the input/output configuration of each pin. It provides the low-order external multiplexed address/data byte lines ADDR[7:0]/DATA[7:0] in the normal expanded wide modes. Data are not placed on these lines in expanded narrow mode.

- *Port E*: Port E pins 0 (PE0) and 1 (PE1) are input pins while pins 2 through 7 are configurable as input or output pins. The PE1 and PE0 may be used to initiate external interrupts via the $\overline{IRQ}$ and $\overline{XIRQ}$ lines, respectively. Port E is also used for mode selection, bus control signals, or general-purpose input/output pins when the B32 is used with external, expanded memory components.

- *Port AD*: Port AD is configured as the analog input pins for the analog-to-digital (ATD) converter system. If the ATD system is not in use, Port AD can be used as a general-purpose input port (PAD[7:0]).

- *Port T*: Port T is used as the input capture and output compare pins for the timing system (TIM). When the TIM is not in use, these pins may also be used as general-purpose input/output pins. It is equipped with an associated data direction register (DDRT) to independently set the input/output configuration of each pin.

- *Port S*: Port S is used with the serial communication interface (SCI) and the serial peripheral interface (SPI) systems. The B32 variant is equipped with one SCI communication channel and one SPI communication channel. Port S may also be used as a general-purpose input/output port. It is equipped with an associated data direction register (DDRS) to independently set the input/output configuration of each pin.

- *Port P*: Port P provides the interface to the pulse width modulation (PWM) system. Port P may also be used as a general-purpose input/output port. It is equipped with an associated data direction register (DDRP) to independently set the input/output configuration of each pin.

- *Port DLC*: Port DLC provides the interface to the byte data link communications (BDLC) system. Port DLC may also be used as a general-purpose input/output port. It is equipped with an associated data direction register (DDRDLC) to independently set the input/output configuration of each pin.

Specialized Port Configuration   As previously discussed, all input/output configurable ports have an associated data direction register (DDRx). In the B32 variant Ports A, B, T, S, P, and DLC can be programmed as bidirectional ports. After each processor reset, the DDRx registers are automatically configured as high-impedance inputs.

Three specialized configuration registers are associated with the port system illustrated in Figure 4.8:

- The pull-up control register (PUCR), which provides the capability to configure the port input pins of ports A, B, and E with pull-up resistors. This

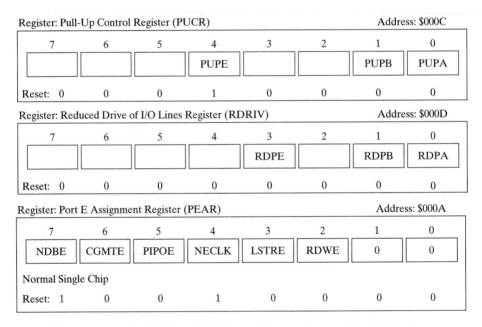

Figure 4.8   The PUCR, RDRIV, and PEAR registers. The PUCR provides the capability to configure the port input pins of the 68HC12 with pull-up resistors. The RDRIV is used to reduce the drive capability of the specified port. The PEAR register provides the capability to choose between the general-purpose digital input/output functions and the alternate bus control functions of PORTE.

is an important feature for hardware interfacing. When a specific port's bit is set in the PUCR, all of the pins of that port configured for input are equipped with pull-up pins. The PUCR features are deactivated when ports are used in expanded operating modes for data and address lines.

- The reduced drive of I/O lines register (RDRIV), which is used to reduce the drive capability of the specified port (A, B, E). This feature provides for reduced power consumption and reduced radio frequency interference. Setting a "1" to the bit associated with a specific port will enable the reduced drive features. We discuss the electrical characteristics of the 68HC12 in Chapter 5. Generally speaking, employing the RDRIV features reduces the current drive capability by approximately one-half.

- The Port E assignment register (PEAR) is used to choose between the general purpose I/O functions and the alternate bus control functions of Port E. When external memory is used with the 68HC12, Port E provides the control and timing signals required in expanded mode memory configurations.

Practice Questions

1. **Question:** How many ports does the B32 have?

   Answer: The B32 variant is equipped with 8 ports (A, B, E, AD, T, S, P, DLC).

2. **Question:** The designers of the B32 were very careful in designating the ports. Their brief descriptors provide a clue to their specialized functions. What are the specialized functions of the AD, T, S, P, and DLC ports?

   Answer: AD: analog-to-digital conversion; T: timer system; S: serial communications; P: pulse width modulation; and DLC: data link communication.

3. **Question:** What is the purpose of the data direction registers?

   Answer: A bidirectional port may be configured as either an input or an output port. To provide complete flexibility, each bit within the port may be separately configured for input or output duties. This is accomplished by setting specific bits within the data direction register. A logic 0 sets a specific port bit as a high impedance input; whereas, a 1 configures the specific port pin as an output.

4. **Question:** What is the reset configuration for the data direction registers?

   Answer: After reset, the data direction registers are set to 0—high-impedance input.

Application Example

In this application, we use Port A to illuminate a set of LEDs. Connect Port A to the eight-channel, tristate logic probe shown in Figure 4.9. Have the even-numbered Port A pins illuminate the green light-emitting diodes (LEDs) with a logic "1" and the odd numbered pins turn on the red LEDs with a logic 0. Hold this configuration for 30 ms and then reverse the red LEDs with the green LEDs and green LEDs with the red LEDs. Repeat this sequence indefinitely.

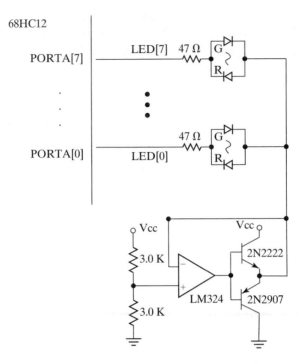

Figure 4.9   The connection between Port A and an LED circuit. The LED circuit acts as an eight-channel, tristate logic probe. When a logic high (1) is provided to LED[n], the green LED illuminates. When a logic low (0) is provided to LED[n], the red LED illuminates. If a high-impedance state is provided to LED[n], neither LED will illuminate.

The LED circuit operates as an eight-channel tristate logic probe. We discuss the operation of the LED circuit in great detail in Chapter 5. The required actions for the algorithm are provided in the form of the UML activity diagram provided in Figure 4.10. As mentioned in Chapter 2, great care must be taken to construct a detailed UML activity diagram. With a complete diagram, you can transition directly to code the algorithm.

Note that we are "pausing" 30 ms between changing the LED sequence. Is their any significance to this delay? This turns out to be a human factors issue. If we used a delay much shorter than 30 ms, the LEDs would appear to not change or to remain stationary. We will use this delay frequently when setting up visible displays. This concept should not be new to you. For example, when you are viewing a "motion" picture you are viewing a sequence of stationary picture frames. The frames change approximately every 33 ms, providing the sensation of continuous motion.

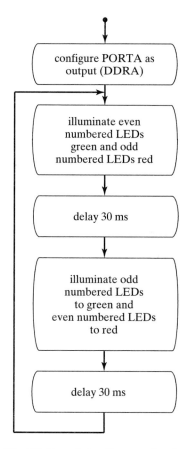

Figure 4.10   The UML activity diagram for the port algorithm.

The 30 ms delay is generated by calling the function to delay 100 microseconds (`delay_100us`) a total of 300 times.

```
/*---------------------------------------------------------------*/
/*MAIN PROGRAM: this program sequences the LEDs on PORTA from   */
/*even LEDs green to odd LEDs to green.                         */
/*---------------------------------------------------------------*/

/*include files*/
#include<912b32.h>

/*function prototypes*/
void delay_100us(void);
void delay_30ms(void);

void main(void){
```

```
DDRA = 0xFF;                      /*PORTA to output*/

while(1){
    PORTA = 0x55;                 /*even numbered to green, odd to red*/
    delay_30ms();                 /*delay*/
    PORTA = 0xAA;                 /*even numbered to red, odd to green*/
    delay_30ms();                 /*delay*/
    }
}
/*-------------------------------------------------------------*/
/*delay_30ms: provides 30 ms delay                            */
/*-------------------------------------------------------------*/

void delay_30ms(void){

int i;                                      /*loop variable*/

for(i=0;i<=299;i++)
  delay_100us();

}

/*-------------------------------------------------------------*/
/*delay_100us: provides approximately 100 us delay - assumes  */
/*8 MHz clock,                                                */
/*-------------------------------------------------------------*/

void delay_100us(void){

int j;                                      /*loop variable*/

for(j=0;j<50;j++)
  asm(''nop\n'');

}
/*-------------------------------------------------------------*/
```

Note that in the above code the function delay_100us provides approximately a 100 μs delay with the processor operating at 8 MHz. You must examine the list file (*.lst) to determine the number of clock cycles to accomplish one iteration of the for loop. For the ICC12 compiler this loop required 16 clock cycles per iteration. This was determined by examining the assembly language instructions associated with the for loop. A total of 800 clock cycles are required to generate a 100 μs delay when the processor is operating at 8 MHz. This then requires 50 loop iterations at 16 clock cycles each to obtain the 800 clock cycle delay. This was experimentally verified with an oscilloscope. For a faster processor such as the DP256 operating at 25 MHz, the loop constant must be adjusted to an appropriate value (156). This too was experimentally verified with an oscilloscope.

4.7 THE B32 MEMORY SYSTEM

The memory system of the 68HC12 consists of the register space, the random access memory, and the EEPROM components. The default memory map for the 68HC12 B32 evaluation board configuration is provided in Figure 4.11; however, each of these memory components can be remapped to other locations in the memory map.

The B32 is intended primarily for single-chip applications. It is equipped with a 32 Kbyte flash EEPROM for program memory, 1 Kbyte of static RAM, and 768 bytes of byte-erasable EEPROM for storing system data.

As its name implies, EEPROM may be quickly erased electronically while it is still resident within its circuit. There are two major variants of the EEPROM: the flash EEPROM and the byte-erasable EEPROM. The flash EEPROM, or simply flash memory, allows electrical erasure of the entire memory or a major block of memory. The byte-erasable EEPROM, or simply EEPROM, allows single bytes within the memory to be erased and reprogrammed. These two EEPROM

```
$0000 ┌──────────────────────────────────────────┐
      │  CPU registers                           │
$01FF ├──────────────────────────────────────────┤
      │                                          │
$0800 ├──────────────────────────────────────────┤
      │  1 Kbytes of on-chip RAM                 │
$0BFF │  • User code/data ($0800–$09FF)          │
      │  • Reserved for D-Bug12 ($0A00–$0BFF)    │
$0D00 ├──────────────────────────────────────────┤
      │  768 bytes of on-chip EEPROM             │
$0FFF │  • User code/data                        │
      ├──────────────────────────────────────────┤
      │                                          │
$8000 ├──────────────────────────────────────────┤
      │  32 Kbytes on-chip FLASH EEPROM          │
      │  • D-Bug12 code ($8000–$F67F)            │
      │  • User-accessible functions ($F680–$F6BF)│
      │  • D-Bug12 customization ($F6C0–$F6FF)   │
      │  • D-Bug12 startup code ($F700–$F77F)    │
      │  • Interrupt vector table ($F780–$F7FF)  │
      │  • Bootloader expansion ($F800–$FBFF)    │
      │  • EEPROM bootloader ($FC00–$FFBF)       │
$FFFF │  • Reset and interrupt vectors ($FFC0–$FFFF)│
      └──────────────────────────────────────────┘
```

Figure 4.11   An evaluation board memory map for the B32.

technologies are used to debug and quickly modify embedded controller software during the development process. Code may be tested and modified within its intended target system. EEPROMs are used within an embedded controller system as a scratch pad memory, for data storage, or for storing end-product characteristics. (Note that developers may prefer to develop programs in RAM and then program the final version of the program in EEPROM.)

Application Example

An embedded control system for electronically controlled gates has been developed at an industrial site. The actual control system for the gate controller was written in C and downloaded into the processor's flash EEPROM memory. As part of the system's requirement, faults that occurred during system operation were to be stored for later analysis. The faults fell into four general categories. Each of these categories were declared as a variable in byte-addressable EEPROM. When a fault occurred, the fault variable was updated by the program. It was important to declare these variables in EEPROM so the fault data would not be lost during a power failure.

Note: Motorola indicates that the B32 EVB's flash EEPROM has a guaranteed program/erase life of 100 cycles, which means the flash EEPROM may be programmed up to 100 times before it may fail. It is advisable to develop, test, and debug your program in RAM memory and then load it into flash EEPROM. This may require using an evaluation board with a larger RAM memory such as the A4 EVB or one of the HCS12 variants. The A4 EVB is configured with 16 Kbytes of RAM, whereas the HCS12 variants have up to 12 Kbytes of RAM. On the other hand, the byte-erasable EEPROM may be programmed/erased 10,000 times. Furthermore, the RAM memory space of the B32 may be expanded with external memory components. We provide an expanded memory design in the Sliding Puzzle Game in Chapter 7.

4.7.1 The B32 Memory Map

A memory map is a tool that tracks how the available memory space is currently configured with different memory components. The 68HC12 B32 variant is configured with a linearly addressable memory space of 64 Kbytes. This means the 68HC12 can access 1 of 65,536 ($2^{\text{address lines}}$ = number of memory locations) memory locations at a given time. These 65,536 (commonly referred to as 64 Kbytes) distinct locations may or may not be occupied with memory components. The first memory location is $0000 while the last location is $FFFF.

Default locations for the 68HC12 register block, RAM, and EEPROM are shown on the memory map in Figure 4.11. The register block spans the memory locations from $0000 to $01FF—that is, for 512 locations. The 1 Kbyte static RAM spans the memory locations from $0800 to $0BFF. The RAM portion from $0800 to $09FF is available for user-written code and data (stack and variables) while the span from \$0A00 to \$0BFF is reserved for use by the D-Bug12 monitor/debugger program for stack and variable storage. The stack is a user-defined portion of RAM used for temporary variable storage during program execution. There are 768 bytes of on-chip EEPROM available for user-written code and data between \$0D00 and \$0FFF. The rest of the memory map consists of 32 Kbytes of on-chip flash EEPROM from \$8000 to \$FFFF. The B32 evaluation board's flash EEPROM is configured as follows:

- \$8000 to \$F67F: D-Bug12 code
- \$F680 to \$F6BF: user-accessible functions
- \$F6C0 to \$F6FF: D-Bug12 customization data
- \$F700 to \$F77F: D-Bug12 startup code
- \$F780 to \$F7FF: interrupt vector jump table
- \$F800 to \$FBFF: reserved for bootloader expansion
- \$FC00 to \$FFBF: EEPROM bootloader
- \$FFC0 to \$FFFF: reset and interrupt vectors

As you can see, the D-Bug12 program takes up most of the 32 Kbytes of flash EEPROM. So where are we supposed to load our programs? The EEPROM bootloader occupies 1 Kbyte of erased-protected flash EEPROM starting at memory location \$FC00. This program is executed when the EVB is started in the BOOTLOAD mode. This bootloader program may be used to program user code into the byte-erasable EEPROM starting at address \$0D00 and the Flash EEPROM starting at address \$8000. *Note:* The D-Bug12 is overwritten when using the flash EEPROM for user code. However, the bootloader program is protected from erasure. User code may occupy the Flash EEPROM memory space from \$8000 to \$F7FF (30 Kbytes).

4.7.2 Memory Resource Remapping

Notice that there are gaps, or unused locations, in the memory map (\$01FF to \$0800, \$0BFF to \$0D00, and \$0FFF to \$8000). These memory spaces are available for expanded, external memory components. During expansion, the internal memory components may not be in convenient locations. These internal resources may be mapped to other locations by setting bits in the three mapping registers: (1) the initialization of internal register position register (INITRG) at memory location \$0011; (2) the initialization of internal RAM position register (INITRM) at memory location \$0010; and (3) the initialization of internal EEPROM position register (INITEE) at memory location \$0012. As their names imply, these registers are used to move the internal register block, the internal RAM memory, and the internal EEPROM memory to new locations. These registers are normally configured during the initialization phase of program execution.

4.8 THE HCS12 DP256 MEMORY SYSTEM

The memory map for the HCS12 DP256 processor is provided in Figure 4.12. It is quite similar to the B32. Its most noticeable difference is the memory paging system that allows more than 64 Kbytes of memory to be addressed. The DP256 processor is equipped with 256 Kbytes of paged flash EEPROM. Memory paging is a concept in which a large portion of memory may be viewed from a fixed-sized memory window. This window is much smaller than the paged memory space and only a single page of memory may be viewed through the window at a given time. For additional information on this topic, see Pack and Barrett (2002, chap. 8).

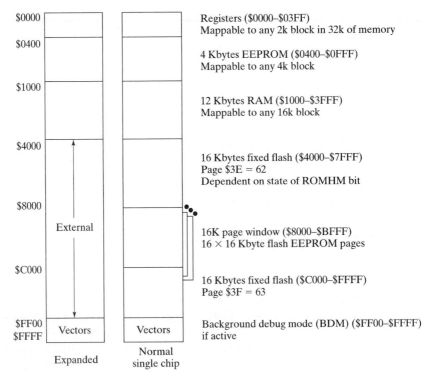

Figure 4.12   A Memory map for the HCS12 DP256.

Practice Questions

1. **Question:** How big is the flash EEPROM in the B32 EVB?

   Answer: The B32 EVB contains 32 Kbytes of flash. It is factory configured with the D-Bug12 monitor/debugger program.

2. **Question:** How is the flash memory reprogrammed with a user-written program?

   Answer: The bootloader program may be used to program user code into the byte-erasable EEPROM starting at address $0D00 and the Flash EEPROM starting at address $8000. The D-Bug12 is overwritten when using the flash EEPROM for user code.

3. **Question:** How many times may the flash EEPROM be reprogrammed?

   Answer: Guaranteed up to 100 cycles.

4. **Question:** How many times may the byte-erasable EEPROM be reprogrammed?

   Answer: Guaranteed up to 10,000 cycles.

5. **Question:** How are flash EEPROM and byte-erasable EEPROM employed in an embedded control system?

   Answer: The B32 EVB is equipped with 32 Kbytes of flash EEPROM memory. Approximately 30 Kbytes of this memory is available to hold user programs. On the other hand, the B32 has a 768 byte EEPROM. This portion of memory is used for frequently accessed static data.

4.9 EXCEPTION PROCESSING—RESETS AND INTERRUPTS

Normally the 68HC12 responds to program steps in an orderly fashion, as specified by the programmer. The 68HC12 processes instructions in a well-defined fetch-decode-execute sequence. The program counter (PC) keeps track of where the next program step is stored in memory. Even when a program deviates from its normal step-by-step sequence in response to a branch or a jump instruction, it is always under a controlled sequence of events.

Exceptions may occur to break out of this orderly flow of events. For example, the 68HC12 may sense high priority software or hardware malfunctions that it must respond to before continuing lower priority, routine processing. We classify a break in normal program flow as an *exception*. Exceptions may be further classified as *interrupts* and *resets*.

Exceptions do not necessarily need to be fault related. Using interrupts is an efficient method of allowing multiple systems to run together on the processor. When polling techniques are used, the processor is tied up waiting for a single flag to occur. However, with interrupts, multiple events can be initiated and easily handled by the processor.

4.9.1 General Interrupt Response

As we discuss the details of a system's response to an exception, we need to keep in mind a few items:

- When an exception occurs, a smooth transition of control from the main program to the interrupt service routine (ISR) must occur. The ISR contains the program steps required to service the specific interrupt.
- All CPU register values at the time of the exception must be temporarily stored. These register values are conveniently stored on the stack—a user-specified portion of RAM that is set aside to temporarily store variables, register contents, etc. The stack "top" should be defined as the last available location of RAM memory plus one for the 68HC12 because the stack pointer points to the last memory location used. When programming in C, the stack location is assigned as a compiler option.
- The condition causing the interrupt must be reset prior to exiting the ISR. Depending on the interrupt source, this may require the programmer (you) to reset the source, such as a Timer Overflow Flag, or it may require a reset by external hardware, such as a low battery indicator connected to the $\overline{IRQ}$ external interrupt pin. If the source of the interrupt is not reset prior to exiting the ISR, the processor will go right back into the ISR.
- At the completion of the ISR, the registers must be restored to their original values at the time of the initial exception reporting.
- A smooth transition of control from the ISR back to the main program at the completion of ISR actions must also occur so the program may resume processing where it left off prior to the interrupt event.
- It must be emphasized that although an exception is an unscheduled event and may occur at anytime, it is still a planned event. A system must be configured to handle a specific exception before it occurs.

With this general concept of exception processing in mind, let's consider the exception processing features aboard the 68HC12.

4.10 RESET AND EXCEPTION SYSTEMS ABOARD THE 68HC12

The 68HC12 is equipped with a very powerful exception processing system. The exceptions that may occur in normal 68HC12 program processing may be categorized into two subdivisions: (1) resets and (2) interrupts. The interrupts may be further subdivided into nonmaskable interrupts and maskable interrupts. These different categories of exceptions are illustrated in Figure 4.13. Listed under each

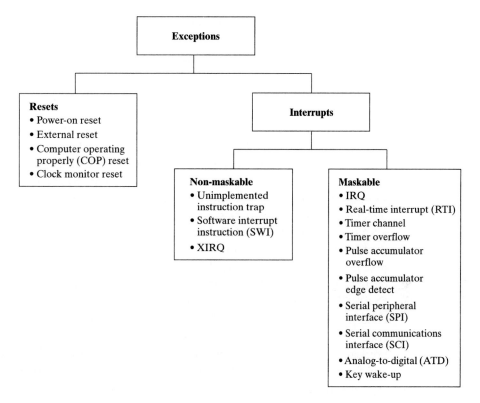

Figure 4.13   68HC12 exception categories.

category are the specific types of exceptions. In the following sections, we discuss each of these major categories and briefly describe the function of each exception.

4.10.1 Resets

The 68HC12 performs a system reset in response to various external events or detected internal system malfunctions. When the 68HC12 detects a reset condition, it sets registers and control bits to known start-up, default values. The overall purpose of the system reset is for fault recovery. That is, when the 68HC12 detects an internal malfunction, it attempts to return itself to a known, well-defined state in an attempt to recover from the fault.

There are four events that can trigger a system reset:

- *External reset:* The 68HC12 is equipped with an active low reset pin designated as RESET. When this pin is driven low, a reset is triggered. On the evaluation boards (EVBs), the reset pin is handily connected to a pushbutton to allow for easy system reset during system development.

- *Power-on reset:* A positive transition on the V_{DD} power pin of the 68HC12 will trigger a power-on reset. This feature ensures that when power is applied to the 68HC12, it starts up in a known, well-defined configuration.
- *Computer operating properly (COP) reset:* We briefly discussed the COP features earlier in this chapter. Here are a few more details. The COP system allows the 68HC12 to detect software execution malfunctions. Normally the COP is disabled during software development. However, it is an important safety feature once a 68HC12 based system is in full operation. Basically, the COP system consists of a user-configurable countdown timer. If the timer expires, a system reset is triggered. To prevent the timer from timing out, it must be repeatedly reset using a timer reset sequence. Specifically, the program under execution must write a $55 followed by a $AA to the arm/reset COP timer register (COPRST) before the countdown timer times out. Should a program stall or get caught in a loop, it will be unable to generate the reset as required and a COP reset will occur. To implement this feature effectively, the code to write a $55 to the COPRST register should be strategically placed in some major portion of code. The code to write $AA should be placed in another major portion of code. That way should the microcontroller get stuck in one major code portion or the other, the required code sequence will not be generated and the COP reset will be triggered. Multiple $55 and $AA pairs may be strategically placed throughout the program to provide for fault recovery.
- *Clock monitor reset:* The clock monitor reset occurs when the system clock frequency falls below a prescribed value or when it is stopped.

When a reset is triggered by any of the above events, the 68HC12 puts a reset vector (memory address) in the program counter and the processor executes a start-up routine. The COP reset and clock monitor reset also have their own associated reset vectors.

Clock Monitor and COP Reset Registers   Two registers are associated with the clock monitor and computer operating properly (COP) resets: (1) the COP control register (COPCTL) and (2) the arm/reset COP timer register (COPRST). These two registers are shown in Figure 4.14.

The COPCTL is used to enable or disable the clock monitor and the COP system. This register can also be used to force one of these two types of resets. Let's take a closer look by examining each bit in the COPCTL register.

- *The clock monitor enable (CME):* The CME bit is the on/off switch for the clock monitor system. When this bit is 0, the clock monitor reset is disabled. When set to 1 a slow or stopped clock will cause a reset to occur.

Register: Computer Operating Properly Control Register (COPCTL)   Address: $0016

7	6	5	4	3	2	1	0
CME	FCME	FCM	FCOP	DISR	CR2	CR1	CR0

Reset: 0 (Normal)	0	0	0	0	0	0	1
Reset: 0 (Special)	0	0	0	1	0	0	1

Register: Arm/Reset COP Timer Register (COPRST)   Address: $0017

7	6	5	4	3	2	1	0
bit 7	bit 6	bit 5	bit 4	bit 3	bit 2	bit 1	bit 0

Reset: 0	0	0	0	0	0	0	0

CR[2:0]	Divide M by:	M = 4.0 MHz Time-out	M = 8.0 MHz Time-out
000	off	off	off
001	2^{13}	2.048 ms	1.024 ms
010	2^{15}	8.192 ms	4.096 ms
011	2^{17}	32.768 ms	16.384 ms
100	2^{19}	131.072 ms	65.536 ms
101	2^{21}	524.288 ms	262.144 ms
110	2^{22}	1.048 s	524.288 ms
111	2^{23}	2.097 s	1.048576 s

Figure 4.14   COP reset registers. These registers are used to configure the clock monitor and computer operating correctly (COP) resets. The CR[2:0] bits are used to specify the time-out interval for the watchdog timer.

- *Force clock monitor enable (FCME) bit*: The FCME bit controls how the clock monitor reset function can be disabled. When set to 1, a slow or stopped clock will cause a clock reset sequence.
- *Force clock monitor reset (FCM) bit*: As its name implies, the FCM can be used to force the 68HC12 into a clock monitor reset by setting this bit to 1 (as long as the clock monitor system is not currently disabled; see DISR bit below).
- *Force COP watchdog reset (FCOP)*: The FCOP bit is similar in operation to the FCM bit except it can force the 68HC12 into a COP reset (as long as the clock monitor system is not currently disabled; see DISR bit below).

- *Disable resets from COP watchdog and clock monitor (DISR)*: The DISR bit turns off the COP and clock monitor reset features of the 68HC12.
- *CR2, CR1, CR0 bits*: The COP watchdog timer rate select bits CR[2:0] are used to specify the time-out interval for the watchdog timer. Recall, the timer is reset by sending a $55 and $AA sequence to the COPRST register at regular intervals. The sequence must occur repetitively at an interval shorter than the timeout interval specified by the CR[2:0] bits or a COP reset will occur. The actual time-out intervals are shown in Figure 4.14.

The COPRST is used to reset the COP time-out register. As previously described, it is a two-step sequence: (1) write $55 to the COPRST register, and (2) write $AA to the COPRST register. Other instructions may be executed between these writes but both steps must be completed, in order, prior to time-out. Writing any other value besides $55 or $AA causes a COP reset to occur.

4.10.2 Interrupts

The other major 68HC12 exception category is interrupts, which may be further categorized as nonmaskable and maskable interrupts. The programming model for the 68HC12 contains the condition code register (CCR), as shown in Figure 4.15. This can be likened to the instrumentation panel on an automobile, which provides visible indicators showing the status of the inaccessible portions of a car's engine. Likewise, the CCR provides accessible indicators (flags) of what is going on inside the inaccessible portions of the processor.

Two of the bits in the CCR—the X bit and the I bit—are associated with interrupts. The X controls the nonmaskable interrupts while the I bit controls the maskable interrupts. These interrupt masking bits are both set to a logic 1 during system reset, which turns off the corresponding interrupt subsystem.

Nonmaskable Interrupts   A nonmaskable interrupt, as its name implies, may not be turned off by the user. As mentioned above, the nonmaskable

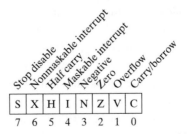

Figure 4.15   Condition code register.

interrupt system is controlled by the X bit in the CCR. This bit is set to 1, turning this interrupt system off, during normal system reset. However, shortly into the system initialization sequence the X bit is set to 0, which re-enables the interrupt system. There are three types of nonmaskable interrupts:

- *Nonmaskable interrupt request ($\overline{XIRQ}$)*: The 68HC12 is equipped with an external pin designated $\overline{XIRQ}$. When taken to logic low, this active low pin generates an interrupt event.
- *Unimplemented instruction trap*: Every instruction in the 68HC12 has an associated numerical operation code (opcode) designator. Due to the coding scheme used for these codes, there are 202 unused numerical opcodes. In the event that the 68HC12 tries to execute one of these unspecified opcodes, an unimplemented instruction trap interrupt is triggered.
- *Software interrupt instruction (SWI)*: The use of the SWI causes a software initiated interrupt to occur.

Maskable Interrupts   Maskable interrupts may be turned on and off by the user under program control. As previously mentioned, the maskable interrupt system is normally turned off during system reset and remains off until enabled by the user within a program. The maskable interrupt system's on/off switch is the I bit in the condition code register. It is turned on (by setting to logic "0") with the clear interrupt mask (CLI) instruction. The system is turned off when the set interrupt mask (SEI) instruction sets the I bit to 1.

Both the CLI and the SEI are assembly language instructions. There are no counterparts in the C language! So how will we turn the maskable interrupt system on and off when programming in C? We can easily insert assembly language instructions into a C program using inline assembly commands. This is accomplished using the following syntax:

```
asm(``<string>'');
```

The assembly language instruction is inserted for `<string>`. Multiple assembly statements can be separated by the newline character \n. For example to turn on the maskable interrupt system, we would use the following:

```
asm(``cli'');
```

68HC12 Maskable Interrupts   The 68HC12 is equipped with an extensive maskable interrupt system. These interrupts are associated with the different hardware systems of the 68HC12. As you read over these interrupts, reflect on how each of the associated hardware systems may be programmed to run more efficiently with an interrupt event as opposed to a polling event.

Remember, when using polling techniques, the processor is tied up waiting for a flag to set. We provide a consolidated list with a brief description of each interrupt here for convenience. The maskable interrupts must be enabled globally with the CLI command and locally with the enable bit associated with the specific interrupt. To get lights in your kitchen, the fuse box switch must be on (global CLI enable) as well as the kitchen wall switch (local enable). These maskable interrupts include the following:

- *Maskable interrupt request ($\overline{IRQ}$)*: The 68HC12 is equipped with an external pin designated $\overline{IRQ}$. When taken to logic low, this active low pin generates an interrupt event. This is the main interrupt pin used to signal an interrupt event to the 68HC12 from the outside world. Although it is only one pin, it can be used to signal multiple external exception events. This can be accomplished by tying the interrupt signals together through combinational logic. When an interrupt event occurs, the 68HC12—as part of the interrupt service routine—could poll the external hardware through an input configured port to determine the specific source of the interrupt event. The interrupt event could then be reset through an output configured port. This concept is illustrated in Figure 4.16.

- *Real-time interrupt (RTI)*: The RTI system generates an interrupt at a user-specified interval. This interrupt is very useful in "reminding" the 68HC12 to perform a regular, repetitive task such as sampling the battery supply level every three minutes. When the interrupt occurs, the interrupt as well as the RTI timer must be reset. We investigate the RTI interrupt in a motor speed control application in Chapter 7.

- *Timer channel*: The timer channel interrupts are associated with the eight input capture/output compare timer channels. An interrupt will be initiated when the user-specified event occurs on the channel. For example, if IOC

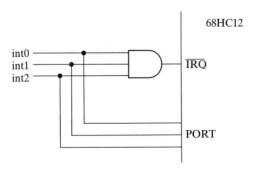

Figure 4.16 Configuring the $\overline{IRQ}$ with multiple interrupts.

channel 5 is configured to monitor for a falling edge, an interrupt will be triggered when this event occurs.

- *Timer overflow*: The timer system is based on a 16-bit free-running counter, which rolls over for every 65,536 counts of the timer clock (time to count up the TCNT register from 0x0000 to 0xFFFF). The timer overflow interrupt may be configured to occur every time this counter rolls over. This interrupt feature is especially useful for timing long events. Rather than keep track of individual pulses with the free-running counter, we could keep track of how many times the counter rolled over. The total elapsed time of the event would be the rollover time of the counter times the number of interrupt overflow events that had occurred.

- *Pulse accumulator overflow*: Much like the free-running counter, the pulse accumulator counter has an interrupt associated with its overflow.

- *Pulse accumulator input edge*: This interrupt is generated every time the user-specified pulse accumulator event occurs.

- *SPI and SCI*: The 68HC12 is equipped with an extensive communications system including the serial peripheral interface (SPI) and the serial communications interface (SCI). Several interrupt events are associated with these communication systems.

- *Analog-to-digital system*: The analog-to-digital (ATD) system is equipped with an interrupt to indicate when a specified ATD conversion sequence is complete.

- *Key wake up*: The key wake up feature of the 68HC12 issues an interrupt that will "wake up" the CPU when it has been placed in the STOP or WAIT mode to conserve battery power. This particular interrupt is useful when we setup a network of 68HC12 controller systems. We discuss this feature in detail later in the chapter.

Practice Questions

1. **Question:** What is the difference between an interrupt and a reset?

   Answer: Both interrupts and resets are considered exceptions—that is, they cause a break in normal program flow. A reset is usually caused by a hardware or software malfunction. When a reset occurs, the processor restarts at a known state. An interrupt is a break in normal program flow. An interrupt may be caused by a software malfunction, an internally generated hardware or software event, or an external hardware or software event. In response to an interrupt, the processor will perform an interrupt service routine specific to the interrupt that occurred.

2. **Question:** What is the difference between a nonmaskable interrupt and a maskable interrupt?

Answer: A nonmaskable interrupt may not be turned off by the user; a maskable interrupt may be turned on and off by the user under program control.

3. **Question:** What is the difference between the $\overline{XIRQ}$ interrupt and the $\overline{IRQ}$ interrupt?

   Answer: Both the $\overline{XIRQ}$ and $\overline{IRQ}$ interrupt systems are connected to external pins on the 68HC12. Both may be used to initiate an interrupt. The $\overline{XIRQ}$ interrupt is nonmaskable whereas the $\overline{IRQ}$ interrupt is maskable.

4. **Question:** How is the $\overline{XIRQ}$ interrupt system enabled?

   Answer: The nonmaskable interrupt system is controlled by the X bit in the condition code register (CCR). This bit is set to 1, turning this interrupt system off, during normal system reset. However, shortly into the system initialization sequence, the X bit is set to 0, which re-enables the interrupt system.

5. **Question:** How are multiple interrupts configured into the $\overline{IRQ}$ pin?

   Answer: The $\overline{IRQ}$ pin is active low. This means a transition from logic high to low on this pin will initiate the interrupt sequence. Multiple interrupts may be tied together via an AND gate. When these multiple interrupts are inactive (logic high), the AND gate will also provide a logic high output. When one of the interrupts becomes active, it will transition to active low and hence create an active low signal on the output of the AND gate, which will initiate the interrupt sequence. As part of the ISR, the source of the interrupt should be determined. This may be accomplished by routing the interrupt sources to a port. Within the ISR, the port can be polled to determine the interrupt source. Also, the source of the interrupt must be reset in the ISR. This concept is illustrated in Figure 4.16.

4.10.3 Exception Vector

When an exception event occurs, the 68HC12 must have a mechanism to begin processing the associated reset sequence for a reset or the associated interrupt service routine for an interrupt. In other words, the 68HC12 needs to know where to go in memory for the required instructions in response to the exception event. This information is contained in the interrupt vector table. The interrupt vector table for the B32 variant of the 68HC12 is shown in Figure 4.17. This table is stored in the upper 128 bytes of the standard 64 Kbyte memory and contains useful information about the entire exception processing system. The first column provides the vector address for the interrupt. In other words, this is where the 68HC12 will find the start address of the interrupt service routine for a specific interrupt event. For example, if the $\overline{IRQ}$ pin goes low, indicating an external interrupt has occurred, the 68HC12 will go to memory location $FFF2 and $FFF3 to find the address of the first instruction in the interrupt service routine associated with the $\overline{IRQ}$ interrupt.

The second column indicates the source of the interrupt. The third column indicates whether the interrupt is maskable or not. We find out shortly that besides enabling the overall maskable interrupt system with the I bit we must also turn

Vector Address	Interrupt Source	CCR Mask	Local Enable		HPRIO Value to Elevate to Highest I Bit
			Register	**Bit(s)**	
$FFFE, $FFFF	Reset	None	None	None	—
$FFFC, $FFFD	COP clock monitor fail reset	None	COPCTL	CME, FCME	—
$FFFA, $FFFB	COP failure reset	None	None	COP rate selected	—
$FFF8, $FFF9	Unimplemented instruction trap	None	None	None	—
$FFF6, $FFF7	SWI	None	None	None	—
$FFF4, $FFF5	XIRQ	X bit	None	None	—
$FFF2, $FFF3	IRQ	I bit	INTCR	IRQEN	$F2
$FFF0, $FFF1	Real-time interrupt	I bit	RTICTL	RTIE	$F0
$FFEE, $FFEF	Timer channel 0	I bit	TMSK1	C0I	$EE
$FFEC, $FFED	Timer channel 1	I bit	TMSK1	C1I	$EC
$FFEA, $FFEB	Timer channel 2	I bit	TMSK1	C2I	$EA
$FFE8, $FFE9	Timer channel 3	I bit	TMSK1	C3I	$E8
$FFE6, $FFE7	Timer channel 4	I bit	TMSK1	C4I	$E6
$FFE4, $FFE5	Timer channel 5	I bit	TMSK1	C5I	$E4
$FFE2, $FFE3	Timer channel 6	I bit	TMSK1	C6I	$E2
$FFE0, $FFE1	Timer channel 7	I bit	TMSK1	C7I	$E0
$FFDE, $FFDF	Timer overflow	I bit	TMSK2	TOI	$DE
$FFDC, $FFDD	Pulse accumulator overflow	I bit	PACTL	PAOVI	$DC
$FFDA, $FFDB	Pulse accumulator input edge	I bit	PACTL	PAI	$DA
$FFD8, $FFD9	SPI serial transfer complete	I bit	SP0CR1	SPIE	$D8
$FFD6, $FFD7	SCI 0	I bit	SC0CR2	TIE, TCIE, RIE, ILIE	$D6
$FFD4, $FFD5	Reserved	I bit	—	—	$D4
$FFD2, $FFD3	ATD	I bit	ATDCTL2	ASCIE	$D2
$FFD0, $FFD1	BDLC	I bit	BCR1	IE	$D0
$FF80–$FFC1	Reserved (not implemented)	I bit	—	—	$80—$C0
$FFC2–$FFC9	Reserved (implemented)	I bit	—	—	$C2—$C8
$FFCA, $FFCB	Pulse accumulator B overflow	I bit	PBCTL	PBOVI	$CA
$FFCC, $FFCD	Modulus down counter underflow	I bit	MCCTL	MCZI	$CC
$FFCE, $FFCF	Reserved (implemented)	I bit	—	—	$CE

Figure 4.17 An Interrupt vector map for the MC68HC912B32. (Copyright of Motorola. Used by permission.)

on the individual interrupt hardware with its associated local enable pin. This information is provided in columns 4 and 5. For example, to enable the $\overline{IRQ}$ interrupt we must accomplish two tasks: (1) set the I bit in the condition code register to 0 using the CLI command, and (2) enable the $\overline{IRQ}$ by setting the IRQEN bit to a logic "1" in the interrupt control register (INTCR) at memory location $001E. This register is illustrated in Figure 4.18. A similar discussion can be made for each of the maskable interrupt systems. The last column indicates the value to load in the HPRIO register to boost the priority of a specific interrupt (described in the next section).

Register: Interrupt Control Register (INTCR)   Address: $001E

7	6	5	4	3	2	1	0
IRQE	IRQEN	DLY	0	0	0	0	0

Reset: 0   1   1   0   0   0   0   0

Figure 4.18   An interrupt control register—INTCR ($001E).

The careful reader will note that we have a bit of a problem here. The 68HC12's interrupt and reset vectors are located in the **erase-protected** area of Flash EEPROM and hence cannot be reprogrammed. To allow the user code to specify interrupt and reset addresses, each entry of the erase protected vector table starting at address $FFC0 contains a pointer to a vector jump table, which is located in user-programmable Flash EEPROM starting at address $F7C0. This information is summarized in Figure 4.19.

Note: Other variants of the 68HC12 and HCS12 have similar RAM vector features built in. However, the RAM-based vector addresses will be different for each variant. These RAM-based vector address tables are available in the documentation for each processor variant.

4.10.4 Exception Priority

Some exception events are more important than others. In general, the nonmaskable interrupts are of higher priority than the maskable events. This means that when two or more interrupts occur simultaneously, the one with the highest priority will be serviced first. In fact, the nonmaskable interrupts are hardwired with the following priorities:

1. Power on reset or $\overline{RESET}$ pin.
2. Clock monitor reset.
3. COP watchdog reset.
4. Unimplemented instruction trap.
5. Software interrupt instruction (SWI).
6. $\overline{XIRQ}$

The maskable interrupts have the priority indicated in the interrupt vector map shown in Figure 4.17. Those higher on the map have higher priority than those appearing lower in the map. However, the priority of a maskable interrupt may be elevated by writing a specific bit sequence to the highest priority I interrupt register (HPRIO). The value that must be written to this register for a specific interrupt is shown in the last column of the interrupt vector map. The

Vector Address	CPU Interrupt	Jump Table Address
$FFC0 - $FFCF	Reserved	$F7C0 - $F7CF
$FFD0	BDLC (J1850)	$F7D0
$FFD2	ATD	$F7D2
$FFD4	Reserved	$F7D4
$FFD6	SCI0	$F7D6
$FFD8	SPI	$F7D8
$FFDA	Pulse accumulator input edge	$F7DA
$FFDC	Pulse accumulator overflow	$F7DC
$FFDE	Timer overflow	$F7DE
$FFE0	Timer channel 7	$F7E0
$FFE2	Timer channel 6	$F7E2
$FFE4	Timer channel 5	$F7E4
$FFE6	Timer channel 4	$F7E6
$FFE8	Timer channel 3	$F7E8
$FFEA	Timer channel 2	$F7EA
$FFEC	Timer channel 1	$F7EC
$FFEE	Timer channel 0	$F7EE
$FFF0	Real-time interrupt	$F7F0
$FFF2	IRQ	$F7F2
$FFF4	XIRQ	$F7F4
$FFF6	SWI	$F7F6
$FFF8	Illegal opcode trap	$F7F8
$FFFA	COP failure reset	$F7FA
$FFFC	Clock monitor fail reset	$F7FC
$FFFE	Reset	$F7FE

Figure 4.19   An Interrupt jump table address for the MC68HC912-B32. (Copyright of Motorola. Used by permission.)

HPRIO register can be changed only when the I bit is set to logic 1, which disables the maskable interrupt system. When a maskable interrupt is elevated in priority, the remaining interrupts will retain their original relative interrupt priority.

Practice Questions

1. **Question:** What value must be written to the highest priority I interrupt register (HPRIO) to boost the priority of the byte data link communications (BDLC) interrupt?

   Answer: The value $D0 must be loaded into the HPRIO register.

2. **Question:** Referring to the previous question, provide the C code to accomplish this.

   Answer: HPRIO = 0xD0;

3. **Question:** Referring to the previous question, what effect will this action have on the nonmaskable interrupt priorities? The maskable interrupt priorities?

   Answer: This will have no effect on the nonmaskable interrupt priorities. The maskable interrupts will be shifted down one level of priority; however, their relative order of priority with one another will not change.

4. **Question:** What actions are required after a reset event to place the $\overline{IRQ}$ maskable interrupt at the highest possible maskable interrupt level?

   Answer: None. After a reset, the $\overline{IRQ}$ maskable interrupt is placed at the highest possible maskable interrupt level.

4.10.5 Interrupt System Associated Registers

There are two 68HC12 registers associated with the 68HC12 interrupt system: (1) the interrupt control register (INTCR) and (2) the highest priority I interrupt register (HPRIO).

The INTCR, illustrated in Figure 4.18, is used to enable the maskable interrupt $\overline{IRQ}$. This is a two-step process. Maskable interrupts must be enabled using the clear interrupt mask (CLI) command and the individual maskable interrupt system must be enabled. For the $\overline{IRQ}$ interrupt, this is accomplished by setting bit 6, the external $\overline{IRQ}$ enable (IRQEN) bit to a logic "1." With this setting the external $\overline{IRQ}$ pin is connected to the interrupt logic. Bit 7 of the INTCR register is the $\overline{IRQ}$ select edge sensitive only (IRQE) bit. When this bit is set to logic 0, the $\overline{IRQ}$ pin is configured for low-level recognition. On the other hand, when this bit is set to logic 1, the $\overline{IRQ}$ pin will respond only to falling edges.

As mentioned previously, the HPRIO is used to "boost" the priority of a maskable interrupt to the highest possible interrupt available for maskable types. (see Figure 4.20 for this register.) The register is configured with values from the right column of Figure 4.17 to boost the priority of the corresponding interrupt. For example, to boost the priority of the timer overflow register, the value $DE is written to the HPRIO register. Note that the reset value for this register is $F2. As expected, this gives the $\overline{IRQ}$ interrupt the highest priority for maskable interrupts.

Register: Highest Priority I Interrupt (HPRIO)							Address: $001F
7	6	5	4	3	2	1	0
1	1	PSEL5	PSEL4	PSEL3	PSEL2	PSEL1	0
Reset: 1	1	1	1	0	0	1	0

Figure 4.20   A highest priority I interrupt register—HPRIO ($001F).

4.11 68HC12 INTERRUPT RESPONSE

Figure 4.21 illustrates a UML activity diagram detailing the actions of the 68HC12 in response to an interrupt. We'll work our way through the diagram to gain an understanding of how the 68HC12 responds and processes an interrupt. Pay close attention to the steps that the user must accomplish versus those that are automatically done by the 68HC12. The user-implemented steps are marked with a small rectangle.

To begin, the interrupt vector jump table must be initialized with the memory address of the first location of the associated interrupt service routine (ISR). Rather than use numerical memory addresses, memory labels are used to specify the beginning of the ISR. This is usually accomplished using assembler directives. Since it is easier to accomplish these steps in assembly language, we use inline assembly commands to accomplish these tasks. (A detailed example is coming up!)

A program containing an interrupt must have the stack pointer initialized. As mentioned earlier in this chapter, the stack is where the 68HC12 will store key register values while an interrupt service routine is being processed. Initialized as a compiler option when programming in C, the stack pointer points to the last memory location used by the stack. Therefore, it should be initialized to the last memory location plus one in user-available RAM.

Next, the maskable interrupt system (if it is to be used) must be enabled. This is a two-step process. First, the enable bit associated with the specific interrupt system must be enabled. (Recall that the enable bits associated with each hardware interrupt system was provided in Figure 4.17.) Second, the overall maskable interrupt system must be enabled by clearing the I bit in the CCR to a logic 0. This is accomplished with the CLI command using inline assembly techniques. Both steps must be accomplished to enable a specific interrupt.

With the stack declared and the maskable interrupt system enabled, the main program must be written as normal. You are also responsible for writing the specific ISR. When the interrupt event occurs, a chain reaction of events is initiated. However, if the interrupt event occurs in the middle of an instruction, the current program step in most cases will be completed. This provides for an orderly transition of control from the main program to the ISR. When programming an ISR in C, it is written like a normal C function. However, other specific configuration actions must be accomplished by the user as we soon will see.

Some of the 68HC12 commands are quite lengthy. In particular, the fuzzy logic rule evaluation (REV), the fuzzy logic rule evaluation—weighted (REVW), and the weighted average (WAV) can require many clock cycles to execute. Rather than wait for these to finish, the 68HC12 has special provisions to interrupt

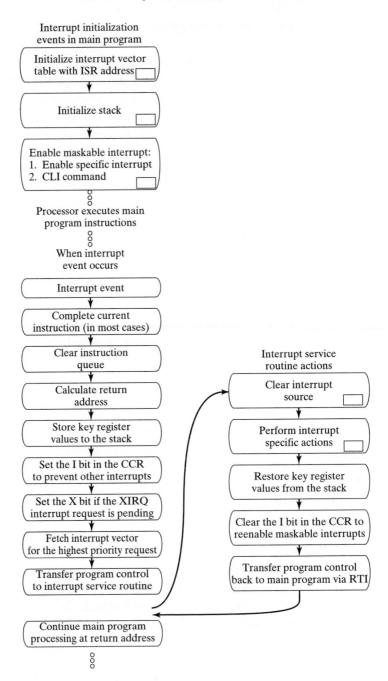

Figure 4.21 The response of a 68HC12 to an interrupt. The user is responsible for programming those activities marked with a small rectangle.

these instructions for an interrupt event. The processing of these instructions is finished after the interrupt service routine is completed.

The 68HC12 is equipped with an instruction queue. The queue normally contains the next two instructions that will be executed during normal program flow. When an interrupt occurs, the normal flow of events is no longer valid. Therefore, the instructions in the queue are useless and the queue must be emptied. After the queue is emptied, the return address back to the main program is calculated. This is usually the address of the next program instruction immediately following the instruction that was executing when the interrupt occurred. With the return address calculated, the 68HC12 will store all key register values on the stack. Accumulators A and B, Index Registers X and Y, the condition code register, and the return address back to the main program are stored on the stack in a specific order. Figure 4.22 illustrates how these registers are placed on the stack. It is important to note that the 68HC12 will accomplish this register stacking automatically. No code is required by the user to accomplish this task.

With the key register values stored on the stack, the 68HC12 will disable the maskable interrupt system by placing a logic 1 in the condition code register I bit. This prevents the 68HC12 from responding to additional interrupts that may occur during the processing of the interrupt service routine. The X bit is also set disabling the $\overline{XIRQ}$ interrupt.

The 68HC12 then retrieves the address associated with the specific interrupt that is active. This address, or interrupt vector, specifies the location of the beginning address of the associated interrupt service routine. Program control is now transferred to the first program step in the interrupt service routine. Figure 4.21 showed this process.

In the next section we discuss in detail how to write an interrupt service routine in C. In general, the interrupt service routine contains specific commands to respond to the interrupt that caused the exception. When the interrupt specific actions are complete, the 68HC12 will automatically restore the key register values from the stack, clear the I bit in the CCR to reenable the maskable interrupt

Memory Location	Stacked Values
Stack Pointer—2	Return address high: Return address low
Stack Pointer—4	Index register Y high: Index register Y low
Stack Pointer—6	Index register X high: Index register X low
Stack Pointer—8	Accumulator B : Accumulator A
Stack Pointer—9	Condition code register

Figure 4.22 Interrupt stacking order on entry to interrupts. Stack pointer (SP) variable in the memory location column refers to the original value of the SP before execution of interrupt service routine.

system, and provide for a smooth transition of control from the interrupt service routine back to the main program. These events are triggered by the return from interrupt (RTI) instruction that concludes a user-written interrupt service routine. In C the compiler will automatically insert the RTI instruction for you, if you declare a function as an interrupt service routine.

Practice Questions

1. **Question:** Listed below are the response of the 68HC12 to an interrupt. Indicate which actions are performed automatically by the 68HC12 and which actions must be programmed by the user.

   Answer:

   - Initialize interrupt vector table with ISR address (user)
   - Initialize the stack pointer via a compiler setting (user)
   - Enable maskable interrupt system (user)
   - Complete current instruction (68HC12)
   - Clear instruction queue (68HC12)
   - Calculate return address (68HC12)
   - Store key register values on stack (68HC12)
   - Set I bit in CCR (68HC12)
   - Fetch interrupt vector for highest priority active interrupt (68HC12)
   - Transfer program control to ISR (68HC12)
   - Clear interrupt source (user/68HC12, depending on specific application)
   - Restore key register values (68HC12)
   - Clear the I bit in the CCR (68HC12)
   - Transfer program control back to the main program (68HC12)

2. **Question:** How does the 68HC12 determine the priority of the pending interrupt events?

   Answer: The interrupt vector table sets the priority of the interrupt events.

3. **Question:** Often the set interrupt (SEI) mask command is used at the beginning of a program containing interrupts. Why?

   Answer: It is good practice to turn off the maskable interrupt features with the SEI command while the interrupt is being configured. Once configured, the maskable interrupt system is enabled with the clear interrupt mask (CLI) command. Realize these are assembly language instructions. To use them in a C program, we must employ inline assembly techniques.

4. **Question:** Why does the 68HC12 flush the instruction queue when an interrupt occurs?

   Answer: The instructions awaiting execution in the queue are no longer valid.

4.12 WRITING INTERRUPT SERVICE ROUTINES IN C

This section focuses on the general details involved in programming an interrupt service routine in C. We provide specific examples when we investigate some of the other systems aboard the 68HC12. Throughout these examples, we use ImageCraft ICC12 C compiler syntax [ImageCraft]. Other C compilers will have similar features.

The following steps should be accomplished to successfully write an interrupt service routine in C.

1. When interrupt handlers are written in C, the interrupt service routine must be preceded by an interrupt handler `#pragma`. A `#pragma` is a preprocessing directive used for implementation-specific guidance to the compiler. A `#pragma` that is not recognized by the compiler is ignored. The `#pragma interrupt_handler` with the ImageCraft compiler has the following format:

   ```
   #pragma interrupt_handler <name>
   ```

   where < name > is the title of the interrupt service routine. This `#pragma` informs the compiler that the named function is an interrupt handler.
2. The interrupt service routine is then defined like a normal C function. The compiler will automatically insert the return from interrupt (RTI) command during the compilation process as a result of the `#pragma` in step 1.
3. You must also initialize the stack, which should be set to the last location (highest RAM memory address) plus one in user-available RAM. This is usually a compiler setting. Therefore, you do not need to include any code to accomplish stack initialization. However, you should check the compiler setting against the memory map of the 68HC12 configuration.
4. You must correctly initialize the interrupt vector table. As we already discussed, the B32 interrupt vector table is stored in write-protected flash EEPROM memory. To allow the user code to specify interrupt and reset addresses, each entry of the erase protected vector table starting at address $FFC0 contains a pointer to a vector jump table, which is located in user-programmable flash EEPROM starting at address $F7C0. This information was summarized in Figure 4.19.
5. The specific interrupt system must be locally enabled. We discuss how to do this when we look at specific examples. In general, recall the enable bits associated with each hardware interrupt system were provided in Figure 4.17.
6. The maskable interrupt must then be globally enabled with the CLI assembly command. As previously discussed, this is easily accomplished by defining the CLI command using inline assembly techniques. This step should

be accomplished last since the interrupt system becomes "hot" with this command. You do not want to enable the interrupt system until all other system parameters are completely configured. This may be accomplished by inserting the following interrupt related commands in an include file:

```
#define CLI() asm(``cli \n''); /*Clear I Bit in CCR -
                                         enables interrupts*/
#define SEI() asm(``sei \n''); /*Set I Bit in CCR -
                                         disables interrupts*/
```

Therefore, when you want to enable the interrupt system within a C program, simply use CLI();

The following is a summary example of initializing an interrupt. We will provide additional detailed examples of writing B32 interrupts after we have discussed the timer system.

```
//function prototype
void toggle_isr(void);

//interrupt pragma
#pragma interrupt_handler toggle_isr

//initializing the vector table
#pragma abs_address: 0xF7EA          //B32 RAM-based vector address
void (*Timer_Channel_2_interrupt_vector[])()={toggle_isr};
#pragma end_abs_address
```

4.13 CLOCK FUNCTIONS

The 68HC12 is equipped with a clock generation module (CGM) circuitry to generate the clock signals used by the CPU, on-chip peripherals, and the external peripheral devices, as illustrated in Figure 4.23. The 68HC12 uses internal clock signals derived from the primary clock signal: the T clock, the E clock, and the P clock. The T clock is used by the CPU; whereas, the E and P clocks are used by the bus interfaces, the serial peripheral interface (SPI) system, and the analog-to-digital (ATD) system. They also drive on-chip modules such as the standard timer module (TIM), the serial communications interface (SCI) system, and the real-time interrupt (RTI) system. The B32 is also equipped with a slow mode clock divider that allows the clock frequency to be significantly slowed down. This allows the timer to be adjusted to specific applications.

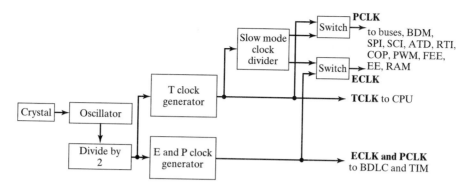

Figure 4.23   An overview of clock generation module (CGM) circuitry. The 68HC12 uses internal clock signals derived from the primary clock signal: T clock, the E clock, and the P clock.

4.13.1 The B32 Evaluation Board Clock System

The B32 evaluation board (EVB) is equipped with a 16 MHz on-board crystal. The crystal frequency is divided by two, which provides for 8 MHz CPU operation. This time base is routed to all of the systems within the processor. Some of these systems have the capability to further reduce the clock frequency. This crystal may be disconnected from the EVB by modifying the factory default jumper configuration. This allows connection of an alternate time base to the EVB via the EXTAL (external crystal) pin. The time base may be a crystal of a different frequency or a ceramic resonator. A ceramic resonator is similar to a crystal; however, its stability characteristics are not usually as precise. However, they are significantly less expensive than a crystal. Throughout this book, we assume an 8 MHz operation.

The bus speed may be further reduced by using the slow mode divider, a features that allows the bus speed to be divided by 1, 2, ... 128. The slow mode divider is configured with the slow mode divider register (SLOW) located at $00E0. The bit configuration and settings are provided in Figure 4.24. The base two raised to the power specified in binary by the SLDV[2:0] bits produce the slow mode frequency divider value.

You may wonder why we would want to change the time base for the processor. Recall, power consumption is proportional to the frequency of operation. Therefore, depending on the application, it might be better to slow down the clock speed to reduce the power consumption. Also, in many situations the processor may be used in an application where it is interfacing and controlling much slower external mechanical devices. In these instances it might be advantageous to operate the processor at a lower frequency. Also, careful choice of the clock

Register: Slow Mode Divider Register (SLOW)   Address: $00E0

7	6	5	4	3	2	1	0
0	0	0	0	0	SLDV2	SLDV1	SLDV0

Reset: 0   0   0   0   0   0   0   0

| | | Bus rate with | | |
SLDV[2:0]	Divider (2^x)	16 MHz oscillator	8 MHz oscillator	4 MHz oscillator
000	1	8 MHz	4 MHz	2 MHz
001	2	4 MHz	2 MHz	1 MHz
010	4	2 MHz	1 MHz	500 KHz
011	8	1 MHz	500 KHz	250 KHz
100	16	500 KHz	250 KHz	125 KHz
101	32	250 KHz	125 KHz	62.5 KHz
110	64	125 KHz	62.5 KHz	31.2 KHz
111	128	62.5 KHz	31.2 KHz	15.6 KHz

Figure 4.24   Slow mode divider register which allows the bus speed to be divided by 1, 2, ... 128.

frequency will allow easy conversion to real-time clock time. For example, if the bus rate is reduced to 62.5 kHz by setting the slow mode divisor selector bits (SLDV[2:0]) to 111, the free running counter (to be discussed shortly) of the timing system will roll over once per second.

4.14 THE TIMING SYSTEM—THE STANDARD TIMER MODULE

The TIM Module of the 68HC12 was designed to accomplish three main functions:

- *Input capture:* The input capture feature allows the characteristics of an input signal to be measured. The input capture system can be programmed to measure the length of an input pulse or used to compute the characteristics of a periodic signal, such as period, duty cycle, and frequency. These definitions are illustrated in Figure 4.25. The duty cycle of a periodic signal is defined as the "on time" of the signal divided by its total period. The period of a repetitive signal is measured from a rising edge to a rising edge (or a falling edge to a falling edge). The frequency of a repetitive signal is simply the reciprocal of the period.
- *Output compare:* The output compare feature allows the generation of an output signal(s) to user specifications. A single active high or low

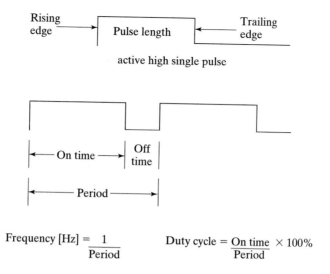

Figure 4.25   Characteristics of signals: duty cycle, period, and frequency.

pulse or a periodic output signal of user-specified frequency and duty-cycle may be generated. This system may also be used to generate PWM signals. However, the B32 configuration is equipped with a dedicated PWM system.

- *Pulse accumulator:* The pulse accumulator feature may be used to count pulses (external events) to the 68HC12. It can also be used to measure the long pulse width of an input signal.

The TIM is equipped with eight complete, individual 16-bit dual function input capture/output compare subsystems called channels. That is, each of these channels is software configurable for either input capture or output compare operation. Although all of these channels use the same time base, they can be configured with interrupt techniques to run simultaneously. The input capture/output compare pins are IOC[7:0] of PORT T. The TIM also contains the hardware components of the 16-bit pulse accumulator. The input for the pulse accumulator is pin IOC7/PAI. Thus pin 7 of Port T can be used as an input pin for an input capture channel, as an input pin for the pulse accumulator subsystem, or as an output pin for an output compare channel.

4.14.1 Components of the Timer Module

The block diagram of the timer module (TIM) is shown in Figure 4.26. Although this diagram may at first appear very complicated, realize there are really

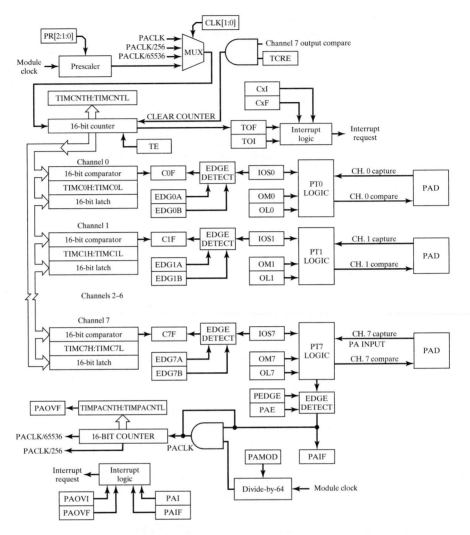

Figure 4.26 A block diagram of the timer module. There are three main components: (1) the 16-bit free running counter and its associated time scaling hardware, (2) eight input capture/output compare channels, and (3) the pulse accumulator hardware. (Copyright of Motorola. Used by permission.)

only three main components to the TIM: (1) the 16-bit free running counter and its associated time scaling hardware, (2) eight input capture/output compare channels, and (3) the pulse accumulator hardware. We shall discuss each of these main components of the TIM in turn. For each component, we provide a simplified block diagram.

4.14.2 Free Running Counter

The heart of the 68HC12 TIM is a 16-bit free running counter (TCNT), illustrated in Figure 4.27. All input capture and output compare functions derive their timing information from this single counter. When the timer system is enabled, by placing a 1 in the TEN bit of the timer system control register, located at memory address $0086, the counter starts at $0000 and is normally incremented for each module clock (P CLOCK) pulse. The counter counts from $0000 to $FFFF and automatically rolls over to $0000 and continues to count. The current value of the 16-bit free running counter is contained in two 8-bit registers: (1) the timer counter register high (TCNTH), located at memory location $0084, and (2) the timer counter register low (TCNTL) at memory location $0085. Together these two registers form the 16-bit TCNT register. Normally this register is defined in the header file as a 16-bit register TCNT.

Free Running Counter Time Base   As can be seen in the free running counter diagram, the frequency of the P clock can be divided by the prescaler hardware. The P clock frequency may be divided (scaled) by different user-programmed divisors. The prescale divisors are determined by bits PR[2:1:0] in the timer mask register 2 (TMSK2). Figure 4.28 presents register details, with the available prescaler divisors shown in the chart. For example, if the prescale divisor is set to 16 (PR[2:1:0] = 100), only one clock pulse is provided to the free running counter for every 16 P CLOCK pulses input to the prescaler.

The prescale factor controls how long it takes for the free running counter to roll over. Since the free running counter contains 16-bits, it requires 2^{16} or 65,536 pulses to rollover. For example, if the P clock's frequency is 2 MHz, the free running counter will roll over every 32.768 milliseconds (2^{16} $pulses$ x $1/(2\ MHz)$). If the prescale divisor is set for 32, only a single pulse will be provided to the free running counter for every 32 input pulses to the prescaler. Hence, the free running counter will roll over every 1.048576 seconds.

Different time bases may be used as the timing source for the free running counter. The PACLK, the PACLK/256, or the PACLK/65,536 may also be used as the free running counter's clock source when the pulse accumulator section of the timer module is enabled. The source is selected via a 4 to 1 multiplexer connected to the input of the free running counter. The desired clock source is selected using bits CLK[1:0] of the pulse accumulator control register (PACTL) located at memory address $00A0.

Timer Overflow Flag   If we are timing a "long" event—an event longer than $FFFF M clock cycles—it is important to monitor how many times the free running counter rolls over. The 68HC12 sets a timer overflow flag (TOF) every time the counter rolls over. The TOF is bit 7 in the timer flag register 2

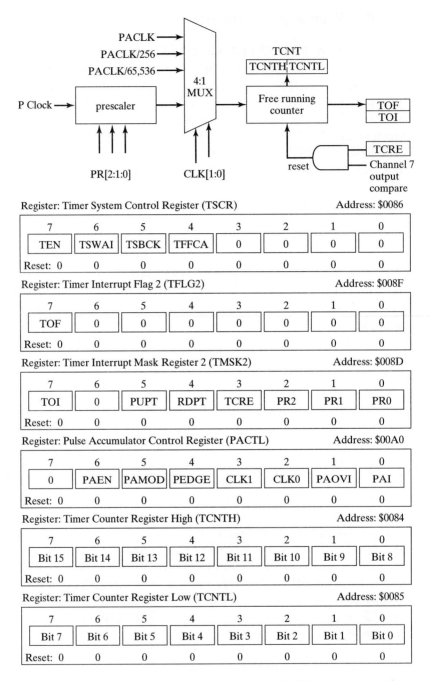

Figure 4.27 Free running counter. The P CLOCK frequency may be divided (scaled) by different user-programmed prescale divisors set by bits PR[2:1:0] located in TMSK2.

PR[2:1:0]	Divisor
000	1
001	2
010	4
011	8
100	16
101	32
110	Reserved
111	Reserved

Figure 4.28   Prescaler selection. The frequency of the P clock may be divided by the prescaler hardware.

(TFLG2) located at memory address $008F. Furthermore, a timer overflow interrupt (TOI) can be employed to signal the rollover of the free running timer. The interrupt approach has a clear advantage over the flag approach. When an interrupt is employed, the 68HC12 will issue an interrupt signal indicating that a significant event has occurred; whereas, with the flag approach, the program must keep polling to see if a significant event has occurred. While polling for a flag, the processor cannot accomplish other actions. This is an extremely inefficient use of a powerful processor.

When a timer overflow occurs, the TOF will be set. The Timer Interrupt Flag 2 (TFLG2) register bit 7 must be reset by the user program prior to the next TOF event. The TOF flag is reset by writing a 1 to the bit. Yes, that's correct; you clear the bit to 0 by writing a 1 to the bit! The TOF flag may also be cleared using fast flag clearing procedures discussed below. To compute a long period, you have to create a TOF counter and it must be incremented to keep track of the total number of timer overflow events.

Calculating Elapsed Time   Although the free running counter (TCNT) may be reset, great caution should be exercised prior to doing so. Remember that all timing channels derive their time base from the TCNT. Therefore, if the TCNT is reset to conveniently start the timer for a specific application at $0000, other timing channels may be affected. You should become comfortable using elapsed time to avoid resetting the timer. That is, the time difference between key events in clock ticks must be calculated. Also, the number of time overflows must be taken into account. This is not a new concept to you. When you purchase a used car, the number of rollovers of the odometer are of great importance to you as the potential buyer.

To calculate elapsed time, the start time is subtracted from the stop time. This is complicated by the nature of the free running counter. Usually the counter is not reset when an event is timed; therefore different timing scenarios will be

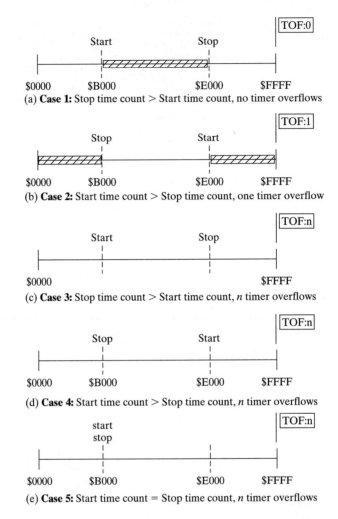

Figure 4.29   Timing examples using the free running counter. To calculate elapsed time, the start time must be subtracted from the stop time.

encountered. In Figure 4.29 (a) the simplest case is shown, with the stop time being a larger number than the start time. Also, no timer overflow has occurred. In this scenario, elapsed time in clock ticks is calculated by simply subtracting the start time from the stop time. To convert the elapsed time in clock ticks to real time, the number of clock ticks is multiplied by the period of the TCNT clock. This is easily accomplished when programming in C.

In Figure 4.29 (b) the start time is larger than the stop time and only one TCNT timer overflow has occurred. Figure 4.29 (c) and (d) provide for events lasting longer than the rollover time of the free running counter. In this case the number of timer overflows must be taken into account. Figure 4.29 (e) provides for events where the stop time and the start time are the same value. In this case the number of rollovers of the free running counter must be taken into account.

At first glance, it might seem that the algorithm to calculate elapsed time for all of these different cases might be quite complex. Luckily, a single equation accounts for all of the cases. Elapsed time may be calculated using the following equations:

$$\text{Elapsed clock ticks} = (n \times 2^{16}) + (\text{Stop count} - \text{Start count}) \ [\text{clock ticks}]$$

$$\text{Elapsed time} = (\text{Elapsed clock ticks}) \times (\text{TCNT clock period}) \ [\text{seconds}]$$

In this first equation n is the number of timer overflow flag (TOF) events that occur between the start and stop events. The equation yields the elapsed time in clock ticks. To convert to seconds the number of clock ticks are multiplied by the period of the clock source of the free running counter.

To compute elapsed time accurately, the timer overflow flag (TOF) must be reset every time it sets since the number of TOF plays a vital role in correctly calculating the elapsed time. This is easily accomplished within an interrupt service routine (ISR) associated with the TOF interrupt.

Resetting the Free Running Counter   To reset the counter, the timer counter reset enable (TCRE) bit in the timer mask register 2 (TMSK2) must be set. Furthermore, the timer channel 7 registers must contain $0000. When these conditions are met, the timer counter registers remain at $0000. Carefully consider whether or not the free running counter needs to be reset in a specific application. Recall, all eight input capture/output compare channels derive their timing from the free running counter.

In the next section we describe TIM system associated registers. We then pull all of these concepts together with several detailed examples.

Practice Questions

1. **Question:** What is the system frequency of the B32 EVB?

   Answer: The B32 EVB is factory equipped and default jumper configured with a 16 MHz crystal. This crystal frequency is divided by two to yield 8 MHz to provide the system frequency.

2. **Question:** Why would you want to possibly operate the B32 EVB at a frequency other than its factory default?

   Answer: Power consumption is proportional to the frequency of operation. Also, the processor may often be used in an application where it is interfacing and controlling much slower mechanical devices. In these instances it might be advantageous to operate the processor at a lower frequency.

3. **Question:** Two input capture events occur at counts $0105 and $EC20 of the free running counter. How many counts (in decimal) have transpired between these two events?

   Answer: $EC20−$0105 = $EB1B = 60,187 counts

4. **Question:** In the preceding question, if the P CLOCK was 2 MHz and the prescaler bits PR[2:1:0] were set to 000, how much time in seconds transpired between the two input capture events?

   Answer: $60,187 \times 1/(2\text{MHz}) = 30.0935$ ms

5. **Question:** Repeat the preceding question if PR[2:1:0] were set to 100.

   Answer: With the prescaler set for "100," the divisor is 16. Therefore, the counter is incremented every 16 E clock pulses. For this example, 481.496 ms have transpired between the two input capture events.

6. **Question:** What are the three primary functions provided by the TIM?

   Answer: (1) Input capture, capturing characteristics of input signals; (2) output compare, generating precision output signals; and (3) pulse accumulator, counting events.

7. **Question:** Why is the TOF flag so important in the timer system?

   Answer: The TOF sets every time the timer rolls over from $FFFF back to $0000. To accurately monitor elapsed time, the number of TOF being set must be tracked.

8. **Question:** Why must great care be exercised prior to resetting the free running counter?

   Answer: All eight channels of the TIM system derive their timing from the TCNT. If the TCNT is reset, it may have an adverse effect on the other timing channels currently in use.

4.14.3 Free Running Counter Associated Registers

In this section the registers associated with the free running counter are discussed. These registers allow the user to tailor the features of the free running counter to the specific application at hand.

Timer System Control Register   The timer system control register (TSCR) is located at memory location $0086, as shown in Figure 4.30. The timer enable (TEN) bit, when set to 1, enables the timer and disables the timer when set to 0. This bit serves as the on/off switch for the TIM system.

The other key component in this register is the timer fast flag clear-all (TFFCA) bit, which controls how fast the flags associated with the input capture/output compare channels will be cleared. When the TFFCA bit is 0, timer system flags are cleared using the standard method of writing a logic 1 to the flag bit. Writing a logic 0 to the flag bit has no effect. When the TFFCA bit is 1,

Register: Timer System Control Register (TSCR)   Address: $0086

7	6	5	4	3	2	1	0
TEN	TSWAI	TSBCK	TFFCA	0	0	0	0
Reset: 0	0	0	0	0	0	0	0

Figure 4.30   Timer system control register (TSCR).

the fast flag clear features are enabled. These features are slightly different for each portion of the timer system as shown here:

- *TFLG1 register*: A read from the input capture or write to the output compare channel causes the corresponding channel flag, CnF, to be cleared in the TFLG1 register.
- *TFLG2 register*: Any access to the TCNT register will clear the timer overflow flag (TOF) in the TFLG2 register.
- *PAFLG register*: Any access to the PACNT or register clears both the PAOVF and PAIF flag bits in the PAFLG register.

The following code shows how to turn on the TIM system using the TEN bit:

```
/*-------------------------------------------------------------*/
/*MAIN PROGRAM                                                 */
/*-------------------------------------------------------------*/
#include<912b32.h>

void main(void){

unsigned char    TSCR_MASK=0x80;            /*TEN mask*/

TSCR=TSCR_MASK;
.
.
.


}
/*-------------------------------------------------------------*/
```

Timer Counter Register   The 16-bit timer counter register (TCNT) is divided into two 8-bit registers: timer counter register high (TCNTH) and timer counter register low (TCNTL). These registers are located at memory locations $0084 and $0085, respectively. The TCNT register contains the current value of the free running counter. The TCNT register should be read all at once. This

Register: Timer Counter Register High (TCNTH)   Address: $0084

7	6	5	4	3	2	1	0
Bit 15	Bit 14	Bit 13	Bit 12	Bit 11	Bit 10	Bit 9	Bit 8

Reset: 0   0   0   0   0   0   0   0

Register: Timer Counter Register Low (TCNTL)   Address: $0085

7	6	5	4	3	2	1	0
Bit 7	Bit 6	Bit 5	Bit 4	Bit 3	Bit 2	Bit 1	Bit 0

Reset: 0   0   0   0   0   0   0   0

Figure 4.31 The timer counter register (TCNT) and its two 8-bit registers.

is easy to accomplish in C. To read the TCNT register, it is set equal to a variable declared as an unsigned integer (16-bits). Figure 4.31 provides register details. For example, if variables start_time and stop_time were declared as an unsigned integer, the current value of the free running counter could be found by using the following code:

```
/*----------------------------------------------------------*/
/*MAIN PROGRAM */
/*----------------------------------------------------------*/
#include<912b32.h>

void main(void){

unsigned int    start_time;          /*start time*/
unsigned int    stop_time;           /*stop time*/

start_time=TCNT;
.

.

.
stop_time=TCNT;


}
/*----------------------------------------------------------*/
```

Timer Mask Register 2   The timer mask register 2 (TMSK2), located at memory location $008D, is illustrated in Figure 4.32. At this time we will describe only the functions for some of the TMSK2 register bits. As previously mentioned, the timer counter reset enable (TCRE) bit allows the free running counter to be reset. The TMSK2 register also contains the timer prescaler select (PR[2:1:0]) bits. These bits are used to set the prescale divisor. The prescale

Register: Timer Interrupt Mask Register 2 (TMSK2)   Address: $008D

7	6	5	4	3	2	1	0
TOI	0	PUPT	RDPT	TCRE	PR2	PR1	PR0
Reset: 0	0	0	0	0	0	0	0

Figure 4.32   The timer mask register 2 (TMSK2).

divisor values were provided in Figure 4.28. The Timer Pull-Up Resistor Enable TPU and Timer Drive Reduction TDRB bits are used to enable PORTT pull up resistors and reduced drive features, respectively.

4.14.4 Input Capture/Output Compare Channels

The TIM is equipped with eight complete, individual 16-bit dual function input capture/output compare channels. A block diagram of one of these dual function channels is provided in Figure 4.33. These eight channels are connected to the outside world via the IOS[7:0] pins (pins PT[7:0]) of PORT T whose memory

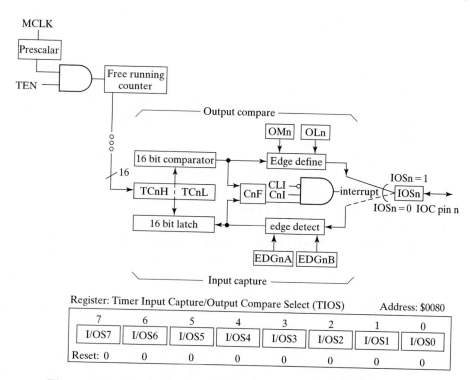

Register: Timer Input Capture/Output Compare Select (TIOS)   Address: $0080

7	6	5	4	3	2	1	0
I/OS7	I/OS6	I/OS5	I/OS4	I/OS3	I/OS2	I/OS1	I/OS0
Reset: 0	0	0	0	0	0	0	0

Figure 4.33   A representative input capture/output compare channel.

location is $00AE. Each specific channel is configured for the input capture or the output compare function with the associated bit in the timer IC/OC select register (TIOS) at memory location $0080. When the IOCx bit is set to logic 1, the corresponding channel is configured for the output compare function. When set to logic 0, the corresponding channel functions as an input capture channel. The 16-bit free running counter provides a reference count to the eight input capture/output compare (IC/OC) channels.

Input Capture   The input capture system is a 16-bit binary stopwatch. It can be configured to capture the current count of the free running timer when a user-specified event occurs. The user-specified event can be a rising edge, a falling edge, or any (rising or falling) edge. Since the free running counter is used for all eight IC/OC channels, it is usually not reset. Instead, elapsed time between key events is used to determine input signal parameters. The input capture system may be used to measure the length of a single pulse whether active high or low or the characteristics of a periodic signal such as period, duty cycle, or frequency.

To capture the characteristics of an input signal, we need to convert the desired parameters to input capture events. For example, to measure the frequency of an input signal, we would capture the free running counter value on two sequential rising (or falling) edges. The period in clock counts would be the difference between the two edges' free running counter values. To convert to real elapsed time, we would multiply the elapsed clock count between the two edges by the period of the free running counter timer.

The calculation of frequency, period, or duty cycle in real clock time is cumbersome when using assembly language. However, when using C as the target language, these values may be readily calculated using standard math functions. Care must be exercised to properly declare the variables associated with these calculations. The key components of the input capture system are illustrated in Figure 4.34. As previously mentioned the free running counter provides a 16-bit binary count to the input capture channel. The input channel is configured to wait for a user-specified event. This event can be a rising signal edge, a falling signal edge, or any signal edge (rising or falling). The user specifies the desired edge characteristics to the edge detection logic using the associated EDGnA and the EDGnB bits of the timer control registers—TCTL3 ($008A) and TCTL4 ($008B). See Figure 4.35 for register details.

When the user-specified event occurs on the configured input capture pin, the following chain reaction of events is set in motion:

1. The current value of the free running counter is latched into the associated timer channel registers (TCnH/L), where *n* represents one of the eight input/output channels. The 16-bit count in the TCnH/L represents the

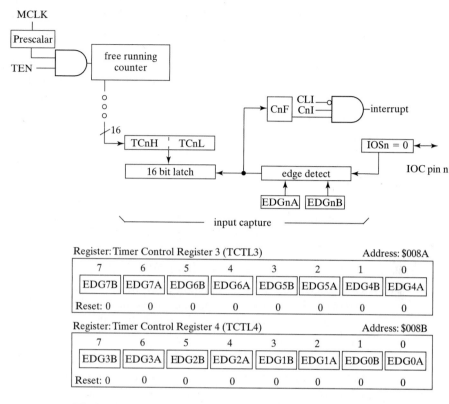

Register: Timer Control Register 3 (TCTL3)   Address: $008A

7	6	5	4	3	2	1	0
EDG7B	EDG7A	EDG6B	EDG6A	EDG5B	EDG5A	EDG4B	EDG4A

Reset: 0   0   0   0   0   0   0   0

Register: Timer Control Register 4 (TCTL4)   Address: $008B

7	6	5	4	3	2	1	0
EDG3B	EDG3A	EDG2B	EDG2A	EDG1B	EDG1A	EDG0B	EDG0A

Reset: 0   0   0   0   0   0   0   0

Figure 4.34   Key components of the input capture system.

EDGnB EDGnA	Configuration
00	Capture disabled
01	Rising Edge
10	Falling Edge
11	Any Edge

Figure 4.35   Input capture edge selection. The input channel is configured to wait for a user-specified event. This event can be a rising signal edge, a falling signal edge, or any signal edge (rising or falling).

value of the free running timer "clock ticks" when the user-specified event occurred. To read the 16-bit value from this register, a 16-bit unsigned integer variable should be used.

2. The associated channel flag (CnF) is set. This flag can be reset by writing a logic 1 to it.

3. If the corresponding channel interrupt enable (CnI) has been set, the channel will generate an interrupt event.

The input capture system may be configured for many applications. Let's examine one such example—capturing the characteristics of a single active high pulse. This example assumes the pulse length is less than the rollover time of the free running counter, and channel 2 (the selection of channel 2 is arbitrary) has been configured as an input capture via the TIOS register. This example also assumes that the pulse width is longer than the time to execute steps 4 through 7. To measure the pulse length of a single active high pulse, the following actions should be taken:

1. Set the input capture edge selection to wait for a rising edge. This is accomplished by setting the associated EDG2B and EDG2A bits to 0 1 in the timer control register (TCTL3, TCTL4).

2. Monitor the associated channel flag (C2F).

3. When the C2F bit is set, indicating the desired second edge action has occurred on the associated input capture pin, the current time in the free running counter is automatically latched into the timer channel register (TC2H/L).

4. Read the value in the TC2H/L register and stored it in a convenient location by assigning the register value to an unsigned integer variable (rising_edge).

5. Reset the C2F flag by writing a logic 1 to it.

6. Set the input capture edge selection to wait for a falling edge. This is accomplished by setting the associated EDG2B and EDG2A bits to 1 0 in the timer control register (TCTL3, TCTL4).

7. Monitor the associated channel flag (C2F).

8. When the C2F bit sets indicating the falling edge has occurred on the associated input capture pin, the current time in the free running counter is automatically latched into the timer channel register (TC2H/L).

9. Read the value in the TC2H/L register again by assigning the register value to an unsigned integer variable (falling_edge).

10. Calculate the elapsed time between the edges (Elapsed time = falling-edge - rising-edge).

11. Convert the elapsed time in "clock ticks" to real time by multiplying the number of clock ticks by the free running counter's period (Elapsed time × Period).

The registers associated with the input capture system will be covered after discussing the output compare system.

Practice Questions

1. **Question:** How must the above steps be modified to measure the pulse length of a single active low pulse?

   Answer: Step 1 must be modified to capture a falling edge. Step 6 must be modified to capture a rising edge.

2. **Question:** How must the above steps be modified to measure the period of a repetitive signal?

   Answer: Step 6 should be deleted; in step 8, look for a rising edge instead of a falling edge. This will have the system capture the time of two rising edges. The period is found by taking the free running count from the second falling edge and subtracting from it the free running count of the first edge. This assumes the period is shorter than the rollover period of the counter.

3. **Question:** How must the steps provided above be modified to measure the time between two input capture rising edge events for time increments greater than the rollover time of the counter.

   Answer: For time increments greater than the rollover time of the free running counter, a counter must be implemented in software to count the number of times rollover occurs.

Output Compare   The output compare function allows the user to generate an output signal to desired specifications. A single active low or active high pulse may be generated or a periodic signal of desired specifications (duty cycle, frequency, etc.) may be generated. The key components of the output compare system are illustrated in Figure 4.36.

Like the input capture system, the free running counter provides the time base for the output compare system. A 16-bit value is loaded into the associated 16-bit timer channel registers (TCnH/L). When the 16-bit count in the free running counter equals the 16-bit value in the TCnH/L, the comparator starts a chain reaction of events.

1. The associated channel flag (CnF) is set. This flag can be reset by writing a logic 1 to it.

2. The corresponding channel interrupt flag (CnI) will be set and generate an interrupt event if it has been previously enabled.

3. The user-specified output event will occur on the associated output pin. The output event is specified by the associated output mode/output level (OMn/OLn) bits. These bits are located in timer control registers 1 (TCTL1— $0088) and 2 (TCTL2—$0089). The specified output event may be a logic level 1 output, a logic level 0 output, or a toggle. Figure 4.37 provides register details.

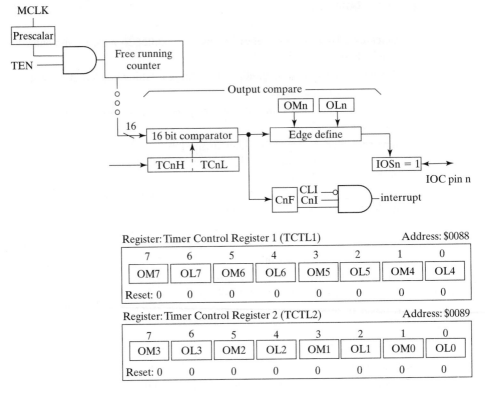

Figure 4.36 Key components of the output compare system.

OMn OLn	Configuration
00	Timer disconnected
01	Toggle OCn output line
10	OCn output line to 0
11	OCn output line to 1

Figure 4.37 Output compare signal selection.

Output compare events are generated in reference to key events. For example, to generate a single active low pulse (assumed to be less than the rollover time of the counter), the following actions must be taken:

1. Obtain the current value of the free running counter (TCNT).
2. Set the desired output pin to low.

3. Calculate the length of the desired pulse duration in clock ticks. That is, the desired pulse length is divided by the period of the free running counter. The resulting fraction is multiplied by $FFFF to complete the conversion to clock ticks.

4. Add the pulse length in clock ticks to the free running counter value obtained in step 1.

5. Store this sum into the associated timer channel register (TCnH/L).

6. Program the associated output pin to set the OCn line. This is accomplished by configuring the associated OMn/OLn bits in the TCTL1,2 registers to 11.

7. When the free running counter value equals the TCnH/L register, the output pin goes high.

Output Compare Channel 7   We next discuss one special output compare channel: output compare channel 7. Output compare channels one through six function identically as we discussed earlier in this section. Output compare 7, however, has an additional capability to control logic states on all output compare pins, once the timer part has been programmed as the output compare pins using the TIOS register. The additional capability is available by configuring two registers associated with the output compare 7 channel: Output Compare Channel 7 Mask (OC7M) register and Output Compare Channel 7 Data (OC7D) register.

When the contents of the free running counter value, updated in the TCNT register, match with the contents of the TC7($009E) register, the logic states of pins OC1-OC7 are controlled by the values pre-stored in the OC7M and the OC7D registers. The OC7M register works as a switch register that turns on or off each output compare pin from being controlled by the OC7 channel. If a bit in the OC7M register contains 1, the logic state on the output compare pin will change based on the corresponding bit in the OC7D register.

For example, suppose the OC7M register contains binary value 10110001 and the OC7D register holds binary value 01010101. When the contents of the TCN7 and the TC7 register match, the value stored in the OC7M register dictates that the logic state on output pins OC0, OC4, OC5, and OC7 to change to logic 1 (bit 0 of OC7D), 1 (bit 4 of OC7D), 0 (bit 5 of OC7D), and 0 (bit 7 of OC7D), respectively.

Using the flexibility of the OC7 channel along with the individual output compare channel functions, you can control the logic states on the output compare pins at two different times during each period of the free running counter, counting from $0000 to $FFFF. For example, pulse width modulated signals can easily be generated on a particular output compare pin by programming the corresponding output compare channel to set logic high/low and the output compare channel 7 to set logic low/high.

The Input Capture/Output Compare Registers   In this section we summarize the registers associated with the input capture (IC)/output compare (OC) system. The registers associated with the pulse accumulator system will be discussed later in this chapter.

Miscellaneous Timer Registers.   The miscellaneous timer registers are illustrated in Figure 4.38.

Timer IC/OC Select Register.   The timer IC/OC select register (TIOS) is located at memory location $0080. This register is illustrated in Figure 4.38. The

Register: Timer Input Capture/Output Compare Select (TIOS)   Address: $0080

7	6	5	4	3	2	1	0
IOS7	IOS6	IOS5	IOS4	IOS3	IOS2	IOS1	IOS0

Reset: 0   0   0   0   0   0   0   0

Register: Timer Compare Force Register (CFORC)   Address: $0081

7	6	5	4	3	2	1	0
FOC7	FOC6	FOC5	FOC4	FOC3	FOC2	FOC1	FOC0

Reset: 0   0   0   0   0   0   0   0

Register: Output Compare 7 Mask Register (OC7M)   Address: $0082

7	6	5	4	3	2	1	0
OC7M7	OC7M6	OC7M5	OC7M4	OC7M3	OC7M2	OC7M1	OC7M0

Reset: 0   0   0   0   0   0   0   0

Register: Output Compare 7 Data Register (OC7D)   Address: $0083

7	6	5	4	3	2	1	0
OC7D7	OC7D6	OC7D5	OC7D4	OC7D3	OC7D2	OC7D1	OC7D0

Reset: 0   0   0   0   0   0   0   0

Figure 4.38   Miscellaneous timer registers.

IOSn bits in this register are used to specify whether a given channel will be configured for input capture or output compare. When a specific IOSn bit is set to 1, the corresponding channel is configured for an output compare operation. When 0, the channel is configured for input capture operations.

Timer Compare Force Register.   The timer compare force register (CFORC) is located at memory location $0081 (see again Figure 4.38 for register details). Setting a specific FOCn bit to 1 causes an immediate output compare action on the corresponding channel. This is a useful technique for initializing the output compare channels.

Timer Output Compare 7 Mask Register.   The timer output compare 7 mask register (OC7M) is located at memory location $0082, as illustrated in Figure 4.38. The bits of the OC7M register correspond with the bits of the PORT T timer port. Setting an OC7Mn bit will set the corresponding port to be an output port regardless of the state of the DDRTn bit when the corresponding TIOS[n] bit is set for the output compare function.

Timer Output Compare 7 Data Register.   The timer output compare 7 data register (OC7D) is located at memory location $0083 (see again Figure 4.38 for register details). The bits of the OC7D register correspond with the bits of the PORT T timer port. When a successful OC7 compare action occurs, for each bit set in the OC7M register, the corresponding data bit in OC7D is placed with the corresponding bit of the timer port.

Timer Control Registers.   The timer control registers are illustrated in Figure 4.39.

Timer Control Register 1 (TCTL1) and Timer Control Register 2 (TCTL2). Timer control registers 1 and 2 are used to specify the output compare actions for a specific output channel. The corresponding OMn and OLn bits specify the output mode for a specific channel. The settings for these two bits were provided earlier in the chapter in Figure 4.37.

Timer Control Register 3 (TCTL3) and Timer Control Register 4 (TCTL4). Timer control registers 3 and 4 are used to specify the input capture actions for a specific input channel. The corresponding EDGnB and EDGnA bits specify the edge to be captured using a specific channel. The settings for these two bits were provided in Figure 4.34.

Timer Mask Registers.   The timer mask registers are illustrated in Figure 4.40.

Timer Mask Register 1.   The timer mask register 1 (TMSK1) is located at memory location $008C. This register is used to selectively turn on the interrupts associated with the input capture/output compare channels. If cleared, the

Register: Timer Control Register 1 (TCTL1)   Address: $0088

7	6	5	4	3	2	1	0
OM7	OL7	OM6	OL6	OM5	OL5	OM4	OL4

Reset: 0   0   0   0   0   0   0   0

Register: Timer Control Register 2 (TCTL2)   Address: $0089

7	6	5	4	3	2	1	0
OM3	OL3	OM2	OL2	OM1	OL1	OM0	OL0

Reset: 0   0   0   0   0   0   0   0

Register: Timer Control Register 3 (TCTL3)   Address: $008A

7	6	5	4	3	2	1	0
EDG7B	EDG7A	EDG6B	EDG6A	EDG5B	EDG5A	EDG4B	EDG4A

Reset: 0   0   0   0   0   0   0   0

Register: Timer Control Register 4 (TCTL4)   Address: $008B

7	6	5	4	3	2	1	0
EDG3B	EDG3A	EDG2B	EDG2A	EDG1B	EDG1A	EDG0B	EDG0A

Reset: 0   0   0   0   0   0   0   0

Figure 4.39 Timer control registers.

corresponding flag is disabled from causing an interrupt. If set, the corresponding flag is enabled to cause an interrupt.

Timer Mask Register 2. The timer mask register 2 (TMSK2) is located at memory location $008D. The timer counter reset enable (TCRE) bit allows the free running counter to be reset. In order for this to occur, the TCRE must be set to 1 and the timer channel 7 register must contain $0000. The TMSK2 register also contains the timer prescaler select (PR[2:1:0]) bits. These bits are used to set the prescale divisor. The timer overflow interrupt enable (TOI) bit is used to turn on the timer overflow Interrupt flag. When this bit is set to logic 1, an interrupt is initiated when the TOF flag is set.

Timer Flag Registers. The timer flag registers are illustrated in Figure 4.41.

Timer Flag Register 1. The timer flag register 1 (TFLG1) is located at memory location $008E. The bits in the TFLG1 register indicate when an interrupt

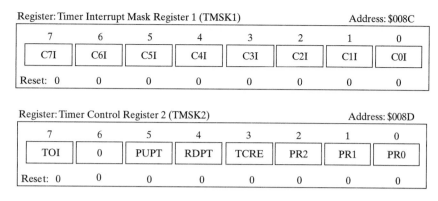

Figure 4.40   Timer mask registers.

condition has occurred. A specific flag bit is reset by writing a 1 to the bit. Writing a zero to a bit will not affect the current status of the bit. When the TFFCA bit in the TSCR register is set, a read from an input capture or a write into an output compare channel will cause the corresponding channel flag (CnF) to be cleared.

Timer Flag Register 2.   The timer flag register 2 (TFLG2) is located at memory location $008F. The timer overflow flag (TOF) bit in the TFLG2 register indicates when the free running counter rolls over. The TOF flag bit is reset by writing a 1 to the bit.

Timer Input Capture/Output Compare Registers High (TCnH) and Low (TCnL).   There are eight separate timer input capture/output compare registers. Figure 4.42 presents register details. Each of these registers is 16-bits long. Depending on the corresponding TIOS channel bit, these registers are used to latch the value of the free running counter during an input capture event or to

Register: Timer Interrupt Flag Register 1 (TFLG1)   Address: $008E

7	6	5	4	3	2	1	0
C7F	C6F	C5F	C4F	C3F	C2F	C1F	C0F

Reset: 0   0   0   0   0   0   0   0

Register: Timer Control Flag 2 (TFLG2)   Address: $008F

7	6	5	4	3	2	1	0
TOF	0	0	0	0	0	0	0

Reset: 0   0   0   0   0   0   0   0

Figure 4.41   Timer flag registers.

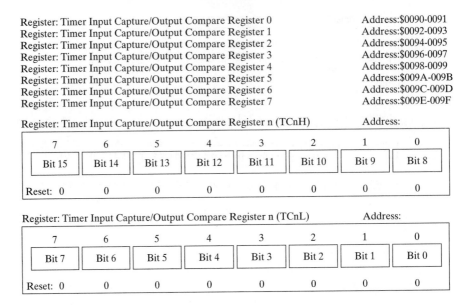

Register: Timer Input Capture/Output Compare Register 0	Address:$0090-0091
Register: Timer Input Capture/Output Compare Register 1	Address:$0092-0093
Register: Timer Input Capture/Output Compare Register 2	Address:$0094-0095
Register: Timer Input Capture/Output Compare Register 3	Address:$0096-0097
Register: Timer Input Capture/Output Compare Register 4	Address:$0098-0099
Register: Timer Input Capture/Output Compare Register 5	Address:$009A-009B
Register: Timer Input Capture/Output Compare Register 6	Address:$009C-009D
Register: Timer Input Capture/Output Compare Register 7	Address:$009E-009F

Register: Timer Input Capture/Output Compare Register n (TCnH)   Address:

7	6	5	4	3	2	1	0
Bit 15	Bit 14	Bit 13	Bit 12	Bit 11	Bit 10	Bit 9	Bit 8

Reset: 0   0   0   0   0   0   0   0

Register: Timer Input Capture/Output Compare Register n (TCnL)   Address:

7	6	5	4	3	2	1	0
Bit 7	Bit 6	Bit 5	Bit 4	Bit 3	Bit 2	Bit 1	Bit 0

Reset: 0   0   0   0   0   0   0   0

Figure 4.42 Timer input capture/output compare Registers High (TCnH) and Low (TCnL).

trigger an output compare event when the TCNT register value matches with values in these registers.

Practice Questions

1. **Question:** Describe two different methods that an interrupt flag (CnF) may be cleared in register TFLG1.

   Answer: A specific flag bit is reset by writing a 1 to the bit. Writing a 0 to a bit will not affect the current status of the bit. When the TFFCA bit in the TSCR register is set, a read from an input capture or a write into an output compare channel will cause the corresponding channel flag (CnF) to be cleared.

2. **Question:** What must the timer input capture/output compare select (TIOS) register be set to configure even-numbered channels for input capture and odd-numbered channels for output compare?

   Answer: $AA

3. **Question:** What must be the contents of the timer control register 1 (TCTL1) to configure output compare channel 7 to logic high?

   Answer: To set channel 7, bits (OM7, OL7) should be set for 1 1.

4. **Question:** What must be the contents of the timer control register 4 (TCTL4) to configure input capture channel 1 to monitor for any edge?

   Answer: To capture any edge on the channel 1, bits (EDG1B, EDG1A) should be set for 1 1.

Timer System Examples   We now provide several examples using the timer system. In the first we use the input capture system to measure the frequency and period of an incoming signal. We show how to capture the key parameters of the signal. As a homework assignment at the end of this chapter, we ask you to calculate the actual parameter values of the signal. In the second example we demonstrate how to generate a precision digital waveform. In the third example we generate a precision waveform using interrupt techniques.

In each example we provide a description of the function, the required theory, a UML activity chart, and well-documented C code.

Input Capture.   Recall from our previous discussion that the input capture feature allows you to measure the characteristics of an input signal. It is possible to measure length of pulses, period, duty cycle, and frequency of a periodic signal by capturing key signal parameters such as a falling edge, a rising edge, or some combination of both.

To configure the input capture system to measure the signal parameters, we must use the following registers. We have already discussed these registers in some detail. They are summarized here for convenience.

IMPORTANT INPUT CAPTURE REGISTERS

- TMSK1 (timer interrupt mask 1) contains timer channel interrupt enable bits (CnI).
- TMSK2 (timer interrupt mask 2) contains timer overflow interrupt enable bit (TOI) and timer prescaler select bits (PR[2:0]).
- TIOS (timer input capture/output compare select) contains input capture/output compare (IOSn) select bits.
- TSCR (timer system control register) contains the timer enable (TEN) bit.
- TCTL3,4 (timer control register 3,4) contains edge control bits for the input capture channels.
- TFLG1 (timer interrupt flag 1) contains CnF interrupt flag for each timer channel.
- TCn (timer input capture/output compare register) stores the signal parameters captured during input capture activities.

In this example we expand a previous example to measure the frequency and period of a square wave generated by a function generator. We assume that the unknown signal period is less than the rollover time of the free running counter. To measure the period and frequency, you must carry out the following steps:

1. Enable the timer.
2. Configure the P CLOCK.

3. Set the input capture to trigger on a rising edge.
4. Save the free running counter value when the first rising edge occurs.
5. Record the free running counter value at the second rising edge.
6. Using the values of the free running counter, calculate the period and frequency of the square wave and store them to memory.

Figure 4.43 contains these steps in the form of a UML activity diagram.

The code to accomplish this input capture task follows below. This program uses the polling method to capture two consecutive rising edges of a periodic signal. Once this information is captured, the frequency and period can be calculated. There are three items to note about the code.

- The main program consists of calls to different functions, each with a specific task.

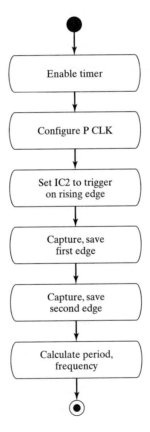

Figure 4.43 Input capture activities to measure frequency and period of an unknown signal.

- The names of the functions and variables have been chosen to reflect their purpose.
- The code is well-documented with comments and "pretty printing" to be read easily.

```
/*------------------------------------------------------------------*/
/*filename: timer1.c                                                */
/*MAIN PROGRAM: This program will measure the period and fre-       */
/*quency of a square wave.  The wave should be input on chan-       */
/*nel 2 (IC2).                                                      */
/*------------------------------------------------------------------*/

/*include files*/
#include<912b32.h>
#include<stdio.h>
#include<math.h>

/*function prototypes*/
void timer_init(void);
void measure_wave(void);
void period_freq(void);

/*global variables*/
unsigned long int rising_1;
unsigned long int rising_2;

void main(void){

timer_init();                       /*initializes timer*/
measure_wave();                     /*polls for two edges*/
period_freq();                      /*calculates freq and period*/
}


/*------------------------------------------------------------------*/
/*Function: timer_init initializes the timer system for input  */
/*capture. Configures channel 2 for input capture to trigger on*/
/*a rising edge. Assume the P clock is operating at 8 MHz.     */
/*------------------------------------------------------------------*/

void timer_init(void){

TMSK1 = 0x00;                       /*Disable interrupts*/
TMSK2 = 0x02;                       /*Prescaler for 2 MHz clock*/
TIOS = 0x00;                        /*Set Ch 2 to input capture*/
TSCR = 0x80;                        /*Enable the timer*/
TCTL4 = 0x10;                       /*Capture rising edges*/
TFLG1 = 0xFF;                       /*Clear Flags*/
}
```

```
/*-------------------------------------------------------------*/
/*Function: measure_wave measures the duty cycle and period of */
/*the wave. Values of the free running counter are stored to   */
/*global variables.                                            */
/*-------------------------------------------------------------*/

void measure_wave(void){

while((TFLG1 & 0x04)==0)
   {
   ;                                    /*wait for first edge*/
   }

rising_1 = TCNT;                        /*store FRC to rising_1*/
TFLG1 = 0x04;                           /*reset flag*/

while((TFLG1 & 0x04)==0)
   {
   ;                                    /*wait for second edge*/
   }

rising_2 = TCNT;                        /*store FRC to rising_2*/
TFLG1 = 0x04;                           /*reset flag*/
}


/*-------------------------------------------------------------*/
/*Function: period_freq calculates the period and frequency of */
/*a wave and displays it to the screen.                        */
/*-------------------------------------------------------------*/

void period_freq (void){

unsigned long int new_rising;
unsigned long int new_falling;
float frequency;
float period;
unsigned int int_period;
unsigned int int_freq, freq_tenths;

if(rising_2 < rising_1)              /*calculate period*/
   {
   new_rising = rising_2 + 0xFFFF;
   period = ((float)new_rising - (float)rising_1)*0.0000005;
   }
else                                /*rising_1 >= rising_2*/
   {                                /*difference * P CLOCK period*/
   period = ((float)rising_2 - (float)rising_1)*0.0000005;
   }
```

```
frequency = 1.0/period;                /*calculate frequency*/
int_freq = (int)(frequency/1000.0);
freq_tenths = (int)((frequency - (float)int_freq*1000)/100.0);

/*print results*/
printf(''Frequency = %d.%d kHz \n\n'', int_freq, freq_tenths);
printf(''Frequency = %f Hz \n\n'', frequency);

int_period = (int)(1000000*period);
printf(''Period = %d us \n\n'', int_period);
printf(''Period = %f ms \n\n'', (period*1000));
}
/*----------------------------------------------------------*/
```

This program does not take into account signal periods lasting longer than the rollover time of the counter. In one of the homework problems, at the end of the chapter (Challenging 8), we ask you to modify the code to detect signals with slower frequencies. How would you do this? To account for signal periods lasting longer than the rollover time of the free running counter, you must track how many times the timer overflow flag (TOF) is set. Recall that this flag sets every time the free running counter rolls over from $FFFF to $0000. If you keep track of the number of TOF occurrences, you can accurately determine elapsed time by multiplying the number of TOFs by the number of clock ticks per rollover (2^{16}) by the period of the free running counter time base. As you solve the problem, consider that you have two methods to do this: (1) monitoring (polling) for the TOF flag to occur, or (2) allowing the TOF interrupt features to keep track of the timer overflows in the background.

At the other extreme, what about signal periods that are very short? How short is short? Your intuition probably tells you that an 8 MHz processor is not fast enough to time signal periods for a 100 MHz signal. How about an 8 MHz signal? A 1 MHz signal? In these cases you must investigate assembly code generated by the compiler for the C source code and actually count clock cycles required to execute specific instructions. This will allow you to determine if the algorithm and processor combination is fast enough to capture the events of a fast signal.

Output Compare   The output compare feature allows you to generate a signal to meet desired specifications. This system may be used to generate precision digital waveforms, active high or low pulses, or even pulse width modulated signals. (The B32 EVB is equipped with a dedicated PWM system.)

In this example, we investigate how to generate a periodic signal of a specified frequency and duty cycle. As before, we list the registers used for this program for convenience.

IMPORTANT OUTPUT COMPARE REGISTERS

- TMSK1 (timer interrupt mask 1) contains timer channel interrupt enable bits (CnI).
- TMSK2 (timer interrupt mask 2) contains timer overflow interrupt (TOI) enable bit and timer prescaler select bits (PR[2:0]).
- TIOS (timer input capture/output compare select) contains input capture/output compare (IOSn) select bits.
- TSCR (timer system control register) contains the timer enable (TEN) bit.
- TCTL2 (timer control register 2) contains edge control bits for the output compare system.
- TFLG1 (timer interrupt flag 1) contains CnF interrupt flag for each timer channel.
- TCn (timer input capture/output compare register) stores the signal parameters captured during input capture activities.

In this example, we use the output compare to generate a precision square wave with a frequency based on the day and month of your birth date and a duty cycle based on the year of your birth. For example: If you were born on May 19, 1977, the square wave you generate will have a frequency of 519 Hz and a duty cycle of 77 percent. To implement this you will need to calculate the number of clock cycles for the high time and the low time of the periodic signal.

To complete this task, you must carry out the following steps:

1. Set up the P CLOCK to operate at 8 MHz.
2. Set the prescaler to divide the P CLOCK by 4 so the clock signal to the output compare system is 2 MHz. This means the period is 0.5 microseconds, which is a convenient value for calculations.
3. The frequency of this signal is 519 Hz, which means the period, T is 1/519 or 0.0019268 s.
4. The 77 percent duty cycle means that the square wave is high 77 percent of the time and low 23 percent of the time.
5. Calculate the high and low time:

High time $= 0.77(0.0019268) = 0.001484$ s
Low time $= 0.23(0.0019268) = 0.0004432$ s

6. Convert the high and low times to number of clock cycles:

High time $= 0.001484/0.5$ μs $= 2968$ clock cycles

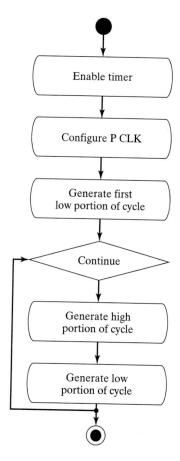

Figure 4.44   Output compare activities to generate a precision square wave.

Low time $= 0.0004432/0.5$ μs $= 886$ clock cycles

Figure 4.44 contains these steps in the form of a UML activity diagram.

The following code will accomplish this output compare task. This program uses the polling method.

```
/*-----------------------------------------------------------------*/
/*filename: timer2.c                                               */
/*MAIN PROGRAM: This program will generate a precision square      */
/*wave with a frequency of 519 Hz and a duty cycle of 77%.  It     */
/*will use output compare channel two (OC2) to generate the        */
/*signal.                                                          */
/*-----------------------------------------------------------------*/

/*include files*/
```

```c
#include<912b32.h>

/*function prototypes*/
void timer_init(void);
void half_cycle(unsigned int time);

void main(void){

unsigned int high_time = 2968;   /*high time*/
unsigned int low_time = 886;     /*low time*/

timer_init();                    /*initializes timer*/
half_cycle(low_time);            /*generate low signal portion*/

while(1)                         /*do this forever*/
  {
  half_cycle(high_time);         /*gen high signal portion*/
  half_cycle(low_time);          /*generate low signal portion*/
  }

}

/*----------------------------------------------------------------*/
/*Function: timer_init initializes the timer system to use out-  */
/*put compare channel two (OC2) and toggle.  Assume P clock is   */
/*operating at 8 MHz.                                            */
/*----------------------------------------------------------------*/

void timer_init(void){

TMSK1 = 0x00;                    /*Disable interrupts*/
TMSK2 = 0x02;                    /*Prescaler for 2 MHz clock*/
TIOS  = 0x04;                    /*Set Ch 2 to output compare*/
TSCR  = 0x80;                    /*Enable the timer*/
TCTL2 = 0x10;                    /*Configure Ch2 to toggle*/
TFLG1 = 0x04;                    /*Clear OC2 flag*/
TC2   = TCNT;                    /*current TCNT to Ch2 ctr*/
}

/*----------------------------------------------------------------*/
/*Function: half_cycle generates either the high or low portion  */
/*of the output compare signal.  It needs to have the desired    */
/*time for the portion of the wave passed to it.                 */
/*----------------------------------------------------------------*/

void half_cycle(unsigned int time){

TC2 += time;                               /*Update timer register*/
```

```
while((TFLG1 & 0x04)==0)                    /*poll for flag*/
  {
  ;
  }

TFLG1 = 0x04;                               /*Clear flag */
}
/*-----------------------------------------------------------*/
```

This program is elegant in its simplicity. However, it has one major problem—the 68HC12 can only generate this single signal. That is, the processor is tied up polling (waiting) for the output compare flags to occur. What happens if you need to generate more than one signal at once? The polling method quickly becomes complicated. To generate multiple signals simultaneously or allow the processor to continue doing other tasks while generating output signals, we need to employ the interrupt capabilities of the timer system. The next example illustrates how to do this.

Output Compare with Interrupts   The purpose of this example is to become familiar with output compare interrupts on the 68HC12. It demonstrates the advantages of running the 68HC12 in an interrupt mode and it also illustrates some complications of running the interrupts out of RAM. Here is a quick review of the registers we use in this example.

IMPORTANT OUTPUT COMPARE REGISTERS

- TMSK1 (timer interrupt mask 1) contains Timer channel interrupt enable bits (CnI).
- TMSK2 (timer interrupt mask 2) contains Timer Overflow Interrupt enable bit (TOI) and Timer Prescaler Select bits (PR[2:0]).
- TIOS (timer input capture/output compare select) contains input capture/output compare (IOSn) select bits.
- TSCR (timer system control register) contains the timer enable (TEN) bit.
- TCTL2 (timer control register 2) contains "edge control" bits for the output compare system.
- TFLG1 (timer interrupt flag 1) contains CnF interrupt flag for each timer channel.
- TCn (timer input capture/output compare register) stores the signal parameters captured during input capture activities.

In this example, we set the 68HC12 to generate a square wave. The frequency in hertz should be the last three digits of your phone number. You should tie the active low IRQ and XIRQ to logic high (Vcc) through a 4.7 KΩ resistor as a safety precaution to prevent accidental interrupts. Prior to reviewing the code, go back and review the steps required to configure an interrupt in C.

Before getting started, remember to ensure that the following interrupt related definitions are contained within your header file. Recall, these definitions allow you to use interrupt-related assembly style commands within your C program.

```
\#define CLI() asm(``cli \n''); /*Clear I Bit in CCR - enables
                                                     interrupts*/
\#define SEI() asm(``sei \n''); /*Set I Bit in CCR - disables
                                                     interrupts*/
```

It should be mentioned that the code to initialize the interrupt service routines may be compiler specific. In this example we use the ImageCraft ICC12 compiler interrupt configuration commands. Other compilers have similar functions.

```
/*----------------------------------------------------------*/
/*filename: timer3.c                                        */
/*MAIN PROGRAM: This program will generate a precision      */
/*square wave using the Timer system interrupt features on  */
/*Channel 2.                                                */
/*----------------------------------------------------------*/

/*include files*/
#include<912b32.h>

/*function prototypes*/
void toggle_isr(void);          /*interrupt_handler toggle_isr*/

//interrupt pragma
#pragma interrupt_handler toggle_isr

//initialize vector table
#pragma abs_address: 0xF7EA
void (*Timer_Channel_2_interrupt_vector[])()={toggle_isr};
#pragma end_abs_address

void initialize(void);          /*Define function initialize*/

/*global variables*/
int c;

void main(void){

c = 100;
initialize();                   /*Init the timer system*/
TMSK1 = 0x04;                   /*Enable Ch2 interrupt*/
TFLG1 = 0xFF;                   /*Clear interrupt flags*/
CLI();                          /*Initialize interrupts*/
```

```
while(1)
   {
   ;                                  /*wait for interrupt*/
   }
}


/*-----------------------------------------------------------*/
/*Function: initialize enables the timer system and          */
/*configures the P CLK.                                      */
/*-----------------------------------------------------------*/

void initialize(void){

TMSK2 = 0x02;                    /*Prescaler for 2 MHz clock*/
TIOS = 0x04;                     /*Set Ch 2 to output compare*/
TSCR = 0x80;                     /*Enable the timer*/
TCTL2 = 0x10;                    /*Configure Ch2 to toggle*/
}


/*-----------------------------------------------------------*/
/*Function: toggle_isr                                       */
/*-----------------------------------------------------------*/

void toggle_isr(void){

TFLG1 = 0xFF;                            /*reset interrupt flag*/
TC2 = TC2+c;                             /*update Ch2 */
c=c+100;                                 /*update c   */
}
/*-----------------------------------------------------------*/
```

Examine the `toggle_isr` function carefully. How do you expect the resulting waveform to appear?

Let's extend this example to simultaneously generate two square waves with different frequencies. For one wave use one-half the frequency obtained using the month and day of your birthday and for the second use one-half the month and day of your friend's birthday. You can verify that the waves are being generated simultaneously and that they have different frequencies with an oscilloscope or logic analyzer.

```
/*-----------------------------------------------------------*/
/*filename: timer4.c                                         */
/*MAIN PROGRAM: This program will generate two precision square*/
/*waves using the Timer system interrupt features.           */
/*-----------------------------------------------------------*/

/*include files*/
#include<912b32.h>
```

```
/*function prototypes*/
void toggle1_isr(void);
void toggle2_isr(void);

/*interrupt pragma*/
#pragma interrupt_handler toggle1_isr
#pragma interrupt_handler toggle2_isr

/*initialize vector table*/
#pragma abs_address: 0xF7E8
void (*Timer_Channel_3_interrupt_vector[])()={toggle2_isr};
void (*Timer_Channel_2_interrupt_vector[])()={toggle1_isr};
#pragma end_abs_address

void initialize(void);                 /*Define function initialize*/

void main(void){

initialize();                          /*Init the timer system*/
TMSK1 = 0x0C;                          /*Enable Ch 3,2 interrupts*/
TFLG1 = 0xFF;                          /*Reset interrupt flags*/
CLI();                                 /*Initialize interrupts*/

while(1)
  {
  ;                                    /*wait for interrupt*/
  }

}

/*----------------------------------------------------------------*/
/*Function: initialize enables the timer system and configures   */
/*the P CLK                                                      */
/*----------------------------------------------------------------*/

void initialize(void){

TMSK2 = 0x02;                          /*Prescaler for 2 MHz clock*/
TIOS = 0x0C;                           /*Set Ch to output compare*/
TSCR = 0x80;                           /*Enable the timer*/
TCTL2 = 0x50;                          /*configure for toggle*/
}

/*----------------------------------------------------------------*/
/*Function: toggle1_isr, birthdate: Feb 19 = 219, generate a     */
/*one-half 219 Hz or 109.5 Hz.  With a 2 MHz clock need to       */
/*toggle TC2 every 9091 clock ticks                              */
/*----------------------------------------------------------------*/
```

```
void toggle1_isr(void){

TFLG1 = 0x04;                          /*reset Ch 2 interrupt*/
TC2 += 9091;                           /*set next interrupt event*/
}


/*----------------------------------------------------------------*/
/*Function: toggle2_isr, birthdate: Apr 12 = 412, generate a     */
/*frequency of one-half 412 Hz or 206 Hz.  With a 2 MHz clock    */
/*need to toggle TC3 every 4854 clock ticks                      */
/*----------------------------------------------------------------*/

void toggle2_isr(void){

TFLG1 = 0x08;                          /*reset Ch 3 interrupt*/
TC3 += 4854;                           /*set next interrupt event*/
}
/*----------------------------------------------------------------*/
```

4.14.5 The Pulse Accumulator

The pulse accumulator (PA) portion of the timer module, as its name implies, is designed to count pulses. The heart of the PA system is a 16-bit counter. This counter can be configured to operate in two modes of operation:

- *Event counter mode*: This mode is used to count user-specified edges that occur on the pulse accumulator input (PAI) pin.
- *Gated time accumulation mode*: In this mode the PA counts pulses using a divide-by 64 clock. It is termed "gated time" because the pulse accumulator will count the divide-by 64 clock pulses while it is enabled and ceases counting while disabled. However, it will maintain the last current count while it is in the disabled mode.

Pulse Accumulator System Description   A block diagram of the pulse accumulator system is provided in Figure 4.45. As you can see, the input pin to the PA system (PAI) shares the same external 68HC12 pin as IC/OC channel 7. To use this pin for the PA system, channel 7 must be turned off. This is accomplished by the following actions:

1. Set the IOS7 bit in the timer IC/OC select register, TIOS ($0080), to 0 to disable output compare channel 7.
2. Set bits OM7 and OL7 to 00 in timer control register 1, TCTL1 ($0088), to disconnect the IC/OC channel from the output logic pin.

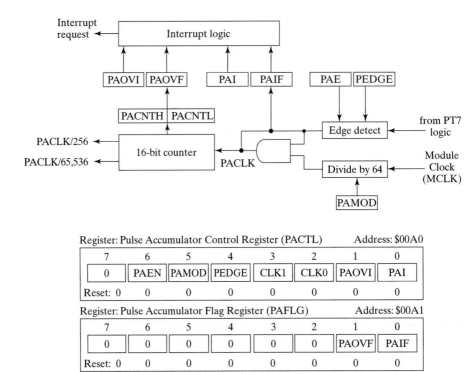

Figure 4.45   A block diagram of a pulse accumulator system. The input pin to the PA system (PAI) shares the same external 68HC12 pin as IC/OC channel 7.

3. Set the OC7M7 bit to 0 in the timer output compare 7 mask register, OC7M ($0082).

The signal from the input pin of the pulse accumulator is then routed to the edge detection circuitry. This functions much like the edge detection circuitry previously described for the input capture system. The edge detection circuitry is controlled by the pulse accumulator enable (PAEN) bit and the pulse accumulator edge (PEDGE) bit. When set to 1, the PAEN enables the pulse accumulator, whereas the PEDGE bit selects falling or rising edges on the PAI pin to increment the counter. In the event counter mode with PEDGE set to 1, the pulse accumulator will count rising edges. With PEDGE set to 0, the pulse accumulator counts falling edges on the PAI pin. The edge detection circuitry has an associated flag called the pulse accumulator input flag (PAIF). This flag is set when the user-specified edge is detected on the PAI pin. The PAIF is located in the pulse accumulator flag register—PAFLG ($00A1).

In the gated time accumulation mode, a PEDGE value of 1 allows a low PAI pin level to enable a P CLOCK/64 pulse train to be the input to the pulse accumulator's 16-bit counter. A PEDGE value of 0 allows a high PAI pin value to enable the P CLOCK/64 pulse train.

Once an input source is selected for the 16-bit counter within the pulse accumulator, it increments for each incoming pulse. The value in the 16-bit counter may be read from the 16-bit pulse accumulator counter register—PACNTH/L ($00A2 and $00A3). The 16-bit count in these registers reflects the number of active input edges on the PAI pin since the last system reset.

The 16-bit pulse accumulator counter has an overflow flag called the pulse accumulator overflow flag (PAOVF). This flag is located in the pulse accumulator flag register—PAFLG ($00A1). As with the other timer module flags, this flag is cleared by writing a logic 1 to it.

The pulse accumulator system has powerful interrupt features. There are two separate interrupts associated with the pulse accumulator system: the pulse accumulator overflow interrupt and the pulse accumulator input interrupt enable.

The pulse accumulator overflow interrupt, when enabled by the PAOVI bit of the PACTL register, initiates an interrupt event when the 16-bit pulse accumulator rolls over from $FFFF to $0000. The pulse accumulator input interrupt, when enabled by the PAI bit of the PACTL register, initiates an interrupt event when the selected edge is detected at the pulse accumulator input pin. When set for the event mode, the event edge triggers the PAIF. When set for the gated time accumulation mode, the trailing edge of the gate signal at the pulse accumulator input pin triggers the PAIF. The PAIF flag is located in the PAFLG register ($00A1).

Pulse Accumulator Registers   In this section we discuss the registers associated with the pulse accumulator system.

Pulse Accumulator Control Register.   The pulse accumulator control register (PACTL) is located at memory location $00A0 (see again Figure 4.45). This register is used to set the operating mode, the edge control, and the timing variables of the pulse accumulator system. The PAEN bit is used to enable the pulse accumulator system. When the PAEN bit is set to 1, the PA system is enabled.

When set to 0, it is disabled. The pulse accumulator mode (PAMOD) bit selects either the event counter mode (0) or the gated time accumulation mode (1) for the pulse accumulator.

The pulse accumulator edge control (PEDGE) bit determines how the PA system will respond to an edge. When the PA system is set for the event counter mode (PAMOD = 0), the PA system will respond to falling edges if the PEDGE bit is programmed to be 0 and to rising edges if the bit is set to 1.

When the PA system is set for the gate time accumulation mode (PAMOD = 1), the system is clocked by the P CLOCK/64 signal. If the PEDGE pin is 0, the falling edge of the clock signal sets the pulse accumulator input edge flag (PAIF) indicating the end of the gated time event (logic high). Similarly, if the PEDGE pin is 1, the rising edge of the clock signal sets the pulse accumulator interrupt flag (PAIF) again signaling the end of the gated time event (logic low).

The CLK1 and CLK0 bits of the PACTL select the clock signal for the PA system. The different available configurations for these pins were provided earlier in Figure 4.27.

Pulse Accumulator Flag Register.   The pulse accumulator flag register (PAFLG) located at memory location $00A1 contains the pulse accumulator system flags (PAOVF and PAIF). Figure 4.45 provides register details. The pulse accumulator overflow flag is set when the 16-bit pulse accumulator counter rolls over from $FFFF to $0000. The pulse accumulator input edge Flag (PAIF) is set when the selected edge event occurs at the pulse accumulator input pin.

Pulse Accumulator Counter Registers.   The 16-bit pulse accumulator counter register (PACNT) contains the current pulse accumulator count value (see Figure 4.45 for details). Since it is a 16-bit register, you should read the register using LDD, LDX, and the LDY type of commands, if the 68HC12 assembly language is used.

Pulse Accumulator Example.   In this example we use the pulse accumulator to derive bicycle speed using a hall effect sensor, a semiconductor device that senses the presence of a magnetic field. Hall effect sensors are available in a variety of configurations including the following:

- *Linear sensor*: Provides an output DC voltage proportional to the field strength of the magnetic field.
- *Bipolar sensor*: Senses the presence of a south magnetic pole; requires a north magnetic pole to reset.
- *Unipolar sensor*: Senses the presence of a south magnetic pole; resets on the absence of a magnetic field.

In this application we mount a magnet to a spoke on the rotating portion of a bicycle wheel. A unipolar hall effect sensor, mounted to the stationary bicycle

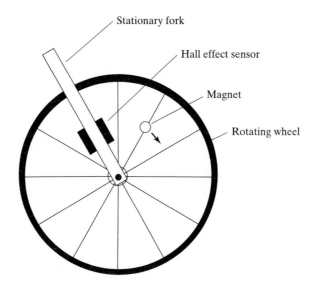

Figure 4.46   Unipolar hall effect sensor. A unipolar hall effect sensor, mounted to the stationary bicycle fork, is connected to a pulse accumulator input (PT7) of the 68HC12 microcontroller.

fork, will be connected to a pulse accumulator input (PT7) of the 68HC12 microcontroller (see Figure 4.46 for details). The hall effect sensor provides a pulse for every rotation of the bicycle tire. If we keep track of the number of pulses in a given amount of time, the distance traveled and the velocity of the bicycle can be determined.

Exercise Problem: Write a program to count the number of pulses for a specified length of time to derive the distance a bicycle has traveled and to compute the bicycle velocity. (This is actually provided as a homework problem at the end of the chapter, Challenging 9.)

Here are some suggestions:

1. Determine the relationship between a single tire rotation and the linear distance traveled by the bicycle. Assume a 66.04 cm (26 in.) tire diameter.
2. Configure the pulse accumulator system:
   (a) The pulse accumulator (PA) system uses pin PT7 of Port T as an input. Configure PT7 for PA use by setting bit 7 of the timer input capture/output compare select register (TIOS) to logic 0. Also, bits 7 and 6 of timer control register 1 (TCTL1) must be set to 0.
   (b) Configure the pulse accumulator control register (PACTL) for proper operation. Examine the required setting for each bit.

3. Obtain the current start count from the 16-bit pulse accumulator count register (PACNT).

4. Delay for the desired amount of time.

5. Obtain the current stop count from the 16-bit pulse accumulator count register (PACNT).

6. Determine distance traveled and velocity.

The following sample code can be used to initialize the pulse accumulator system.

```
//*************************************************************
//initialize_PA: initializes 68HC12 pulse accumulator system
//*************************************************************

void initialize_PA(void)
{
TIOS  = 0x00;               //Turn off timer channel 7 to use pulse
TCTL1 = 0x00;               //accumulator - 3 step process
OC7M  = 0x00;
TSCR  = 0x80;               //Turn on timer enable bit
PACTL = 0x70;               //Enable pulse accumulator, rising edge,
}                           //event count mode
```

4.15 THE REAL-TIME INTERRUPT

The 68HC12 has built-in features to perform required actions on a regular basis. This can be accomplished using the real-time interrupt (RTI) features of the 68HC12 illustrated in Figure 4.47. In this section we describe the features of this clock-related system.

The RTI system consists of two registers: (1) the real-time interrupt control (RTICTL) register, and the real-time interrupt flag (RTIFLG) register. The RTICTL is used to enable and set the interrupt rate of the RTI. The RTI system is enabled by setting the real-time interrupt enable (RTIE) bit to logic 1 and the interrupt rate is set using bits RTR[2:0]. The RTIFLG register contains the RTI flag (RTIF) in bit 7. This flag is set when the RTI occurs. It is cleared by writing a 1 to the RTIF bit in the RTIFLG register.

The time base for the RTI system is the P CLOCK (see again Figure 4.23 for clock system details). The P CLOCK is divided by a divisor determined by bits RTR[2:0], bits 2-0, of the RTICTL. As you can see in the table provided in Figure 4.47, different P CLOCK divisors may be chosen to establish the timeout value of the RTI. For example, if the P CLOCK is operating at 8 MHz and bits RTR[2:0] are set to 111, the RTI will occur 65.536 ms after the RTIF of the RTIFLG has been cleared. The RTI system aboard the DP256 processor is similar but uses slightly different registers (RTICTL, CRGINT, and CREFLE).

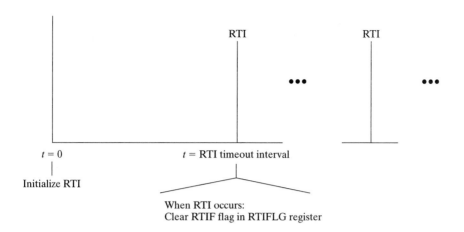

Register: Real-Time Interrupt Control Register (RTICTL)   Address: $0014

	7	6	5	4	3	2	1	0
	RTIE	RSWAI	RSBCK	0	RTBYP	RTR2	RTR1	RTR0
Reset:	0	0	0	0	0	0	0	0

Register: Real-Time Interrupt Flag Register (RTIFLG)   Address: $0015

	7	6	5	4	3	2	1	0
	RTIF	0	0	0	0	0	0	0
Reset:	0	0	0	0	0	0	0	0

RTR[2:0]	Divide E by	E = 4.0 MHz Timeout	E = 8.0 MHz Timeout
000	Off	Off	Off
001	2^{13}	2.048 ms	1.024 ms
010	2^{14}	4.096 ms	2.048 ms
011	2^{15}	8.192 ms	4.096 ms
100	2^{16}	16.384 ms	8.196 ms
101	2^{17}	32.768 ms	16.384 ms
110	2^{18}	65.536 ms	32.768 ms
111	2^{19}	131.072 ms	65.536 ms

Figure 4.47   Real-time interrupt (RTI) registers. The RTI system consists of two registers: (1) the real-time interrupt control (RTICTL) register, and (2) the real-time interrupt flag (RTIFLG) register.

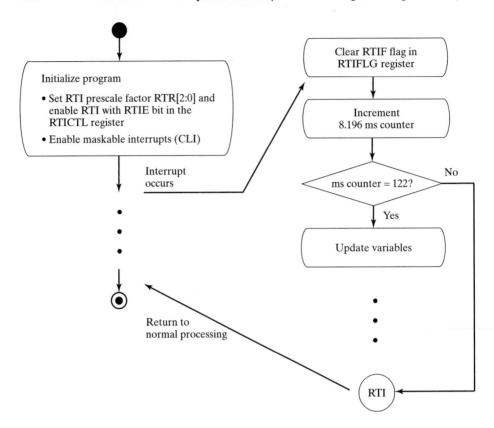

Figure 4.48   Programming the real-time interrupt.

Real Time Interrupt Example.   In this example, we use the real-time interrupt system to keep track of clock time. We accomplish this by having the RTI system generate an interrupt every 8.196 ms. When the interrupt occurs we update variables that are used to keep track of elapsed time as illustrated in Figure 4.48.

```
/*--------------------------------------------------------------*/
/*filename: realtime.c                                          */
/*MAIN PROGRAM: This program keeps track of clock time using    */
/*the Real Time Interrupt.  The RTI generates an interrupt      */
/*every 8.192 ms.  The RTI_isr keeps track of elapsed time.     */
/*--------------------------------------------------------------*/

/*include files*/
#include<912b32.h>

/*function prototypes*/
```

```
void RTI_isr(void);                    /*Real Time Interrupt - ISR*/

/* interrupt pragma */
#pragma interrupt_handler RTI_isr

/*initialize vector table*/
#pragma abs_address: 0xF7F0
void (*RTI_interrupt_vector[])()={RTI_isr};
#pragma end_abs_address

/*global variables*/
unsigned int ms_ctr, sec_ctr, mins_ctr, hrs_ctr, days_ctr;

void main(void){
ms_ctr   = 0;                          /*initialize timer variables*/
sec_ctr  = 0;
mins_ctr = 0;
hrs_ctr  = 0;
days_ctr = 0;

RTICTL = 0x84;                         /*Enable RTI int, 8.196ms RTI*/
CLI();                                 /*Initialize interrupts*/

while(1)
   {
   ;                                   /*wait for interrupt*/
   }
}

/*-------------------------------------------------------------*/
/*Function: RTI_isr: RTI interrupt occurs every 8.196 ms       */
/*-------------------------------------------------------------*/

void RTI_isr(void)
{
RTIFLG = 0x80;                    /*reset RTI Interrupt Flag*/

/*update milliseconds*/
ms_ctr = ms_ctr+1;               /*increment ms counter */

/*update seconds*/

if(ms_ctr == 122)                /*counter equates to 1000 ms at 122*/
   {
   ms_ctr = 0;                   /*reset millisecond counter*/
   sec_ctr = sec_ctr +1;         /*increment seconds counter*/
   }
```

```
/*update minutes*/
if(sec_ctr == 60)
  {
  sec_ctr = 0;                          /*reset seconds counter*/
  mins_ctr = mins_ctr + 1;              /*increment minutes counter*/
  }

/*update hours*/
if(mins_ctr == 60)
  {
  mins_ctr = 0;                         /*reset minutes counter*/
  hrs_ctr = hrs_ctr + 1;                /*increment hours counter*/
  }

/*update days*/
if(hrs_ctr == 24)
  {
  hrs_ctr = 0;                          /*reset hours counter*/
  days_ctr = days_ctr +1;               /*increment days counter*/
  }
}
/*------------------------------------------------------------*/
```

4.16 THE ENHANCED CAPTURE TIMER: MC68HC12BE32 AND HCS12 VARIANTS

One variant of the 68HC12, the MC68HC12BE32, and variants of the HCS12 are equipped with an enhanced capture timer (ECT). The ECT module has many of the same features of the standard timer module (TIM) but it also has a number of additional features. The ECT system is equipped with eight input capture/output compare channels, and these dual-use channels may be configured for either input capture (measuring parameters of an input signal) or output compare (generating precision output signals) as was the case for the 68HC12 configuration.

With the ECT configuration, however, four of the input channels are equipped with an additional holding register. This allows the input channel to capture two different capture values prior to activation of a timer related (CnF) interrupt. These are referred to as buffered channels. These buffered channels may be used in either a latch or a queue mode. The remaining input capture channels are referred to as nonbuffered channels. These channels function in a manner similar to the input capture channels found in the standard TIM. The ECT hardware functions are illustrated in Figure 4.49.

The ECT is also equipped with four 8-bit pulse accumulators (PACN3–PACN0). These pulse accumulators may be configured in pairs (PACN3:PACN2 and PACN1:PACN0) to form 16-bit pulse accumulators. With this brief overview, let's take a closer look at the ECT system in more detail.

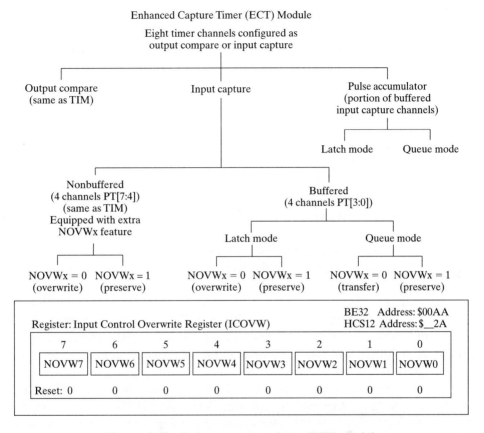

Figure 4.49   Enhance capture timer (ECT) module.

4.16.1 Nonbuffered Input Capture Channels

The nonbuffered input capture channels function similarly to those in the standard timer module (TIM). However, they are also equipped with an additional control signal, the no input capture overwrite (NOVWx) bits contained in the input control overwrite register (ICOVW). When the NOVWx bit is set (logic 1) for a specific nonbuffered IC channel, the corresponding IC register cannot be overwritten until read. This prevents the captured value from being overwritten before its value has been read and stored. If the NOVWx bit is cleared (logic 0), the IC register is overwritten when a new input capture event occurs.

4.16.2 Buffered Input Capture Channels

The four buffered input capture channels are equipped with an additional holding register. This permits the register to store two input captured values prior to initiation of an interrupt. The input capture register is considered empty when it has been read or latched into a holding register. A holding register is considered empty when it has been read. The buffered IC channels may be configured for either a latch or a queue mode.

IC Latch Mode   A buffered IC channel is configured in the latch mode by setting the input control latch or queue mode enable (LATQ) bit in the input control system control register (ICSYS) to a logic 1. In this mode, the time from the free running counter is captured in the IC capture register when a pre-defined signal event occurs at the corresponding input capture pin. The captured value is then latched to the corresponding holding register when one of three events occur: (1) the 16-bit modulus down counter (MCCNT) reaches $0000, (2) a $0000 is written to the MCCNT, or (3) a logic 1 is written to the input capture force latch action bit (ICLAT) in the 16-bit modulus down-counter control register (MCCTL). (See Figure 4.50.)

In the IC latch mode, the NOVWx bits operate the same way as described for the nonbuffered IC channels.

IC Queue Mode   As shown in Figure 4.51, when the LATQ bit is set to logic 0, the buffered IC channel is placed in the queue mode, where a specified IC transition will cause the value in the free running counter to be stored. When the NOVWx is set to logic 0, the value of the IC register will be transferred to its corresponding holding register and the IC register will store the value currently present in the free running counter. When the NOVWx is set to logic 1, the IC capture register and its corresponding holding register cannot be written until they are empty (read).

4.16.3 Pulse Accumulator Features

The ECT is also equipped with a complement of pulse accumulator (PA) registers. Specifically, the ECT PA is equipped with four 8-bit pulse accumulators. These pulse accumulators may be concatenated in pairs to form two 16-bit pulse accumulators. The PA may also be configured for Latch or Queue Modes. (See Figure 4.52.)

4.16.4 ECT Related Registers

Some of the ECT related registers are provided in Figure 4.53. Register addresses are provided for both the BE32 and also the HCS12 series of processors. The address for the BE32/HCS12 registers indicate off-set values from the start of the central register block. The default start address of the control register block is $0000. A brief explanation of each register is provided.

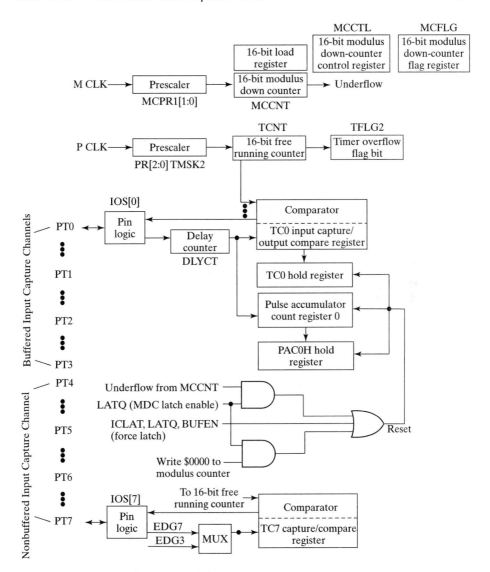

Figure 4.50   ECT buffered IC—latch mode.

Input Control Overwrite Register   The input control overwrite (ICOVW) register contains a no input capture overwrite (NOVWx) bit for each channel of the ECT. When this bit is set to logic "0" for a specific input capture channel, the contents of the associated input capture register may be overwritten. When set to a logic 1, the related registers may not be overwritten unless they are empty (read or latched into another register).

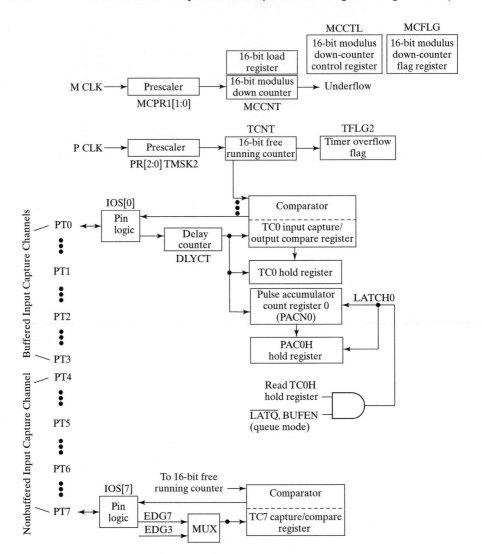

Figure 4.51 ECT buffered IC—queue mode.

Input Control System Control Register The input control system control (ICSYS) register contains the IC buffer enable (BUFEN) bit and the input control latch or queue mode enable (LATQ) bit. The BUFEN bit are used to enable the input capture and pulse accumulator holding registers when set to logic 1. The LATQ bit determines if the buffered input capture channels will be used in the queue mode (0) or latch mode (1).

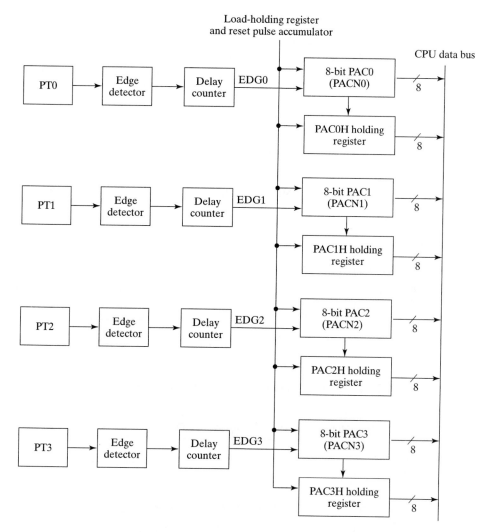

Figure 4.52 ECT pulse accumulator.

Delay Counter Control Register The delay counter control (DLYCT) register allows insertion of a delay between detection of an input capture edge and activation of associated input capture events. Such an event will be activated after the delay only if the level of the input signal at the end of the delay is opposite to what it was at delay activation. This feature provides some level of noise immunity from narrow input pulses. The length of the delay pulse is determined using the DLY[1:0] bits. A value of 00 disables the feature

Register: Input Control Overwrite Register (ICOVW)

BE32 Address: $ 00AA
HCS12 Address: $002A

	7	6	5	4	3	2	1	0
	NOVW7	NOVW6	NOVW5	NOVW4	NOVW3	NOVW2	NOVW1	NOVW0
Reset:	0	0	0	0	0	0	0	0

Register: Input Control System Control Register (ICSYS)

BE32 Address: $00AB
HCS12 Address: $002B

	7	6	5	4	3	2	1	0
	SH37	SH26	SH15	SH04	TFMOD	PACMX	BUFEN	LATQ
Reset:	0	0	0	0	0	0	0	0

Register: Delay Counter Control Register (DLYCT)

BE32 Address: $00A9
HCS12 Address: $0029

	7	6	5	4	3	2	1	0
	0	0	0	0	0	0	DLY1	DLY0
Reset:	0	0	0	0	0	0	0	0

Register: 16-bit Modulus Down-Counter Control Register (MCCTL)

BE32 Address: $ 00A6
HCS12 Address: $0026

	7	6	5	4	3	2	1	0
	MCZI	MODMC	RDMCL	ICLAT	FLMC	MCEN	MCPR1	MCPR0
Reset:	0	0	0	0	0	0	0	0

Register: Modulus Down-Counter Count Registers (MCCNT)

BE32 Address: $00B6,7
HCS12 Address: $0036,7

	15	14	13	12	11	10	9	8
	7	6	5	4	3	2	1	0
Reset:	1	1	1	1	1	1	1	1

Register: 16-bit Modulus Down-Counter Flag Register (MCFLG)

BE32 Address: $00A7
HCS12 Address: $0027

	7	6	5	4	3	2	1	0
	MCZF	0	0	0	POLF3	POLF2	POLF1	POLF0
Reset:	0	0	0	0	0	0	0	0

Figure 4.53   ECT related registers.

while 01 selects a delay of 256 P clock cycles, 10 selects a delay of 512 P clock cycles, and 11 selects a delay of 1024 P clock cycles.

Sixteen-bit Modulus Down-Counter Control Register   The 16-bit modulus down-counter (MCCTL) register is used to control the modulus down-counter. When the modulus mode enable (MODMC) bit is set to logic 0, the counter counts down from its loaded value and stops at $0000. When set to logic 1, the counter is loaded with the value written to the modulus count register when it reaches the $0000 count.

Modulus Down-Counter Count Registers   The modulus down-counter (MCCNT) contains the count of the modulus counter.

Sixteen-bit Modulus Down-Counter Flag Register   The 16-bit modulus down-counter flag register (MCFLG) contains the modulus counter underflow flag (MCZF). The flag is set to logic 1 when the modulus down-counter reaches $0000. The flag is cleared by writing a logic 1 to it.

4.17 SERIAL COMMUNICATIONS: THE MULTIPLE SERIAL INTERFACE

Serial communications is a hardware-efficient method of communicating between the controller and other devices. A single transmission line is used as a communication link. Data are then sent or received a single bit at a time. Although parallel communication of data is much faster, multiple parallel transmission paths are required.

The serial communications features of the 68HC12 allow for serial transmission and reception. Strict communication protocol and timing schemes must be followed to ensure reliable communications.

The 68HC12 serial communications features are provided by the multiple serial interface (MSI) module. This module consists of two independent serial I/O systems: (1) the serial communication interface (SCI) and (2) the serial peripheral interface (SPI). Each serial pin shares functions with the general-purpose port pins of port S. The SCI systems are nonreturn to zero (NRZ) type systems that are compatible with standard RS-232 systems. The SCI allows easily configurable two-way communications, and it is asynchronous—that is, it does not use a common clock to maintain synchronization between the transmitter and receiver, as shown in Figure 4.54.

The SPI allows the 68HC12 to communicate synchronously with peripheral devices and other microcontrollers. In addition, it requires an additional clock signal to maintain synchronization between the transmitter and receiver. At the

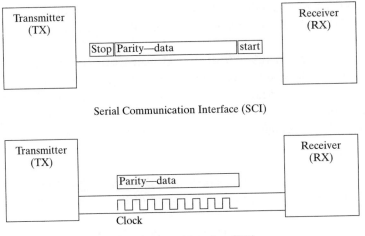

Figure 4.54   Serial communications interface versus serial peripheral interface.

expense of the additional clock signal, the SPI may be used at much higher data rates than the SCI system. The 68HC12 SPI system can be configured to act in the master or the slave mode. The master mode device controls the timing of the data transfer. The SPI system may also be used to extend the features of the 68HC12. There is a plethora of peripheral devices compatible with the SPI system.

Example

John Davis, one of our graduate students, is developing an autonomous vehicle capable of maneuvering in and about an unknown environment containing obstacles. John has equipped the vehicle with passive infrared (IR) sensors. A passive sensor is one that collects information from the environment without first probing the environment with a signal. For example, a nonpassive, or active, IR sensor would send an IR beam into the environment and monitor the return signal to detect the presence of objects. Instead, the passive sensor collects existing light from the environment and determines how the detected light changes in the presence of objects.

John has been very successful in developing such a passive sensor system and has equipped a motorized platform (a radio-controlled car minus the radio) with an array of these sensors. The sensors experience a slow drift requiring John to periodically adjust them. John developed a compensation system employing the SPI to periodically measure the offset with the ATD system aboard the processor and send out an analog correction signal to each sensor via the SPI. Recall, the 68HC12 does not have a built-in digital-to-analog conversion (DAC) system. Therefore, DACs may be connected to the processor in two ways: (1) by using a parallel port

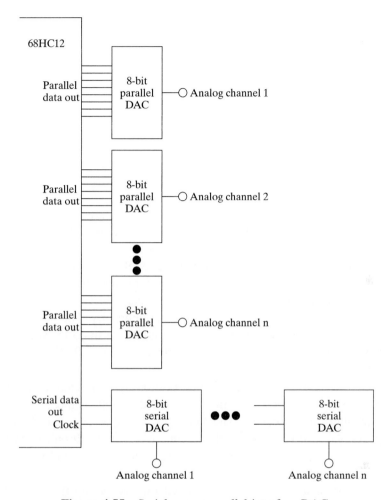

Figure 4.55   Serial versus parallel interface DACs.

for each DAC or (2) by connecting any number of DACs to the SPI system, as shown in Figure 4.55. For this application, John needed 16 DACs—one for each analog sensor. The SPI provided a two-wire interface for the 16 DAC channels to the 68HC12. Several manufacturers provide DAC peripheral chips compatible with the SPI system.

To ensure correct synchronization between a serial transmitter and receiver, a number of different methods are employed. In an asynchronous system, such as the 68HC12's serial communications interface (SCI), information is transmitted using American Standard Code for Information Interchange (ASCII) code. Also, a parity bit may or may not be used. To synchronize the transmitter to the receiver, a start bit and a stop bit are used to frame the ASCII coded character, as shown

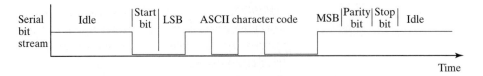

Serial bit stream | Idle | Start bit | LSB | ASCII character code | MSB | Parity bit | Stop bit | Idle

Time

Figure 4.56 Synchronizing an asynchronous transmitter/receiver. In an asynchronous system, such as the serial communication interface, information is transmitted using ASCII code. A parity bit may or may not be used. To synchronize the transmitter to the receiver, a start bit and a stop bit are used to frame the character.

in Figure 4.56. The 68HC12 may also be configured to set the transmit (TxD) pin to logic 1, an idle signal, when the transmitter is not transmitting a character frame.

On the receiving end, the receiver looks for a falling edge on the receive (RxD) line. When one is detected, it samples the bit several times to ensure it is truly a logic low. If a valid low bit is received, it is interpreted as the start bit and the system begins sampling the incoming bits. The data bits are sampled at three different points on the incoming bit and a majority vote system is used to determine if the incoming bit is a logic 1 or a logic 0. This technique allows the information bits to be extracted from some level of noise.

A synchronous serial communication system, such as the 68HC12's serial peripheral interface (SPI), may use two different methods of synchronizing the transmitter and receiver. The first uses a unique code word as a "sync" pulse. When the receiver receives this unique word, it synchronizes itself to the incoming data. The second method provides a separate "shift clock" (SCK) signal. As data are output on the serial output line by the transmitter, the SCK signal pulses once for each bit output on the serial line. Although this technique requires an extra signal line, data may be transmitted and received at a much greater rate than the asynchronous technique. The SPI system in the 68HC12 uses the SCK signal technique.

4.17.1 Serial Communication Terminology

Figure 4.57 provides an illustration of some of the key terms associated with serial communications. These terms are briefly described here:

clock: A signal that establishes the rate of data transfer. As you can see in Figure 4.57, a single bit is sent on each clock pulse.

bit rate: The number of bits transmitted/received per second. The rate in bits per second (bps) is numerically equal to the clock signal in hertz.

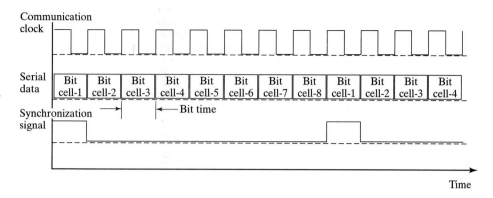

Figure 4.57   Serial communication terminology (adapted from Wakerly).

bit time: The reciprocal of the bit rate: (Bit time [s] = 1/Bit rate [Hz]) This term describes the time increment required to transmit a single bit.

bit cell: The time required to transmit a single bit; also referred to as the *bit time*.

baud rate: (pronounced "bod") The rate at which bits are transmitted per second. For example, if a serial channel is transmitting at 9600 baud, it is transmitting 9600 bps.

line code: The format used to transmit each information bit. There are many different types of line codes. The 68HC12 communication system employs the nonreturn-to-zero (NRZ) line code format. To transmit a 1, a 1 is placed on the transmission line for the entire bit cell, whereas to transmit a 0, a 0 fills the entire bit cell, as shown in Figure 4.58.

American Standard Code for Information Interchange (ASCII) coding: A character code used to encode uppercase and lowercase letters, punctuation,

Figure 4.58   Nonreturn to zero (NRZ) serial communications format, the communication system employed by the 68HC12. To transmit a 1, a 1 is placed on the transmission line for the entire bit cell. To transmit a 0, a 0 fills the entire bit cell. In this figure a 1 0 1 0 1 1 0 1 is being transmitted using NRZ code.

		Most Significant Digit							
		$0_	$1_	$2_	$3_	$4_	$5_	$6_	$7_
	$ _0	NUL	DLE	SP	0	@	P	`	p
	$ _1	SOH	DC1	!	1	A	Q	a	q
	$ _2	STX	DC2	"	2	B	R	b	r
	$ _3	ETX	DC3	#	3	C	S	c	s
	$ _4	EOT	DC4	$	4	D	T	d	t
	$ _5	ENQ	NAK	%	5	E	U	e	u
	$ _6	ACK	SYN	&	6	F	V	f	v
Least Significant Digit	$ _7	BEL	ETB	'	7	G	W	g	w
	$ _8	BS	CAN	(	8	H	X	h	x
	$ _9	HT	EM	)	9	I	Y	i	y
	$ _A	LF	SUB	*	:	J	Z	j	z
	$ _B	VT	ESC	+	;	K	[	k	{
	$ _C	FF	FS	,	<	L	\	l	|
	$ _D	CR	GS	-	=	M	]	m	}
	$ _E	SO	RS	.	>	N	^	n	~
	$ _F	SI	US	/	?	O	_	o	DEL

Figure 4.59 American Standard Code for Information Interchange (ASCII). (Figure adapted from information provided by Motorola.)

numbers, and control characters into a 7-bit binary code representation. A table of the ASCII code is provided in Figure 4.59.

parity bit: A bit used to detect a single error in a character transmission. When an odd parity is employed, the parity bit is set to a value (either 1 or 0) such that there is an odd number of bits at logic 1 in the character code. Conversely, when a system employs even parity, the parity bit is set to a value such that there is an even number of bits at logic 1 in the character code.

simplex communication: A link that can either transmit or receive data.

half-duplex communication: A link that can either transmit or receive data at any one time.

full-duplex communication: A link that provides a simultaneous two-way communication path.

Practice Questions

1. **Question:** What is the ASCII coding for B32-EVB? (Assume a 7 bit ASCII character code is used, as illustrated in Figure 4.59.)
   Answer: $42 $33 $32 $2D $45 $56 $42.

2. **Question:** In the question above, if the most significant bit (MSB) was used as an even parity bit, what would the ASCII coding be for B32-EVB?
   Answer: $42 $33 $B2 $2D $C5 $56 $42.

3. **Question:** Assuming that the MSB is used as an odd parity bit, what character stream is represented by the ASCII code $C1, $F7, $E5, $73, $EF, $6D, $E5, $A1?

   Answer: Awesome!

4. **Question:** Describe the key similarities and differences between the SCI and the SPI communication systems.

   Answer: Both the SCI and SPI systems are serial systems—that is, they transmit a single bit at a time. The SCI system is an asynchronous system in that a common clock signal is not used to maintain synchronization between the transmitter and the receiver. Instead, distinctive framing bits (start and stop bits) are used to maintain synchronization. Fewer control signals are required in the SCI system at the expense of the transmission of these additional overhead bits. The SPI system uses a separate clock synchronization signal to maintain sync between the transmitter and receiver and is therefore designated as a synchronous system. An extra control signal line is required between the transmitter and receiver; however, the transmission rate may be significantly higher in a synchronous configured system.

5. **Question:** Sketch the NRZ ASCII code character for SCI transmission using one start bit, a stop bit, and even parity for the letter J.

   Answer: Figure 4.56 illustrates the SCI transmission of the character J.

4.18 THE 68HC12 SERIAL COMMUNICATIONS INTERFACE

The serial communications interface (SCI) is an asynchronous serial communications system. As we have previously discussed, the asynchronous system does not use a separate shift clock line to maintain synchronization between the transmitter and the receiver. Instead, it employs a start bit and a stop bit to frame each transmitted character. Provided below is a list of characteristics for the SCI system. Several SCI related registers are mentioned in this list. We discuss these registers in detail in an upcoming section.

full-duplex operation: An operation that provides for simultaneous transmission and reception.

nonreturn to zero (NRZ) format: As previously described, a format that fills the entire bit cell with either a logic 1 or 0 for the entire bit time.

baud rate selection: A rate that is set by configuring the SCI baud rate control registers (SC0BDH/SC1BDH and SC0BDL/SC1BDL). The 68HC12 SCI system allows for the selection of many different baud rates.

programmable 8-bit or 9-bit data format: An SCI system that may be configured for either an 8-bit or 9-bit data word. The specific format is configured using the mode (M) bit in SCI control register 1.

Two receiver wake-up methods: idle line and address mark. An important feature for systems that may contain multiple receivers. The SCI receiver
evaluates the first character of each message. If the message is not addressed for
that specific receiver, the receiver is placed in a sleep mode. A receiver may be
put "asleep" by setting the receiver wake-up control (RWU) bit in the SCI status
register to logic 1. The receiver can be "awakened" using one of two methods:
(1) wake up by IDLE line recognition, or (2) wake up by address mark. In the
wake-up by idle line method, a sleeping receiver wakes up as soon as its receive
(RxD) line becomes idle. When a wake-up by address mark is selected, the SCI
system uses the most significant bit signal to wake up the receiver. When the
wake-up condition is detected, the 68HC12 resets the RWU bit back to logic 0,
which wakes the receiver.

Interrupt-Generation Capability. The SCI system has two associated
interrupt sets, one set for SCI0 and another set for SCI1. Associated with each
of these interrupts are four separate interrupts:

- *Transmit interrupt enable (TIE)*: SCI interrupt is requested whenever the
  transmit data register empty (TDRE) flag is set.
- *Transmit complete interrupt enable (TCIE)*: SCI interrupt is requested
  whenever the transmit complete (TC) flag is set.
- *Receiver interrupt enable (RIE)*: SCI interrupt is requested whenever the
  receive data register full (RDRF) flag is set.
- *Idle line interrupt enable (ILIE)*: SCI interrupt is requested whenever the
  IDLE status flag is set.

Receiver Noise Error Detection. As mentioned previously, the 68HC12
uses a majority vote system to determine if a received bit is a logic 1 or 0. This
is accomplished by sampling the received bit at three different locations. If the
majority vote is not unanimous (3 for 3), the noise error flag (NF) is set in the
SCI status register 1.

Framing Error Detection. We have already established how important
it is to maintain synchronization between a serial transmitter and receiver. If
synchronization is lost, it is important to detect this condition as soon as possible.
The 68HC12 monitors for a logic 1 stop bit at the end of a character frame. If a
stop bit is not detected as expected, the 68HC12 sets the framing error (FE) bit
in the SCI status register 1.

Receiver Parity Error Detection. The 68HC12 is equipped with a user-
configured parity checking system. The user may elect to use the system and

also elect whether to use even or odd parity. If a parity error is detected by the receiver, the parity error flag (PF) is set in the SCI status register 1.

Now that we have covered the features of the serial communications interface, let's take a closer look at the SCI transmitter and receiver hardware. Due to the complexity of the hardware, we will discuss the transmitter and receiver separately. But first, a few questions.

Practice Questions

1. **Question:** What is the importance of a parity bit?

   Answer: A parity bit provides for detection of transmission error. With a single parity bit, a single error can be detected. However, a single parity bit does not allow for error correction. To both detect and correct errors, a more sophisticated parity system employing more parity bits is required.

2. **Question:** What is the difference between even and odd parity?

   Answer: When even (odd) parity is used, the parity bit is configured so that there are an even (odd) number of ones in a frame.

4.18.1 Hardware Description: The SCI Transmitter

Transmit Shift Register.   The main component of the SCI transmitter, illustrated in Figure 4.60, is the 11-bit transmit shift register. As you can see in the diagram, the actual data are contained in bits 0-6 (recall that the ASCII code requires only 7 bits). The transmit shift register is preconfigured with a logic low START bit and a logic high STOP bit. The mode bit (M) is user-configured to select either an eight-bit or nine-bit data word. A detailed description of each register is provided in section 4.18.3.

The 68HC12 is equipped with automatic parity generation hardware. If the parity hardware is enabled (PE bit = 1), a parity bit is generated and inserted into bit 7 of the transmit shift register. Either even or odd parity may be selected by the user.

Transmitter Control.   The transmitter control hardware generates all of the required signals to control SCI transmission. The user controls this hardware using the transmitter enable (TE) and the send break (SBK) bits. When the TE bit is set to logic 1, the SCI transmit logic is enabled and the TxD pin is set for transmitter use. The transmitter control logic also generates SCI associated interrupts.

Baud Divider.   The transmission baud rate is set by the SBR[12:0] bits in the SCI baud rate control registers. The time base for the SCI transmitter is derived from the module clock (P CLOCK).

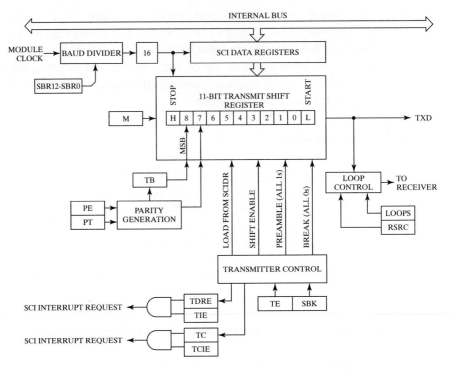

Figure 4.60   The SCI transmitter. (Copyright of Motorola. Used by permission.)

SCI Data Register.   The SCI data register is the portal through which the user accesses the transmit shift register. When using a standard 7- or 8-bit data word, the user sends the character to be transmitted to the SCI data register low. The 68HC12 transfers the contents of the SCI data register to the transmit shift register for transmission.

Loop Control.   The loop control hardware allows the output of the transmitter to be connected to the input of the receiver. This is accomplished by setting the LOOPS bit and the receiver source (RSRC) bit to logic 1. This is a handy setting for system troubleshooting.

4.18.2 Hardware Description: The SCI Receiver

The SCI receiver hardware, illustrated in Figure 4.61, contains much of the same hardware already discussed for the SCI transmitter. Furthermore, we have discussed many of the flags and hardware associated with the SCI transmitter. The primary difference between the transmitter and receiver is the direction of the data flow. We examine only the hardware not previously discussed.

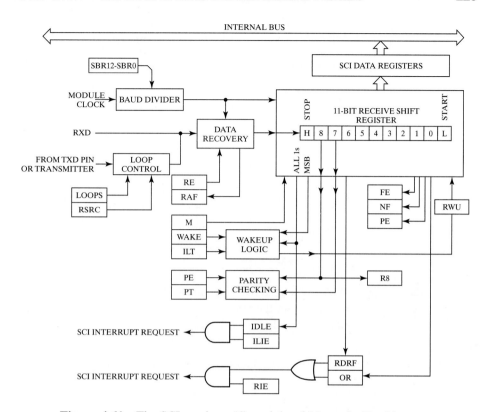

Figure 4.61   The SCI receiver. (Copyright of Motorola. Used by permission.)

Data Recovery.   The data recovery hardware contains the majority vote generator to determine if a received bit is either a logic 1 or 0. If a unanimous vote is received (3 for 3), the received bit is determined to be a logic 1 or 0. If the vote is not unanimous (2 for 3), the received bit is determined to be a logic 1 or 0 and the noise flag (NF) bit in the SCI status register 1 (SC0SR1) is set.

RDRF Flag.   The receive data register full (RDRF) flag is set when a received character is ready to be read from the serial communications data register (SC0DR).

The remaining registers and their associated bits are discussed in the next section.

4.18.3 SCI Registers

The SCI has a dedicated set of registers to control the operation of the SCI system. The SCI registers may be grouped into baud rate control registers, control

Desired SCI Baud Rate	BR Divisor for M = 4.0 MHz	BR Divisor for M = 8.0 MHz
110	2273	4545
300	833	1667
600	417	833
1200	208	417
2400	104	208
4800	52	104
9600	26	52
14400	17	35
19200	13	26
38400	--	13

Figure 4.62   SCI baud rate generation. The SCI baud rate control registers are used to set the rate of SCI transmission and reception using bits SBR[12:0]. The divisors are specified in the table as decimal values.

registers, status registers, and data registers. We discuss each of these registers in turn. We then discuss how to program these registers for SCI transmission and reception.

SCI Baud Rate Control Registers   The SCI baud rate control registers are used to set the rate of SCI transmission and reception. The SCI baud rate is set using bits SBR[12:0]. These values are determined using the following relationship:

$$SBR = PCLOCK/(16 \cdot SCI \text{ baud rate})$$

The SBR value for different desired SCI baud rates are shown in Figure 4.62.

It is important to note that SBR[12:0] bits are distributed between the two SCI baud rate control registers: SC0BDH and SC0BDL. The SCI baud rate settings, BR Divisor, in Figure 4.62 are provided in decimal. To configure the SCI system for a desired baud rate, the appropriate value from Figure 4.62 is loaded to the SC0BDH and SC0BDL registers shown in Figure 4.63.

Example

If the PCLOCK is 8 MHz and it is desired to set the serial communications interface 1 (SCI0) to 9600 baud, a 52 ($34) must be loaded into SC0BDH and SC0BDL.

Register: SCI Baud Rate Control Register (SC0BDH)   Address: $00C0

7	6	5	4	3	2	1	0
BTST	BSPL	BRLD	SBR12	SBR11	SBR10	SBR9	SBR8

Reset: 0   0   0   0   0   0   0   0

Register: SCI Baud Rate Control Register (SC0BDL)   Address: $00C1

7	6	5	4	3	2	1	0
SBR7	SBR6	SBR5	SBR4	SBR3	SBR2	SBR1	SBR0

Reset: 0   0   0   0   0   1   0   0

Figure 4.63   SCI baud rate control register—SC0BDH/SC0BDL ($00C0, $00C1).

The following code fragment will accomplish this baud rate setting:

```
/*-------------------------------------------------------------*/
/* PROGRAM */
/*-------------------------------------------------------------*/
\#include<912b32.h>

void main(void){


SC0BDH=0x00;
SC0BDL=0x34;
.
.
.


}
/*-----------------------------------------------------------*/
```

SCI Control Register

SCI Control Register 1.   The SCI control register 1 (SC0CR1) is used to set different features for the SCI communications system. See Figure 4.64.

LOOPS: The SCI LOOP mode/single wire mode enable bit configures the SCI system for loop operation when set to 1. In LOOP operation, the RxD pin is disconnected from the SCI system and the transmitter output is routed internally to the receiver input. Since both the receiver and transmitter are used in LOOP mode, both the receiver and the transmitter must be enabled.

Register: SCI Control register 1 (SC0CR1)   Address: $00C2

7	6	5	4	3	2	1	0
LOOPS	WOMS	RSRC	M	WAKE	ILT	PE	PT

Reset: 0   0   0   0   0   0   0   0

Figure 4.64   SCI control register 1—SC0CR1 ($00C2).

WOMS: The wired-OR mode for serial pins bit allows the TxD and RxD pins to operate in an open drain configuration when set to logic 1. Open drain configured gates allow the outputs from several gates to be tied directly together and then connected to an external pull-up resistor. (This is usually forbidden in other gate configurations!) When the TxD and RxD pins are configured for WOMS operation, the TxD pins may be tied together in a multiple-transmitter system. The TxD pins of nonactive transmitters follow the logic level of an active transmitter.

RSRC: The receiver source bit determines the internal feedback path for the receiver when used in conjunction with the LOOPS bit. When the LOOPS bit is set to logic 1, a RSRC bit set to 1 connects the receiver output to the transmitter input pin (TxD).

M: The mode bit is used to select the character format. When $M = 0$, the character format is one start, eight data, and one stop bit. When $M = 1$, the character format is one start, nine data, and one stop bit.

WAKE: As previously discussed, the SCI system can be awakened once put to sleep. When WAKE = 0, the 68HC12 is awakened using the IDLE line method. When WAKE = 1, the 68HC12 is awakened by the address mark method.

ILT: The idle line type (ILT) bit determines when the SCI receiver starts counting logic 1's as idle character bits. Recall that an idle character contains all logic 1's and has no start, stop, or parity bit. The idle line character counting begins either after the start bit or after the stop bit. If the count begins after the start bit, then a string of logic 1's preceding the stop bit may cause false recognition of an idle character. Beginning the count after the stop bit avoids false recognition of an idle character. When $ILT = 1$, the idle character bit count starts after the stop bit; whereas, if $ILT = 0$, the idle character bit count begins after the start bit.

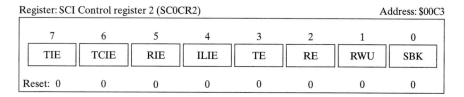

Figure 4.65   SCI control register 2—SC0CR2 ($00C3).

PE: The parity enable (PE) bit is the on/off switch for the parity generation system. A logic 1 turns the parity system on.

PT: The parity type (PT) bit is used to select even (0) or odd (1) parity.

SCI Control Register 2   The SCI control register 2 (SC0CR2), shown in Figure 4.65, is used to set different features for the SCI communications system. The first four bits of this register (TIE, TCIE, RIE, and ILIE) are used to enable different maskable interrupts associated with the SCI system. Recall from our discussion in the interrupt and reset section (4.9) that maskable interrupts must be turned on by (1) enabling the I bit in the condition code register, and (2) locally enabling the interrupts using their respective enable bits. The first four bits of the SC0CR2 registers (TIE, TCIE, RIE, and ILIE) are the local enable bits for different SCI associated interrupts.

Transmit interrupt enable (TIE):   This interrupt is requested whenever the transmit data register empty (TDRE) flag is set.

Transmit complete interrupt enable (TCIE):   This interrupt is requested whenever the transmit complete (TC) flag is set.

Receiver interrupt enable (RIE):   This interrupt is requested whenever the receive data register full (RDRF) flag is set.

Idle line interrupt enable (ILIE):   This interrupt is requested whenever the IDLE status flag is set.

Transmitter enable (TE):   The on/off switch for the SCI transmitter. A logic 1 turns the SCI transmitter on.

Receiver enable (RE):   The on/off switch for the SCI receiver. A logic 1 turns the SCI receiver on.

Receiver wake-up control (RWU):   When the RWU bit is set to logic 1, the SCI receiver is placed in the sleep mode. It is awakened by hardware as previously described.

Register: SCI Status register 1 (SC0SR1)   Address: $00C4

7	6	5	4	3	2	1	0
TDRE	TC	RDRF	IDLE	OR	NF	FE	PF

Reset: 1   1   0   0   0   0   0   0

Figure 4.66   SCI status register 1—SC0SR1 ($00C4).

Send break (SBK):   When the SBK bit is set to logic "1," the transmitter sends zeros to the receiver.

SCI Status Registers

SCI Status Register 1.   As its name implies, SCI status register 1 provides detailed status on the SCI system. The flags within this register, shown in Figure 4.66, are set in response to different events that occur in the SCI system. The receive related flag bits are cleared by a read of the SC0SR1 register followed by a read of the transmit/receive data register low byte.

Transmit data register empty flag (TDRE):   A flag that is set to a logic 1 when the data register associated with the SCI transmission system is empty.

Transmit complete flag (TC):   A flag that is set to logic 1 when the transmitter is idle.

Receive data register full flag (RDRF):   A flag that is set to logic 1 when a received character is ready to be read from the SCI data register (SC0DR).

Idle line detected flag (IDLE):   A flag that is set to logic 1 when 10 consecutive logic 1's appear on the receiver input when the Mode (M) bit is set to zero. (Recall that an idle character contains all logic 1's and has no start, stop, or parity bit.) When $M = 0$, the SCI is configured for 8-bit data words. The IDLE flag is also set to logic 1 when 11 consecutive logic 1's are received for $M = 1$ (SCI configured for 9-bit data words).

Overrun error flag (OR):   A flag that is set to logic 1 when the SCI data register is not read before the receive shift register receives the next frame. As its name implies, the new received character has overrun the preceding character.

Noise error flag (NF):   As previously discussed, the SCI system uses a majority vote system to detect reception of a logic 1 or 0. If an unanimous vote (3 of 3) is not received, the NF is set to a logic 1 indicating that noise is present.

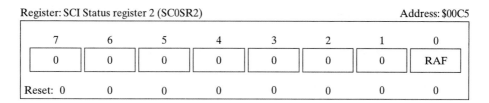

Register: SCI Status register 2 (SC0SR2)   Address: $00C5

7	6	5	4	3	2	1	0
0	0	0	0	0	0	0	RAF

Reset: 0   0   0   0   0   0   0   0

Figure 4.67   SCI status register 2—SC0SR2 ($00C5).

Framing error flag (FE):   A flag that is set when a logic 0 is accepted as the stop bit. Recall that the stop bit should be a logic 1. A framing error indicates that the transmitter and receiver are out of synchronization with one another. Therefore, when the FE bit is set, data reception is inhibited until the FE bit is cleared.

Parity error flag (PF):   A bit that is set when a parity error is detected. Recall that no, even, or odd parity may be used with the SCI system. A parity error indicates an error has occurred in transmission of a character.

SCI Status Register 2.   The SCI status register 2, shown in Figure 4.67, contains only a single flag, the receiver active flag (RAF). This flag is active (logic 1) when a character is being received.

SCI Data Registers   The SCI data registers (SC0DRH and SC0DRL), shown in Figure 4.68, contain the transmitted/received data. The SC0DRL register contains bits [7:0], whereas the eighth bit is contained in SC0RDH. The

Register: SCI Data Register High (SC0DRH)   Address: $00C6

7	6	5	4	3	2	1	0
R8	T8	0	0	0	0	0	0

Reset: -   -   0   0   0   0   0   0

Register: SCI Data Register Low (SC0DRL)   Address: $00C7

7	6	5	4	3	2	1	0
R7T7	R6T6	R5T5	R4T4	R3T3	R2T2	R1T1	R0T0

Reset: -   -   -   -   -   -   -   -

Figure 4.68   SCI data register high/low—SC0DRH/SC0DRL ($00C6, $00C7).

SC0DRL register is used for the 8-bit data format. Both SC0DRH and SC0DRL are used for the 9-bit data format.

This completes our discussion of the transmitter and receiver hardware and the SCI associated registers. We now discuss how information is transmitted and received by this hardware. We then discuss how to program the SCI for transmission and reception. But first, some review questions.

Practice Questions

1. **Question:** What is the difference between the TDRE bit and the RDRF bit?

   Answer: Both bits are flags that indicate the status of the SCI system. The TDRE bit, transmit data register empty flag, is set to logic 1 when the SCI data registers are empty. This indicates transmission of a character. On the other hand, the receive data register full flag (RDRF) bit is set to logic 1 when the SCI data registers are full. This indicates reception of a character.

2. **Question:** What is the purpose of the PF flag? Why is it important?

   Answer: The Parity error flag (PF) is set to indicate a parity error has occurred. A parity error indicates that the character received is incorrect.

3. **Question:** Are there any interrupts associated with the SCI system? If so, describe them.

   Answer: There are actually four interrupts associated with the SCI system.

   - Transmit interrupt enable (TIE): An interrupt that is requested whenever the transmit data register empty (TDRE) flag is set.
   - Transmit complete interrupt enable (TCIE): An interrupt that is requested whenever the transmit complete (TC) flag is set.
   - Receiver interrupt enable (RIE): An interrupt that is requested whenever the RDRF flag is set.
   - Idle line interrupt enable (ILIE): An interrupt that is requested whenever the IDLE status flag is set.

   The enable bits for each of these interrupts are located in SCI Control Register 2.

4.18.4 SCI Transmitter and Receiver Operation

There are three distinct operations used by the SCI communications system: (1) SCI system initialization, (2) SCI transmission, and (3) SCI reception. The required steps for these operations are illustrated in the UML activity diagram provided in Figure 4.69.

   SCI System Initialization.   In order to properly initialize the SCI system, the following actions must be completed: (1) set the SCI system baud rate,

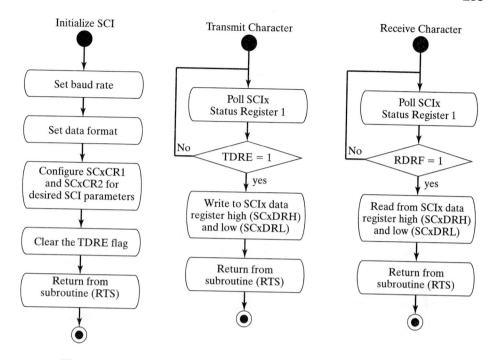

Figure 4.69 An activity diagram for three operations used by the serial communications interface: (1) SCI system initialization, (2) SCI transmission, and (3) SCI reception.

(2) initialize the SCI system for an 8-bit or 9-bit data format, (3) configure SC control registers (SC0CR1 and SC0CR2) for desired parameters, (4) clear the TDRE flag using the two-step process of first reading the SC0SR1 register and then writing to the SC0DR register. The SCI transmitter and the intended SCI receiver must be initialized identically for proper reception. That is, they must both (transmitter and receiver) be configured for the same baud rate, parity, and end data format.

SCI Transmission.   To transmit a character, you must wait for the TDRE flag to set, indicating that the transmit data register is empty and is therefore ready for another character. Once the flag is set, the character to be sent must be transferred to the serial communications data register (SC0DRH and L). This transfer of data sets the TDRE bit and may generate an interrupt if the transmit interrupt is enabled. For all data, the least significant bit (LSB) is transmitted first. Upon completion of data transmission, the transmission complete (TC) bit of the SCSR is set, and an interrupt may be generated if the transmit complete interrupt is enabled.

SCI Reception.   To receive a character, the RDRF flag is monitored. It sets to logic 1 when the receive data register is full, which can cause an interrupt if the receiver interrupt is enabled. The received character can then be read from the SC data registers (SC0DRH and L).

4.18.5 Programming the Serial Communications Interface

This example illustrates the operation of the serial communications interface on the 68HC12.

Recall from our previous discussion that the serial communications interface allows the 68HC12 to communicate *asynchronously* with peripheral devices. A single transmission line is required for a communication link. Bits are sent or received a single bit at a time and, since the SCI is an asynchronous device, it is not clock dependent. The SCI on the 68HC12 uses parity for error detection. When odd parity is used, the parity bit is set to a logic high(1) or low(0) to make the total number of logic highs in the signal to an odd number. When even parity is used, the parity bit is set to a logic high(1) or low(0) to make the total number of logic highs in the signal to an even number. The SCI communicates with the outside world via Port S. The 68HC12 B32 EVB has a single SCI on board.

IMPORTANT REGISTERS

- SC0BDH—SCI 0 BAUD rate control register high ($00C0) is used to set the baud rate.
- SC0BDL—SCI 0 BAUD rate control register low ($00C1) is used to set the baud rate.
- SC0CR1—SCI control register 1 ($00C2) is used to enable the parity system (PE), select odd or even parity (PT), and to select 8-bit or 9-bit mode using the M mode.
- SC0CR2—SCI control register 2 ($00C3) is used to enable the transmitter (TE) or the receiver (RE) bit.
- SC0DRL—SCI data register low ($00C7) is used to hold SCI data for transmission and reception.
- SC0SR1—SCI status register 1 ($00C4) is used to monitor for transmission complete via the TDRE bit or reception complete using the RDRF bit.

In this example we configure the SCI system to continually output an ASCII character through the SCI transmit pin (TxD, PORTS[0]). We employ subroutines to initialize the SCI and transmit the ASCII character. We configure the baud rate to 9600, normal operations, one start, eight data, one stop bit, and even parity. The output from the SCI may be viewed on an oscilloscope or logic analyzer.

```
/*----------------------------------------------------------*/
/*filename: SCI.c                                           */
/*MAIN PROGRAM: This program initializes the SCI to 9600 BAUD */
/*with even parity.  It then transmits a single character    */
/*continuously for observation via an oscilloscope or logic  */
/*analyzer.                                                  */
/*----------------------------------------------------------*/

/*include files*/
#include<912b32.h>

/*function prototypes*/
void sci_init(void);
void sci_trans(void);

void main(void){

sci_init();
while(1)                            /*initializes SCI*/
   {
   sci_trans();                     /*transmit character via SCI*/
   }
}

/*----------------------------------------------------------*/
/*Function: sci_init initializes the sci                    */
/*----------------------------------------------------------*/

void sci_init(void)
{
unsigned char clear;

SC0BDL=0x34;                        /*BAUD:9600*/
SC0BDH=0x00;
SC0CR1=0x03;                        /*start,8 data,stop, parity, odd*/
clear=SC0SR1;                       /*clear TDRE flag-2 step process*/
                                    /*Step 1: read SC0SR1         */
                                    /*Step 2: write to SC0DRL      */
                                    /*accomplished in sci_trans    */
}

/*----------------------------------------------------------*/
/*Function: sci_trans                                       */
/*----------------------------------------------------------*/

void sci_trans(void){

SC0CR2=0x08;                        /*enable SCI transmitter*/
```

```
SCODRL='S';                          /*send letter for transmission*/
while(SC0SR1 != 0x80)                /*wait for TDRE*/
   {
   ;
   }
}
/*------------------------------------------------------------*/
```

If we were to connect two 68HC12s together via their SCI TxD and RxD pins, we could communicate between the two processors. We leave the writing of an SCI receive function as a homework exercise at the end of the chapter (Challenging 11).

4.19 SERIAL PERIPHERAL INTERFACE

The serial peripheral interface (SPI) is a synchronous serial communications system. That is, a common clock signal is shared between the transmitter and the receiver for data synchronization purposes. Before we begin a detailed discussion of the SPI system, let's review concepts related to the SPI system.

4.19.1 SPI Concepts

An interface diagram of an SPI system is illustrated in Figure 4.70. Let's first look at some new terminology associated with SPI communications:

Master mode: A 68HC12 configuration that generates the serial shift clock (SCK) signal and initiates data transmission actions. Basically, it is in charge of all slave-configured peripheral components.

Slave mode: A 68HC12 configuration that depends on a master-configured component (another 68HC12 or a peripheral component) to synchronize and initiate transmission. As the name implies, the slave mode is submissive to the master mode configured component.

Serial shift clock (SCK): A signal that serves as the synchronization clock between the master and slave component and controls the rate of data transmission. A single bit is transmitted for each cycle of the SCK. As we shall see in a later section, the polarity and phase of the SCK are fully programmable by the user.

Master out slave in (MOSI)/Master in slave out (MISO): The two data connections between the master and slave components, both defined from the point of view of the master component. As its name implies, the MOSI connection is the output data line from the master component, which is

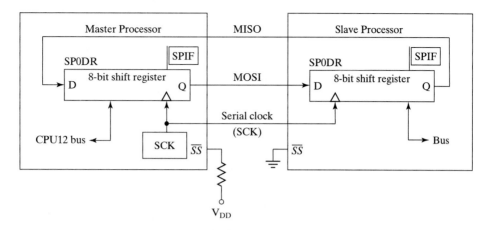

Figure 4.70   Serial peripheral interface diagram. There are two data connections between the master and slave components, both defined from the point of view of the master component. As its name implies, the MOSI connection is the output data line from the master component that is connected to the input data line of the slave component. Similarly, the MISO connection is the output data line from the slave component to the input data line to the master component. The serial shift clock (SCK)—the synchronization clock between the master and slave component—controls the rate of data transmission. A single bit is transmitted for each cycle of the SCK. The configuration of the slave select pin ($\overline{SS}$) determines if the 68HC12 is configured for master mode ($\overline{SS} = 1$) or slave mode ($\overline{SS} = 0$) in a system containing a single slave-configured device.

connected to the input data line of the slave component. Similarly, the MISO connection is the output data line from the slave component to the input data line to the master component.

Slave select ($\overline{SS}$):   A slave select input pin that determines if the 68HC12 is configured for master mode ($\overline{SS} = 1$) or slave mode ($\overline{SS} = 0$) in a system containing a single slave configured device.

4.19.2 SPI General Description

In this section we provide a general description of an SPI data transfer and some of the features related to the SPI system. We also introduce the function of the SPI associated registers. In the section that follows, we discuss these registers in detail describing the function of each register bit. After becoming comfortable with the SPI system hardware, we show how to program the SPI system.

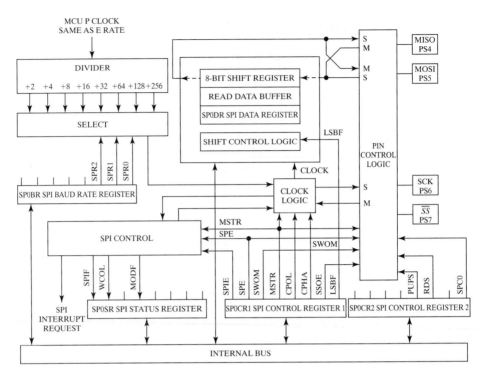

Figure 4.71   SPI block diagram. The clock source for the SPI system is the P clock, which consists of a set of dividers. The output from each of these dividers may be selected by the SPI baud rate register bits SPR[2:1:0] to establish the clock source for the SPI. The main component of the SPI system is the SPI data register (SP0DR). The SP0DR is configured for SPI operation by SPI control registers 1 and 2. The SPI status register sets flags to indicate the status of the SPI system. (Copyright of Motorola. Used by permission.)

Figure 4.71 provides a block diagram of the serial peripheral interface (SPI). Let's start with the clock source for the SPI system illustrated in the upper-left corner of the diagram. The clock source for the SPI system is the P clock, a clock that has the same frequency as the E clock. The P clock consists of a set of dividers. The output from each of these dividers may be selected by the SPI baud rate register bits SPR[2:1:0] to establish the clock source for the SPI. The main component of the SPI system is the SPI data register (SP0DR), which is configured for SPI operation by SPI control registers 1 and 2 (SP0CR1 and SP0CR2). The SPI status register (SP0SR) sets flags to indicate the status of the SPI system. Finally, the SPI system is interfaced to other peripheral devices via the pins of Port S (MISO, MOSI, SCK, and $\overline{SS}$).

In the SPI system the 8-bit data register (SP0DR) in the master component and the 8-bit data register (SP0DR) in the slave component are linked to form a distributed 16-bit shift register. (We introduced this concept in Figure 4.70). When a data transfer operation is performed, this 16-bit register is serially shifted by the common SCK clock. For each SCK clock cycle, a single bit is shifted from the master component to the slave component. Simultaneously, as each bit is transferred from master to slave, a bit is also transferred from slave to master. After eight SCK clock cycles have occurred, data in the master component are effectively exchanged with data in the slave component.

To initialize an SPI data transfer, there are a series of steps that must be completed. Port S must first be configured for SPI operation by setting the appropriate bits in the data direction for Port S (DDRS) register. We discuss the details of this configuration step in the next section. The baud rate and phase of the SCK clock signal must then be set. The SCK clock source is derived from the P-clock. We discussed the P-clock earlier in the chapter. A clock divider in the SPI hardware produces eight divided P-clock signals. The P-clock divisors are 2, 4, 8, 16, 32, 64, 128, and 256. The SPI clock rate select bits, SPR[2:1:0], in the SPI baud rate register (SP0BR) select one of the divided P-clock signals to serve as the SCK signal. The SCK signal controls the rate of the shifting from master to slave. The SCK clock can be tailored with four different combinations of serial clock phase and polarity combinations. We discuss these combinations when we discuss the details of the SPI registers.

After setting the baud rate, the SPI control registers (SP0CR1 and SP0CR2) must be configured for desired SPI parameters. For example, both the master component and the slave component must be properly configured for SPI transmission. The SPI operates in the master mode when the master mode bit (MSTR) in the SPI Control Register 1 (SP0CR1) is set to logic 1. In contrast, when the MSTR bit is set to logic 0, the SPI component is set for slave operation. Therefore, these bits must be properly configured by the user in both the master and the slave SPI components. In addition to properly setting the MSTR bit, the slave select ($\overline{SS}$) pin must also be configured on both the master and the slave component. Recall, the configuration of this pin determines whether the 68HC12 is configured for master mode ($\overline{SS} = 1$) or slave mode ($\overline{SS} = 0$) in a system containing a single master-configured component and a single slave-configured component. The $\overline{SS}$ pin may be controlled via register settings as discussed in the next section for systems containing more than one slave-configured component. Once the $\overline{SS}$ pins are configured for proper operation, the SPI flag in register SP0CR1 must be cleared.

Once both SPI modules have been properly configured as a master or a slave component, they must be enabled. The master component must be enabled before the slave-configured component. Components are enabled for SPI operation using the SPI enable (SPE) bit in the SP0CR1 register. When SPI actions are complete, the slave component should be disabled before disabling the master component.

When initialization actions are complete, SPI data transmission can commence. An SPI data transmission from the master component to the slave component is initiated by writing the character to be transmitted to the SPI data register (SP0DR) in the master component. If the master shift register is empty, the data byte is immediately transferred to the shift register. The byte begins shifting out on the MOSI pin under the control of the SCK. As the data byte shifts out on the MOSI pin one bit at a time, a byte shifts in from the slave on the MISO pin one bit at a time. On the eighth serial clock cycle, the transmission ends and sets the SPI flag (SPIF) in the SPI status register (SP0SR) indicating that transmission is complete. At the same time that the SPIF becomes set, the byte from the slave transfers from the shift register to the slave's SPI data register (SP0DR). If the $\overline{SS}$ pin is under software control, the $\overline{SS}$ must be de-asserted to stop transmission. This two-way communication between the master and slave component provides for a full-duplex serial communication system, as shown in Figure 4.71. In the slave-configured device, the SPIF sets to indicate receipt of a character. When the flag is set, the character may be read from the SP0DR.

The SPI system in the 68HC12 is also equipped with several interrupts. The SPIF generates an interrupt request if the SPI interrupt enable (SPIE) bit in the SPI control register 1 is set to logic 1. Like the SPIF flag, the interrupt indicates transmission complete. The other interrupt is related to mode fault detection. It is also enabled by the SPIE bit. The mode fault interrupt flag (MODF) is set and an interrupt occurs when a mode fault is detected. Mode fault conditions occur when contention occurs between master and slave mode settings.

Practice Questions

1. **Question:** What is the difference between the SPI master and slave modes?

   Answer: A 68HC12 configured for master mode generates the serial shift clock (SCK) and initiates data transmission actions. Basically, it's in charge of all slave configured peripheral components. A 68HC12 configured in slave mode depends on a master configured component (another 68HC12 or a peripheral component) to synchronize and initiate transmission. The slave mode configured component is submissive to the master mode configured component.

2. **Question:** What is the purpose of the SCK signal?

   Answer: The SCK signal is the synchronization clock between the master and slave component. It controls the rate of data transmission. A single bit is transmitted for each cycle of the SCK. As we shall see in section 4.19.3, the polarity and phase of the SCK are fully programmable by the user.

4.19.3 SPI Registers

The SPI is controlled and configured with associated registers. In this section, we discuss these registers and describe the function of each bit. In section 4.19.4 we discuss how to configure these registers for proper SPI operation.

SPI Baud Rate Control Registers   The SPI baud rate register is used to select the frequency of the SPI clock (SCK) and hence the rate of SPI data transmission. Recall that a single bit is transmitted with each clock cycle of the SCK. The SPI baud rate is set by configuring the SPR[2:1:0] bits as shown in Figure 4.72. The most important thing to note from this figure is how much faster SPI transmission rates are compared to SCI transmission rates discussed in section 4.18. Recall that the maximum baud rate possible with the serial communications interface (SCI) system was 38,400 baud. Compare this to the maximum baud rate of the SPI system illustrated in Figure 4.72.

SPI Control Register 1   The SPI system contains two control registers, designated SP0CR1 and SP0CR2, to configure the system for a specific application, as shown in Figure 4.72. The SPI control register 1 (SP0CR1) contains the following configuration bits:

SPI interrupt enable (SPIE):   A bit that allows a hardware interrupt sequence (described in the Interrupt and Reset section (4.9)) to occur each time the SPIF (SPI Interrupt Request) and the MODF (SPI Mode Error Interrupt Status Flag) in the SPI Status Register (described below) are set.

SPI system enable (SPE):   A bit that serves as the on/off switch for the SPI system. When this bit is logic 0, the SPI system is placed in a low-power disabled state. When the SPE bit is set to logic 1, bits 4-7 of Port S are dedicated to the SPI function.

Port S wired-OR mode (SWOM):   A bit that allows Port S[7:4] pins to operate in an open drain configuration when set to logic 1. Open drain configured gates allow the outputs from several gates to be tied directly together and then connected to an external pull-up resistor. (Again, this is usually forbidden in other gate configurations!)

Master/slave mode (MSTR):   A bit that configures the SPI hardware for master mode (MSTR = 1) or slave mode (MSTR = 0).

Clock polarity (CPOL):   An SPI clock (SCK) that may be configured in several different variations using the CPOL and the CPHA bits. Together these two bits are used to specify the clock format to be used in SPI operations. To transmit between SPI modules, both modules must have identical CPOL

SPR[2:1:0]	E Clock Divisor	Frequency at E Clock = 4.0 MHz	Frequency at E Clock = 8.0 MHz
[0:0:0]	2	2.0 MHz	4.0 MHz
[0:0:1]	4	1.0 MHz	2.0 MHz
[0:1:0]	8	500 KHz	1.0 MHz
[0:1:1]	16	250 KHz	500 KHz
[1:0:0]	32	125 KHz	250 KHz
[1:0:1]	64	62.5 KHz	125 KHz
[1:1:0]	128	31.3 KHz	62.5 KHz
[1:1:1]	256	15.6 KHz	31.3 KHz

Register: SPI Baud Rate Register (SP0BR)   Address: $00D2

7	6	5	4	3	2	1	0
0	0	0	0	0	SPR2	SPR1	SPR0

Reset: 0   0   0   0   0   0   0   0

Register: SPI Control Register 1 (SP0CR1)   Address: $00D0

7	6	5	4	3	2	1	0
SPIE	SPE	SWOM	MSTR	CPOL	CPHA	SSOE	LSBF

Reset: 0   0   0   0   0   1   0   0

Register: SPI Control Register 2 (SP0CR2)   Address: $00D1

7	6	5	4	3	2	1	0
0	0	0	0	PUPS	RDS	0	SPC0

Reset: 0   0   0   0   1   0   0   0

Figure 4.72   SPI control registers.

and CPHA values. When the CPOL bit is cleared and data are not being transferred, the SCK pin of the master device is low. When CPOL is set, the SCK idles high.

Clock phase (CPHA):   A bit that determines whether a falling $\overline{SS}$ edge or the first SCK edge begins the transmission. When CPHA = 0, a falling edge $\overline{SS}$ signals the slave to begin transmission. After transmission of all eight bits, the slave $\overline{SS}$ pin must toggle from low to high to low again to begin another character transmission. This format is preferable in systems having more than one slave-configured device. When CPHA = 1, the master begins driving its MOSI pin and the slave begins driving its MISO pin on the first serial clock edge. The $\overline{SS}$ pin can remain low between transmissions. This format may be preferable in systems having only one slave driving the master MISO line.

Slave select output enable (SSOE):   An $\overline{SS}$ output feature that is enabled only in the master mode by asserting the SSOE and DDRS7 bits.

Least significant bit first (LSBF):   An SPI enable bit that controls the direction that data are shifted out of the SPI system. When the LSBF bit is set to 0, data are shifted out of the SPI system most significant bit first. On the other hand, when the LSBF bit is set to 1, data are shifted out of the SPI system least significant bit first. Normally data are transferred most significant bit first.

SPI Control Register 2   The serial peripheral interface control register 2 (SP0CR2) has three configurable bits:

Pull-up Port S enable (PUPS):   When set to logic 1, this bit configures all Port S input pins with active pull-up devices.

Reduce drive of Port S (RDS):   When set to logic 1, this bit configures Port S output pins for reduced drive capability. This configuration reduces power consumption.

Serial pin control (SPCO):   In conjunction with the MSTR control bit (previously described), this bit determines serial pin configurations, as illustrated in Figure 4.73

As mentioned previously, bits within the SPI control registers (SP0CR1 and SP0CR2) specify the operation of the SPI hardware. Specifically, the SPC0 bit in register SP0CR2 and the MSTR bit in SP0CR1 specify the operational configuration of the SPI, as illustrated in Figure 4.73. For example, if the SPC0 is set to 0 and the MSTR to 1, the MISO pin will be configured as the master input pin and the MOSI pin as the master output pin. Furthermore, the SCK pin is configured as the SCK output signal and the $\overline{SS}$ pin is configured for input or output. Notes 1–5 in Figure 4.73 provide further guidance on using additional DDRS pins for enabling the signals. We illustrate the use of these features in the programming examples in section 4.19.4.

As can be seen in Figure 4.73, the SPI system may be configured for normal or bidirectional modes. In the bidirectional mode, the SPI system uses only one serial pin for external device interface connections.

Pin Mode		SPCO[1]	MSTR	MISO[2]	MOSI[3]	SCK[4]	$\overline{SS}$[5]
#1	Normal	0	0	Slave Out	Slave In	SCK In	$\overline{SS}$ In
#2	Normal	0	1	Master In	Master Out	SCK Out	$\overline{SS}$ I/O
#3	Bidirectional	1	0	Slave I/O	GPI/O	SCK In	$\overline{SS}$ In
#4	Bidirectional	1	1	GPI/O	Master I/O	SCK Out	$\overline{SS}$ I/O

[1]The serial pin control 0 bit enables bidirectional configurations.
[2]Slave output is enabled if DDRS4 = 1, SS = 0, and MSTR = 0 (#1, #3).
[3]Master output is enabled if DDRS5 = 1 and MSTR = 1 (#2, #4).
[4]SCK output is enabled if DDRS6 = 1 and MSTR = 1 (#2, #4).
[5]$\overline{SS}$ output is enabled if DDRS7 = 1, SSOE = 1 and MSTR = 1 (#2, #4).

$\overline{SS}$ Output Selection

DDRS7	SSOE	Master Mode	Slave Mode
0	0	$\overline{SS}$ input with MODF feature	$\overline{SS}$ input
0	1	Reserved	$\overline{SS}$ input
1	0	General-purpose output	$\overline{SS}$ input
1	1	$\overline{SS}$ output	$\overline{SS}$ input

Normal Mode and Bidirectional Mode

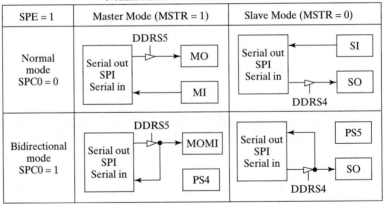

Figure 4.73 SPI mode selection. Bits within the SPI control registers specify the operation of the SPI hardware. Specifically, the SPC0 bit in register SP0CR2 and the MSTR bit in SP0CR1 specify the operational configuration of the SPI.

Register: SPI Status Register (SP0SR)   Address: $00D3

7	6	5	4	3	2	1	0
SPIF	WCOL	0	MODF	0	0	0	0

Reset: 0   0   0   0   0   0   0   0

Figure 4.74   SPI status register—SP0SR ($00D3).

SPI Status Register   The SPI status register (SP0SR), shown in Figure 4.74, contains the following flag bits:

SPI interrupt request (SPIF):   A flag bit that is set to indicate the transmission of eight bits of peripheral data transmission. It is set after the eighth clock of the SCK cycle in a data transfer, and it is cleared by reading the SP0SR register followed by a read or write to the SPI data register.

Write collision status flag (WCOL):   A flag bit that is set to logic 1 to indicate that a serial transfer was in progress when the 68HC12 tried to write new data into the serial peripheral data register (SP0DR).

Mode error interrupt status flag (MODF):   A flag bit that is set automatically by the SPI hardware if the MSTR bit is set and the slave select input pin ($\overline{SS}$) becomes zero. Basically, the MSTR bit is trying to place the SPI system in master mode while the $\overline{SS}$ pin is trying to place the SPI system in slave mode.

SPI Data Registers   The SPI data register (SP0DR), shown in Figure 4.75, serves as both the input and output data register for the SPI system. As previously discussed, the data register in the master-configured device is serially linked to the data register in the slave-configured device to form a 16-bit shift register. When a data transfer operation is initiated, this shift register is shifted eight times (once for each pulse of the SCK clock). This results in a data exchange between the master- and slave-configured devices. Note that some of the more simple slave-configured peripheral devices either accept data from

Register: SPI Data Register (SP0DR)   Address: $00D5

7	6	5	4	3	2	1	0
Bit 7	Bit 6	Bit 5	Bit 4	Bit 3	Bit 2	Bit 1	Bit 0

Reset: 0   0   0   0   0   0   0   0

Figure 4.75   SPI data register—SP0DR ($00D5).

Register: Port S Data Register (PORTS)   Address: $00D6

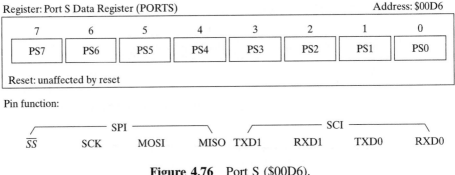

Figure 4.76   Port S ($00D6).

the master and do not return data or pass data to the master without requiring input data from the master-configured device.

Port S Data Register   The Port S data register (called Port S) may be used as a general-purpose input port. However, it also provides the input and output pins for the SCI (TXD1, RXD1, TXD0, and RXD0) system and the SPI ($\overline{SS}$, SCK, MOSI, and MISO) system, as illustrated in Figure 4.76.

Data Direction Register for Port S   As mentioned previously, Port S may be used as a general purpose input/output port. The data direction register for Port S (DDRS), shown in Figure 4.77, configures the different pins on Port S for either an input or an output. When a specific bit in the DDRS register is set to logic 0, the corresponding pin in Port S is configured as an input pin. On the other hand, when a specific bit in the DDRS register is set to logic 1, the corresponding pin in Port S is configured as an output pin. When used as SCI and SPI input and output pins, the following restrictions apply:

DDRS2, DDRS0: If the SCI receiver is configured for two-wire SCI operation, corresponding port S pins will be designated as input pins regardless of the state of these bits.

Register: Ports S Data Direction Register (DDRS)   Address: $00D7

7	6	5	4	3	2	1	0
DDRS7	DDRS6	DDRS5	DDRS4	DDRS3	DDRS2	DDRS1	DDRS0

Reset: 0   0   0   0   0   0   0   0

Figure 4.77   DDRS ($00D7).

DDRS3, DDRS1: If the SCI receiver is configured for two-wire SCI operation, corresponding port S pins will be designated as output pins regardless of the state of these bits.

DDRS[6:4]: If the SPI is enabled and expects the corresponding Port S to be an input, it will be an input regardless of the state of the DDRS bit. If the SPI is enabled and expects the bit to be an output, it will be an output only if the DDRS bit is set.

DDRS7: In the SPI slave mode, DDRS7 has no meaning or effect; Port S pin 7 is dedicated as the $(\overline{SS})$ input pin. In SPI master mode, DDRS7 determines whether Port S pin 7 is an error detect input to the SPI, a general-purpose line, or a slave select output line.

Practice Questions

1. **Question:** What is the minimum frequency for SPI transfer when the ECLK = 8 MHz?

   Answer: When SPR[2:1:0] bits are set for 111, the SPI frequency is 31.3 kHz.

2. **Question:** What is the highest frequency for SPI transfer when the ECLK = 4 MHz?

   Answer: When SPR[2:1:0] bits are set for 000, the SPI frequency is 2.0 MHz.

3. **Question:** Provide the C language code to set the SPI to the lowest frequency.

   Answer: `SP0BR = 0x07;`

4. **Question:** What is the purpose of the SPIF bit?

   Answer: The SPI interrupt request bit is set to indicate the transmission of eight bits of peripheral data transmission. It is set after the eighth clock of the SCK cycle in a data transfer and it is cleared by reading the SP0SR register followed by a read or write to the SPI data register.

5. **Question:** How do the settings for the master- and slave-configured SPI system compare?

   Answer: The systems are configured identically except one device is designated as the master while the other one is designated the slave device. The other configuration settings must be the same to provide for accurate transmission of information.

4.19.4 Programming the SPI

Earlier in this chapter we discussed required actions to initiate SPI transmission. These actions are summarized in the form of a UML activity diagram provided in Figure 4.78. We illustrate in this section how to program the SPI for initialization and character transmission.

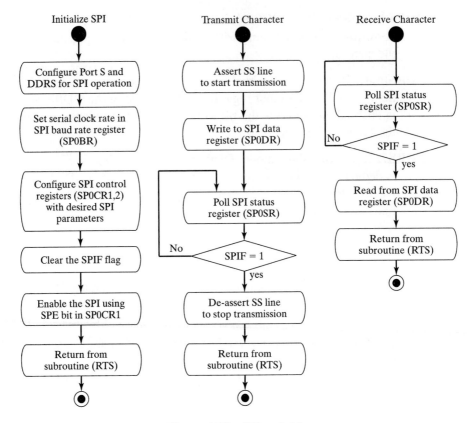

Figure 4.78   SPI activities.

Serial Peripheral Interface Example.   The serial peripheral interface (SPI) allows the 68HC12 to communicate synchronously with peripheral devices. The SPI system on the 68HC12 allows the microprocessor to act as either a master or a slave. In the master mode, data are transferred serially from the 68HC12 to the slave-designated device.

The SPI system is accessible via PORT S on the 68HC12. The pins in PORT S that relate to the SPI are PORT S [7:4]. The function of each pin is described below.

- PORT S[7]: This is the slave select line SS. When the SS line is set low, data in the SPI data register will be transferred out serially.
- PORT S[6]: This pin is the serial clock, SCK.
- PORT S[5]: This pin is the Master Out Slave In (MOSI) line. Data are transferred out of the SPI to the slave device when the 68HC12 is in master mode.

- PORT S[4]: This pin is the Master In Slave Out (MISO) line. Data are transferred from the slave to the master via this connection.

IMPORTANT SERIAL PERIPHERAL INTERFACE REGISTERS

- **Data direction register for Port S (DDRS):** Configures DDRS[7:4] for output in master mode.
- **SPI Baud Rate Register (SPOBR):** Sets the SPI baud rate via the SPR[2:0] bits.
- **SPI Control Register 1 (SPOCR1):** One of the main SPI configuration registers. In this example, we configure for no interrupts, normal operation, master mode, CPOL = 0, CPHA = 0, and SS0E = 0.
- **SPI Control Register 2 (SP0CR2):** Use default settings.
- **SPI Status Register (SP0SR):** Provides status of data transmission.
- **SPI Data Register (SP0DR):** Provides data for SPI system.

In this example we use the SPI system in the master mode. We then send out the hex number $F0 in a continuous loop and examine the results with an oscilloscope or logic analyzer. As an alternative, the SPI test configuration illustrated in Figure 4.79 may be used. The test configuration consists on an 8-bit serial-to-parallel converter. The SPI will shift out the data word serially. The

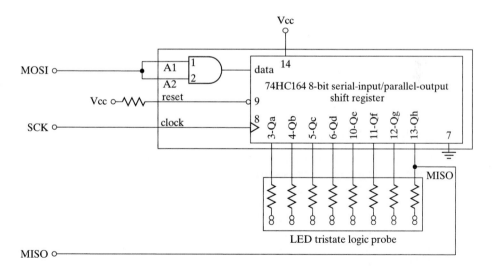

Figure 4.79 SPI test configuration. The test configuration consists of an 8-bit serial-to-parallel converter. The SPI will shift out the data word serially. The results will be shown on the LED tristate logic probe.

results will be shown on the 8-channel, tristate logic probe discussed earlier in the chapter. Here is the code to accomplish SPI testing.

```
/*----------------------------------------------------------*/
/*filename: SPI.c                                           */
/*This code initializes the SPI system to Master mode       */
/*----------------------------------------------------------*/

#include <912b32.h>
#include <stdio.h>

/*Functions*/
void initialize_SPI(void);     /*function to initialize SPI
                                                    settings*/
void send_data(unsigned int); /*transmits data and checks
                                                    for flag*/


void main(void){

int i,j;
unsigned int data;
initialize_SPI();
data = 0xF0;

while(1){
   PORTS = PORTS & 0x7F;       /*Set SS to 0, turn on*/
   send_data(data);
   PORTS = PORTS | 0x80;       /*Set SS 1, turns off*/
   }
}


/*----------------------------------------------------------*/
/*Functions                                                 */
/*----------------------------------------------------------*/

void initialize_SPI(void)
{
PORTS = 0x80;     /*Set SS line high to disable*/
DDRS = 0xE0;      /*DDRS pins 7,6,5 high for output and SS*/
SP0BR = 0x04;     /*Sets clock/baud rate*/
SP0CR1 = 0x18;    /*No interrupts, enable SPI, normal, master*/
                  /*CPOL/CPHA 0 SSOE 0, MSB first*/
SP0CR2 = 0x08;    /*PUPS 0, RDS 0, SPC0 0*/
SP0DR = 0x00;     /*Clears data register*/
SP0SR = 0x00;     /*Initializes SPI Status Register*/
SP0CR1 = 0x58;    /*Enable SPI*/
}


/*----------------------------------------------------------*/
```

```
void send_data(unsigned int data)
{
unsigned int status;

SP0DR = data;
while((SP0SR&0x80) == 0x00){ /*wait for flag*/
  ;
  }
status = SP0SR;
}
/*-------------------------------------------------------------*/
```

That completes our discussion of programming the synchronous serial peripheral interface system of the 68HC12. In the programming example we purposely did not discuss details of the slave device. In this next section we show a list of devices that can be used to extend the features of the 68HC12.

4.19.5 SPI Applications

The SPI system can be used to extend the features of the 68HC12. There are many systems that can be added to the processor via the SPI, including the following:

- memory components
- additional ports
- real-time clock
- phase-locked loop
- frequency modulated (FM) transmitter/receiver set
- higher resolution (more than 8-bit) analog-to-digital converters
- light-emitting diode (LED) and liquid crystal display (LCD) drivers
- multiple channel digital-to-analog converters
- digital compass

4.20 ANALOG-TO-DIGITAL CONVERSION BACKGROUND THEORY

The 68HC12 is frequently used in systems where physical, measurable system parameters are sampled. Based on the values of these parameters, the 68HC12 will make decisions using the user-written program resident within the controller. The program then activates outputs in response to the algorithm-directed actions.

The physical parameters of interest might be light intensity, temperature, pressure, strain, stress, etc. What all of these parameters have in common is that they are all continuous type variables. The 68HC12, being a digital-based processor, only understands 1's and 0's. Therefore, an analog-to-digital conversion system is required to convert the physical variables into digital variables.

The analog-to-digital conversion process is simply sampling an analog (continuous) signal at regular intervals and then converting each of these analog samples into a corresponding binary code.

There are many different types of analog-to-digital converter designs. We concentrate on the successive approximation converter design since this is the type implemented within the 68HC12.

The analog-to-digital conversion process consists of three steps:

1. Determining the sampling rate
2. Encoding the different analog voltage levels into a corresponding binary code
3. Determining the required resolution of the converter

We discuss each of these steps in turn.

4.20.1 Sampling Rate

Adequately reconstructing a continuous analog signal from discrete (or digital) "snapshots" requires an adequate sampling rate. Considerable analysis has been accomplished to determine just what is an adequate sampling rate. In the 1920s, Harry Nyquist at Bell Laboratories was able to quantify the minimum sampling rate required for adequate reconstruction. His work led to the Nyquist criterion, which stipulates that we must sample a signal at a minimum frequency of twice the highest frequency component contained in the signal to be sampled. This can be concisely stated as

$$f_s >= 2f_h$$

where f_s is the sampling frequency and f_h is the highest expected frequency component in the sampled signal.

The sampling frequency chosen provides a discrete sample of the signal at regular time intervals given by

$$T_s = 1/f_s$$

where T_s is the time interval between samples and is called the sampling period, as shown in Figure 4.80.

For a simple sinusoidal signal containing a single frequency, the sampling frequency f_s will be twice the frequency of the sinusoid. For a more complex signal, harmonic analysis must be used to estimate the highest expected frequency component of the signal.

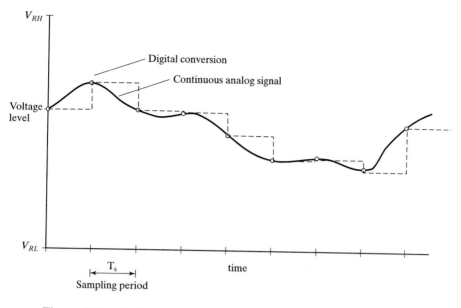

Figure 4.80   Analog-to-digital conversion process. This process simply samples an analog signal at regular intervals and then converts
each of these analog samples into a corresponding binary code. The
digital representation remains constant between samples (dotted line
waveform).

Example

The human voice spectrum has an approximate upper frequency bound of approximately 4 kHz. The telephone company digitizes the analog human voice using a
sampling frequency of 8 kHz.

A low pass filter (LPF) is employed to condition the signal prior to conversion. The filter is referred to as an anti-aliasing filter. The LPF reduces unwanted
electrical interference noise, electronic noise from the signal, and unwanted high
frequency components. If unwanted frequency components cause the Nyquist criterion to be violated, frequency folding or aliasing will occur. In the process of
recovering the signal, the folded part of the spectrum causes distortion in the
recovered signal, which cannot be removed by filtering from the recovered signal
because the folded frequency is in the same frequency band as the desired information frequency. Frequency folding is eliminated by using a LPF, which has a cutoff
frequency corresponding to f_h, the expected highest frequency content of the signal.

4.20.2 Encoding

The overall purpose of the analog-to-digital conversion process is to convert each
of the voltage samples provided at regular time intervals into a corresponding

unsigned binary value. The step referred to as *encoding* provides an unique binary code for each voltage step between the two reference voltages that we describe below. Since a binary code is used, the following equation describes how many binary bits (*b*) are required to uniquely specify different voltage levels

$$n = 2^b$$

where *n* equals the number of discrete encoded events and *b* is the number of bits used for encoding. Figure 4.81 illustrates details. The number of bits in the binary code used to specify each converted value is a design parameter of the analog-to-digital converter.

Example

The 68HC12 has an 8-bit analog-to-digital converter system. This means that each analog sample provided to the 68HC12 ATD system is converted to an unsigned, 8-bit binary representation. Therefore, these 8 bits generate $2^8 = 256$ different voltage levels. The B32 version of the 68HC12 has the option of employing a 10-bit converter. These 10 bits generate $2^{10} = 1024$ different voltage levels.

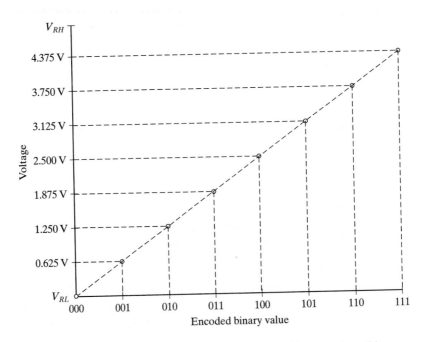

Figure 4.81   Encoding. The encoding step provides a unique binary code for each voltage step between the two reference voltages. This figure illustrates the encoding for a 3-bit ATD converter. With 3 bits, $2^3 = 8$ different voltage levels may be encoded.

4.20.3 Quantizing and Resolution

After the proper sampling frequency and the number of bits available for encoding are determined for the analog-to-digital conversion process, we must establish the levels of quantization—which is nothing more than establishing how many discrete levels the analog signal will be divided into between its two reference voltage levels. An ATD converter must have an established lower voltage reference level V_{RL} and a higher voltage reference level V_{RH}. These references are applied to the 68HC12 via external hardware pins. All signals applied to the ATD converter must fall between these two extremes. Quantization provides multiple levels between the two references. If more levels are provided, a better representation of the sampled voltage will result.

For illustration purposes, let us assume that the two reference levels chosen for our ATD converter are 5.0 volts for V_{RH} and 0 volts for V_{RL}. If we divide the voltage span between these two references into 256 identically spaced levels, the voltage difference (quantum) represented by each step is

$$(5 \ V - 0 \ V)/(256 \text{ steps}) = 19.53 \text{ millivolts/step}$$

Furthermore, the first step corresponds to 0 volts, the tenth step to 175.78 millivolts, and the 256th step to 4.980 volts (5.0 volts–19.53 mV). Intuitively, if we increase the number of steps between the two voltage references, the individual voltage steps will become smaller, or the converter resolution will improve. In general, resolution may be described by

$$\text{Resolution} = (V_{RH} - V_{RL})/(\text{Number of steps})$$

We can tie together all of these concepts with

$$\text{Resolution} = (V_{RH} - V_{RL})/2^b$$

where b represents the number of bits used in the ATD conversion.

Another helpful expression which ties these concepts together is:

$$V_x = V_{RL} + x(V_{RH} - V_{RL})/2^b$$

where V_x is the sample voltage, x is its converted digital encoded value, and b is the number of bits used for the conversion.

Another related specification of a converter is the dynamic range in decibels (dB). This range provides a measure of how well the converter operates over a range of voltage inputs from very small values to very large values. The dynamic range is given by

$$DR(\text{dB}) = 20 \log 2^b = 20b \log 2 = 20b(0.301) = 6.02b$$

where the *DR* is the dynamic range and *b* is the number of bits produced by the converter.

Example

What is the dynamic range of an 8-bit converter?

$$DR(\text{dB}) = 6.02b = 6.02\,(8) = 48.16 \text{ dB}$$

4.20.4 Data Rate

The data rate (d)—the amount of data generated by an ATD converter—may be calculated by multiplying the sampling frequency by the number of bits required to represent each sample. This is given by

$$d = f_s b$$

The f_s term describes how many conversions are completed per second while b describes the number of bits generated per conversion. The overall data rate (d), or the bits generated per second, is simply the product of f_s and b.

Practice Questions

1. **Question:** An analog signal has a spectrum (frequency content) that varies from 10 Hz to 4.2 kHz. It is to be sampled at a rate of 10,000 samples per second. Is the sampling rate adequate to allow reconstruction of the signal?

   Answer: The minimum sampling rate as determined by

   $$f_s \geq 2f_h$$

   is 8.4 kHz. Therefore, the sampling rate of 10,000 samples per second or 10 kHz is adequate.

2. **Question:** The 68HC12 ATD system converts each analog signal sample to an 8-bit unsigned binary value. What is the resolution of the converter? Assume that the reference voltages for the 68HC12 designated as V_{RH} and V_{RL} are 5 volts and 0 volts, respectively.

   Answer: The resolution is given by

   $$\text{Resolution} = (V_{RH} - V_{RL})/(2^b) = (5 - 0)/(256) = 19.53 \text{ mV}$$

3. **Question:** If the 68HC12 is configured so that each analog conversion yields an unsigned, 10-bit binary value, what will be the resolution of the converter? Assume that the reference voltages for the 68HC12 designated as V_{RH} and V_{RL} are 5 volts and 0 volts, respectively.

   Answer: The resolution is given by

   $$\text{Resolution} = (V_{RH} - V_{RL})/(2^b) = (5 - 0)/(1024) = 4.88 \text{ mV}$$

4. **Question:** A 2 kHz square wave is to be sampled using an ATD conversion system. Harmonic analysis of the signal indicates that harmonic content up to 20 kHz should be sampled. What should the sampling frequency be?

   Answer:

   $$f_s >= 2f_h >= 2(20 \cdot 10^3) >= 40 \text{ kHz}$$

5. **Question:** In the preceding question, how many bits of binary data are generated per second assuming an 8-bit ATD converter?

   Answer: In the preceding example, 40,000 analog samples are converted per second. Each sample requires 8 bits for an unsigned, binary representation. Therefore, the total number of bits generated per second is

   $$40,000 \text{ samples/s} \cdot 8 \text{ bits/sample} = 320,000 \text{ bps}$$

6. **Question:** Assume that music consists of frequencies from 20 Hz to 20 kHz. A compact disc converts stereo analog music signal using a 16-bit analog converter at a sampling frequency of 44 kHz. Is the Nyquist criterion maintained? What is the data rate of an audio compact disc?

   Answer: Yes, the Nyquist Criterion is maintained. The music is sampled at a frequency of 44 kHz which is more than double the highest expected frequency (20 kHz) of the music signal. If a 16-bit analog converter is used to digitize the left and right (stereo) channels, the bit rate is given by

   Bit rate = Sample rate ∗ Bits/channel ∗ Number of channels

   Bit rate = 44K samples/second ∗ 16 bits/channel ∗ 2 channels = 1.41 Mbps

Note: In an actual compact disc storage protocol, additional bits are used for error-correcting procedures.

4.21 ANALOG-TO-DIGITAL CONVERTER TECHNOLOGIES

There are several different types of technologies used to convert an analog sample into a corresponding digital representation. Most of the converter types require a sample and hold circuit at the input to keep the analog sample under conversion constant during the conversion process. Some of the more common techniques include the following:

- Successive-approximation converters
- Integration-based converters
- Counter type converters
- Parallel converters

We discuss only the successive-approximation converter as this is the type used by the 68HC12. Those interested in other converters are referred to Pack and Barrett [2002].

4.21.1 Successive-Approximation Converters

The operation of this converter is best illustrated with an example.

Example

Let us assume our converter has V_{RH} set at 5.0 V and V_{RL} set to 0 V. Each analog sample will be converted to an 8-bit binary representation. These 8 bits will provide 256 distinct conversion levels and a corresponding resolution of

$$\text{Resolution} = (5.0 - 0.0)/(256) = 19.53 \text{ mV}$$

As a first guess, the converter sets the most significant bit (MSB) of the result register to 1 and the rest of the bits to 0 (see Figure 4.82 for details). This corresponds to a binary value of 128 or 128/256 or 1/2 full scale or 2.5 volts. The comparator—an analog component that compares an unknown input signal to a known voltage reference—indicates whether the unknown analog sample is higher or lower than 2.5 volts. If the unknown signal is higher than the reference voltage, the comparator's output is a logic high. If the unknown signal is lower than the reference voltage, the comparator's output is a logic low. If the unknown sample is higher than 2.5 volts, the next guess will be 11000000, which corresponds to 192/256 or 3/4 full scale or 3.75 volts. If the unknown sample is lower than 2.5 volts, the next guess will be 01000000, which corresponds to 64/256 or 1/4 full scale or 1.25 volts. This process continues for six more guesses—that is, one guess for each bit.

The successive-approximation converter has a number of distinct advantages and disadvantages:

- *Advantage.* The conversion time is fixed and independent of the magnitude of the unknown analog sample. This is an especially important advantage in a synchronous machine such as the 68HC12 since the time of the conversion process is fixed and precisely known.
- *Advantage.* Since the internal logic clears at the end of each conversion, each conversion is independent and unique of the results of previous conversions.
- *Disadvantage.* The hardware implementation of this converter is quite complex.
- *Disadvantage.* Relative to other conversion techniques, successive approximation is slower.

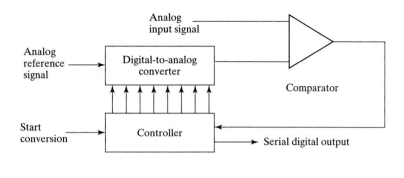

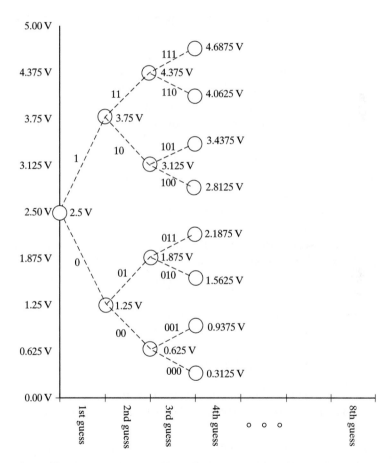

Figure 4.82   Successive-approximation converter process. This method approximates an unknown analog sample using an *n*-bit code in *n* guesses.

Practice Question

1. **Question:** Does the maximum value of a converter's digital output (all 1's) correspond to the maximum analog full scale (FS) of the converter?

Answer: The maximum value of the digital code (all 1's) corresponds with one LSB less than full scale, or $FS(1 - 2^{-n})$ — *not* the analog full scale value. Therefore a 12-bit converter with a 0 to +10 V analog range has a maximum digital code of 1111 1111 1111 and a maximum analog value of $10(1 - 2^{-12}) = 9.99756\ V$. In other words, the maximum analog value of the converter corresponding to all 1's in a code, never quite reaches the point defined as analog full scale.

4.22 THE 68HC12 ANALOG-TO-DIGITAL CONVERSION SYSTEM

In this section, we discuss the 68HC12 analog-to-digital (ATD) conversion system in detail. The block diagram of the ATD system is shown in Figure 4.83. We begin by providing a brief overview of the system, followed by a discussion of the system block diagram. We then discuss the ATD associated registers and conclude by discussing how to program the ATD for proper configuration and operation.

The 68HC12's ATD system contains 8 channels. Each channel converts its input into an unsigned, 8-bit binary representation. The eight inputs are multiplexed so that only a single input signal is fed to the input of the successive approximation ATD converter at a time. This converter is accurate to ± 1 least significant bit (LSB).

The ATD system may be configured for a single conversion sequence or continuous conversions. Additionally, the user has the flexibility to configure the ATD to perform conversions on a single channel or multiple sequential channels. The user tailors ATD system operation for a specific application using a 16-word (32-byte) memory mapped control register bank and by proper selection of the high V_{RH} and low V_{RL} reference voltages.

4.22.1 68HC12 ATD System

The eight ATD system analog inputs from the outside world are located on pins AN0/PAD0 through AN7/PAD7. The analog input signals are fed into an analog multiplexer. The multiplexer selects which signals are routed to the successive approximation ATD converter as specified by the ATD control registers. An ATD conversion sequence is initiated by writing to one of the ATD control registers (ATDCTL5). At the completion of the ATD conversion process, the results are placed in the corresponding ATD converter result register (ADR0H through ADR7H) and the corresponding flags are set in the ATD status register (ATDSTAT). Timing for the conversion process is provided by the P clock.

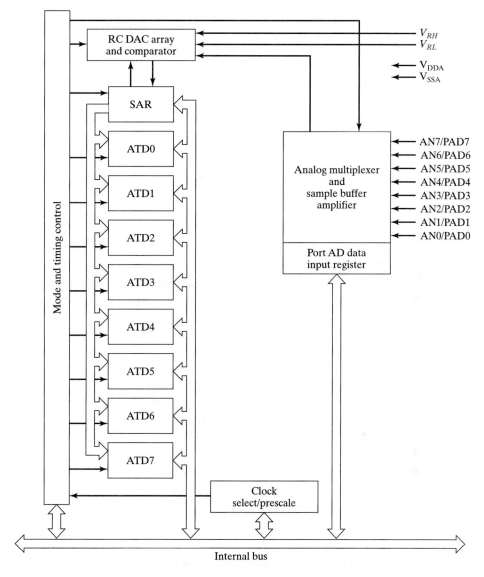

Figure 4.83 Analog-to-digital block diagram. (Copyright of Motorola. Used by permission.)

Two dedicated lines—V_{RH} and V_{RL}—are used as reference voltage levels for the high voltage and the low voltage, respectively. If an input voltage value is equal to V_{RL}, it is converted to \$00 whereas if the input voltage is equal to V_{RH}, it is represented as \$FF. The results are represented as unsigned binary values.

It may seem like there are too many steps to keep straight here. We like to compare the ATD voltage conversion to making brownies. To make brownies (and to convert ATD voltage) the following steps must be accomplished:

- Turn on the oven. (The ADPU bit in ATDCTL2 must be set to 1 to turn on the ATD system.)
- Preheat the oven to come up to the appropriate baking temperature. (You must wait 100 μs after setting the ADPU bit to allow the ATD system to stabilize.)
- Decide what else you will add to the brownies you are baking—walnuts, pecans, no nuts, etc. (You must decide what type of ATD conversion you will accomplish using control registers ATDCTL4 and ATDCTL5.)
- Place the brownies in the oven (setting ATDCTL5). They will be done at the end of the prescribed baking time or when the timer buzzer (the SCF bit in the ATDSTAT register) is active.
- When the brownies are fully cooked, place them on a cooling rack (ATD result registers). They are ready to eat. Enjoy! (Use the results.)

4.22.2 68HC12 ATD System Control Registers

As mentioned previously, the user tailors ATD system operation for a specific application using a 16-word (32-byte) memory-mapped control register bank. Listed below are the different type of registers found in the control bank. We discuss each of these register types in turn.

- *Control registers*: Registers that are used to tailor an ATD conversion sequence to user specifications.
- *Status register*: A 2-byte register containing a series of flags that indicate the status of the ATD system.
- *Result registers*: Eight identical 8-bit result registers. After the specified conversion(s) take place in the ATD system, the results are placed into the corresponding result register (ADR0H through ADR7H).
- *Test registers*: A 2-byte ATD test register (ATDTEST) that can only be read from or written to in special modes. In normal operating modes reads and writes have no effect. Due to the special nature of this register, we will not discuss it any further.

In the next several subsections we review each of the 16 registers associated with the ATD system.

ATD Control Registers   The ATD control registers are used to tailor an ATD conversion sequence to user specifications. There are six ATD control registers named ATDCTL0 through ATDCTL5. One of these control registers allows you to turn the ATD system "on" (ATDCTL2) since it is shut off after processor reset to conserve power. Once the ATD system is "powered up," you must wait 100 μs for the ATD system to stabilize prior to starting a conversion. You also use these control registers to specify whether you perform a single conversion or continuous conversions. Finally, these registers are used to specify which of the ATD channels is used to perform the conversion. You may configure the ATD converter to perform conversions on a single channel or scan through multiple channels. Control registers 0, 1, and 3 are used infrequently and are mentioned only briefly. Control registers 2, 4, and 5 allow the user to completely tailor the operation of the ATD system to a specific application.

ATD Control Registers 0 (ATDCTL0) and 1 (ATDCTL1).   The ATD-CTL0 is located at memory address $0060. This register is used to abort a conversion sequence. This is accomplished by writing a value to the register. In normal operation you will not use this register. The ATDCTL1 is located at memory address $0061. It is only used in special test cases, so we will not discuss it further.

ATD Control Register 2 (ATDCTL2).   The ATDCTL2 is located at memory address $0062. This register is used to power up the ATD conversion system. It also contains flags and interrupt enable bits associated with the ATD system. Figure 4.84 provides register details. The function of each bit follows:

ADPU: Bit 7 of ATDCTL2 is the on/off switch for the ATD system. This bit, called ATD Powerup Bit or ADPU, is set to 0 after the processor is reset. To power up the ATD system, this bit must be set to 1. Once the ADPU is set, you must wait 100 μs for the ATD system to become stable.

AFFC: The ATD fast flag clear all bit controls how the ATD system related flags are cleared. When the AFFC bit is set to 0, the ATD system flags are cleared in the normal manner. When the AFFC bit is set to 1, all of the

Register: Analog-to-Digital Converter Control Register 2 (ATDCTL2)   Address: $0062

7	6	5	4	3	2	1	0
ADPU	AFFC	AWAI	0	0	0	ASCIE	ASCIF

Reset: 0   0   0   0   0   0   0   0

Figure 4.84   ATD control register 2 (ATDCTL2).

ATD conversion complete flags are set for a fast clear sequence. Both the normal mode and fast clear mode of flag clearing are discussed below.

AWAI: The ATD wait mode bit determines whether or not the ATD continues to operate when the 68HC12 is in the wait mode. If AWAI is set to 0, the ATD continues to operate while the 68HC12 is in the wait mode. However, if the AWAI is set to 1, ATD system operation is halted while the 68HC12 is in the wait mode to conserve power.

ASCIE: Bit 1 contains the ATD sequence complete interrupt enable (ASCIE) bit. When this bit is set to 1, interrupt requests generated by the ATD sequence complete interrupt flag (ASCIF) are enabled.

ASCIF: Bit 0 contains the ATD sequence complete interrupt flag (ASCIF). This flag is set when a conversion sequence is finished. If the ASCIE bit described above is set, the ASCIF will also generate an interrupt.

The interrupt features allow the CPU to continue to process other tasks while waiting for an interrupt to occur. For example, when the ATD interrupt features are enabled (by setting the ASCIE bit to logic 1), the 68HC12 can initiate an ATD conversion sequence and then continue to process other program steps. When the specified conversion is complete, an interrupt is generated and the 68HC12 can then process interrupt-related events. The alternative to using an interrupt is to initiate an ATD conversion sequence and then poll the conversion complete flag(s) (CCF), which signals conversion completion. While polling the CCF, the 68HC12 cannot perform any other operations.

ATD Control Register 3 (ATDCTL3).   The ATDCTL3 is located at memory address $0063. This register contains two freeze bits: FRZ1 and FRZ0. As the name implies, these bits are used to suspend ATD operation for background debugging. Like control registers 0 and 1, control register 3 is not used in normal operation and therefore will not be discussed further.

ATD Control Register 4 (ATDCTL4).   The ATDCTL4 is located at memory address $0064. This register is used to control the sample timing for the ATD system. The total conversion time for an 8-bit conversion consists of four components. Three of these components are fixed while one may be set by the user. Figure 4.85 provides register details. These components include the following:

- Initial sample time, which consists of 2 ATD clock periods.
- Transfer time, which consists of 4 ATD clock periods.
- Final sample time, which is programmable using bits 6 (SMP1) and 5 (SMP0) in the ATDCTL4 register.
- Resolution time consisting of 10 ATD clock periods.

Register: ATD Converter Control Register 4 (ATDCTL4)   Address: $0064

7	6	5	4	3	2	1	0
S10BM	SMP1	SMP0	PRS4	PRS3	PRS2	PRS1	PRS0

Reset: 0   0   0   0   0   0   0   0

Figure 4.85   ATD control register 4 (ATDCTL4).

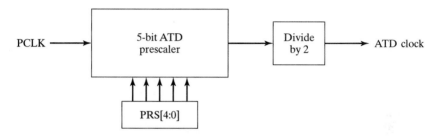

Figure 4.86   The P clock, the time base for the ATD system. A prescalar value is used to further divide the P clock frequency. The P clock goes through two divider stages: The first divide factor is set by the binary value written to PRS[4:0] (bits 4 to 0 of the ATDCTL4 register) plus one; the second is always two.

The time base for the ATD system is the P clock, as shown in Figure 4.86. A prescalar value is used to further divide the P clock frequency. The P clock goes through two different divider stages. The first stage divide factor is set by the binary value written to PRS[4:0] (bits 4 to 0 of the ATDCTL4 register) plus one. For example, if you set PRS[4:0] to 00101, the first divider stage divides the P clock by 6 (that is 5+1). The second divide stage is always 2. Therefore, the total division factor when PRS[4:0] is set to 00101 is 12.

The select sample time bits (SMP1 and SMP2) are used to select one of four sample times. As previously mentioned, three of the four time components of the ATD conversion are fixed and total 16 ATD clock periods. The final sample time is variable and is set by the user. Figure 4.87 lists the different settings for these two bits. The S10BM bit is the ATD 10-bit mode control bit. When this bit is set to 0, the ATD performs an 8-bit conversion. When set to 1, the ATD performs a 10-bit conversion.

ATD Control Register 5 (ATDCTL5).   The ATDCTL5 control register is used to select the conversion mode of the ATD system, specify the channels for conversion, and initiate the actual conversion process. It is located at memory address $0065, as shown in Figure 4.88.

SMP1 SMP2	Final Sample Time	Total 8-bit Conversion Time
0 0	2 ATD clock periods	18 ATD clock periods
0 1	4 ATD clock periods	20 ATD clock periods
1 0	8 ATD clock periods	24 ATD clock periods
1 1	16 ATD clock periods	32 ATD clock periods

Figure 4.87   Sample time selection.

Register: Analog-to-Digital Converter Control Register 5 (ATDCTL5)   Address: $0065

7	6	5	4	3	2	1	0
0	S8CM	SCAN	MULT	CD	CC	CB	CA
Reset: 0	0	0	0	0	0	0	0

Figure 4.88   ATD control register 5 (ATDCTL5).

Conversions are completely specified by the user by the following bit settings:

- The S8CM (select 8 channel mode) bit is used to select a conversion sequence of four conversions (0) or eight conversions (1).
- The SCAN (enable continuous channel scan) bit allows the user to choose between a single conversion sequence (0) or a continuous conversion sequence (1). In a single conversion sequence, the ATD performs a single conversion and stops.
- The MULT (enable multichannel conversion) bit when set to 0 specifies the ATD system to perform all specified conversions on a single input channel. When the MULT bit is set to 1, the ATD system performs conversions on sequential channels as specified by the CD, CC, CB, and CA bits.
- The CD, CC, CB, and CA bits are used to specify the channels for conversion to the ATD system.

Figure 4.89 shows how to properly set the S8CM and the CD, CC, CB, and CA bits for proper multichannel mode operation. Note that when the S8CM and CD bits are both set to 1, reference signals associated with the ATD system, V_{RH} and V_{RL}, may be converted and analyzed.

S8CM	CD	CC	CB	CA	Channel Signal	Result in ADRx if MULT = 1
0	0	0	0	0	AN0	ADR0
			0	1	AN1	ADR1
			1	0	AN2	ADR2
			1	1	AN3	ADR3
0	0	1	0	0	AN4	ADR0
			0	1	AN5	ADR1
			1	0	AN6	ADR2
			1	1	AN7	ADR3
0	1	0	0	0	Reserved	ADR0
			0	1	Reserved	ADR1
			1	0	Reserved	ADR2
			1	1	Reserved	ADR3
0	1	1	0	0	V_{RH}	ADR0
			0	1	V_{RL}	ADR1
			1	0	$(V_{RH} + V_{RL})/2$	ADR2
			1	1	Test/reserved	ADR3
1	0	0	0	0	AN0	ADR0
		0	0	1	AN1	ADR1
		0	1	0	AN2	ADR2
		0	1	1	AN3	ADR3
		1	0	0	AN4	ADR4
		1	0	1	AN5	ADR5
		1	1	0	AN6	ADR6
		1	1	1	AN7	ADR7
1	1	0	0	0	Reserved	ADR0
		0	0	1	Reserved	ADR1
		0	1	0	Reserved	ADR2
		0	1	1	Reserved	ADR3
		1	0	0	V_{RH}	ADR4
		1	0	1	V_{RL}	ADR5
		1	1	0	$(V_{RH} + V_{RL})/2$	ADR6
		1	1	1	Test/reserved	ADR7

Note: Shaded bits are "don't care" if MULT = 1 and the entire block of four or eight channels makes up a conversion sequence. When MULT = 0, all four bits (CD, CC, CB, and CA) must be specified and a conversion sequence consists of four or eight consecutive conversions of the single specified channel.

Figure 4.89 Multichannel mode result register assignment. (Copyright of Motorola. Used by permission.)

Before proceeding to the other ATD registers, let's look at a few questions that illustrate the proper use of the ATD control registers.

Practice Questions

1. **Question:** Specify the contents of the ATDCTL2 register to power up the ATD system and set the ATD for normal flag-clearing operations.

   Answer: Recall the ADPU (ATD power up) bit is bit 7 of the ATDCTL2 register, and the flag-clearing parameters are set by the AFFC (ATD fast flag clear all) bit, bit 6 of the ATDCTL2 register. To power up the ATD, the ADPU bit should be set to 1. Upon 68HC12 reset, the AFFC bit is reset to 0. This is the same setting required for normal flag-clearing operations. Therefore, to configure the ATDCTL2 register, a 1000 0000 or $80 must be written to memory location $0062.

2. **Question:** Specify the code to accomplish the actions of question 1.

   Answer: ATDCTL2 = 0x80;

3. **Question:** Specify the contents of the ATDCTL5 register to configure the ATD system for a continuous sequence of conversions with eight conversions per sequence.

   Answer: To properly configure the ATD to these specifications, the S8CM bit (bit 6) should be set to 1, the SCAN bit (bit 5) to 1, and the MULT bit (bit 4) to 1. According to the register assignments shown in Figure 4.89, the CD bit (bit 3) should also be set to 1 while the CC, CB, and CA bits are "don't care." Therefore, to configure the ATDCTL5 register, a 0111 1000 or $78 must be stored in memory location $0065.

4. **Question:** Specify the C code to accomplish the actions of question 3.

   Answer: ATDCTL5 = 0x78;

5. **Question:** What are the advantages in using the ATD system in the 10-bit versus the 8-bit conversion mode?

   Answer: Recall from our previous discussion that the ATD system aboard the B32 can be set for either a 10-bit or 8-bit conversion. This is accomplished using the S10BM bit of the ATDCTL4 control register. In the 10-bit mode, the resolution of the system would be 4.88 mV; with the 8-bit mode, the resolution is 19.53 mV. Thus, with 10 bits, we can obtain finer resolution.

ATD Status Register   The ATD status register (ATDSTAT) is a 2-byte register located at memory locations $0066 and $0067. It contains a series of flags, which indicate the status of the ATD system. Figure 4.90 provides register details.

The sequence complete flag (SCF) indicates when the ATD system has completed the specified conversion. If a single conversion sequence was specified by the user, the SCF bit is set at the end of the conversion sequence. If the ATD system is configured for continuous mode, the SCF bit is set at the end of the first conversion sequence. As discussed earlier, the AFFC bit in ATD control register 2 specifies how the flags will be reset. If the AFFC bit is 0, the SCF

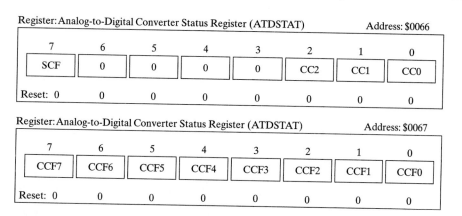

Figure 4.90   The ATD status register (ATDSTAT).

is cleared when a write is performed to ATDCL5 to initiate a new conversion sequence. On the other hand, if the AFFC bit is 1, the SCF is cleared after the first result register is read.

The CCx bits CC[2:0] form a 3-bit conversion counter. This counter indicates which channel is currently undergoing conversion and hence which result register will be written to next in a four- or eight-channel conversion sequence.

There are eight conversion complete flags, CCF[7:0], in the ATDSTAT register, each associated with an individual ATD result register. Each bit is set upon completion of the conversion associated with a given channel. Each flag will remain set until the associated result register for that channel is read. It is cleared when the register is read, if the AFFC bit (previously discussed) is set. If the AFFC bit is not set, the status register must be read to clear the flag. The conversion complete flags may be continuously polled to see if a specific channel conversion is complete.

ATD Input Register   Input signals are provided to the ATD conversion system via the Port AD data input register (PORTAD), as shown in Figure 4.91. PORTAD may also be used as a general-purpose digital input port. When POR-TAD is read, the digital signal levels currently connected to each of the PORTAD pins are sensed. The PORTAD register is mapped to memory location $006F.

ATD Result Registers   After the specified conversion(s) takes place in the ATD system, the results are placed into the corresponding result register (ADR0H through ADR7H). These are eight identical, 8-bit wide, result registers located at memory locations $0070 through $007E. Figure 4.92 provides register details.

The results of the conversion are 8-bit, unsigned binary values between 0 and 255. To interpret the result as a decimal voltage, the binary value must be

Register: Port AD Data Input Register (PORTAD)   Address: $006F

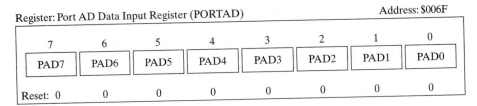

Figure 4.91   Port AD data input register (PORTAD).

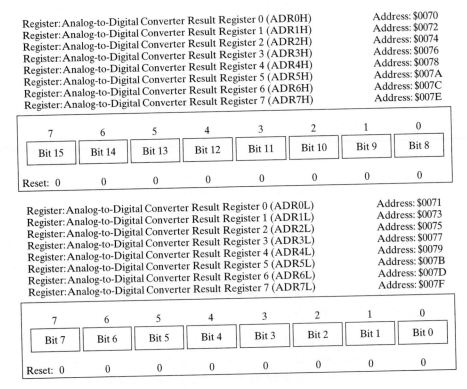

Figure 4.92   ATD result registers.

scaled by $2^{\#bits}$—in this case, 256—and then multiplied by the difference of the two ATD system reference voltages V_{RH} and V_{RL}.

Practice Questions

1. **Question:** An 8-bit analog converter, with $V_{RH} = 5$ V and $V_{RL} = 0$ V, converts an unknown voltage to an unsigned binary representation of 1000 1010. What is the

unknown voltage assuming the converter has rounded down to the nearest unsigned binary representation?

Answer: The decimal equivalent of 1000 1010 is 138. This value must be scaled and then multiplied by the difference between the reference voltages.

$$(138/256) \cdot 5.0 = 2.69 \text{ volts}$$

ATD Test Registers   The ATD test register (ATDTEST) is a 2-byte register at memory locations $0068 and $0069. It can only be read from or written to in special modes. In normal operating modes, reads and writes have no effect.

4.22.3 Programming the 68HC12 ATD System

To configure and program the ATD for successful operation, follow these simple steps:

1. Connect the appropriate reference voltage sources to 68HC12 external pins V_{RH} and V_{RL}. The reference voltage for pin V_{RH} cannot exceed 5 V and the reference voltage for pin V_{RL} cannot be less than 0 V. In addition, the difference between these two reference voltages must be at least 2.5 volts.
2. Connect the analog signal(s) for conversion to the appropriate A/D input pin(s): PAD0 through PAD7.
3. Write 1 to the ADPU bit in the ATDCTL2 register located at memory address $0062.
4. After the ADPU bit is set, wait 100 μs before using the ATD system. In the upcoming code example we show how to provide a 100 μs software delay.
5. Configure the ATD for proper operation using the ATD control registers.
6. Initialize the ATD conversion process by writing to ATD control register 5 (ATDCTL5).
7. Monitor for ATD conversion completion using the ATD status registers.
8. Use the results of the conversion, which are located in the corresponding result register (ADR0H through ADR7H).
9. If processor power consumption is an issue, the ATD system may be powered down after conversion completion using the ADPU bit in the ATDCTL2 register.

ATD Example.   The ATD converter on the 68HC12 can be configured to be an 8-bit converter. It takes in an analog signal and converts it to a binary representation. One application of an ATD converter is a digital voltmeter. In this example we program a simple voltmeter using the ATD system onboard the 68HC12.

Recall that the conversion produces a weighted binary value, not simply the voltage expressed in binary. Some method is necessary to convert the weighted binary value to a representation suitable for display. If you are programming in C, this is a fairly straightforward process. The voltage can be found using the following formula:

$$\text{Voltage} = (\text{Weighted binary value}/0xFF) * (V_{RH} - V_{RL})$$

This will give the value of the analog signal passed to the converter, which can then be used for other tasks.

When creating a digital voltmeter, there must be some method to display the voltage to the user. In this example we display the result to the host PC screen. In Chapter 7, we revisit this example and display the result on a liquid crystal display (LCD).

In this example, we make a conversion on a single ATD channel. We set the ATD to convert in 2 ATD clock periods. Initializing the ATD and performing the conversions will take place in separate functions. We find the average value of the conversion (mean of the ATD result registers) and convert it to a floating-point value. We then display the result to the host PC via the `printf` function.

Here is the step-by-step summary of the approach discussed here:

1. Connect the appropriate reference voltage sources to 68HC12 external pins V_{RH} and V_{RL}. The reference voltage for pin V_{RH} cannot exceed 5 V and the reference voltage for pin V_{RL} cannot be less than 0 V. For this example, let's set V_{RH} to 5 V and V_{RL} to 0 V.

2. Connect the analog signal(s) for conversion to the appropriate ATD input pin(s): PAD0 through PAD7. For this example, the unknown analog voltage will be connected to 68HC12 pin PAD6.

3. Write 1 to the ADPU bit in the ATDCTL2 register located at memory address $0062.

4. After the ADPU bit is set, wait 100 μs before using the ATD system.

5. Configure the ATD for proper operation using the ATD control registers.

6. Initialize the ATD conversion process by writing to ATD control register 5 (ATDCTL5).

7. Monitor for ATD conversion completion using the ATD status registers.

8. Use the results of the conversion, which are located in the appropriate result register (ADR0H through ADR7H).

9. If processor power consumption is an issue, the ATD system may be powered down after conversion completion using the ADPU bit in the ATD-
CTL2 register.

In this example we leave the ATD power on. The following sample code
"voltmeter.c" illustrates how to use the ATD system to collect and display analog
data.

```
/******************************************************************/
/* filename: voltmeter.c                                        */
/* This program will create a simple voltmeter using the on-    */
/* board analog-to-digital converter in the 68HC12.  It will    */
/* perform one conversion and then the user will have to man-   */
/* ually restart the program to convert another voltage.        */
/******************************************************************/

#include <912b32.h>
#include <stdio.h>

#define DECIMAL 0x2E          /*macro: decimal point in ASCII*/
#define V 0x56                /*macro:  "V" in ASCII*/

/*function prototypes*/
void delay_100us(void);
void ADC_convert(void);
void delay_5ms(void);

void main(void)
{
printf("HELLO\n");
ATDCTL2 = 0x80;               /*power up ADC, disable interrupts*/
printf("ADC2\n");
delay_100us();                /*wait for ADC to warm up*/
printf("warmed up\n");
ATDCTL3 = 0x00;               /*select active background mode*/
ATDCTL4 = 0x01;               /*sample time 2 ADC clk, prescale 4 */
printf("ready\n");
ADC_convert();                /*perform conv, convert value*/
}

/******************************************************************/
/* void ADC_convert(void): function to perform a single con-    */
/* version and stores it for user access. The function then     */
/* converts the floating point result to an integer value such  */
/* that each individual integer may be isolated, converted to   */
/* ASCII and sent out to an LCD for display.  This code will    */
/* prove very helpful.                                          */
/******************************************************************/
```

```
void ADC_convert(void)
{
unsigned int sumadr;
unsigned int avg_bin_voltage;
unsigned int int_voltage;
unsigned int ones_int;
unsigned int tenths_int;
unsigned int hundreths_int;
char ones;
char tenths;
char hundreths;

ATDCTL5 = 0x06;                              /*perform 4 conv, ch 6*/
/*Wait for conversion to finish*/
while((ATDSTAT & 0x8000) != 0x8000)
   {
   ;
   }

/*print results to PC screen for verification           */
printf("%x %x %x %x\n", ADR0H, ADR1H, ADR2H, ADR3H);

/*average four results for noise reduction              */
sumadr = ADR0H + ADR1H + ADR2H + ADR3H;
avg_bin_voltage = sumadr/4;

/*convert result to voltage between 0.00 and 5.00        */
/*convert result to all integer value between 000 and 500 */
int_voltage = (100*avg_bin_voltage/255)*5;

/*isolate and convert most significant digit to ASCII     */
/*decimal value + 48 yields ASCII code                    */
ones_int = int_voltage/100;
ones = (char)(ones_int + 48);

/*isolate and convert next most significant digit to ASCII*/
/*decimal value + 48 yields ASCII code                    */
tenths_int = (int_voltage - ones_int*100)/10;
tenths = (char)(tenths_int + 48);

/*isolate and convert next most significant digit to ASCII*/
/*decimal value + 48 yields ASCII code                    */
hundreths_int = (int_voltage - ones_int*100 - tenths_int*10)/1;
hundreths = (char)(hundreths_int + 48);

/*print results to PC screen an ASCII character at a time */
/*this is good practice for sending results to LCD display*/
```

```
printf("%c.%c%cV\n", ones, tenths, hundreths);
}

/*****************************************************************/
/*100us delay based on an 8MHz clock                           */
/*****************************************************************/

void delay_100us(void)
{
int i;

for (i=0; i<50; i++)
  {
  asm("nop");
  }
}

/*****************************************************************/
/*5 ms delay based on an 8MHz clock                            */
/*****************************************************************/

void delay_5ms(void)
{
int i;

for (i=0; i<50; i++)
  {
  delay_100us();
  }
}
/*****************************************************************/
```

4.22.4 Programming the ATD System Using Interrupts

In the previous programming examples, the ATD system has been used in a polling mode. That is, the ATD was configured for an analog conversion event and the completion of the event was signaled by either the setting of the sequence complete flag (SCF bit) in the ATD status register or by the conversion complete flags (within the ATD status register) associated with each channel of the ATD.

The ATD system is equipped with an interrupt that is triggered when the ATD sequence is complete. The ATD sequence complete interrupt is enabled with the ASCIE bit in ATD control register 2 (ATDCTL2). When enabled, the ASCIF (ATD sequence complete interrupt bit) in the ATDCTL2 register will set and cause an interrupt event.

4.23 HCS12 ANALOG-TO-DIGITAL CONVERSION SYSTEM

The HCS12 family of microcontrollers are equipped with an ATD system similar to the 68HC12; however, it has some enhanced features. In this section we discuss these powerful enhanced features, which include the following:

- Selectable 8- or 10-bit resolution
- Left/right justified and signed/unsigned result data
- External trigger control
- Flexible 1 to 8 conversion sequence length configuration
- Multiple ATD channels

We examine each enhanced feature in turn.

4.23.1 Selectable 8-Bit or 10-Bit Resolution

The ATD systems aboard the HCS12 can be configured for either 8-bit or 10-bit operation. The extra two bits of resolution increases the sensitivity from approximately 19.53 mV to 4.88 mV. The resolution is selected using the A/D resolution select (SRES8) bit in ATD control register 4 (ATDCTL4). You should examine the specific application to determine required system resolution.

4.23.2 Left/Right Justified and Signed/Unsigned Result Data

With the HCS12 system, the format of the resulting ATD data is under the control of the user. The result register data justification (DJM) and the result register data signed or unsigned representation (DSGN) bits are used to select right (1) or left justified (0) data and signed (1) and unsigned (0) data representation in the result registers.

4.23.3 External Trigger Control

The HCS12 ATD system is equipped with an external trigger feature. The external trigger is applied to analog input channel 7 (AN7/ETRIG/PAD7). This feature allows a signal external to the HCS12 to determine when an analog conversion is initiated.

External trigger signal parameters are set using the external trigger level/edge control (ETRIGLE), the external trigger polarity (ETRIGP), and the external trigger mode enable (ETRIGE) bits in the ATD control register 2 (ATDCTL2). This register is illustrated in Figure 4.93.

Register: ATD Control Register 2 (ATDCTL2)   HCS12 Address: $0002

7	6	5	4	3	2	1	0
ADPU	AFFC	AWAI	ETRIGLE	ETRIGP	ETRIGE	ASCIE	ASCIF
Reset: 0	0	0	0	0	0	0	0

Register: ATD Control Register 3 (ATDCTL3)   HCS12 Address: $0003

7	6	5	4	3	2	1	0
0	S8C	S4C	S2C	S1C	FIFO	FRZ1	FRZ0
Reset: 0	0	1	0	0	0	0	0

Register: ATD Control Register 4 (ATDCTL4)   HCS12 Address: $0004

7	6	5	4	3	2	1	0
SRES8	SMP1	SMP0	PRS4	PRS3	PRS2	PRS1	PRS0
Reset: 0	0	0	0	0	1	0	1

Register: ATD Control Register 5 (ATDCTL5)   HCS12 Address: $0005

7	6	5	4	3	2	1	0
DJM	DSGN	SCAN	MULT	0	CC	CB	CA
Reset: 0	0	0	0	0	0	0	0

Register: ATD Status Register 0 (ATDSTAT0)   HCS12 Address: $0006

7	6	5	4	3	2	1	0
SCF	0	ETORF	FIFOR	0	CC2	CC1	CC0
Reset: 0	0	0	0	0	0	0	0

Register: ATD Status Register 1 (ATDSTAT1)   HCS12 Address: $000B

7	6	5	4	3	2	1	0
CCF7	CCF6	CCF5	CCF4	CCF3	CCF2	CCF1	CCF0
Reset: 0	0	0	0	0	0	0	0

Register: ATD Input Enable Register (ATDDIEN)   HCS12 Address: $000D

7	6	5	4	3	2	1	0
IEN7	IEN6	IEN5	IEN4	IEN3	IEN2	IEN1	IEN0
Reset: 0	0	0	0	0	0	0	0

Figure 4.93   HCS12 ATD registers.

The [ETRIGLE:ERIGP] bit pattern determines what kind of external trigger signal will initiate an ATD conversion. A [0:0] selects a falling edge trigger, a [0:1] a rising edge trigger, a [1:0] a low level trigger, and a [1:1] a high level trigger. When set to logic 1, the ETRIGE bit enables the external trigger.

4.23.4 Flexible 1 to 8 Conversion Sequence Length Configuration

The HCS12 ATD system has complete flexibility to select which channels will be chosen for ATD conversion. The multi-channel sample mode, when the MULT bit is set to logic 1, samples across several channels. When set to logic 0, the ATD system obtains samples only from a single channel. The actual number of channels sampled is determined by the binary value set into the [S8C:S4C:S2C:S1C] bits of ATD control register 3 (ATDCTL3). For example, if these bits are set to [0:1:0:1], there will be five channels converted per conversion sequence. The [CC:CB:CA] bits of ATD control register 5 (ATDCTL5) determine which specific channel will be sampled (MULT = 0) or the first channel to be sampled in a sequence (MULT = 1).

The result register First In First Out mode (FIFO) bits provide additional flexibility. If the FIFO bit is set to logic 0 (non-FIFO mode), the results are mapped into result registers based on the specified conversion sequence. If the FIFO bit is set to logic 1, conversion results are placed in consecutive result registers and wrap around from ATD Result Register 7 to ATD result register 0 if required.

4.23.5 Multiple ATD Channels

The HCS12 series of processors may be equipped with more than one ATD subsystem. For example the DP256 is equipped with two complete ATD subsystems (ATD0, ATD1).

4.23.6 HCS12 ATD Registers

The HCS12 ATD related registers are illustrated in Figure 4.93. The registers for the most part function the same way as the ones for the 68HC12 ATD converter. We have discussed the special features of the HCS12 in the previous sections. We complete our discussion here with a few remaining registers.

ATD Status Register 0 (ATDSTAT0)   Register ATDSTAT0 contains the sequence complete flag (SCF) bit. This flag is set upon completion of the specified conversion sequence. The flag may be cleared by (1) writing a logic 1 to the SCF bit, (2) starting a new conversion sequence by writing a value to ATDCTL5, or (3) reading a result register when the ATD fast flag clear all (AFFC) bit in the ATDCTL2 register has been set to logic 1.

ATD Status Register 1 (ATDSTAT1)   The ATD status register 1 (ATDSTAT1) contains conversion complete flags (CCFx) for each conversion channel. A flag sets to indicate that a conversion on a specific channel has been completed.

ATD Input Enable Register (ATDDIEN)   The ATD input enable register (ATDDIEN) contains an ATD digital input enable on channel x (IENx) bit for each channel. When the corresponding bit is set to logic 1, the digital input buffer for the corresponding channel is enabled.

4.24 THE PULSE WIDTH MODULATION SYSTEM

The 68HC12 B32 configuration and the HCS12 series of processors is equipped with a pulse width modulation (PWM) system. A PWM signal is a convenient method to control motor speed by varying the average voltage applied to the motor. The signals are also used to control the direction of motor turns in radio control cars and airplanes.

The average voltage applied to the motor is adjusted by varying the "on" time of the signal to the total period of the signal (duty cycle). For example, a duty cycle of 80% means that the signal is logic high for 80% of its period and logic low for 20% of its period. The overall effect of this duty cycle is to provide 80% of the motor's source voltage to the motor. Using this method, a motor's speed is precisely controlled. A 100% duty cycle means that the switch is closed at all times while 0% duty cycle means that the switch is open at all times. Figure 4.94 shows the waveforms with 20% and 80% duty cycles, and Figure 4.95 shows a simplified view of how such a waveform can control a DC motor.

Aside from controlling the speed of DC motors, PWM techniques can be also used to control servo motors, which are used in a variety of applications. For example, the steering system of a radio control car uses a servo motor to steer the vehicle. The motor rotates with a precision angular displacement consistent with the duty cycle of the control signal sent to the motor. A typical motor requires a 50 Hz control signal to operate. By varying the duty cycle while maintaining a constant control signal frequency, a turn may be rendered. The servo may displace from one angular extreme to another by varying the duty cycle from 4.5 to 10 percent. Figure 4.96 illustrates a PWM steering control system.

Note: The 68HC12 B32 does not have the capability to drive a DC motor or a servo motor directly. A device such as a buffer is used to interface the

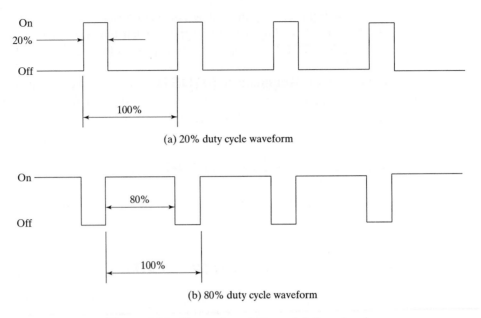

(a) 20% duty cycle waveform

(b) 80% duty cycle waveform

Figure 4.94   Two pulse width modulation signals.

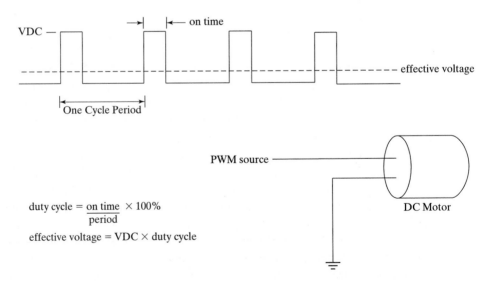

$$\text{duty cycle} = \frac{\text{on time}}{\text{period}} \times 100\%$$

$$\text{effective voltage} = \text{VDC} \times \text{duty cycle}$$

Figure 4.95   A pulse width modulation signal controlling a DC motor.

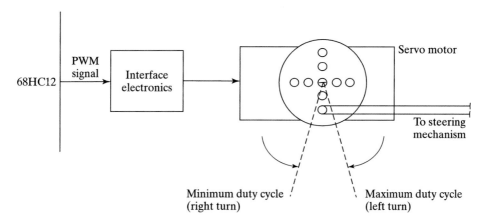

Figure 4.96   Using PWM to steer a radio control car.

controller with a motor. In Chapter 5, we discuss the electrical characteristics of the processor in detail and how to interface different devices to the controller. We next take a closer look at the PWM features of the B32.

4.24.1 Fundamentals and Features

To generate a PWM signal, the signal characteristics must be specified in terms of PWM clock ticks. We show how to specify PWM signal characteristics in a detailed example provided in section 4.24.5. Once these values are converted, the duty cycle and the period must be stored in appropriate registers: for duty cycle, use PWM channel duty register x (PWDTYx); for period, use PWM channel period register x (PWPERx).

The PWM system generates a signal by comparing the duty cycle value to the PWM channel counter x (PWCNTx). When the value in the PWDTYx register and the PWCNTx match, the active portion of the signal is de-asserted. In other words, if the duty cycle was active high, the signal will transition to logic low. The signal will remain low until the value in the PWCNTx register equals the value in the PWPERx register. It is a good idea to reset the PWCNTx at the beginning of the PWM cycle. The PWCNTx increments on every PWM clock tick. This procedure repeats continually to generate the PWM signal. This process is illustrated in Figure 4.97.

The time base for the PWM system is provided by the E clock. The PWM clock system is equipped with a complement of divider circuits that provide the capability to generate a range of signals from high frequency, short duty cycle signals to low frequency, long duty cycle signals. Again, the signal characteristics must be converted to clock ticks and stored in the appropriate registers.

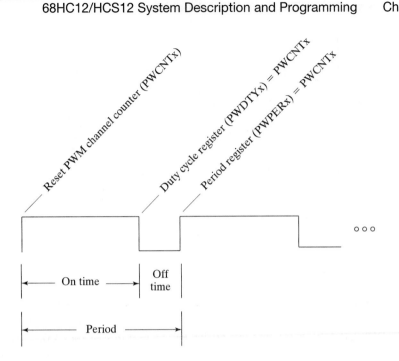

Figure 4.97 Generating a PWM signal. The PWM system generates a signal by comparing the duty cycle value to the PWM channel counter x (PWCNTx). When the values in the PWDTYx register and the PWCNTx match, the active portion of the signal is de-asserted. The signal will remain de-asserted until the value in the PWCNTx register equals the value in the PWPERx register.

The PWM system aboard the B32 and the HCS12 provides four independent 8-bit PWM waveforms. These channels may be configured by the user as follows:

- Four 8-bit channels (HCS12: eight 8-bit channels)
- Two 16-bit PWM waveforms (HCS12: four 16-bit channels)
- A combination of one 16-bit and two 8-bit PWM waveforms

With an 8-bit channel, duty cycle and period counts may range from 0 to 255 clock ticks ($2^8 - 1$). The 16-bit channels are formed by concatenating (joining together) two of the 8-bit channels. The 16-bit channels may store counts from 0 to 65,535 ($2^{16} - 1$).

However the channels are configured, there are certain features that are common to all of them. The channels may be programmed with the PWM period

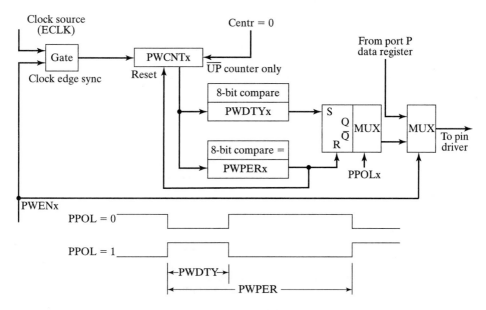

Figure 4.98   MC68HC912B32 left-aligned output channel. (Copyright of Motorola. Used by permission.)

and duty cycle. The duty cycles may range from 0 to 100 percent. Also, the signals may be programmed for left-aligned or center-aligned output.

4.24.2 PWM Channel Alignment

A left-aligned signal is illustrated in Figure 4.98. As its name implies, the signal is active on the left (leading edge) of the signal. As you can see in the diagram both the duty cycle (PWDTY) and period (PWPER) are set by placing values in the corresponding registers. The signal may be selected for either active high duty (PPOL = 1) or active low duty (PPOL = 0) using the polarity bit.

The duty cycle and period for the left-aligned waveform are found using the following equations:

```
Duty cycle = [(PWDTYx +1)/(PWPERx +1)] x 100%    (for PPOLx = 1)
Duty cycle = [(PWDPERx - PWDTYx)/(PWPERx +1)] x 100%
                                              (for PPOLx = 0)
Period = Channel-Clock-Period x (PWPER + 1)      (CENTR = 0)
```

A center-aligned signal is illustrated in Figure 4.99. As its name implies, the signal is active in the center of the signal. As you can see in the diagram,

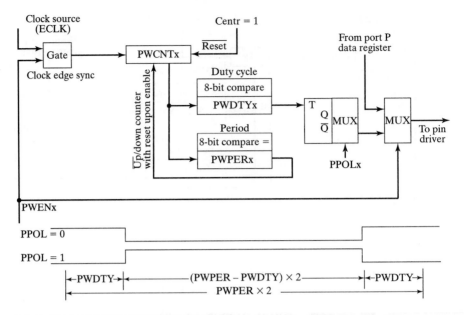

Figure 4.99 MC68HC912B32 center-aligned output channel. (Copyright of Motorola. Used by permission.)

both the duty cycle (PWDTY) and period (PWPER) are set by placing values in the corresponding registers. Note that the period specified in the PWPER register is actually one-half the period of the signal. Verify this by carefully examining Figure 4.99. The signal may be selected for either active high duty (PPOL = 1) or active low duty (PPOL = 0) using the polarity bit.

The duty cycle and period for the center-aligned waveform is found using the following equations:

```
Duty cycle = (PWDTYx/PWPERx) x 100%        (for PPOLx = 1)
Duty cycle = [(PWDPERx - PWDTYx)/PWPERx] x 100%  (for PPOLx = 0)
Period = Channel-Clock-Period x PWPER x 2   (CENTR = 1)
```

4.24.3 PWM Clock System

The clock system for the pulse width modulation system is illustrated in Figure 4.100. The PWM time base is provided by the E clock. The E clock may be divided down by setting appropriate prescaler bits (PCKA[2:0] and PCKB[2:0]) in the PWM clocks and concatenate register (PWCLK). Clock channel A is the time base used for PWM channels 0 and 1; clock channel B is the time base used for PWM channels 2 and 3. Figure 4.101 provides the clock scaling factors for the E clock.

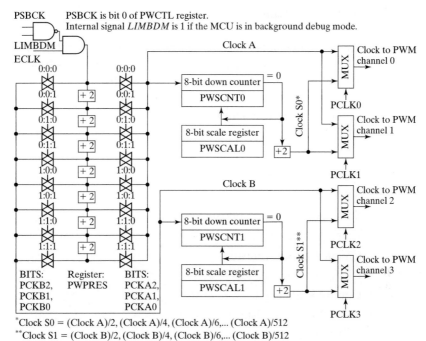

Figure 4.100   MC68HC912B32 PWM clock sources. (Copyright of Motorola. Used by permission.)

PCKA2 (PCKB2)	PCKA1 (PCKB1)	PCKA0 (PCKB0)	Value of Clock A (B)
0	0	0	E
0	0	1	E + 2
0	1	0	E + 4
0	1	1	E + 8
1	0	0	E + 16
1	0	1	E + 32
1	1	0	E +64
1	1	1	E + 128

Figure 4.101   MC68HC912B32 PWM clocks A and B prescaler. (Copyright of Motorola. Used by permission.)

4.24.4 PWM Registers

At first glance there appears to be an overwhelming number of PWM related registers. These registers may be conveniently set into the following groups. We cover each of these register (register groups) in turn.

* Clocks and concatenate register
* Clock select and polarity register
* Enable register
* Prescale counter
* Scale registers
* Scale counter value register
* Channel counters
* Channel period registers
* Channel duty registers
* Control register
* Special mode register
* Port P related registers

Clocks and Concatenate Register   As mentioned previously, the PWM system consists of four 8-bit PWM waveform channels. These four channels may be concatenated (connected together) to form two 16-bit PWM waveform channels. This allows for very long periods and duty cycles.

The PWM clocks and concatenate register (PWCLK), shown in Figure 4.102, has two distinct functions: (1) controls how the different channels may be concatenated together, and (2) it sets the E clock divider for the A and B clocks. Clock A serves PWM channels 0 and 1. Clock B serves PWM channels 2 and 3.

The CON23 bit controls how PWM channels are concatenated together. When CON23 is set to 0, channels 2 and 3 are separate 8-bit PWM channels. When CON23 is set to 1, channels 2 and 3 are concatenated together to form a single 16-bit PWM channel. The CON01 bit performs the same function as the

Register: PWM Clocks and Concatenate Register (PWCLK)   Address: $0040

7	6	5	4	3	2	1	0
CON23	CON01	PCKA2	PCKA1	PCKA0	PCKB2	PCKB1	PCKB0

Reset: 0   0   0   0   0   0   0   0

Figure 4.102   PWM clocks and concatenate register (PWCLK).

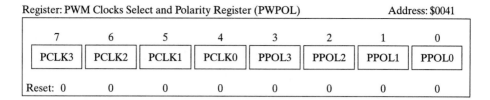

Register: PWM Clocks Select and Polarity Register (PWPOL)   Address: $0041

7	6	5	4	3	2	1	0
PCLK3	PCLK2	PCLK1	PCLK0	PPOL3	PPOL2	PPOL1	PPOL0

Reset: 0   0   0   0   0   0   0   0

Figure 4.103   PWM clock select and polarity register (PWPOL).

CON23 bit for PWM Channels 0 and 1. When concatenated, the output signals are provided on Port P[0] for channels 0, 1 and Port P[2] for channels 2, 3. Furthermore, the polarity is set by using the polarity control bits for channel 1 for channels 0, 1 and channel 3 for channels 2, 3. Figure 4.103 provides register details.

The PCKA[2:0] and the PCKB[2:0] bits set the E clock divider, as shown in Figure 4.101.

Clock Select and Polarity Register   The clock select and polarity register (PWPOL) selects the clock source and clock polarity for PWM channels 0 to 3. Each PWM channel has a corresponding PCLKn and PPOLn bit.

The PCLKn bit selects the clock source for the channel. When PCLKn is set to 0, the clock source is clock A (channels 0, 1) and clock B (channels 2, 3); when set to 1, the PCLKn bit routes the clock source through additional divider hardware (PWSCNTx, PWSCALx).

The PPOLn bit selects the polarity of the waveform, as previously discussed and illustrated in Figures 4.98 and 4.99.

Enable Register   The PWM enable register (PWEN) is used to activate a specific PWM channel. When the corresponding bit is set to 1, a PWM signal becomes available at the corresponding PORT P bit. When set to 0, the channel is disabled. Figure 4.104 provides register details.

Prescale Counter   This register is used only in special modes of operation. Figure 4.105 provides register details.

Register: PWM Enable Register (PWEN)   Address: $0042

7	6	5	4	3	2	1	0
0	0	0	0	PWEN3	PWEN2	PWEN1	PWEN0

Reset: 0   0   0   0   0   0   0   0

Figure 4.104   PWM enable register (PWEN).

Register: PWM Prescale Counter (PWPRES)   Address: $0043

7	6	5	4	3	2	1	0
0	Bit 6	Bit 5	Bit 4	Bit 3	Bit 2	Bit 1	Bit 0

Reset: 0   0   0   0   0   0   0   0

Figure 4.105   PWM prescale counter (PWPRES).

Before discussing the next two registers, refer again to the PWM clock source diagram provided in Figure 4.100. Note that the clocks are all derived from the E clock. Clock A serves PWM channels 0 and 1; whereas, clock B serves channels 2 and 3. Note that clocks A and B may be directly routed to their respective channels or they may be routed through additional division circuitry. The next two registers (scale registers and scale counter value) provide this division circuitry.

Scale Registers and Scale Counter Value   The PWM channels can select a scaled value of the clock as its clock source. When this option is selected, using the previously discussed PWPOL register, the clock frequency is formed by dividing the clock source by the value loaded into the PWM scale register plus 1 divided by 2:

$$\text{Frequency} = ((\text{PWSCALx} + 1)/2).$$

Figure 4.106 provides register details.

The PWM scale counter register determines when the value will be loaded into the PWSCALx register. PWSCNTx is a down-counter that loads PWSCALx when it reaches $00. Figure 4.107 provides register details.

Channel Counters   As previously discussed, each PWM channel is equipped with a dedicated PWM channel counter (PWCNTx), as shown in Figure 4.108. Normally this counter is reset at the beginning of the PWM cycle. It then is used to determine the length of the duty cycle and the period. The PWM system generates a signal by comparing the duty cycle value to the PWCNTx. When the value in the PWDTYx register and the PWCNTx match, the active

Register: PWM Scale Register 0/1 (PWSCAL0/PWSCAL1)   Address: $0044/$0046

7	6	5	4	3	2	1	0
Bit 7	Bit 6	Bit 5	Bit 4	Bit 3	Bit 2	Bit 1	Bit 0

Reset: 0   0   0   0   0   0   0   0

Figure 4.106   PWM scale register 0 and 1 (PWSCALx).

Register: PWM Scale Counter Register 0/1 (PWSCNT0/PWSCNT1) Address: $0045/$0047

7	6	5	4	3	2	1	0
Bit 7	Bit 6	Bit 5	Bit 4	Bit 3	Bit 2	Bit 1	Bit 0

Reset: 0   0   0   0   0   0   0   0

Figure 4.107   PWM scale counter register 0 and 1 (PWSCNTx).

Register: PWM Channel Counter 0/1/2/3 (PWCNT0/PWCNT1/PWCNT2/PWCNT3)
Address: $0048/$0049/$004A/$004B

7	6	5	4	3	2	1	0
Bit 7	Bit 6	Bit 5	Bit 4	Bit 3	Bit 2	Bit 1	Bit 0

Reset: 0   0   0   0   0   0   0   0

Figure 4.108   PWM channel counter 0 to 3 (PWCNTx).

Register: PWM Channel Period Register 0/1/2/3 (PWPER0/PWPER1/PWPER2/PWPER3)
Address: $004C/$004D/$004E/$004F

7	6	5	4	3	2	1	0
Bit 7	Bit 6	Bit 5	Bit 4	Bit 3	Bit 2	Bit 1	Bit 0

Reset: 0   0   0   0   0   0   0   0

Figure 4.109   PWM channel period register 0 to 3 (PWPERx).

portion of the signal is de-asserted. The signal remains de-asserted until the value in the PWCNTx register equals the value in the PWPERx register. Figure 4.109 provides register details. The PWCNTx increments on every PWM clock tick.

Channel Period Registers   The value in the period register determines the period of the associated PWM channel. The value is determined using the equations presented in section 4.24.2. (See Figure 4.109 for register details.)

Channel Duty Registers   The value in each duty register determines the duty cycle of the associated PWM channel. The value is determined using the equations in section 4.24.2. When the duty cycle value is equal to the counter value, the output changes state. The duty register is shown in Figure 4.110.

Control Register   The PWM control register (PWCTL) is the main control register for the PWM system. Figure 4.111 provides register details. We discuss only the center-aligned output mode bit (CENTR) at this time. When set

Register: PWM Channel Duty Register 0/1/2/3 (PWDTY0/PWDTY1/PWDTY2/PWDTY3)

Address: $0050/$0051/$0052/$0053

7	6	5	4	3	2	1	0
Bit 7	Bit 6	Bit 5	Bit 4	Bit 3	Bit 2	Bit 1	Bit 0
Reset: 0	0	0	0	0	0	0	0

Figure 4.110   PWM channel duty register 0 to 3 (PWDTYx).

Register: PWM Control Register (PWCTL)   Address: $0054

7	6	5	4	3	2	1	0
0	0	0	PSWAI	CENTR	RDPP	PUPP	PSBCK
Reset: 0	0	0	0	0	0	0	0

Figure 4.111   PWM control register (PWCTL).

Register: PWM Special Mode Register (PWTST)   Address: $0055

7	6	5	4	3	2	1	0
DISCR	DISCP	DISCAL	0	0	0	0	0
Reset: 0	0	0	0	0	0	0	0

Figure 4.112   PWM special mode register (PWTST).

to logic 0, this bit provides left-aligned PWM signals. When set to 1, the PWM system provides center-aligned PWM signals.

Special Mode Register   This register is used only in special modes. Figure 4.112 provides register details.

Port P Related Registers   The PWM signals are output on Port P pins [3:0]. The PWM functions take priority over the general-purpose input/output functions of the pins. The data direction register for Port P (DDRP) determines whether a specific pin is an output or input when used as a general-purpose input/output pin. Figure 4.113 provides register details.

4.24.5 Programming the PWM

The steps below are required for programming the pulse width modulation system. We discuss each of the steps in turn and then apply them to a specific example—programming the steering control for a radio-controlled car. As a homework problem at the end of the chapter (Challenging 12) we ask you to

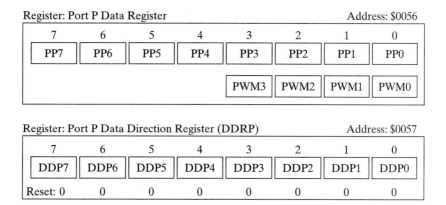

Figure 4.113   Port P related registers.

construct the UML activity diagram and write the entire program. We provide a guideline to complete that task next.

The following steps must be accomplished to program the PWM system:

1. For your specific application, determine the number of clock ticks required for the desired duty cycle and period.
2. Determine the clock source frequency and scaling factors that will allow the duty cycle and period counts to fit in either an 8-bit or 16-bit register.
3. Select the 8-bit or 16-bit mode. Register: PWCLK; bits: CON23, CON01.
4. Select the left-aligned or center-aligned mode of operation. Register: PWCTL; bit: CENTR.
5. Determine which signal polarity you will use. Register: PWPOL; bits: PPOL[3:0].
6. Select the clock source for the channel(s) that will be used in your application. Register: PWPOL; bits: PCLK[3:0].
7. Set the desired E clock divider. Register: PWCLK; bits PCKA[2:0], PCKB [2:0].
8. Set the period count in the PWPERx register and the duty cycle count in the PWDTYx register. Use the following equations:

   The duty cycle and period for the left-aligned waveform are found using the following equations:

```
Duty cycle = [(PWDTYx +1)/(PWPERx +1)] x 100%  (for PPOLx = 1)
Duty cycle = [(PWDPERx - PWDTYx)/(PWPERx +1)] x 100%
                                               (for PPOLx = 0)
Period = Channel-Clock-Period x (PWPER + 1)    (CENTR = 0)
```

The duty cycle and period for the center-aligned waveform is found using the next three equations:

```
Duty cycle = (PWDTYx/PWPERx) x 100%              (for PPOLx = 1)
Duty cycle = [(PWDPERx - PWDTYx)/PWPERx] x 100%
                                                (for PPOLx = 0)
Period = Channel-Clock-Period x PWPER x 2       (CENTR = 1)
```

9. Enable the specific PWM channels using the PWEN register.

PWM Example 1   Let's set the PWM system for a 976 Hz output and a 66.7 % PWM duty cycle. We have arbitrarily chosen these values to illustrate the flexibility of the PWM system.

To use a 976 Hz PWM control signal, we need to divide the PWM clock source of 8 MHz by 32. This provides a 250 kHz (period = 4 μs) clock source to the PWM system. With our period set at 256 counts, the resulting PWM control signal frequency is 976 Hz (period = 4 μs pulse × 256 pulses).

To achieve a 66.7 % PWM duty cycle, we set the PWM period to 256 counts and the PWM duty cycle to 171 counts. Recall from our previous discussion of the PWM system that this is accomplished using the PWPER0 and the PWDTY0 registers, respectively.

The following sample code can be used to achieve these values of PWM frequency and duty cycle:

```
/****************************************************************/
/*init_pwm(): initializes 68HC12 pulse width modulation system  */
/****************************************************************/

void init_pwm()
{
PWTST = 0x00;                /*Sets PWM port for normal operation  */
PWCTL = 0x00;                /*Set to left aligned signal          */
PWCLK = 0x28;                /*no concatenation, ECLK/128          */
PWPOL = 0x01;                /*set pins high then low transition   */
DDRP = 0xFF;                 /*Port P set to output                */
PWEN = 0x01;                 /*forces output for PWM pins          */
PWPER0 = 255;                /*sets PWM signal period to 250Hz     */
PWDTY0 = 171;                /*set duty cycle                      */
}
/****************************************************************/
```

PWM Example 2   At the beginning of section 4.24, we discussed how PWM signals may be used to control servo motors. The servo motor diagram is provided here again for convenience (see Figure 4.114). The motor rotates with a precision angular displacement consistent with the duty cycle of the control

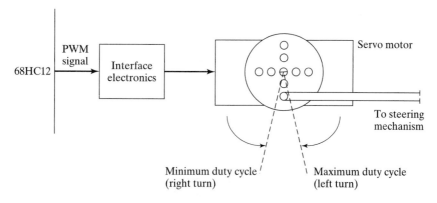

Figure 4.114   Using PWM to steer a radio control car.

signal sent to the motor. The steering system of a radio-controlled car uses a servo motor to steer the vehicle. The motor requires a 50 Hz control signal sent to it. By varying the duty cycle while maintaining a constant control signal frequency, a turn may be rendered. The servo may displace from one angular extreme to another by varying the duty cycle from 4.5 to 10 percent. Figure 4.114 provides steering control details.

Let's convert this period and duty cycle specifications to clock ticks. Assume for our calculations that the E clock is operating at 8 MHz. We begin by calculating the number of clock ticks required for the PWM period.

We first calculate the period of the E Clock:

$$E \text{ clock period } = 1/E \text{ clock frequency } = 1/8 \text{ MHz } = 125 \text{ ns}$$

Let's now calculate the period of the PWM signal:

$$PWM \text{ clock period } = 1/PWM \text{ clock frequency } = 1/50 \text{ Hz } = 20 \text{ ms}$$

Now express the PWM clock period in terms of E clock frequency clock ticks:

$$E \text{ clock ticks} = PWM \text{ clock period}/E \text{ clock period } = 20 \text{ ms}/125 \text{ ns}$$
$$= 160{,}000 \text{ clock ticks}$$

This number is too large to fit in either a 16-bit or 8-bit register. The maximum value we can prescale the E clock by is 128. This prescaler would provide a PWM period count of 160,000 clock ticks/128 = 1,250 clock ticks. This count is still too large for an 8-bit PWM channel (max count 255) but it will fit nicely in a 16-bit PWM channel. Therefore, we have to concatenate two channels together.

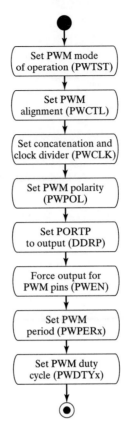

Figure 4.115   Pulse width modulation UML activity diagram.

In a similar manner you should calculate the duty cycle counts required for a duty cycle of 4.5 and 10 percent. Remember to use the scaled E clock frequency in your calculations (8 MHz/128 = 62.5 kHz).

Use the steps provided above as a checklist to write your code. These steps are summarized in the UML activity diagram shown in Figure 4.115. How will you know if your code is correct? Connect an oscilloscope or logic analyzer to the PWM pins of the 68HC12 EVB and examine the waveform.

4.25 POWER LIMITING FEATURES

Have you ever noticed that your cell phone goes into a battery save mode automatically after you have finished using it. Many cell phones have an illuminated LCD display. However, once a call is completed, the display illumination goes out and remains that way until a key is pressed on the phone's keypad. When the key is depressed, the LCD automatically re-illuminates and stays that way until the phone call is completed.

As you might imagine this feature conserves precious battery power when the phone is not in use. The phone goes into a low current drain "sleep" mode and remains there until interrupted from its slumber by a keypress. In Chapter 6 we take a detailed look at battery capacity and how to conserve power. We shall see that the power consumption of a CMOS device (such as the 68HC12) is directly related to the processor clock speed. Some current drain parameters are provided in Figure 4.116. As you can see, the current drain increases dramatically for an increase in processor operating speed. Also, note that the processor reduces its current drain and hence its power dissipation if the processor is placed into a WAIT or STOP state when not in use. Note the dramatic decrease of current drain when the processor is in the STOP state.

4.25.1 How to "Pause" the 68HC12

The 68HC12 is placed in the WAIT state when the assembly language instruction WAI is executed. Upon entry to the WAI state, the processor stores all key register values and a return address on the stack. While in the WAIT state, the CPU clocks are stopped, but other system clocks may continue to run. The CPU exits the WAIT state when it senses an interrupt. When the interrupt occurs, the CPU leaves the wait state and restores key register values. It then executes the interrupt service routine for the corresponding interrupt.

The 68HC12 is placed in the standby or STOP state by executing the assembly language STOP instruction. The STOP instruction is executed as long as the

	Processor Operating Frequency		
Maximum Total Supply Current	**2 MHz**	**4 MHz**	**8 MHz**
Run			
Single-chip Mode	15 mA	25 mA	45 mA
Expanded Mode	25 mA	45 mA	70 mA
Wait (all peripheral functions shut down)			
Single-chip Mode	1.5 mA	3 mA	5 mA
Expanded Mode	4 mA	7 mA	10 mA
Stop			
Single-chip Mode, no clocks			
-40 to $+85$ (°C)	10 uA	10 uA	10 uA
$+85$ to $+105$ (°C)	25 uA	25 uA	25 uA
$+105$ to $+125$ (°C)	50 uA	50 uA	50 uA

Figure 4.116   68HC12 supply current.

stop bit S in the condition control register is not set. Upon entering standby mode, the processor places key register values on the stack and stops all system clocks. In the standby mode, the processor has minimal current drain, as previously discussed. The processor exits standby mode when the active low RESET, IRQ, or XIRQ processor pins are asserted.

4.25.2 How to Wake Up the Processor

68HC12 A4 Configuration. Once the processor is in one of its slumber modes, it may be awakened by applying a falling edge signal to any pin on Port D, H, or J. However, the specific pin must be properly configured for key wakeup action by setting appropriate bits in the key wakeup related registers. Ports D, H, and J are all equipped with these related registers; however, we take a closer look only at Port D as a representative example. Figure 4.117 provides register details.

Register: Port D Data Register (PORTD)   Address: $0005

7	6	5	4	3	2	1	0
PD7	PD6	PD5	PD4	PD3	PD2	PD1	PD0
Reset: 0	0	0	0	0	0	0	0

Alternate pin function:

KWD7	KWD6	KWD5	KWD4	KWD3	KWD2	KWD1	KWD0

Register: Port D Data Direction Register (DDRD)   Address: $0007

7	6	5	4	3	2	1	0
Bit 7	Bit 6	Bit 5	Bit 4	Bit 3	Bit 2	Bit 1	Bit 0
Reset: 0	0	0	0	0	0	0	0

Register: Key Wakeup Port D Interrupt Enable Register (KWIED)   Address: $0020

7	6	5	4	3	2	1	0
Bit 7	Bit 6	Bit 5	Bit 4	Bit 3	Bit 2	Bit 1	Bit 0
Reset: 0	0	0	0	0	0	0	0

Register: Key Wakeup Port D Flag Register (KWIFD)   Address: $0021

7	6	5	4	3	2	1	0
Bit 7	Bit 6	Bit 5	Bit 4	Bit 3	Bit 2	Bit 1	Bit 0
Reset: 0	0	0	0	0	0	0	0

Figure 4.117 Port D key wakeup features.

The key wakeup related registers are the Key Wakeup Port D Interrupt Enable Register (KWIED) and the Key Wakeup Port D Flag Register (KWIFD). A key wakeup interrupt is generated when a falling edge occurs on a key wakeup configured pin and the pin's corresponding bits in the KWIED and KWIFD registers are set. The key wakeup interrupt associated with Port D shares an interrupt vector with the IRQ interrupt. The IRQ interrupt enable (IRQEN) must also be enabled for the Port D key wakeup features to work. The port J and H key interrupts have their own dedicated key wakeup interrupt vectors.

Once the processor is awakened from its slumber, it executes the interrupt service routine assigned to the specific interrupt vector.

All Other Variants.   The processor exits standby mode when the active low RESET, IRQ, or XIRQ processor pins are asserted.

There are other methods of slowing down the processor, including using the slow mode divider features (B32) described earlier in the chapter or employing the phase-locked loop (PLL) features of the 68HC12.

4.26 APPLICATION

In this final section of this chapter, we describe the configuration of the B32 EVB and how to interface input and output signals to the B32.

4.26.1 EVB Overview

Throughout this chapter we have been referring to the M68EVB912B32 evaluation board or B32 EVB except as noted. In this section we provide a brief look at this board, its features, and how to interface external components to the board.

The B32 EVB is manufactured by Motorola to allow a user to quickly get a 68HC12-based system up and operating. It consists of a MC68HC192B32 embedded controller and associated communication and timing hardware. An EVB layout and component placement diagram is provided in Figure 4.118.

The B32 is factory default configured to communicate via an RS-232C interface on connector P1 with a host PC. The EVB's P1 connector is wired as data circuit-terminating equipment (DCE) via a standard DB-9 connector. The host PC is normally configured as a data terminal equipment (DTE) via a DB-9 or DB-25 connector. With this DCE to DTE connection, normal straight-through

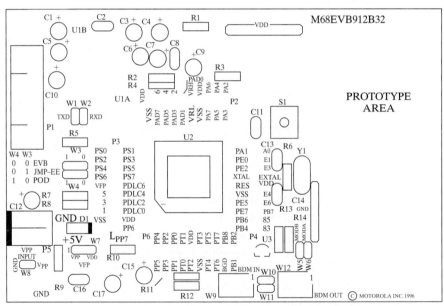

Figure 4.118 MC68HC912B32 EVB layout diagram. (Copyright of Motorola. Used by permission.)

cabling is used between the EVB and the host PC. Both the host and the B32 must be configured for communications at a baud rate of 9600, with 8 data bits, 1 stop bit, and no parity. If the communication parameters between the PC and EVB do not match, communications between them is not possible.

In normal operation, code will be generated by a software package such as the ImageCraft ICC12 on the host PC. The code will be compiled, assembled, and linked. The result of these steps is a machine code file that is downloaded to the B32 embedded controller resident on the EVB. When the EVB is reset, the embedded controller will begin executing the code resident on the EVB without any assistance from the host PC.

The B32 is equipped with the D-Bug12 monitor program. This program is useful for program development and troubleshooting. However, it resides within the B32's flash memory. To load a program of substantial size to the B32 flash, the D-Bug12 program must first be erased and then the user program may then be loaded in its place.

The MC68HC912B32 embedded controller resident aboard the EVB is of the HC CMOS family of logic components. Great care must be exercised in interfacing external components to the EVB. In general, careful interface analysis must be accomplished prior to connecting any component to the EVB. We discuss interface techniques in Chapter 5.

A convenient prototype area is provided on the EVB for additional external hardware. Access may be gained to selected MC68HC912B32 embedded controller pins via four 2×10 male header pin blocks. The blocks are soldered to the EVB via the predrilled holes. Connections are then made to the male header pins using female crimp connectors, as shown in Figure 4.119. Insure the proper D-Sub terminal crimping tool is used (for example, Jameco #159265). Jameco part numbers are provided in the diagram; however, the connectors are available from a number of electronic supply houses.

Lew Sircin a master engineering technician in the Department of Electrical and Computer Engineering at the University of Wyoming, has further extended this idea. Lew developed a technique that allows a printed circuit board (PCB) to be connected to the EVB via a female header block (Digikey #929975-01-ND or Jameco #70826). To mate the EVB to the PCB, the male header pins (Jameco #67820) are mounted to the bottom of the EVB. The pins of the header pin then mate to the female header block of the PCB.

The B32 is factory configured with the memory mapped components described earlier in this chapter. The B32 memory system may be expanded with additional RAM and ROM components.

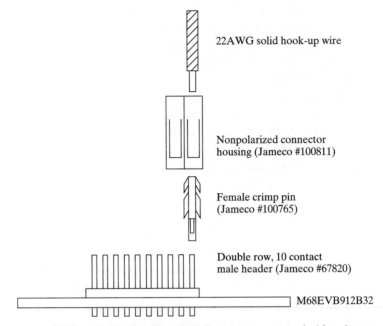

(a) Nonpolarized female crimp style connectors are used with male header pins to interface to the B32 leads on the EVB.

(b) The 22 AWG solid hook-up wire is crimped on to the female crimp connector. The female connector is then slid into the non-polarized connector housing.

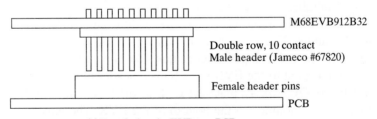

(c) Interfacing the EVB to a PCB.

Figure 4.119   Connecting the B32 to the EVB fabrication area. The B32 processor pins in part (a) are connected to the fabrication area by using a combination of male header pins and female crimp connections. Connections between the hook-up wire and crimp connector are shown in (b). The interface between the B32 EVB and a printed circuit board is shown in (c).

4.27 SUMMARY

This chapter provided an overview of the 68HC12 and HCS12 hardware configuration. Sections described each of the following hardware systems: timing system, memory system, interrupts and resets, serial communications, port system, and the data conversion system. The timing system has the capability to measure the parameters of an incoming signal, generate digital waveforms, and count pulse events. The memory system consists of the components required to support the controller including RAM, ROM, and flash memory. The interrupt system allows the microcontroller to respond to high-priority, unscheduled but planned events. The 68HC12/HCS12 is also equipped with two different types of serial communication systems: the synchronous serial peripheral interface and the asynchronous serial communications interface. We also examined the analog-to-digital (ATD) conversion system. This system allows an analog signal to be converted to a weighted binary representation. We also presented the PWM system, which is used to generate flexible pulse width modulated signals. For each system, we provided supporting tutorial information, register descriptions, and programming examples.

4.28 FURTHER READING

Motorola. *68HC12 M68EVB912B32 Evaluation Board User's Manual* (68EVB912B32-UM/D). Motorola Inc., 1997.

Motorola. *HC12 M68HC12B Family Advance Information*, (M68HC12B/D), Motorola Inc., 2000.

ImageCraft. *ImageCraft C Compiler and Development Environment for Motorola HC12, Version 6*. Palo Alto, CA: ImageCraft, Inc.

Pack, Daniel, and Steven Barrett. *68HC12 Microcontroller: Theory and Application*, Upper Saddle River, NJ: Prentice Hall, 2002.

Wakerly, John. Digital Design Principles and Practices, Upper Saddle River, NJ: Prentice Hall, 2001.

4.29 PROBLEMS

Fundamental

1. Sketch a block diagram of the 68HC12 B32 architecture. Briefly describe the function of each system.

2. The 68HC12 consists of several variants. What features distinguish one variant from another?

3. How much memory space does the 68HC12's register block require? Where can the register block be placed in memory?

4. What is the function of Port AD?

5. What is the size of the flash EEPROM in the 68HC12 B32 configuration?

Advanced

1. What is the difference between a maskable and nonmaskable interrupt? Which has a higher priority?

2. What is an interrupt? Briefly explain how the 68HC12 responds to an interrupt.

3. What is the accuracy (resolution) of the 68HC12's analog-to-digital converter system?

4. What is the purpose of the data direction registers?

5. The standard timer module consists of a 16-bit counter. What is the maximum count of the counter?

6. If the counter is incremented every 2 µs, how often does the counter roll over?

7. Complete the real-time interrupt example provided in section 4.15 to display the time on an LCD display.

Challenging

1. In the description of the input capture features of the TIM, we provided an algorithm in a step-by-step format to measure the pulse length of a single active high pulse. The pulse length was assumed to be less than the rollover time of the free running counter. Construct a Unified Modeling Language (UML) activity diagram for this algorithm.

2. Provide the C program to accomplish the algorithm in the preceding question. Include code to initialize the TIM. Assume the unknown signal is connected to timer channel 2. Also, use and configure a 2 MHz clock for the timer system.

3. In the description of the output compare features of the TIM, we provided an algorithm in a step-by-step format to generate a single active low pulse assumed to be less that the rollover time of the free running counter. Construct a Unified Modeling Language (UML) activity diagram for this algorithm.

4. Provide the C program to accomplish the algorithm in the preceding question. Include code to initialize the TIM. Assume timer channel 2 is used for the output pulse. Pass in the desired pulse length as a variable. Use and configure the timer system for 2 MHz operation.

5. Write a program in C to send an incrementing binary value to Port A of the B32. The count should be incremented every 30 ms.

6. Write a program in C to send a "rain gauge" indicator to Port A of the B32. The output of Port A should be incremented every 30 ms. *Hint:* The output of Port A should start out with 0x00..0x01..0x03..0x07... ...0xFF..0x7F... ...0x00.

7. In the input capture example code provided in the chapter, we assumed the period of the incoming signal was less than the rollover time of the free running counter.

Modify the algorithm to handle periods longer than the rollover time of the counter. *Hint:* Employ the timer overflow interrupt features of the timer to track how many times the free running counter overflows between the first and second rising edge of the unknown signal.

8. In the preceding question, are there any limits to the algorithm? What is the shortest period that can be measured accurately by the input capture system? The longest?

9. In the pulse accumulator section (4.14.5) of the chapter, we presented a scenario of deriving the bicycle velocity by counting the number of tire rotations. The rotations were sensed using a unipolar hall effect sensor. Construct the UML activity diagram and structure chart for this scenario and write the C code to accomplish this task.

10. In the real-time interrupt example (section 4.15), we equated 122 occurrences of a 8.196 ms interrupt to 1000 ms. How much will our example be off in the course of a 24-hour period?

11. In the serial communications interface (SCI) section (4.18) of the chapter, we provided functions to initialize the SCI and transmit an ASCII character. Assume that we connect two 68HC12's together via their SCI TxD and RxD pins. Provide a diagram of this connection, a structure chart, and a UML activity diagram for the SCI receive function, and the corresponding C code to implement the activity diagram.

12. In the pulse width modulation section (4.24) we discussed how PWM signals may be used to control servo motors. The motor requires a 50 Hz control signal sent to it. By varying the duty cycle while maintaining a constant control signal frequency, a turn may be rendered. The servo may displace from one angular extreme to another by varying the duty cycle from 4.5 to 10 percent. Construct the UML activity diagram for this application and write the C code to accomplish this task. Verify your results with an oscilloscope or logic analyzer. *Hint:* Recall that we provided considerable background information for this application in the PWM section of the chapter.

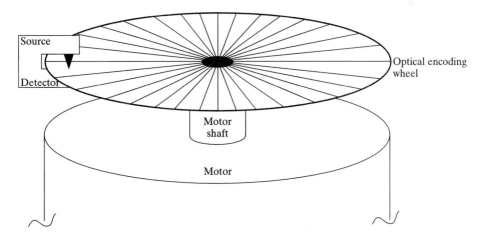

Figure 4.120   Motor equipped with an optical tachometer.

13. Many motors are equipped with an optical tachometer subsystem. The subsystem consists of a plastic disk connected to the shaft of the motor, as shown in Figure 4.120. The disk is transparent with black lines etched in the disk. As the motor rotates so does the disk. The disk is sandwiched between an optical source and detector. The output signal generated by the optical source/detector pair generates a logic pulse every time a black line on the disk passes through the pair. Assume that a motor is equipped with a disk that generates 200 pulses per motor revolution. Write a function in "C" to convert the pulses to revolutions per minute using the pulse accumulator system. Provide an UML activity diagram for your solution.

5

Basic Input/Output Interfacing Concepts

Objectives: After reading this chapter, you should be able to

- Describe the electrical current and voltage specifications/requirements for the 68HC12's digital inputs and outputs.
- Describe what occurs when the current and voltage specifications/requirements are violated.
- Apply 68HC12 electrical specifications/requirements to interface various input/output devices to the 68HC12.
- Connect hardware input devices (e.g., switches, keypads) to the 68HC12.
- Program the interface between hardware input devices and the 68HC12.
- Discuss the requirement for mechanical switch debouncing.
- Properly apply hardware and software debouncing techniques.
- Connect hardware output devices (e.g., LEDs, LCD character displays, 2D LCD graphics display) to the 68HC12.
- Program the interface between hardware output devices and the 68HC12.

- Design a transducer interface circuit at the block diagram level to link a transducer of specific parameters to the 68HC12.
- Describe the RS-232 communications interface.

What devices can you safely connect to the 68HC12 without additional interface circuitry? Your intuition may indicate you could probably connect a logic device from the same logic family as the 68HC12 without additional interface circuitry. For example, you could connect a single NAND gate (74HC00) to the microprocessor without additional interface components. What about multiple devices from the same family? For example, could you connect 20, 30, or 50 of these NAND gates? What about a different logic family? Could you connect a single NAND gate (74LS00) to the 68HC12 without additional interface circuitry? Your intuition probably also leads you to think that some type of interface circuitry is required to have the 68HC12 control a motor. In this chapter we answer these questions. We begin by investigating the electrical characteristics of the 68HC12 in some detail. You must thoroughly understand these electrical parameters to properly interface an external device to the 68HC12. This sets the stage to discuss the topic of interfacing. We then describe how to configure external hardware and software devices to communicate with the 68HC12. We tie the chapter concepts together by providing the complete hardware and software description of a 68HC12-controlled combination lock. Throughout this chapter we generically refer to the 68HC12 processor. Realize that all interface concepts discussed in this chapter equally apply to the HCS12 series of processors.

5.1 VOLTAGE AND CURRENT CHARACTERISTICS OF THE 68HC12

The 68HC12 is a member of Motorola's HC, or high-speed Complementary Metal Oxide Semiconductor (CMOS), family of chips. As long as all components in a system are also of the "HC" family, electrical compatibility issues are minimal. If the 68HC12 is connected to some component not in the HC family, electrical compatibility analysis must be completed.

Manufacturers readily provide the electrical characteristic data necessary to complete this analysis. There are eight electrical specifications required for electrical compatibility analysis, as illustrated in Figure 5.1:

- V_{OH}: Lowest guaranteed output voltage for a logic high
- V_{OL}: Highest guaranteed output voltage for a logic low
- I_{OH}: Maximum allowable output current for a V_{OH} logic high
- I_{OL}: Maximum allowable output current for a V_{OL} logic low
- V_{IH}: Lowest input voltage guaranteed to be recognized as a logic high
- V_{IL}: Highest input voltage guaranteed to be recognized as a logic low

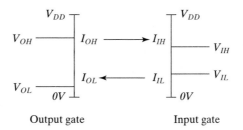

Output gate   Input gate

Figure 5.1 Electrical compatibility. There are eight electrical specifications required for electrical compatibility analysis. The arrows indicate the direction of current flow.

- I_{IH}: Input current for a V_{IH} logic high
- I_{IL}: Input current for a V_{IL} logic low

These electrical characteristics are required for both the 68HC12 and the external components. The 68HC12 values for these characteristics are (assuming $V_{DD} = 5.0$ volts and $V_{SS} = 0$ volts) as follows:

- $V_{OH} = 4.2$ volts
- $V_{OL} = 0.4$ volts
- $I_{OH} = -0.8$ milliamps
- $I_{OL} = 1.6$ milliamps
- $V_{IH} = 3.5$ volts
- $V_{IL} = 1.0$ volt
- $I_{IH} = 10$ microamps
- $I_{IL} = -10$ microamps

Note: The minus sign on several of the currents indicates a current flow out of the device. A positive current indicates current flow into the device. Here's an easy way to remember this sign convention: Money coming into your bank account is a positive event, whereas money going out of your bank account is a negative event!

5.1.1 Loading Curves

If external circuitry is connected to the 68HC12 such that the current parameters specified above are exceeded, the voltage levels will also be affected. We need to examine two cases: (1) the current source case and (2) the current sink case.

In the sink case, an output voltage V_{OL} is provided at the output pin of the 68HC12 processor when the load connected to this pin delivers a current

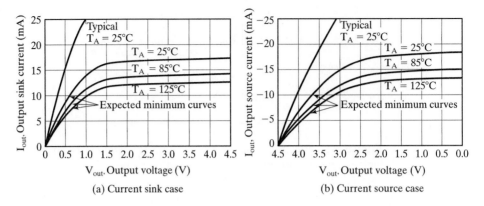

Figure 5.2 Standard output characteristics for the HC CMOS logic family. (Used by permission of ON Semiconductor, Inc.)

of I_{OL} to this logic pin. Recall that the plus sign indicates that current is going into the specific logic pin (sink). If a load delivers more current to the output pin of the 68HC12 than the I_{OL} specification, the value of V_{OL} increases. If the load current becomes too high, the value of V_{OL} rises above the value of V_{IL} for the subsequent logic circuit stage and may not be recognized as an acceptable logic low signal. When this occurs, erratic and unpredictable circuit behavior results. The characteristic curves for the current sink case are shown in Figure 5.2(a).

In the current source case, an output voltage V_{OH} is provided at the output pin of the 68HC12 processor when the load connected to this pin draws a current of I_{OH}. Recall that the minus sign indicates that current is coming out of the specific logic pin (source). If a load draws more current from the output pin than the I_{OH} specification, the value of V_{OH} is reduced. If the load current becomes too high, the value of V_{OH} falls below the value of V_{IH} for the subsequent logic circuit stage and may not be recognized as an acceptable logic high signal. When this occurs, erratic and unpredictable circuit behavior results. The characteristic curves for the current source case is shown in Figure 5.2(b).

Motorola clearly indicates in the Electrical Specifications for the 68HC12 that the maximum current rating for each pin is ± 25 mA. However, and this is a very important however, they also clearly state *"This device is not guaranteed to operate properly at the maximum ratings."*

In many applications the 68HC12 needs to control loads that exceed its voltage and current specifications. What should be done now? The answer is quite straightforward. You must complete a thorough and detailed interface analysis where you must ensure that the specifications of the 68HC12 are not exceeded and the external load device receives its required voltage and current specification.

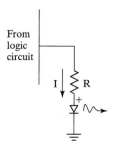

Figure 5.3   Poor LED logic indicator design.

5.1.2 What Happens If You Do Not Complete a Detailed Interface Analysis?

Case Study: Let's examine what happens when you wind up with a poor design. We have a close friend, Dr. Jim Rasmussen (J.R.), who has been an engineer for over 20 years and was an engineering technician for 10 years before completing his engineering studies. An engineer's engineer, J.R. has a phenomenal combination of hands-on practical experience coupled with a thorough understanding of engineering theory. When he retired from the U.S. Air Force, he went to work for a renowned defense contractor. The first project he was assigned at his new job was to troubleshoot a faulty logic indicator board. The board had several digital logic outputs with light-emitting diodes (LED) connected as logic indicators. A schematic of one logic indicator channel is illustrated in Figure 5.3. Let's assume the logic circuit output is from an HC CMOS device. Can you spot the problem? We briefly discussed LED theory in an earlier chapter. Let's examine some additional theory on LED operation to "shed some light" on the current situation.

Background Theory: LED indicators are now available in a multitude of colors (red, green, yellow, blue, white, and orange) and intensities. These LEDs typically have a low power requirement coupled with long lifetime characteristics. The LED has two leads: (1) the anode ($+$) and (2) the cathode ($-$). The LED must be forward-biased for illumination.

The LED has two specifications: (1) forward voltage drop and (2) operating current. Both specifications must be met to illuminate the LED. A typical value of forward voltage drop for an LED is 1.5 volts while a typical value of operating current is 15 mA.

So what is the problem with the LED indicator design provided in Figure 5.3? When the LED is connected as shown in the figure, the forward voltage drop requirement is met. When the logic circuit outputs a logic high, the LED anode will be at least 1.5 volts higher than the cathode. However, this is a current source problem scenario. The LED requires 15 mA of current sourced from the logic circuit to illuminate the LED. At this current level V_{OH} will be significantly reduced and the LED may not illuminate. Furthermore, any logic circuitry connected to the logic output receives a voltage level below the specification for V_{IH}. As previously mentioned, erratic circuit behavior results since this voltage level is not guaranteed to be recognized as a valid logic high signal.

So how did J.R. remedy this situation? We describe how to properly interface an LED indicator to a logic output in section 5.3.1, but we first examine how to properly interface logic families.

5.1.3 Interface Analysis—Interfacing Logic Families

In this section we examine how to successfully interface one logic family with another. To complete a thorough electrical analysis, the following steps must be taken:

- Ensure that the output voltages, both logic high and low, are compatible with the input voltages.
- Ensure that the output currents, both logic high and low, are compatible with the input currents.
- Determine fanout, the maximum number of devices that can be connected to a chip's pin. As before, two cases must be analyzed: (1) output logic high and (2) output logic low.

Let's illustrate the electrical analysis process with an example.

Example

Two new logic families (DP1 and SB2) have been developed. Key parameters for each logic family are as follows:

DP1

$$V_{IH} = 2.0 \text{ V}, \; V_{IL} = 0.8 \text{ V}, \; I_{OH} = -0.4 \text{ mA}, \; I_{OL} = 16 \text{ mA}$$
$$V_{OH} = 3.4 \text{ V}, \; V_{OL} = 0.2 \text{ V}, \; I_{IH} = 40 \text{ uA}, \; I_{IL} = -1.6 \text{ mA}$$

SB2

$$V_{IH} = 2.0 \text{ V}, \; V_{IL} = 0.8 \text{ V}, \; I_{OH} = -0.4 \text{ mA}, \; I_{OL} = 8 \text{ mA}$$
$$V_{OH} = 2.7 \text{ V}, \; V_{OL} = 0.4 \text{ V}, \; I_{IH} = 20 \text{ uA}, \; I_{IL} = -0.4 \text{ mA}$$

Can the DP1 logic family drive SB2 logic family? If so, what is the fanout?

Solution. To correctly answer this question, you must compare voltage levels for compatibility and current for fanout calculations. The fanout must be calculated for both the logic high and logic low level cases. The worst case value is then chosen.

- The high voltage levels must be compared. The V_{OH} value of DP1 must be compared with the V_{IH} of SB2 for compatibility. DP1's V_{OH} is 3.4 volts while SB2's $V_{IH} = 2.0$ V. These levels are compatible since by definition V_{OH} is the lowest guaranteed output voltage for a logic 1 while V_{IH} sets the lower threshold for interpreting an input voltage as being a logic high.
- The low voltage levels must be compared. The V_{OL} value of DP1 must be compared with the V_{IL} of SB2 for compatibility. DP1's V_{OL} is 0.2 V while SB2's $V_{IL} = 0.8$ V. These levels are compatible since by definition V_{OL} is the highest guaranteed output voltage for a logic zero while V_{IL} sets the upper threshold for interpreting an input voltage as being a logic low.
- Fanout must now be calculated for the logic high level case:

$$\text{Fanout} = I_{OH}/I_{IH} = -400\,\text{uA}/20\,\text{uA} = 20 \text{ chips}$$

- Fanout must now be calculated for the logic low level case:

$$\text{Fanout} = I_{OL}/I_{IL} = 16 \text{ mA}/-0.4 \text{ mA} = 40 \text{ chips}$$

- The worst case fanout is then chosen as the smaller of these two numbers: fanout = 20 chips

Example

Let's determine the fanout for an HC series component connected to another HC series component. Recall that:

$$V_{IH} = 3.5 \text{ V}, \quad V_{IL} = 1.0 \text{ V}, \quad I_{OH} = -0.8 \text{ mA}, \quad I_{OL} = 1.6 \text{ mA}$$

$$V_{OH} = 4.2 \text{ V}, \quad V_{OL} = 0.4 \text{ V}, \quad I_{IH} = 10 \text{ uA}, \quad I_{IL} = -10 \text{ uA}$$

Solution. As in the previous example, you must compare voltage levels for compatibility and current for fanout calculations. The fanout must be calculated for both the logic high and logic low level cases. The worst case value is then chosen.

- The high voltage levels must be compared. The V_{OH} value of HC must be compared with the V_{IH} of HC for compatibility. HC's V_{OH} is 4.2 V while HC's V_{IH} is 3.5 V. These levels are compatible since by definition V_{OH} is the lowest guaranteed output voltage for a logic 1 while V_{IH} sets the lower threshold for interpreting an input voltage as being a logic high.
- The low voltage levels must be compared. The V_{OL} value of HC must be compared with the V_{IL} of HC for compatibility. HC's V_{OL} is 0.4 V while HC's V_{IL} is 1.0 V. These levels are compatible since by definition V_{OL} is the highest guaranteed output voltage for a logic zero while V_{IL} sets the upper threshold for interpreting an input voltage as being a logic low.

- Fanout must now be calculated for the logic high level case:

$$\text{Fanout} = I_{OH}/I_{IH} = -0.8 \text{ mA}/10 \text{ uA} = 80 \text{ chips}$$

- Fanout must also be calculated for the logic low level case:

$$\text{Fanout} = I_{OL}/I_{IL} = 1.6 \text{ mA}/-10 \text{ uA} = 160 \text{ chips}$$

- The worst case fanout is then chosen: Fanout = 80 chips.

This section provided a brief introduction on connecting the 68HC12 to another logic family. We provide additional information on interfacing the 68HC12 to other external devices throughout the chapter. For an exhaustive treatment of interfacing logic families, the interested reader is referred to *The Art of Electronics* by P. Horowitz and W. Hill. This source provides information on adjusting voltage and current levels such that virtually any logic family can be interfaced to another logic family.

5.2 INPUT DEVICES: SWITCHES, DIP SWITCHES, AND KEYPADS

An embedded controller typically processes data from the outside world, makes decisions based on this data, and produces outputs. Often these inputs are user-activated switches, and the outputs are various types of displays. In this section we present a brief overview on how to interface switches, keypads, and indicators to the 68HC12. In section 5.6 we provide a detailed example on how to interface a liquid crystal display (LCD) panel to the 68HC12.

5.2.1 Switches

Figure 5.4(a) is a switch configuration for a momentary contact push-button type switch. This type of switch is used to momentarily introduce a logic 0 to an external pin of the 68HC12. When the switch is in the open position, a logic 1 is provided to the 68HC12. When the switch is depressed, the input to the 68HC12 is grounded through the switch and thus provides a logic 0. The resistor limits current flow when the switch push-button is depressed.

Ideally, the logic level connected to the switch push-button is normally at logic high, and it transitions to logic low when depressed. In actual switches, the switch has a tendency to bounce. That is, due to the nonideal mechanical characteristics of the switch, the switch makes and breaks contact multiple times. Since, the 68HC12 is operating in the range of MHz, it is fast enough to register these switch bounces as multiple switch open and closures. To prevent this phenomena, switch debouncing techniques should be employed. Switches may

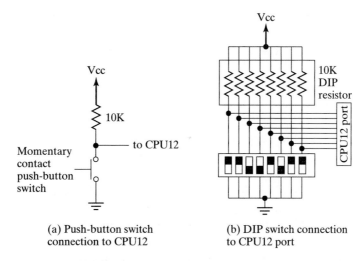

Figure 5.4   Switch interface circuits.

be debounced using hardware or software techniques. To debounce a switch in software, the first switch contact is read and then a 100–200 ms software delay is executed. During this short delay, switch bouncing is effectively locked out. We examine hardware and software techniques to eliminate switch debouncing phenomena in section 5.5.

5.2.2 DIP Switches

In Figure 5.4(b) we have extended the single switch idea further to a bank of multiple switches. These switch banks are typically manufactured in a dual in line (DIP) style package. In this case, slide switches are used instead of push-button switches. The individual switch inputs are connected to the individual input lines of a 68HC12 port. As before, a resistor is used to limit current for each switch. Resistors are conveniently packaged with eight resistors in a single DIP for this type of application. Resistors are also available in single in line (SIP) package. In this configuration, one lead from each resistor in the package is tied to a common pin.

In section 5.8 we introduce the use of multiple debounced momentary contact switches to select different operations for an embedded controller to perform.

5.2.3 Keypads

To introduce different numerical values to the 68HC12, a hexadecimal keypad may be used. An example of this type of switch array is illustrated in Figure 5.5.

Examine this figure in close detail. Note how port pins PORTx[3:0] are used to assert a specific row of the keypad. Keypad row 0 consists of switches 0, 1, 2, and 3. Keypad row 1 consists of switches 4, 5, 6, and 7, etc. The code rendered by the keypad is read on port pins PORTx[7:4]. These pins are at a logic 1 (high) state when a switch is not depressed. This is due to the 10 k ohm pull-up resistor connected to each of these port pins.

When PORTx[0] is set to a logic low during user program execution, the first row of the keypad is asserted low. If one of the switches in this row is depressed, the logic low signal from PORTx[0] is routed to the corresponding pin on PORTx[7:4]. When this value is read by the microprocessor, the keypad switch depressed can be determined. The user-written program continually asserts each keypad row in sequential order.

The table at the bottom of Figure 5.5 describes the connections made when each key is pressed. When a single key is pressed, an electrical connection is made between two of the eight pins on the keypad. Each key has its own unique combination. For example, if the F switch is depressed on the keypad, a connection is rendered between pins 3 and 7.

These keypad values may be converted to usable values—such as those issued by American Standard Code for Information Interchange (ASCII)—using combinational logic external to the 68HC12 or they may be converted in software by a user-written program. The combinational logic can be implemented in discrete combinational logic or in programmable logic.

The keypad can also be used to select a function for the embedded controller to perform. For example, if the keypad is used to implement a gas pump controller, the numbered keys can be relabeled with a specific function such as select payment type (cash, debit, or credit) or select the grade of gasoline (regular, mid, or supreme). Again, the program must convert the information provided to the microprocessor from the keypad into the required embedded controller actions.

Figure 5.6 provides an abbreviated UML activity diagram for obtaining key press information from a keypad. The basic algorithm is to assert a specific row of the keypad and then immediately read the result from the keypad. If the assertion pattern matches the value read from the port, then no key was depressed on the keypad. On the other hand, if there is a mismatch, this means that a keypad switch was depressed in the asserted switch row. If a keypad switch was depressed, then a switch statement is used to determine the ASCII representation of or the specific activity associated with the depressed key. The algorithm continually cycles from asserting row 0, to row 1, to row 2, etc. Again, we have provided only a bare bones activity diagram at this time. We are also providing only the bare bones code. We provide additional details on this algorithm later in the chapter after a presentation on liquid crystal display technology and code.

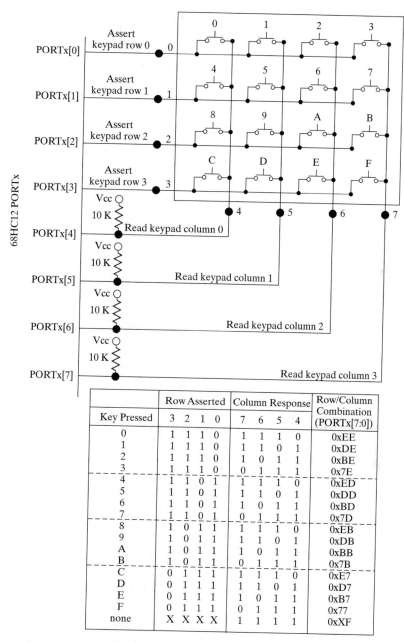

	Row Asserted				Column Response				Row/Column Combination (PORTx[7:0])
Key Pressed	3	2	1	0	7	6	5	4	
0	1	1	1	0	1	1	1	0	0xEE
1	1	1	1	0	1	1	0	1	0xDE
2	1	1	1	0	1	0	1	1	0xBE
3	1	1	1	0	0	1	1	1	0x7E
4	1	1	0	1	1	1	1	0	0xED
5	1	1	0	1	1	1	0	1	0xDD
6	1	1	0	1	1	0	1	1	0xBD
7	1	1	0	1	0	1	1	1	0x7D
8	1	0	1	1	1	1	1	0	0xEB
9	1	0	1	1	1	1	0	1	0xDB
A	1	0	1	1	1	0	1	1	0xBB
B	1	0	1	1	0	1	1	1	0x7B
C	0	1	1	1	1	1	1	0	0xE7
D	0	1	1	1	1	1	0	1	0xD7
E	0	1	1	1	1	0	1	1	0xB7
F	0	1	1	1	0	1	1	1	0x77
none	X	X	X	X	1	1	1	1	0xXF

Figure 5.5 A keypad. When PORTx[0] is set to a logic low during user program execution, the first row of the keypad is asserted low. If one of the switches in this row is depressed, the logic low signal from PORTx[0] is routed to the corresponding pin on PORTx[7:4]. When this value is read by the microprocessor, the keypad switch depressed can be determined. The user-written program continually asserts each keypad row in a sequential order.

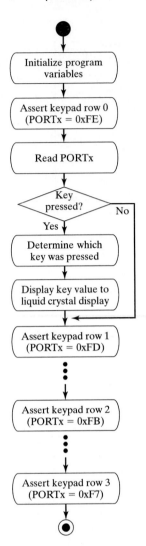

Figure 5.6   A keypad UML activity diagram.

The following code implements portions of the keypad processing software.

```
/****************************************************************/
/*filename: keypad.c                                          */
/*This program processes keypad switch presses.  We will as-  */
/*sume that the keypad has been connected to PORTB.  PORTB[3:0] */
/*will be used to assert corresponding rows of the keypad.    */
/*PORTB[7:4] will be used to determine which key (if any) was */
/*depressed in a specific column.                             */
/****************************************************************/
```

```c
/*include files*/
#include <hc12.h>
#include <stdio.h>
#include <math.h>

/*Function prototypes*/
char which_key(unsigned char keypress); /*Function to select key*/
char keypad(unsigned char keypress, unsigned char row);

void main(void)
{
/*initialize row assertion variables - assert with active low
                                                     signal*/
unsigned char keypress;
unsigned char first = 0xFE;    /*comparison variable 1st row*/
unsigned char second = 0xFD;   /*comparison variable 2nd row*/
unsigned char third = 0xFB;    /*comparison variable 3rd row*/
unsigned char fourth = 0xF7;   /*comparison variable for 4th row*/

DDRB = 0x0f;                   /*PORTB[3:0] output, [7:4] input*/

while(1){
  PORTB = 0xFE;                    /*assert keypad row0-PORTB[0]*/
  keypress = PORTB;                /*get value of PORTB*/
  key = keypad(keypress, first);

  PORTB = 0xFD;                    /*assert keypad row1-PORTB[1]*/
  keypress = PORTB;                /*get value of PORTB*/
  key = keypad(keypress, second);

  PORTB = 0xFB;                    /*assert keypad row2-PORTB[2]*/
  keypress = PORTB;                /*get value of PORTB*/
  key = keypad(keypress, third);

  PORTB = 0xF7;                    /*assert keypad row3-PORTB[3]*/
  keypress = PORTB;                /*get value of PORTB*/
  key = keypad(keypress, fourth);
  }

}


/******************************************************************/
/*keypad: determines if a key has been depressed by comparing   */
/*the value that was just sent to PORTB (row) with the current   */
/*value of PORTB (keypress).  If these two values are the same, */
/*no key was pressed.                                           */
/******************************************************************/
```

```
char keypad(unsigned char keypress, unsigned char row)
{
char key1;
int i;

if(keypress != row)
  {                                    /*a key was pressed....*/
  key1 = which_key(keypress);          /*find out the key depressed*/
  putchars(key1);                      /*display depressed key to LCD*/
  }
else if(keypress == row)               /*a key was not depressed*/
  {
  key1 = 'Z';
  }

return(key1);
}

/***************************************************************/
/*which_key: determines which keypad switch was depressed by   */
/*examining the combination of which keypad row was asserted   */
/*PORTB[3:0] and what was read from PORTB[7:4].  For example,   */
/*if PORTB[0] was asserted low and key 0 was depressed a logic  */
/*0 would be read from PORTB[4]. PORTB[7:5] would be logic one. */
/***************************************************************/

char which_key(unsigned char keypress)
{
char key;

switch(keypress){
  case 0xEE: key = '0';             /*this is key '0'*/
          break;

  case 0xDE: key = '1';             /*this is key '1'*/
          break;

  case 0xBE: key = '2';             /*this is key '2'*/
          break;

  case 0x7E: key = '3';             /*this is key '3'*/
          break;

  case 0xED: key = '4';             /*this is key '4'*/
          break;

  case 0xDD: key = '5';             /*this is key '5'*/
          break;
```

```
        case 0xBD: key = '6';           /*this is key '6'*/
                break;

        case 0x7D: key = '7';           /*this is key '7'*/
                break;

        case 0xEB: key = '8';           /*this is key '8'*/
                break;

        case 0xDB: key = '9';           /*this is key '9'*/
                break;

        case 0xBB: key = 'A';           /*this is key 'A'*/
                break;

        case 0x7B: key = 'B';           /*this is key 'B'*/
                break;

        case 0xE7: key = 'C';           /*this is key 'C'*/
                break;

        case 0xD7: key = 'D';           /*this is key 'D'*/
                break;

        case 0xB7: key = 'E';           /*this is key 'E'*/
                break;

        case 0x77: key = 'F';           /*this is key 'F'*/
                break;

    default:    key ='Z';
                }//end switch
return (key);
}


/****************************************************************/
```

We need to emphasize that there are some timing and debouncing issues lurking in the code. We also need to discuss how to interface an LCD display to the 68HC12. These details are coming up later in section 5.6.

5.3 OUTPUT DEVICES: LEDS, SEVEN-SEGMENT DISPLAYS, TRISTATE INDICATORS

In this section we discuss how to properly interface a light-emitting diode to the 68HC12. Recall earlier in the chapter we provided a poor design. The basic concept of LED interfacing is easily extended to bar configured LEDs and seven-segment display LEDs. We also investigate how to interface with a large seven-segment display. We conclude the section by discussing the operation of the 8-channel, tristate indicator circuit provided earlier in the text.

5.3.1 Light-Emitting Diodes

It is often helpful to monitor different signals from the 68HC12. Figure 5.7 illustrates various LED indicator circuits. One method of monitoring a 68HC12 output pin is with light-emitting diodes (LEDs), which typically have a low power requirement coupled with long lifetime characteristics. The LED has two leads: the anode (+) and the cathode (−). The LED must be forward-biased for illumination.

The LED has two specifications: (1) forward voltage drop and (2) operating current. Both specifications must be met to illuminate the LED. Recall that a typical value of forward voltage drop for an LED is 1.5 V while a typical value

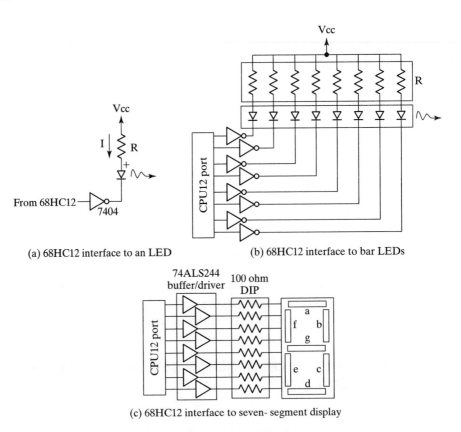

(a) 68HC12 interface to an LED

(b) 68HC12 interface to bar LEDs

(c) 68HC12 interface to seven- segment display

Figure 5.7 Indicator interface circuits.

of operating current is 15 mA. When an LED is connected to the 68HC12, great care must be taken to ensure that a limiting resistor is used to maintain current through the LED to a safe operating level. Furthermore, the device to which the LED is connected must also be rated at a current value consistent with the operating current of the LED. To establish a forward bias, the voltage of the anode must be higher than the cathode by the forward voltage parameter of the diode.

Recall from our previous discussion that the current specification I_{OL} for the 68HC12 is 1.6 mA. This is the current that the 68HC12 can safely sink (current into a 68HC12 pin). The electrical specifications provided by Motorola indicate the maximum current is ±25 mA per pin. However, the device is not guaranteed to operate properly at these maximum ratings. Therefore, another logic family (e.g., the 74xx) with sufficient current sink capability is used as an intermediate interface between the 68HC12 and the LED. The 74xx family has an I_{OL} value of 16 mA.

The configuration to equip a 68HC12 with an LED indicator is illustrated in Figure 5.7(a). When a logic high is presented on the 68HC12 output pin, the inverter (7404) inverts the logic high to a logic low. Current flows from the power supply (5 VDC) through the current limiting resistor R, and the LED to the output pin of the inverter. The LED will then illuminate. On the other hand, when a logic low is present on the 68HC12 output pin, there is not a sufficient potential difference between the logic high of the inverter and the supply voltage to satisfy the forward voltage drop requirement of the LED, and hence the LED will not illuminate.

Example

To calculate the value of resistance R to limit the current I to the operating current of the LED, Ohm's law is employed. Let's assume that the LED has a current rating of 15 mA and a forward voltage drop of 1.5 V. The voltage drop across the resistor is $5V - 1.5 - V_{OL}$ of the TTL inverter (0.4 V) while the current flowing through the resistor is 15 mA. This provides a resistance value of 206 ohms. We could use a convenient value of 220 ohms as the resistor value.

As we did for switches, the basic circuit for the LED may be extended to 8 bits. In fact, LEDs are readily available in a bar type display that consists of 8 LEDs provided in the same DIP package as that shown in Figure 5.7(b). We must also duplicate the limiting resistor and inverter configuration hardware. This configuration allows examination of a port's output.

5.3.2 Seven-Segment Displays

It is often useful to have some type of an alphanumeric display. One common type of display is a seven-segment LED display. The display consists of seven individual bar LEDs that have been configured to display decimal or hexadecimal values. The LED segments are labeled *a* through *g*, as shown in Figure 5.7(c). As with our previous discussion of LEDs, current through the LEDs must be limited to safe values. To illuminate a 0 on the display, segments *a* through *f* are illuminated. In Figure 5.7(c) we used the 74ALS244, an interface chip that provides the necessary drive current to illuminate the individual segments. A 100 ohm resistor limits current to a safe value. In this example we used a common cathode (CC) display. The CC designator indicates that all of the cathodes (negative leads) of all LEDs in the display share a common pin. Seven-segment displays are also available in common anode (CA) configurations.

5.3.3 Tristate Logic Indicator Circuit

In this section we describe the theory of operation of the 8-channel, tristate indicator circuit. Let's first briefly review tristate logic.

Tristate Logic   A tristate output may be a logic 1, a logic 0, or a high-impedance (Z) state, as illustrated in Figure 5.8. For example, a memory chip is placed in the high-impedance Z mode when its output enable ($\overline{OE}$) pin is deactivated. When in the high Z state, the memory chip is not electrically connected to the bus although it retains its physical bus connection. This allows multiple chips to be connected to the bus simultaneously. Since only one memory chip is allowed to be output enabled at a time, only one memory chip is electrically connected to the bus at any instant of time. This prevents simultaneous data bus access by more than one memory chip. Without a tristate output, memory chips could not be connected simultaneously to the bus. If multiple memory chips are connected without the benefit of the tristate output configuration, severe damage to the bus and memory components would result.

Theory of Operation   An 8-channel, tristate indicator circuit is illustrated in Figure 5.9. The circuit consists of eight independent tristate logic indicators. If a specific PORTx pin has a logic high level present, the green LED is forward-biased and illuminates. On the other hand, if a specific PORTx pin

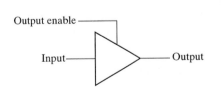

Output Enable	Input	Output
L	L	High-Z
L	H	High-Z
H	L	L
H	H	H

Figure 5.8   Tristate logic. A tristate output may be a logic 1, a logic 0, or a high impedance (Z) state.

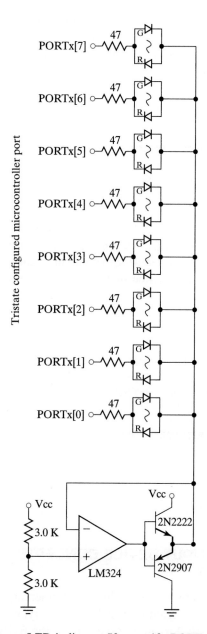

Figure 5.9 Tristate LED indicator. If a specific PORTx pin has a logic high level present, the green LED is forward-biased and illuminates. On the other hand, if a specific PORTx pin has a logic low level present, the red LED is forward-biased and it illuminates. In the high-Z case, neither LED is properly biased for illumination.

has a logic low level present, the red LED is forward-biased and illuminates.
When the processor is in the High-Z case, neither LED is properly biased for
illumination. The resistor limits the current to a safe value for the LED. The
PNP-NPN push-pull transistor configuration provides a voltage reference at the
emitter junction of the two transistors. Variations of this circuit have existed for
a number of years [Furlow, 1975].

5.4 PROGRAMMING INPUT AND OUTPUT DEVICES

In the following example, we tie together the concepts of reading a logic value
from a PORT and then writing the value to another PORT.

Example

An eight-position DIP switch is connected to Port A of the 68HC12. The pins of
Port B are connected to the tristate indicator circuit of Figure 5.9. The following
code reads the position of the DIP switches connected to Port A and sends the
value to Port B.

```
    .
    .
    .
unsigned char INMASK = 0x00;          /*set port for input*/
unsigned char OUTMASK = 0xff;         /*set port for output*/
unsigned char PORTA_value;

DDRA = INMASK;
DDRB = OUTMASK;
PORTA_value = PORTA;                   /*read Port A*/
PORTB = PORTA_value;                   /*display to Port B*/
    .
    .
    .
```

5.5 ADVANCED INPUT DEVICE CONCEPTS—SWITCH DEBOUNCING

Earlier in the chapter we introduced a momentary contact push-button type switch
configuration (see again Figure 5.4a). This type of switch is used to momentarily
introduce a logic 0 to an external pin of the 68HC12. When the switch is in the
open position, a logic 1 is provided to the 68HC12. When the switch is depressed,
the input to the 68HC12 is grounded through the switch and thus provides a logic
0. The resistor limits current flow when the switch push-button is depressed.

Ideally, the switch push-button is normally at logic high and transitions
to logic low when depressed. In actual switches, the switch has a tendency to

bounce. That is, due to the nonideal mechanical characteristics of the switch, the switch makes and breaks contact multiple times. Since, the 68HC12 is operating in the range of MHz, it is fast enough to register these switch bounces as multiple switch open and closures. To prevent this phenomena, switch debouncing techniques may be employed. Switches may be debounced using hardware or software techniques. In this section we investigate these debouncing techniques.

5.5.1 Hardware Debouncing Techniques

Figure 5.10 illustrates a hardware switch debounce circuit [Horowitz and Hill, 1989]. The key circuit components are resistors, a capacitor, a HC Schmitt-Trigger inverter (74HC14), and an optional HC inverter (74HC04).

The Schmitt-Trigger has what is known as hysteresis—different input thresholds when transitioning from logic high to low and when transitioning from logic low to high. This feature allows the Schmitt-Trigger to "square up" slow input transitions and also to provide some level of immunity from input noise occurring around the threshold values.

The inverter is an optional component. If the inverter is not used, a transition from logic low to high occurs at the output of the Schmitt-Trigger when the push-button switch is depressed. When the inverter is included, the logic is "flipped," and a transition from logic high to logic low is provided when the push-button switch is depressed. With this overview of components complete, let's take a closer look at the overall circuit operation.

Since the capacitor is tied to the supply voltage (Vcc) through the resistors, it is normally charged to 5 V when the switch is in its normally open position. Since the capacitor voltage is the input to the Schmitt-Trigger, the output is normally at logic low.

When the switch is depressed, the capacitor is now connected to ground via the 470 kΩ resistor. The capacitor begins to discharge at a rate determined by the time constant of the 470 kΩ resistor and the capacitor. When the capacitor voltage reaches the input threshold voltage of the Schmitt-Trigger, this action provides a logic high output.

Any bouncing action caused by the mechanical action of the switch is minimized by the capacitor. Recall from basic circuits that the voltage across a capacitor cannot change instantaneously. Furthermore, the hysteresis action of the Schmitt-Trigger further minimizes bounce effects.

5.5.2 Software Techniques

There are several methods to debounce a switch in software. Here is a brief explanation of two common methods.

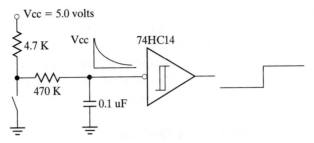

(a) Active high bounceless transition

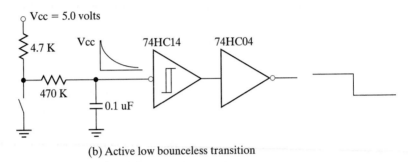

(b) Active low bounceless transition

Figure 5.10   Hardware debounce circuit. (a) Since the capacitor is tied to the supply voltage (Vcc) through the resistors, it is normally charged to 5 V when the switch is in its normally open position. Since the capacitor voltage is the input to the Schmitt-Trigger, that output is normally at logic low. When the switch is depressed, the capacitor discharges. When the capacitor voltage reaches the input threshold voltage of the Schmitt-Trigger, this action provides a logic high output. (b) The inverter is listed as an optional component. If the inverter is not used, a transition from logic low to high occurs at the output of the Schmitt-Trigger when the push-button switch is depressed. When the inverter is included, the logic is "flipped," and a transition from logic high to low is provided when the push-button switch is depressed.

- The first switch contact is read and then a 100 to 200 ms software delay is inserted. During this short delay, switch bouncing is effectively locked out. The delay time may be adjusted to suit the specific parameters of the switch employed.
- When a switch transition is detected by the microprocessor, the switch may be monitored for some amount of time. During this monitoring period, the switch value is continually read. If the value changes during the monitoring period, it is assumed to be noise rather than an actual switch transition at the specific microprocessor pin.

5.5.3 A Programming Example: Menu Software with LED Output Test Circuit

To tie some of these concepts together, let's connect a bank of eight debounced push-button switches to PORTB of the 68HC12. PORTC is connected to the tristate indicator circuit. This configuration is illustrated in Figure 5.11. When a switch is depressed, it is debounced and the corresponding LED connected to PORTC is illuminated. Note we have elected to use an active low debounced switch configuration in hardware and also the second software debounce technique.

```
//A bank of eight debounced push-button switches are connected to
//PORTB of the 68HC12.  PORTC will be connected to the tri-state
//indicator circuit. When a switch is depressed, it will be de-
//bounced and the corresponding LED on PORTC will be illuminated.
//Note we have elected to use an active low debounced switch con-
//figuration in hardware and software debounce techniques.

//function prototypes*****************************************
int process_valid_input(unsigned char input_value);
                                            //process switch input
void initialize_ports(void);                //initializes ports
void timer_init(void);                      //initialize timer

//main program***********************************************

//global variables
int             keep_going= 1;     //loop variable
unsigned char   old_PORTB = 0xff;  //present value of PORTB
unsigned char   new_PORTB;         //new values of PORTA, PORTB

//include files
#include<hc12.h>

void main(void)
{
initialize_ports();                //initialize ports
timer_init();                      //initialize timer

while(keep_going){                 //menu processing
  new_PORTB = PORTB;               //read PORTB
  if(new_PORTB != old_PORTB){      //process change in PORTB input
     switch(new_PORTB){            //PORTB asserted low
        case 0xFE:                 //PB0 (1111_1110)
           if(process_valid_input(new_PORTB))//debounce input
              {
               :                   //perform actions associate
               :                   //with this switch selection
```

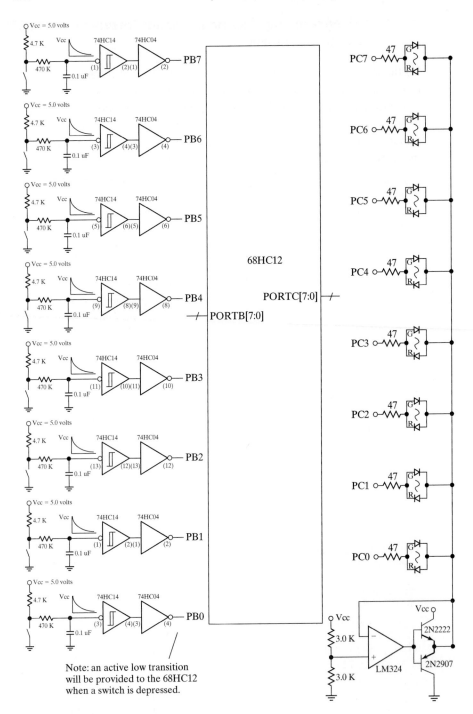

Note: an active low transition
will be provided to the 68HC12
when a switch is depressed.

Figure 5.11 Test circuit. A bank of eight debounced push-button
switches is connected to PORTB of the 68HC12. PORTC is connected
to the tristate indicator circuit.

```
                    PORTC = 0x01;          //illuminate green LED PORTC[0]
                    keep_going=1;
                    }
                    break;

            case 0xFD:                     //PB1 (1111_1101)
                if(process_valid_input(new_PORTB))//debounce input
                    {
                    :                      //perform actions associate
                    :                      //with this switch selection
                    PORTC = 0x02;          //illuminate green LED PORTC[1]
                    keep_going=1;
                    }
                    break;
                    :


                    :

            case 0x7F:                     //PB7 (0111_1111)
                if(process_valid_input(new_PORTB))//debounce input
                    {
                    :                      //perform actions associate
                    :                      //with this switch selection
                    PORTC = 0x80;          //illuminate green LED PORTC[7]
                    keep_going=1;
                    }
                    break;

                    default:;              //all other cases
            }//end switch(new_PORTB)
        }//end if new_PORTB
        old_PORTB=new_PORTB;     //update PORTB
    }//while(keep_going)
}//end main

//function definitions*****************************************

//*************************************************************
//initialize_ports: provides initial configuration for I/O ports *
//*************************************************************

void initialize_ports(void)
{
DDRC=0xff;                               //set PORTC as output
PORTC=0x00;                              //illuminate Red LEDs
DDRB=0x00;                               //set PORTB as input
}
```

```
/*****************************************************************/
/process_valid_input: insures switch depression lasts at least  */
/as long as the rollover time of the counter                    */
/*****************************************************************/

int process_valid_input(unsigned char portx)
{
int    valid_input;         //set valid input flag
int    int_value;           //capture current value of TCNT

valid_input = TRUE;         //initialize flag
int_value = TCNT;           //get initial free running counter value

while(int_value != TCNT){ //does input remain stable for rollover
   if(portx==PORTB)
     valid_input = TRUE;    //PORTB remains stable
   else
     valid_input = FALSE;   //PORTB does not remain stable
   if (!valid_input)
     break;                 //get out of while loop
   }                        //end while

return valid_input;
}

/*****************************************************************/
/*Function: timer_init initializes the timer system for input  */
/*capture.  Assume the P clock is operating at 8 MHz.          */
/*****************************************************************/

void timer_init(void)
{
TMSK1 = 0x00;               //Disable interrupts
TMSK2 = 0x02;               //Prescaler for 2 MHz clock
TSCR = 0x80;               //Enable the timer
}
/*****************************************************************/
```

5.6 ADVANCED OUTPUT DEVICE CONCEPTS: LIQUID CRYSTAL DISPLAYS

In this section we provide a detailed example of how to connect a liquid crystal display (LCD) to the 68HC12. We begin by providing some basic background information on LCD displays. We then provide a detailed case study on how to provide a hardware and software interface to the LCD. In this example we use an AND671GST 16 character by one line display. Given only as a representative sample, this study can be adapted to other manufacturers' displays and other display types.

5.6.1 LCD Overview

A liquid crystal display (LCD) is an output device. It is a handy method of providing a low-power consumption user interface. LCDs are everywhere. You probably have seen them as displays in watches, calculators, cellular phones, and even as a color television type monitor on a video camera. LCDs are available in monochrome as well as color displays. They are also available in two general categories: (1) character display and (2) graphic dot matrix style display.

In general, a LCD display consists of two panes of polarized glass with a liquid suspended between the two panes. The liquid between the two panes of glass may be of either the twisted nematic (TN) or super twisted nematic (STN) type. In general, the TN technology is less expensive, but it has poorer contrast and a narrower viewing angle than the STN technology. Whichever technology is employed, characters and graphics are formed within the display by arranging the liquid crystals into segments. When the individual liquid crystal segments are properly excited, their optical properties may be adjusted to transmit or reflect light such that characters or graphics are formed.

Features available on LCDs include different color panels, backlit displays for easier viewing, many different configurations of characters per line, number of lines, and a number of dot matrix formats. All intelligent LCDs are controlled by a microprocessor that is provided with and affixed to the backside of the LCD display. The microprocessor converts the input provided to the LCD module into the proper excitation to display the input. The microprocessor is equipped with a ROM to store a character library and a RAM that holds characters currently being displayed. So when you establish an interface between the 68HC12 and the LCD display, you are actually establishing an interface between two processors.

In the next section we provide a detailed case study of interfacing an AND671GST LCD character display to the 68HC12.

5.6.2 A Case Study: The AND671GST LCD Character Display Interface

The AND671GST is an intelligent 16 characters by 1 line alphanumeric display. (Actually the display is divided into two 8-character, side-by-side lines). The intelligence for the display is provided by an HD44100H and HD44780 microprocessor chip set. The chip set shares a printed circuit board (PCB) host with the actual display. The interface between the LCD's PCB and the 68HC12 is via a 14-pin connector. The pin numbers are from 1 to 14 starting on the top left PCB corner, as shown in Figure 5.12. The function of each pin is also shown in the diagram.

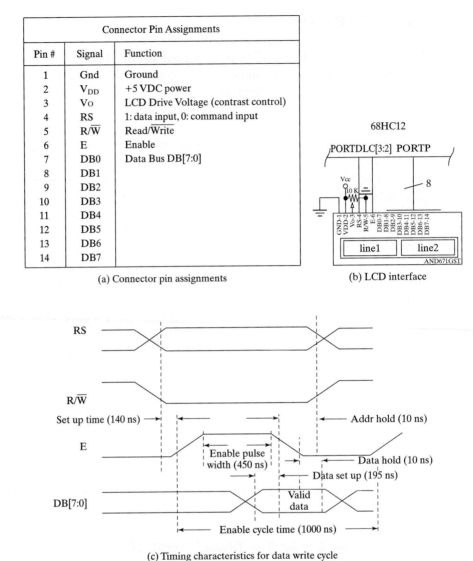

(a) Connector pin assignments

(b) LCD interface

(c) Timing characteristics for data write cycle

Figure 5.12 Liquid crystal display.

Hardware Interface The interface between the LCD and the 68HC12 is shown in Figure 5.12(b). As you can see, a 68HC12 port must be dedicated for the LCD 8-bit data path (LCD pins DB[7:0]). Two additional lines are required between the 68HC12 and the LCD, the enable line (E) and the RS line. The LCD's $R/\overline{W}$ control line is grounded. This allows only one-way communication between the 68HC12 and the LCD—what is known as a write operation. The

V_O pin is the contrast control. In the configuration shown, we have connected the V_O pin to the wiper connection on a 10 kΩ trimmer potentiometer (pot). The other two pins on the trim pot are connected between V_{cc} and ground. This configuration provides a variable contrast control. In this example we use the 68HC12's PORTDLC[3:2] for the control lines (E, RS) and PORTP[7:0] for the LCD's data connection DB[7:0]. With the hardware interface established, let's investigate the timing requirements for the LCD write cycle.

Timing Interface   Two-way communication is possible between the 68HC12 and the LCD. The 68HC12 can either write commands or data to the LCD. The 68HC12 can also read faults from the LCD. In this application, we will write only to the LCD.

Technical documentation for a specific LCD is available from the LCD's manufacturer. This documentation will contain the timing diagrams for the LCD, hardware connections, the initialization sequence, and available LCD commands.

The timing characteristics for the LCD write cycle are shown in Figure 5.12(c). The timing constraints are established by the LCD. The LCD actually has a small processor attached to it. Therefore, when the 68HC12 is communicating with the LCD, it is actually communicating with another microprocessor.

The timing diagram illustrates the relationships between the different control signals for the 68HC12 and the LCD. The manufacturer's data provide these timing relationships in the form of definitions and an associated timing diagram. Here is a summary of the timing relationships between the 68HC12 and the LCD when configured in the Write mode:

- The RS line must be asserted (1: data input, 0: command input).
- The RS signal must be asserted 140 ns (set-up time) before assertion of the Enable (E) signal.
- The Enable pulse width must be a minimum of 450 ns in length.
- The data to be sent to the LCD must be present 195 ns before the Enable signal is de-asserted. This is known as the data set-up time.
- The data lines must remain stable for at least 10 ns (data hold time).
- The rise time of the Enable signal must be greater than 25 ns.
- The Enable signal must not be repeated any sooner than 1000 ns.

Based on these timing requirements, the basic algorithm to write to the LCD is as follows:

1. Configure the RS line (1: writing data to the LCD, 0: writing a command to the LCD).

2. Assert the Enable line.

3. Provide the data (or command) to the DB[7:0] pins.

4. De-assert Enable for the data (or command) to be processed.

The timing requirements shown in the diagram are met by the coding that we shall examine shortly.

Software Interface A structure chart for the LCD-related functions is shown in Figure 5.13(a). As you can see, separate functions are required for LCD initialization, sending commands, sending characters, and required timing delays. Figure 5.13(b) contains the UML activity diagram for the initialization sequence for the LCD. The initialization sequence is provided in the manufacturer's data.

```
/**************************************************************/
/* filename: lcd.c contains liquid crystal display support   */
/* functions                                                 */
/**************************************************************/


/**************************************************************/
/*The initialize function sends the LCD the correct start-up se-*/
/*quence. The command sequence for initialization is provided  */
/*in the manufacturer's technical data for the display.        */
/**************************************************************/

void initialize_lcd(void)
{
delay_5ms();
delay_5ms();
delay_5ms();                         /*wait 15 ms for LCD to turn on*/

putcommands(0x38);                   /*sets interface*/
delay_5ms();
putcommands(0x38);
delay_100us();
putcommands(0x38);
putcommands(0x38);
putcommands(0x0C);
putcommands(0x01);                   /*Display clear*/
putcommands(0x06);                   /*Sets mode to increment by one*/
putcommands(0x0E);                   /*Turn on display, cursor, blink*/
putcommands(0x02);                   /*Return home*/
}


/**************************************************************/
/*The putchar function initializes the data port, the RS and  */
/*Enable and sends it to the correct port                     */
/**************************************************************/
```

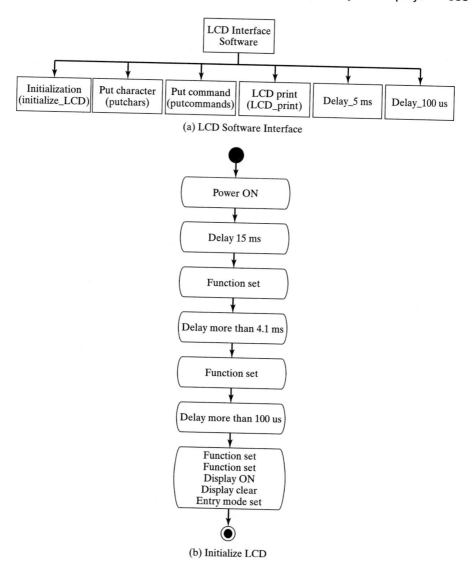

(a) LCD Software Interface

(b) Initialize LCD

Figure 5.13 LCD software interface. The command sequence for initialization is provided in the manufacturer's data.

```
void putchars(unsigned char c)
{
DDRP = 0xFF;                       /*set Port P to output*/
DDRDLC = DDRDLC|0x0C;              /*set PORTDLC[3:2] to output*/
PORTP = c;                         /*assign char C to data port*/
PORTDLC = PORTDLC|0x08;            /*set RS to 1 for DATA*/
```

```
PORTDLC = PORTDLC|0x04;          /*set E to 1 ( PORTDLC[5] = 1 ) */
PORTDLC = 0;                     /*set E and RS to 0*/
delay_5ms();                     /*wait 5 ms*/
}

/********************************************************************/
/*The putcommand function sends the data in the data Port          */
/*to the LCD                                                       */
/********************************************************************/

void putcommands(unsigned char d)
{
DDRP = 0xFF;                     /*set PORTP to output*/
DDRDLC = DDRDLC|0x0C;            /*PORTDLC[3:2] to output*/
PORTDLC = PORTDLC & 0xF7;        /*RS = 0 for Command */
PORTP = d;                       /*assign command to LCD*/
PORTDLC = PORTDLC|0x04;          /*E = 1*/
PORTDLC = 0;                     /*E = 0 */
delay_5ms();                     /*wait 5 ms*/
}

/********************************************************************/
/*The lcd_print function sends a string to the lcd                 */
/********************************************************************/

void lcd_print(char *string)
{
putcommands(0x02);               /*put cursor on first line*/
                                 /*putcommand to select line*/

while(*(string) != '\0')
  {
  putchars(*string);
  string++;
  }
}

/********************************************************************/
/*5 ms delay based on an 8MHz clock                                */
/********************************************************************/

void delay_5ms(void)
{
int i;

for(i=0; i<50; i++)
  {
  delay_100us();
  }
```

```
}
/*****************************************************************/
/*100us delay based on an 8MHz clock                            */
/*****************************************************************/

void delay_100us(void)
{
int i;

for(i=0; i<50; i++)
   {
   asm("nop");                  /*Assembly language nop, takes 2 cycles*/
   }
}
/*****************************************************************/
```

5.6.3 2D LCD Graphics Display

In this section we investigate a two-dimensional liquid crystal display (2D LCD) in detail. Following the same approach as we did in the previous section, we investigate the electrical interface, the timing interface, and finally the software interface for the display. At the end of this section, we provide a "toolbox tray" of useful 2D LCD support functions. We base our discussion on the AND1391ST LCD module. As before, this information may be adapted to a wide range of similar displays. In Chapter 7 we provide a detailed example employing a 2D LCD display.

2D LCD Overview   The AND1391ST is a 128 × 128 pixel dot matrix liquid crystal display. The display may be used in either a character mode, a graphics mode, or a combination of both. When used in a character mode, the display consists of 16 character rows with 16 characters per row, as shown in Figure 5.14. Each character that may be displayed is described by an 8 × 8 dot matrix configuration, as shown in Figure 5.15. The display can also be configured for 21 characters and 16 rows when a 6 × 8 font is selected. The font size is selected by the FS pin on the LCD display. The font configurations are stored within the LCD module's support ROM.

Each character location within the array is associated with a specific memory location in the LCD module's support RAM. During initialization, you set the Text Home Address. This corresponds to the top left corner of the display. In this specific example, the Text Home Address was set for $1000. Also, during initialization you set the number of characters per row. In this specific example we use 16 characters per row. We also use an 8 × 8 dot font (FS pin tied to ground). The value to be displayed in each character position is stored in RAM starting at the Text Home Address. Each subsequent character location is stored in the subsequent RAM memory location, as shown in Figure 5.14.

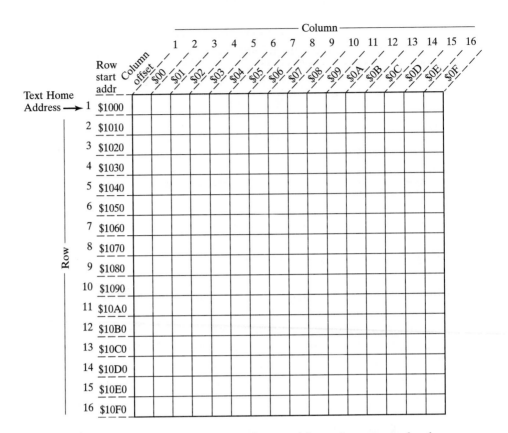

Figure 5.14   2D LCD matrix. When used in a character mode, the display consists of 16 character rows with 16 characters per row.

LSB / MSB	0	1	2	3	4	5	6	7	8	9	A	B	C	D	E	F
0		!	"	#	$	%	&	'	(	)	*	+	,	-	.	/
1	0	1	2	3	4	5	6	7	8	9	:	;	<	=	>	?
2	@	A	B	C	D	E	F	G	H	I	J	K	L	M	N	O
3	P	Q	R	S	T	U	V	W	X	Y	Z	[	\	]	^	_
4	`	a	b	c	d	e	f	g	h	i	j	k	l	m	n	o
5	p	q	r	s	t	u	v	w	x	y	z	{	|	}	~	

Figure 5.15   Character code related to character font.

Electrical Interface   The electrical interface between the 68HC12 and the AND1391ST is shown in Figure 5.16(a). The pin definitions and assignments for the interface are shown in Figure 5.16(b). Let's begin by investigating the power supply needs of the LCD. As you can see in Figure 5.16(a) the LCD requires both a positive and a negative supply. The actual negative supply voltage is adjustable since it controls the contrast.

For this specific example, we interface the LCD to the 68HC12 using PORT P and PORT DLC. As you can see in Figure 5.16(a), PORT P is used to pass data back and forth between the processor and the display. PORT DLC[3:0] is used to provide the associated control signals to the LCD. A description of each LCD control signal is provided in Figure 5.16(b). The inset to this figure provides the control signal combinations to set different command modes for the LCD.

Timing Considerations   The 2D LCD has similar timing requirements to the 1D LCD previously discussed. These timing requirements are provided in Figure 5.17. As before, we handle the timing requirements within our coded functions.

A "Toolbox Tray" of 2D LCD Functions   In this section we provide a "toolbox tray" of 2D LCD Functions. We describe each function and then provide the code. We also provide documentation and discussion within the code. Figure 5.18 provides a structure chart of the 2D LCD support functions. As a homework assignment at the end of the chapter (Advanced 7), we ask you to construct the UML activity diagram for each of these functions.

```
// -------------------------------------------------------------
// filename: 2D_LCD.c   Contains 2D LCD support functions
// -------------------------------------------------------------
// initialize_LCD: initializes the AND1391ST per manufacturer's
//                                                         data
// 68HC12 microcontroller to AND1391ST 2D LCD interface:
// - PORTDLC[3] to C/D'
// - PORTDLC[2] to CE'
// - PORTDLC[1] to RD'
// - PORTDLC[0] to WR'
// - PORTP[7:0] to D[7:0]
// - AND1391ST RESET' to logic high via 4.7K resistor
// - AND1391ST font select (FS) to ground to select 8x8 dot
//                                                    character
// -------------------------------------------------------------

void initialize_LCD(void)
{
char temp = 0x00;
```

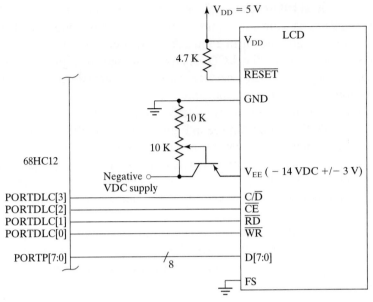

(a) Electrical interface

Connector Pin Assignments		
Pin #	Signal	Function
1	FGND	Frame Ground (connect to bezel)
2	GND	Ground (signal)
3	V_{DD}	5 V
4	V_{EE}	−14 V +/− 3 V
5	$\overline{WR}$	Data Write
6	$\overline{RD}$	Data Read
7	$\overline{CE}$	Chip Enable
8	C/$\overline{D}$	Command/Data →
9	NC	
10	$\overline{RESET}$	Controller reset
11	DB0	Data
12	DB1	
13	DB2	
14	DB3	
15	DB4	
16	DB5	
17	DB6	
18	DB7	
19	FS	Font select. V_{DD}: 6x8 dot, Gnd: 8x8 dot
20	NC	

WR = "L", C/D = "H": Command Write
WR = "L", C/D = "L": Data Write
RD = "L", C/D = "H": Status Read
RD = "L", C/D = "L": Data Read

(b) Connector pin assignments

Figure 5.16   2D LCD electrical interface.

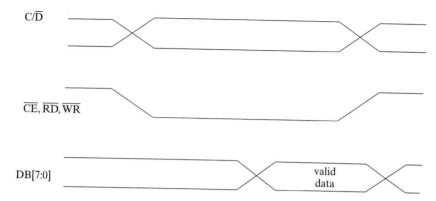

Figure 5.17   2D LCD timing requirements.

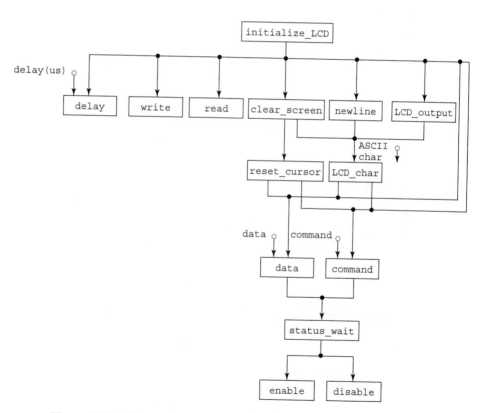

Figure 5.18   2D LCD structure chart. Recall that a directed arrow indicates the data are passed to the called function.

```
PORTDLC = 0xFF;            //all 1 (disabled, command)
PORTDLC = PORTDLC&0xEF;    //reset screen (RESET = 0)
delay(2000);              //delay 2 msec
PORTDLC = 0x7F;            //turn off reset (=1)

write();                   //turn on write (WR=0)
command(0x80);             //mode set: text

data(0x00);                // control word set
data(0x10);
command(0x40);             //set Text Home Address

data(0x10);                //number of text area set 16 decimal
data(0x00);
command(0x41);             //set Text Area Set

command(0x94);             //turn text display, cursor, blink on 97
command(0xA7);             //cursor is 8x8 dot
data(0x01);                //set cursor position
data(0x01);
command(0x21);
}


// ----------------------------------------------------------------
// read: configures PORTP to input data from the LCD. Also enables
// the Read line.
// ----------------------------------------------------------------

void read()
{

DDRP = 0x00;               //make Port P input

}


// ----------------------------------------------------------------
// clearscreen: clears LCD screen by sending a " " to every
// character space on LCD screen.
// ----------------------------------------------------------------

void Clearscreen()
{

int i,j;

Reset_cursor();
```

```
//do for number of lines (i), chars/line (j)
for(i=0;i<16;i++)
  for(j=0;j<16;j++)
    LCD_char(' ');

Reset_cursor();
}



// --------------------------------------------------------------
// newline: writes a new line to LCD screen by displaying a
// line of " "
// --------------------------------------------------------------

void newline()
{
int i;

for(i=0;i<16;i++)
  LCD_char(' ');

}



// --------------------------------------------------------------
// LCD_output: outputs string to LCD screen
// character by character.
// --------------------------------------------------------------

void LCD_output(char s[])
{
int n = 0;

while(s[n] != '\0')
  {
  LCD_char(s[n]);
  ++n;
  }
}



//--------------------------------------------------------------
// delay: approximates delay argument in microseconds
//--------------------------------------------------------------

void delay(int usec)
{
int i,j;
```

```
for(i=0;i<usec; i++)
  {
  for(j=0; j < 7; j++)
    {
    }
  }
}



// ------------------------------------------------------------
// write: sets LCD's command lines so PORTP outputs data to
// the LCD. Also enables the Write line.
// ------------------------------------------------------------
void write()
{

DDRP = 0xFF;                                    //output

}

// ------------------------------------------------------------
// data: sends data to LCD, with the proper control signals. Waits
// for status register flag to indicate LCD ready for another
// instruction.
// ------------------------------------------------------------

void data(unsigned char n)
{
status_wait();
PORTP = n;
PORTDLC = 0xFF;
PORTDLC = PORTDLC&0xF7;              //C/D low
PORTDLC = PORTDLC&0xFE;              //WR low
PORTDLC = PORTDLC&0xFB;
enable();
disable();
}



// ------------------------------------------------------------
// command: sends command to LCD, with the proper control signals.
// Waits for status register flag to indicate LCD ready for an-
// other instruction.
// ------------------------------------------------------------

void command(unsigned char n)
{
status_wait();
```

```
  PORTP = n;
  PORTDLC = 0xFF;
  PORTDLC = PORTDLC&0xFE;                      //write low
  enable();                                    //make CE low
  disable();                                   //make CE high
  }


// -------------------------------------------------------------
// status_wait: called after each command/data. Reads Status
// register to determine when LCD is ready for another
// instruction.
// -------------------------------------------------------------

void status_wait()
{
char temp = 0x00;

DDRP = 0x00;                            //make PortP input port
PORTDLC = PORTDLC|0x0F;                 //turn everything off, C/D high
PORTDLC = PORTDLC&0xFD;                 // make RD low
enable();                               //make CE low

while((temp&0x03) != 0x03)
   {
   temp = PORTP;
   }
disable();
DDRP = 0xFF;                            //write();
}


// -------------------------------------------------------------
// enable: turns on chip enable for the start of an instruction.
// -------------------------------------------------------------

void enable(void)
{
PORTDLC = PORTDLC|0x04;                      //turn enable off (=1)
PORTDLC = PORTDLC&0xFB;                      //turn enable on (=0)
}


// -------------------------------------------------------------
// disable: turns off chip enable after data has been sent for an
// instruction.
// -------------------------------------------------------------

void disable(void)
{
PORTDLC = PORTDLC|0x04;                      //turn enable off (=1)
}
```

```
// ------------------------------------------------------------
// Reset_cursor: resets cursor to home position--top left corner
// of screen
// ------------------------------------------------------------

void Reset_cursor()
{
data(0x00);                                 //set cursor position
data(0x10);
command(0x24);
}




// ------------------------------------------------------------
// LCD_char: takes ASCII char as input and outputs corresponding
// LCD character.
// ------------------------------------------------------------

void LCD_char(unsigned char n)
{
data(n - 0x20);
command(0xC0);
}

// ------------------------------------------------------------
```

5.7 A MOTOR EXAMPLE: INTERFACING TO OTHER DEVICES

In Chapter 4 we discussed pulse width modulation (PWM) techniques. Recall that PWM provides a method to adjust the average voltage applied to a motor by varying the duty cycle of the source voltage. In our discussion we indicated that the 68HC12 does *not* have sufficient voltage/current capability to drive a motor directly. Some type of an interface circuit is required between the 68HC12 and the motor. In this example, we discuss several different methods of interfacing the 68HC12 to motors.

5.7.1 Electronic Switching Device

Since the 68HC12 does not have sufficient capability to drive a motor directly, some form of interface electronics is required. The interface may be implemented with mechanical relays, solid state relays, bipolar transistors, unipolar transistors, etc. In this section we provide a representative sample using an N-channel enhancement MOSFET (metal oxide semiconductor field-effect transistor). We have chosen this example due to the wide range of high-power MOSFETs available to switch substantial loads.

Enhancement MOSFET Theory   Before discussing the interface between the 68HC12 and a motor using a MOSFET, let's review some background information on MOSFETs. A MOSFET is a unipolar, voltage controlled device. It has the advantage of an extremely high-input impedance (hence no current drain from 68HC12) and a low-offset voltage when used as a switch. The MOSFET may be configured as an amplifier or a switch. We use the MOSFET as a switch to turn a motor on and off consistent with an applied 68HC12 PWM control signal.

The MOSFET has three leads: (1) the drain, (2) the source, and (3) the gate. The schematic representation of an N-channel enhancement MOSFET is provided in Figure 5.19(a). Normally, no channel exists between the drain and source leads. Application of a positive gate voltage above a certain threshold (V_t) establishes a channel between the source and the drain leads. With the channel established, current may flow between the drain and source. When the gate voltage is removed, the channel disappears between the source and drain; thus no current flows—we have an electronic switch!

In our specific example we have employed an International Rectifier IRF530. This is an N-channel enhancement MOSFET. It has a rated drain current (I_D) of 14 amps! This means we can switch a 14 A load on and off with a HC CMOS control signal. Realize that this style of MOSFETs are readily available in N-channel or P-channel configurations with substantial (100+ A) current ratings.

The actual interface is provided in Figure 5.19(b). We have included a 10 kΩ resistor between the gate and ground to allow charge from the gate to bleed off when the gate voltage goes to zero. There is also a protection diode provided in parallel to the motor for protection. We discuss the function of the diode in the next section when we discuss the H bridge configuration. When a gate voltage of 5 V is applied to an IRF530, approximately 4 A can flow through the device. To allow a load current of 14 A, a larger gate voltage is required. The motor employed in this example required a 12 VDC source and drew 1 A of current.

5.7.2 Optical Isolation

Motors are a notorious source of electronic noise. Noise is produced by the motor itself as well as the motor power supply. The power supply provides noise because as the motor is turned on and off consistent with the pulse width modulated control signal, large transients occur within the supply, resulting in noise.

To isolate the 68HC12 from the noise produced by the motor and its supply, another interface stage is required. Specifically, an optical isolation stage is required. It is placed between the 68HC12 and the enhancement MOSFET. Optical isolators come in a variety of configurations. What they all have in common is an input source stage optically isolated from an output load stage. When the input stage is activated, an optical link is established between the input and output.

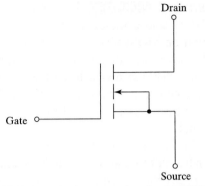

(a) N-channel enhancement interface MOSFET.

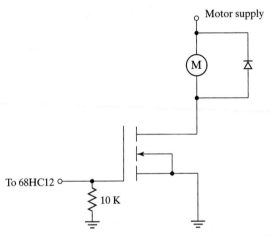

(b) 68HC12 to motor interface using an enhancement MOSFET.

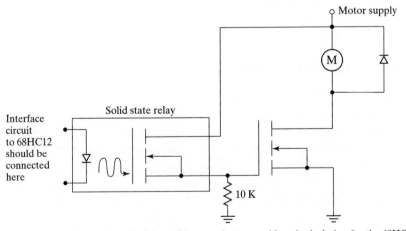

(c) Interface enhanced with a solid state relay to provide noise isolation for the 68HC12.

Figure 5.19   Enhancement MOSFET interface.

One such device that provides optical isolation is a solid state relay (SSR). It consists of a light-emitting diode in the same DIP package as an optical detector. The detector activates a low power enhancement MOSFET, which is connected to the gate of the high-power enhancement MOSFET, as shown in Figure 5.19(c). An interface circuit similar to a standard LED may be used to interface the SSR to a processor. As a homework assignment, later in the chapter we ask you to properly interface the SSR to the 68HC12 (Advanced 8).

5.7.3 H-bridge

In the previous section we described how to control a motor using a MOSFET "switch." This is an effective method to control motor speed. What about motor direction? If we have an application where we need to control not only motor speed but also direction, the previous configuration will not work. However, we could use several MOSFET "switches" to dynamically change the polarity of the voltage applied to the motor and hence its direction. You might think that this would be complicated to do. However, this is a common switch configuration called an H bridge (see Figure 5.20). It gets this designation because the switches form a letter H.

The basic H bridge configuration consists of four electronically controlled switch devices. The DC motor is connected to the two legs of the H. When switches 1 and 4 are closed, the motor rotates in a clockwise direction, as shown in Figure 5.20(b). When switches 2 and 3 are closed, the motor rotates in a counterclockwise direction. If switches 1 and 2 are closed, the motor is braked. What would happen if switch 1 and 3 or 2 and 4 were closed at the same time? Let's not find out. This configuration would cause short through—a shorting out of the power supply.

An actual H bridge configuration has additional circuitry to protect the switching devices. They are normally rated by the maximum motor supply voltage and current that they can safely switch. The inputs to the switch are normally HC CMOS compatible so they may be driven directly from the 68HC12.

As a case study, let's examine the Texas Instruments SN754410NE 1 amp dual H-bridge. This is an amazing chip! Within a 16-pin DIP package, it contains two complete H bridge configurations. The bridge is rated at 1 A and can safely handle motor supply voltages from 4.5 to 36 V. A simplified schematic of one of the H bridges within the chip is provided in Figure 5.21.

5.8 A CONCLUDING EXAMPLE: A COMBINATION PIN CODE

We now provide an example that pulls together some of the main concepts discussed. Note that throughout the chapter we have provided interface information

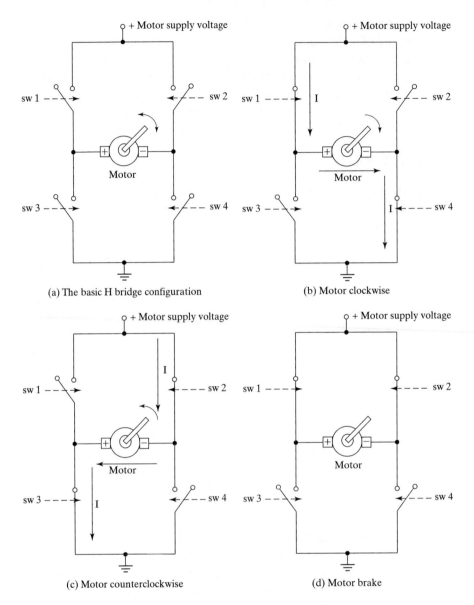

Figure 5.20 H bridge switch configuration.

for a number of input and output devices, discussing each of these devices in a separate section. This has allowed you to use the hardware descriptions and supporting software code as reusable tools in many different projects.

In this example, we use a keypad to enter a pin access code. If this pin access code matches the pre-stored program's pin code, access is allowed. If the

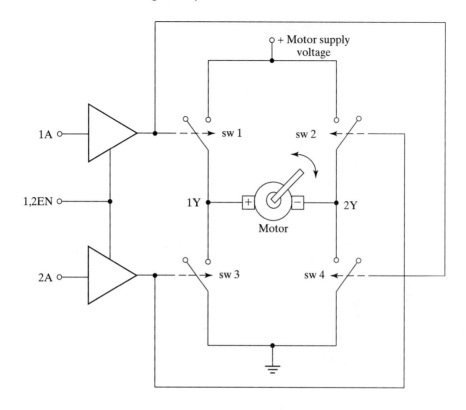

Inputs		Motor Action
1A	2A	
0	0	Free wheel
0	1	CCW
1	0	CW
1	1	Forbidden

Figure 5.21   A simplified schematic of one of the H bridges within the SN 754410NE.

pin access code does not match, access is denied. We employ a LCD display to provide program status.

In order to fully explain this example, we provide details of the hardware interface and the software description. We also provide the actual code for your review, but more importantly we provide a UML activity diagram to describe program operation.

5.8.1 Hardware Description

The hardware interface for this project is illustrated in Figure 5.22. As you can see, PORTB is used for the keypad, PORTP is used for LCD data, and PORTDLC[3:2] is used for the LCD control signals.

5.8.2 Software Description

Figure 5.23 provides an activity diagram to describe program flow for a combination pin code. The actual code to implement the activity diagram is provided below.

```c
/****************************************************************/
/*This program allows the user to enter a pin code into the    */
/*keypad for verification.                                     */
/*Port assignments                                             */
/* - PORTB: keypad                                             */
/* - PORTP: LCD data                                           */
/* - PORTDLC[3:2]: LCD control                                 */
/****************************************************************/

#include <hc12.h>
#include <stdio.h>
#include <math.h>

/*Function prototypes*/
char which_key(unsigned int keypress);/*Function to select key*/
void delay_100us(void);             /*Function to delay 100 us*/
void delay_5ms(void);               /*Function to delay 5 ms*/
void initialize_lcd(void);          /*Initializes LCD*/
void initialize_key(void);          /*Initialize keypad*/
void putchars(unsigned char c);     /*putchar Function*/
void putcommands(unsigned char d);  /*putcommand Function*/
void lcd_print(char *string);       /*Function to print a string*/
char keypad(unsigned int keypress, int row);

void main(void)
{
int first = 0x01;         /*comparison variable for first row*/
int second = 0x02;        /*comparison variable for second row*/
int third = 0x04;         /*comparison variable for third row*/
int fourth = 0x08;        /*comparison variable for fourth row*/

int i,j,k, count = 0;
unsigned int keypress;
char key;
```

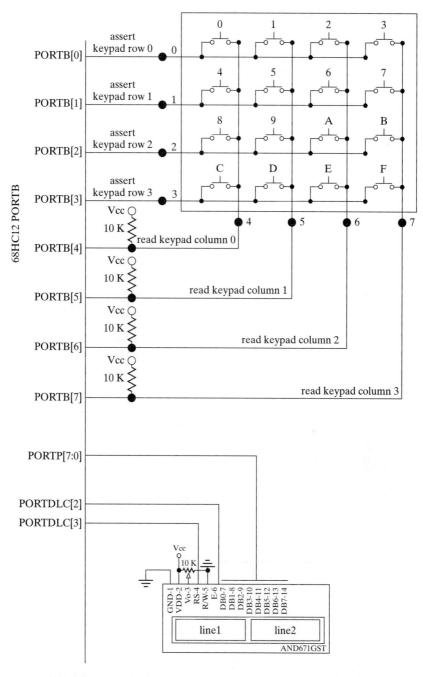

Figure 5.22   The hardware interface for an electronic combination pin code. PORTB is used for the keypad, PORTP is used for LCD data, and PORTDLC[3:2] is used for the LCD control signals.

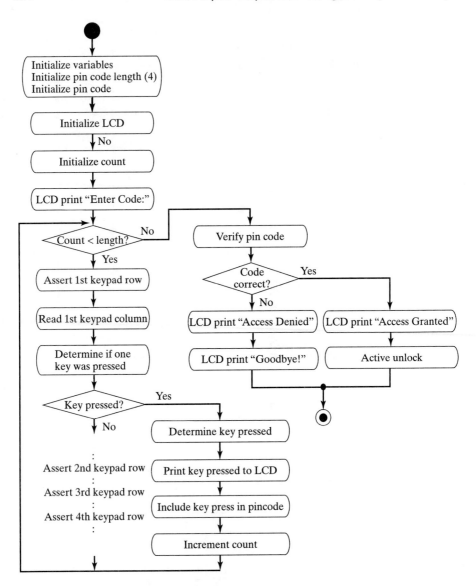

Figure 5.23   Electronic combination code lock activity diagram.

```
int length=4;                 /*length of pin code*/

char pin[] = {'C','9','6','3'};  /*character array for pin code*/
char code[4];                 /*character array for pin code entered*/

initialize_lcd();             /*initialize lcd*/
initialize_key();             /*initialize keypad*/
```

```c
for(k=0;k<4;k++)
 {                               /*Allow four entries of the pin code*/
 count = 0;
 putcommands(0x01);
 lcd_print("Enter Code:");

 while(count < length){        /* loop statement*/

   for(i=0;i<=50;i++)          /*Hold output pin high*/
     {
     PORTB = 0x01;             /*sets PortB[0] high, polls 1st row*/
     keypress = PORTB;         /*get value of PORTB*/
     key = keypad(keypress, first);

     if(key != 'Z')
       {
       printf("%c", key);
       code[count] = key;
       count++;
       }
     }

   for(i=0; i<= 50; i++)
     {                         /*Same process as above*/
     PORTB = 0x02;             /*sets PortB[1] high,polls 2nd Row*/
     keypress = PORTB;
     key = keypad(keypress, second);

     if(key != 'Z'){
       printf("%c", key);
       code[count] = key;
       count++;
       }
     }

   for(i=0; i<= 50; i++)       /*Same process as above*/
     {
     PORTB = 0x04;             /*sets PortB[2] high, polls 3rd row*/
     keypress = PORTB;
     key = keypad(keypress, third);

     if(key != 'Z'){
       printf("%c", key);
       code[count] = key;
       count++;
       }
     }
```

```
   for(i=0; i<= 50; i++)
     {
     PORTB = 0x08;                /*sets PortB[3] high, polls 4th row*/
     keypress = PORTB;
     key = keypad(keypress, fourth);

     if(key != 'Z'){
       printf("%c", key);
       code[count] = key;
       count++;
       }
     }
}

/*After the pin code has been entered into the keypad, it is
  verified */

j = 0;
for(i=0;i<3;++i){                /*step through the array*/
  if(pin[i]==code[i])
    {                            /*compare each element*/
    j++;                         /*if correct increment j*/
    }
  else
    {
    j--;                         /*if incorrect decrement j*/
    }
  }

if(j==(length - 1))
  {                              /*all digits entered correctly?*/
  putcommands(0x01);
  lcd_print("Access Granted");
  }
else
  {
  putcommands(0x01);
  lcd_print("Access Denied");
  }
 }
 putcommands(0x01);
 lcd_print("Goodbye!");
}

/****************************************************************/
/*Functions: function bodies were provided earlier in the
                                                chapter.*/
/*Provided here are a list of functions used by the main program*/
```

```
/*    char which_key(unsigned int keypress)                      */
/*    void delay_5ms(void)                                       */
/*    void delay_100us(void)                                     */
/*    void initialize_lcd(void)                                  */
/*    void putchars(unsigned char c)                             */
/*    void putcommands(unsigned char d)                          */
/*    void lcd_print(char *string)                               */
/*    void initialize_key(void) - function body is provided below*/
/*    char keypad(unsigned int keypress, int row)                */
/****************************************************************/


/****************************************************************/
/*initialize_key: initializes the keypad                        */
/****************************************************************/

void initialize_key(void)
{
DDRB= 0x0F;     /*PORTB[3:0] output, PORTB[7:4] input*/
PORTB = 0x00;    /*initialize PORTBB */
}


/****************************************************************/
```

In the next section, we investigate interfacing techniques from a different point of view. We discuss how signals external to the processor should be conditioned for compatibility with the 68HC12. Specifically, we investigate how to condition an external signal for compatibility to the 68HC12's analog-to-digital (ATD) conversion subsystem.

5.9 TRANSDUCER INTERFACE DESIGN

A transducer is a mechanical and/or electronic component that converts a physical variable such as temperature, pressure, or displacement into an electrical signal. In the weather station example provided in Chapter 2, the weather parameter transducers conveniently transduced the physical phenomena into electronic signals compatible with the 68HC12. In the ideal weather station example, we did not have to concern ourselves with conditioning the signal. Often this is not the case. The output signal from the transducer may require scaling (amplification or attenuation), filtering of undesired frequency components, and/or the addition of a DC bias signal. It is beyond the scope of this book to cover the myriad details of signal conditioning. Several excellent references are listed in the Further Reading section at the end of this chapter. In this section we provide the basic concept of transducer interface design at a block diagram level.

A block diagram of a basic transducer interface design is shown in Figure 5.24. The transducer converts a physical variable X into an electronic

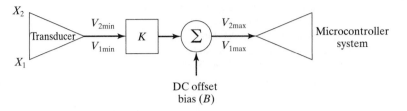

Figure 5.24   Transducer interface design.

signal. Generally speaking, the transducer output X is scaled by a factor K and then has a DC bias (B) applied. In our discussion we assume that the output from the transducer is linear. That is, when the physical variable X_1 is provided to the transducer, the transducer generates an output voltage of $V_{1\,min}$. Likewise, when the physical variable X_2 is provided to the transducer, the transducer generates an output voltage of $V_{2\,min}$. When physical variables between the extremes of X_1 and X_2 are provided to the transducer, a corresponding linearly related value is generated at the transducer's output.

Ideally, we would like our transducer to provide a voltage of 5 VDC to the input of the microcontroller's ATD converter when X_2 is applied to the transducer and 0 VDC to the input of the microcontroller's ATD converter when X_1 is applied to the transducer. To accomplish this conversion, the output from the transducer $V_{2\,min}$ and $V_{1\,min}$ may require scaling and the addition of a DC bias. In our block diagram we have designated the scaling operation with a K and the addition of the bias with a summation.

In general, we can develop two equations with two unknowns to describe the operation of our transducer interface design. These equations are given as

$$V_{2\,max} = V_{2\,min} * K + B$$

and

$$V_{1\,max} = V_{1\,min} * K + B$$

Usually, the specifications of our transducer dictate the values of $V_{2\,min}$ and $V_{1\,min}$ while the specifications of the 68HC12's ATD converter govern the values of $V_{2\,max}$ and $V_{1\,max}$. Substitution of these values results in a set of two equations and two unknowns (K and B). Therefore, the desired values of scaling (K) and the DC bias (B) may be determined for a specific interface. The scaling and addition of DC bias is easily implemented with basic operational amplifier (op amp) circuitry. (See the sources provided at the end of this chapter for implementation details.) Let's illustrate the approach to transducer interface design with an example.

Example

Let's consider a barometer on a weather station that provides a signal that ranges from 0 to 5 V depending on the sensed barometric pressure. Let's assume it provides a 0 V output for 64 cm of mercury and 5 V for 81 cm of mercury (the normal range for barometric pressure). For values between these two extremes, there is a linear relationship between output voltage and barometric pressure. In this case, no interface is required between the transducer and the ATD system.

Let's now suppose that the barometer we have chosen provides a -100 mV output for 64 cm of mercury and 300 mV output for 81 cm of mercury. As before, for values between these two extremes, there is a linear relationship between output voltage and barometric pressure. We would like to interface this barometric sensor to the 68HC12's ATD converter so that 0 V is provided for 64 cm of mercury and 5 V for 81 cm of mercury.

By interpreting these specifications, we can determine that $V_{1\,min}$ is -100 mV and $V_{2\,min}$ is 300 mV while $V_{1\,max}$ is 0 V and $V_{2\,max}$ is 5 V. Substituting these values provides the following equations:

$$5\ V = 300\ mV * K + B$$

and

$$0\ V = -100\ mV * K + B$$

Simultaneously solving these equations provides a scale factor (K) of 12.5 and a DC bias (B) of 1.25 V. Check these values! Do you agree? As previously mentioned, it is easy to implement an op amp circuit to scale the transducer's output by a factor of 12.5 and add an offset of 1.25 V.

This transducer interface procedure may be used for a wide variety of transducers. Note that the signal may require further conditioning, such as using a filter circuit to remove undesired frequency components.

5.10 THE RS-232 INTERFACE

In Chapter 4 we discussed the serial communications capability of the 68HC12. Recall that the processor is equipped with both an asynchronous (SCI) and a synchronous (SPI) serial communications channels. Both of these systems output a 5 V signal for a logic 1 and a 0 V signal for a logic 0. If these systems are connected to an RS-232 compatible signal source, some interfacing is required.

The RS-232 is an Electronic Industries Alliance (EIA) standard. The current EIA-232-D standard has evolved from the original 1960s era standard. This standard governs four aspects of the communication interface: (1) the electrical specifications, (2) the functional specification for each signal, (3) the mechanical specification, and (4) the procedural specifications.

Although this may seem complicated, the electrical portion of the standard is easily implemented using a single chip solution. For example, MAXIM-IC incorporated manufactures a full line of multichannel RS-232 drivers/receivers. Generally speaking, the CMOS signals from the 68HC12 may be converted to an RS-232 compatible level with these chips. These chips invert the logic and represent a logic 1 with a −10 VDC level, and a logic 0 may be implemented with a +10 VDC level. Similarly, incoming signals from an RS-232 compatible device must be converted back to CMOS compatible logic levels. It is interesting to note that these RS-232 compatible chips are powered from a single 5 VDC supply as shown in Figure 5.25.

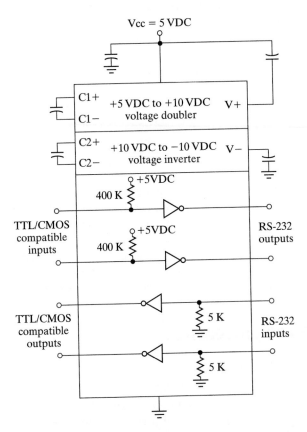

Figure 5.25 RS-232 interface chip. MAXIM-IC incorporated manufactures a full line of multichannel RS-232 drivers/receivers. The CMOS signals from the 68HC12 may be converted to an RS-232 compatible level. Similarly, incoming signals from an RS-232 compatible device must be converted back to CMOS compatible logic levels. These RS-232 compatible chips are powered from a single 5 VDC supply.

5.11 SUMMARY

We began this chapter by reviewing the electrical characteristics of the HC CMOS family of the 68HC12. It is important to thoroughly understand these characteristics so proper interfaces may be designed and implemented. We then investigated the interface of different input and output devices to the 68HC12. We showed how to interface LEDs, keypads, and 1D and 2D LCD displays with the 68HC12. We also investigated some real world issues such as switch debouncing techniques and motor noise isolation techniques. We concluded the chapter with a discussion on how to properly interface an input signal for the 68HC12. We also discussed the RS-232 communication interface. We shall continue to investigate real-world design issues in Chapter 6.

5.12 FURTHER READING

Horowitz, P., and W. Hill. *The Art of Electronics*, 2nd ed. Cambridge, England: Cambridge University Press, 1989.

Furlow, Bill. *Circuit Design Idea Handbook*. Boston: Cahners, 1975.

Sheingold, Daniel H., ed. *Analog-Digital Conversion Handbook*. Norwood, MA: Analog Devices, 1976.

"Transducers," Omega Engineering Inc., 1 Omega Drive, Stamford, CT, 06907

Stout, David F., and Milton Kaufman. *Handbook of Operational Amplifier Circuit Design*. New York: McGraw-Hill, 1976.

Hollander, M. A. *Electrical signals and systems*. New York: McGraw-Hill.

5.13 PROBLEMS

Fundamental

1. What does the HC designator stand for in the 68HC12 part number?

2. Provide the definition of the eight voltage and current parameters for a logic family. Include a diagram with your answer.

3. What are the eight electrical parameters for the 68HC12? Provide a diagram with your answer with each of the parameters clearly labeled.

4. What is the maximum current rating for the 68HC12 digital input/output pins?

5. What happens to V_{OH} and V_{OL} at the maximum current ratings?

6. What two requirements must be met to properly bias a light-emitting diode?

7. What was the problem with the poor LED interface design of Figure 5.3? Provide a correct design, assuming $V_{LED} = 1.7$ V and $I_{LED} = 15$ mA.

8. Describe in detail two different methods of switch debouncing.

9. What is tristate logic? What is it used for?

10. What is the function/purpose of a solid state relay?

Advanced

1. Two new logic families (DP1 and SB2) have been developed. Key parameters for each logic family are provided below:

DP1

$$V_{IH} = 2.0 \text{ V}, \quad V_{IL} = 0.8 \text{ V}, \quad I_{OH} = -0.4 \text{ mA}, \quad I_{OL} = 16 \text{ mA}$$
$$V_{OH} = 3.4 \text{ V}, \quad V_{OL} = 0.2 \text{ V}, \quad I_{IH} = 40 \text{ uA}, \quad I_{IL} = -1.6 \text{ mA}$$

SB2

$$V_{IH} = 2.0 \text{ V}, \quad V_{IL} = 0.8 \text{ V}, \quad I_{OH} = -0.4 \text{ mA}, \quad I_{OL} = 8 \text{ mA}$$
$$V_{OH} = 2.7 \text{ V}, \quad V_{OL} = 0.4 \text{ V}, \quad I_{IH} = 20 \text{ uA}, \quad I_{IL} = -0.4 \text{ mA}$$

Can a SB2 logic family drive a DP1 logic family? If so, what is the fanout?

2. Can a HC system drive a DP1 logic family?

3. Can a HC system drive a SB2 logic family?

4. In Figure 5.5 pull-up resistors of 10 kΩ were connected from the keypad column pins to Vcc. If we modified the design so that the resistors were pull-down resistors (connected from the keypad column pins to ground), how must the table contained in the figure be modified?

5. Look again at Figure 5.5. You have been asked by your boss to investigate decoding the keypad switch depressions in hardware. That is, when the F key is depressed the ASCII code for F is provided. You have decided to use combinational logic to implement this keypad decoder. Provide the truth table for the decoder. Assume 10 kΩ pull-up resistors were connected from the keypad column pins to Vcc as described in the chapter. Are there other issues that need to be considered?

6. Describe in your own words how the switch debounce configurations of Figure 5.10 provide switch debouncing.

7. Construct the UML activity diagrams for each of the functions provided in Sections 5.6.2 and 5.6.3 to support the liquid crystal display.

8. The solid state relay of Figure 5.19 (c) requires 1.7 V and 20 mA of current to activate the MOSFET switch on the load side of the SSR. Provide an interface from the 68HC12 to the SSR. Be careful! Remember the current ratings of the 68HC12.

9. Describe the operation of an enhancement mode MOSFET.

10. Conduct a literature search on available MOSFET switches. Write a one-page point paper on MOSFET availability, power ratings, etc. *Hint*: Check out the Web site for International Rectifier www.irf.com.

11. A transducer produces a signal of 30 mV corresponding to 0 RPM and 500 mV at 5000 RPM. Provide a design to interface this transducer to the 68HC12.

12. Repeat the problem with a transducer that provides 500 mV a 0 RPM and −30 mV at 5000 RPM.

Challenging

1. In Figure 5.5 pull-up resistors of 10 kΩ were connected from the keypad column pins to Vcc. If we modified the design such that the resistors were pull-down resistors (connected from the keypad column pins to ground), how must the software be modified?

2. Look again at Figure 5.11. Write a program that illuminates the green LED on PC0 when the switch connected to PB0 is depressed. The remainder of the LEDs should be red. When the PB1 switch is depressed, the green LEDs connected to PC0 and PC1 are illuminated and the remaining LEDs will be red, etc. Provide an activity diagram of your code. As you know, the activity diagram should be accomplished first!

3. Modify the pin access code example provided in section 5.8.2 to accept a 6 digit pin code.

6

Welcome to the Real World!

Objectives: After reading this chapter, you should be able to

- Identify real-world design constraints that may prevent a microcontroller-based system from operating correctly.
- Define CMOS handling and design guidelines.
- Identify sources of both internal and external noise to a microcontroller system.
- List key agencies responsible for providing electromagnetic compatibility (EMC) directives and guidance.
- Identify design techniques to minimize noise susceptibility.
- Apply defensive programming techniques to minimize noise susceptibility.
- Describe techniques to detect noise.
- Apply power management techniques to minimize the power consumption of a microcontroller-based system.
- Understand the trade-offs involved when choosing a battery supply for a microprocessor system.

365

- Identify the key features of microprocessor supervisory circuits.
- Identify and apply power conservation measures.

What is this chapter all about? When you first look at the chapter objectives, you might think the chapter is a collection of "cat and dog" topics—that is, topics that do not fit conveniently in any other chapter. We agree that the chapter covers many diverse topics; however, they all have a common thread. If any of these real-world design considerations are ignored, a system may not operate at all. Worse yet, it may exhibit sporadic, unpredictable, or unreliable behavior. In this chapter we deal with the real-world design issues that must be overcome. We provide a comprehensive list of source material in the Further Reading section for those readers seeking additional information.

6.1 HORROR STORIES ABOUT DESIGN FAILURES

We begin with several "horror stories" about designs that did not operate correctly. Pay close attention to the specific causes of these design failures. We then present many techniques to translate a good paper design into a functioning system.

6.1.1 The Case of the Quadrature Generator

Before we discuss the first case, we provide some background information on signal reconstruction. A useful technique to generate an analog signal of a specific waveshape is to divide the signal into a series of analog data points. The individual data points are then converted into a binary value from $00 to $FF, which corresponds to 0 volts ($00) at one extreme and the full-scale value such as 5 volts ($FF) at the other extreme. Analog data points between the two extremes are linearly encoded with corresponding 8-bit weighted binary values. Does this technique sound vaguely familiar? This is the process of analog-to-digital (ATD) conversion that we discussed in Chapter 4.

To reconstruct the analog signal, the individual binary data points are sequentially sent to a digital-to-analog converter (DAC). Before going any further, let's quickly review DAC concepts.

Digital-to-Analog Converter   A digital-to-analog converter (DAC) translates a multibit binary input into a corresponding analog output (see Figure 6.1). We will not discuss the different methods of DAC conversions. We simply treat the DAC as a "black box" and describe its function with a block diagram. The analog output is provided by summing the weighted binary inputs, as shown in the figure.

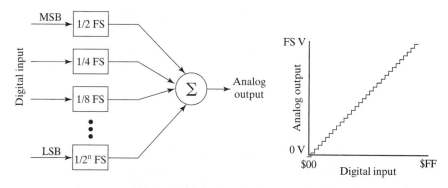

Figure 6.1   A digital-to-analog converter. A DAC translates a multibit binary input into a corresponding analog output. The analog output is provided by summing the weighted binary inputs. Symbol FS stands for full scale voltage.

For example, when $CA is presented to the DAC, the most significant binary bit is multiplied by one-half of the FS value. The next most significant bit is multiplied by one-fourth of the FS value and so on. The result from each weighted bit is summed to provide the analog value.

Let us assume the full-scale (FS) voltage (where FS $= V_{RH} - V_{RL}$) of an 8-bit DAC is 5 V with the high and low reference voltages of 5 V and 0 V. With a binary input of $CA, what is the corresponding analog output voltage?

This voltage is determined by using the following weighted sum for the $CA input:

$$V_{out} = 5[(1 \cdot 1/2) + (1 \cdot 1/4) + (0 \cdot 1/8) + (0 \cdot 1/16) + (1 \cdot 1/32) + (0 \cdot 1/64)$$
$$+ (1 \cdot 1/128) + (0 \cdot 1/256)] = 3.945V$$

An analog signal may then be constructed by sequentially presenting digital data points to a DAC to obtain an analog reconstruction. The technique of reconstructing the analog signal from individual binary points may be used on many different types of signals [Barrett 1979, Welch 1997].

We now discuss the design failure of a quadrature generator. Figure 6.2 illustrates how this technique can be used to generate quadrature-related signals (a sine wave and a cosine wave). The circuit consists of a Statek CMOS PXO1000 programmable crystal oscillator. The oscillator's frequency is set by DIP switch settings. The oscillator provides the timebase for an 8-bit binary CMOS counter, which continually counts from $00 to $FF. The output from this counter is fed into two separate NMOS 2048 by 8 memory EPROMS, which store the data points for the sine wave and the cosine wave. The output from the memory chips are fed into separate 8-bit CMOS digital-to-analog converters (DACs), which reconstruct the individual binary data points back into an analog signal. Following the DACs are operational amplifiers to shift the output signal from the DACs to be centered about zero volts and also to provide gain control.

On paper, the design performed very well. However, when the circuit was constructed, it appeared to be a good noise generator. What was the problem? In the initial design the 4.7 k resistors at the outputs of the NMOS memory devices were not present. In Chapter 5 we indicated that we can usually connect chips of the same family without significant interface issues. However, when connecting dissimilar families, we must be very careful. Note in this design we go from a CMOS counter to NMOS memory and then back to a CMOS DAC. We have to carefully examine the interface between the CMOS and the NMOS and then the NMOS interface to the CMOS. In order for this circuit to properly operate, pull-up resistors must be included at the NMOS outputs. This allows the NMOS outputs to be recognized properly by the CMOS DAC's inputs. The pull-up resistors are shown in Figure 6.2.

From this example you can see the importance of carefully examining the interface between all components within a circuit. Be especially careful at interfaces between dissimilar families.

6.1.2 The Case of the Laser Irradiation Timer

Let's now consider a research project that involved a method of recording laser irradiation time. In the experiment, a laser was controlled by a TTL compatible pulse issued from a PC. When the pulse was high, the laser shutter was opened; when it was low, the laser shutter closed. The purpose of the experiments was to study the effects of the laser on tissue for eye surgery studies. Ideally, we wanted to time stamp the video recording of the experiment. Commercially available "time stamping" equipment was checked and found to be cost prohibitive for a project on a small budget.

A visit to the parts room to construct a digital timer from 74LSXX components was accomplished. The components were used to construct a five-stage counter that drove several seven-segment displays via display driver chips. Optically, the readout from the seven-segment displays was projected into the camera lens field of view recording the experiment. The counter/display electronics were mounted in a plastic box and a portal was cut so that the display readout was visible, as shown in Figure 6.3.

The camera field of view, the display readout, and the laser path were all optically co-aligned. A "chopping wheel" alternately provided the laser and then the camera exposure to the tissue target. Without this arrangement, the high intensity of the laser would saturate the video camera. The chopping wheel had portals staggered from one another to alternate between the camera and the laser. The motor spinning the chopping wheel was speed stabilized such that a portal

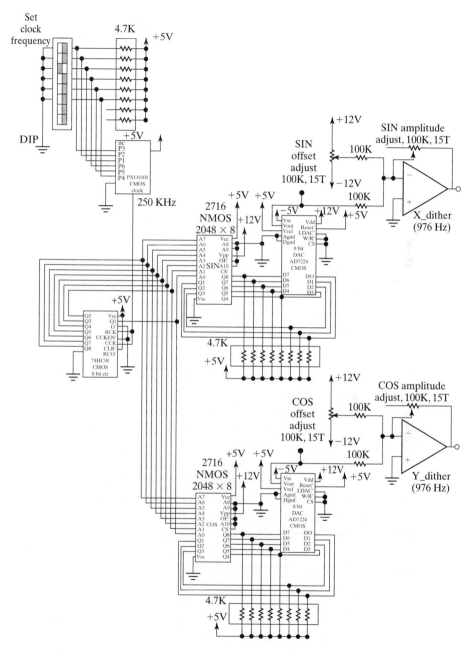

Figure 6.2   Quadrature generator.

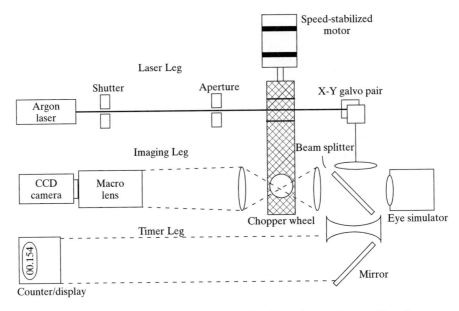

Figure 6.3 A laser "chopping wheel," which alternately provides the laser and then the camera exposure to the tissue target. The camera field of view, the counter/display readout, and the laser path are all optically co-aligned.

was provided to the camera at a harmonic of the camera's frame rate. This produced a stable image.

In theory, the shutter "on" pulse from the PC was also used to enable the clock for the shutter timer through an AND gate. Thus the counter would count while the shutter was enabled.

The counter/display circuit worked very well on the bench in the fabrication lab. However, when introduced into the laser lab environment, its operation became very erratic. Suspecting a noise problem, we then painstakingly tried to isolate the source of the noise. We had made no attempt to provide the counter/display circuit with standard noise minimization countermeasures until the problem occurred. It was difficult to add these countermeasures after the circuit had been constructed. What do you think the problem might have been? What corrective measures should be taken?

Knowing that motors are a notorious source of noise, we suspected that the noise source was the chopper wheel motor. Often microcontrollers are used to control motors. In Chapter 5, we showed how to optically isolate a control circuit from a motor. However, in this example, the counter/display circuit had no direct electrical connection to the motor. In fact, the counter/display circuit and the motor were powered from separate DC supplies. Solving this type of motor noise problem was a bit more challenging. We used the following techniques to isolate the motor noise from the counter/display circuit:

- The control signal line from the PC to the timer/circuit was replaced with a shielded cable. The shield on the cable was grounded. The cable was routed around and away from the motor.
- Noise suppression (bypass) capacitors were installed on every chip between power and ground within the timer/display circuit. Additionally, noise suppression capacitors were installed on the power leads of the timer/display board.
- The plastic enclosure for the timer/display board was lined with copper tape. The copper tape was then grounded. Also, a copper screen was installed on the display portal of the enclosure. The copper screen was also connected to the copper tape. The screen with the tape provided a shielded enclosure for the counter/display circuit.

After applying these noise suppression countermeasures, the circuit worked as designed and the experiments were completed without further difficulty.

What was the lesson learned in this scenario? A considerable number of problems were encountered because a thorough analysis of the operating environment was not conducted. This should be accomplished as a matter of course when requirements are first established for a project. Also, as a matter of course, noise countermeasures should be included in any circuit design. There are many standard techniques to minimize the effects of noise both internal and external to a circuit. Finally, it is extremely costly to install noise countermeasures after a product has been shipped. In the above scenario, the problem arose in a rush to collect research data.

We presented the two case studies to illustrate the following common problems in microprocessor-based systems:

- Improper interface techniques
- Noise problems associated with external and internal sources
- Noise problems associated with analog electronics

Now that we have identified some common real-world problems, we now devote the rest of the chapter to describing methods that will effectively translate a paper design into a good operating design while avoiding real-world pitfalls.

6.2 68HC12 HANDLING AND DESIGN GUIDELINES

All data books contain considerable information that is often overlooked. This information may be the most important in the data book—how to properly handle

CMOS devices and device guidelines. If you are a design engineer, you may not typically get involved with the fabrication process. On the other hand, if you are a senior design student or you have the pleasure of fabricating prototypes, these handling guidelines should be committed to memory.

6.2.1 CMOS Handling Guidelines

The CMOS "HC" family of chips by design have an extremely high input imped-ance. This is due to the insulated gate at the device inputs. This gate is suscepti-ble to damage if the chips are not handled correctly. Although the CMOS gates have built-in protection circuits, common CMOS handling procedures have been developed to minimize the chance of causing damage. These handling procedures are based on preventing a large static voltage from being presented to the gate's inputs. Here is a brief review of these handling procedures:

- Wear a grounded wrist strap while handling CMOS devices. These straps are readily available from a number of electronic supply companies.
- Keep CMOS devices in their original shipping container until ready for use. These containers have been designed to prevent exposure to static electricity.
- Use CMOS devices on a grounded test bench.
- Ensure that a grounded soldering tip is used when soldering.
- Do not remove or replace a CMOS device in a circuit while the circuit is powered.

If these handling procedures are conscientiously followed, accidental damage to CMOS circuits is minimized. Aside from handling procedures, there are also several design guidelines to follow.

6.2.2 CMOS Design Guidelines

Let's review some design guidelines to help ensure a solid CMOS-based circuit design.

- Frequently when designing an embedded system, there are several unused processor inputs. You cannot ignore these inputs. They must be properly terminated by either connecting them to the processor supply voltage via a resistor (4.7 kΩ) or by grounding them. Later in the chapter, we inves-tigate what problems occur when these inputs are not properly handled.
- A CMOS-based embedded system is often contained on a printed circuit board (PCB) that is then connected to another PCB via a connector.

When external connectors to a PCB are connected directly to the input or output of a CMOS device, a series resistor should be employed. This series resistor helps minimize damage due to static electricity when the PCB is connected to or removed from the connector.

- As we saw in the previous chapter, CMOS devices should only be used within their specified electrical parameter envelope. When used outside these design specifications, erratic circuit behavior may result.

You are probably feeling pretty comfortable now. You understand and can apply CMOS design techniques and you feel comfortable with the concepts of interfacing from the previous chapter. However, you might follow all of these good design practices and your system might still not operate correctly. This brings us to our next topic, system noise and how to prevent and minimize its effects.

6.3 NOISE CONSIDERATIONS

In this section we carefully examine the designer's nemesis—noise! We answer the following questions: What is noise? Where does it come from? What are some good design practices to minimize noise susceptibility?

6.3.1 Understanding Noise

In the simplest sense, noise is any undesired signal that does not belong in a system. Realize that the origins of these undesired signals may be external or internal to a system. For example, the crystal based timer for a processor is a required system component. However, when the clock signal shows up in other portions of the system where it does not belong, it is considered noise. Corp [1990] has done a good job placing noise in specific source categories. It is a good idea to know the source of noise in any circuit, because this knowledge helps you determine the best way to get rid of it. Figure 6.4 provides a brief review of noise sources.

- *Electrostatic discharge (ESD):* ESD can basically be defined as static electricity. As previously mentioned, CMOS devices are susceptible to gate damage when exposed to static electricity. Static electricity is caused when two objects of different charge come in close proximity of one another.
- *Radio frequency interference (RFI):* RFI is caused by radiated energy. In this case, the noise may be from a radio, cellular phone, etc. Although it might be emanating from a bona fide signal source, if it is an undesired signal in your system, it is considered noise. The first author describes

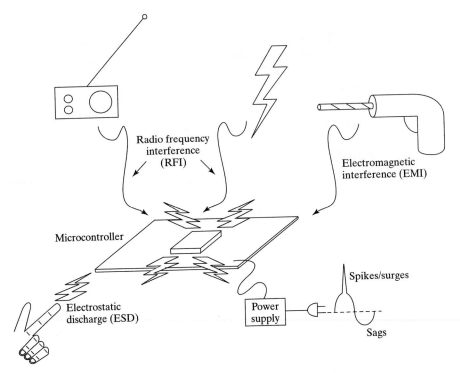

Figure 6.4 Sources of noise.

a period when he lived in Omaha, Nebraska, for a number of years: "We used to get some fairly serious 'thunder boomers'—rainstorms with considerable thunder and lightning. We could also tell when a such a storm was coming near because the lightning discharges would cause our doorbell to ring. The first time it happened we were quite surprised. 'Who is ringing the doorbell at 2 A.M. in the middle of a big rainstorm?' Once I figured out the RFI generated by the lightning was inducing a voltage in our doorbell circuit, I used it as a sentry for oncoming storms." Aside from external noise, note that the microcontroller itself may be a source of noise. The clock frequency on the 68HC12 is 8 MHz. Harmonic analysis of the clock pulses indicates that significant harmonics exist at frequencies up to ten times this value or 80 MHz! If a printed circuit board is not properly designed to minimize RFI effects, these frequencies may be radiated and manifest themselves as noise.

• *Electromagnetic interference (EMI):* There are two categories of EMI: radiated and conducted. Both types are due to noise caused by electromechanical equipment such as motors. In radiated EMI, the noise source is not necessarily in close proximity to a system. In fact, this type of EMI is often classified as RFI. In the conducted type of EMI, noise is induced in a conductor when the conductor passes through the noise flux of the source. Recall from Faraday's law, a voltage is induced in a conductor when it cuts lines of magnetic flux. You have probably experienced this phenomena when using an electric razor, a power drill, or a kitchen mixer. If you are watching television without a cable connection and one of these appliances is used nearby, often you observe noise on your television.

- *Voltage sags:* Voltage sags or "brownouts" are caused by a decrease in the alternating current (AC) supply. These occur when a large load is put on the AC distribution grid. Picture a hot, humid day. You have been at work all day long. Your first reaction when you get home is to turn up the air conditioner to cool your home. If many people do this at the same time, it puts a tremendous stress on the power grid and a brownout may occur. Brownouts can wreak havoc on an unprotected system. Remember CMOS devices have a very specific operating envelope. The supply voltage is specified at 5.0 volts $\pm 10\%$. A brownout could cause the supply voltage to go outside this operating envelope. When this occurs, logic lows and highs are no longer correct. Voltage sag protection is provided by supervisory circuits, discussed in section 6.6.5 of this chapter.

- *Voltage surges:* Voltage surges are similar to voltage sags; however, they are an increase in AC supply voltage. A voltage surge can cause severe damage to an unprotected system. Surge protection can be provided by a well-filtered power supply cord and power supply.

6.3.2 Electromagnetic Compatibility

Now that we have a good handle on what exactly noise is, here's some bad news. As system designers, we must protect our embedded controller system from these noise sources. Electromagnetic compatibility (EMC) is the technical term that defines a product operating correctly within its assigned and intended electromagnetic spectrum. If a product emits signals outside of its defined spectrum, it is considered a noise source. It should not emanate signal frequencies outside of its allotted spectrum. Aside from being concerned about emanations, we also need to be concerned about the susceptibility of a finished product to external noise sources as described above. We could consider EMC from either point of view—emanation or susceptibility. As it turns out, countermeasures for one also serve as countermeasures for the other.

As you might suspect, EMC is a serious topic in product development. There are a number of national and international governing agencies that provide guidance and regulations on EMC compliance. We provide a brief overview of these agencies and their regulations later in the chapter.

In the next section, we begin to investigate how to systematically provide for noise protection both external and internal to a circuit. This information was culled from a number of manufacturers' application notes and lessons learned from practicing engineers. Full reference citations are provided in the Further Reading section at the end of the chapter.

6.3.3 Noise-System Specification—Not an Afterthought!

For starters, we may need to rearrange our thinking on noise. As we saw in the cases discussed earlier in the chapter, it is very difficult to provide common noise counter-measures to an already completed design. We observed that noise considerations or electromagnetic compatibility should be a design requirement for each embedded control system. During the development of system specifications, a complete inventory of expected operating conditions should be accomplished. The specifications should then be developed to encompass these expected operating conditions.

6.3.4 Checklist

We provide in this section a checklist of noise minimization techniques. This list is based on work provided by M. Glenewinkel [1995] and supplemented with additional information from a number of applications notes and advice provided by practicing engineers. Some of these techniques are illustrated in Figure 6.5.

- **a.** *Surface mount components:* In general, surface mount components are less susceptible to noise than leaded components. If you have recently constructed a PCB design, you have probably observed that leaded components are becoming more difficult to obtain. Integrated circuits, processors, resistors, capacitors, etc., are readily available in surface mount packages.
- **b.** *Power conditioning:* Power supplies may be a source of noise. Embedded processors can generate power spikes due to current transients. Realize that a spike resembles a pulse and a pulse has significant high frequency Fourier spectral components. If transients from the power supply are not properly decoupled from the embedded system, EMI problems may occur. As a matter of course, you should include decoupling capacitors to minimize these transients. Generally a 0.1 µF capacitor is used for frequencies up to 15 MHz. These capacitors should be an axial glass, multilayer ceramic construction. A 0.01 µF capacitor should be used for operating frequencies greater than 15 MHz. These capacitors should be placed between the power and ground pin of each integrated circuit (IC) package. The capacitors should be placed as close as physically possible to each IC. In addition to these capacitors, a 10-470 µF capacitor should be included between

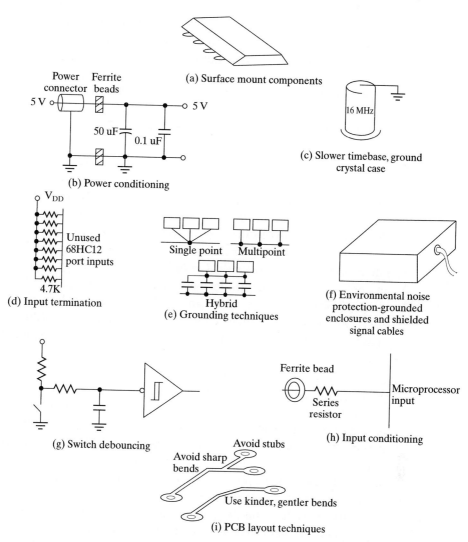

(a) Surface mount components

(b) Power conditioning

(c) Slower timebase, ground crystal case

(d) Input termination

(e) Grounding techniques

(f) Environmental noise protection-grounded enclosures and shielded signal cables

(g) Switch debouncing

(h) Input conditioning

(i) PCB layout techniques

Figure 6.5   Noise minimization techniques.

the power and ground leads at the supply line entry point of the PCB. Additionally, it is recommended that a ferrite bead be added between the coupling capacitor and the power supply. Note that a typical microprocessor chip may have multiple power connections. For example, the analog-to-digital (ATD) system requires reference voltages (V_{RH} and V_{RL}). These voltage supplies should also be decoupled.

c. *Clock frequency:* When designing an embedded control system, the lowest frequency clock allowed by the system requirements should be used.

The clock is a notorious source of noise if not properly isolated; it will generate significant harmonic frequencies well above the frequency of the clock signal. The 68HC12 employs a 16 MHz crystal to generate the 8 MHz time base. Note that significant harmonics may exist at frequencies up to 160 MHz. Normally the time base for the processor is provided by a crystal. The crystal should be placed in the center of the printed circuit board and mounted flush to it. Additionally, the crystal case should be grounded.

d. *Input termination:* A notorious source of noise is found in improper terminating of both digital and analog component inputs. In a digital circuit, an unused input tends to self-bias into the transistor's active region. These nonterminated inputs also act as "mini-antennas" for noise. Such inputs should be either tied to the source voltage (V_{DD}) through a 4.7 kΩ resistor or to ground (V_{SS}). Resistors are readily available in either a single inline package (SIP) or a dual inline package (DIP) to easily terminate an unused embedded controller port. Aside from port inputs, the hardware interrupt pins should also be similarly terminated if they are not being used. Otherwise, inadvertent interrupts may be initiated. Additionally, any unused gates in an integrated digital circuit should have their inputs terminated.

e. *Grounding techniques:* In any embedded control system, there are multiple points in the circuit that require connection to ground. It is assumed that "ground" is an equipotential value equal to zero volts. You can imagine the problems that occur in a circuit if this is not true. It is therefore extremely important to ensure that all of these various circuit points are indeed at the same potential. Your intuition might lead you to believe that merely connecting all the ground points together solves the problem. This technique, which is called a *single point ground*, works well at low frequencies. An alternative is to have multiple connection points to a ground plane. Called a *multipoint ground*, this works well at high frequencies. The real answer is a mixture of the two techniques referred to as a *hybrid ground*. It is also important to separate digital, analog, input/output devices, and switching components from one another on a PCB. A combination of grounding techniques is then employed for each subsystem. For example, each subsystem may all share a single point ground with the power supply ground but then a combination of multipoint and hybrid grounds may be used in each subsystem.

f. *Environmental noise protection:* There are a number of methods to shield an embedded control system from environmental noise. As we saw in the cases discussed earlier in the chapter, a shielded enclosure and shielded cables may be used to minimize the susceptibility to environmental noise by shunting the noise to ground. For cables containing low frequency signals, the shield should be grounded at one end. For cables containing high frequency signals, the shield should be connected at both ends to ground. An instrument case should be connected to ground. That way induced noise is shorted to ground.

g. *Switch debouncing:* In Chapter 5 we discussed switch debouncing as an interface technique. This can also be viewed as a method to minimize noise transients. Recall that, ideally, a switch pushbutton is normally at logic high, and it transitions to logic low when depressed. In actual switches, the switch has a tendency to bounce. That is, due to the nonideal mechanical characteristics of the switch, the switch makes and breaks contact multiple times. Since, the 68HC12 is operating in the range of MHz, it is fast enough to register these switch bounces as multiple switch open and closures. To prevent this phenomena, switch debouncing techniques may be employed. Switches may be debounced using hardware or software techniques. To debounce a switch in software, the first switch contact is read and then a 100–200 ms software delay is inserted. During this short delay, switch bouncing is effectively locked out. This debouncing technique also works to minimize noise transients at circuit inputs. Hardware and software debouncing techniques were discussed in detail in Chapter 5, Section 5.5.

h. *Input conditioning:* Signals entering and exiting a board should be protected from noise. To prevent static discharge damage, a series resistor should be placed inline with an input pin. It is also a good idea to include an inline filter with the input. This is easily accomplished by passing the input lead through a ferrite bead, which acts as a filter for high-frequency switching transients. You might think that it would be difficult to include these beads. The ferrite "beads" are available in a wide variety of configurations including filters that may be clamped on to an existing ribbon cable or even a single line. There are also ferrite filters available for printed circuit board (PCB) mounting.

i. *Printed circuit board layout techniques:* Since your finished product will most likely be manufactured on a multilayer PCB, it is important to understand how to lay out a PCB to minimize noise effects. If a multilayer PCB is used, the outermost opposite layers should consist of power and ground. The signal lines are routed in the layers between the power and ground layers. The signal lines on adjacent layers should be routed perpendicular to one another. Unused space on a PCB should be occupied by ground planes. In addition to these techniques, clock-associated circuitry should be grouped closely together. Also, abrupt changes (90 degree angles) in PCB traces should be avoided. Instead, gentler changes in direction should be employed. Similarly, PCB stubs—short runs branching off of the main PCB run—should be avoided. As we mentioned earlier, all circuits—digital, analog, etc.—should be separated from one another. Also, signal traces should be spaced as far as possible to prevent coupling between parallel runs.

6.4 DEFENSIVE PROGRAMMING

In the previous section we discussed "tried and true" hardware design techniques to minimize noise effects. In this section we investigate effective software techniques to mitigate noise susceptibility. This information was adapted from Motorola application notes. Full citations are provided in the Further Reading section at the end of this chapter.

- *Refreshing port pins:* In many applications the microcontroller system is used to take in external inputs and then generate appropriate output responses. It is good practice to periodically update the data direction registers and the port outputs associated with these ports.
- *Polling:* In this technique an input pin is polled for some period of time to ensure that a valid input rather than a spurious noise event has occurred. Earlier we discussed switch debouncing techniques. Recall that one of the techniques was to monitor a specific switch input and ensure it did not change within a prescribed amount of time.
- *Token passing:* This technique ensures that key pieces of an algorithm have been executed in the correct order. This is accomplished by setting aside a memory location as a token collection site. As an algorithm is executed, tokens are placed in the collection site in numerical order. Upon entering a new section of software, the token collection site is examined to ensure that the preceding portions of software have already been executed in the correct order. If the correct tokens are not in place, the software has reached the new area incorrectly. For example, let's say you have eight functions that are called in sequential order. When the first function is called, a token is placed in the first token location. When the second function is called, the first token location is checked to ensure a token is properly in place. If it is, a second token is now placed to indicate that the second function has been initiated. This procedure is followed for each subsequent function.
- *Unused Memory:* The B32 is equipped with 32 Kbytes of flash EEPROM memory to store programs. It would be quite coincidental to write programs that are always exactly 32 Kbytes in length. What is an effective method to use the unused memory space? A good software design technique is to place multiple Software Interrupt (SWI) instructions in the

remaining space. Therefore, if the processor should incorrectly end up in this space, a software interrupt is generated. This provides for fault recovery.

- *Computer operating correctly (COP) watchdog timer:* When an embedded-based system is fielded, it is essential that it continues to operate correctly. In the event of an error, the processor should have the capability to recover. The COP watchdog timer is one method that allows a processor to recover from being "stuck." This timer must be continually reset during normal program execution. If the COP watchdog timer expires, a COP reset is generated. To reset the timer on a regular basis, the arm/reset COP timer register (COPRST) must sequentially be sent a $55 followed by an $AA. Intervening instructions may be sent between the commands for 68HC12 controllers; however, they must be sent close enough together to prevent the COP watchdog timeout during normal program execution. Multiple reset sequences of $55 and $AA pairs may be strategically placed throughout key portions of a program. Should the program incorrectly get "stuck," the COPRST will not receive its required reset sequence of $55 and $AA. Hence, the controller experiences a COP reset. The reset might then clear the fault that originally caused the "stuck" condition.

6.5 NOISE-TESTING TECHNIQUES

Even if you conscientiously follow the techniques described in the previous sections, there is no guarantee that your design would not be susceptible to noise or would not radiate noise. Prior to sending a design into full-scale testing and production, it would be helpful to test its noise characteristics using some low-cost tests. In the next two sections we discuss some low-cost techniques to test a microcontroller system for noise emission and noise susceptibility. These techniques are from Gerry O. (he wishes to remain anonymous), who has worked as an electronics designer for over 35 years and is now the president and head designer for an international electronics design and fabrication firm.

6.5.1 Detecting Noise

To determine if a prototype embedded control system is emanating noise, the following technique may be used: "I (Gerry O.) usually tune to Channel 2 on a television (with no cable connection) to see if there is radiated radio frequency interference (RFI). I also tune across the AM band on an AM radio. AM radio is usually the best test for "hash" that is radiated via power circuits. The TV is best for high frequency radiation. Note that the sound on the TV is usually not affected, as that is FM, but the video is AM. So, look for noise in the picture. I read somewhere that if there is a tornado nearby, Channel 2 will pick this up by going blank due to overloading the automatic gain control (AGC) circuit. Some computer programs will also cause Channel 2 to have noise hash if the TV is too close to the computer."

6.5.2 Testing for Noise Susceptibility

A low-cost method for testing a microcontroller system for noise susceptibility is to use a high-power videotape bulk eraser as shown in Figure 6.6. The purpose of the test is to see if a strong alternating magnetic field could induce signals into the microprocessor or surrounding circuitry. The induced signals could lead to undesired operation. Although this is no way to duplicate lightning or electromagnetic pulse events, it is a good quick test for susceptibility. Gerry indicated that several years ago there was a lightning "blast" right outside his office window. His computer was turned off yet several files were erased from his computer. It also destroyed the LPT1 printer driver circuit on the PC's motherboard.

Dr. Jerry Hamann (University of Wyoming) indicated another method of testing for noise susceptibility. He suggests moving your hand over a completed circuit. As you know, your body is an infamous source of static electricity. As your hand is brought in close proximity to the circuit, circuit operation should remain stable.

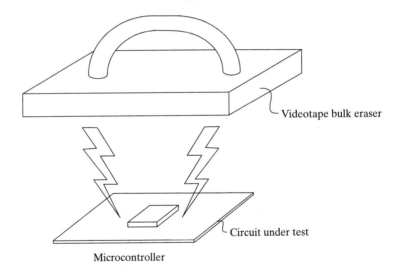

Videotape bulk eraser

Circuit under test

Microcontroller

Figure 6.6   A low-cost method for detecting the noise susceptibility in a circuit. The videotape bulk eraser provides a low cost source for strong alternating magnetic fields to test microprocessor susceptibility to interference.

If there are changes in circuit operation when your hand is moved about the circuit, you should investigate the circuit for improperly terminated inputs.

Again, these tests are not considered a complete noise test battery. However, they do provide a quick check on the noise characteristics of prototype circuits.

6.5.3 Noise Testing

Prior to manufacturing, a completed embedded controller based product must be tested for EMC. Regulations and guidelines governing these tests are provided by the Federal Communications Commission (FCC) in the United States and in the European Economic Community (EEC). Furthermore, the Food and Drug Administration (FDA) provides standards for medical devices. Our intent here is not to provide the details of these tests. Quite frankly, the regulations are constantly evolving, and any information provided here would be quickly out of date. Instead, we provide an overview of the regulations with pointers in the Further Reading section to obtain the most up-to-date information.

The FCC Rules and Regulations Part 15 Radio Frequency Devices provides regulations and guidelines governing radio (RF) devices capable of emitting RF energy in the range of 9 kHz to 200 GHz. FCC Part 15 currently has three procedures for showing EMC conformance:

- *Verification:* The product manufacturer files an EMC compliance report.
- *Certification:* The FCC reviews the EMC application.
- *Declaration of conformity:* A laboratory certified by the National Institute of Standards and Technology (NIST) performs designated testing. For example, Underwriters Laboratory (UL) performs EMC testing for a number of manufacturers.

International standards concerning EMC are primarily developed by the International Electrotechnical Commission (IEC). The standards provided by the IEC can be categorized into the following groups:

- Electrostatic discharge (publication IEC 61000-4-2)
- Radiated, radio frequency electromagnetic fields (publication IEC 61000-4-3)
- Electrical fast transients/burst (EFT) (publication: IEC 61000-4-4)
- Surges (publication IEC IEC 61000-4-5)
- Immunity to conducted disturbances (publication IEC 61000-4-6)
- Immunity to magnetic fields (publication IEC 61000-4-9)
- Voltage dips, short interruptions, and voltage variations (publication IEC 61000-4-11)

That completes our investigation of noise. The most important lesson to take away from our discussion is that EMC considerations must be part of the product requirements and specifications from the beginning of the product design cycle.

In the next section we investigate how to manage power in an embedded system.

6.6 POWER MANAGEMENT

Often microcontroller-based systems are portable or remote units. Providing a suitable voltage source for the system becomes a major issue—an issue that can be a double-edged sword. On one edge, a suitable power system must be designed to supply the proper voltage and current requirements for the system for a reasonable amount of time. On the other edge, the designer needs to employ measures to reduce the power consumption of the embedded controller system. Furthermore, the system should have protection against a low-voltage supply condition. All of these design considerations are covered in this section. We limit our discussion to battery-operated systems.

6.6.1 68HC12 Power Consumption Parameters

To design a power system for an embedded controller system, there are several design parameters that must be determined:

- The supply voltages required by the embedded controller, its peripherals, and all system components
- The current drain of each component in the system
- The expected operational system life between battery replacement or recharge
- The temperature of the operating environment

Once these parameters are determined, the design of a suitable battery supply can commence. These values may be determined by carefully examining the technical data for each component in the system. In all calculations, a worst-case scenario should be employed—in other words, the most extreme conditions of current drain and operating temperature.

6.6.2 Battery Types

Once the parameters of the system have been determined, battery selection may begin. Figures 6.7 and 6.8 both present a brief summary of common battery types. We have only provided parameters for common battery configurations. Note that there is a plethora of battery types, voltages, and capacities. A thorough review of an electronic supply catalog is highly recommended. This provides a good education on the variety of batteries. Let's first summarize the characteristics of the four main battery types:

- *Alkaline:* Alkaline batteries are a relatively low-cost, high-capacity variety available in many standard sizes. The battery's terminal voltage gracefully degrades when discharged; its capacity increases when warmed and significantly decreases at low temperatures. Most alkaline batteries cannot be recharged but some manufacturers provide a rechargeable variant of the alkaline battery.

- *Nickel-cadmium:* Nickel-cadmium batteries may be recharged. However, their terminal voltage when fully charged is lower than a similarly sized alkaline cell. Also note that the capacity of this battery type is significantly less than the alkaline type battery. The discharge profile is flatter than the alkaline battery, as shown in Figure 6.8.

- *Nickel-metal hydride:* Nickel-metal hydride (Ni-MH) batteries may be recharged. This type of battery provides moderate capacity at a moderate cost.

- *Lithium:* The lithium battery has a 3.6 V terminal voltage and a correspondingly high capacity. This battery type also exhibits a fairly flat voltage discharge profile. These features come at a relatively high cost when compared with the other battery types.

6.6.3 Battery Capacity

What exactly is battery capacity? Note that the unit for capacity is milliamphour (mA-hr). This unit tells the entire story. If the current drain of the battery is known, its operating life may be calculated. For example, if a 9 V, 500 mA-h

Type	Nonrechargeable Alkaline		Rechargeable Nickel-Cadmium		Rechargeable Nickel-Metal Hydride		Nonrechargeable Lithium	
Size	Voltage	Capacity	Voltage	Capacity	Voltage	Capacity	Voltage	Capacity
D	1.5 V	15,000 mA-hr	1.2 V	1,200 mA-hr	1.2 V	8,000 mA-hr	3.6 V	16,500 mA-hr
C	1.5 V	7,000 mA-hr	1.2 V	1,200 mA-hr	1.2 V	4,500 mA-hr	3.6 V	7,200 mA-hr
AA	1.5 V	2,250 mA-hr	1.2 V	500 mA-hr	1.2 V	2,250 mA-hr	3.6 V	2,100 mA-hr
AAA	1.5 V	1,000 mA-hr	1.2 V	180 mA-hr	1.2 V	600 mA-hr	—	—
N	1.5 V	650 mA-hr	1.2 V	150 mA-hr	1.2 V	—	---	---
9 V transistor	9.0 V	550 mA-hr	—	—	9.0 V	170 mA-hr	---	---
6 V lantern	6.0 V	11,000 mA-hr	---	---	—	---	---	---

Figure 6.7   Capacity characteristics for different battery types.

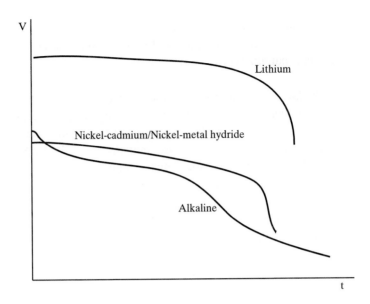

Figure 6.8 Battery discharge characteristics. These are generic battery discharge profiles. Detailed battery profiles with current drain and temperature dependent characteristics are provided in the manufacturers' literature.

transistor battery is used to power a circuit that has a 5 mA current drain, the circuit should operate for approximately 100 hours. However, the capacity value degrades for high current drains and low operating temperatures.

6.6.4 Voltage Regulation

Recall that the supply voltage (V_{DD}) for the 68HC12 has a fairly tight tolerance. The electrical specifications for the controller indicate the supply voltage should be maintained at 5 VDC ±10%. To maintain this relatively constant voltage under varying conditions, a regulator circuit is used to condition the input voltage. A typical regulator circuit is the front end of the microprocessor supervisory circuit shown in Figure 6.9.

The regulator circuit consists of the regulator component equipped with noise suppression capacitors at its input and output terminals. Regulator devices are usually a three-terminal device—input (I), output (O), and common (C). These regulator devices are specified by their output voltage and current rating. It is a good engineering practice to choose a regulator with at least twice the current rating as the maximum anticipated current load. A common regulator line is the 78XX series. The XX indicates its rated output voltage value. For

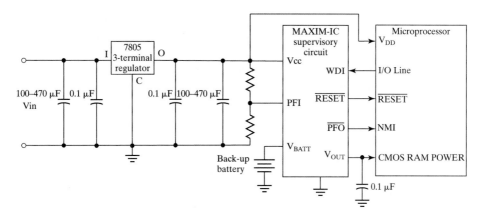

Figure 6.9   Microprocessor supervisory circuit.

example, in Figure 6.9 we have used a 7805 (+5 VDC) regulator. The 7805 regulator comes in a wide variety of current ratings. The 79XX regulator series are negative voltage regulators.

The regulator's input and output are equipped with noise suppression capacitors. A 0.1 μF decoupling capacitor is used at the input and output to suppress high frequency noise. Bypass capacitors in the range of 100 to 470 μF are also included to reduce output ripple.

The input for the regulator circuit could be provided by a DC power supply or a suitable battery configuration. Whichever source is chosen, the input voltage to the regulator must usually be at least 3 V greater than the regulator's specified output voltage.

In the event of a power failure or burned-out battery, a back-up supply must be provided to the processor. This is easily implemented using a microprocessor supervisory circuit.

6.6.5 Microprocessor Supervisory Circuits

There is a wide variety of microprocessor supervisory circuits available from several manufacturers. We briefly review the functions of those provided by MAXIM manufacturing.

The microprocessor supervisory circuits provide the following functions:

* A reset output during power-up, power-down, and brownout conditions.
* Battery backup switching for CMOS RAM, CMOS microprocessor, or other low-power logic.
* A reset pulse if the optional watchdog timer has not been toggled within a specified time.

- A 1.3V threshold detector for power failure warning, low battery detection, or monitoring a power supply other than +5 VDC.

A sample circuit employing a supervisor circuit is shown in Figure 6.9. The supervisory circuit constantly compares the voltage at the V_{cc} input with the back-up battery voltage at V_{BATT}. It connects whichever voltage is greater to the V_{OUT} output pin. The comparison circuit has built in hysteresis to prevent rapidly switching back and forth between V_{cc} and V_{BATT} when they are close in value.

The supervisory circuit is also equipped with a watchdog timer. Recall that the 68HC12 has a computer operating properly (COP) watchdog system. The supervisory circuit's system is quite similar. The watchdog timer generates a reset if the watchdog input (WDI) is not reset by the microprocessor within the timeout period of the timer. Like the COP system of the 68HC12, the programmer (you) must strategically place commands in your program to regularly send out a signal to the WDI. Should your program get "stuck," the WDI will not receive its periodic reset, and a reset signal will be issued by the supervisory circuit on the RESET line.

6.6.6 Power Conservation Measures

The system designer can employ several techniques to reduce the power consumption of an embedded control system:

- *Operating frequency:* The embedded controller should be operated at the lowest frequency possible for the specific application. The CMOS configuration consumes power when switching from one logic level to another. Therefore, at lower operating frequencies, fewer transitions take place and hence reduce power consumption.
- *STOP and WAIT Instructions:* The 68HC12 instruction set contains both the STOP and WAIT instructions, Both instructions put the 68HC12 in an inactive state that reduces power consumption. For example, when the B32 is operating at 8 MHz, it normally draws 45 mA of current in the single chip mode. In the WAIT mode, current draw is reduced to 5 mA and to 10 µA in the STOP mode. Both instructions cause the 68HC12 to place a return address on the stack and also the contents of the CPU registers. The STOP instruction halts all system clocks while the WAIT instruction allows the system clocks to continue to operate. Both instructions require either an interrupt or reset event to occur to resume normal system operation. Note that in many applications the 68HC12 is placed in an interrupt driven mode. That is, the processor is initialized and then it waits for interrupt events to occur.
- *Subsystem activation:* Several subsystems aboard the 68HC12 have "on/off" switches. For example, the timer subsystem has the timer enable

(TEN) bit in the timer system control register (TSCR). Also, the analog-to-digital (ATD) converter subsystem has the ATD power up (ADPU) bit in ATD Control Register 2 (ATDCTL2). This allows the systems to be powered up when needed and powered down to conserve power when not in use.

6.7 SUMMARY

We have discussed CMOS considerations, external and internal sources of noise in a circuit, methods to minimize noise, noise testing techniques, and current noise guidelines. We also discussed power considerations for an embedded system including battery types, capacity, power supervisory circuits, and conservation measures. Although these issues come from a wide variety of sources, they all have a common thread—they may prevent a good solid paper design from operating correctly in the "real world."

6.8 FURTHER READING

Atmel, Inc. "EMC Design Considerations." Application Note AVR040. 2004.

Atmel, Inc. "External Brown-out Protection." Application Note AVR180. 2002.

Barrett, S. F. "Heart Arrhythmia Simulator." Senior Design Project presented at the annual Nebraska Academy of Science, Lincoln, NE, 1979.

Campbell, D. "Designing for Electromagnetic Compatibility with Single-Chip Microcontrollers." Application Note AN1263/D. Motorola, Inc., 1995.

Catherwood, M. "Designing for Electromagnetic Compatibility." Application Note AN1050/D. Motorola, Inc., 2000.

Corp, M. Bruce. *ZZAAP! Taming ESD, RFI, and EMI.* Academic Press, 1990.

Federal Communication Commission. Rules and Regulations Part 15 Radio Frequency Devices. www.fcc.gov, 2004.

Glenewinkel, M. "System Design and Layout Techniques for Noise Reduction in MCU-Based Systems." Application Note AN1259/D. Motorola, Inc., 1995.

Horowitz, Paul, and Winfield Hill. *Art of Electronics*, 2nd ed. Cambridge, England: Cambridge University Press, 1989.

International Electrotechnical Commission. IEC 61000 Series Guidelines. www.iec.ch.

Johnson, Howard. *High-Speed Digital Design: A Handbook of Black Magic.* Upper Saddle River, NJ: Prentice Hall, 1993.

Kobeissi, I. "Noise Reduction Techniques for Microcontroller-Based Systems." Application Note AN1705/D. Motorola, Inc., 1999.

Lun, T. C. "Designing for Board Level Electromagnetic Compatibility." Application Note AN2321/D. Motorola, Inc., 2002.

Maxim Integrated Products, "MAXIM Microprocessor Supervisory Circuits." MAX 690-695. April 1995.

Motorola, Inc. "High-Speed CMOS Logic Data." 1989.

Welch, T. B. "Teaching Three Phase Power—A Low Voltage Approach." Paper presented at the ASEE Annual Conference, Milwaukee, WI, June 1997.

Welch, T. B., and J. N. Berry. "Teaching Three-Phase Electrical Power Using a Low-Voltage Power Supply." Paper presented at the ASEE Annual Conference, Seattle, WA, 1998.

6.9 PROBLEMS

Fundamental

1. Describe methods to properly handle CMOS devices.

2. What happens if CMOS devices are not handled properly?

3. What is switch "bouncing"? How are the effects of switch bounce minimized?

4. Describe methods to reduce power consumption in an embedded controller system.

5. Construct a selection chart of different types of batteries commonly available. Include selection factors such as type, physical size, capacity, and cost factors.

6. What is voltage regulation? Why is it important to employ voltage regulation techniques in an embedded controller system?

Advanced

1. Describe the difference between ESD, RFI, EMI, sags, and surges. Provide an example of each type.

2. Why is the clock time base for an embedded controller system a notorious source of noise? What techniques may be employed to control undesired emanations from the clock source?

3. Why is it important to terminate unused port inputs in an embedded controller system? How should these inputs be properly terminated?

4. Why is it important to terminate unused hardware interrupt inputs in an embedded controller system? How should these inputs be properly terminated?

5. Summarize defensive programming techniques.

Challenging

1. Design a 5 VDC power supply system for the 68HC12. The system should have a lithium battery back-up supply and also be equipped with a MAXIM microprocessor supervisory circuit. Provide a block diagram of the circuit and a detailed description of how the circuit operates.

2. Write a two-page point paper on design techniques to minimize noise susceptibility.

3. Research IEC 6100-4-2 through 6100-4-9 guidelines. Provide a brief description of each test.

7

Embedded Control Systems

Objectives: After reading this chapter, you should be able to

- Employ a structured systems approach to embedded controller system design.
- Generate a detailed project description.
- Determine a required 68HC12 system or systems to accomplish a specific application.
- Describe the structure of an embedded controller software system using a structure chart and an UML activity diagram.
- Implement the required C code for a specific application.

Picture a beautiful, heirloom quality, oak tool chest similar to the one shown in Figure 7.1. Each drawer in the chest is partitioned to hold valuable tools in a separate bin. Each of the felt-lined bins is carefully labeled with the tool's name. An instruction sheet for each tool is also kept within the tool's bin. In previous chapters we have developed good hardware, software, and systems development tools. These together provide a "chest" of tools to design, develop, and implement embedded control systems. In this chapter we demonstrate through multiple examples how

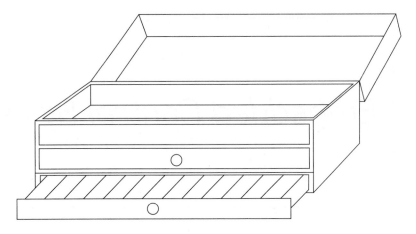

Figure 7.1 A tool chest partitioned to hold tools in separate bins.

to develop different systems. We have carefully chosen projects to demonstrate how many of the different systems aboard the 68HC12 and the HCS12, which may be employed to accomplish the tasks. Through multiple project examples, we demonstrate how these systems are used together. For each example, we provide a detailed project description, a list of the 68HC12 systems employed in the application, additional background theory where required, a detailed structure chart, an accompanying UML activity diagram, and well-documented code.

The following applications are presented in this chapter:

Wall-following mobile robot system

Laser light show

Digital voltmeter

Motor speed control with optical tachometer

Flying robot

Fuzzy-logic-based security system

Electronic sliding puzzle game

We also include the procedure to program the Flash EEPROM on the "B32" evaluation board at the end of the chapter.

7.1 WALL-FOLLOWING MOBILE ROBOT SYSTEM

7.1.1 Project Description

For this project, we have been asked to design an autonomous robot that navigates through an unknown maze. The robot must move through the maze, detect

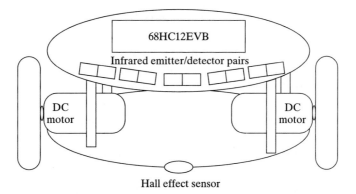

Figure 7.2   A diagram for a wall-following robot. The robot is equipped with two main wheels powered by DC motors. As the robot rolls forward, it constantly monitors for walls using IR emitter-detector pairs and land mines using a Hall effect sensor.

maze walls with infrared emitter-detector pairs, and make decisions to move forward or turn appropriately as the robot makes its way through the maze. As the robot moves through the maze, it should also avoid "land mines" (magnets) in the maze floor. The robot senses the land mines with a Hall effect sensor. If a magnet is sensed, the robot stops, backs up, and takes evasive actions to steer around the "land mine."

A diagram of the robot is provided in Figure 7.2. The robot's body consists of two lightweight aluminum platforms that have been connected together. The lower platform is equipped with two direct current (DC) motors that are used to drive the two large wheels mounted on either side of the robot's body. Using this two-wheel configuration, the robot may be steered like a tank. That is, in order to render a turn, equal but opposite (clockwise and counterclockwise) signals are issued to the motors. Two small caster wheels are used at either end of the robot's body to provide balance and stability. The robot rests in a tripod configuration. The top platform is equipped with five sets of infrared emitter and detector pairs to sense walls in front of and to either side of the robot. The top platform also contains the 68HC12 evaluation board (EVB), which is used to input signals, make decisions based on these inputs, and issue signals to control external events. The Hall effect sensor is mounted to the bottom plate of the robot body to detect magnet "land mines."

To navigate through an unknown maze, the robot is placed at the start coordinate located near an entrance door to the maze. The overall goal for the robot is to proceed through the maze while avoiding collisions with the maze walls and contact with land mines. The robot rolls forward by issuing identical signals simultaneously to each of its DC motors. As the robot rolls forward powered by its DC motors, it constantly monitors for walls and magnets using its five sets of IR emitter-detector pairs and the Hall effect sensor.

The maze walls are painted with a highly reflective white paint so that the signals emitting from the IR sources are reflected off of the walls back to the detectors. If the robot is within proximity to a wall, its presence is detected by the appropriate IR emitter-detector pair(s). For example, if the robot approaches a corner on its right side, it senses a wall in front of it with its front IR emitter-detector pair and a wall to its right with its right IR emitter-detector pair. The robot then responds to these inputs by turning left to avoid colliding with the walls. (See Figure 7.3.)

A natural reaction when given a new project such as this is to panic. However, if we employ a top-down design approach, we can subdivide the overall requirement into doable subsystems. We begin by constructing a list of required functions the robot's operating system would be required to execute in order to accomplish the overall mission of the robot:

- Analog-to-digital (ATD) conversion of the infrared sensor outputs.
- Comparison of the infrared (IR) sensor output to a wall-detection threshold.

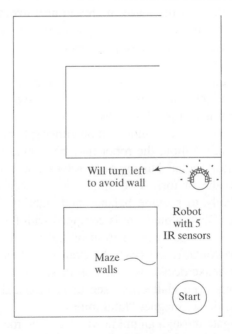

Figure 7.3 A wall-following robot designed to sense nearby walls. Using a complement of five infrared sensors, the robot is getting ready to make a left turn to avoid walls to its front and right.

- Robot turn algorithm to determine which direction the robot should turn in response to the infrared sensor pair outputs.
- Functions to turn the robot left or right, or to proceed forward.
- A mechanism to process the output from the Hall effect sensor.
- A function to stop, back up, and steer around a detected land mine.
- Liquid crystal display (LCD) related functions.

7.1.2 68HC12 Systems Employed

From the list of required functions, we can identify which 68HC12 systems we will use and which other tasks associated external devices will be needed.

- Infrared (IR) sensors and Hall effect sensors
- 68HC12 ATD system to perform conversions for the infrared sensors as well as the Hall effect sensor
- 68HC12 pulse width modulation (PWM) system
- LCD display interface and support functions
- 68HC12 interface to the IR sensors
- 68HC12 interface to the Hall effect sensor
- Motor drive interface
- Motor selection
- Rechargeable battery system to provide power for the motors, sensors, and the 68HC12B32 evaluation board

7.1.3 Background Theory

Let's first see what tools are available to accomplish the list of required functions. In previous chapters (our tool chest) we have investigated the following:

- 68HC12 ATD system
- 68HC12 PWM system
- LCD interface and support software
- Motor drive interface
- Battery operated systems

If you are not comfortable with these concepts, go back and review each of them at this time. We have not investigated IR emitter-detector pairs or Hall effect sensors yet. We now take a closer look at these two topics.

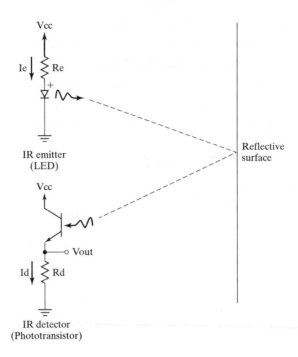

Figure 7.4   An infrared emitter-detector pair. The resistor (Re) limits
the IR emitter current to the rated value (Ie). The resistor Rd forms a
detectable voltage drop (Vout) with the detector current (Id).

Infrared Emitter-Detector Pairs   The infrared (IR) emitter-detector
pair consists of an infrared (above red) wavelength light-emitting diode (emitter)
circuit and an infrared sensitive phototransistor (detector) circuit, as shown in
Figure 7.4. The IR diode is biased using techniques previously described for an
LED. A phototransistor has a light sensitive base-emitter junction. When light of
the proper wavelength impinges on the junction, base current is generated. The load
resistor in the emitter leg of the transistor is chosen to provide a suitable output
voltage. Frequently a 10-turn trimmer potentiometer is used in place of a fixed
resistor to allow the sensitivity of each emitter to be adjusted separately. A range
to maze wall distance versus output voltage plot may be obtained experimentally.
The output from each IR emitter circuit is provided to a channel of the 68HC12's
ATD converter.

Hall Effect Sensors   As its name implies, a Hall effect sensor employs
the Hall effect principle to generate a voltage that is proportional to a detected
magnetic field. Two types of Hall effect–based sensors are available: (1) switches
and (2) linear sensors. A switching-style sensor detects the presence of a magnetic
field and latched to an "on" position. The sensor remains activated even when

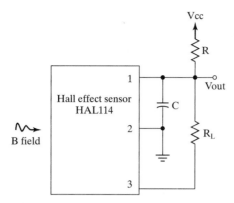

Figure 7.5   A Hall effect Micronas HAL114 sensor.

the magnetic field is no longer present. A linear style sensor provides an analog output voltage that is proportional to the applied magnetic flux. We employed the linear style sensor for the "land mine" detection application.

There are several manufacturers that provide Hall effect sensors. We chose to use a Micronas HAL114, a simple three-terminal sensor that is biased for proper operation with two resistors (R, R_L) and a capacitor, (C) as shown in Figure 7.5. As before, a range to output voltage characteristic plot may be determined experimentally. The output from the sensor is provided to a 68HC12 ATD converter channel. The overall interface diagram for the 68HC12 to the associated robot hardware is provided in Figure 7.6. With this overview of hardware complete, we'll review the software system for the robot.

7.1.4 Structure Chart and UML Activity Diagram

Tom Schei, a former undergraduate student at the University of Wyoming, developed the software operating system for this project. His code was developed using the ImageCraft ICC12 compiler. Before providing the code, let's review the structure chart and the UML activity diagram for the main program provided in Figure 7.7. We ask you to develop the UML activity diagram for each of the functions as a homework assignment (Advanced 1).

7.1.5 Code

```
/*******************************************************************/
/*filename: robot.c                                              */
/*Wall-Following Robot Operating System:  This is the operating */
/*system for the wall-following robot. The robot uses five      */
/*infrared emitter-detector sensor pairs to determine maze wall */
```

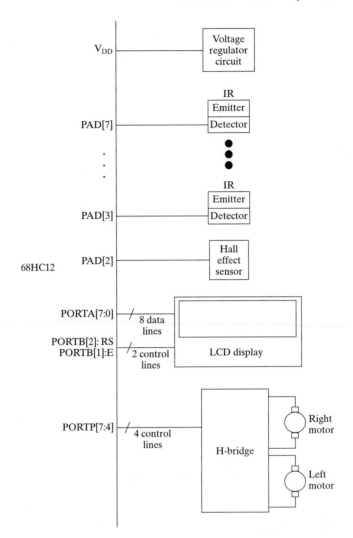

Figure 7.6   Interface between robot hardware and the 68HC12.

```
/*locations.  The robot determines wall locations based on in-  */
/*formation received from the sensors. If the infrared receiver */
/*exceeds a set threshold, a wall is in close proximity to the  */
/*robot. The wall is assumed to be directly in front of the in- */
/*frared emitter-detector pair.  Based on the returns from the  */
/*five sensors, the robot can determine which direction to turn */
/*to avoid maze walls.  A Hall effect sensor allows the robot to*/
/*detect magnets or "land mines" mounted in the maze floor. It  */
/*is also equipped with a liquid crystal display to output user */
/*information. The program uses the polling technique to read   */
/*results from the ATD system and output a pulse width modu-    */
```

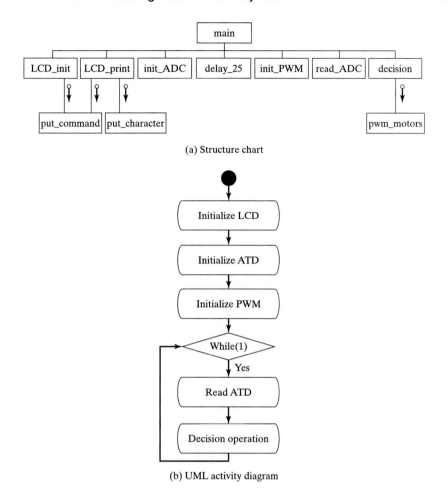

(a) Structure chart

(b) UML activity diagram

Figure 7.7   Software diagrams for a wall-following robot.

```
/*lated signal to drive the robot motor wheels.                  */
/*Author: Thomas Schei                                           */
/*Created: Oct 18, 2002                                          */
/*Last revised: Dec 4, 2002                                      */
/*************************************************************/

/*include files*/
#include <912b32.h>
#include <stdio.h>

/*label definitions - thresholds were determined experimentally */
#define opto_threshold 0x50      /*optical sensor threshold     */
#define hes_threshold 0x80       /*Hall Effect Sensor threshold */
#define forward 0
```

```
#define half_left 1
#define half_right 2
#define left_turn 3
#define right_turn 4
#define back_up 5

/*global variables*/
unsigned int i=0,j=0;                  /*16 bit loop delays        */
unsigned char sens[6]={0,0,0,0,0,0}; /*array for ATD conversion
                                                     results  */

/*function prototypes*/
void init_adc(void);         /*initialize ATD converter*/
void read_adc(void);         /*read ATD values          */
void decision(void);         /*render a turn decision based on ATD*/
void init_pwm(void);         /*initialize pulse width modulation  */
void pwm_motors(const char a); /*activate PWM system to render
                                                     action*/
void lcd_init(void);         /*initialize LCD                   */
int putchar(char c);         /*put ASCII character out to LCD    */
int putcommand(char c);      /*put command out to LCD           */
void delay_25(void);         /*2.5 second delay subroutine       */
void lcd_print(char *string); /*prints string to LCD display     */

void main()
{

asm(" .area vectors(abs)\n"/*code to initialize B32 reset vector*/
    " .org 0xFFF8\n"
    " .word 0x8000, 0x8000, 0x8000, 0x8000\n"
    " .text");

lcd_init();                  /*initialize LCD                   */
lcd_print("LCD initialized");
delay_25();                  /*delay 2.5s                       */
init_adc();                  /*initializes ATD converter system */
lcd_print("ADC initialized");
delay_25();                  /*delay 2.5s                       */
init_pwm();                  /*initialize pulse width modulation */
lcd_print("PWM initialized");
delay_25();                  /*delay 2.5s                       */

while(1)                     /*infinite loop                    */
  {
  read_adc();                /*obtain current value from ATD    */
  decision();                /*decide on required turn          */
  }
}/*end main*/
```

```
/*****************************************************************/
/*initialize_adc: initializes ATD 68HC12 system                 */
/*****************************************************************/

void init_adc()
{

ATDCTL2 = 0x80;              /*Set ADPU bit to power up ATD system */
ATDCTL3 = 0x00;              /*ignore ATD freeze features          */
ATDCTL4 = 0x7F;              /*P clock to 125 kHz samples,         */
                            /*conversion time: 32 ATD CLKs,       */
                            /*1 sample per every 256 us           */
for(i=0; i<67; i++)         /*wait 100 microseconds 8 MHz ECLK    */
 {
 ;
 }
}


/*****************************************************************/
/*read_adc: read results from ATD converter                     */
/*****************************************************************/

void read_adc()
{
ATDCTL5 = 0x50;             /*Set ATD 8 ch, multichannel conversion */

while((ATDSTAT & 0x8000)==0)     /*test SCF bit for conversion
                                                      complete */
  {
  ;
  }
                            /*store results to global array       */
  sens[0] = ADR7H;          /*far left sensor                     */
  sens[1] = ADR6H;          /*inner left sensor                   */
  sens[2] = ADR5H;          /*middle sensor                       */
  sens[3] = ADR4H;          /*inner right sensor                  */
  sens[4] = ADR3H;          /*far right sensor                    */
  sens[5] = ADR2H;          /*Hall Effect sensor                  */
}


/*****************************************************************/
/*decision(): turn decision based on information obtained from  */
/*five sensors. The Hall effect sensor threshold (hes_threshold)*/
/*and the optical threshold (opto_threshold) is determined      */
/*experimentally.                                               */
/*****************************************************************/

void decision()
```

```
{

if(sens[5] < hes_threshold){ /* detect Hall effect sensor, avoid*/
   pwm_motors(back_up);         /*'landmine' by having robot backup*/
                                /* after robot backed up determine */
                                /*next action                      */
  if(sens[0] > opto_threshold)
    pwm_motors(right_turn);
  else
    pwm_motors(left_turn);

  for(i=0; i<0xFFFF; i++){    /*delay for motor turn            */
   for(j=0; j<15; j++){
     ;
     }
   }

 }
                                /*if three walls detected - backup */
else if((sens[2]>opto_threshold)&&(sens[0]>opto_threshold)
                       &&(sens[4]>opto_threshold)){
  pwm_motors(back_up);}

                                /*if wall to left and in front,   */
                                /*turn the robot right            */
else if((sens[0]>opto_threshold)&&(sens[2]>opto_threshold)){
  pwm_motors(right_turn);}

                                /*if wall to right and in front,  */
                                /*turn the robot left             */
else if((sens[2]>opto_threshold)&&(sens[4]>opto_threshold)){
  pwm_motors(left_turn);}

                                /*if wall in front of half right  */
                                /*sensor then navigate half right */
else if(sens[1]>opto_threshold){
  pwm_motors(half_right);}

                                /*if wall in front of half left   */
                                /*sensor then navigate half left  */
else if(sens[3] > opto_threshold){
  pwm_motors(half_left);}

                                /*if nothing detected, then       */
                                /*default to forward motion       */
else{
  pwm_motors(forward);}

}
```

```
/******************************************************************/
/*init_pwm(): initializes 68HC12 pulse width modulation system  */
/******************************************************************/

void init_pwm()
{
PWTST = 0x00;              /*Sets PWM port for normal operation */
PWCTL = 0x00;              /*Set to left aligned signal         */
PWCLK = 0x3F;              /*no concatenation, ECLK/128         */
PWPOL = 0x0F;              /*set pins high then low transition  */
DDRP = 0xFF;               /*Port P set to output               */
PWEN = 0x0F;               /*forces output for PWM pins         */
PWPER0 = 250;              /*sets PWM signal period to 250 Hz   */
PWPER1 = 250;
PWPER2 = 250;
PWPER3 = 250;
PWDTY0 = 0;                /*init set PWM output for no motion  */
PWDTY1 = 0;
PWDTY2 = 0;
PWDTY3 = 0;
}


/******************************************************************/
/*pwm_motors: renders a turn based on specified action.         */
/******************************************************************/

void pwm_motors(const char a)
{
for(i=0;i<2000;i++)     /*3 ms delay to allow motors to respond */
 {
 ;
 }

switch(a){              /*render turn based on specified action */

  case 0: /*forward*/
          PWDTY0 = 200; /*PWM channel duty registers          */
          PWDTY1 = 250;
          PWDTY2 = 250;
          PWDTY3 = 200;
          lcd_print("Forward\n");
          break;

  case 1: /*half left turn */
          PWDTY0 = 0;   /*PWM channel duty registers          */
          PWDTY1 = 250;
          PWDTY2 = 250;
          PWDTY3 = 125;
```

```
            lcd_print("Half Left\n");
            break;

    case 2: /*half right turn*/
            PWDTY0 = 125;   /*PWM channel duty registers          */
            PWDTY1 = 250;
            PWDTY2 = 250;
            PWDTY3 = 0;
            lcd_print("Half Right\n");
            break;

    case 3: /*left turn*/
            PWDTY0 = 125;   /*PWM channel duty registers          */
            PWDTY1 = 250;
            PWDTY2 = 0;
            PWDTY3 = 125;
            lcd_print("Left Turn\n");
            break;

    case 4: /*right turn*/
            PWDTY0 = 125;   /*PWM channel duty registers          */
            PWDTY1 = 0;
            PWDTY2 = 250;
            PWDTY3 = 125;
            lcd_print("Right Turn\n");
            break;

    case 5: /*back up*/
            PWDTY0 = 125;   /*PWM channel duty registers          */
            PWDTY1 = 0;
            PWDTY2 = 0;
            PWDTY3 = 125;

            for(i=0; i<0xFFFF; i++)   /* 1.25 s delay for backup  */
              {
              for(j=0; j<15; j++)
                {
                ;
                }
              }
            lcd_print("Back Up\n");
            break;

    default:                    /*default to forward, reduced speed */
            PWDTY0 = 63;        /*PWM channel duty registers        */
            PWDTY1 = 250;
            PWDTY2 = 250;
            PWDTY3 = 63;
```

```
        lcd_print("Error\n");
        break;
   }
}


/*****************************************************************/
/*lcd_init(): initialization sequence for LCD - provided in    */
/*manufacturers data                                           */
/*PORTA: data port, PORTB[2:1]: LCD R/S line, enable line      */
/*****************************************************************/

void lcd_init()
{
DDRA=0xff;                      /*PORTA output                 */
DDRB=0x06;                      /*PORTB [2:1] output           */

                                /*command string to initialize LCD */
putcommand(0x38);
putcommand(0x38);
putcommand(0x38);
putcommand(0x38);
putcommand(0x0f);
putcommand(0x01);
putcommand(0x06);
putcommand(0x00);
                                /*clear display, cursor at home   */
putcommand(0x00);
}


/*****************************************************************/
/*putchar(char c): puts ASCII character out to LCD             */
/*****************************************************************/

int putchar(char c)
{

PORTA=c;
PORTB= PORTB|0x04;
PORTB= PORTB|0x02;
PORTB= PORTB&0xfd;
for (i=0; i<100; i++);  /*150 us delay to allow LCD to respond */

return c;
}


/*****************************************************************/
/*putcommand(char c): puts command out to LCD                  */
/*****************************************************************/
```

```c
int putcommand(char c)
{

PORTA= c;
PORTB= PORTB&0xfb;
PORTB= PORTB|0x02;
PORTB= PORTB&0xfd;
for (i=0; i<100; i++);   /* 150 us delay to allow LCD to respond*/

return c;
}

/*****************************************************************/
/*delay_25(): provides 2.5 second delay                         */
/*****************************************************************/

void delay_25()
{

for(i=0; i<0xFFFF; i++)
  {
  for(j=0; j<30; j++)
    {
    ;
    }
  }
}

/*****************************************************************/
/*lcd_print(): prints character string argument to LCD until    */
/*null character.                                               */
/*****************************************************************/

void lcd_print(char *string)
{
putcommand(0x02);               /*put LCD cursor on first line   */

while (* (string) != '\0')
  {
   putchar(*string);
   string++;
   }
}
/*****************************************************************/
/*****************************************************************/
```

7.2 LASER LIGHT SHOW

In this section, we design and implement an embedded control system for a laser light show. You have probably seen such a system used at a concert or a planetarium. The same concepts can be used for precision laser pointing for medical applications and industrial techniques such as those used to control a laser for precision engraving.

7.2.1 Project Description

The system has seven precoded patterns that are traced by a laser onto a wall or a projection screen. We choose one of the precoded patterns for tracing by selecting its corresponding push button. Once a pattern is selected, a corresponding LED illuminates to indicate the pattern selected. The control system then opens the laser shutter to allow the laser light to pass through to a pair of galvanometer-steered mirrors. The 68HC12 generates the control signals to steer the mirrors to the appropriate locations to trace the selected pre-stored pattern via peripheral digital-to-analog converters (DACs). The selected pattern is traced once. A diagram of the system is provided in Figure 7.8.

7.2.2 68HC12 Systems Employed

Based on the brief project description provided, we can identify the 68HC12 and external systems that will be used:

- A debounced eight-switch input bank connected to an input configured 68HC12 port
- An eight-position LED display connected to an output configured 68HC12 port
- A two-channel DAC connected to the 68HC12's serial peripheral interface (SPI) or two 68HC12 output configured ports
- A laser source
- A shutter and shutter controller
- Two galvanometer steered mirrors

7.2.3 Background Theory

As before, we consider the available tools in our tool chest and see what is available to accomplish the list of required functions. In previous chapters (our

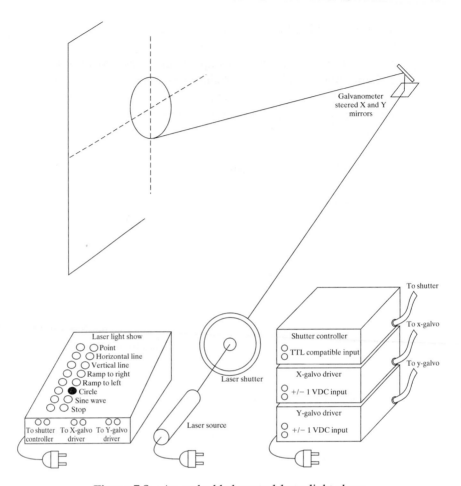

Figure 7.8 An embedded control laser light show.

tool chest), we have investigated the following:

- Debounced switch techniques
- An eight LED tristate indicator
- DAC converters

We have not investigated lasers, laser mirrors, laser shutters, and galvanometer-steered mirrors. We now take a closer look at these topics. We also take a closer look at DAC technology.

    Digital-to-Analog Converters   In Chapter 6 we discussed the theory behind digital-to-analog converters (DACs). Since the 68HC12 is not equipped with a DAC, what are we to do? In this application we actually need two separate

DAC channels to generate the control signals for the X and Y channel galvanometers. There are a wide variety of single-chip DACs that can be connected to the 68HC12 for this application. They fall into two categories: serial input and parallel input DACs. Serial input DACs are normally interfaced with the serial peripheral interface (SPI) system of the 68HC12. The interested reader is referred to Pack and Barrett [2002, ch. 10] for details on this type of interface. In this example, we use two 8-bit parallel input DACs. There is a wide variety of these types of DACs. In this project we use a Motorola MC1408P8 (a.k.a. National DAC0808LCN). A typical DAC circuit for the MC1408P8 is provided in Figure 7.9. The DAC output voltage is determined by V_{ref}, R14, Ro, and the values of A1 through A8. The values of the first three variables are fixed while the values of A1 through A8 are either a logic high or low provided by the 68HC12. This particular DAC is directly compatible with the 68HC12 without additional circuitry.

If we desire the output voltage to be ± 1 V, we could choose the following values for each variable:

- $V_{ref} = 5.0$ VDC
- $R14 = R15 = 1$ kΩ

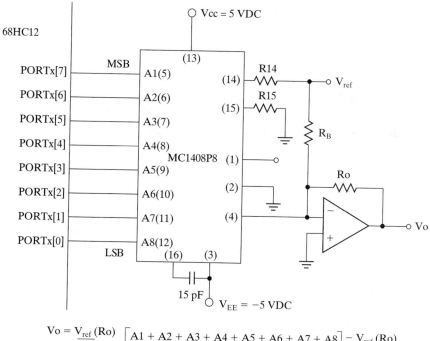

$$Vo = \frac{V_{ref}(Ro)}{R14}\left[\frac{A1}{2} + \frac{A2}{4} + \frac{A3}{8} + \frac{A4}{16} + \frac{A5}{32} + \frac{A6}{64} + \frac{A7}{128} + \frac{A8}{256}\right] - \frac{V_{ref}(Ro)}{R_B}$$

Figure 7.9   A typical DAC circuit for the MC1408P8.

- Ro = (2/5) R14 = 400Ω
- R_B = 2 (R14) = 2 kΩ

These values were obtained by solving the output voltage equation provided in Figure 7.9 for two different cases: (1) when the output voltage is +1 V, and (2) when the output voltage is 0 V. The reference voltage V_{ref} is conveniently chosen to be 5 V. These component values yield an output voltage of −1.0 VDC for a binary input of $00 and an output voltage of 0.992 VDC for a binary input of $FF. Binary values between these two extremes would provide a corresponding linearly related analog output.

Lasers   The laser (a word derived from the acronym for light amplification by stimulated emission of radiation) is a light source with several special properties and characteristics. It is said to be monochromatic (a single wavelength or a small group of wavelengths), coherent (wave fronts in phase with one another), and nondivergent. What does all of this mean? Basically, a laser provides a single color light source in a small, pencil-like beam. Since its inception, the laser has found applications in virtually every area of industry and medicine [Vij and Mahesh, 2002]. The interested reader is referred to the Further Reading section of this chapter for additional information on this fascinating topic. For this application, we use a low-power (less than 3 mW) laser in a visible wavelength. Lasers of this type are available in several different technologies. The helium-neon (HeNe) laser is readily available in several different colors. However, these laser tubes are typically 25 cm in length and 5 cm in diameter. A newer technology is the diode pumped solid state (DPSS) laser, a low-power laser available in several visible wavelengths. Measuring approximately 5 cm in length and 1.5 cm in diameter, they are powered from a small AC adapter [Edmund Industrial Optics, 2004]. We use this style of laser for this application. These lasers are simple to operate. You plug them in and a beam of light is immediately available.

Laser Safety   ANSI standard Z136.1, entitled "Safe Use of Lasers," governs the safe handling of laser-based products. If you plan to implement this experiment, we encourage you to obtain a copy of this document and review it thoroughly. It divides lasers into different categories (Class 1 to 4) based on their inherent danger to the user and those in proximity to the laser. The higher the class number, the greater the danger. The laser we are using in this application is designated as a Class 3a. That is, it has a visible wavelength with an output power of 1-5 mW. This is the same class of laser as a laser pointer. Although this is considered a relatively low power, the laser should be handled and operated with extreme care and respect. Also, you should exercise extreme caution when aligning the optics associated with the laser system to prevent an inadvertent eye exposure to the laser source. Under no circumstances should you look directly into the laser source. The ANSI standard also provides other safety requirements for using this class of laser, including the posting of warning signs, protective laser housing, education and training on the safe use of lasers, and limiting access to the laser.

Mirrors   Optical mirrors are available in a wide variety of shapes, sizes, thickness, and wavelength compatibility. For this application, we require a front (or first) surface mirror. This means the mirror has its reflective coating on the first glass surface. This prevents multiple reflections from occurring between the front and rear surface of the mirror. Aside from being on the first surface, the reflective coating should have the proper wavelength characteristics. That is, it should properly reflect the wavelength of interest. For this application, we use a laser in the visible wavelengths (400–700 nm). A wide range of mirrors are available from a wide variety of manufacturers and suppliers [Edmund Industrial Optics, 2004]. The optical mirrors are mounted to the galvanometer rotors by a low mass mirror holder.

Laser Shutters   A laser shutter is simply an aperture for the laser to pass through. The shutter is normally in a closed position with shutter blades covering the laser aperture. The shutter blades are coated with a heat resistant coating to withstand high laser energy. The shutter is controlled by a laser shutter driver. The driver takes a transistor-transistor logic (TTL) compatible logic input and generates a shutter compatible signal. The shutter opens with a logic "1" and closes with a logic "0." Shutters and shutter drivers are available from several different manufacturers. They are available in a wide variety of aperture diameters, from 2 to 45 mm [Vincent Associates, 2004].

Galvanometers   Galvanometers, also known as optical scanners, are an effective method of redirecting a laser beam. Galvanometers provide a precise angular rotation for a given direct current voltage (VDC) input. Ideally, there is a linear relationship between the input voltage and the output angular rotation. One galvanometer specification is the maximum and minimum angular rotation. Galvanometers are readily available [GSI Lumonics, 2004] to scan angles up to ±30 degrees.

Galvanometers are driven by external driver amplifiers. Typically, such amplifiers are solid-state variable output impedance amplifiers. These amplifiers accept a DC voltage input in the range of ±1.0 V and provide a compatible galvanometer drive current proportional to the input voltage. Typically, zero-offset and gain controls are provided to the user on the driver amplifier.

Manufacturer configured X-Y scanning systems are available. These systems use two mirrors and two galvanometers separately driven to provide an

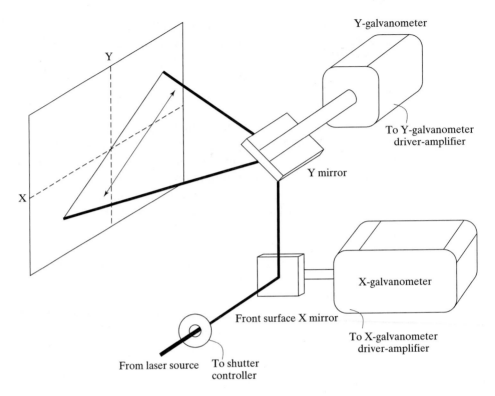

Figure 7.10   X-Y scanning system.

optical scan in an X-Y plane. The mirrors are placed orthogonally. The laser beam follows the path to the target, as illustrated in Figure 7.10. Drive signals are separately provided to the X and Y scanner drivers to position the laser at any point in the X-Y plane. Different patterns may be created by sequentially drawing a series of points.

7.2.4 Hardware Interface

The external hardware interface with the 68HC12 is provided in Figure 7.11. This diagram may seem a bit overwhelming. However, since we are already familiar with each of the different subsystems, understanding the overall system becomes quite straightforward. The bank of eight, debounced momentary contact switches connected to PORTA of the 68HC12 is used to select which pattern to trace with the laser. When a pattern is selected, the corresponding LED on PORTB is also illuminated. For example, if we depress the switch connected to PORTA[4], a right ramp pattern is traced. This illuminates the LED connected to PORTB[4].

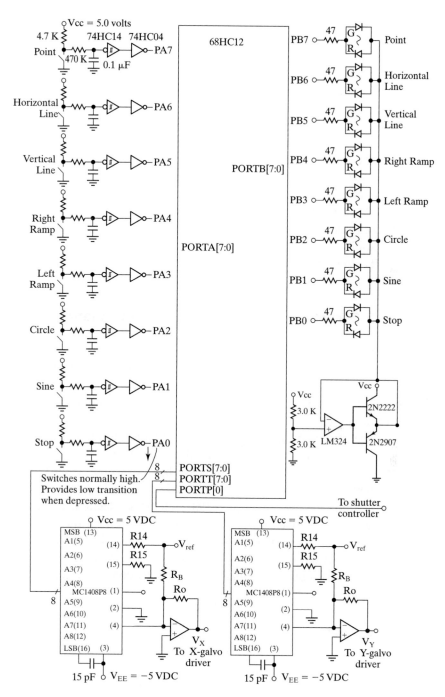

Figure 7.11   The external hardware interface for the 68HC12.

We are using the tristate LED indicator bank to indicate which pattern has been selected.

When a pattern is selected, the appropriate binary values to trace the pattern are issued on PORTS[7:0] for the X galvanometer and PORTT[7:0] for the Y galvanometer. These binary values are routed to the DAC for the X channel and the DAC for the Y-channel, respectively. The DAC converts each of the binary values into a corresponding analog signal to drive the galvanometers via the galvanometer driver-amplifiers.

The shutter control signal to open and close the shutter is provided on PORTP[0]. A logic "1" opens the shutter and a logic "0" closes the shutter. The shutter, like the galvanometers, requires a controller to convert the logic signal from the 68HC12 to a signal capable of opening and closing the shutter. The controller takes a TTL compatible input signal and converts it into a signal compatible to drive the shutter.

That completes our discussion of the hardware for the system. In the next section we discuss the system control software in detail.

7.2.5 Structure Chart and UML Activity Diagram

A UML activity diagram and a structure chart are provided for the system control software in Figure 7.12. Both diagrams are fairly self-explanatory. An interface diagram is provided to illustrate the conversion required between the binary code provided by the 68HC12 and the ±1 VDC signal required by the galvanometer driver amplifiers.

The system is first initialized by configuring the ports to their required setting (input or output) and closing the laser shutter. The software system then reads PORTA to determine if a switch has been depressed. If it has, a switch statement is used to determine the selected pattern. The code to generate a specific pattern is provided within each switch statement selection. To generate a pattern, the laser is first moved to its required starting position for a specific trace. The laser shutter is then opened and the proper trace is provided by sequentially plotting a laser dot over time. We provide a few representative examples and then we ask you to finish the remaining trace selections as a homework assignment (Challenging 3).

7.2.6 Code

```
//***********************************************************
//file name: laser.c
//function: program provides control of laser light show
//target controller: Motorola 68HC12B32 evaluation board (EVB)
//
```

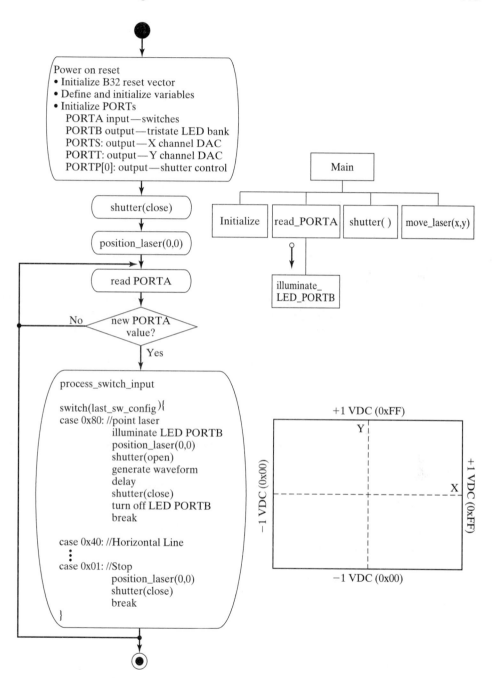

Figure 7.12   Laser control diagrams. UML activity diagram (left), structure chart (top right), hexadecimal value to voltage conversion interface diagram (bottom right).

```
//Motorola 68HC12B32 EVB Controller Pin Assignments
//Port A: Configured as digital inputs, active low debounced
//         switch connected to each pin
//Port B: Configured as digital outputs, 8-channel tristate LED
//         indicator
//Port S: Configured as digital outputs, provides binary code
//         to X ch DAC
//Port T: Configured as digital outputs, provides binary code
//         to Y ch DAC
//Port P[0]: Configured as digital output, provide TTL com-
//            patible shutter control signal.
//author: Steve Barrett and Daniel Pack
//created: Feb 20, 2003
//last revised: Mar 3, 2004
//***********************************************************

//include files*********************************************
#include<912b32.h>

//function prototypes***************************************
void initialize_ports(void);          //initializes ports
void shutter(int);                     //open/closes laser shutter
//positions laser
void position_laser(unsigned char, unsigned char);
void delay(void);

#define open 1
#define close 0

//main program**********************************************

//global variables
unsigned char new_PORTA, old_PORTA = 0xFF;
int i;
int go;

void main(void)
{
//initialize B32 reset vector
asm(" .area vectors(abs)\n"
    " .org 0xFFF8\n"
" .word 0x8000, 0x8000, 0x8000, 0x8000\n"
" .text");

go = 1;                                //enter the while loop
initialize_ports();                    //initialize ports
shutter(close);                        //close shutter
position_laser(0x80,0x80);             //center laser
```

```
while(go){                                      //process loop until Stop sw
                                                                 depressed
  new_PORTA = PORTA;                            //read PORTA input switches
  if(new_PORTA != old_PORTA){
    switch(new_PORTA){                          //PORTA asserted low
        case 0x7F:                              //PA7 Point Laser center
                    PORTB = 0x80;//illuminate LED on PORTB
                    position_laser(0x80,0x80);
                    shutter(open);
                    delay();
                    shutter(close);
                    PORTB=0x00;   //turn on red LEDs on tri-state
                                                               indicator
                    break;

        case 0xBF:                      //PA6 Horizontal Line
                    PORTB = 0x40;//illuminate LED on PORTB
                    position_laser(0x00,0x80);
                    shutter(open);
                    for(i=0; i<=255; i++)
                      {
                      i = (unsigned char)(i);
                      position_laser(i, 0x80);
                      delay();
                      }
                    shutter(close);
                    PORTB=0x00;   //turn on red LEDs on tri-state
                                                               indicator
                    break;

        case 0xDF:                      //PA5 Vertical Line
                    PORTB = 0x20;//illuminate LED on PORTB
                    position_laser(0x80,0x00);
                    shutter(open);
                    for(i=0; i<=255; i++)
                      {
                      i = (unsigned char)(i);
                      position_laser(0x80,i);
                      delay();
                      }
                    shutter(close);
                    PORTB=0x00;   //turn on red LEDs on tri-state
                                                               indicator
                    break;

        case 0xEF:                      //PA4 Right Ramp-45 degree
                                                        angle SW to NE
```

```
                    PORTB = 0x10;//illuminate LED on PORTB
                    position_laser(0x00,0x00);
                    shutter(open);
                    for(i=0; i<=255; i++)
                      {
                      i = (unsigned char)(i);
                      position_laser(i, i);
                      delay();
                      }
                    shutter(close);
                    PORTB=0x00;  //turn on red LEDs on tri-state
                                                     indicator
                    break;

   case 0xF7:                     //PA3 Left Ramp-45 degree angle
                                                        SE to NW
                    PORTB = 0x08;//illuminate LED on PORTB
                    delay();
                    PORTB=0x00;  //turn on red LEDs on tri-state
                                                     indicator
                    break;

   case 0xFB:                     //PA2 Circle
                    PORTB = 0x04;//illuminate LED on PORTB
                    delay();
                    PORTB=0x00;  //turn on red LEDs on tri-state
                                                     indicator
                    break;

   case 0xFD:                     //PA1 Sine
                    PORTB = 0x02;//illuminate LED on PORTB
                    delay();
                    PORTB=0x00;  //turn on red LEDs on tri-state
                                                     indicator
                    break;

   case 0xFE:                     //PA0 Stop
                    PORTB = 0x01;//illuminate LED on PORTB
                    position_laser(0x00,0x00);
                    shutter(close);
                    delay();
                    PORTB=0x00;  //turn on red LEDs on tri-state
                                                     indicator
                    go = 0;
                    break;

   case 0xFF:    break;
```

```
        default:                ;           //all other cases

        }//end switch(new_PORTA)
        old_PORTA = new_PORTA;
    }//end if(new_PORTA != old_PORTA)
  }//end while(go)
}//end main

//function definitions****************************************

//****************************************************************
//****************************************************************
//initialize_ports: provides initial configuration for I/O ports
//****************************************************************

void initialize_ports(void)
{
DDRA=0x00;              //set PORTA as input
DDRB=0xFF;              //set PORTB as output
PORTB=0x00;             //turn on red LEDs on tristate indicator
DDRS=0xFF;              //set PORTS as output
DDRT=0xFF;              //set PORTT as output
DDRP=0xFF;              //set PORTP as output
}


//****************************************************************
//****************************************************************
//shutter(int action):   opens and closes laser shutter
//****************************************************************

void shutter(int action)
{
if (action == open)
   PORTP = 0x01;
if (action == close)
   PORTP = 0x00;
}


//****************************************************************
//****************************************************************
//position_laser(unsigned char x_pos, unsigned char y_pos): sends
//control signals for X and Y channel galvanometer out of PORT S
//and T respectively.
//****************************************************************

void position_laser(char x_pos,char y_pos)
{
PORTS = x_pos;
```

```
PORTT = y_pos;
}


//*********************************************************************
//*********************************************************************
//delay(void): provides delay
//*********************************************************************

void delay(void)
{
int j;

for(j=0x0000;j<0x1000;j=j+0x01)
  {
  asm("nop");
  }
}


//*********************************************************************
//*********************************************************************
```

7.2.7 Testing

Prior to connecting the system components to the 68HC12, we should thoroughly test the circuit. In Chapter 5 we provided test circuits to simulate system inputs with switches and outputs with LEDs. Our project configuration already provides the switches and LEDs to do this. However, how do we test the analog signals? There are two methods readily available to test two-channel X and Y signals that are related to one another: (1) use an X-Y pen plotter or (2) use a classic instrumentation technique called Lissajous patterns.

In the first technique, the analog X-channel galvanometer signal from the X-channel DAC is connected to the X-channel on an X-Y pen plotter. Similarly, the analog Y-channel galvanometer signal from the Y-channel DAC is connected to the Y-channel on an X-Y pen plotter. The shutter control signal can be connected to the plotter pen up/down control. The specifications of a specific plotter being used need to be checked to determine if an interface circuit is required between the TTL compatible shutter control signal from the 68HC12 and the pen up/down control. Once the connections are made between the 68HC12 and the plotter, each of the different patterns may be thoroughly tested.

The second testing technique employs Lissajous patterns, a classical method of testing X and Y related signals. To generate a Lissajous pattern, the X-channel galvanometer signal from the X-channel DAC is connected to the X-channel connection on an oscilloscope. Similarly, the analog Y-channel galvanometer signal from the Y-channel DAC is connected to the Y-channel on an oscilloscope.

Once the connections are made between the 68HC12 and the oscilloscope, each of the different patterns may be thoroughly tested. (Additional information on Lissajous patterns is found in Cooper [1970]).

7.2.8 Final Assembly

Once the software has been thoroughly tested, it can be connected to the laser control hardware. The actual hardware to provide a stable mounting platform for the laser, shutter, and galvanometers is not discussed here. The interested reader is referred to optical hardware manufacturers' literature for tutorial information on optical assembly [Newport Corporation, 2004; Edmund Industrial Optics, 2004; LINOS phototonics, 2004].

7.3 DIGITAL VOLTMETER

7.3.1 Project Description

For this project we need to develop a digital voltmeter (DVM) that can take an analog DC input from +10 VDC to −10 VDC. The voltage sensed is displayed on a liquid crystal display to one-hundredth of a volt.

   This is quite a feat since the 68HC12's analog-to-digital (ATD) converter system typically has a range of values from 0 to 5 VDC. External signal conditioning is required to sense a voltage input over a wider range. We employ transducer interface design techniques discussed earlier in the text (Section 5.9) to condition the ±10 VDC input signal to a 0 to 5 VDC range.

7.3.2 68HC12 Systems Employed

The following subsystems are required to complete the project described above.

- 68HC12 ATD system
- LCD display
- Transducer interface
- Algorithm to convert sensed voltage for ASCII display on the LCD

We review a few items prior to developing the software.

7.3.3 Background Theory—Transducer Interface Design Revisited

In Section 5.9 we described how to interface an analog input device with the 68HC12 using a transducer interface design method. We apply this material to

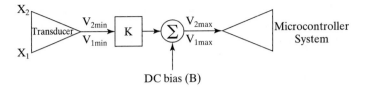

Figure 7.13   Transducer interface design.

developing an interface to scale the input voltage from ± 10 VDC to a 0 to 5 VDC range that is compatible with the 68HC12's ATD system.

A block diagram of a basic transducer interface design is provided in Figure 7.13. Ideally, we would like to send a voltage of 5 VDC to the microcontroller's ATD input when 10 VDC is applied to the input of the voltmeter. Similarly, we would like 0 VDC presented to the microcontroller's ATD input when -10 VDC is applied to the voltmeter input. To accomplish this conversion, voltages must be scaled and a DC offset bias voltage must be added. In our block diagram, we have designated the scaling operation with a K and the addition of the bias with a summation.

Recall, we can develop two equations with two unknowns to describe the operation of our transducer interface design, as shown in Figure 7.13. These equations are given as

$$V_{2max} = V_{2min} * K + B$$

and

$$V_{1max} = V_{1min} * K + B$$

By interpreting the DVM specifications, we can determine that V_{1min} is -10 VDC and V_{2min} is $+10$ VDC while V_{1max} is 0 V and V_{2max} is 5 V. These values can be substituted into our two equations:

$$5\ V = 10\ V * K + B$$

and

$$0\ V = -10\ V * K + B$$

Simultaneously solving these equations provides a scale factor (K) of 0.25 V/V and a DC offset bias (B) of 2.5 V. It is straightforward to implement an op amp circuit to scale the input voltage by a factor of 0.25 V/V and add an offset of 2.5 V. Once the input voltage is converted by the ATD system, we have to reverse the process to obtain the actual sensed input voltage for display. This is accomplished through the software.

7.3.4 Structure Chart and UML Activity Diagram

We have been providing a software structure chart and a UML activity diagram for each of the projects presented. We leave the DVM structure chart and UML activity diagram for this project as a homework assignment for you (Advanced 6).

7.3.5 Code

```c
/*****************************************************************/
/* filename: voltmeter2.c                                        */
/* This program will create a simple voltmeter using the onboard*/
/* analog to digital converter in the HC12.  It will perform one*/
/* conversion and then the user will have to manually restart   */
/* the program to convert another voltage.                      */
/*****************************************************************/

#include <912b32.h>
#include <stdio.h>

/*function prototypes*/
void delay_100us(void);
void ADC_convert(void);
void delay_5ms(void);


void main(void)
{

asm(" .area vectors(abs)\n"/*code to initialize B32 reset vector*/
    " .org 0xFFF8\n"
    " .word 0x8000, 0x8000, 0x8000, 0x8000\n"
    " .text");

initialize_LCD();               /*initialize liquid crystal display */
ATDCTL2 = 0x80;                 /*power up ADC, disable interrupts   */
delay_5ms();                    /*wait for ADC to warm up            */
ATDCTL3 = 0x00;                 /*select active background mode      */
ATDCTL4 = 0x01;                 /*8-bit result, sample time 2 ADC    */
                                /*clk, prescale 4                    */
ADC_convert();                  /*perform conv, convert value        */
}


/*****************************************************************/
/* void ADC_convert(void): function to perform a single con-    */
/* version and to store it for user access. The function then   */
/* converts the floating point result to an integer value such  */
```

```
/* that each individual integer may be isolated, converted to    */
/* ASCII and sent out to an LCD for display.                      */
/****************************************************************/

void ADC_convert()
{
unsigned int sumadr;
unsigned int avg_bin_voltage;
unsigned int int_voltage;
unsigned int tens_int;
unsigned int ones_int;
unsigned int tenths_int;
unsigned int hundreths_int;
double   voltage, abs_voltage;
char tens;
char ones;
char tenths;
char hundreths;

ATDCTL5 = 0x06;                      /*perform 4 conv, ch 6        */

while((ATDSTAT & 0x8000) != 0x8000)
  {                                  /*Wait for conversion to finish */
  ;
  }
                                     /*average four results        */
sumadr = ADR0H + ADR1H + ADR2H + ADR3H;
avg_bin_voltage = sumadr/4;

/*convert result to voltage between 0.00 and 5.00               */
voltage = (avg_bin_voltage/256)*5;

/*rescale voltage to -10.00 to +10.00                           */
/*reverse analog hardware interface process                     */
abs_voltage = (fabs)((voltage - 2.5) * 4);

/*convert result to all integer value between -1000 and +1000   */
int_voltage = (100*voltage);

/*isolate and convert most significant digit to ASCII           */
/*decimal value + 48 yields ASCII code                          */
tens_int = int_voltage/1000;
tens = (char)(tens_int + 48);

/*isolate and convert next most significant digit to ASCII      */
/*decimal value + 48 yields ASCII code                          */
ones_int = int_voltage/100;
ones = (char)(ones_int + 48);
```

```
/*isolate and convert next most significant digit to ASCII     */
/*decimal value + 48 yields ASCII code                         */
tenths_int = (int_voltage - ones_int*100)/10;
tenths = (char)(tenths_int + 48);

/*isolate and convert next most significant digit to ASCII     */
/*decimal value + 48 yields ASCII code                         */
hundreths_int = (int_voltage - ones_int*100 - tenths_int*10)/1;
hundreths = (char)(hundreths_int + 48);

/*print results to LCD                                         */
if (voltage < 0)
   putchars('-');                  /*provide negative sign     */
else
   putchars('+');                  /*provide positive sign     */

putchars(tens);
putchars(ones);
putchars('.');
putchars(tenths);
putchars(hundredths);
putchars(' ');
putchars('V');
}

/****************************************************************/
/*100 us delay based on an 8 MHz clock                         */
/****************************************************************/

void delay_100us(void)
{
int i;

for (i=0; i<50; i++)
   {
   asm("nop");
   }
}

/****************************************************************/
/*5 ms delay based on an 8 MHz clock                           */
/****************************************************************/

void delay_5ms(void)
{
int i;

for (i=0; i<50; i++)
```

```
 {
 delay_100us();
 }
}
/****************************************************************/
/*The initialize function sends the LCD the correct start-up    */
/*sequence.  The command sequence for initialization is provided*/
/*in the manufacturer's technical data for the display.         */
/****************************************************************/

void initialize_lcd(void)
{
delay_5ms();
delay_5ms();
delay_5ms();                        /*wait 15 ms for LCD to turn on  */

putcommands(0x38);                  /*sets interface                 */
delay_5ms();
putcommands(0x38);
delay_100us();
putcommands(0x38);
putcommands(0x38);
putcommands(0x0C);
putcommands(0x01);                  /*Display clear                  */
putcommands(0x06);                  /*Sets mode to increment by one  */
putcommands(0x0E);                  /*Turn on display, cursor, blink */
putcommands(0x02);                  /*Return home                    */
}


/****************************************************************/
/*The putchar function initializes the data port, the RS and    */
/*Enable and sends it to the correct port                       */
/****************************************************************/

void putchars(unsigned char c)
{
DDRP = 0xFF;                        /*set Port P to output           */
DDRDLC = DDRDLC|0x0C;               /*set PORTDLC[3:2] to output     */
PORTP = c;                          /*assign char C to data port     */
PORTDLC = PORTDLC|0x08;             /*set RS to 1 for DATA           */
PORTDLC = PORTDLC|0x04;             /*set E to 1 ( PORTDLC[5] = 1 )  */
PORTDLC = 0;                        /*set E and RS to 0              */
delay_5ms();                        /*wait 5 ms                      */
}


/****************************************************************/
/*The putcommand function sends the data in the data Port to     */
/*the LCD                                                        */
/****************************************************************/
```

```
void putcommands(unsigned char d)
{
DDRP = 0xFF;                        /*set PORTP to output           */
DDRDLC = DDRDLC|0x0C;               /*PORTDLC[3:2] to output        */
PORTDLC = PORTDLC & 0xF7;           /*RS = 0 for Command            */
PORTP = d;                          /*assign command to LCD         */
PORTDLC = PORTDLC|0x04;             /*E = 1                         */
PORTDLC = 0;                        /*E = 0                         */
delay_5ms();                        /*wait 5 ms                     */
}


/******************************************************************/
/*The lcd_print function sends a string to the LCD               */
/******************************************************************/

void lcd_print(char *string)
{
putcommands(0x02);                  /*put cursor on first line      */
                                    /*putcommand to select line     */
while(*(string) != '\0')
  {
  putchars(*string);
  string++;
  }
}



/******************************************************************/
/*5 ms delay based on an 8 MHz clock                            */
/******************************************************************/

void delay_5ms(void)
{
int i;

for(i=0; i<50; i++)
  {
  delay_100us();
  }
}

/******************************************************************/
/*100 us delay based on an 8 MHz clock                          */
/******************************************************************/

void delay_100us(void)
{
int i;
```

```
for(i=0; i<50; i++)
  {
  asm("nop");                    /*Assem lang nop takes one cycle */
  }
}
/***********************************************************/
```

7.3.6 Extending the DVM to a Generic Instrumentation System

Temperature Sensor. With a basic voltmeter operating, it is straight-forward to connect a transducer to the 68HC12 and measure some physical, external parameter. For example, we can connect a National Semiconductor LM34 Precision Fahrenheit Temperature Sensor to the 68HC12. This sensor has a linear +10 mV per degree Fahrenheit scale factor, and it has a −50 to +300 degree Fahrenheit range. The interface circuit for the LM34 is shown in Figure 7.14. The interface circuit consists of the LM34 sensor and a filtering network consisting of the 75Ω resistor and the capacitor. The interface circuit allows a direct conversion of the sensed temperature. For example, if a 70 degree temperature is sensed, the LM34 outputs 700 mV. This voltage is multiplied by 100 to provide a direct conversion from volts to Fahrenheit degrees for display. This value must then be converted to ASCII for display on the LCD.

Humidity/Moisture Sensor. Honeywell manufactures the HIH-3610 series of humidity/moisture sensors [Honeywell 2004]. These sensors are calibrated to a 5 VDC supply voltage. The sensors provide a linear DC voltage output from 0.8 VDC to 4.07 VDC for sensed relative humidity (%) from 0 to 100, respectively. These sensors may be connected directly to the 68HC12's ATD system without an interface.

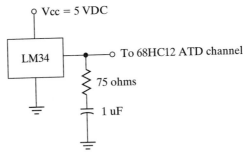

Figure 7.14 The interface for the National Semiconductor LM34 Precison Fahrenheit Temperature Sensor.

7.4 MOTOR SPEED CONTROL WITH OPTICAL TACHOMETER

7.4.1 Project Description

For this project, we need to stabilize a motor so that it operates at a constant speed. We use closed-loop control techniques to stabilize the motor. That is, we constantly monitor motor speed during motor operation and make adjustments to the motor supply voltage to speed up or slow down the motor. We also display motor speed in revolutions per minute (RPM) on an LCD display.

We have decided to use an Electro-Craft Corporation permanent magnet DC motor equipped with a Servo-tek optical encoder [Servo-Tek 2004]. This motor has the following specifications:

- Supply voltage: 12 VDC
- No load speed: 2,500 RPM at 12 VDC (determined experimentally)
- Start current: 2 A (determined experimentally)
- No load running current: 370 mA (determined experimentally)
- Moderate load current: 600 mA (determined experimentally)
- Stall current: 4 A (determined experimentally)
- Motor is equipped with a single channel optical encoder (Servo-Tek # PMBX-60-05). The encoder provides 60 TTL compatible pulses per motor revolution.

This brief project description raises several questions.

1. How will we monitor motor speed?
2. How can we easily vary the motor supply voltage to adjust motor speed?
3. The 68HC12 is a 5 volt system with minimal current drive capability. How can we drive a 12 VDC, high current load motor?
4. How can we monitor the motor speed and still accomplish other system related tasks?
5. What systems aboard the 68HC12 should be employed to accomplish this task?

As before, we first go to our "toolbox" to find out which tools we have already developed to accomplish the project requirements and which ones we might have to develop. Let's do this by considering each of the questions below. Please refer to Figure 7.15, a motor speed control interface diagram, as we discuss these questions.

1. How will we monitor motor speed? As previously mentioned, we equip the motor with an optical encoder that provides 60 pulses per motor revolution.

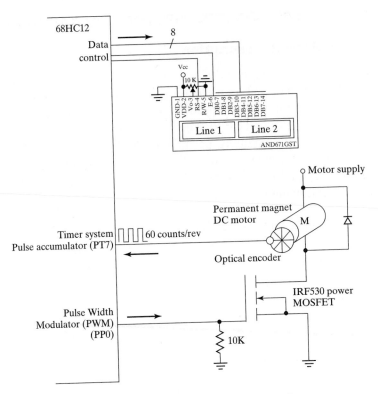

Figure 7.15   Motor speed control interface.

By counting the number of pulses in a fixed time interval, the motor speed can be determined. The number of pulses occurring within a given time interval may be measured by using the 68HC12's real-time interrupt (RTI) system and also the pulse accumulator (PA) system. Both systems were discussed in Chapter 4. Recall the RTI system generates an interrupt at regular user-specified intervals to "remind" the processor to accomplish a periodic task. The PA may be configured to count pulses. If we combine these two systems, we can count the number of optical encoder pulses occurring within a given time interval and hence calculate motor speed in RPM.

Let's look at an example. Suppose we have configured the RTI to generate an interrupt every 32.768 ms, and during this interval the PA counts 52 pulses. What is the speed of the motor in RPM? Let's perform some unit analysis to calculate the motor speed:

$$(52 \text{ pulses}/32.768 \text{ ms})(1 \text{ rev}/60 \text{ pulses})(1{,}000 \text{ ms}/1 \text{ sec})(60 \text{ sec }/1 \text{ min})$$

$$= 1{,}586 \text{ RPM}$$

2. How can we easily vary the motor supply voltage to adjust motor speed? In Chapter 4 we discussed the pulse width modulation (PWM) concept.

Recall that the average voltage delivered to a motor can be adjusted by varying the duty cycle of the motor supply voltage. The duty cycle was defined as the "on" time of the periodic signal divided by its total period. If we employ PWM techniques, the supply voltage and hence motor speed may be adjusted. For simplicity, we assume that the motor supply voltage is linearly related to motor speed. We experimentally verify this assumption shortly. PWM signals may be generated with the output compare features of the timer system (A4 and B32 configuration) or with the pulse width modulation system (B32 configuration only and all HCS12 variants). For this project, we use the B32 configuration PWM system that was discussed in Chapter 4. Recall that we also employed the PWM concept earlier in this chapter to generate motor control signals for the wall-following robot.

3. The 68HC12 is a 5 V system with minimal current drive capability. How can we drive a 12 VDC, high current motor load? In Chapter 5, we discussed how a motor may be driven from the 68HC12 by using a power Metal Oxide Semiconductor Field Effect Transistor (MOSFET) interface. The PWM control signal is provided to the gate of the MOSFET. The motor load is connected between the motor supply voltage and the drain of the MOSFET, as illustrated in Figure 7.15. For this specific project, we use an International Rectifier IRF530N HEXFET Power MOSFET. This MOSFET is provided in a TO-220AB (three-legged tab case) and is rated for a 100 V, 17 A load. Note: Do not forget to place a reverse-biased diode across the motor load.

4. How can we monitor the motor speed and still accomplish other system related tasks? If we used normal sequential processing techniques, our processor would be tied up constantly monitoring motor speed, adjusting the motor supply voltage, and displaying the current motor speed on the LCD display. However, as we mentioned in the answer to question 1, we use the RTI system to accomplish these motor control related tasks at approximately 33 ms intervals. In between these periodic interrupts, the processor is available to perform other tasks. This periodic interrupt concept is illustrated in Figure 7.16 for a motor control application. We investigate related concepts in the next chapter.

5. What systems should be employed to accomplish this task? This question has already been answered in the previous questions. However, for completeness here is a list of required systems to implement the project:

- Liquid crystal display
- Pulse accumulator
- Pulse width modulation
- Motor interface
- Optical encoder
- Real-time interrupt

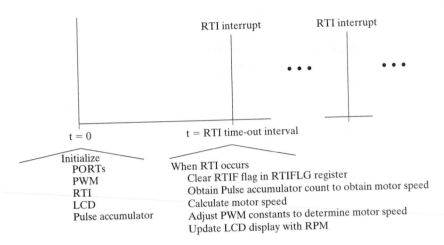

Figure 7.16 Motor control overview.

7.4.2 Background Theory

In this section we investigate some of the project-related concepts in more detail. We take a closer look at motor requirements, the operation of the optical encoder, and configuring the real-time interrupt in C as well as the pulse accumulator in C.

Motor Requirements   The specific motor we use in this project is the Electro-Craft Corporation permanent magnet DC servo motor. We have already provided available motor specifications. However, there are several additional specifications required for this project, such as the motor speed characteristics as well as some of the related motor currents. Since these are not provided, we measure them experimentally. In the laboratory, we vary the supply voltage provided to the motor and then measure the corresponding speed using the optical encoder. We connect a frequency counter to the optical encoder output to determine the number of pulses at a given motor supply voltage and then calculate motor speed. During this experiment, we also measure motor-related currents. The results from the motor tests are provided in Figure 7.17.

Optical Encoder   There is a wide variety of optically based shaft encoders. These encoders "snap on" to the shaft of a motor or they may be coupled to the motor shaft via coupling hardware. When mounted to a rotating shaft, the encoder provides a square wave output. The encoders require a 5 VDC supply and are rated at a maximum motor speed of 12,000 RPM. We use the optical encoders to provide an indication of motor speed as described previously [Servo-Tek, 2004]. Figure 7.18 illustrates the motor speed control testing mount.

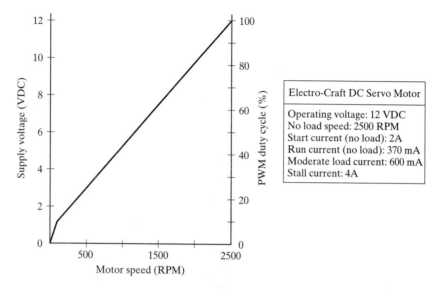

Figure 7.17 Motor testing results.

Real-Time Interrupt   We use the 68HC12's real-time interrupt (RTI) system to periodically interrupt the 68HC12 to check motor speed and adjust PWM constants if needed to stabilize motor speed. Before examining the RTI sample code, we recommend that you review the information on resets and interrupts. Here is a brief review of required actions to initialize an RTI interrupt:

- Initialize RTI interrupt vector.
- Set RTI prescale factor RTR[2:0].
- Enable RTI with RTIE bit in the RTICTL register.
- Enable maskable interrupts (CLI).
- Clear RTIF flag in RTIFLG register.

The following sample code will help you to become familiar with RTI operation. In this example, we have the RTI interrupt service routine (ISR) toggle a pin on PORTP. If you observe the resulting waveform, as shown in Figure 7.19, on an oscilloscope or logic analyzer, you can verify the periodic interrupt feature of the RTI system.

```
//****************************************************************
//file name: RTI_test.c
//
//Port P[0]: Configured as digital output, provide TTL compatible
//           shutter control signal.
//author: Steve Barrett and Daniel Pack
```

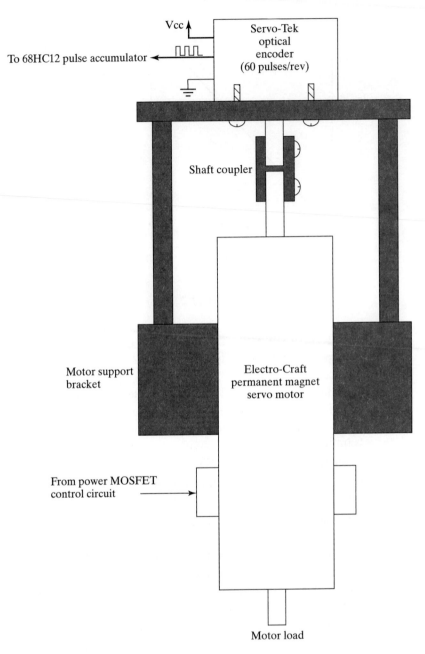

Figure 7.18 Motor speed control testing mount.

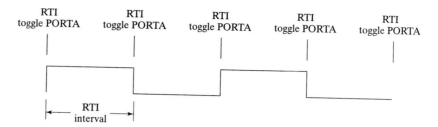

Figure 7.19   Real-time interrupt test.

```
//created: Mar 10, 2003
//last revised: Mar 10, 2004
//***********************************************************

//include files*********************************************
#include<912b32.h>

#pragma interrupt_handler RTI_isr

//function prototypes***************************************
void initialize_ports(void);          //initializes ports
void RTI_isr(void);
void initialize_RTI(void);

//main program**********************************************

void main(void)
{
//initialize B32 reset vector
asm(" .area vectors(abs)\n"
    ".org 0xFFF0\n"               //initialize RTI interrupt vector
".word _RTI_isr\n"
    " .org 0xFFF8\n"              //initialize B32 reset vector
" .word 0x8000, 0x8000, 0x8000, 0x8000\n"
" .text");
initialize_RTI();                    //initialize RTI system
initialize_ports();                  //initialize ports
PORTP = 0x01;                        //enable PORTP pin 0
asm("cli");                          //enable global maskable interrupts
.
.
.
}



//function definitions**************************************

//***********************************************************
```

```
//*****************************************************************
//initialize_ports: provides initial configuration for I/O ports
//*****************************************************************

void initialize_ports(void)
{
DDRP=0xFF;                                      //set PORTP as output
}


//*****************************************************************
//*****************************************************************
//RTI_isr: interrupt service routine associated with Real Time
//          Interrupt
//          -resets RTI flag
//- toggles PORTP[0] to generate square wave signal on output pin
//*****************************************************************

void RTI_isr(void)
{
RTIFLG = 0x80;                                  //reset RTI flag
PORTP = ~(PORTP);                               //toggle PORTP
}


//*****************************************************************
//*****************************************************************
//initialize_RTI: configures RTI related registers
//- RTI Control Register (RTICTL):
//  -- enable RTI with RTIE bit
//  -- set RTI time-out for 32.768 ms
//- reset RTI with RTIF bit in the RTI Flag Register (RTIFLG)
//*****************************************************************

void initialize_RTI(void)
{
RTICTL = 0x86;                                  //set RTI countdown timer
RTIFLG = 0x80;                                  //reset RTI flag
}


//*****************************************************************
```

Pulse Accumulator   We use the pulse accumulator (PA) to count the number of pulses from an optical encoder. We initialize the PA at the beginning of our program and then capture its current value during every RTI interrupt. Since we know the time interval between RTI interrupt events (32.768 ms) and we can determine the number of PA counts between RTI events, we can then obtain an indication of motor speed.

Here is some sample code to configure the PA system.

```
//***********************************************************
//initialize_PA: initializes 68HC12 pulse accumulator system
//***********************************************************

void initialize_PA(void)
{
TIOS  = 0x00;          //Turn off timer channel 7 to use pulse
TCTL1 = 0x00;          //accumulator - 3 step process
OC7M  = 0x00;
TSCR  = 0x80;          //Turn on timer enable bit
PACTL = 0x70;          //Enable pulse accumulator, rising edge,
}                      //event count mode
```

Let's now combine this code with our RTI code to count the number of optical encoder pulses occurring during the RTI interval. We take these results and convert them to RPM and display them on the liquid crystal display.

```
//***********************************************************
//file name: motor.c
//author: Steve Barrett and Daniel Pack
//created: Mar 10, 2003
//last revised: Mar 25, 2004
//***********************************************************

//include files*********************************************
#include<912b32.h>

#pragma interrupt_handler RTI_isr //declare Real Time Interrupt
                                                          (RTI)
                                  //Interrupt Service Routine (ISR)

//function prototypes***************************************
void initialize_ports(void);      //initializes ports
void RTI_isr(void);               //RTI Interrupt Service
                                                        Routine
void initialize_RTI(void);        //initialize RTI system
void initialize_PA(void);         //initialize Pulse
                                              Accumulator (PA)
void initialize_LCD(void);        //initialize Liquid Crystal
                                                   Display (LCD)
void display_count_LCD(unsigned int);//display elapsed PA count
                                                         to LCD
void putchars(unsigned char);     //LCD support function - put
                                                       character
void putcommands(unsigned char);  //LCD support function - put
                                                        command
void delay_5ms(void);             //5 millisecond delay
void delay_100us(void);           //100 microsecond delay
```

```
//global variables*************************************************
unsigned int old_count;            //last Pulse Accumulator (PA) count
int RTI_int_count =0;              //used to count RTI interrupts


//main program****************************************************

void main(void)
{
asm(" .area vectors(abs)\n"    //inline assembly statement
     ".org 0xFFF0\n"           //initialize RTI interrupt vector
 ".word _RTI_isr\n"
     " .org 0xFFF8\n"          //initialize 68HC12 B32 reset vector
" .word 0x8000, 0x8000, 0x8000, 0x8000\n"
" .text");

initialize_ports();            //initialize ports
initialize_LCD();              //initialize LCD
initialize_RTI();              //initialize RTI system
initialize_PA();               //initialize pulse accumulator
asm("cli");                    //enable global maskable interrupts

while(1)                   //continuous loops to wait for interrupts
  {
  ;
  }
}



//***********************function definitions*******************
//***************************************************************
//initialize_ports: provides initial configuration for I/O ports
//***************************************************************

void initialize_ports(void)
{
DDRP   = 0xFF;  //set PORTP as output - Pulse Width Modulation
DDRT   = 0x00;  //set PORT as input   - PORTT[7] as Pulse
                //Accumulator input
DDRB   = 0xFF;  //set PORTB as output - data port for LCD
DDRDLC = 0xFF;  //PORT DLC as output  - control signals for LCD
}



//*****************************************************************
//*****************************************************************
//RTI_isr: interrupt service routine associated with Real Time
//         Interrupt - resets RTI flag
//*****************************************************************
```

```
void RTI_isr(void)
{
unsigned int new_count;
unsigned int pulse_count;
float max_count = 65535.0;

new_count = PACNT;                   //get current pulse
                                              accumulator count
if (new_count > old_count)        //determine elapsed count
  pulse_count = new_count - old_count;
else
  pulse_count = (unsigned int)(max_count-(float)
                                     (old_count +new_count));

RTI_int_count = RTI_int_count + 1;//update RTI interrupt counter
if(RTI_int_count == 10)              //update LCD every 10 RTI
                                                     interrupts
  {
  display_count_LCD(pulse_count); //update LCD
  RTI_int_count = 0;                //reset RTI interrupt counter
  }
old_count = new_count;
RTIFLG = 0x80;                      //reset RTI
}

//****************************************************************
//****************************************************************
//initialize_RTI: configures RTI related registers
//- RTI Control Register (RTICTL):
//   -- enable RTI with RTIE bit
//   -- set RTI time-out for 32.768 ms
//- reset RTI with RTIF bit in the RTI Flag Register (RTIFLG)
//****************************************************************

void initialize_RTI(void)
{
RTICTL = 0x86;          //set RTI countdown timer for 32.768 ms
RTIFLG = 0x80;          //reset RTI
}

//****************************************************************
//initialize_PA: initializes 68HC12 pulse accumulator system
//****************************************************************

void initialize_PA(void)
{
TIOS  = 0x00;           //Turn off timer channel 7 to use pulse
TCTL1 = 0x00;           //accumulator - 3 step process
```

```
OC7M  = 0x00;
TSCR  = 0x80;                 //Turn on timer enable bit
PACTL = 0x50;                 //Enable pulse accumulator, rising edge,
}                             //event count mode


/******************************************************************/
/*initialize_LCD: This initialize function sends the LCD the    */
/*correct start-up sequence.  The command sequence for initial-*/
/*ization is provided in the manufacturer's technical data for  */
/*the display.                                                   */
/*   - PORTDLC[3]: LCD RS control line                           */
/*   - PORTDLC[2]: LCD E control line                            */
/*   - PORTB : data lines LCD                                    */
/******************************************************************/

void initialize_LCD(void)
{
delay_5ms();
delay_5ms();
delay_5ms();                  /*wait 15 ms for LCD to turn on    */

putcommands(0x38);            /*interface data length 8 bits     */
delay_5ms();                  /*delay                            */
putcommands(0x38);            /*interface data length 8 bits     */
delay_100us();                /*delay                            */
putcommands(0x38);            /*interface data length 8 bits     */
putcommands(0x38);            /*8 bits, 2 lines, font size        */
putcommands(0x0C);            /*display on                        */
putcommands(0x01);            /*Display clear                     */
putcommands(0x06);            /*Sets mode to increment by one     */
putcommands(0x00);
putcommands(0x00);
putcommands(0xC0);            /*line 2 char 1                     */
putchars('R');                /* display RPM on LCD line 2        */
putchars('P');
putchars('M');
}



/******************************************************************/
/*putchars: the putchar function sends an ASCII character to    */
/*the LCD for display.  It generates the RS and Enable LCD      */
/*control signal and sends them and the ASCII character to the */
/*correct ports for display.                                     */
/******************************************************************/

void putchars(unsigned char c)
{
PORTB = c;                    /*assign char C to data port        */
```

```
PORTDLC = PORTDLC|0x08;      /*set RS to 1 for DATA            */
PORTDLC = PORTDLC|0x04;      /*set E to 1                      */
PORTDLC = 0x00;              /*set E and RS to 0               */
delay_100us();  delay_100us();
}



/*************************************************************/
/*putcommands: the putcommands function sends a command to the */
/*LCD. It generates the RS and Enable LCD control signal and   */
/*sends them and the control signal to the correct ports for   */
/*display.                                                      */
/*************************************************************/

void putcommands(unsigned char d)
{
PORTDLC   = PORTDLC & 0xF7; /*RS = 0 for Command               */
PORTB = d;                  /*assign command to LCD            */
PORTDLC   = PORTDLC|0x04;   /*E = 1                            */
PORTDLC   = 0x00;           /*E = 0                            */
delay_100us();  delay_100us();
}

/*************************************************************/
/*5 ms delay based on an 8 MHz clock                          */
/*************************************************************/

void delay_5ms(void)
{
int i;

for(i=0; i<50; i++)
  {
  delay_100us();
  }
}



/*************************************************************/
/*100 us delay based on an 8 MHz clock                       */
/* - assembly language NOP function requires 1 clock cycle or */
/* 125 ns (at 8 MHz) to execute.  Executing this instruction  */
/* 800 times will provide an approximate 100 microsecond delay.*/
/*************************************************************/

void delay_100us(void)
{
int i;
```

```
for(i=0; i<800; i++)
  {
  asm("nop");              /*Assembly language nop, takes 1 cycle*/
  }
}

/*************************************************************/
/*display_count_LCD: converts integer count to ASCII character*/
/*                   for LCD display                         */
/*************************************************************/

void display_count_LCD(unsigned int count)
{
unsigned int thousands_int;
unsigned int hundreds_int;
unsigned int tens_int;
unsigned int ones_int;
char thousands;
char hundreds;
char tens;
char ones;

/*isolate and convert most significant digit to ASCII        */
/*decimal value + 48 yields ASCII code                       */
thousands_int = count/1000;
thousands = (char)(thousands_int + 48);

/*isolate and convert next most significant digit to ASCII   */
/*decimal value + 48 yields ASCII code                       */
hundreds_int = (count - thousands_int*1000)/100;
hundreds = (char)(hundreds_int + 48);

/*isolate and convert next most significant digit to ASCII   */
/*decimal value + 48 yields ASCII code                       */
tens_int = (count - thousands_int*1000 - hundreds_int*100)/10;
tens = (char)(tens_int + 48);

/*isolate and convert next most significant digit to ASCII   */
/*decimal value + 48 yields ASCII code                       */
ones_int = (count-thousands_int*1000-hundreds_int*100
                                        -tens_int*10);
ones = (char)(ones_int + 48);

/*print results to LCD                                       */
putcommands(0x80);          /*LCD cursor to line 1, char 1   */
putchars(thousands);
putchars(hundreds);
```

```
putchars(tens);
putchars(ones);
}
```

```
/********************************************************************/
/********************************************************************/
```

7.4.3 Supporting Analysis

In the previous section we were able to measure and display motor speed in RPM. In this section we close the loop. That is, we compare the instantaneous motor speed to desired motor speed and then adjust the PWM constants to stabilize the motor at the desired speed under varying motor loads.

Let's stabilize the motor at 1,600 RPM. To do this we need to determine the required PWM duty cycle for 1,600 RPM. Earlier we measured PWM duty cycle versus motor speed in RPM. From the graph of results (Figure 7.17) we see a 8 VDC motor supply voltage is required to achieve a motor speed of approximately 1,600 RPM. Let's assume we use a 12 VDC supply to power the motor. The corresponding PWM duty cycle is therefore 66.7% (8 VDC/ 12 VDC).

To achieve a 66.7% PWM duty cycle, we initially set the PWM period to 256 counts and the PWM duty cycle to 172 counts. Recall from our previous discussion of the PWM system that this is accomplished using the PWPER0 and the PWDTY0 registers, respectively.

We use a 976 Hz PWM control signal. This requires us to divide the PWM clock source of 8 MHz by 32. This provides a 250 KHz (period = 4 μ s) clock source to the PWM system. With our period set at 256 counts, the resulting PWM control signal frequency is 976 Hz (period = 4 μ s per pulse × 256 pulses).

Provided below is sample code to set the PWM constants to 1,600 RPM. This function is used to initially set the speed of the motor.

```
/********************************************************************/
/*init_pwm(): initializes 68HC12 pulse width modulation system  */
/********************************************************************/

void init_pwm()
{
PWTST = 0x00;              /*Sets PWM port for normal operation  */
PWCTL = 0x00;              /*Set to left aligned signal          */
PWCLK = 0x28;              /*no concatenation, ECLK/128          */
PWPOL = 0x01;              /*set pins high then low transition   */
DDRP = 0xFF;               /*Port P set to output                */
PWEN = 0x01;               /*forces output for PWM pins          */
```

```
PWPER0 = 255;                  /*sets PWM signal period to 976 Hz     */
PWDTY0 = 171;                  /*init set PWM output for no motion     */
}
/***************************************************************/
```

During the RTI interrupt service routine the motor speed is checked using the optical encoder data. If the motor's speed is faster than 1,600 RPM, the PWM duty cycle is reduced by one count. On the other hand, if the motor's speed is less than 1,600 RPM, the PWM duty cycle is incremented by one count. Each increment or decrement of the PWM duty cycle corresponds to a 8.5 change in RPM. We ask you to calculate this change as a homework assignment (Advanced 8).

The code to compare desired motor RPM with actual motor RPM and to adjust motor speed is provided in the RTI interrupt service routine (RTI_ISR). In this code listing, LCD support functions have been placed in the include file LCD.h with their function prototypes.

7.4.4 Structure Chart and UML Activity Diagram

Figure 7.20 illustrates the UML activity diagram and motor speed control structure chart for this project. In the next section we provide the entire code for this project. We ask you to provide the UML activity diagram for each project support function as a homework assignment (Advanced 9).

7.4.5 Code

In this section we have employed top-down design—bottom-up implementation techniques to design, implement, and document a motor speed control system. The entire code for the project is provided in this section. If we had provided this code in its entirety at the beginning of the section, you might have been overwhelmed with its complexity. However, since we used bottom-up implementation techniques, you will be comfortable with each function within the code and how it relates to other functions.

```
//**************************************************************
//file name: motor.c
//author: Steve Barrett and Daniel Pack
//created: Mar 10, 2003
//last revised: Mar 25, 2004
//**************************************************************

//include files**********************************************
#include<912b32.h>
#include<LCD.h>                    //LCD support functions
```

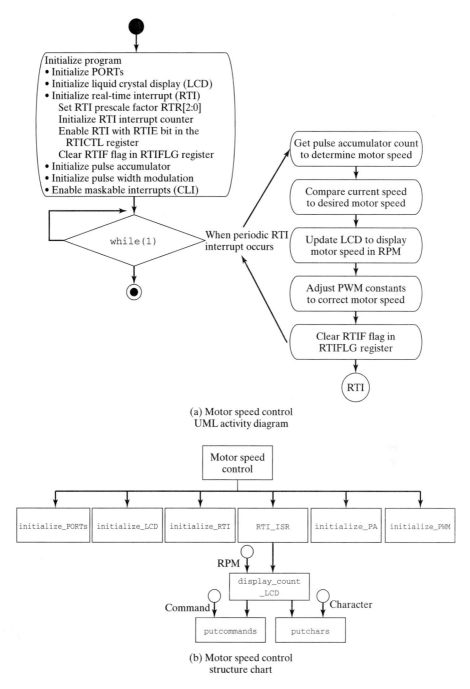

(a) Motor speed control
UML activity diagram

(b) Motor speed control
structure chart

Figure 7.20 Motor speed control project support documentation.

```
#pragma interrupt_handler RTI_isr
                            //declare Real Time Interrupt (RTI)
                            //Interrupt Service Routine (ISR)

//function prototypes**********************************************
void initialize_ports(void);    //initializes ports
void RTI_isr(void);             //RTI Interrupt Service Routine
void initialize_RTI(void);      //initialize RTI system
void initialize_PA(void);       //initialize Pulse Accumulator (PA)
void initialize_PWM(void);      //initialize PWM system

//global variables*************************************************
unsigned int old_count;         //last Pulse Accumulator (PA) count
int RTI_int_count =0;           //used to count RTI interrupts
unsigned char PWM_duty_cycle = 172;    //initial PWM duty cycle
unsigned int desired_motor_RPM = 1600; //target motor RPM
//main program****************************************************

void main(void)
{
asm(" .area vectors(abs)\n"  //inline assembly statement
    ".org 0xFFF0\n"          //initialize RTI interrupt vector
 ".word _RTI_isr\n"
    " .org 0xFFF8\n"         //initialize 68HC12 B32 reset vector
" .word 0x8000, 0x8000, 0x8000, 0x8000\n"
" .text");

initialize_ports();        //initialize ports
initialize_LCD();          //initialize LCD
initialize_RTI();          //initialize RTI system
initialize_PA();           //initialize pulse accumulator
initialize_PWM();          //initialize PWM system
asm("cli");                //enable global maskable interrupts

while(1)                   //continuous loops to wait for interrupts
  {
  ;
  }
}

//*********************function definitions********************
//************************************************************
//initialize_ports: provides initial configuration for I/O ports
//************************************************************

void initialize_ports(void)
{
DDRP   = 0xFF;  //set PORTP as output - Pulse Width Modulation
```

```
DDRT    = 0x00;
//set PORT as input    - PORTT[7] as Pulse Accumulator input
DDRB    = 0xFF;  //set PORTB as output - data port for LCD
DDRDLC = 0xFF;  //PORT DLC as output -  control signals for LCD
}


//****************************************************************
//****************************************************************
//RTI_isr: interrupt service routine associated with Real Time
//          Interrupt - resets RTI flag
//****************************************************************

void RTI_isr(void)
{
unsigned int new_count;
unsigned int pulse_count;
unsigned int current_RPM;
float max_count = 65535.0;

new_count = PACNT;            //get current pulse accumulator count

if (new_count > old_count) //determine elapsed count
  pulse_count = new_count - old_count;
else
  pulse_count = (unsigned int)(max_count-(float)
                                        (old_count +new_count));
                            //convert optical encoder count to RPM
current_RPM = (unsigned int)(pulse_count/0.032768);

RTI_int_count = RTI_int_count + 1;  //update RTI interrupt counter
if(RTI_int_count == 5)      //update LCD every 10 RTI interrupts
  {
  display_count_LCD(current_RPM);   //update LCD
  RTI_int_count = 0;                //reset RTI interrupt counter
  }
//update motor speed
if(current_RPM < desired_motor_RPM)
  PWM_duty_cycle = PWM_duty_cycle + 1; //speed motor up
else
  PWM_duty_cycle = PWM_duty_cycle - 1; //slow motor down
                              //update motor speed by adjusting PWM
PWDTY0= PWM_duty_cycle;     //duty cycle

old_count = new_count;
RTIFLG = 0x80;             //reset RTI interrupt flag
}


//****************************************************************
```

```
//******************************************************************
//initialize_RTI: configures RTI related registers
//- RTI Control Register (RTICTL):
//  -- enable RTI with RTIE bit
//  -- set RTI time-out for 32.768 ms
//- reset RTI with RTIF bit in the RTI Flag Register (RTIFLG)
//******************************************************************

void initialize_RTI(void)
{
RTICTL = 0x86;              //set RTI countdown timer for 32.768 ms
RTIFLG = 0x80;             //reset RTI
}


//******************************************************************
//initialize_PA: initializes 68HC12 pulse accumulator system
//******************************************************************

void initialize_PA(void)
{
TIOS  = 0x00;              //Turn off timer channel 7 to use pulse
TCTL1 = 0x00;             //accumulator - 3 step process
OC7M  = 0x00;
TSCR  = 0x80;             //Turn on timer enable bit
PACTL = 0x50;            //Enable pulse accumulator, rising edge,
}                          //event count mode


/*****************************************************************/
/*initialize_PWM: generate PWM signal of 976 Hz at 67.2%         */
/*****************************************************************/

void initialize_PWM(void)
{
PWTST = 0x00;              /*set PWM for normal operation       */
PWCTL = 0x00;              /*set to left aligned signal         */
PWCLK = 0x28;             /*no concatenation, divide clk by 32  */
PWPOL = 0x01;             /*polarity: high then transition to low*/
DDRP  = 0xFF;             /*set PORTP for output               */
PWEN  = 0x01;             /*enable PWM channel 0               */
PWPER0= 0xFF;             /*set period to 256 counts           */
PWDTY0= PWM_duty_cycle;  /*set duty cycle to 172 counts        */
}


/*****************************************************************/
/*****************************************************************/
```

7.4.6 Testing

A test configuration for the motor speed control is provided in Figure 7.18. This is a very complex system involving many components and 68HC12 systems. To guarantee system operational success, the bottom-up testing approach discussed in Chapter 2 is highly recommended. With the entire system up and operating, it is now possible to place the motor under a moderate load and see the system stabilize the motor speed at 1,600 RPM.

7.5 FLYING ROBOT

7.5.1 Project Description

The flying robot we develop here is a hovering robot that possesses the capability to remain directly over an area of interest until a designated mission is complete. Over the past two decades a variety of researchers in universities and research laboratories have studied and developed flying robots of various sizes and shapes for a number of applications. Some used existing model airplanes and helicopters, some used ingeniously designed mechanical systems that flap wings, and others used blimp systems. Such efforts have been made because of the enormous benefits flying robots can bring to both the military and industry, including distant planet exploration, indoor and outdoor surveillance, and target recognition and localization for the military.

We first describe the overall objective of the system, followed by a list of project requirements. We next present the hovering robot system design that meets all of the requirements. The system description is followed by the hardware interface diagram, a software structure chart, and the UML activity diagram. Sample C code follows the structure chart section.

The goal of this project was to design and build an autonomous hovering robot system based on the 68HC9S12 microcontroller. The most challenging aspect of the system is the inherent stability problem of the aircraft that must constantly be maintained by the controller. Figure 7.21 shows a photo of the hovering robot frame. This project was completed by a student in a senior design capstone course.

To meet the project objectives, we must first identify all system requirements. There are a number of challenging problems that must be solved: (1) creation of a sturdy, yet light, air frame that meets the lift requirements, (2) sensor integration, (3) actuator selection, (4) design of the power system, and (5) stability control.

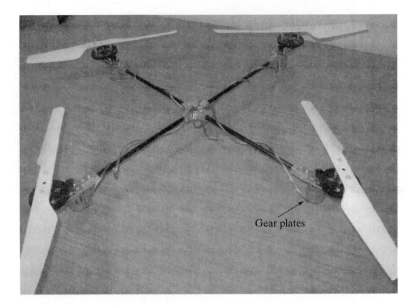

Gear plates

Figure 7.21   The hovering robot frame.

The hovering robot must meet the following system requirements:

1. Be autonomous.
2. Fit within a 16×16 in. (40.6×40.6 cm) box.
3. Weigh no more than 2.5 lb (1.14 kg).
4. Take off and land on its own.
5. Use DC motors.
6. Lift up to 4.5 lb (2.05 kg) including its own weight.
7. Maintain level hover.
8. Have the ability to move in all directions.
9. Avoid obstacles.
10. Have room for upgrades.
11. Cost no more than $500.00.

7.5.2 HCS12 Systems Employed

The following HCS12 systems will be employed in this project:

- Input capture system
- ATD converter
- Pulse width modulation system

7.5.3 Background Theory

For the hardware frame, a simple airframe was designed, similar to a pre-existing, commercially available, radio-controlled product, as shown in Figure 7.21. It is made of four rods that span out from the center of the frame and form an X-shaped airframe. Attached to each rod is a DC motor and gear assembly for a propeller. The pitch of adjacent propellers is reversed to compensate for counter rotation, making two propellers rotate clockwise and the other two rotate counterclockwise. The counter rotation is controlled by a tail rotor in conventional helicopters.

For the microcontroller, a 68HCS12 T-board from ImageCraft (Figure 7.22) was used. The controller has a 25 MHz clock, 256 Kbyte on-chip flash memory, 12 Kbyte RAM, and 4 Kbyte of EEPROM. The compact size of the board is highly desirable for the on-board circuitry. The built-in pulse width modulation module is used to control the DC motors. For sensors, piezo gyros placed on three axes of rotation provide the yaw, pitch, and roll angles of the hovering robot for control. The gyro sensor outputs are fed to the timer input capture port

Figure 7.22   ImageCraft 68HCS12 microcontroller T-board.

of the controller and are used to adjust the speed of the four motors to control the flying robot. In addition to the gyro sensors, four infrared sensors are also placed on the robot. These sensors detect obstructions when and if the robot approaches walls or obstacles. The sensors' outputs are fed to the ATD converter input port to trigger the flight control algorithm to avoid crashing into walls or obstacles.

For the gyro sensors, three Futaba GYA350 piezo gyros were used. We selected this specific gyro since it is specially made for model airplanes. The gyro weighs 26 g and fits in a 27 mm × 27 mm × 20 mm box. The sensors provide PWM signals at 55 Hz, and the change of the pulse widths indicate the orientation of the sensor, thus the orientation of the hovering robot. This gyro can also function in heading-hold mode, a feature that lets the microcontroller know the pulse width of gyro output when the hovering robot is flying level. Using the input capture function of the controller, the robot checks its orientation by evaluating the gyro output PWM signals.

In addition to the gyro sensors, four Sharp GP2D12 distance-measuring infrared transmitter/detector pairs were used by the robot to avoid any approaching objects. The particular sensor can provide a range of voltages corresponding to 10 to 80 cm distance from the robot. The input voltages are then converted to corresponding digital values with the help of the controller's ATD converter. The sensor is light and can fit in a 45 mm × 14 mm × 20 mm box.

Four Graupner Speed300 6V DC motors were used to propel the hovering robot off the ground. Each motor weighs 50 g and has a 2 mm shaft diameter. The motor can draw up to 5 A. The motor shaft is connected to a small plastic gear plate, which in turn is connected to a larger gear plate, as shown in Figure 7.21.

7.5.4 Structure Chart and UML Activity Diagram

The interface diagram in Figure 7.23 shows the hardware components of the hovering robot and how each component is connected to the controller. Figure 7.24 shows the robot with all its components. Note that the speed control PWM signals are fed to motor drive chips that provide sufficient current to DC motors. A pack of batteries is used to provide all necessary power to the system. Signals flow into the controllers from the sensors and flow out of the controllers to the actuators via motor driver chips.

Figure 7.25 provides the software structure chart for the hovering robot, which shows the directions for signal flows between software modules. Figure 7.26 correspondingly shows the UML activity diagram for control of the robot.

7.5.5 Code

In this section, we present a sample C program for control of the hovering robot. The program was initially written by Joel Perlin, one of our students, and modified by the authors.

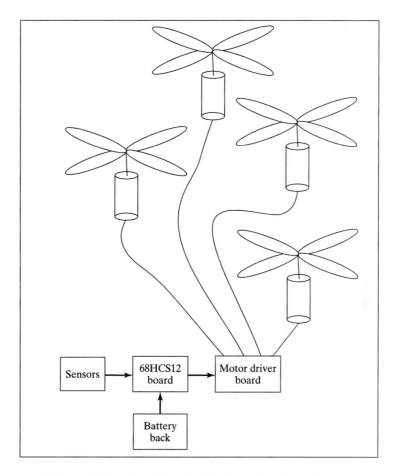

Figure 7.23   Hovering robot hardware interface diagram.

```
//------------------------------------------------------------------
// filename: flying.c
// Program Description: This program starts four motors and speeds
// them up for a takeoff.  Once airborne, the program checks each
// onboard sensor for robot status.  If an obstruction or a tilt
// is detected, the motor speeds will be adjusted to correct the
// error.
//
// Name: Joel Perlin, Daniel Pack, and Steve Barrett
// Date: 27 July 2004
//
// Memory use: Program - 0x1000, Data - 0x3000 and Stack - 0x4000
//------------------------------------------------------------------
#include <stdio.h>
#include ``hcs12dp256.h''
```

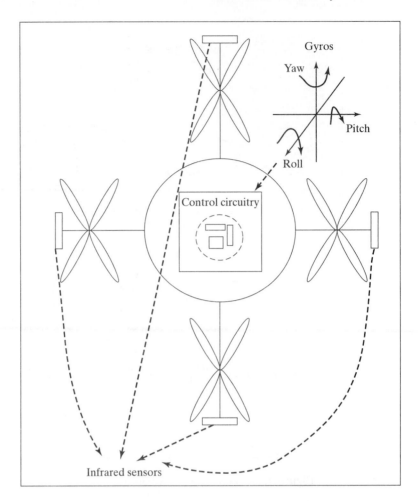

Figure 7.24 A diagram of the hovering robot with all components on board.

```
#pragma abs_address 0x3000
unsigned int count1;        //counter variables
unsigned int count2;
unsigned int sensor;
char sensoravg;             //store sensor value as an 8-bit number
volatile unsigned p;        //a counter
#pragma end_abs_address

//------------------------------------------------------------
// Main Program
//------------------------------------------------------------
```

Software Structure Chart

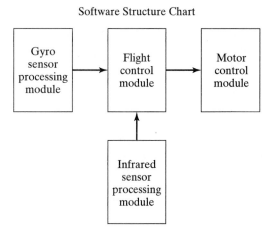

Figure 7.25   Software structure chart for the hovering robot.

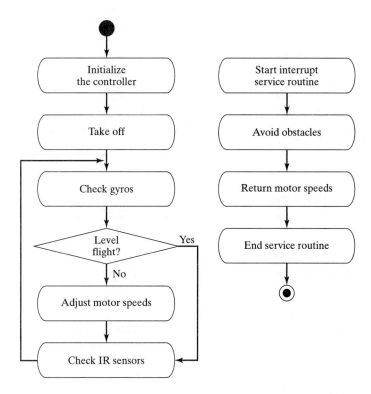

Figure 7.26   UML activity diagram for the hovering robot.

```
void main(void){

   //Initialize robot
   PWME = 0x00;            //disable PWM
   DDRA = 0xFF;            //configure ports A and B as outputs
   DDRB = 0xFF;
   PORTA = 0xAA;           //power up the sensors
   PORTB = 0xFF;           //shows program mode on a bank of LEDs

   //Initialize ATD
   PORTAD1 = 0x00;         //set ports as inputs
   ATD1CTL2 = 0xC2;        //initialize ATD with fast complete flag
   ATD1CTL3 = 0x00;        //set the ATD function
   ATD1CTL4 = 0x80;        //set to 8 bit mode
   PORTB = 0xFE;           //show LED completion

   //Input Capture set up
   TSCR1 = 0x80;           //turn on timer (normal mode)
   TSCR2 = 0x80;           //set overflow rate to 8.192 ms
                           //(prescale factor = 1)
   TIOS = 0x00;            //set timer channels as input capture
   TIE = 0xE0;             //enable TFLG1 interrupt ports T[7:5]
   TFLG1 = 0xE0;           //clear TFLG1
   PORTB = 0xFC;           //show LED completion

   //initialize PWM
   PWMCTL = 0x00;          //choose 8 bit mode
   PWMCAE = 0x10;          //choose left-aligned 0-4 and 6
   PWMPOL = 0x5F;          //choose high polarity

   //select PWM clock for channels 0,1,2,3,4, and 6

   PWMCLK = 0x50;          //ch 0,1,4  = A and ch 2,3,6 = B
   PWMSCLA = 0x20;         //scale 0x20 = 4.1 ms
   PWMSCLB = 0x04;         //scale 0x02 = 255 us
                           //select full period for all channels
   PWMPER0 = 255;
   PWMPER1 = 255;
   PWMPER2 = 255;
   PWMPER3 = 255;

   //Start motors
   PWME = PWME | 0x5F;     //enable PWM on channels 0,1,2,3,4, and 5
   PWMDTY0 = 80;           //set duty cycle on channels 0,1,2, and 3
   PWMDTY1 = 80;
   PWMDTY2 = 80;
   PWMDTY3 = 80;
```

```
//Take off
while (PWMDTY0 < 200)
  {
  PWMDTY0 = PWMDTY0 + 1;
  PWMDTY1 = PWMDTY1 + 1;
  PWMDTY2 = PWMDTY2 + 1;
  PWMDTY3 = PWMDTY3 + 1;
  }

p = 20;

// adjust motor duty cycles for level flight
while (battery == 1)     //check battery level
  {

  // motor 1
  ATD0CLT5 = 0x04;        //left justified, unsigned, multi-ch
  while ((ATD0STAT0 & 0x80) == 0);
  sensoravg = ATD0DR4H; //store PAD00 to sensor 1
  if((int)sensoravg > 80)
    {
    PWMDTY0 = PWMDTY0 + 20;
    delay2();
    for (i=0; i<p; i++)
     PWMDTY0--;
    }

  // motor 2
  ATD0CLT5 = 0x04;        //left justified, unsigned, multi-ch
  while ((ATD0STAT0 & 0x 80) == 0);
  sensoravg = ATD0DR5H; //store PAD00 to sensor 2
  if((int)sensoravg > 80)
    {
    PWMDTY1 = PWMDTY1 + 20;
    delay2();
    for (i=0; i<p; i++)
     PWMDTY1--;
    }

  // motor 3
  ATD0CLT5 = 0x04;        //left justified, unsigned, multi-ch
  while ((ATD0STAT0 & 0x 80) == 0);
  sensoravg = ATD0DR6H; //store PAD00 to sensor 3
  if((int)sensoravg > 80)
    {
    PWMDTY2 = PWMDTY2 + 20;
    delay2();
```

```
        for (i=0; i<p; i++)
          PWMDTY2--;
        }

    // motor 4
    ATD0CLT5 = 0x04;        //left justified, unsigned, Multi channel
    while ((ATD0STAT0 & 0x 80) == 0);
    sensoravg = ATD0DR7H;//store PAD00 to sensor 4
    if((int)sensoravg > 80)
        {
        PWMDTY7 = PWMDTY7 + 20;
        delay2();
        for (i=0; i<p; i++)
          PWMDTY7--;
        }
    }//end while

    // slow down motors for landing
    while (PWMDTY0 > 80)
        {
        PWMDTY0--;
        PWMDTY1--;
        PWMDTY2--;
        PWMDTY3--;
        delay1();
        }

    // stop motors
    PWME = 0x00;
}
//-------------------------------------------------------------
```

7.5.6 Some Comments

The above program is a bare-bones version of the flying robot program; readers will notice that it contains only a simple control algorithm. Furthermore, due to drifting problems experienced with the gyros, the program uses only IR sensors for obstacle avoidance.

7.6 FUZZY-LOGIC-BASED SECURITY SYSTEM

7.6.1 Project Description

In this section, we present a fuzzy-logic-based computer security system that can be used to protect your computer from external intruders. In particular, the system is designed to detect Hypertext Transfer Protocol (HTTP) tunneling activities on a computer network bus using the built-in fuzzy logic engine of the 68HC12/HCS12 controllers. A tunneling activity is defined as an authorized establishment of communication sessions between a host computer within a computer network and a computer external to the network. An intruder uses a computer external to a computer network to establish a clandestine session by encapsulating messages within packets of an approved protocol such as HTTP. To prevent such activities, the computer information security community has been developing information assurance systems over the past decade. The goal of our microcontroller-based security system is not to replace existing commercial systems but to aid such systems by evaluating network traffic data for one particular type of activity: HTTP tunneling activity.

Our objective in this project is to build a portable microcontroller-based HTTP tunneling activity detection system. In particular, we are interested in building a system that detects both malicious and unauthorized HTTP tunneling activities: (1) interactive tunneling sessions, (2) scripted tunneling sessions, and (3) unauthorized video and audio streaming sessions.

The security system must meet the following system requirements:

1. Use a HCS12 microcontroller.
2. Have a display unit (LCD) to display the status of web traffic.
3. Detect interactive tunneling sessions.
4. Detect scripted attack tunneling sessions.
5. Detect unauthorized video and audio streaming sessions.
6. Use a fuzzy logic engine to determine the status of web traffic.

7.6.2 HCS12 Systems Employed

This project will extensively use the built-in fuzzy logic features of the HCS12.

7.6.3 Background Theory

Figure 7.27 shows the overall process that the microcontroller-based security system must follow in order to identify undesired network traffic. The system takes a set of six inputs generated by a PC and processes them using a fuzzy engine. (For a review of 68HC12-based fuzzy logic concepts, see Pack and Barrett [2002]). The inputs are in the form of matching scores; a score of zero means no matching, while a maximum score represents a perfect match. The first three inputs are the behavior profile matching scores. A behavior profile is made up of session attributes, such as packet size, number of packets for a session, session duration, ratio between large and small packets, data directions, average packet size, change of packet size pattern, and the size of total packets received. By comparing each behavior file

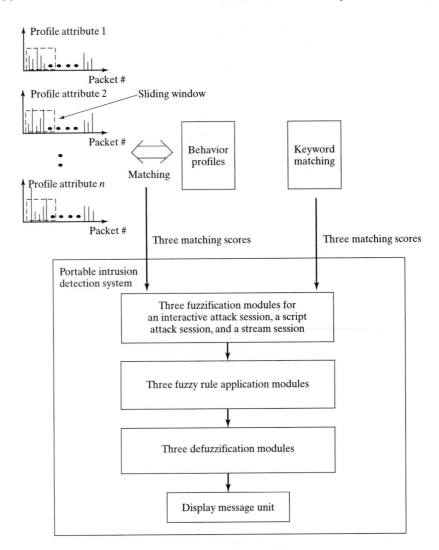

Figure 7.27 Three sets of two matching scores (six inputs) on behavior profiles and keyword matching. Corresponding scores for interactive tunneling, scripted tunneling sessions, and unauthorized video and audio streaming sessions are delivered to the fuzzy-logic-based detection system. The net traffic session is evaluated using these scores.

(we have three such files that describe the three HTTP tunneling activities: interactive tunneling sessions, scripted tunneling sessions, and stream sessions) with the bus traffic data profile, a designated PC with an intrusion detection system provides a matching score to the HTTP tunneling activity detection (TAD) system. The other three inputs to the system are the matching scores of keywords.

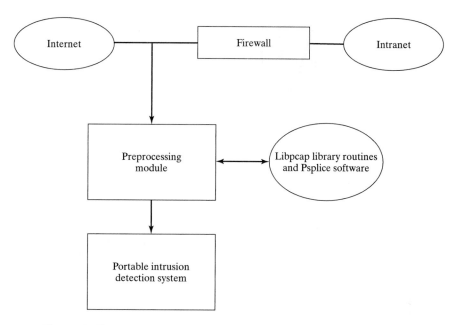

Figure 7.28   The location of the portable intrusion detection system within the overall network structure.

In an HTTP tunneling session, the data contents of packets contain one or more keywords, which can be used to identify tunneling activities. The designated PC compares 40 keywords to the words that appear in session data. A matching score is provided to the portable system as the second data input.

Figure 7.27 shows the overall system and the inputs that it requires. Figure 7.28 shows the placement of the portable intrusion detection system in an overall network environment. In a wireless network, the portable system can be connected to an individual computer. The Libpcap library routines are used to collect session packets from raw Internet data, the Psplice software parses individual packets, and the preprocessing module compares the packet data with three behavior profiles and score keyword matching. For further details on the library routines, Psplice software, and the preprocessing module, see Pack and Barrett [2002].

7.6.4 Structure Chart and UML Activity Diagram

Figure 7.29 provides the hardware interface diagram for the HTTP-based system. The software structure chart for the security system is relatively simple. We have three fuzzy engines running one at a time as a single software module, as was shown in Figure 7.27. To improve speed, we can use three HCS12 boards to detect the three undesired bus activities. Figure 7.30 shows the corresponding UML activity diagram for the security system.

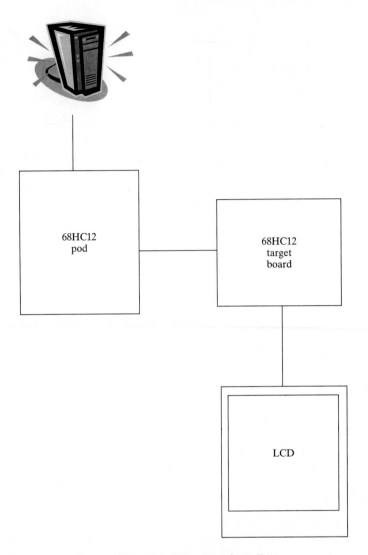

Figure 7.29   Hardware interface diagram.

7.6.5 System Description

Figure 7.31(a) shows the overall portable system at work. The liquid crystal display (LCD) screen shows the following initial message:

```
Portable HTTP

TAD System

version 1.0
```

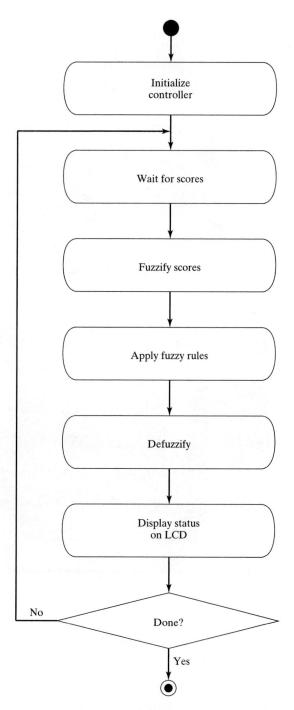

Figure 7.30   UML activity diagram for the security system.

(a) Overall portable system

(b) LCD

Figure 7.31   Microcontroller-based HTTP TAD system: (a) Components that make up the controller system. The left bottom shows a 68HC12 controller board used to interface a PC with the target board, shown in the right bottom corner of the photo. The target board uses the 68HC129S12DP256B microcontroller, a member of the 68HC12 controller family. (b) Picture of the LCD, displaying a sample message.

Part (b) of the same figure shows the following sample screen after a session is evaluated:

```
IA: 60 Med Alert
SA: 40 Low Alert
S : 40 Low Alert
```

The message shows the raw scores of the current session for the three HTTP tunneling activities and their corresponding messages.

The process structure for each of the three fuzzy-logic-based subsystems is identical within the portable microcontroller-based HTTP TAD system. Each subsystem is made of a fuzzifier module, a rule-based engine, and a defuzzifier module, and it uses two matching scores—one from behavior profile matching and the second from keyword matching—to determine the security status of a session. This status is scored in three categories and appropriate messages are displayed on a two-dimensional LCD for the user.

In the preprocessing module, pregenerated profiles are compared with session data to compute matching scores for the fuzzy-logic-based interactive TAD subsystem, the script TAD subsystem, and the stream TAD subsystem. Similarly, three sets of keywords—corresponding to an interactive HTTP tunneling session, a scripted HTTP tunneling session, and a stream HTTP tunneling session—are also searched in the transcript to generate three keyword matching scores. The six numerical scores are then sent to the microcontroller-based system.

Once the portable HTTP TAD system receives a set of six matching scores, the scores are forwarded to three fuzzy-rule-based subsystems. Each HTTP TAD subsystem is now responsible for generating a score for a particular tunneling activity. We next describe the fuzzy subsystems.

The three HTTP TAD fuzzy-logic-based subsystems are responsible for detecting and identifying HTTP interactive tunneling sessions, scripted tunneling sessions, and streaming sessions. Since all three subsystems have the same structure, we describe only a single system, pointing out the differences for the other two subsystems. Once two session scores generated by the preprocessing module are sent to one of the subsystems, the subsystem first fuzzifies the numerical values to a set of corresponding linguistic variables, also called membership functions, with appropriate membership values. The conversion is necessary since the fuzzy-logic engine maps the input linguistic variables to the output linguistic variables. Once all input variables are mapped to the output variables, the subsystem executes the defuzzification process to compute a numerical value that indicates the security status of a particular session.

We start with input linguistic variables. Each subsystem has the same input variable definition. There are three variables describing the level of behavior profile matches: (1) low match, (2) medium match, and (3) high match. The input membership functions are shown in Figure 7.32. Notice that the shape of

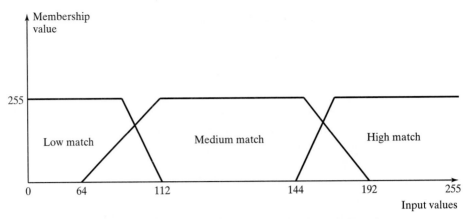

Input Behavior Profile and Keyword Match Membership Functions

Figure 7.32 Input membership functions for the interactive HTTP TAD subsystem.

the functions are chosen to take advantage of the built-in fuzzy functions of the HCS12 microcontroller. The range of values in the y-axis indicates that the maximum membership function value cannot exceed 255, a limiting value for an 8-bit register used in the controller. The values on the x-axis correspond to matching scores received from the preprocessing module: score 0 indicates no match and score 255 signifies the perfect match. The particular range of numerical values is used to make matching scores compatible to the 8-bit number format used in the microcontroller system.

In addition to the behavior profile matching score, the subsystem also receives a keyword matching score ranging from 0 to 255. The input fuzzy membership function definition for the keyword matching score is also shown in Figure 7.32. As shown in the figure, we used the identical input membership function definition. Again, the y axis represents the level of membership, ranging 0 to 255, and the x axis value specifies the input keyword matching score.

Due to the overlaps in the definition of the input membership functions, one numerical score can correspond to multiple input membership functions. The process of identifying an input membership function and the corresponding membership value for all possible input membership functions is called the fuzzification process.

At the end of the fuzzification process, we have one or more input fuzzy membership functions with corresponding membership values. The next step in the process is to map the fuzzy input functions to the fuzzy output functions using a set of predefined rules. Before we discuss the mapping process in the fuzzy engine, we must first define the output fuzzy membership functions. There

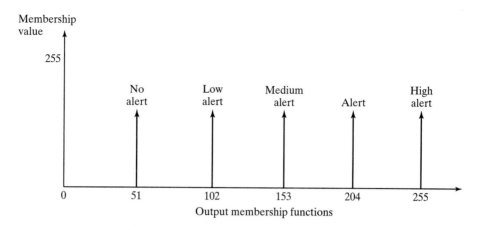

Figure 7.33   Output membership functions for the interactive HTTP TAD subsystem.

are five of them, as shown in Figure 7.33: (1) no alert, (2) low alert, (3) medium alert, (4) alert, and (5) high alert.

The output linguistic variable membership functions in Figure 7.33 may look peculiar to astute fuzzy logic experts. As we will show shortly, the designers of the Motorola HCS12 controller simplified the defuzzifying process by requiring each output fuzzy function to hold a single value. For the current subsystem, we apply the nine rules shown in Table 7.1 to map input functions to the output functions.

Table 7.1   Fuzzy Rules to Map the Input Variables to Output Variables

Profile Match	Keyword Match	Output Variable
Low	Low	No alert
Low	Medium	Low alert
Low	High	Alert
Medium	Low	Low alert
Medium	Medium	Medium alert
Medium	High	Alert
High	Low	Medium alert
High	Medium	Alert
High	High	High alert

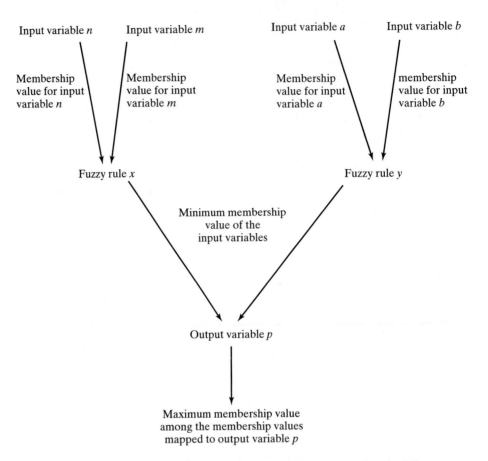

Figure 7.34 Procedure to transfer membership values using the Min-Max method.

We used the common min-max method, shown in Figure 7.34, to assign the membership values for the output function variables. That is, the maximum membership value of the two input functions is mapped to the corresponding output function. Once all rules are applied, and if one output function was mapped more than once by multiple rules, a minimum output membership value is assigned for that particular output membership function. To defuzzify the output values, all output functions and their membership values are used to compute the centroid of the output numerical value. The assigned output function values (x-axis) shown in Figure 7.33 are multiplied by the computed membership values from the nine rules, their results are added, and the sum is divided by the total number of the output membership functions. The final numerical value and an appropriate message is printed out on the LCD screen to inform the user the status of a session. Thus, for each session, the LCD displays a set of three numerical scores for the current session indicating the status of HTTP tunneling activities as an interactive session, a scripted session, and a streaming session.

7.6.6 Background Material

Recently, detecting HTTP tunneling activities has received a considerable amount of interest from the intrusion detection community. The primary reason for the attention is the pervasiveness of HTTP traffic on the Internet. Most firewalls do not perform extensive tests to check for any HTTP tunneling activities, which is very troublesome since the HTTP traffic makes up the bulk of incoming and outgoing traffic of any large organization.

The microcontroller-based system takes partial responsibility for the overall intrusion detection system's function by providing the computation associated with testing HTTP tunneling activities. The system uses the session features to test the Internet traffic data, which are made up of Internet sessions—software connections between two computers for transfer of data. A good example of a session occurs when you type in a Web address in a browser. Your computer is requesting a session to a host computer that contains a Web page that you want to see. Once you close that Web site and move on to another site, you are closing a session and starting another one.

7.6.7 Code

```
//===================================================================
// File: micro.c
// Func: Takes a set of six IDS matching scores and generates
//       alarm results
// Authors: Daniel Pack, Barry Mullins, and Steve Barrett
// Date: 6-17-04
// Setting: Program=0x1000, Data=0x3000, Stack=0x4000
//===================================================================

#include <stdio.h>
#include "hcs12dp256.h"


//===================================================================
//support functions

//===================================================================
// _HC12Setup: turn off the COP watchdog
//===================================================================
```

```
void _HC12Setup(void)
{
COPCTL = 0x00;                      //turn off the COP watchdog
}


//================================================================
// delay: time delay routines
//================================================================

void delay(void)
{                                   //Time delay routines
volatile unsigned n, m;
m = 10;
  do
   {
   n = 0;
   do
    {
    n--;
    }while(n);
   m--;
   } while(m);
}


//================================================================
// status_wait: time interface routine with the LCD
//================================================================

void status_wait(void)
{                                   //time interface routine with the LCD
char temp = 0x00;

DDRA = 0x00;
PORTB = 0xF9;
while((temp & 0x03) != 0x03)
   {
   PORTB = 0xFF;
   temp = PORTA;
   PORTB = 0xF9;
   }
PORTB = 0xFF;
DDRA = 0xFF;
}


//================================================================
// command: sending commands to the LCD
//================================================================
```

```c
void command(unsigned char n)
{                           //sending commands to the LCD
status_wait();
PORTA = n;
PORTB = 0xFF;
PORTB = PORTB & 0xFA;
PORTB = 0xFF;
}


//=================================================================
// data: sending data to the LCD
//=================================================================

void data(unsigned char n)
{                           //sending data to the LCD
status_wait();
PORTA = n;
PORTB = PORTB & 0xF2;
PORTB = 0xFF;
}



//=================================================================
// LCD_char: function to send a character to the LCD
//=================================================================

void LCD_char(unsigned char n)
{                           //function to send a character to the LCD
data(n - 0x20);
command(0xC0);
}



//=================================================================
// newline: send a new line to the LCD
//=================================================================

void newline(void)
{                           //send a new line to the LCD
int i;

for(i=0; i<16; i++)
  LCD_char(' ');
}

//=================================================================
// LCD_output: send a string of characters to the LCD
//=================================================================
```

```
void LCD_output(char s[])
{                           //send a string of characters to the LCD
int n = 0;

while (s[n] != '\0')
  {
  LCD_char(s[n]);
  ++n;
  }
}


//================================================================
// Reset_cursor: reposition the cursor
//================================================================

void Reset_cursor(void)
{                           //reposition the cursor
data(0x00);
data(0x10);
command(0x24);
}


//================================================================
// Clearscreen: clear LCD screen
//================================================================

void Clearscreen(void)
{                           //function to clear LCD screen
int i,j;

Reset_cursor();

for(i=0; i<16; i++)
    for(j=0; j<16; j++)
        LCD_char(' ');

Reset_cursor();
}


//================================================================
// Initlcd: initialize LCD
//================================================================

void Initlcd(void)
{                           //initialize LCD

PORTB = 0xEF;               //hard reset
delay();
```

```
PORTB = 0xFF;                    //all command lines high
status_wait();

command(0x80);                   //set mode to text
data(0x00);                      //set text home address L
data(0x10);                      //set text home address H
command(0x40);                   //set text home command

data(0x10);                      //set text area
data(0x00);
command(0x41);
command(0x94);                   //turn text display on
command(0xA7);                   //cursor is 8 x 8 dot
Clearscreen();
Reset_cursor();
}


//================================================================
// InitMes: initial message
//================================================================

void InitMes(void)
{                                //initial message

unsigned char k;

for(k=0; k<3; k++)
  newline();

LCD_output(" Portable HTTP  ");
newline();
LCD_output("   TAD System   ");
newline();
LCD_output("   version 1.0  ");
}


//================================================================
// numdisplay: display numerical numbers on LCD
//================================================================

void numdisplay(char s)
{                                //display numerical numbers on LCD
char k;

newline();
k = s;
s = s>>4;
```

```
if(s > 0x08)
  data(s + 0x17);
else
  data(s + 0x10);

command(0xC0);
k = k & 0x0F;

if(k > 0x08)
  data(k + 0x17);
else
  data(k + 0x10);

command(0xC0);
}

//-------------------------------------------------------------------
// Data Section
//-------------------------------------------------------------------

#pragma abs_address 0x3000

char BeP[12] = {0x00, 0x70, 0x00, 0x10,
                0x40, 0xC0, 0x10, 0x10,
                0x90, 0xFF, 0x10, 0x00};

char KeM[12] = {0x00, 0x70, 0x00, 0x10,
                0x40, 0xC0, 0x10, 0x10,
                0x90, 0xFF, 0x10, 0x00};

char OT[5]  =  {0x40, 0x60, 0x80, 0xA0, 0xC0};

char IMV[6] =  {0x00, 0x00, 0x00,
                0x00, 0x00, 0x00};

char OMV[5] =  {0x00, 0x00, 0x00, 0x00, 0x00};

// rules
char rules[45] =  {0x00, 0x03, 0xFE, 0x06, 0xFE,
                   0x00, 0x04, 0xFE, 0x07, 0xFE,
                   0x00, 0x05, 0xFE, 0x08, 0xFE,
                   0x01, 0x03, 0xFE, 0x07, 0xFE,
                   0x01, 0x04, 0xFE, 0x08, 0xFE,
                   0x01, 0x05, 0xFE, 0x09, 0xFE,
                   0x02, 0x03, 0xFE, 0x08, 0xFE,
                   0x02, 0x04, 0xFE, 0x09, 0xFE,
                   0x02, 0x05, 0xFE, 0x0A, 0xFF};
```

```
char result[3] =   {0x00, 0x00, 0x00};
#pragma end_abs_address


//---------------------------------------------------------------
// Main Program
//---------------------------------------------------------------

void main(void)
{
int index;
char temp = 0x00;

                                /* Interactive Tunneling Detection */
asm("LDX #$3000");
asm("LDY #$301D");
asm("LDAA $4000");              //behavior profile score
asm("MEM");
asm("MEM");
asm("MEM");                     //fuzzify

asm("LDAA $4001");              //keyword matching score
asm("MEM");
asm("MEM");
asm("MEM");                     //fuzzify

asm("LDY #$301D");
asm("LDX #$3028");
asm("LDAA #$FF");               //initialize min and V bit
asm("REV");                     //apply fuzzy rules

asm("LDX #$3018");              //defuzzify
asm("LDY #$3023");
asm("LDAB #$05");
asm("WAV");
asm("EDIV");
asm("TFR Y,D");
asm("STAB $3055");              //store result

PORTB = 0xff;
DDRB = 0xff;

delay2();
PORTB = 0x7F;                   //check board using the LEDs
delay2();
PORTB = 0xFF;


                                /*Script Tunneling Detection */
```

```
asm("LDX #$3000");
asm("LDY #$301D");
asm("LDAA $4002");                //behavior profile score
asm("MEM");
asm("MEM");
asm("MEM");                       //fuzzify

asm("LDAA #$FF");                 //keyword matching score
asm("MEM");
asm("MEM");
asm("MEM");                       //fuzzify

asm("LDY #$301D");
asm("LDX #$3028");
asm("LDAA $4003");                //initialize min and V bit
asm("REV");                       //apply fuzzy rules

asm("LDX #$3018");                //defuzzify
asm("LDY #$3023");
asm("LDAB #$05");
asm("WAV");
asm("EDIV");
asm("TFR Y,D");
asm("STAB $3056");                //store result

PORTB = 0xff;
DDRB = 0xff;

delay2();
PORTB = 0x7F;                     //check board using the LEDs
delay2();
PORTB = 0xFF;

                                  /*Stream Detection */
asm("LDX #$3000");
asm("LDY #$301D");
asm("LDAA $4004");                //behavior profile score
asm("MEM");
asm("MEM");
asm("MEM");                       //fuzzify

asm("LDAA $4005");                //keyword matching score
asm("MEM");
asm("MEM");
asm("MEM");                       //fuzzify

asm("LDY #$301D");
asm("LDX #$3028");
```

```
asm("LDAA $4003");              //initialize min and V bit
asm("REV");                     //apply fuzzy rules

asm("LDX #$3018");              //defuzzify
asm("LDY #$3023");
asm("LDAB #$05");
asm("WAV");
asm("EDIV");
asm("TFR Y,D");
asm("STAB $3057");              //store result

PORTB = 0xff;
DDRB = 0xff;

delay2();
PORTB = 0x7F;                   //check board using the LEDs
delay2();
PORTB = 0xFF;


                                //LCD configuration
DDRA = 0xFF;
PORTB = 0xFF;

Initlcd();                      //Initialize LCD
InitMes();                      //Initialize message

delay2();

Clearscreen();                  //Clear LCD screen
Reset_cursor();                 //Reset LCD cursor

newline();                      //Generate newline on LCD
newline();

LCD_output("IA: ");
numdisplay(result[0]);

if (result[0] > 0xA0)           //Display alert status
  LCD_output(" High Alert");
else if (result[0] > 0x60)
  LCD_output(" Med Alert");
else
  LCD_output(" Low Alert");

newline();

LCD_output("SA: ");
numdisplay(result[1]);
```

```
if (result[0] > 0xA0)
  LCD_output(" High Alert");
else if (result[1] > 0x60)
  LCD_output(" Med Alert");
else
  LCD_output(" Low Alert");

newline();

LCD_output("S: ");
numdisplay(result[2]);

if (result[2] > 0xA0)
  LCD_output(" High Alert");
else if (result[0] > 0x60)
  LCD_output(" Med Alert");
else
  LCD_output(" Low Alert");
}

//================================================================
```

7.6.8 Some Comments

You may be wondering about the reason to have a separate microcontroller-based HTTP TAD system. Why not include the function of the HTTP TAD system within an intruder detection system? The purpose of the exercise is to show the powerful features of the HCS12 controller and its application to a variety of projects. Certainly, the system described in this section can be incorporated within a large intruder detection system. One advantage of having a separate system is portability. It provides information security administrators with a flexible tool to modify a single portable system and test multiple units within a network. To probe further on the information security issues and research, we refer our readers to the Further Reading Section at the end of this chapter.

7.7 ELECTRONIC SLIDING PUZZLE GAME

7.7.1 Project Description

It is very likely that you have played the sliding puzzle game shown in Figure 7.35. The game has been used to entertain kids at home, in summer camps, and traveling in the backseats of cars. Over the years, we have witnessed a variety of games such as the sliding puzzle game be transformed into electronic form. In this section, we present an electronic version of the sliding puzzle game. The project was created by Scott Lewis as his senior project design.

Figure 7.35   The sliding puzzle game.

1	5	15	▨
11	3	6	4
10	12	2	7
9	8	13	14

1	2	3	4
5	6	7	8
9	10	11	12
13	14	15	▨

Figure 7.36   A sliding puzzle game board. The left frame shows a start state of the board and the right frame shows the desired ending state of the board when the game is finished.

The objective of the sliding puzzle game is as follows: Given a set of 15 randomly arranged consecutive numerical number pieces and a blank slot in a 4 × 4 array, the objective of the game is to slide number pieces to an open slot, one at a time, and to rearrange the number pieces in proper numerical order. Typically, numbers from 1 to 15 are shown on the puzzle pieces, and a player must put the numbers in an increasing order, starting with 1 on the top-left corner of the 4 × 4 array and placing the remaining numbers in the proper order, as shown in Figure 7.36.

Our objective for this project is to create an electronic version of the game with proper input devices to move each piece of the puzzle and a display device to show the current locations of the puzzle pieces.

The system requirements for the sliding puzzle game system are as follows:

1. Use a microcontroller.
2. Allow a user to identify a number piece using an input device.
3. Allow a user to move a selected piece to a blank slot.
4. Display the current locations of all number pieces.

7.7.2 68HC12 Systems Employed

This project uses various parts of the 68HC12 to interface various switches and a two-dimensional liquid crystal display.

7.7.3 Background Theory

The system uses the 68HC12B32EVB, an AND 1391 two-dimensional LCD, an external RAM 6264 chip, an EPROM 27256 chip, a programmable GAL16V8 chip, a set of input buttons, and a 74HC373 latch chip. Figure 7.37 shows a block diagram of the sliding puzzle system.

Although we could have used the internal memory of the 68HC12, for the benefit of the reader we used external memory devices and operated the microcontroller in an expanded mode. To send appropriate control signals and provide

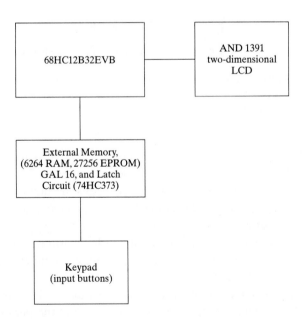

Figure 7.37   A block diagram showing the components of the sliding puzzle system.

memory address decoding, we need to program a GAL16V8 chip and place it between the memory chips and the microcontroller. The GAL chip is programmed so that the external RAM chip is placed at memory locations $2000 through $3FFF and the external EPROM chip is placed at memory locations $4000 through $7FFF. As you will see, the program shown in this section runs using the RAM chip. The EPROM chip can be used to make the system stand-alone.

Here are the program equations for the 16V8:

```
CHIP PAL16V8
Pins 1    2     3     4     5     6     7     8     9     10
     NC   A15   A14   A13   E     R_W   A12   NC    NC    GND

Pins 11   12    13    14    15    16    17    18    19    20
     NC   NC    NC    NC    NC    /WE   /OE   /RAM  /ROM  VCC

Equations
; The following equation uses A15, A14, and A13
; to place the SRAM chip at $2000-$3FFF

RAM = /A15 * /A14 * A13

; The following equation uses A15 and A14
; to place the EPROM chip at $4000-$7FFF

ROM = /A15 * A14

; The following equation creates the output enable
; signal for the memory chips by ANDing the E clock
; with the read/write line form the 68HC12

OE = E * R_W

; The following equation creates the write enable signal
; for the SRAM by ANDing the E clock with an inverted
; read/write line form the 68HC12

WE = E * /R_W
```

7.7.4 Game Schematic, Structure Chart and UML Activity Diagram

Figure 7.38 shows a hardware interface diagram for the sliding puzzle game system. The built-in ports of the 68HC912B32 board are used to receive and send data from a keypad and an LCD display unit.

The game schematic for the sliding puzzle circuit with memory expansion is provided in Figure 7.39.

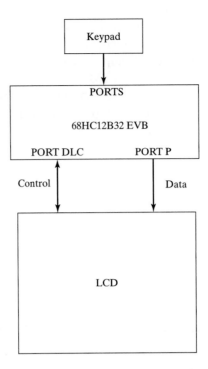

Figure 7.38   Sliding puzzle hardware interface diagram.

Figure 7.40 shows the software structure chart of the sliding puzzle game system. The main program calls on six submodules to perform the task. For each submodule, a number of associated functions are provided in the figure.

The corresponding UML activity diagram is shown in Figure 7.41.

7.7.5 Background Material

The AND 1391ST dot intelligent graphics display is a full dot matrix LCD with a built-in LCD controller module and RAM-based display. It can display 21 characters on each of the 18 display lines. For a refresher on this display and its supporting functions, see Chapter 5.

7.7.6 Code

```
//****************************************************************
//filename: sliding.c
//Program: Sliding Puzzle Game
//Authors: Scott Lewis, Daniel Pack, and Steve Barrett
//Date: Started 27 April 2004
//       Ended 7 May 2004
```

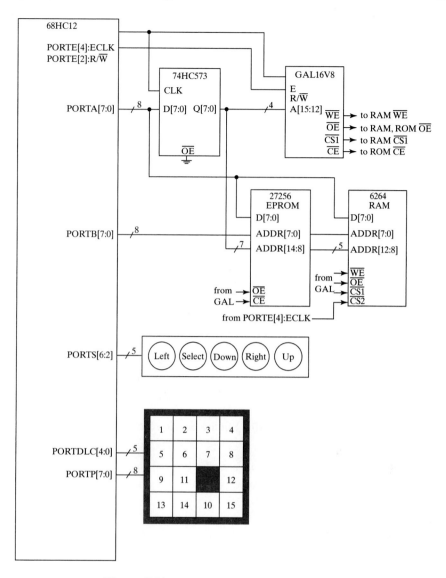

Figure 7.39   Sliding puzzle game schematic.

```
//Description: This program implements the sliding puzzle game.
//            The objective of the game is to move number pieces
//            so that they end up in order.  You can only move a
//            piece where there is an empty slot.  The program
//            resides in location $2000 of the system memory.
//            The program displays an introduction, then shows
//            the configuration needed to win.  The program
//            places all number pieces randomly, displays their
```

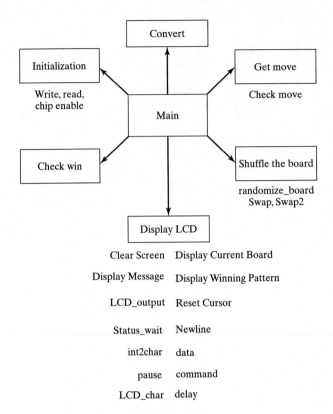

Figure 7.40   Sliding puzzle software structure chart.

```
//              positions, and then allows the user to start
//              playing.
//
//Hardware configuration
//    Program: 0x2000
//    Data:    0x3500
//    Stack:   0x4000
//
//    PDLC0: /WR      PP0: Data 0      PS0: NC
//    PDLC1: /RD      PP1: Data 1      PS1: NC
//    PDLC2: /CE      PP2: Data 2      PS2: Left Button
//    PDLC3: C/D      PP3: Data 3      PS3: Select Button
//    PDLC4: /Reset   PP4: Data 4      PS4: Down Button
//    PDLC5: NC       PP5: Data 5      PS5: Right Button
//    PDLC6: NC       PP6: Data 6      PS6: Up Button
//    PDLC7: NC       PP7: Data 7      PS7: NC
//
//    LCD Pin connections
//    GND  -  2    1 - GND
```

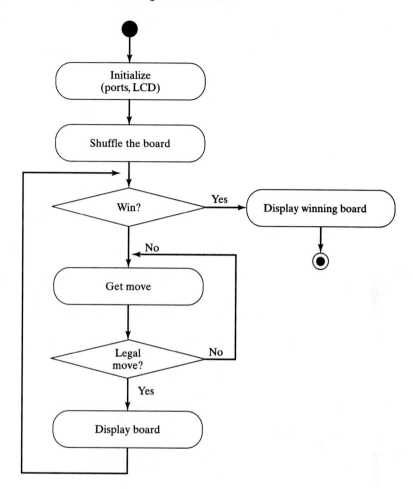

Figure 7.41   Sliding puzzle UML activity diagram.

```
//    -14V  -   3     4 - +5V
//    /WR   -   5     6 - /RD
//    /CE   -   7     8 - C/D
//    NC    -   9    10 - /Reset
//    D0    - 11    12 - D1
//    D2    - 13    14 - D3
//    D4    - 15    16 - D5
//    D6    - 17    18 - D7
//    GND   - 19    20 - NC
//***************************************************************

#include <912b32.h>              // port description - header file
                                 // provided in appendix
```

```
//*****************************************************************
// CONSTANTS
//*****************************************************************
#define ARRAY_MAX 15
#define ZERO    0x00

#define L_BUTTON 0x04                        // button signals
#define R_BUTTON 0x20
#define U_BUTTON 0x40
#define D_BUTTON 0x10
#define S_BUTTON 0x08

#define LEFT 1                               // select direction
#define RIGHT 2
#define UP 3
#define DOWN 4
#define SELECT 5

#define SIZE 4                               // size of row/col


//*****************************************************************
// FUNCTION PROTOTYPES
//*****************************************************************

int check_win(int array[ARRAY_MAX+1]);

void convert_multi_single(int A[SIZE][SIZE], int B[SIZE][SIZE]);
void convert_single_multi(int A[ARRAY_MAX+1], int B[SIZE][SIZE]);
void display_board
            (int A[SIZE][SIZE], int row, int col, int direction);
void display_board2(int board_array[ARRAY_MAX+1]);
void display_error(int n);
void display_intro(void);
void display_win(void);
void get_move(int *direction, int *row, int *col, int *select);
void randomize_board(int board_array[]);
void swap(int row, int col, int new_row, int new_col,
                                    int array[SIZE][SIZE]);
void swap2(int from, int to, int array[ARRAY_MAX+1]);
void try_move(int move, int row, int col, int array[SIZE][SIZE]);
unsigned char mode(unsigned char num, int modulus);
void LCD_output(char s[]);
void int2char(int i);
void pause(void);
void delay(int usec);
void enable(void);
void initialize_LCD(void);
void command(unsigned char n);
```

```
void data(unsigned char n);
void write(void);
void read(void);
void status_wait(void);
void LCD_char(unsigned char n);
void Clearscreen(void);
void newline(void);
void Reset_cursor(void);


//*****************************************************************
// VARIABLES
//*****************************************************************

#pragma abs_address 0x3600
static int win_array[ARRAY_MAX+1]
                    = {1,2,3,4,5,6,7,8,9,10,11,12,13,14,15,0};
#pragma end_abs_address

#prama abs_address 0x3500
int board_array_single[ARRAY_MAX+1];
int board_array_multi[SIZE][SIZE];
int win;                              //used as boolean
int direction;                        //moving direction
int row;                              //row selected
int col;                              //col selected
int select;                           //if button selected
int i;                                //temporary variable
#pragma end_abs_address


//*****************************************************************
// MAIN PROGRAM
//*****************************************************************

void main()
{
win = 0;                   //initialize all variables
direction = 0;
row = 1;
col = 1;
select = 0;
i = 0;
DDRDLC = 0x1F              //configure DDRDLC as output pins
DDRP = 0xFF               //configure all port P pins as output
DDRS = 0x00               //configure all port S pints as input
TSCR = 0x80               //turn on timer
initialize_LCD();         //initialize LCD
Clearscreen();
Reset_cursor();
```

```
display_intro();
for(i=0; i<ARRAY_MAX+1; i++)
  board_array_single[i] = win_array[i];
convert_single_multi(board_array_single, board_array_multi);
display_board(board_array_multi,row,col, direction);
pause();                          // wait for user to push X button
LCD_output(''Now the board is");    // display message
LCD_output(''randomized. You ");
LCD_output(''may begin by     ");
LCD_output(''choosing a piece");
LCD_output(''to move, and its");
LCD_output(''direction.      ");
newline();
pause();
randomize_board(board_array_single); // randomize the board
convert_single_multi(board_array_single, board_array_multi);
display_board(board_array_multi, row, col, direction);

while(win ==0)
  {                          //loop until the game is won

  while (select == 0)
    {                        //if anything but X button is pressed
                             //get the move direction, row and col
                             //of selected
    get_move(&direction, &row, &col, &select);
    Reset_cursor();          // put cursor at top
    if(select == 0)
      display_board(board_array_multi,row,col, direction);
    }
                             //check legal move, take it if valid, or
                             //display error

    try_move(direction,row-1,col-1,board_array_multi);
    select = 0;
    convert_multi_single(board_array_multi, board_array_single);
    win = check_win(board_array_single);
    Clearscreen();
                             // display the current board
    display_board(board_array_multi,row,col, direction);
  }
  display_win();             //display winding screen
}

//*************************************************************
// DISPLAY INTRO MESSAGE
//*************************************************************
```

```
void display_intro()
{
newline();
LCD_output(''    WELCOME     ");
LCD_output(''       TO       ");
LCD_output('' SLIDING PUZZLE ");
new_line();
pause();
LCD_output(''The object of  ");
LCD_output(''this game is to ");
LCD_output(''move each #'ed  ");
LCD_output(''puzzle piece so ");
LCD_output(''that you end up ");
LCD_output(''in the order    ");
LCD_output(''seen below. The ");
LCD_output(''star shows the  ");
LCD_output(''current piece   ");
LCD_output(''selected. You   ");
LCD_output(''can choose a    ");
LCD_output(''different piece ");
LCD_output(''by using the    ");
LCD_output(''arrow buttons   ");
newline();
pause();
LCD_output(''and select the  ");
LCD_output(''piece you want  ");
LCD_output(''to move by      ");
LCD_output(''pressing the X  ");        // 'select' button
LCD_output(''button. Choose  ");
LCD_output(''the direction to");
LCD_output(''move that piece ");
LCD_output(''with the arrows.");
new_line();
LCD_output(''WINDING         ");
LCD_output(''CONFIGURATION:  ");
newline();
}


//*************************************************************
// DISPLAY WINNING MESSAGE
//*************************************************************

void display_win()
{
LCD_output(''   YOU WIN!!!   ");
LCD_output(''CONGRATULATIONS ");
}
```

```
//****************************************************************
// GET MOVE: gets the position the user chooses and the direction
//           to move
//****************************************************************
void get_move(int *direction, int *row, int *col, int *select)
{
int n = 0;
int button = 0;
unsigned char temp = ZERO;
newline();
LCD_output(''Choose move or  ");
LCD_output(''select piece:   ");

while(button == 0)
  {                              // keep looping until button is pressed
  temp = PORTS;
  temp = temp & 0x7C

  switch (temp)               //respond to switch depression
    {
    case L_BUTTON:
        button = LEFT;
        break;

    case R_BUTTON:
        button = RIGHT;
        break;

    case U_BUTTON:
        button = UP
        break;

    case D_BUTTON:
        button = DOWN;
        break;

    case S_BUTTON:
        button = SELECT;
        break;
    } // end switch
  }//end while

n = 0;
switch (button)               //respond to switch input
  {
  case UP:
        if (*row > 1)
          *row -= 1;
```

```
           else
              display_error(UP);
           break;

   case DOWN:
           if (*row < SIZE)
             *row += 1;
           else
             display_error(DOWN);
           break;

   case LEFT:
           if (*col > 1)
             *col -= 1;
           else
             display_error(LEFT);
           break;

   case RIGHT:
           if (*col < SIZE)
             *col += 1
           else
             display_error(RIGHT);
           break;

   case SELECT:
           *select = 1;
           LCD_output(''Pick a direction");
           *direction = 0;

           while (*direction == 0)
             {
             temp = PORTS;
             temp = temp & 0x7C;

             switch(temp)
               {
               case L_BUTTON:
                    *direction = LEFT;
                     break;

               case R_BUTTON:
                    *direction = RIGHT;
                    break;

               case U_BUTTON:
                    *direction = UP;
                    break;
```

```
                case D_BUTTON:
                      *direction = DOWN;
                      break;
                }
            }
          break;
        }
    }
```

```
//****************************************************************
// RANDOMIZE BOARD
//****************************************************************

void randomize_board(int board_array[])
{
int temp = 0;
int i;
unsigned char temp2 = 0x00;

for(i=0; i<ARRAY_MAX+1; i++)
  {
  temp2 = TCNTL;
  temp = mod(temp2,15);        //random value using the TCNT counter
  swap2(i,temp, board_array);
  }
}

//****************************************************************
// MATHEMATICAL MOD FUNCTION
//****************************************************************

unsigned char mod(unsigned char num, int modulus)
{
while ((num - modulus) > 0)
  num = num -modulus;

return num;
}

//****************************************************************
//Display Board2: Displays the board as a single row values
//****************************************************************

void display_board2(int board_array[ARRAY_MAX+1])
{
int = 0;
int n;
```

```
for (i=0; i<ARRAY_MAX+1; i++)
  {
  n = board_array[i];
  int2char(n);
  }
LCD_output(''\n");
}


//************************************************************
//Display Board: Displays the board as a proper 4 x 4 array
//************************************************************

void display_board(int A[SIZE][SIZE], int row, int col,
                                      int direction)
{
#pragma abs_address 0x0800
int i;
int j;
int num;
#pragma end_abs_address

newline();
LCD_output(''    |   Column   ");
LCD_output(''    | 1  2  3  4 ");
LCD_output(''----------------");

for (i=0; i < SIZE; i++)
  {
  j=0;
  switch(i)
    {
    case 0: LCD_output(''R 1|");
            break;

    case 1: LCD_output(''o 2|");
            break;

    case 2: LCD_output(''w 3|");
            break;

    case 3: LCD_output(''  4|");
            break;
    }

    for (j=0; j < SIZE; j++)
      {
      num = A[i][j];
      if (num == 0)
```

```
      LCD_output('' ");
    else
      int2char(num);
    if ((i+1 == row) && (j+1) == col))
      LCD_output(''*");
    else
      LCD_output('' ");
     }
    }
  newline();
  LCD_output(''You are at (R,C)");
  LCD_output(''   (");
  int2char(row);
  LCD_output(",");
  int2char(col);
  LCD_output('') =");
  int2char(A[row-1][col-1]);
  LCD_output(''   ");
  newline();
 }

//******************************************************************
// INT2CHAR: takes an integer and  outputs it to the LCD as
//           2 characters
//******************************************************************

void int2char(int i)
{
if (i > 9)
  {
  LCD_output(''1");
  i -= 10;
  }
else
  {
  LCD_output('' ");
  }

switch(i)
  {
  case 0: LCD_output(''0");
          break;

  case 1: LCD_output(''1");
          break;

  case 2: LCD_output(''2");
          break;
```

```
   case 3: LCD_output (''3");
           break;

   case 4: LCD_output (''4");
           break;

   case 5: LCD_output (''5");
           break;

   case 6: LCD_output (''6");
           break;

   case 7: LCD_output (''7");
           break;

   case 8: LCD_output (''8");
           break;

   case 9: LCD_output (''9");
           break;
   }
}


//******************************************************************
//Check_Win: This function checks each cell on the board to see if
//the board is in the wining configuration. win = 1, 0 otherwise
//******************************************************************

int check_win(int array[ARRAY_MAX+1])
{
int i;
int win = 1;
for (i=0; i<ARRAY_MAX+1; i++)
  {
  if (array[i] != win_array[i])
    win = 0;
  }
return win;
}


//******************************************************************
//Convert_multi_single: This function converts a 2D array into a
//1D array.
//******************************************************************

int convert_multi_single(int A[SIZE][SIZE], int B[ARRAY_MAX+1])
{
int n = 0;
int i = 0;
```

```
int j = 0;
for (i=0; i<SIZE; i++)
  {
  for (j=0; j<SIZE; j++)
    {
    B[n] = A[i][j];
    n++;
    }
  }
}


//********************************************************************
//Convert_single_multi: This function converts a 1D array into a
//2D array.
//********************************************************************

void convert_single_multi(int A[ARRAY_MAX+1], int B[SIZE][SIZE])
{
B[0][0] = A[0];
B[0][1] = A[1];
B[0][2] = A[2];
B[0][3] = A[3];
B[1][0] = A[4];
B[1][1] = A[5];
B[1][2] = A[6];
B[1][3] = A[7];
B[2][0] = A[8];
B[2][1] = A[9];
B[2][2] = A[10];
B[2][3] = A[11];
B[3][0] = A[12];
B[3][1] = A[13];
B[3][2] = A[14];
B[3][3] = A[15];
}


//********************************************************************
//Try_move: This function checks to see if a user specified move
//is valid. If legal, it executes the move, else displays an
//appropriate message.
//********************************************************************

void try_move(int move, int row, int col, int array[SIZE][SIZE])
{
switch(move)
  {
  case UP:
            if ((row-1 >=0) && (array[row-1][col] == 0))
```

```
                    swap(row,col, row-1,col,array);
                else
                    display_error(UP);
                break;

        case DOWN:
                if ((row+1 <= SIZE) && (array[row+1][col] == 0))
                    swap(row,col, row+1,col,array);
                else
                    display_error(DOWN);
                break;

        case LEFT:
                if ((col-1 >=0) && (array[row][col-1] == 0))
                    swap(row,col, row,col-1,array);
                else
                    display_error(LEFT);
                break;

        case RIGHT:
                if ((col+1 <= SIZE) && (array[row][col+1] == 0))
                    swap(row,col, row,col+1,array);
                else
                    display_error(RIGHT);
                break;
    }
}


//******************************************************************
//Swap: This function swaps two values in a 2D array.
//******************************************************************
void swap(int row, int col, int new_row, int new_col,
                                    int array[SIZE][SIZE])
{
int temp;

temp = array[row][col];
array[row][col] = array[new_row][new_col];
array[new_row][new_col] = temp;
}


//******************************************************************
//Swap2: This function swaps two values in a 1D array.
//******************************************************************

void swap2(int from, int to, int array[ARRAY_MAX+1])
{
int temp = array[from];
array[from] = array[to];
```

```
array[to] = temp;
}

//*************************************************************
//ERROR: This function displays an error message.
//*************************************************************

void display_error(int n)
{
LCD_output(''ERROR: ");

switch(n)
   {
   case LEFT:
              LCD_output(''no move L");
              break;

   case RIGHT:
              LCD_output(''no move R");
              break;

   case UP:
              LCD_output(''no move U");
              break;

   case DOWN:
              LCD_output(''no move D");
              break;
   }

pause();
}

//*************************************************************
//LCD_output: This function displays a string to the LCD screen.
//*************************************************************

void LCD_output(char s[])
{
int n = 0;

while (s[n] != '\0')
   {
   LCD_char(s[n]);
   ++n;
   }
}
```

```
//****************************************************************
//Pause: This function waits for the user to press the select
//        button.
//****************************************************************

void pause()
{
unsigned char c = ZERO;
LCD_output(''(Please press X)");

while (c != S_BUTTON)
  {
  c = PORTS;
  c = c& 0x7C;
  }

Clearscreen();
Reset_cursor();
}


//****************************************************************
//Delay: This function causes n microseconds delay, where n is an
//input value.
//****************************************************************

void delay(int usec)
{
int i,j;

for (i=0; i<usec; i++)
  {
  for (j=0; j < 7; j++)
    {
    }
  }
}


//****************************************************************
//Initialize_LCD: This function sets up the LCD.
//****************************************************************

void initialize_LCD(void)
{
char temp = 0x00;
PORTDLC = 0xFF;
PORTDLC = PORTDLC & 0xEF;    // reset screen (RESET = 0)
delay(2000)                 // delay 2 msec
PORTDLC = 0x7F;             // turn off reset
```

```
write();                        // turn on write
command(0x80);                  // mode set: text

data(0x00);                     // control word set
data(0x10);                     // = 0x1000
command(0x40);

data(0x10);                     // number of text area set (1E)
data(0x00);                     // = 0x1000
command(0x41);

                                //turn text display on, cursor, blink off
command(0x94);
command(0xA7);                  //cursor is 8 x 8 dot
}


//****************************************************************
//Enable: This function turns on the chip enable
//****************************************************************

void enable(void)
{
PORTDLC = PORTDLC | 0x04;   // turn enable off
PORTDLC = PORTDLC & 0xFB;   // turn enable on
}


//****************************************************************
//Disable: This function turns off the chip enable.
//****************************************************************

void disable(void)
{
PORTDLC = PORTDLC | 0x04;
}


//****************************************************************
//Command: This function sends a command out to the LCD.
//****************************************************************

void command(unsigned char n)
{
status_wait();
PORTP = n;
PORTDLC = 0xFF;
PORTDLC = PORTDLC & 0xFE;              // write low
enable();                              // make CE low
delay(10)                              // delay at least 80 ns
disable();                             // make CE high
}
```

```c
//*******************************************************************
//Data: This functions sends data out to the LCD.
//*******************************************************************

void data(unsigned char n)
{
status_wait();
PORTP = n;
PORTDLC = 0xFF;
PORTDLC = PORTDL>C & 0xF7;              // make C/D low
PORTDLC = PORTDLC & 0xFE;               // make WR low
PORTDLC = PORTDLC & 0xFB;
delay(10);
disable();
}


//*******************************************************************
//Write: This function sets up PORT P as output.
//*******************************************************************

void write()
{
DDRP = 0xFF;
}


//*******************************************************************
//Read: This function sets up port P as input.
//*******************************************************************

void read()
{
DDRP = 0x00;
}


//*******************************************************************
//Status_wait: Provides an appropriate delay between LCD
//             instructions.
//*******************************************************************

void status_wait()
{
char temp = 0x00;
DDRP = 0x00;
PORTDLC = PORTDLC | 0x0F;               // turn everything off
PORTDLC = PORTDLC & 0xFD;               // make RD low
enable();
delay(10);
```

```
while ((temp & 0x03) != 0x03)
  {
  temp = PORTP;
  }

disable();
DDRP = 0xFF;
}

//****************************************************************
//LCD_char: This function writes an ASCII character to the
//          LCD screen.
//****************************************************************

void LCD_char(unsigned char n)
{
data(n-0x20);
command(0xC0);
}

//****************************************************************
//Clearscreen: This function clears the LCD screen.
//****************************************************************

void Clearscreen()
{
int i,j;

Reset_cursor();

for (i=0; i < 16; i++)
  for (j=0; j<16; j++)
    LCD_char(' ');
Reset_cursor();
}

//****************************************************************
//Newline: This function writes a blank line to the LCD screen.
//****************************************************************

void newline()
{
int i;

for (i=0; i<16; i++)
  LCD_char(' ');
}
```

```
//**************************************************************
//Reset_cursor: Resets the cursor to the beginning of the
//              LCD display.
//**************************************************************

void Reset_cursor()
{
data(0x00);
data(0x10);
command(0x24);
}


//**************************************************************
```

7.7.7 Some Comments

The sliding puzzle game uses five keypad buttons to move puzzle pieces: (1) up arrow, (2) down arrow, (3) right arrow, (4) left arrow, and (5) select button. In addition, puzzle piece locations are specified by row and column numbers using keyboard input. Once packaged, the system can make a great game for both adults and kids.

7.8 APPLICATION: PROGRAMMING THE FLASH EEPROM ON THE B32 EVB

In Chapter 4 we discussed the memory configuration of the B32 variant of the 68HC12. Recall the B32 EVB was equipped with 32K of flash EEPROM beginning at memory location $8000. Normally the flash has the D-Bug12 monitor program resident within it. If you would like to store a program in the flash memory, you must first erase the D-Bug12 program from the flash. It is a good idea to have the D-Bug12 file available in the event you would like to restore it to flash later.

There are several methods available to reprogram the flash. These methods normally require two B32 configured processors to accomplish the programming actions. If two processors are used, one is designated as the pod and the other as the target. Detailed instructions of this technique are available [Lind].

In this section we describe how to program flash memory using P&E Microcomputer Systems' CABLE12 BDM Interface Cable for the CPU12 and their PROG12Z FLASH/EEPROM Programmer Software. The CABLE12 serves as the pod during programming activities.

The programming configuration using these tools is provided in Figure 7.42. As you can see, the CABLE12 is connected to the host PC via a standard 25 pin parallel cable. The CABLE12 is connected to the B32 EVB via the six-conductor

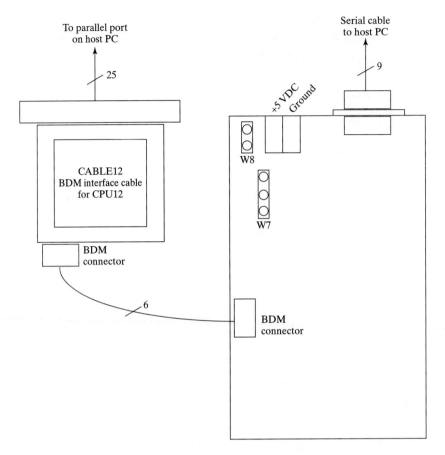

Figure 7.42   Flash EEPROM programming configuration.

BDM cable supplied with the CABLE12. The BDM cable plug mates with the W9 header pins on the B32 EVB card. The cable's red conductor corresponds to pin 1 on the W9 header.

The B32 EVB is also connected to the host PC via a serial cable. It should have its normal power connections (+5 VDC, ground). Additionally, a +12 VDC supply (V_{pp}) and ground connection should be connected to the W8 header pins during programming. Be careful to observe the polarity markings on the header. Also, the W7 header pin should be configured for V_{pp}.

Once the hardware is configured, follow these steps to program the flash EEPROM:

1. Apply power to the B32 (both +5 VDC and +12 VDC).
2. Find the location of the PROG12Z software on your computer (`c:\pemicro\prog12z\prog12z`).

3. Double click on `prog12z`.

4. A `Connect Assistant` window appears to help establish connection with the CABLE12 BDM interface pod.

- Check window settings, then click `OK`.
- In the `Status Window` the message `BDM Interface cable detected` appears if connection has been established between the `prog12z` software and the CABLE12 BDM interface pod.
- If the connection between the PC and the CABLE12 BDM interface pod is not established, troubleshooting information is provided.

5. A `Specify Programming Algorithm to Use!` pop-up window should appear.

- Choose the correct `'*.12P'` P&E Program Algorithm for the desired programming activity. For example, to program the 32K flash EEPROM on the B32 EVB, select `912b32_32K.12P`.
- The `Status Window` indicates the device has been detected.

6. A `Base Address` window then appears.

- You must provide the base address of the flash EEPROM component.
- The base address information is provided in the factory-configuration memory map, shown in *68HC12 M68EVB912B32 Evaluation Board User's Manual* (Table 3-5, pages 3–55)
- The flash EEPROM memory begins at location $8000.
- Insert this value and click `OK`.

7. Click `SM Show Module` to display module contents.

8. Erase the module prior to programming the flash EEPROM memory. *Caution*: The D-BUG12 monitor program is currently in the flash EEPROM. Once you erase the module, D-BUG12 features are no longer available for use. Erase the module.

9. Choose `SS Specify Record` to choose the `*.S19` record for downloading.

10. Choose `PM` to `Program Module`.

7.9 SUMMARY

In this chapter we presented a variety of embedded systems using the 68HC12 and HCS12 controllers. In particular, we showed a wall-following mobile robot system, a laser light show, a digital voltmeter, a motor speed control with optical tachometer, a flying robot, a fuzzy-logic-based security system, and an electronic sliding puzzle game. For each system, we included a project description, system requirements, background information, a software structure chart, a UML activity diagram, and C code. Although the functions of the embedded systems differ, we have illustrated the same common process involved in creating all of them.

7.10 FURTHER READING

American National Standards Institute (ANSI) Z136.1, *Safe Use of Lasers* (ANSI Z136.1), 1993.

Cooper, W. D. *Electronic Instrumentation and Measurement Techniques.* Upper Saddle River, NJ: Prentice-Hall, 1970.

Edmund Industrial Optics, Barrington, NJ, www.edmundoptics.com, 2004.

GSI Lumonics, "General Scanning Scanners and Drivers." www.gsilumonics.com, 2004.

Honeywell Sensing and Control, www.honeywell.com/sensing, 2004.

Lind, Magnus. *Motorola M68HC912B32EVB Evaluation Board: PC-POD-Target Set Up*, Western Washington University Electronics Engineering Technology, Bellingham, WA, http://eet.etec.www.edu.

68HC12 M68EVB912B32 Evaluation Board User's Manual, 68EVB912B32 UM/D, Motorola Inc., 1997.

LINOS Photonics, Milford, MA, www.linos.com.

Newport Corporation Irvine, CA, www.newport.com, 2004.

Pack, D. J. and S. F. Barrett. *68HC12 Microcontroller: Theory and Applications.* Upper Saddle River, NJ: Prentice-Hall, 2002.

Pack, D. J., W. Strelein, S. Webster, and R. Cunningham. "Detecting HTTP Tunneling Activities." Paper presented at the annual Information Assurance Workshop, West Point, NY, June 2002.

Servo-Tek, "Encoders and Other Position/Velocity Sensors for Motion Control. www.servotek.com, 2004.

Vij, D. R. and K. Mahesh. *Medical Applications of Lasers.* Kluwer Academic Publishers, 2002.

Vincent Associates, "Uniblitz Electronic Drive Equipment and Shutters." www.uniblitz.com, 2004.

7.11 PROBLEMS

Fundamental

1. Describe the theory of operation for the infrared emitter-detector pairs used for maze wall detection.

2. Describe the purpose of the Hall effect sensor.

3. Describe the theory of operation of a parallel input DAC and a serial input DAC.

4. What is a laser?

5. What is a galvanometer?

6. Describe two methods of improving the resolution of a the 68HC12's ATD system.

7. Describe the theory of operation of an optical encoder.

8. What is the purpose of the 68HC12's real-time interrupt (RTI) system?

9. What are the benefits of having a hardware interface diagram, software structure chart, and UML activity diagram?

10. In designing an embedded system, what is the difference between system requirements and system specifications?

11. Given the variety of 68HC12 microcontrollers, what is the proper procedure to select a particular controller to meet design requirements?

Advanced

1. Construct the UML activity diagrams for each function used by the wall-following robot operating system provided in Section 7.1.5.

2. Devise an experiment to precisely determine the length of the time delay provided by the function delay in the laser light show project.

3. Investigate the differences between laser classes.

4. If the 74HC04 inverters were removed from the input switch configuration of the laser control interface, how would the software supporting the interface change?

5. Recalculate the values of resistances and the V_{ref} required to provide for a ± 4 VDC DAC0808LCN operation.

6. Develop the structure chart and the UML activity diagram for the DVM support functions.

7. What is the resolution of the 8-bit DVM described in Section 7.3 of the text? What determines this resolution? Describe a method to improve the resolution. *Hint*: Examine the S10BM bit in the ATDCTL4 register. What is the improved resolution?

8. In the motor speed control project, we indicated that each incremental change in the PWM duty cycle resulted in an approximate 8.5 RPM change in motor speed. Do you agree with this analysis? Support your answer with calculations.

9. Construct the UML activity diagrams for each function used by the motor speed control project provided in Section 7.4.5 of the chapter.

10. Develop a test plan based on bottom-up implementation techniques for the motor speed control project.

Challenging

1. Replace the parallel input DAC0808LCN of the laser light show with a DAC connected to the serial peripheral interface (SPI). Provide a wiring diagram for the DAC and also a support function to replace `move_laser(x,y)`.

2. Modify the code contained in `laser.c` (Section 7.2.6) such that a waveform is traced continuously until another waveform is selected.

3. Write a function for each waveform selection in `laser.c`. provided in Section 7.2.6.

4. Modify the DVM software for a 10-bit ATD converter operation.

5. Design and implement a three-channel weather station to measure environmental temperature, relative humidity, and barometric pressure. Display each of the sensed values at 3 second intervals on a LCD display. Provide a structure chart, UML activity diagram, code, and test plan to implement the weather station.

8

Real-Time Operating Systems

Objectives: After reading this chapter, you should be able to

- Describe in detail the concepts and terms related to a real-time operating system (RTOS).
- Differentiate between a polling and an event-driven (interrupt) RTOS.
- Differentiate between a hard, firm, and soft RTOS.
- Describe fundamental features of a record, a linked list, stacks, and queues.
- Define dynamic memory allocation and its associated advantages and disadvantages.
- Explain the role of heaps and stacks in dynamic memory allocation.
- Identify concerns of using a heap and stack in an embedded controller system with limited dynamic memory resources.
- Define a task and how to control one using a task control block (TCB).
- Describe the required change in thinking (paradigm shift) to program a multitasking system using tasks as opposed to standard sequential programming.

- Explain the importance of systems tables, device control blocks, and the dispatcher in the implementation of a RTOS.
- Explain the differences between types of RTOS scheduling algorithms.
- Identify the appropriate RTOS for a given application.
- Describe the process and steps to follow in designing a RTOS system.
- Identify the issues associated with a RTOS.
- Understand the operation of a RTOS.

8.1 A PARABLE: THE "REAL" REAL-TIME OPERATING SYSTEM

In this chapter we will expose you to the concepts associated with Real-Time operating systems. We begin with a parable to illustrate same key RTOS points and concepts.

I (sfb) have a phenomenal and genuine respect for the waitron (waitress/waiter) profession. I have been accused of being a generous tipper. (I think there is a connection between these two statements!) I admire the skills associated with a difficult, often thankless, busy occupation. I witnessed the challenge of this profession firsthand as a sophomore in high school. I had a job evenings and weekends as a busboy/dishwasher/cook's aid/extraordinaire at the Officer's Open Mess (military dinner club) at Minot Air Force Base, North Dakota.

I used to watch the waitrons in action with awe. Somehow they were able to keep multiple tables of demanding people happy all at the same time. Somehow they seemed to be able to do everything at once. If something out of the ordinary occurred such as a general and his entourage showing up for dinner or a child spilling his glass of milk all over a table, they adjusted their activities on the fly to handle these unexpected events. Again, even with these additional demands on their precious time, somehow they were able to keep up with all of the events at once. They were also required to keep track of the status of multiple tables of customers and inventory in the kitchen (e.g., how many of the daily specials were still available). This required considerable communication between the serving and kitchen staff.

When things slowed down, the waitrons handled some of the preparations for the following day, such as rolling silverware in napkins, folding napkins, etc. These talented individuals must have really slept well at night because they certainly worked extremely hard.

Several years later while working at the Pizza Haven in Bellevue, Nebraska (a chain of one!), I was given the opportunity to forgo my pizza cooking duties to be a waitron at the restaurant. I lasted two days as a waitron. I asked the manager if it would be okay to return to my cooking duties. It was far less challenging to me to serve as a cook instead of a waitron.

The waitron is a classic example of a real-time operating system (RTOS)—a system that must have the capability to respond to multiple events using limited resources. In an embedded control-based RTOS system, we have a single, sequential processor that must detect, prioritize, and respond to multiple events (tasks). However, the processor cannot execute the highest priority event to completion, while ignoring all other events. It must somehow respond to the highest priority event for some amount of time and then switch over to another event of high priority. Imagine the disaster of a waitron who gives all of his or her energy and attention to a single table and ignores all other assigned tables.

As the processor switches from task to task, it must remember (store) the key details of the executing event such as key register values, program counter values, and so on. We refer to this information as the task's *context*. Similarly, as waitrons switch their attention from table-to-table, they must remember the status of each table—its context.

As already pointed out, when an unscheduled, higher priority event occurs, the processor (and waitron) must respond to this new event in a timely manner but not completely ignore everything else. Furthermore, there must be communication between tasks, a process called *intertask communication*.

Our goal in this chapter is to make you comfortable with the concepts and challenges of developing a RTOS system. We assume that you have no background in this concept and begin with a review of associated RTOS concepts. We are not advocating that you write your own RTOS rather than buy a commercial version. Our goal is to present the concepts and complexities of RTOS. We leave the decision about developing your own system or purchasing a commercial system up to you.

8.2 WHAT IS AN RTOS?

In this section we introduce the concept of an RTOS. Once you have a good fundamental understanding of what an RTOS is, we begin a review of fundamental concepts necessary to design such a system.

So what is a real-time operating system? At its most fundamental definition, an RTOS is a computer or processor operating system that must handle multiple activities in a timely manner with limited resources. In the RTOS of an embedded control system, multiple events are handled by a single, sequential processor. The operating system must handle multiple, often simultaneous events that all require precious processing time. Since we are using a single, sequential processor, the processor can execute only a single program step at a time. We investigate methods that allow prioritization of the events so that the highest priority events are handled first, but other lower priority events are not ignored and all events appear as if they are running simultaneously. (Although we must emphasize again that this is not actually occurring since we are using a single, sequential processor.)

The events that a RTOS handles may be periodic, asynchronous, or occurring at any time. For example, if we develop a RTOS to control the overall operation of your home, certain events—such as monitoring the internal temperature of your home—will occur on a regular periodic basis, while others—such as a fire or security alarm—may be unscheduled and occur at anytime.

We will investigate here a wide range of RTOS systems—from simple polling loop systems to complex, multiple interrupt systems—and we will also look at hybrid systems that are a combination of both types. In a simple polling scheme, the operating system regularly sequences through a series of tasks. For example, the operating system monitoring home security could sequentially poll the status of each security sensor within your house in a round-robin fashion. Basically, the security system would question each sensor in turn asking, "Is it safe?" A system consisting of multiple interrupts would instead respond to events as they occur. For example, an activated security sensor would alert the operating system via an interrupt that some important event requiring action had just occurred. The difference between the two operating systems is this: in polling, the operating system is sequentially asking status questions; in an interrupt-driven system, the operating system is alerted when some key event has occurred. It is important to emphasize that one technique is not better than the other. Each has its own advantages and disadvantages. The real importance is matching a specific operating system technique to the application at hand.

Example

> Here's an example illustrating that an operating system has a critical function but still uses polling techniques to accomplish its activities. The first author (sfb) worked for an electronics firm in his later high school years and all through college. A product developed by the firm was a television security system for a motel or hotel. The system would interrogate (poll) the television set in each room to ensure that it was still present. The system would continually sequence through all television sets in the hotel/motel. If a television set did not respond, an alarm would sound in the main hotel office and illuminate the offending room number on a seven-segment light-emitting diode (LED) display. Again, polling was used because all activities were of equal priority. Furthermore, it was a simple technique that was fairly easy to implement.

And now back to RTOS theory . . . Each system activity in a RTOS is called as a *task*. Since the system is designed to handle multiple tasks, it is called a *multitasking system*. These multiple tasks are said to run concurrently. That is, a specific task runs to some specific point within the task's associated function or for some fixed amount of time. The operating system then shifts control to another task awaiting execution. Control is returned to the first task some time later, and it resumes executing its associated activities from where it left off. Since the operating system shifts control from task to task, it is important that all key registers associated with the task are stored for safekeeping while other tasks are being executed. The task's key register values are called its *context*. This is no different than our earlier parable about a waitron. As the waitron shifts attention from one table of customers to another, he or she must remember the status (context) of each table.

A real-time operating system may be placed in different subcategories relating to the risk imposed upon the system should it not complete its assigned task within bounded response time constraints. An RTOS fails if it does not complete its assigned task within the time constraint. Even though it completes its assigned task, if it does not do so when required, it is considered a failure. For example, if we have an RTOS calculating in-flight course corrections for a missile system, the system is considered a failure if the calculations are not calculated quickly enough to affect the course of the missile. The RTOS may be subdivided into categories based on the criticality of meeting time constraints [Laplante 1993].

- *Hard real-time system:* A system where failure to meet time constraints leads to system failure.
- *Firm real-time system:* A system with deadlines where a low occurrence of missing a deadline can be tolerated.
- *Soft real-time system:* A system whose performance is degraded by failure to meet time constraints but continues to function.

An RTOS is responsible for all activities related to a task, including the following:

- Task management, including scheduling and dispatching
- Communication between tasks (intertask communication)
- Memory system management
- Input/output (I/O) system management
- Memory system management
- Timing
- Error management
- Message management

In an embedded system RTOS, we usually concern ourselves only with what is called the *kernel* —the smallest portion of the operating system that provides the key functions of task scheduling, dispatching, and intertask communication. We investigate these concepts later in this chapter.

Practice Questions

Question: What is a task?

 Answer: Each activity within an RTOS is defined as a task.

Question: What is meant by context?

 Answer: The current value of the key registers associated with a task.

Question: What is meant by intertask communication?

 Answer: Communication between different tasks.

Question: What is the difference between a hard, firm, and soft real-time system?

 Answer: In a hard system, a failure to meet time constraints leads to system failure; in a firm system, a low occurrence of missing a deadline can be tolerated; in a soft system, performance is degraded by a failure to meet time constraints.

Question: What is a kernel?

 Answer: A kernel is the smallest portion of the operating system that provides the key functions of task scheduling, dispatching, and intertask communication.

Before going any further in our study of the RTOS, we need to review some prerequisite RTOS-related concepts.

8.3 REVIEW OF CONCEPTS

In this section we review some of the important background topics related to RTOS. Several authors have clearly (and adamantly) indicated that an RTOS should be written in an assembly language to maximize system responsiveness. We do not necessarily disagree with this point of view; however, we present our examples in C to clearly illuminate the concepts and the important details of the RTOS. In that vein, we review some C associated concepts along with some data structure fundamentals. An RTOS consists of these basic data structures working together to accomplish the system requirements.

We encourage you to take some time and go back and review the following concepts: pointers (Chapter 3), global versus local variables (Chapter 3), stack features of the 68HC12 (Chapter 4), and interrupt features of the 68HC12 (Chapter 4). Once you are comfortable with these topics, you can move on to dynamic memory allocation.

8.3.1 Dynamic Memory Allocation RAM Requirement

In Chapter 4 we discussed the memory system aboard the evaluation board (EVB) of the B32, which is intended primarily for single-chip applications. It is equipped with a 32 Kbyte flash electrically erasable programmable read-only memory

$0000 $01FF	CPU registers
$0800 $0BFF	1 Kbyte of on-chip RAM • User code/data ($0800-$09FF) • Reserved for D-Bug12 ($0A00-$0BFF)
$0D00 $0FFF	768 bytes of on-chip EEPROM • User code/data
$8000 $FFFF	32 Kbytes on-chip FLASH EEPROM • D-Bug12 code ($8000-$F67F) • User-accessible functions ($F680-$F6BF) • D-Bug12 customization ($F6C0-$F6FF) • D-Bug12 start-up code ($F700-$F77F) • Interrupt vector table ($F780-$F7FF) • Bootloader expansion ($F800-$FBFF) • EEPROM bootloader ($FC00-$FFBF) • Reset and interrupt vectors ($FFC0-$FFFF)

Figure 8.1   B32 memory map.

(EEPROM), 1 Kbyte of static random access memory (RAM), and 768 bytes of byte-erasable EEPROM for storing system data. The memory map for the B32 EVB is provided in Figure 8.1. Note that the majority of memory is flash EEPROM while the random access memory (RAM) is only 1 Kbyte. In fact only 512 bytes are available for your use ($0800 to $9FFF).

What exactly is this RAM used for? Primarily it is used for local variables for each function. Placed on the stack, the variables are in existence only when a function is called. The variables are removed from the stack, which frees up stack memory space when the function is exited. You can imagine that you could potentially use up the RAM stack rather quickly if your embedded controller employed a recursive routine (one that calls itself, such as the Fibonacci series or the calculation of the factorial operation) or if functions are heavily nested. That is, a function calls a function, that calls a function, etc. Since all of the functions are active in these situations, so are their associated local variables.

A key tool of the RTOS is the use of abstract data types such as the record, linked list, and queue. We'll be discussing these shortly. These data types normally use RAM dynamic memory allocation. Where shall we get the RAM for these data types? If we choose to use the 512 bytes for both abstract data types and the stack we could potentially run into the "show stopping" situation when the stack overwrites the memory-containing data structures or vice versa. This results in a catastrophic system malfunction. We need to prevent this at all costs. Ideally, we need to add additional RAM memory to the B32 memory map. It would also be helpful to physically separate this memory from the RAM memory aboard the B32. This allows us to have separate RAM spaces for the stack and the heap. This isn't always possible. If both the stack and the heap reside in the same memory space, you should ensure that one does not override the other during program execution. The 68HC12 does not have automatic features to check for this situation. It is your responsibility as the system programmer to provide these features.

In section 4.7.1 we discussed the memory system onboard the B32. At this time, we provide a system schematic in Figure 8.2 and then begin to use the

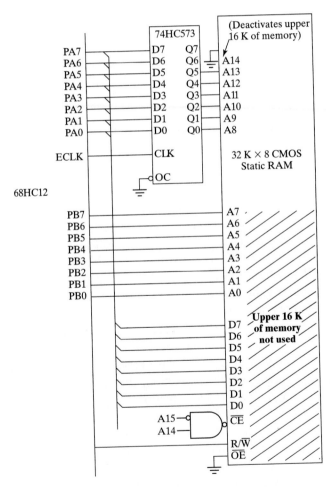

Figure 8.2   "B32" RAM expansion.

extra RAM space. It is highly recommended that you review the basic concepts of memory expansion in Pack and Barrett [2002, Ch. 8]. We are only providing a schematic here. We are glossing over the issues of memory layout design, electrical interfacing, and timing issues. These are all extremely important concepts but not necessary for our discussion on dynamic memory allocation.

Before we start to use this additional RAM space at face value, let's get comfortable with its design. We want to insert 16 Kbytes of static random access memory (SRAM) into the memory map of the B32 EVB. We place this memory at locations $4000 to $7FFF. As luck would have it, all we have available in the parts room is a 32 Kbyte × 8 SRAM. If we tie the most significant address line of this memory A[14] to ground, the upper 16 Kbytes of the memory chip are not accessible. Recall from Chapter 4 that PORTA provides multiplexed data lines D[7:0] and the upper address lines A[15:8] in the expanded memory mode. PORTB provides the lower address lines A[7:0]. We use address lines A[15:14] with a NAND gate to generate the active low chip enable signal for the SRAM memory.

An alternative to expanding the memory is to use a HCS12 variant with a larger complement of RAM. Refer to the different available variants described in Chapter 1, Sections 1.3 and 1.4, and Chapter 4, Section 4.8. These variants are equipped with RAM memory from 4 to 12 Kbytes.

Before continuing our discussion on dynamic memory allocation, let's review a few concepts. Refer to Figure 8.2 to answer these questions.

Practice Questions

Question: What is the purpose of the NAND gate?

Answer: The NAND gate is asserted low and generates the chip enable ($\overline{CE}$) signal for the SRAM memory when A15 is low and A14 is high.

Question: What is the purpose of the 74HC573?

Answer: The 573 acts as a latch to demultiplex the address/data lines from Port A.

Question: What is the span of memory addresses of the RAM memory?

Answer: $4000 to $7FFF or 16 Kbytes of RAM memory.

Question: What is the size of the SRAM memory?

Answer: Memory size: 2^{15} or 32 K locations with a single byte at each location. We just happen to be using only the lower 16 Kbytes of memory.

Question: Provide an updated memory map with these new memory components.

Answer: Refer to Figure 8.3 for the memory map.

8.3.2 Dynamic Memory Allocation

Pointers are used in C for effective dynamic storage management. They allow the declaration of many different types of variables of various sizes. When storage

$0000 $01FF	CPU registers
$0800 $0BFF	1 Kbyte of on-chip RAM • User code/data ($0800-$09FF) • Reserved for D-Bug12 ($0A00-$0BFF)
$0D00 $0FFF	768 bytes of on-chip EEPROM • User code/data
$4000 $7FFF	16 Kbytes of external RAM ($4000-$7FFF)
$8000 $FFFF	32 Kbytes on-chip FLASH EEPROM • D-Bug12 code ($8000-$F67F) • User-accessible functions ($F680-$F6BF) • D-Bug12 customization ($F6C0-$F6FF) • D-Bug12 start-up code ($F700-$F77F) • Interrupt vector table ($F780-$F7FF) • Bootloader expansion ($F800-$FBFF) • EEPROM bootloader ($FC00-$FFBF) • Reset and interrupt vectors ($FFC0-$FFFF)

Figure 8.3   B32 memory map expanded with external flash and RAM.

is dynamically allocated for the variable in RAM, a pointer may be assigned to lead you to the memory resource for the variable.

Dynamic memory allocation is accomplished using `malloc()`, a memory allocation command. This command is contained in the `stdlib.h` header file, which is a part of any C compiler. The `malloc()` command is normally used in conjunction with the `sizeof()` function. This function combination is extremely useful in dynamically allocating memory. The general form of this function combination is

```
ptr = (variable_type *) malloc( sizeof(variable_type));
```

Most data structures are declared and allocated using this technique. When the variable is no longer needed, the memory space it was using is returned to the system via the `free()` function. This is dynamic memory allocation at its best. We create variables on the fly (during program execution) as we need them and we get rid of the variables when they are no longer needed.

With this memory allocation and deallocation occurring during program execution, we need an effective memory management system. The heap is a portion of RAM memory used for dynamic memory allocation. As we mentioned before, it is important to keep the stack and the heap separate from one another.

Now that we have two separate RAM spaces in our memory map, we can easily allocate one for the stack and one for the heap. We recommend use of the smaller space for the stack and the larger one for the heap. There are user-configurable settings in a given compiler to set the start address for the stack and the memory span of the heap.

With the ability to dynamically allocate memory, we can now create data structures for use in our RTOS. In the next section we review the common data structures used in RTOS: the structure (or record), the linked list, the queue, and the circular queue. Once we are comfortable with each of these basic types, we combine them into the more complex data structures used to implement an RTOS.

8.3.3 Data Structures

In this section we review the common data structures used in a real-time operating system. We review each data structure separately and then combine them to accomplish different operations within an RTOS.

Structure   We use the terms *record* and *structure* interchangeably. Structures allow programmers to custom design a data type to their specifications using other fundamental data types. This allows them to keep track of related information that may be of different data types. For example, if you were developing an inventory system for an automobile dealer, you might develop a structure to document the key details of a given automobile such as year, make, model, vehicle identification number (VIN), and mileage, as shown in Figure 8.4.

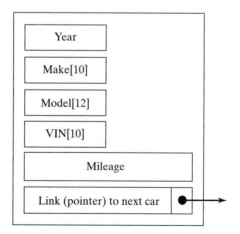

Figure 8.4   The record for an automobile. The record contains data fields that collectively describe a car.

Each of the constituent data types within the record is referred to as a field. We declare a record or structure using the following syntax:

```
struct car
{
int  year;                  /*year of manufacture                */
char make[10];              /*BWM, Hummer, Saturn                */
char model[12];             /*coupe, convertible, SUV, pickup    */
char VIN[10];               /*combination of numbers, characters*/
float mileage;              /*odometer reading: 0 to 500,000+    */
struct car *next;           /*pointer to next car in list        */
};
/*typedef provides compiler an alternate*/
typedef    struct car  ELEMENT;    /*for a variable type         */
typedef    ELEMENT  *car_temp_ptr; /*defines pointer to car      */
```

As you can see, all of the record fields are related in that they describe different parameters of a given vehicle. We have provided an abbreviated list of parameters. Realize the structure can contain as many fields as necessary. We have chosen the data type for each field that best fits the type of data to store the parameter.

Structures are created using dynamic memory allocation techniques. Recall from our previous discussion that the `malloc()` command is a dynamic memory allocation technique for determining the proper amount of memory for the data structure. For example, to create a new car record we would use the following code:

```
car_temp_ptr new_car_entry;

new_car_entry = (car_temp_ptr) malloc(sizeof(ELEMENT));
```

In Chapter 3, we described how to access different fields within the record. In this example, we are initializing the newly created car record with information on a specific vehicle. Note that we have used the $->$ operator to access a specific field within the structure.

```
/*initializes new car entry fields  */
new_car_entry->year = 1981; /*year of manufacture               */
strcpy(new_car_entry->make,"Chevy");  /*BWM, Hummer, Saturn      */
strcpy(new_car_entry->model,"Camaro");
/*coupe, convertible, SUV, pickup   */
strcpy(new_car_entry->VIN, "12Z367");
/*combination of numbers, characters*/
new_car_entry->mileage = 37456;/*odometer reading: 0 to 500,000+*/
new_car_entry->next = NULL;    /*pointer to next car in list    */
```

To print out the different fields of the record, we could use the following code:

```
printf("\nyear: %4d", new_car_entry->year);    /*year of mfg     */
printf("\nmake: %s", new_car_entry->make);      /*car make        */
printf("\nmodel: %s", new_car_entry->model);    /*model           */
printf("\nVIN: %s", new_car_entry->VIN);        /*VIN             */
printf("\nMileage: %6.0f", new_car_entry->mileage);
/*odometer reading*/
```

Let's put all of these pieces together with an example. We highly encourage you to compile and execute this code.

```
#include <stdio.h>            /*standard input/output functions  */
#include <stdlib.h>           /*library and memory allocation     */

void main(void)
{
                              /*define structure                  */
struct car
{
int  year;                    /*year of manufacture               */
char make[10];                /*BWM, Hummer, Saturn               */
char model[12];               /*coupe, convertible, SUV, pickup   */
char VIN[10];                 /*combination of numbers, characters*/
float mileage;                /*odometer reading: 0 to 500,000+   */
struct car *next;             /*pointer to next car in list       */
};
                              /*defines pointer to car            */
typedef    struct car   ELEMENT;
typedef    ELEMENT  *car_temp_ptr;

car_temp_ptr new_car_entry; /*creates car entry                   */
new_car_entry = (car_temp_ptr) malloc(sizeof(ELEMENT));

/*initializes new car entry fields  */
new_car_entry->year = 1981; /*year of manufacture                 */
strcpy(new_car_entry->make,"Chevy");    /*BWM, Hummer, Saturn     */
strcpy(new_car_entry->model,"Camaro");
/*coupe, convertible, SUV, pickup   */
strcpy(new_car_entry->VIN, "12Z367");
/*combination of numbers, characters*/
new_car_entry->mileage = 37456;/*odometer reading: 0 to 500,000+*/
new_car_entry->next = NULL;    /*pointer to next car in list     */

printf("\nyear: %4d", new_car_entry->year);    /*year of mfg     */
printf("\nmake: %s", new_car_entry->make);      /*car make        */
```

```
printf("\nmodel: %s", new_car_entry->model);    /*model        */
printf("\nVIN: %s", new_car_entry->VIN);         /*VIN          */
printf("\nMileage: %6.0f", new_car_entry->mileage);
/*odometer reading*/
}
```

When this program is compiled and executed, the following message is printed on your PC screen:

```
year: 1981
make: Chevy
model: Camaro
VIN: 12Z367
Mileage: 37456
```

At this point the use of dynamic memory allocation does not seem very powerful. In the next section we begin to explore the power of dynamic memory allocation when we link the records we have declared into a list that we can dynamically update during program execution. That is, we can add new elements to the list, change an element from one list to another, delete elements from a list, etc. A word of warning: Let's not get lost in the woods of detail here. Let's refocus our intent and stay on the path through the woods. We are studying basic data structures to see how they may be employed in the construction and implementation of a real-time operating system.

Linked List   A linked list is a powerful data structure that can be created, added to, and deleted from dynamically during program execution. The linked list consists of a node that contains two parts: the data portion and the link field portion. The data portion stores information about the node (or item) in the list. For example, if we were to create a list of cars in stock, available for sale, the data portion of the item would be the structure (or record) car we developed in the previous section. The link field would be a pointer (the memory location) to the next car (record) in the list. The beginning of a list is called the *head*. The end of the list is called the *tail* and is designated with a null character ('ø') in the link field. This concept is illustrated in Figure 8.5. Provided here is the declaration of different lists to track the status of cars at an automobile dealership.

```
car_temp_ptr head_ptr;        /*initiates list of car status    */
car_temp_ptr in_stock_list; /*cars in stock                     */
car_temp_ptr repair_list;
/*cars in repair shop - not avail for sale*/
car_temp_ptr paint_shop_list;
/*cars in paint shop - not avail for sale */
car_temp_ptr sold_list;       /*sold cars - not avail for sale   */
```

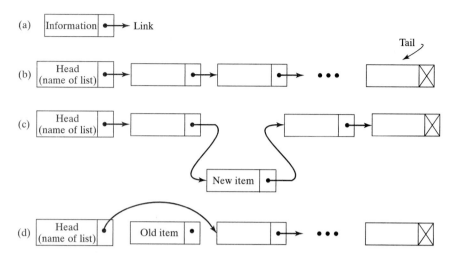

Figure 8.5 List operations. (a) List consists of node with a data and link portion. (b) The beginning of a list is called the head. The end of the list is called the tail. (c) List node insertion. (d) Node deletion.

You can imagine that the world of car sales is quite dynamic. The car dealership is constantly selling cars, taking in cars as trade-ins, placing cars in the shop for repairs, or even having cars repainted. If we were to create a list for each of these activities, we would be constantly adding and deleting items from each of the lists. These activities are illustrated in Figure 8.5(c) and (d). To insert a new car into the list, we would have to find the appropriate place for the car in the existing list. For example, if we want to place the cars in alphabetical order by make, we would proceed down the links until we found the proper place to insert the car in the list, as shown in Figure 8.6. Once the proper insertion point was found, the predecessor node's link would need to be changed to point to the new car and the new car's link would need to be changed to point to the successor car in the list.

When a car is sold, it is no longer available for sale. It should then be deleted from the "for sale" list. To do this, the car's record would need to be located in the list. The predecessor's link would need to now point to the successor car. The car that was sold would now be effectively deleted from the "for sale" list and could be added to the "sold" list. If we did not have a "sold" list, we could de-allocate the dynamic memory for that car and return it to the heap. This is accomplished using the free(argument) command.

If you were searching for a particular car in the list, you would have to follow the chain of links (pointers) until the desired car was found. We would accomplish the search by examining the contents of a specific field of each record in the linked list.

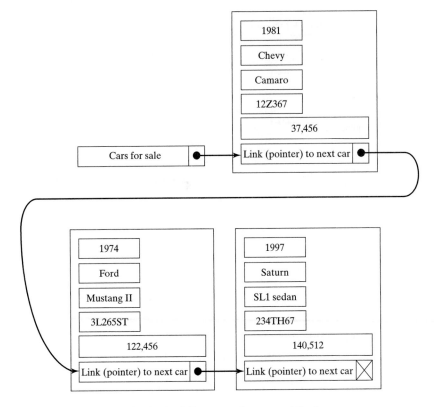

Figure 8.6   Linked list to track automobile inventory.

Figure 8.7   Common functions associated with a linked list.

Figure 8.7 illustrates the common functions associated with a linked list. The following code implements each of these functions:

```
/****************************************************************/
/*filename: linklist.c                                         */
/****************************************************************/

/*include files*/
#include <stdio.h>          /*standard I/O library            */
#include <stdlib.h>         /*standard library-dynamic allocation */
```

```
/*global variables - put these global declarations in a header  */
/*file. They are provided here to illustrate the program flow.   */

/*define structure*/
struct car
{
int  year;                    /*year of manufacture               */
char make[10];                /*BWM, Hummer, Saturn               */
char model[12];               /*coupe, convertible, SUV, pickup   */
char VIN[10];                 /*combination of numbers, characters */
float mileage;                /*odometer reading: 0 to 500,000+   */
struct car *next;             /*pointer to next car in list       */
};
/*defines pointer to car              */
typedef    struct car  ELEMENT;
typedef    ELEMENT  *car_temp_ptr;


/*function prototypes*/
void initialize_link_list(void);
void print_link_list(car_temp_ptr);
void insert_link_list(car_temp_ptr);
void delete_link_list(car_temp_ptr);
void search_link_list(car_temp_ptr);

/*variables*/
/*create lists to track car status    */
car_temp_ptr in_stock_list;/*cars in stock                        */
car_temp_ptr repair_list;  /*cars in repair-not avail for sale  */
car_temp_ptr paint_shop_list; /*cars in paint-not avail for sale*/
car_temp_ptr sold_list;    /*sold cars - not avail for sale     */
car_temp_ptr new_car_entry;/*new car to add to list             */
int TRUE=1,FALSE=0;        /*logic flags                         */

void main(void)
{
                           /*terminate empty lists with NULL     */
in_stock_list = NULL;      /*cars in stock                       */
repair_list = NULL;        /*cars in repair-not avail for sale   */
paint_shop_list = NULL;    /*cars in paint-not avail for sale    */
sold_list = NULL;          /*sold cars - not avail for sale      */
new_car_entry = NULL;

initialize_link_list();          /*construct for sale list       */
print_link_list(in_stock_list); /*print the list                 */
insert_link_list(in_stock_list);/*insert a new car into the list*/
print_link_list(in_stock_list); /*print the list                 */
delete_link_list(in_stock_list);/*delete car from for sale list */
```

```
print_link_list(in_stock_list); /*print the list                    */
search_link_list(in_stock_list);
/*searches list for specific item     */


}


/********************************************************************/
/*void initialize_link_list(car_temp_ptr):initializes car for    */
/*sale list used in inventory control.  Note that this linked    */
/*list was declared as a global variable.                        */
/*global variables.                                              */
/********************************************************************/

void initialize_link_list(void)
{
car_temp_ptr new_car_entry1, new_car_entry2;
/*creates car entry             */
new_car_entry = (car_temp_ptr) malloc(sizeof(ELEMENT));
/*initializes new car entry fields*/
new_car_entry->year = 1981;    /*year of manufacture          */
strcpy(new_car_entry->make,"Chevy");  /*BWM, Hummer, Saturn    */
strcpy(new_car_entry->model,"Camaro");
/*coupe, convertible, SUV, pickup */
strcpy(new_car_entry->VIN, "12Z367");
/*combination of numbers, chars    */
new_car_entry->mileage = 37456;/*odometer reading: 0 to 500,000+*/
new_car_entry->next = NULL;    /*pointer to next car in list     */

in_stock_list = new_car_entry;

new_car_entry1 = (car_temp_ptr) malloc(sizeof(ELEMENT));
/*initializes new car fields  */
new_car_entry1->year = 1974;  /*year of manufacture         */
strcpy(new_car_entry1->make,"Ford");/*BWM, Hummer, Saturn    */
strcpy(new_car_entry1->model,"MustangII");
/*coupe, convertible, SUV, PU */
strcpy(new_car_entry1->VIN, "3L265ST");
/*combination of numbers, char*/
new_car_entry1->mileage = 122456; /*odometer: 0 to 500,000+ */
new_car_entry1->next = NULL;  /*pointer to next car in list */

new_car_entry->next = new_car_entry1;

new_car_entry2 = (car_temp_ptr) malloc(sizeof(ELEMENT));
/*initializes new car fields  */
new_car_entry2->year = 1997;  /*year of manufacture        */
strcpy(new_car_entry2->make,"Saturn"); /*BWM, Hummer, Saturn*/
```

```
strcpy(new_car_entry2->model,"SL1");
/*coupe, convertible, SUV, PU */
strcpy(new_car_entry2->VIN, "234TH67");
/*combination of numbers, char*/
new_car_entry2->mileage = 140512; /*odometer: 0 to 500,000+ */
new_car_entry2->next = NULL;  /*pointer to next car in list */

new_car_entry1->next = new_car_entry2;
}


/****************************************************************/
/* print_link_list: prints fields of designated linked list    */
/****************************************************************/

void print_link_list(car_temp_ptr print_list)
{
car_temp_ptr temp_ptr;              /*declare temporary pointer    */

printf("\nCars available in stock for sale:");
/*advance along list        */
for(temp_ptr=print_list;temp_ptr!=NULL;temp_ptr=temp_ptr->next){
   printf("\n\nyear: %4d", temp_ptr->year);    /*year of mfg     */
   printf("\nmake: %s",   temp_ptr->make);     /*car make        */
   printf("\nmodel: %s", temp_ptr->model);     /*model           */
   printf("\nVIN: %s",    temp_ptr->VIN);      /*VIN             */
   printf("\nMileage: %6.0f", temp_ptr->mileage);
                                               /*odometer reading*/
   }
}


/****************************************************************/
/*insert_link_list(in_stock_list) - insert new car into desig-  */
/*nated list. Car is inserted in alphabetical order of car make.*/
/****************************************************************/

void insert_link_list(car_temp_ptr in_stock_list)
{
car_temp_ptr new_car_entry, list, ptr;
int place_found;

list = in_stock_list;
                            /*creates car entry                 */
new_car_entry = (car_temp_ptr) malloc(sizeof(ELEMENT));
                            /*initializes new car entry fields  */
new_car_entry->year = 2002;  /*year of manufacture              */
```

```
strcpy(new_car_entry->make,"Hummer");/*BWM, Hummer, Saturn       */
strcpy(new_car_entry->model,"H2");
/*coupe, convertible, SUV, pickup   */
strcpy(new_car_entry->VIN, "73H2L7");
                                /*combination of numbers, characters*/
new_car_entry->mileage = 13;/*odometer reading: 0 to 500,000+   */
new_car_entry->next = NULL; /*pointer to next car in list       */

if(list==NULL)
    {                               /*inserting into an empty list     */
    list=new_car_entry;
    }
else
    {                               /*inserting first element into list*/
    if(strcmp(new_car_entry->make, list->make) <1)
      {
      new_car_entry->next=list;
      list = new_car_entry;
      }
    else                        /*inserting into non-empty lists   */
      {
      ptr = list;               /*look for insertion location      */
      place_found = FALSE;
      while((ptr->next != NULL) && (!place_found))
        {
        if(strcmp(new_car_entry->make, ptr->next->make) >=1)
                        /*compare     */
    {
        ptr=ptr->next;          /*advance along list               */
    }
        else                    /*insert after pointer             */
    {
    place_found = TRUE;
    }
        }/*end while*/

                                /*connect pointers to complete     */
                                /*the link list insertion          */
    new_car_entry->next = ptr->next;
    ptr->next = new_car_entry;
      }/*end else*/
    }/*end else*/
}/*end insert_link_list*/

/*************************************************************/
/*delete_link_list(car_temp_ptr): deletes specified node     */
/*from list                                                  */
/*************************************************************/
```

```
void delete_link_list(car_temp_ptr in_stock_list)
{
car_temp_ptr current,backup,temp; /*temporary list pointers    */
char delete_make[10];
/*determine make for deletion  */
printf("\n\nDelete car from for sale list.");
printf("\nEnter make of car for deletion from list.");
scanf("%s", delete_make);
                                /*Initiate pointers for search */
current = in_stock_list;
backup=NULL;
/*Search for node containing the car make value              */
while(strcmp(current->make, delete_make) !=0){
  backup = current;
  current = current -> next;
  }
                               /*Was car for deletion in the  */
                               /*first node?                   */
if (backup==NULL){             /*remove first node from list   */
  in_stock_list = in_stock_list->next;
  }
else{                          /*remove element from list      */
  backup->next = current -> next;
  }
free(current);                 /*de-allocate dynamic memory    */
}


/*************************************************************/
/*void search_link_list(car_temp_ptr) - searches for specified */
/*make of car in list.  Prints info on cars of specified make. */
/*************************************************************/

void search_link_list(car_temp_ptr search_list)
{
char search_make[10];
car_temp_ptr temp_ptr;         /*declare temporary pointer     */
/*determine make of car for search*/
printf("\n\nSearch for car in stock.");
printf("\nEnter make of car to search for in list.");
scanf("%s", search_make);
/*advance along list            */
for(temp_ptr=search_list;temp_ptr!=NULL;temp_ptr=temp_ptr->next)
  {
  if(strcmp(temp_ptr->make, search_make) == 0)
    {
    printf("\n\nyear: %4d", temp_ptr->year); /*year of mfg    */
    printf("\nmake: %s",  temp_ptr->make);   /*car make       */
```

```
    printf("\nmodel: %s", temp_ptr->model);   /*model        */
    printf("\nVIN: %s",    temp_ptr->VIN);     /*VIN          */
    printf("\nMileage: %6.0f", temp_ptr->mileage);
    /*odometer reading*/
    }
  }
}
/***********************************************************/
/***********************************************************/
```

When the program is executed, the following will occur.

```
year: 1981
make: Chevy
model: Camaro
VIN: 12Z367
mileage: 37456

year: 1974
make: Ford
model: MustangII
VIN: 3L265ST
mileage: 122456

year: 1997
make: Saturn
model: SL1
VIN: 234TH67
Mileage: 140512

year: 1981
make: Chevy
model: Camaro
VIN: 12Z367
mileage: 37456

year: 1974
make: Ford
model: MustangII
VIN: 3L265ST
mileage: 122456

year: 2002
make: Hummer
model: H2
VIN: 73H2L7
Mileage: 13
```

```
year: 1997
make: Saturn
model: SL1
VIN: 234TH67
Mileage: 140512


Delete car from for sale list.
Enter make of car for deletion from list.Hummer

year: 1981
make: Chevy
model: Camaro
VIN: 12Z367
mileage: 37456

year: 1974
make: Ford
model: MustangII
VIN: 3L265ST
mileage: 122456

year: 1997
make: Saturn
model: SL1
VIN: 234TH67
Mileage: 140512


Search for car in stock.
Enter make of car to search for in list.Saturn

year: 1997
make: Saturn
model: SL1
VIN: 234TH67
Mileage: 140512
```

This is a very simple, contrived example to illustrate the basic activities related to linked list processing. We have purposely chosen the bare bones approach to concentrate on link list operation. If we were developing an actual inventory program based on linked lists, we would have a user-friendly menu that would allow the functions to be called in any order. Also, we would initially load the data to form each list from a file. We would also have the capability to store the linked list data in a file.

Queue   The queue is a specially configured linked list. It is also known as a first-in-first-out (FIFO) buffer. Elements are added to the queue at its rear

Figure 8.8   The queue—a first-in-first-out (FIFO) data structure.

and extracted from the queue at its front end, as shown in Figure 8.8. Now back to our car sales analogy. Once you purchase your car, you must register it at the Department of Motor Vehicles (DMV). I was recently at the DMV with my son who needed a new driver's license. Upon our arrival we got in a line (a queue) to await service. We got into the line at its rear. After a short wait we reached the front of the line. At that time we were able to get assistance to obtain the new license. We were serviced in the order in which we entered the queue. During peak busy times—for example, during lunch hours on days near the end of the month—the line at the DMV may be quite long. At other nonpeak times the line may be quite short. Both cases illustrate that the queue does not have a fixed number of elements. Its length, or number of elements, is dynamic and changes based on program activity.

Circular Queue   In a circular queue, which has the same basic structure as the queue, the null pointer of the last record in the queue is replaced by a pointer that points to the first record. The circular queue is illustrated in Figure 8.9. As we shall soon see, this is an effective data structure for moving from one task to another.

Stack   The stack is a last-in-first-out (LIFO) data structure as shown in Figure 8.10. It too may be created using linked-list techniques. In an embedded controller system such as the 68HC12, the stack is a user-specified portion of RAM that is set aside during normal program execution to temporarily store variables, register contents, etc. The stack "top" is usually defined at the last location of RAM memory plus one for the 68HC12. The stack pointer for the 68HC12 contains the address of the last used stack location. As items are placed on the stack (push), the stack pointer is decremented. When items are retrieved from the stack (pulled), the stack pointer is incremented. When programming in C, the stack location is assigned as a compiler option. If an embedded controller system requires only a single stack, using the built-in features of the processor may be the best choice. However, as we shall soon see, in an RTOS we may require multiple stacks, one for each task. In this case the system developer is required to provide for multiple stacks. If dynamic memory allocation techniques are used, the stacks are created and used within the heap. We have left the development of the stack data structure using dynamic memory allocation techniques as a homework assignment (Challenging 1). Instead, we develop a stack structure using a fixed array size. A stack implemented with a fixed array is used when

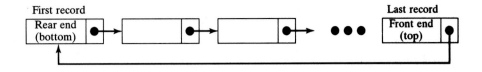

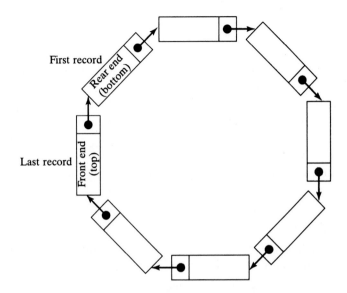

Figure 8.9   The circular queue.

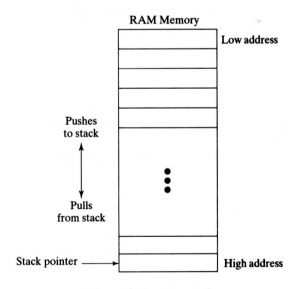

Figure 8.10   The stack.

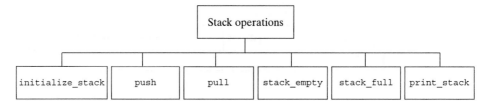

Figure 8.11 Stack operations.

the size of the stack is known and fixed. As we shall soon see, we have fixed stacks in our task control blocks.

A stack data structure, whether it is developed using dynamic allocation techniques or using a fixed array, has the following constituent functions:

- initialize_stack: Initializes a stack.
- push: Places an item on the stack.
- pull: Retrieves an item from the stack.
- stack_empty: Checks to see if the stack is empty. It is called prior to using the Pull function.
- stack_full: Checks to see if the stack is full. It is called prior to using Push function.
- print_stack: Prints the contents of the stack.

The basic stack operations are shown in Figure 8.11.

The following basic code will implement a stack in a fixed array.

```
/******************************************************************/
/*filename: stack.c                                             */
/******************************************************************/

/*include files*/
#include <stdio.h>              /*standard I/O library            */
#include <stdlib.h>             /*standard library-dynamic allocation*/

/*global variables - put these global declarations in a header  */
/*file. They are provided here to illustrate the program flow.   */

/*define structure*/
struct stack_struct
{
int   stack_top;               /*next avail location  in stack     */
int   stack_item[10];          /*items stored on stack - fixed size */
};

                               /*typedef declaration causes the com */
```

```
typedef struct stack_struct stack;
                                /*piler to recognize different name  */
                                /*for variable type                  */
typedef stack *stack_ptr;   /*definition of pointer to stack     */

/*function prototypes*/
void initialize_stack(stack);
void push(stack *, int);    /*Call by Reference techniques used  */
int  pull(stack *);         /*since stack contents will change   */
int  stack_empty(stack);
int  stack_full(stack);
void print_stack(stack);

/*variables*/
int YES=1,NO=0;             /*logic flags                        */
stack   stack1;             /*declare stack                      */
char *filename;
FILE *outputfile;

void main(void)
{
int response;
int stack_item;
                            /*print results to file              */
printf("\n\nEnter a filename for output.");
scanf("%s", filename);
outputfile = fopen(filename, "a");

initialize_stack(stack1);
response = stack_empty(stack1); /*Call by Value                  */
response = stack_full(stack1);
print_stack(stack1);
push(&stack1, 11);          /*Call by Reference                  */
push(&stack1, 12);
push(&stack1, 13);
push(&stack1, 14);
print_stack(stack1);
pull(&stack1);
pull(&stack1);
pull(&stack1);
pull(&stack1);
pull(&stack1);
fclose(outputfile);         /*close output file                  */
}

/**************************************************************/
/*initialize_stack: sets stack top to 0                       */
/**************************************************************/
```

```c
void initialize_stack(stack a_stack)
{

a_stack.stack_top=0;          /*sets stack pointer to 0            */

}


/****************************************************************/
/*stack_empty: returns YES if stack is empty, otherwise NO      */
/****************************************************************/

int stack_empty(stack a_stack)
{

fprintf(outputfile, "\n\nStack top: %d", a_stack.stack_top);

if(a_stack.stack_top == 0)    /*check for empty stack            */
  {
  fprintf(outputfile, "\nStack Empty!");
  return YES;
  }
else
  {
  fprintf(outputfile, "\nStack is not empty.");
  return NO;
  }
}

/****************************************************************/
/*stack_full: returns YES if stack is full, otherwise NO        */
/****************************************************************/

int stack_full(stack a_stack)
{

if(a_stack.stack_top == 10)    /*check for full stack           */
  {                            /*stack limit arbitrarily chosen */
  fprintf(outputfile, "\n\nStack Full!");
  return YES;
  }
else
  {
  fprintf(outputfile, "\n\nStack is not full.");
  return NO;
  }
}
```

```
/******************************************************************/
/*print_stack: prints elements currently on stack from top     */
/******************************************************************/

void print_stack(stack a_stack)
{
int  i;

if(!(stack_empty(a_stack)))/*check for empty stack before print*/
   {                          /*proceed down stack printing items */
   for(i=a_stack.stack_top;i>=0;i=i-1)
   fprintf(outputfile, "\nStack item: %d", a_stack.stack_item[i]);
   }
else
   fprintf(outputfile,"\nCannot print - stack is empty!");
}


/******************************************************************/
/*push(stack *, int): pushes item to stack                     */
/******************************************************************/

void push(stack *a_stack, int item)
{
fprintf(outputfile, "\n\nBefore push - stack pointer: %d",
                                        a_stack->stack_top);

if(!(stack_full(*a_stack)))  /*check for full stack before push*/
   {
   a_stack->stack_item[a_stack->stack_top] = item;
   fprintf(outputfile, "\nstack item after push: %d",
                        a_stack->stack_item[a_stack->stack_top]);
   a_stack->stack_top = a_stack->stack_top + 1;
   fprintf(outputfile, "\nstacktop after push: %d",
                                        a_stack->stack_top);
   }
else
   fprintf(outputfile, "\nCannot push - stack is full!");
}


/******************************************************************/
/*pull(stack *): pulls item from stack                         */
/******************************************************************/

int pull(stack *a_stack)
{
int item;
```

```
fprintf(outputfile,"\n\nBefore pull - stack pointer: %d",
                                        a_stack->stack_top);

if(!(stack_empty(*a_stack)))/*check for empty stack before pull*/
  {
  item = a_stack->stack_item[a_stack->stack_top-1];
  fprintf(outputfile, "\nstack item pulled: %d",  item);
  a_stack->stack_top = a_stack->stack_top - 1;
  fprintf(outputfile,"\nstacktop after pull: %d",
                                        a_stack->stack_top);
  return item;
  }
else
  fprintf(outputfile, "\nCannot pull - stack is empty!");
}


/****************************************************************/
/****************************************************************/
```

We have illustrated the operation of this example in Figure 8.12.
When this program is executed, the following code will be issued:

```
Stack top: 0
Stack Empty!

Stack is not full.

Stack top: 0
Stack Empty!
Cannot print - stack is empty!

Before push - stack pointer: 0

Stack is not full.
stack item after push: 11
stacktop after push: 1

Before push - stack pointer: 1

Stack is not full.
stack item after push: 12
stacktop after push: 2

Before push - stack pointer: 2

Stack is not full.
stack item after push: 13
stacktop after push: 3
```

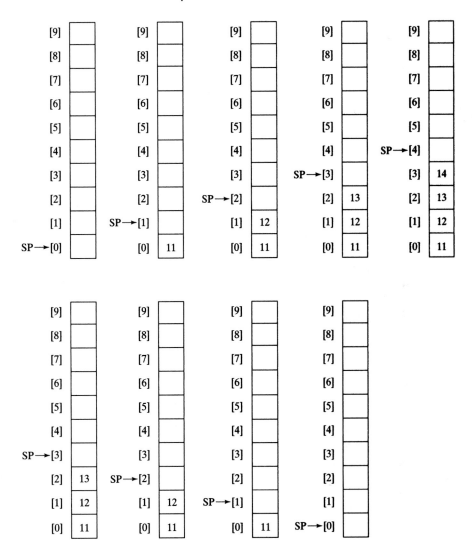

Figure 8.12 Pushing and pulling from the stack.

```
Before push - stack pointer: 3

Stack is not full.
stack item after push: 14
stacktop after push: 4

Stack top: 4
Stack is not empty.
Stack item: 0
Stack item: 14
```

```
Stack item: 13
Stack item: 12
Stack item: 11

Before pull - stack pointer: 4

Stack top: 4
Stack is not empty.
stack item pulled: 14
stacktop after pull: 3

Before pull - stack pointer: 3

Stack top: 3
Stack is not empty.
stack item pulled: 13
stacktop after pull: 2

Before pull - stack pointer: 2

Stack top: 2
Stack is not empty.
stack item pulled: 12
stacktop after pull: 1

Before pull - stack pointer: 1

Stack top: 1
Stack is not empty.
stack item pulled: 11
stacktop after pull: 0

Before pull - stack pointer: 0

Stack top: 0
Stack Empty!
Cannot pull - stack is empty!
```

Multiple Stacks.   Normally a microprocessor system is equipped with a single stack. This stack is normally declared within RAM and the processor is equipped with many functions such as declaring the stack location (LDS), pushing data to the stack (PUSH), pulling data from the stack (PULL), etc. Furthermore, as we discovered in Chapter 4, there are many stack-related functions "hardwired" into the processor, such as storing the program counter and key registers. In a real-time operating system we require a stack for each task that we employ to store its context. Therefore, we must have multiple stacks in operation during execution of an RTOS-based system. In these cases, we use the stack concepts that we have developed in this section. We could easily declare additional stacks using the code above. Furthermore, the stack operations we developed could be used by any of the stacks that we declared.

That completes our review of the basic constructs that are used in the implementation of a real-time operating system. We are now going to shift gears and discuss additional RTOS concepts in the next section. We conclude the section with constructs and concepts to describe how to program different RTOS variations.

8.4 BASIC CONCEPTS

Earlier in this chapter we said an RTOS is a computer operating system that must handle multiple activities in a timely manner with limited processor resources. Our investigation of the RTOS begins with defining a task. This requires a radical change (paradigm shift) in the way we think about programs. In a single, sequential processor system, we are used to visualizing a program being a single thread of steps that the processor executes one after the other as defined by an algorithm. In an RTOS, our program consists of independent, asynchronous (occurring at any time), and interacting tasks that will all be competing for precious (and sparse) processing time. Our program consists of mechanisms to keep track of the status of each task, to schedule the tasks for execution, and to make sure each task is receiving its fair share of processor time.

In this section, we begin by getting a good handle on defining a task and how we represent it in a program. We then investigate how the status of each task is updated and tracked using a task control block (TCB). We investigate how the status of other system-related information is tracked using device control blocks. We see how the dispatcher keeps track of the status of all tasks and determines which task gets to be executed next. Finally, we also investigate the different scheduling algorithms that may be employed within an RTOS.

8.4.1 What Is a Task?

A task is an independent, asynchronous activity that is performed by an RTOS system. Because tasks are asynchronous, we do not know exactly when their events occur during program execution. Each task may be visualized as a small, independent program that completes a specific activity. Since we have multiple tasks competing for the use of the same processor, the task must have the capability to store its context (key register values, program counter, etc.) in the event it is preempted by the execution of another task. Therefore, each task is equipped with a stack to store the task context. Even if a task is preempted by another task, eventually the original task will be scheduled to finish execution.

In the next several sections we investigate the different states a task may be in and how all of the information relating to a task is maintained in a task control block. Before moving on to this material, let's consider the tasks associated with a wall-following robot.

Example

In Chapter 7 we investigated the design of a wall-following autonomous robot that had to navigate through an unknown maze. The robot moved through the maze, detecting maze walls with infrared emitter-detector pairs, and made decisions to move forward and turn appropriately to make its way through the maze. Also, as the robot processed through the maze, it was to avoid "land mines" (magnets in the maze floor). Recall that the robot was to sense the land mines with a Hall effect sensor. If a magnet was sensed, the robot must stop, back up, and take evasive actions to steer around the "land mine." The robot was also equipped with a liquid crystal display (LCD) indicating robot status during program execution.

Let's construct a list of required functions the robot's operating system is required to execute in order to accomplish the overall mission of the robot:

- Initialization functions for the LCD, the ATD converter, and the pulse width modulation (PWM) system.
- ATD conversion of the infrared sensor outputs.
- Comparison of the infrared sensor output to a wall-detection threshold.
- Robot turn algorithm to determine which direction the robot should turn in response to the infrared sensor pair outputs.
- Functions to turn the robot left and right and to proceed forward.
- A method of processing the output from the Hall effect sensor.
- A function to perform evasive action—stop, back up, and steer around a detected land mine.
- LCD-related functions.

These functions are illustrated in the structure chart provided in Figure 8.13.

If we want to implement the autonomous robot operating system using real-time operating concepts, these functions would become tasks. Recall from our previous discussion that tasks are independent, asynchronous, and interacting processes

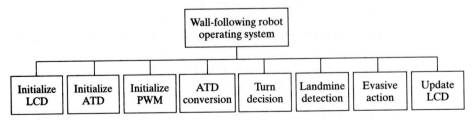

Figure 8.13 Wall-following robot structure chart.

competing for precious CPU time. Let's investigate a scenario with the robot system to illustrate these points.

Scenario

The robot is placed at a starting point in an unknown, unmapped maze containing land mines. The operating system initializes the LCD, the ATD converter system, and also the PWM system. In Chapter 4, we discussed the initialization requirements for each of these robot systems.

Once initialization is complete, the robot proceeds through the unknown maze by processing inputs from its infrared sensor array and its Hall effect sensor. What happens if the robot is about to collide with a wall and at the same time run over a land mine? The robot cannot process both events at the same time because it only has a single processor. Both events are critical, although not to the same degree. If we process the wall information first, the robot avoids collision with the wall but runs the risk of running over the land mine if the wall-processing event is not completed quickly enough. On the other hand, if we respond to the land mine event first, which appears to be the higher priority task, we run the risk of potentially colliding with a wall. On top of all of this, both events are related to one another. We do not want to process wall information in the event we run over a land mine. Also, we do not want to evasively take action to move away from the land mine without knowing the location of nearby walls.

In the sections that follow we investigate how to resolve the above issues using an RTOS. In the next section we become more familiar with concepts relating to tasks.

8.4.2 Controlling a Task

In this section we investigate how an individual task is controlled by the operating system. We begin by defining the different states that a task may be in. We also investigate how a task transitions from one state to another and also provide a software function to model the task states and their relationship to one another. This discussion sets the stage for our discussion on the task control block.

Task States   A task may be in only one defined state at any given instant in time. These different task states are illustrated in Figure 8.14. It is the responsibility of the operating system to track and update the status of each defined task. Keep in mind that all tasks are independent and asynchronous. In addition, the tasks all compete for precious processor execution time. Therefore, the operating system must provide for effective scheduling of this precious resource.

A task is in one of the following states:

- Dormant (D): The task has no need for computer time. It is considered a deleted or a nonactive task, and it transitions into the ready state when so directed by the operating system.

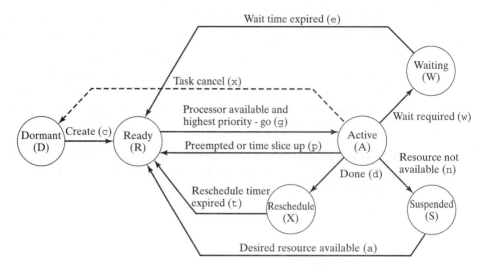

Figure 8.14　Task states.

- `Ready (R)`: The task is fully capable of entering the active or running state; however, another task is currently using the processor. A task may enter the ready state from either the dormant or the active state. A task is moved from the active state to the ready state when a priority task that requires the use of the processor occurs. The preempted, lower priority task (now in the ready state) reenters the active state once processor time is available and the state is given the go-ahead by the operating system.

- `Executing/active/running (A)`: The task is executing its associated activities on the processor. Since our system contains only a single processor, only one task may be in the active state at any given time. A task remains in the active state until one of three things happen: (1) it completes its associated activities, (2) it is preempted by a higher priority task, or (3) it relinquishes control back to the operating system. In these cases the task transitions from the active state to the ready state. These alternatives become more clear when we discuss different types of RTOS systems in section 8.5. From the active state a task may also transition to the waiting or suspended states.

- `Waiting (W)`: The task has been delayed from execution. It remains in the waiting state for a designated amount of time and then transitions back to the ready state to await processor time. A task is placed in the wait state temporarily to allow lower priority tasks an opportunity to execute.

- Suspended (S): The task is waiting for some resource. Once the resource is available the task transitions to the ready state and awaits processor time.
- Rescheduling (X): This state is entered whenever a task runs to completion but does not need to be repeated and enter the ready state right away. In this case, the task remains in the reschedule state until its reschedule interval (RSI) has expired. Once the RSI has expired, the task reenters the ready state.

The following task state diagram may be implemented with a software function. We implement the function using a switch statement. This allows us to carefully control transitions from state to state.

```
/******************************************************************/

char task_state_diagram(char present_state, char action)
{
char   next_state;

switch(present_state){
   case 'D': /*if in dormant (D) state, transition to ready (R)   */
             /*state if create (c) action specified, else stay in*/
             /*dormant state (D)                                  */
             if(action == 'c')
                next_state = 'R';
             else
                next_state = 'D';
             break;

   case 'R': /*if in ready (R) state, task will transition to     */
             /*active (A) state if processor is available and if */
             /*task is highest priority ready task.  These con-  */
             /*ditions are designated with a go signal (g)        */

             if(action == 'g')
                next_state = 'A';
             else
                next_state = 'R';
             break;

   case 'A': /*if in active state (A), the task can transition to*/
             /*a number of states depending on action specified. */

             if(action == 'p')
             /*time slice has expired or task pre-empted*/
                next_state = 'R';              /*return to ready state*/
             else if (action == 'w')
             /*task will enter waiting state*/
```

```
                next_state = 'W';                       /*waiting state*/
            else if (action == 'n')   /*resource is not available*/
               next_state = 'S';
                                /*task will enter suspended state*/
            else if (action == 'd')
                                /*task has completed execution*/
               next_state = 'X';
                                /*only required to run once, goes*/
                                      /*to reschedule state*/
            else if (action == 'x')              /*task cancelled*/
               next_state = 'D';  /*task re-enters dormant state*/
            else next_state = 'A';              /*default case*/
            break;

   case 'X': /*if in reschedule (X) state transition to ready (R)*/
            /*state when reschedule timer expired (t).          */

            if(action == 't')         /*reschedule timer expired*/
               next_state = 'R';/*task will re-enter ready state*/
            else
               next_state = 'X';
            break;


   case 'W': /*if in wait (W) state transition to ready (R) state*/
            /*when wait timer expired (e).                       */

            if(action == 'e')         /*reschedule timer expired*/
               next_state = 'R';/*task will re-enter ready state*/
            else
               next_state = 'W';
            break;


   case 'S': /*if in suspended (S) state transition to ready (R) */
            /*state when desired resource is available (a)       */

            if(action == 'a')       /*desired resource available*/
               next_state = 'R';/*task will re-enter ready state*/
            else
               next_state = 'S';
            break;

return next_state;
}

}
/*******************************************************************/
```

The Task Control Block   Recall from our previous discussion that tasks are independent, asynchronous, and interacting processes requiring the same processor to complete their associated actions. Let's revisit our fearless waitron from earlier in the chapter. The waitron (the processor) must contend and satisfy multiple customers (tasks) using limited resources. As the waitron (processor) switches from serving one table of customers (tasks) to another, he or she must remember the status (context) of each one of the tables (tasks) to provide quality service worthwhile of a good tip.

In this section we investigate how an RTOS "remembers" and tracks the status of each task as it allows each task to complete its process. We know what you are thinking, "What's the big deal? Let a process, once active, run to completion." As we have illustrated with the robot example this is not possible. Also, in a system with a large number of competing tasks, some lower-priority tasks would never get to use the processor. Imagine what would happen if our waitron (processor) devoted all of his or her time to a single table (process) until completing all tasks associated with the table and ignored all of the other customers (tasks).

We do not know exactly how a good waitron keeps track of multiple tables simultaneously. On the other hand, an RTOS typically uses a task control block (TCB) to track the status of each task. Each task in an RTOS has its own associated TCB, which contains the most up-to-date information on the task. This information is used and updated by the RTOS kernel to effectively track, schedule, and execute multiple tasks within a given system. We need to emphasize that the RTOS updates the TCB. The actual task does not have direct contact with the TCB, although the TCB contains the most up-to-date information about the task.

A TCB is illustrated in Figure 8.15. As the RTOS switches from one task to another, all of the key information concerning the currently executing task must be safely stored before switching to the next task. That way, when the task later obtains processor time, it can pick up where it left off when it was preempted by the RTOS. As mentioned earlier, we term this key task information as its context.

Pause for a second and think about what information would be important to a task. Also, consider how you might implement a TCB in software. At a minimum the TCB should contain the task's name, its current state, its priority, its current context (key register values), and where it left off in processing its associated task-related activities.

At first, it might appear daunting to develop a TCB in software. The pieces of information concerning each task are of different types. Earlier in the chapter we discussed the record or structure, an abstract data type well suited for TCB implementation duty. Recall, the structure is a user-defined collection of different

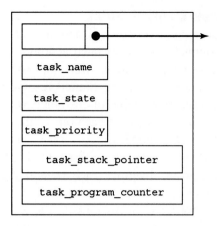

Figure 8.15   Task control block.

but related data types. We can conjoin these different data types together as a structure. We use the structure to implement a TCB. Earlier in the chapter we developed a structure for a car and kept track of all the diverse details concerning a specific car in the structure's fields. We do the same thing for a TCB. (Actually, we ask you to do this as a homework problem (Challenging 4). Use the car record as an example and develop a similar structure for a TCB.)

Let's take a closer look at the individual fields for the TCB and determine the data type for each field.

- *Task name:* The task name consists of a character array. We limit the task name to 20 characters for the robot example. This allows us to store each task's name without using cryptic abbreviations. We allow this memory use extravagance for readability.

- *Task current state:* Recall from the previous section that a task can be in one of six states—Dormant (D), Ready (R), Active (A), Waiting (W), Suspended (S), or Rescheduling (X)—at a given time. We have designated each task with a single alphanumeric character. We can therefore store the current task state with a *char* variable within our TCB structure.

- *Task priority:* Indicating the relative ranking of tasks within a system, the task priority is assigned by the system developer. In our robot example, we use fixed priority values. It is possible to implement RTOS systems in which the priority of a task may change during program execution. The task priority is represented with an unsigned integer number. We illustrate how to assign task priority in an upcoming example.

- *Task context:* All of the key registers associated with a task comprise the task context. The interrupt system aboard the 68HC12 uses a stack to store all of its context when an interrupt occurs. We also use the stack to store the context of a task. Each task has its own stack. Therefore, an RTOS has multiple stacks in existence at the same time. As a system programmer, you must ensure that these stacks will not collide with one another in the memory space. For simplicity, we use the fixed stack structure developed earlier in the chapter for TCB context storage. Since all key registers and memory locations within the 68HC12 are either 8 or 16 bits, we use a fixed array of integers for our TCB stack.

- *Task activity status:* The task activity status is the next program step that is executed once the task becomes active. Upon initialization, the task starts at the beginning of its associated activities. However, during program execution a given task may be preempted by a higher priority task before it finishes its associated task. Therefore, the TCB needs to remember the next step the task executes.

- *Task link:* Since we will be linking these TCB structures in linked lists, we need a pointer to the next TCB in the list. The task link is the pointer to the next TCB in the list.

You should begin feeling more comfortable with the concept of tasks and task control blocks. However, we have uncovered some disconcerting problems. You are probably uncomfortable with the idea of breaking out of the middle of program execution even if it is for a higher priority event. We investigate this topic in the next section. You can imagine the complications that result if we initiate an ATD conversion and are preempted by a higher priority event before the conversion is complete. Imagine the complications if the higher priority event also used the ATD converter. We see it is up to the operating system developer to determine when it is safe for a task to relinquish control of the processor. Before investigating these concepts, let's return to our robot example and see how to assign task priorities.

Scenario

In the wall-following robot example we had multiple tasks to support the operation of the robot. We must assign a numerical priority to each task. We use a lower numerical value to indicate a higher priority task. For example, the highest priority task is given a priority of one. We use our understanding of the robot scenario to assign task priorities. Since our robot is deactivated if it runs over a land mine, we assign the Land Mine Detection task a priority of 1. The next highest priority would be taking Evasive Action should a land mine be detected. We therefore assign it a priority of 2. We assign priority 3 to the ATD Conversion task since it supplies information concerning the proximity of maze walls. The Turn Decision task is given the next highest priority (4) since it processes the information necessary to avoid maze walls. We assign a priority of 5 to Update LCD. It is lower in priority to the tasks discussed thus far; however, it is of higher priority than the remaining tasks. The remaining tasks are of low priority. They are active during the early portion of our operating system execution and then go into the dormant state. We therefore assign them the lowest priority, giving them a priority of 6 (Initialize LCD), 7 (Initialize ATD), and 8 (Initialize PWM).

Partitioning Tasks   Earlier in this section we raised the issue of how to partition task-related activities (code) into pieces or phases with convenient exit points. This is important because in an RTOS with multiple tasks with similar priority, a task will rarely be able to complete its associated activities from beginning to end. Most often a task will complete some portion of its associated activities and then be preempted by a higher priority task or tasks. Just because a higher priority task is ready does not mean we immediately transfer from the currently active task to the ready higher priority task. We must provide an orderly transition from one task to another at a convenient break point in the code. As we write the task-associated activity code, we must keep this in mind. For example, we may subdivide a task-related function into three pieces. The first time the task becomes active, the processor executes the first third of the code until a convenient break point (as defined by you, the programmer). When the code reaches this break point, its context is saved in the TCB and the task relinquishes control of the processor. The higher priority task is then executed. When the original task again obtains precious processor time for execution, it picks up where it left off and continues with the processing of the second portion of the task-related functions. This process continues until the task completes its task-related activities.

Let's illustrate this concept with an example.

Example

Suppose that we have equipped a robot with five infrared sensor pairs, as shown in Figure 8.16. Furthermore, suppose that we have a function called `process_turn` that initializes the 68HC12 ATD system, initiates a conversion sequence to collect the analog signal from the five sensors (0 to 4) that are connected to ATD channels 7 to 3. Also, the Hall effect sensor to detect land mines (magnets) is mounted to the bottom of the robot. Its output is connected to ATD channel 2. *Note:* This is a contrived example illustrating how to subdivide code at convenient break points.

The code for the `process_turn` function is provided below.

```
void process_turn()
{
                              /*Initialize ATD system        */
ATDCTL2 = 0x80;              /*Set ADPU to power up ATD system */
ATDCTL3 = 0x00;              /*ignore freeze                 */
```

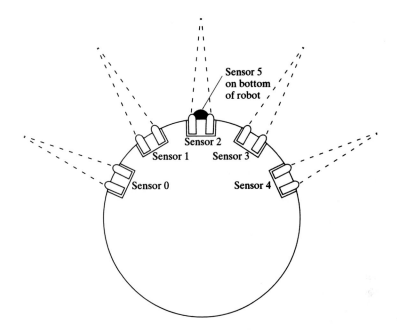

Figure 8.16 Robot equipped with five Infrared sensors and a Hall effect sensor. The Infrared sensor detects the presence of maze walls while the Hall effect sensor detects the presence of land mines (magnets) in the floor.

```
ATDCTL4 = 0x7F;                    /*Slow down P clock to 125kHz    */
                                   /*samples, conv time = 32 ATD CLKs*/
                                   /* 1 sample per every 256 us     */
for(i=0; i<67; i++){               /* wait 100 microseconds 8MHz ECLK*/
  ;
}

                                   /*Initiate ATD conversion sequence*/
ATDCTL5 = 0x50;                    /*Starts the ATD for 8 channel   */
                                   /*multichannel conversion        */
while((ATDSTAT & 0x8000) == 0){ /*test SCF bit for conv complete*/
  ;
}
                                   /*store ATD results in global    */
                                   /*character array                */
sens[0] = ADR7H;                   /*far left sensor                */
sens[1] = ADR6H;                   /*inner left sensor              */
sens[2] = ADR5H;                   /*middle sensor                  */
sens[3] = ADR4H;                   /*inner right sensor             */
sens[4] = ADR3H;                   /*far right sensor               */
sens[5] = ADR2H;                   /*Hall Effect sensor             */
```

```
/*process sensor data for turn decision.  Note: The threshold    */
/*for the Hall Effect sensor(hes_threshold) and the infrared     */
/*detector (opto_threshold) are global variables and are         */
/*determined experimentally                                      */

if(sens[5] < hes_threshold){  /*detect Hall effect Sensor, avoid*/
  pwm_motors(back_up);        /*'land mine' by having robot backup*/
                              /*after robot backed up determine */
                              /*next action                     */
  if(sens[0] > opto_threshold)
    pwm_motors(right_turn);
  else
    pwm_motors(left_turn);

  for(i=0; i<0xFFFF; i++){     /*delay for motor turn           */
   for(j=0; j<15; j++){
    ;
    }
   }

 }
                              /*if three walls detected - backup*/
else if((sens[2]>opto_threshold)&&(sens[0]>opto_threshold)
                      &&(sens[4]>opto_threshold)){
  pwm_motors(back_up);}

                              /*if wall to left and in front,  */
                              /*turn the robot right           */
else if((sens[0]>opto_threshold)&&(sens[2]>opto_threshold)){
  pwm_motors(right_turn);}

                              /*if wall to right and in front, */
                              /*turn the robot left            */
else if((sens[2]>opto_threshold)&&(sens[4]>opto_threshold)){
  pwm_motors(left_turn);}

                              /*if wall in front of half right */
                              /*sensor then navigate half right*/
else if(sens[1]>opto_threshold){
  pwm_motors(half_right);}

                              /*if wall in front of half left  */
                              /*sensor then navigate half left */
else if(sens[3]>opto_threshold){
  pwm_motors(half_left);}

                              /*if nothing detected, then      */
                              /*default to forward motion       */
```

```
else{
  pwm_motors(forward);}


}
```

If we want to subdivide this code into three sections for processing by an RTOS, we can insert break points after the ATD initialization sequence and after the ATD data collection sequence. This would allow the function to relinquish control of the processor and return control to the RTOS. To implement these changes we need to introduce a variable we will call code_section. This variable will allow us to track which portion of the task-related function should be executed next.

```
int process_turn(int code_section)
{

switch(code_section){

  case 0:

                                      /*Initialize ATD system          */
      ATDCTL2 = 0x80;                 /*Set ADPU to power up ATD system */
      ATDCTL3 = 0x00;                 /*ignore freeze                   */
      ATDCTL4 = 0x7F;                 /*Slow down P clock to 125kHz     */
                                      /*samples, conv time = 32 ATD CLKs*/
                                      /* 1 sample per every 256 us      */
      for(i=0; i<67; i++){            /* wait 100 microseconds 8MHz ECLK*/
        ;
        }

      code_section = 1;              /*update code_section variable     */
      break;


  case 1:
                                      /*Initiate ATD conversion sequence*/
      ATDCTL5 = 0x50;                 /*Starts the ATD for 8 channel    */
                                      /*multichannel conversion         */
      while((ATDSTAT & 0x8000) == 0){
                                      /*test SCF bit for conv complete  */

        ;
        }
                                      /*store ATD results in global     */
                                      /*character array                 */
      sens[0] = ADR7H;                /*far left sensor                 */
      sens[1] = ADR6H;                /*inner left sensor               */
      sens[2] = ADR5H;                /*middle sensor                   */
      sens[3] = ADR4H;                /*inner right sensor              */
```

```
   sens[4] = ADR3H;          /*far right sensor              */
   sens[5] = ADR2H;          /*Hall Effect sensor            */

   code_section = 2;         /*update code_section variable  */
   break;


 case 2:

/*process sensor data for turn decision.  Note: The threshold */
/*for the Hall effect sensor(hes_threshold) and the infrared  */
/*detector (opto_threshold) global variables and are deter-   */
/*mined experimentally                                        */

if(sens[5] < hes_threshold){
                             /*detect Hall effect sensor, avoid */
   pwm_motors(back_up);      /*'landmine' by having robot backup*/
                             /*after robot backed up determine  */
                             /*next action                      */
   if(sens[0] > opto_threshold)
     pwm_motors(right_turn);
   else
     pwm_motors(left_turn);

   for(i=0; i<0xFFFF; i++){ /*delay for motor turn              */
     for(j=0; j<15; j++){
       ;
      }
     }

 }
                             /*if three walls detected - backup*/
else if((sens[2]>opto_threshold)&&(sens[0]>opto_threshold)
                          &&(sens[4]>opto_threshold)){
   pwm_motors(back_up);}

                             /*if wall to left and in front,  */
                             /*turn the robot right           */
else if((sens[0]>opto_threshold)&&(sens[2]>opto_threshold)){
  pwm_motors(right_turn);}

                             /*if wall to right and in front, */
                             /*turn the robot left            */
else if((sens[2]>opto_threshold)&&(sens[4]>opto_threshold)){
  pwm_motors(left_turn);}

                             /*if wall in front of half right */
                             /*sensor then navigate half right*/
```

```
    else if(sens[1]>opto_threshold){
      pwm_motors(half_right);}

                                 /*if wall in front of half left  */
                                 /*sensor then navigate half left */
    else if(sens[3]>opto_threshold){
      pwm_motors(half_left);}

                                 /*if nothing detected, then       */
                                 /*default to forward motion       */
    else{
      pwm_motors(forward);}


    code_section = 0;            /*update code_section variable    */
    break;

    }/*end switch*/
return code_section;

}
```

When the task associated with the `process_turn` function transitions from the ready to the active state, the RTOS calls the function with an argument of 0. The function `process_turn` then executes up to the first break point in the code. At that time the function returns processor control back to the RTOS. The RTOS updates the TCB associated with `process_turn` to reflect that the second portion of code should be executed the next time the task enters the active state. The task then reverts back to the ready state and awaits processor time as allocated by the RTOS. Again, the reason that we subdivide the code into logical pieces is to allow a portion of a task to run to completion and then allow another task to run a portion of its associated code, etc. This allows multiple tasks to appear to be executing simultaneously although only a single task is actually being executed by the processor at any instant in time.

In this example we used global variables to store information between different calls to the `process_turn` function. Using global variables may not be the best use of our precious RAM memory resources. Later in the chapter we investigate alternative methods of passing information between tasks.

As you might have surmised from this example, the RTOS kernel must be fairly sophisticated to efficiently track multiple tasks, schedule processor time efficiently, and complete the overall intent of the application. In the next section we investigate the component portions of the RTOS kernel and how they interact with one another to complete the overall required activities of the specific application.

8.4.3 Multitasking System Components

To implement a multitasking operating system, the system developer (you) must view the application as a group of independent but interacting tasks. Each task has its associated activities that must be accomplished. The multitasking system's objective is to accomplish the requirements of the application by scheduling, updating, tracking, and deconflicting tasks using only a single processor. As you might imagine, the multitasking system may become quite complex. However, we break the system into its constituent parts and investigate each one separately.

In general the operating system must keep track of the status of every task within its system. Recall from the automobile dealership example how we employed multiple linked lists to keep track of the status of each car as a car was traded in, reconditioned, placed on the lot for sale, sold, etc.; we would remove it from one list and add it to another as its status changed. The RTOS uses similar techniques to track the status of each task.

In general the RTOS allows a task to execute for some limited amount of time. When the task's allotted time has expired, the RTOS collects and stores the current context of the task within its associated TCB. The RTOS then decides which task will be executed (obtain processor time) next. A variety of scheduling algorithms may be employed to make this decision. Whichever scheduling algorithm is chosen, its basic premise is the same. That is, every task must obtain its fair share of processor execution time.

Before a task can transition to the ready state, the RTOS must ensure that all resources required by the task are available. Resources may be defined as specific data, hardware subsystems, etc. For example, if a task will be using one of the 68HC12's subsystems, the RTOS must ensure that the resource is available prior to the task entering the ready state. A task that is awaiting a resource is placed in the suspended state.

The processor must also have the capability to suspend a task for some specified amount of time. This allows lower priority tasks a chance to obtain processor time. For example, if we took a simplistic approach to RTOS scheduling which selected the highest priority ready task to execute, lower priority tasks might not get a chance to run. To prevent this situation, an active high priority task may be temporarily placed in the waiting state to allow lower priority tasks in the ready state a chance to execute. The operating system must also have mechanisms to respond to the highest priority critical tasks when they occur. This implies the use of interrupts in RTOS processing.

To accomplish these activities the RTOS kernel uses a variety of tools including system tables to track status and a dispatcher/scheduler to assimilate system data to determine which task should execute next. The RTOS also provides for intertask communication capability that we investigate later in the chapter.

System Tables   The operating system uses a variety of tables/blocks to track the status of tasks, input/output devices, and system services. We have already discussed the TCB in some detail earlier in Section 8.4. Aside from the TCB, the operating system also maintains a device control block (DCB) to track the status of system-associated devices. This allows the operating system to ensure that all task-required resources are available for use prior to allowing a task to transition to the ready state. Depending on the number of devices/resources in a system, the DCB may be implemented with a simple two-dimensional array that can be dynamically updated as device status changes.

Example

> We were watching the phenomenal Tiger Woods play golf on television and became intrigued by how the golf course staff was able to track the status of multiple golfers (tasks) throughout the tournament involving multiple holes (resources). During the course of the broadcast, we had a glimpse of a large status board that tracked both the golfers and the holes status. At a glance, the golf course staff could tell the status of a given player or hole. The status board was constantly updated during the course of the tournament. An RTOS uses the exact same techniques (TCB and DCB) to track the status of tasks, resources, and services during program execution.

Dispatcher/Scheduler   The dispatcher/scheduler is the other key portion of the RTOS kernel. Its primary function is to determine which task executes next. The scheduler may employ a variety of algorithms to make this decision. The different algorithms and their inherent disadvantages and advantages are discussed in the next section.

8.5 TYPES OF REAL-TIME OPERATING SYSTEMS

Typically, real-time operating systems are categorized by the type of algorithm used by the scheduler/dispatch portion of the RTOS kernel. The name for each RTOS type does a fairly good job of describing the fundamental premise of how the algorithm operates. We review the different types in turn. We need to emphasize that a specific RTOS scheduling algorithm is not better than another type. It is your job as an RTOS system programmer to match a specific application with the best suited RTOS scheduling algorithm.

8.5.1 Polled Loop Systems

The polled loop system is the simplest real-time scheduling kernel to design and implement. As its name implies, it uses a polling mechanism to sequentially determine if a specific task requires processor time. When a task requires processing time, it executes from beginning to end. Once the task associated actions are complete, the operating system continues polling for tasks requiring processor time.

The polled loop system is used in systems that contain multiple tasks with equal priority. It should also be used for systems with tasks that will not likely require processor time simultaneously. Since a single task runs to completion with the polled loop mechanism, intertask communication is usually not required.

The primary advantage of the polled loop system is its simplicity. With this type of system it is easy to determine the response time of a specific task, the system is easy to write, and it is also easy to debug. The primary disadvantage of the polled loop system is also its simplicity. A polled loop system cannot handle a burst of events—that is, more than one task requiring processor time simultaneously. Also, due to its simplicity it is not well suited for complicated systems involving multiple tasks competing for the same precious processor time. It needs to be emphasized that the polled loop system is not a poor choice for an RTOS scheduling algorithm. It has its limitations; however, it is ideally suited for certain applications, as we shall see in the following example.

Example

In Chapter 2 we discussed an embedded control system to process inputs from a remote control or from a panel input for a stereo amplifier. In this specific example, the operating system would initiate the amplifier system and then continually poll for input changes from the remote control and the front panel switches. The remote control interface was connected to Port A while the front panel switches were connected to Port B. In this application, polling was the preferred method for the operating system implementation. It was chosen over other alternatives because (1) once the amplifier was initialized there was nothing else for the operating system to do except to poll for input changes, (2) the inputs from the remote control and the front panel switches are of equal importance (priority), and (3) response to the inputs were not time sensitive.

8.5.2 Polled Loop with Interrupts

What happens if you have an application that appears to be a good match for a polling scheme but there are several tasks that require immediate processor access? Are you required to abandon the polled scheme in favor of a much more complicated RTOS scheduling algorithm? The answer is no. As we discussed in Chapter 4, the 68HC12 is equipped with a powerful, flexible, and priority-driven interrupt system. A polling algorithm may be used to handle the normal mundane day-to-day tasks of the operating system, whereas the interrupt system may be employed to handle the time-sensitive tasks that require processor time.

These types of scheduling algorithms are also known as a foreground/background system. The polling algorithm is considered the background portion of the operating system, whereas the interrupt is considered the foreground portion of the system. Normally, these systems are written in two stages. The background portion is designed, implemented, and tested first and then the foreground interrupt is added as a second stage.

Example

> Let's revisit our stereo amplifier controller. The transistor-based amplifiers used in our stereo design are quite expensive. A good design prevents the transistors from overheating during normal amplifier use to prevent damage or destruction of the transistors. Let's suppose that the amplifier designer adds temperature transducers to each transistor to constantly monitor their operating temperature. If the temperature of any transistor reaches an unacceptably high level, the designer would like the operating system to activate an auxiliary cooling fan to reduce transistor temperature.
>
> This design modification would not require us to abandon the polling scheme. We would instead use the polling scheme in a background mode to process normal day-to-day activity of the stereo controller. In the foreground portion of the system, the transistor temperature-monitoring transducers could be interfaced to the interrupt system. An interrupt would be activated when the temperature of the transistor(s) reached an unacceptably high temperature level. At that time the processor could issue a control signal to activate the cooling fan. We investigate this design in the applications Section 8.9 and a homework problem later in the chapter (Challenging 2).

8.5.3 Round-Robin Systems

In a round-robin RTOS system, the kernel sequences from one active task to another. When it reaches the last task in the system, it begins again with the first task. In a round-robin system, tasks are often allowed to run to completion before sequencing to the next task. If this provides an unacceptable update cycle for a single pass through all of the tasks, time-slicing techniques may be used. Time-slicing provides each round-robin task a fixed access time internal to the processor. When the time-slicing increment has expired, the context of the active task is stored in its associated TCB and the next task in the round-robin sequence goes active while the current task is returned to the ready state. The round-robin operating system may be easily implemented using a circular queue data structure. In this case, the TCBs could be linked in a circular queue. The operating system would sequence from one task to another within the queue. The real-time interrupt (RTI) features of the 68HC12 could be used if time-slicing was desired.

Example

> In a previous professional life I (sfb) was an Air Force missileer. My crew partner and I were responsible for monitoring the status of our assigned missiles, which

we fondly referred to as our missile "patch." We were remotely separated from the missiles (order of kilometers). Missile status was monitored via a computer within our control center. The computer sequentially polled the status from each assigned missile in a round-robin fashion. I was not involved in the design of the control center's computer operating system; however, I speculate that a round-robin polling scheme was used because the status from each missile was of equal importance.

8.5.4 Hybrid Systems

As we saw with the polling system, a round-robin scheduling algorithm can also be equipped with interrupt capabilities. This type of a round-robin system with interrupts is referred to as a hybrid system. In this case, the round-robin algorithm forms the background portion of the operating system while the interrupt portion forms the foreground portion of the system.

Example

In the missile "patch" monitoring scenario, we would be interested in being immediately notified if there was a catastrophic event involving one of our assigned missiles, such as flooding of the launch tube, a fire in the missile silo, a security breach, etc. In these conditions the operating system could be equipped with interrupts to break out of the normal round-robin sequence, handle the higher priority events, and then return to the normal round-robin processing once the higher priority events had been handled.

8.5.5 Interrupt-Driven Systems

In Chapter 4 we discussed the powerful, flexible, and priority-driven interrupt system aboard the 68HC12. An RTOS operating system may be developed around this interrupt system. In this type of implementation the main program consists of initialization activities to configure the system and then the system enters an infinite "jump to self" loop. Within the loop, the processor simply waits for interrupt events to occur. When the individual interrupts occur, the processor executes the interrupt service routine associated with each task (interrupt). When multiple interrupts simultaneously occur, the internal 68HC12 priority mechanisms may be employed to determine which task should be executed first. The stack mechanisms within the 68HC12 interrupt system ensure that the tasks' context is stored and restored correctly. An interrupt-driven operating system of this type is easy to write. It also has the added advantage of having a quick response time to an interrupt event. It is essential that the system writer carefully evaluates each task in the system to determine its associated priority.

Example

Throughout this chapter we have discussed a wall-following robot with the capability to steer through an unknown maze while searching for land mines. The operating system for this robot could be implemented using interrupt techniques. In this case the initialization tasks (LCD, ATD, and PWM) would be called upon at the initiation of the operating system and then enter the dormant state. The operating system would then enter a continuous jump to self loop awaiting interrupt-driven tasks. The tasks associated with detecting land mines, detecting and steering around maze walls, and updating the LCD display would each be assigned an individual interrupt and associated interrupt service routine (ISR). For example, when a land mine was detected, it would trigger an interrupt event. The ISR associated with the land mine detection task would then be executed. If multiple interrupts were to occur simultaneously, the interrupt priority hardware of the 68HC12 would ensure that the highest priority interrupt would be executed first. If a higher priority interrupt were to occur while a lower priority interrupt is executing, the 68HC12 could be configured to respond to the higher priority interrupt and then return to service the lower priority interrupt.

8.5.6 Cooperative Multitasking

In a cooperative multitasking RTOS, the highest priority ready task is executed for some amount of processor time. The task then relinquishes control of the processor back to the operating system at a convenient break point in the task-associated activities. Prior to relinquishing control, the task updates its associated TCB with the task's current context. The task then reenters the ready state. The operating system then allows the highest priority ready task to enter the active state. The task entering the active state restores its context extracting the information from its associated TCB. This task then executes its associated activities until it reaches a break point. It will update its TCB with its current context and relinquish control back to the operating system. This process continues. It is important to emphasize in the cooperative multitasking system, the task relinquishes control back to the operating system. Should a task not relinquish control, lower priority tasks may never obtain processor time. As you might imagine, intertask communication is very important in this type of operating system. This is accomplished using global variables.

This style of operating system may be implemented with a series of linked lists of system tasks. That is, a linked list exists for each of the different states that a task could be in. This concept is illustrated in Figure 8.17. During system operation, tasks are moved from list-to-list in response to system activity. Earlier in this chapter we moved the car record from one linked list to another linked list in response to activity occurring at the car dealership. In like manner, a task, which is implemented as a record, is moved from list to list depending on the activity of your specific application.

8.5.7 Preemptive Priority Multitasking Systems

A preemptive priority multitasking system (PPMS) is very similar to the cooperative multitasking system, the primary difference between the two being who is

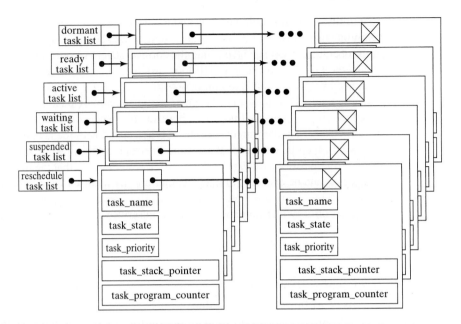

Figure 8.17   Multiple lists of records.

in charge of the processor time. In the cooperative multitasking system, the task relinquishes control of the processor back to the operating system. In a PPMS, the processor decides what task is active next and if a lower priority task will be preempted. With the PPMS, each task within the system is assigned a priority. The operating system examines the linked list containing all ready tasks and chooses the task with the highest priority to place in the active state. When a higher priority task is ready, the operating system will then preempt the lower priority task. The lower priority task updates its TCB and then transitions from the active to the ready state. The higher priority task is then allowed to enter the active state. In this type of RTOS, task priorities may either be fixed or they may be dynamically changed during program execution.

That completes our discussion of different types of RTOS. We need to emphasize that one RTOS technique is not better than the others. It is incumbent on the system designer to choose the best-suited RTOS configuration for the specific requirements of the application. In the next section we discuss the techniques necessary to implement an RTOS.

8.6 RTOS ISSUES

As we have discussed the theory and operation of an RTOS in previous sections, concerns may have been raised in your mind. The RTOS solves a lot of problems but it also creates a number of challenges. In this section we investigate some of the issues you might encounter in an RTOS-based embedded control system. We also discuss methods to avoid, mitigate, or correct these situations. We investigate the issues regarding concurrency, reentrancy, intertask communication, and safety, and we explore the big question about whether to write your own RTOS or buy one.

8.6.1 Concurrency

Another Parable

I spend a lot of time on the road driving. While driving from Laramie to Fort Collins on beautiful and scenic U.S. 287 for a conference planning meeting, I came upon a stretch of road under repair. This highway is a two-lane blacktop road. The construction crew had one highway lane closed for repair while the other was open for traffic. Flag persons were posted on either end of the open lane to alternately allow a group of southbound vehicles to use the open lane and then a group of northbound vehicles to do the same. The flag persons maintained synchronization with one another via radio. To maintain traffic flow and avoid collisions, one flag person would provide a "stop" sign to oncoming traffic while the other would provide a "proceed with caution" sign to oncoming traffic.

This parable illustrates the concurrency issue that occurs in some types of RTOS. In this case we have a critical resource (the single highway lane) that requires use simultaneously by two different tasks (northbound and southbound traffic). The goal of the two flag persons is to prevent these two tasks from simultaneously accessing the critical resource so that a collision will not occur. In this section we investigate how the critical resource competing situation occurs in an RTOS and how collisions might be prevented.

As we have seen in our discussions, the basic RTOS premise is to allow multiple tasks, competing for the same processor resource, time to complete their assigned activities. We investigated a large number of scheduling algorithms to perform this basic concept. Some algorithms allowed switching from task-to-task to occur at well-defined times (round-robin, cooperative multitasking), but some algorithms—in particular, those that employed interrupt mechanisms or preemptive scheduling—could switch from task-to-task without warning.

A concurrency issue occurs when a lower priority task is performing some critical portion of its coded activity or is using a critical resource. If interrupted, the lower priority task will not complete its required actions correctly even if it obtains sufficient processing time later to do so. For example, imagine if a task is using the 68HC12's ATD to perform an analog-to-digital conversion. If the task initiates a conversion and is interrupted before the conversion is complete, errors will occur. This situation could be further complicated if the higher priority interrupting task uses the ATD converter.

In general, we term these portions of program code or resources as critical. The key to solving the concurrency issue is to prevent it from happening in the first place. A number of techniques may be employed to prevent simultaneous access to critical resources, including the following:

- *Disable interrupts:* Interrupts are disabled when a task is performing a critical portion of its associated code. This is accomplished in the 68HC12 with the SEI (set interrupt mask) command. Once the critical portion of code is complete, interrupts can be re-enabled using the CLI (clear interrupt mask) command.
- *Employ semaphores or locks:* A semaphore or lock can be used to indicate that a critical resource is not available for use because it is currently in use by another task. The flag persons on the highway employed semaphores (the "stop" and "proceed with caution" signs) to prevent or allow access to a critical resource. Before a program portion can use a critical portion of code, it must check to see if the resource is available.

8.6.2 Reentrancy

Closely related to the concept of concurrency is the issue of reentrancy. A function is said to be reentrant if it always works correctly and preserves its data even if interrupted and restarted. Again, problems occur when the lower priority task is interrupted before it completes its associated function. Should the higher priority task use the same function, the function is restarted before it was finished by the lower priority task.

The following techniques can be used to create a reentrant function:

- *Disable interrupts:* Interrupts are disabled during critical portions of certain function.
- *Employ local variables:* Recall that local variables are implemented on the stack. If a higher priority task preempts a lower priority task, its variables are safely stored on the stack.
- *Use microprocessor registers:* Microprocessor registers can be used to store critical variables within a reentrant function. If the function is interrupted, the variables are stored automatically to the stack by the microprocessor.
- *Combine techniques:* A combination of these techniques can be used to create a reentrant function.

8.6.3 Intertask Communication

Intertask communication is a key requirement of an RTOS employing interrupts. This is not a critical issue with a cooperative multitasking RTOS since the tasks determine when they relinquish control back to the operating system. Therefore, the task activities can ensure that all data have been properly updated before relinquishing task control.

The simplest method of transferring data between tasks is through the use of global variables. As we have seen in the previous discussion, this simple technique may break down if a lower priority task is preempted by a higher priority task before it has a chance to update these variables.

To prevent this from happening, we can use a mailbox—a mutually agreed upon location in memory that tasks may share. The mailbox may contain a single variable, a group of variables, or even data structures. To ensure that the data are current in the mailbox, a task may perform a post operation—an operation that is secured with a key—and may write information to the mailbox. Another task may then read (pend operation) the mailbox contents if it has access to the key. The key is provided to only a single task at a given time to prevent multiple tasks having access to the mailbox. This is very similar to the semaphore technique previously discussed.

8.6.4 Safety, Verification, and Fail-Safe Operation

One of the most critical issues involving RTOS operation is safety. We have already discussed some of the testing and safety standards. Depending on where the RTOS is employed (communications, medical product, commercial product, aviation, etc.), there are different safety standards that must be met. The software system must be proved safe through documentation and testing. Furthermore, in the event of system failure, the system must enter a fail-safe condition—that is, it should enter a condition to prevent harming people or equipment.

Example

> If we were to employ an RTOS to control the traffic lights at a busy intersection, a fail-safe condition would be for all traffic lights to go red in the event of system failure. You can imagine the catastrophe if the system were to allow lights to go green during a system failure.

The issue of safety is a key factor when deciding to write your own operating system or purchase a commercially available product.

8.6.5 The Big Question

We have been careful in our discussion of real-time operating systems not to answer a key question you might have: Should you write your own system or purchase a commercial variety? We believe that this decision is up to you, the system designer. To help make this decision, we have identified the following three factors for consideration:

- *Application:* What will the system be used for? If it is used in a system where safety is a critical issue, it might be wiser to use a system that has already been certified for use in safety-critical applications. This does not imply a high cost. Safety-Critical RTOS packages are available for a low to moderate cost [Labrosse 2002].
- *Criticality:* A respected computer engineering colleague purposefully chose not to use a commercially available RTOS package when developing a critical RTOS application involving nuclear safety. He indicated that he wanted to write each line of code and thoroughly understand the operation of the system. He felt that some system details would be hidden from him in a commercial package.
- *Cost:* You may think that writing your own RTOS will render a large cost savings in system development since commercially available varieties on the order of $5,000 may seem cost prohibitive. However, you can easily expend that amount in labor costs when writing your own system.

Whichever route you decide to pursue, the next section provides some guidelines to follow when implementing an RTOS.

8.7 IMPLEMENTING A REAL-TIME OPERATING SYSTEM

We present here a brief summary of how to go about implementing a real-time operating system:

1. Understand all system requirements thoroughly. Determine if an RTOS is actually required. If you are developing a simple control algorithm, a standard sequential program may suffice; if you are developing an application with multiple events, the RTOS is the appropriate choice.
2. Determine the appropriate scheduling algorithm to employ for task management. Remember, one is not better than the other. It is your job as the system developer to find the scheduling algorithm that best fits the application.
3. Partition your system into independent tasks.
4. Implement the operating system—the system that controls and schedules tasks—first.
5. Write the tasks. Ensure that tasks do not compete for the same memory locations and that they are independent of one another. Also ensure that the task implementation agrees with the type of scheduling algorithm you have decided to use.

6. If you are developing a foreground/background style system, implement the background portion first and then the foreground portion.

7. Most importantly, test, test, test! Use the sound testing techniques that were discussed in Chapter 2.

8.8 A FUNDAMENTAL APPLICATION: STEREO AMPLIFIER CONTROLLER AND A POLLED LOOP SYSTEM

In this section we discuss different real-time operating systems. We begin with a fundamental polled loop system followed by a polled loop system with an interrupt. We then present a hardware simulator to develop and test more complex scheduling algorithms.

8.8.1 Project Overview

We examine here a fundamental polled loop system used to control a stereo amplifier. We looked at this stereo amplifier in Chapter 2 when we discussed system design and then earlier in this chapter as an example of a polled loop system. Figure 8.18 presents an overview of the amplifier system. Six front chassis panel switches or a remote control are used to select one of six audio sources. Only one audio source is routed to the amplifier at any given time.

8.8.2 Sample Code

The code that follows, which is used to control the amplifier, consists of initialization code followed by a polling loop. The polling loop continually checks for a change in status on the chassis front panel (PORTB) or the remote control (PORTA). The UML activity diagram is provided in Figure 8.19.

```
//******************************************************************
//file name: amp12.c
//function: program provides control of amplifier
//target controller: Motorola 68HC912B32 evaluation board (EVB)
//   - 32 K Flash EEPROM available at $8000
//   - Compiler options:
//        - Program Memory: 0x8000
//        - Data Memory:    0x0800
//        - Stack Pointer:  0x09FF
//
//This program provides the control of an audio amplifier.  The
//amplifier may accept an audio source from a number of selec-
//tions. The user may select the audio source for amplification
//using either front panel switches on the amplifier chassis
```

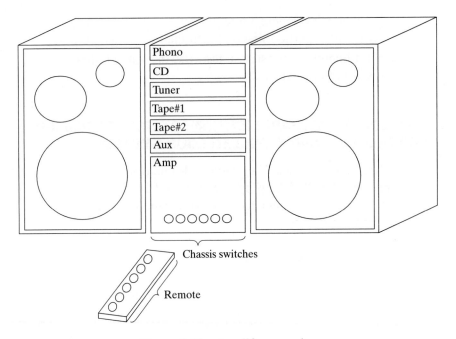

Figure 8.18   Amplifier overview.

```
//(connected to Port B) or from a remote control (connected to
//Port A).  The processor will provide active outputs for front
//panel LEDs (connected to Port P) and also activate relays to
//connect the audio source to the amplifier (connected to Port T).
//
//Chip Port Function I/O Source/Dest Asserted Notes
//
//Port A input - input from remote control - requires 100 ms
//active high pulse
//PA7 R-MUTE In Remote Control High ~100ms Pulse
//PA6 R-AUX In Remote Control High ~100ms Pulse
//PA5 R-TAPE#2 In Remote Control High ~100ms Pulse
//PA4 R-TAPE#1 In Remote Control High ~100ms Pulse
//PA3 R-TUNER In Remote Control High ~100ms Pulse
//PA2 R-CD In Remote Control High ~100ms Pulse
//PA1 R-Phono In Remote Control High ~100ms Pulse
//PA0 R-PREAMP-PWR In Remote Control High ~100ms Pulse
//
//Port B input - Chassis Panel Input Switches
//PB0 S-PREAMP-PWR In Front Panel
//Switch Low Internal Pull Ups = ON
//PB1 S-PHONO In Front Panel Switch Low Internal Pull Ups = ON
//PB2 S-CD In Front Panel Switch Low Internal Pull Ups = ON
//PB3 S-TUNER In Front Panel Switch Low Internal Pull Ups = ON
```

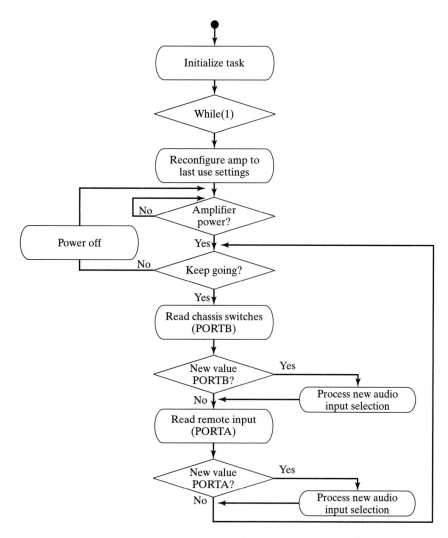

Figure 8.19   UML activity diagram for an amplifier.

```
//PB4 S-TAPE#1 In Front Panel Switch Low Internal Pull Ups = ON
//PB5 S-TAPE#2 In Front Panel Switch Low Internal Pull Ups = ON
//PB6 S-AUX In Front Panel Switch Low Internal Pull Ups = ON
//PB7 S-MUTE In Front Panel Switch Low Internal Pull Ups = ON
//
//Port P output - Chassis Panel LEDs
//PP0 LED-PWR-RELAY Out Pwr Relay & LED Low Signal to Buffer
//PP1 LED-PHONO Out LED Low Sink ~ 10mA
//PP2 LED-CD Out LED Low Sink ~ 10mA
//PP3 LED-TUNER Out LED Low Sink ~ 10mA
```

```
//PP4 LED-TAPE#1 Out LED Low Sink ~ 10mA
//PP5 LED-TAPE#2 Out LED Low Sink ~ 10mA
//PP6 LED-Aux Out LED Low Sink ~ 10mA
//PP7 LED-MUTE-RELAY Out Mute Relay & LED Low Signal to Buffer
//
//Port T output - relay drive
//PT0 RELAY-RESET Out Reset Relay High ~5 ms Pulse
//PT1 RELAY-PHONO Out Phono Relay Select High ~5 ms Pulse
//PT2 RELAY-CD Out CD Relay Select High ~5 ms Pulse
//PT3 RELAY-TUNER Out Tuner Relay Select High ~5 ms Pulse
//PT4 RELAY-TAPE#1 Out Tape 1 Relay Select High ~5 ms Pulse
//PT5 RELAY-TAPE#2 Out Tape 2 Relay Select High ~5 ms Pulse
//PT6 RELAY-AUX Out Aux Relay Select High ~5 ms Pulse
//PT7 10 ms active high pulse to drive optical isolator LED and
//in turn the main power amplifier
//
//Power ON RESET (plugged in, or 5V power supplies coming on):
//Set up ports:
//1. Port A: Configured as inputs, pull-ups DISABLED
//2. Port B: Configured as inputs, pull-ups ENABLED
//3. Port P: Configured as outputs, DE-Assert all lines
//                                      (make all pins HIGH)
//4. Port T: Configured as outputs, DE-Assert all lines
//                                      (make all pins LOW)
//5. Assert "RELAY-RESET" (PT0) with 5ms asserted high pulse
//6. Assert "RELAY-CD" (PT2) with 5ms asserted high pulse
//7. Set "WHICH-INPUT" storage location = "CD"
//8. Cycle the PP1-PP6 (Asserted low) LEDs to show controller
//   is working.
//9. GOTO "PREAMP ON" Sequence
//
//Logic of operation:
//"PREAMP ON" Sequence
//1. Await "S-PREAMP-PWR" (PB0) OR "R-PREAMP-PWR" (PA0) assertion
//2. Assert "LED-MUTE-RELAY" (PP7)
//3. Assert "LED-PWR-RELAY" (PP0)
//4. Read "WHICH-INPUT" storage location
//5. Assert "LED-xxxxx" = "WHICH-INPUT" storage location
//6. Assert PT7(1) for 10 ms
//7. DE-Assert "LED-MUTE-RELAY" (PP7) after ~3 sec.
//8. GOTO "SCAN"
//
//"SCAN" Mode:
//1. Await Assertion of any input signal (PB0-PB7) OR (PA0-PA7)
//2. IF = "x-PREAMP-PWR" GOTO - "PREAMP OFF" Sequence
//3. IF = "x-MUTE" GOTO - "MUTE" Sequence
//4. IF = different input signal select (PB1-PB6) or (PA1-PA6)
//GOTO "CHANGE
```

```
//INPUT" sequence
//
//"CHANGE INPUT" Sequence:
//1. Assert "LED-MUTE-RELAY" (PP7)
//2. Assert "RELAY-RESET" (PT0) with 5ms asserted high pulse
//3. Assert "RELAY-xxxxx" (PT1-PT6) (according to which input
//selection #) - 5 ms pulse asserted high
//4. Assert "LED-xxxxx" (PP1-PP6) (according to which input
//selection #)
//5. Clear Old/Input New "WHICH-INPUT" storage location
//6. DE-Assert "MUTE-RELAY" (PP7) after ~3 sec.
//7. GOTO "SCAN"
//
//"MUTE" Sequence:
//1. Toggle "LED-MUTE-RELAY" (PP7)
//2. GOTO "SCAN"
//
//"PREAMP OFF" - Sequence:
//1. Assert "LED-MUTE-RELAY" (PP7)
//2. DE-Assert "LED-PWR-RELAY" (PP0)
//3. DE-Assert all LEDs (PP1-PP6)
//4. Assert PT7(1) for 10 ms
//5. DE-Assert "LED-MUTE-RELAY" (PP7) after ~3 sec
//6. GOTO "PREAMP ON" Sequence
//
//author: Steven Barrett and Daniel Pack
//created: June 19, 2004
//last revised: June 20, 2004
//****************************************************************

//include files*************************************************
#include<912b32.h>          //B32 EVB header file
#include"func_def.h"        //function prototypes, global variables


//main program**************************************************

//global variables
int             which_input;        //amplifier input
int             keep_going;         //loop variable
int             mute;               //mute control flag
unsigned char   old_PORTB = 0xff;   //present value of PORTB
unsigned char   old_PORTA = 0x00;   //present value of PORTA
unsigned char   new_PORTB, new_PORTA;//new values of PORTA, PORTB

void main(void)
{
asm(" .area vectors(abs)\n"
    " .org 0xFFF8\n"                //initialize 68HC12 B32 reset vector
```

```
" .word 0x8000, 0x8000, 0x8000, 0x8000\n"
" .text");

initialize_task();
                              //main loop
while(1){                     //wait for power-up signal
  if ((PORTB==0xFE)||(PORTA==0X01))
                              //PORTB asserted low, PORTA asserted high
    {                         //we've got power! proceed pre-amp on seq
    keep_going = 1;           //loop_variable
    PORTP=0x7E;               //assert LED-MUTE-RELAY PP7(0
                              //LED-PWR-RELAY PP0(0) (0111_1110)

    which_input_task();
    activate_power_relay_task();
    delay_3s();               //delay 3 seconds
    PORTP |= 0x80;            //de-assert PD7(1) - turns mute off

    while(keep_going)         //menu processing - main polling loop
       {
       process_PORTB_input_task();
       process_PORTA_input_task();
       }

    }//end if - waiting for power up signal - no power yet!
  }//end while(1)
}//end main

//****************************************************************
//function definitions********************************************
//****************************************************************

//****************************************************************
//initialize_task: initializes amplifier to start up state
//****************************************************************

void initialize_task(void)
{
mute = on;                 //turn mute on
initialize_timer();        //initialize timer
initialize_ports();        //initialize ports
initialize_pins();         //initialize specific pins
which_input = 2;           //default to CD(2) input
                           //flash LEDs on front panel
PORTP = 0x81;              //set LEDs PD1-PD6 active low (1000_0001)
delay_3s();                //delay 3s
PORTP = 0xff;              //turn off LEDs
}
```

```
//*****************************************************************
//which_input_task: remembers and processes previous input in use
//*****************************************************************

void which_input_task(void)
{

  switch(which_input){      //illuminate LED for input in use
                            //default to CD - input 2 during init
    case 1: //PHONO
      phono_task();
            break;

    case 2: //CD
      CD_task();
            break;

    case 3: //TUNER
      tuner_task();
            break;

    case 4: //TAPE#1
            tape1_task();
            break;

    case 5: //TAPE#2
            tape2_task();
            break;

    case 6: //AUX
            aux_task();
            break;

    default:;
    }//end switch
}

//*****************************************************************
//phono_task: configures phono input
//*****************************************************************

void phono_task(void)
{
//PHONO
PORTT |= 0x02;                            //assert PT1(1) (0000_0010)
delay_5ms();
PORTT &= ~0x02;                           //turn off PT1(0)
PORTP |= 0x7E;                            //turn all LEDs off
```

```
PORTP &= ~0x02;                              //turn on LED1 (0)
}


//****************************************************************
//CD_task: configures CD input
//****************************************************************

void CD_task(void)
{
//CD
PORTT |= 0x04;                               //assert PT2(1) (0000_0100)
delay_5ms();
PORTT &= ~0x04;                              //turn off PT2(0)
PORTP |= 0x7E;                               //turn all LEDs off
PORTP &= ~0x04;                              //turn on LED2 (0)
}


//****************************************************************
//tuner_task: configures tuner input
//****************************************************************

void tuner_task(void)
{
//TUNER
PORTT |= 0x08;                               //assert PT3(1) (0000_1000)
delay_5ms();
PORTT &= ~0x08;                              //turn off PT3(0)
PORTP |= 0x7E;                               //turn all LEDs off
PORTP &= ~0x08;                              //turn on LED3 (0)
}


//****************************************************************
//tape1_task: configures tape1 input
//****************************************************************

void tape1_task(void)
{
//TAPE#1
PORTT |= 0x10;                               //assert PT4(1) (0001_0000)
delay_5ms();
PORTT &= ~0x10;                              //turn off PT4(0)
PORTP |= 0x7E;                               //turn all LEDs off
PORTP &= ~0x10;                              //turn on LED4 (0)
}


//****************************************************************
//tape2_task: configures tape2 input
//****************************************************************
```

```
void tape2_task(void)
{
//TAPE#2
PORTT |= 0x20;                          //assert PT5(1) (0010_0000)
delay_5ms();
PORTT &= ~0x20;                         //turn off PT5(0)
PORTP |= 0x7E;                          //turn all LEDs off
PORTP &= ~0x20;                         //turn on LED5 (0)
}


//*****************************************************************
//aux_task: configures tape1 input
//*****************************************************************

void aux_task(void)
{
//AUX
PORTT |= 0x40;                          //assert PT6(1) (0100_0000)
delay_5ms();
PORTT &= ~0x40;                         //turn off PT6(0)
PORTP |= 0x7E;                          //turn all LEDs off
PORTP &= ~0x40;                         //turn on LED6(0)
}


//*****************************************************************
//activate_power_relay_task(): activates main power relay
//*****************************************************************

void activate_power_relay_task(void)
{
PORTT |= 0x80;                          //assert PT7(1) 10 ms
delay_5ms();
delay_5ms();
PORTT &= ~0X80;                         //turn off PT7
}


//*****************************************************************
//process_PORTB_input_task(): processes input from PORTB
//*****************************************************************

void process_PORTB_input_task(void)
{
new_PORTB = PORTB;                  //read PORTB
if(new_PORTB != old_PORTB){         //process change in PORTB input
  switch(new_PORTB){                //PORTB asserted low

      case 0xFE:                    //PB0 "S-PREAMP-PWR" (1111_1110)
```

```
                if(process_valid_input_PORTB(new_PORTB))
                  {
                  preamp_off();
                  keep_going=0;
                  }
                break;

      case 0xFD:                      //PB1 "S-PHONO" (1111_1101)
                if(which_input !=1){
                if(process_valid_input_PORTB(new_PORTB))
                  {
                  which_input = 1;
                  change_input();
                  }}
                break;

      case 0xFB:                      //PB2 "S-CD" (1111_1011)
                if(which_input !=2){
                if(process_valid_input_PORTB(new_PORTB))
                  {
                  which_input = 2;
                  change_input();
                  }}
                break;

      case 0xF7:                      //PB3 "S-TUNER" (1111_0111)
                if(which_input !=3){
                if(process_valid_input_PORTB(new_PORTB))
                  {
                  which_input = 3;
                  change_input();
                  }}
                break;

      case 0xEF:                      //PB4 "S-TAPE#1" (1110_1111)
                if(which_input !=4){
                if(process_valid_input_PORTB(new_PORTB))
                  {
                  which_input = 4;
                  change_input();
                  }}
                break;

      case 0xDF:                      //PB5 "S-TAPE#2" (1101_1111)
                if(which_input !=5){
                if(process_valid_input_PORTB(new_PORTB))
                  {
                  which_input = 5;
```

```
                        change_input();
                        }}
                  break;

        case 0xBF:                         //PB6 "S-AUX" (1011_1111)
                  if(which_input !=6){
                  if(process_valid_input_PORTB(new_PORTB))
                    {
                    which_input = 6;
                    change_input();
                    }}
                  break;

        case 0x7F:                         //PB7 "S-MUTE" (0111_1111)
                  if(process_valid_input_PORTB(new_PORTB))
                    {
                    mute_toggle();
                    }
                  break;
        default:;                   //all other cases
        }                           //end switch(new_PORTB)
   }                                //end if new_PORTB
   old_PORTB=new_PORTB;             //update PORTB
}

//****************************************************************
//process_PORTA_input_task(): processes input from PORTA
//****************************************************************

void process_PORTA_input_task(void)
{
new_PORTA = PORTA;                  //read PORTA
if(new_PORTA != old_PORTA){         //process change in PORTA input
  switch(new_PORTA){                //PORTA asserted high

        case 0x01:                         //PA0 "R-PREAMP-PWR" (0000_0001)
                  if(process_valid_input_PORTA(new_PORTA))
                    {
                    preamp_off();
                    keep_going=0;
                    }
                  break;

        case 0x02:                         //PA1 "R-PHONO" (0000_0010)
                  if(which_input !=1){
                  if(process_valid_input_PORTA(new_PORTA))
                    {
                    which_input = 1;
```

```
                            change_input();
                            }}
                  break;

    case 0x04:                      //PA2 "R-CD" (0000_0100)
                  if(which_input !=2){
                  if(process_valid_input_PORTA(new_PORTA))
                     {
                     which_input = 2;
                     change_input();
                     }}
                  break;

    case 0x08:                      //PA3 "R-TUNER" (0000_1000)
                  if(which_input !=3){
                  if(process_valid_input_PORTA(new_PORTA))
                     {
                     which_input = 3;
                     change_input();
                     }}
                  break;

    case 0x10:                      //PA4 "R-TAPE#1" (0001_0000)
                  if(which_input !=4){
                  if(process_valid_input_PORTA(new_PORTA))
                     {
                     which_input = 4;
                     change_input();
                     }}
                  break;

    case 0x20:                      //PA5 "R-TAPE#2" (0010_0000)
                  if(which_input !=5){
                  if(process_valid_input_PORTA(new_PORTA))
                     {
                     which_input = 5;
                     change_input();
                     }}
                  break;

    case 0x40:                      //PA6 "R-AUX" (0100_0000)
                  if(which_input !=6){
                  if(process_valid_input_PORTA(new_PORTA))
                     {
                     which_input = 6;
                     change_input();
                     }}
                  break;
```

```
        case 0x80:                      //PA7 "R-MUTE" (1000_0000)
                if(process_valid_input_PORTA(new_PORTA))
                  {
                  mute_toggle();
                  }
                break;

        default:;                       //all other cases
}                                       //end switch(new_PORTA)
   }                                    //end if new_PORTA
  old_PORTA=new_PORTA;                  //update PORTA
}


//****************************************************************
//initialize_timer:initializes time base prescaler serving counter
//****************************************************************

void initialize_timer(void)
{
TMSK2 = 0x05;                           //set prescalar for 250 KHz
TSCR =  0x80;                           //enable the timer
}


//****************************************************************
//initialize_ports: provides initial configuration for I/O ports
//****************************************************************

void initialize_ports(void)
{
DDRA=0x00;                              //set PORTA as input
PORTA=0x00;                             //disable PORTA pull-up resistors
DDRB=0x00;                              //set PORTB as input
PORTB=0xff;                             //enable PORTB pull-up resistors
DDRT=0xff;                              //set PORTT as output
PORTT=0x00;                             //initialize low
DDRP=0xff;                              //set PORTD as output
PORTP=0xff;                             //initialize high
}


//****************************************************************
//initialize_pins: set specific output pins to start up values
//****************************************************************

void initialize_pins(void)
{
PORTT=0x01;                             //reset relay PT0(1) w/5ms active
                                        //high pulse (0000_0001)
delay_5ms();
```

```
PORTT=0x00;
}

//*****************************************************************
//delay_5ms: 5ms delay based on 250 KHz clock
//*****************************************************************

void delay_5ms(void)
{
int i;
for(i=0; i<1250; i++)
  asm("nop");              //requires one clock pulse
}

//*****************************************************************
//delay_3s: 3s pause
//*****************************************************************

void delay_3s(void)
{
int i;

for(i=0;i<600;i++)
  delay_5ms();
}

//*****************************************************************
//change_input: processes change in input
//*****************************************************************

void change_input(void)
{
PORTP &= ~0x80;           //assert LED-MUTE-RELAY PP7(0) 1000_0000
PORTT |= 0x01;            //assert relay-reset PT0(1) 5 ms
delay_5ms();
PORTT &= ~0X01;           //turn off PT0
switch(which_input)
  {
  case 1: //PHONO
          phono_task();
          break;

  case 2: //CD
          CD_task();
          break;

  case 3: //TUNER
          tuner_task();
          break;
```

```
  case 4: //TAPE#1
          tape1_task();
          break;

  case 5: //TAPE#2
          tape2_task();
          break;

  case 6: //AUX
          aux_task();
          break;

  default:;//all other inputs
  }//end switch
  delay_3s();
  PORTP |= 0x80;               //de-assert PP7(1) LED-MUTE-RELAY
}

//*****************************************************************
//mute_toggle: toggles mute on and off
//*****************************************************************

void mute_toggle(void)
{
if (mute==off){
  PORTP &= ~0x80;              //assert LED-MUTE-RELAY PP7(0)
  mute = on;}
else{
  PORTP |= 0x80;              //de-assert LED-MUTE-RELAY PP7(1)
  mute = off;}
}//end mute_toggle

//*****************************************************************
//preamp_off: turn amplifier off
//*****************************************************************

void preamp_off(void)
{
PORTP &= ~0x80;               //assert LED-MUTE-RELAY PP7(0)
PORTP |= 0x01;               //de-assert LED-PWR-RELAY PP0(1)
PORTP |= 0x7e;               //de-assert LEDs PP1-PP6(1)(0111_1110)
                             //assert PT7 for 10 ms
PORTT |= 0x80;               //assert PT7(1) 10 ms
delay_5ms();
delay_5ms();
PORTT &= ~0X80;              //turn off PT7
delay_3s();
PORTP |= 0x80;               //de-assert PP7(1) LED-MUTE-RELAY
```

```
keep_going=0;
}


//***************************************************************
//process_valid_input_PORTA: ensures remote signal lasts
//at least 50 ms
//***************************************************************

int process_valid_input_PORTA(unsigned char portx)
{
int   valid_input;                    //set valid input flag
unsigned int current_count;

valid_input = TRUE;
current_count = TCNT;                  //get current count
while(TCNT < (current_count+12500)){   //monitor input for 50 ms
  if(portx==PORTA) valid_input = TRUE; else valid_input = FALSE;
  if (!valid_input) break;             //get out of while loop
  }//end while
return valid_input;
}


//***************************************************************
//process_valid_input_PORTB: ensures switch depression lasts
//at least 50 ms
//***************************************************************

int process_valid_input_PORTB(unsigned char portx)
{
int   valid_input;                    //set valid input flag
unsigned int current_count;

valid_input = TRUE;
current_count = TCNT;                  //get current count
while(TCNT < (current_count+12500)){   //monitor input for 50 ms
  if(portx==PORTB) valid_input = TRUE; else valid_input = FALSE;
  if (!valid_input) break;             //get out of while loop
  }//end while
return valid_input;
}


//***************************************************************
//***************************************************************
```

8.8.3 Amplifier Controller Testing

To test the software, it is wise to implement an amplifier simulator, as we
discussed in Chapter 2. The simulator is provided again for convenience in

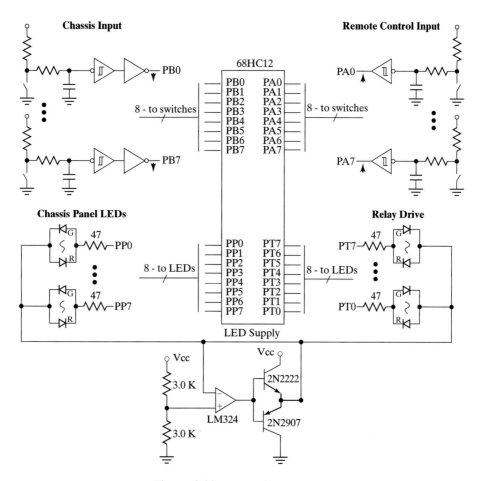

Figure 8.20   Amplifier simulator.

Figure 8.20. This allows thorough testing of the control algorithm on an inexpensive simulator. The algorithm should be thoroughly tested under every conceivable scenario.

8.9 ANOTHER APPLICATION: POLLED LOOP WITH INTERRUPTS

In this next application we develop the foreground portion of a polling foreground/background system to handle a transistor overheat condition in the stereo amplifier. The system is shown in Figure 8.21. The transistor's temperature is constantly monitored by an LM34 temperature sensor (plastic body) bonded to the metal case of the TO-220 power transistors. This sensor provides a linearly related output voltage for an applied temperature (10 mV/degree).

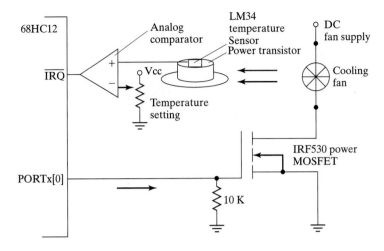

Figure 8.21   Transistor temperature overheat detection system.

The output from the LM34 is fed to one input of an analog comparator operational amplifier configuration. The other input is used to set the trip temperature of the interrupt. When the power transistor's temperature reaches the preset trip temperature, the active low IRQ interrupt pin is presented with an active low signal.

In response to the interrupt, an active high pulse should be sent out on PORTx[0] to activate the cooling fan via an IRF530 power MOSFET. You might consider inserting a delay in the interrupt service routine and then deactivating the fan after the delay. When the transistor temperature falls below the preset trip temperature, the IRQ pin is provided a high logic signal.

As the processor exits the interrupt service routine, it resumes normal processor operation if the transistor has returned to a safe temperature (as indicated by a high-level signal on the IRQ pin) or it reinitiates the interrupt (continued low level on the IRQ pin). We leave the program for the system using interrupts as a homework problem (Challenging 2).

8.10 A CHALLENGING APPLICATION: AN RTOS SIMULATOR

8.10.1 Project Overview

It is very challenging to implement some of the advanced real-time scheduling algorithms. Part of the challenge is that the internal operation of these programs is not visible. The RTOS simulator in Figure 8.22 can be used as an aid in RTOS development.

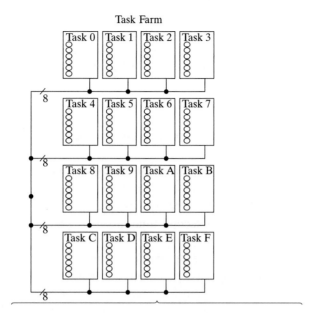

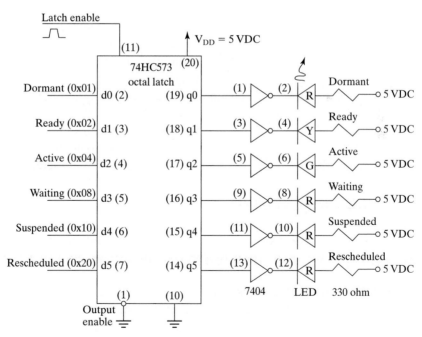

Figure 8.22   RTOS simulator.

The simulator consists of a "farm" of 16 tasks labeled Task 0 to Task F. Each task is implemented with a 74HC573 latch. Status is sent to the latch where it is held until updated. The status of a specific task is provided by an array of light-emitting diodes. Only one LED is illuminated for a specific task. We have used the LED driver circuit provided in Chapter 5 at each latch output.

The hardware interface diagram for the task farm is provided in Figure 8.23. A 4-to-16 line decoder (74HC154) is used to select a specific task. The task's binary "address" is provided by the microprocessor on the input lines to the decoder. Only a single output of the decoder is active low at any given time and therefore only one task is selected.

Normally, all tasks are initialized to the dormant state. A keypad is used to choose different actions to simulate the activities of the RTOS system. The keypad is depressed once to select the specific activity, such as activating a task. The keypad is depressed a second time to select which task the activity will be performed on.

To aid in an understanding of RTOS concepts, think again about a highly volatile, rapidly changing, easy to visualize scenario such as a used car dealership, a waitron handling multiple customers in a restaurant, or even the security system in a large hotel. Any one of these may be used to illustrate different scheduling algorithms.

For example, a used car (task) can have its inherent context such as year, make, model, vehicle identification number (VIN), and odometer reading. The car (task) can be in a variety of states similar to the task states of ready, dormant, etc. In the case of a used car, it may be ready for sale (ready), out for a test drive (active), unavailable due to maintenance (waiting), dormant (sold), etc. The status of up to 16 cars (tasks) may be displayed on the RTOS visual simulator. New scenario status may be injected by an user with the hexadecimal keypad. The new status may be shown on the LCD and the contents of the linked lists in response to the status changes may be displayed on the PC screen [Barrett 2004].

8.10.2 Sample Code

A detailed treatment of the RTOS simulator is outside the scope of the text. In this section we simply provide the code to access and update the status of a specific task in the farm.

The function `update_task_status` requires the specific task and the desired change of task status as arguments. The specific task is used to configure `PORTA[3:0]` with the correct four-bit binary code to feed to the 74HC154 4-to-16 decoder. When the decoder is enabled via `PORTA[7]` connected to the decoders enable pins, the selected task's latch enable pin is activated. This allows the updated task status present on PORT T of the 68HC12 to be latched to the

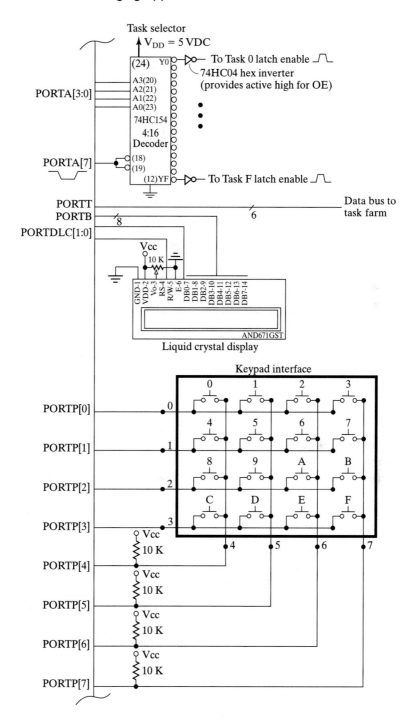

Figure 8.23 RTOS hardware simulator.

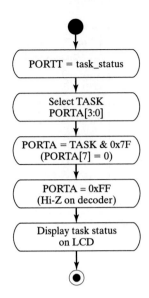

Figure 8.24 UML activity diagram for the function
update_task_status.

LEDs and hence update the task status display. The UML activity diagram for
this function is provided in Figure 8.24.

```
//****************************************************************
//file name: realtime.c
//author: Steve Barrett and Daniel Pack
//created: July 1, 2004
//last revised: July 1, 2004
//****************************************************************

//include files************************************************
#include<912b32.h>

//function prototypes******************************************
void initialize_ports(void);//initializes ports
void initialize_LCD(void);
                            //initialize Liquid Crystal
                                                Display (LCD)
void putchars(unsigned char);
                            //LCD support function - put character
void putcommands(unsigned char);
                            //LCD support function - put command
void delay_5ms(void);       //5 millisecond delay
void delay_100us(void);     //100 microsecond delay
void update_task_status(unsigned char task, char task_status);
                            //update task
```

```c
//global variables*******************************************

//main program**********************************************

void main(void)
{
asm(" .area vectors(abs)\n"    //inline assembly statement
    " .org 0xFFF8\n"           //initialize 68HC12 B32 reset vector
    " .word 0x8000, 0x8000, 0x8000, 0x8000\n"
    " .text");

initialize_ports();            //initialize ports
initialize_LCD();              //initialize LCD
update_task_status(0x00, 'R');//update task
:
:
:

}

//**********************function definitions*****************
//**********************************************************
//initialize_ports: provides initial configuration for I/O ports
//**********************************************************

void initialize_ports(void)
{
DDRA   = 0xFF;  //set PORTA as output - control lines for decoder
DDRT   = 0xFF;  //set PORT as output  - task status
DDRB   = 0xFF;  //set PORTB as output - data port for LCD
DDRDLC = 0xFF;  //PORT DLC as output -  control signals for LCD
DDRP   = 0x0F;  //set PORTP[3:0] output, PORT[7:4] input - keypad
PORTA  = 0xFF;  //set PORTA all 1's - Hi-Z decoder output
}

/**************************************************************/
/*update_task_status: updates specified task with specified  */
/*status                                                      */
/**************************************************************/

void update_task_status(unsigned char task, char task_status)
{

                        //set PORTT with task status
switch(task_status){
  case 'D': //dormant (D)
          PORTT = 0x01;
          break;
```

```
case 'R': //ready (R)
        PORTT = 0x02;
        break;

case 'A': //active (A)
        PORTT = 0x04;
break;

case 'W': //wait (W)
        PORTT = 0x08;
        break;

case 'S': //suspended (S)
        PORTT = 0x10;
        break;

case 'X': //reschedule (X)
        PORTT = 0x20;
        break;
}

PORTA = task & 0x7F;        /*select task, activate decoder   */
PORTA = 0xFF;               /*Hi-Z decoder                    */
}
/*****************************************************************/
/*****************************************************************/
```

8.11 SUMMARY

In this chapter we have exposed you to the concepts of real-time operating systems. Our intent was not to provide a sample RTOS and then dissect its operation. Instead, we focused on the concepts associated with RTOS and the key issues associated with implementing an RTOS-based application. We introduced RTOS terminology, data structures, scheduling algorithms, and complex RTOS issues.

8.12 FURTHER READING

Barrett S. F, D. J. Pack, C. Straley, L. Sircin, and G. Janack. "Real-Time Operating Systems: A Visual Simulator." Paper presented at the annual meeting of the American Society for Engineering Educations, June 2004.

Ganssle, J. "Writing a Real-Time Operating System—Part I: A Multitasking Event Scheduler for the HD64180." *Circuit Cellar Ink* (January/February 1989): 41–51.

Ganssle, J. "Writing a Real-Time Operating System—Part II: Memory Management and Applications for the HD64180." *Circuit Cellar Ink* (March/April 1989): 30–33.

Ganssle, J. "An OS in a CAN." *Embedded Systems Programming* (January 1994): 1–6.

ImageCraft Creations, Inc. "ICC12, ImageCraft C Compiler and Development Environment for Motorola HC12." 2001.

Korsch, J. F., and L. J. Garrett. *Data Structures, Algorithms, and Program Style Using C*. Boston: PWS-Kent Publishing Company, 1988.

Labrosse, J. J. *Micro C/OS-II The Real-Time Kernel*, 2nd ed. Lawrence, KS: CMP Books, 2002.

Lafore, R. *The Waite Group's Microsoft C Programming for the PC*, 2nd ed. Carmel, IN, Howard W. Sams and Company, 1990.

Laplante, P. *Real-Time Systems Design and Analysis: An Engineer's Handbook*. New York: IEEE Computer Society Press, 1993.

Miller, G. H. *Microcomputer Engineering*, 2nd ed. Englewood Cliffs, NJ: Pearson Education, 1998.

Moore, R. *How to Use a Real-time Multitasking Kernels in Embedded Systems*, Costa Mesa, CA: Micro Digital Associates, 2001.

Motorola Inc. "68HC12 M68EVB912B32 Evaluation Board User's Manual." Motorola Document 68EVB912B32 UM/D, 1997.

Motorola Inc. "HC12 M68HC12B Family Advance Information." Motorola Document M68HC12B/D, 2000.

Pack, D. J., and S. F. Barrett. *68HC12 Microcontroller: Theory and Applications*. Upper Saddle River, NJ: Prentice Hall, 2002.

8.13 PROBLEMS

Fundamental

1. What is an RTOS?
2. What is a task?
3. What is a task's context? Provide specific examples of what would be in a task's context.
4. Describe the activities that an RTOS must accomplish in relation to a task.
5. What is an RTOS kernel? What key features must the RTOS kernel provide?
6. What are the differences between a global and a local variable?
7. What is meant by dynamic memory allocation?
8. What type of memory (RAM, ROM, etc.) is employed in dynamic memory allocation? Explain.
9. Describe the following data structures and where they are commonly used:

   Structure/record
   Linked list
   Queue

Circular queue

Stack

Advanced

1. Define the difference between hard, firm, and soft real-time systems. Provide an example of each.

2. Compare and contrast the heap versus the stack. Where are they typically located in a memory system? Why?

3. What programming techniques should be avoided to conserve RAM memory? Why?

4. Define each of the different states that a task may be in. How many states may a task be in at any given instant of time?

5. What is a task control block (TCB)? What should be contained within a TCB? What data structure would be a good choice for a TCB? Why?

6. What is the function of the dispatcher/scheduler in an RTOS kernel? Define each of the different types of scheduling algorithms and their inherent advantages and disadvantages.

7. What is concurrency? How does it occur? How is it prevented?

8. What is reentrancy? How does it occur? How is it prevented?

9. What is meant by fail-safe RTOS operation? Why is this a critical issue in RTOS development?

10. An interrupt-driven RTOS is to be implemented on the 68HC12. You have decided that you want the system to always respond to higher priority interrupts when they occur. How can this be accomplished? Recall that the 68HC12 automatically disables the interrupt system while responding to an interrupt. *Hint:* Review the 68HC12 CLI and SEI assembly language commands.

Challenging

1. Develop a stack and its associated functions using a linked-list dynamic memory allocation techniques.

2. Develop the foreground portion of a polling foreground/background system to handle the transistor overheat condition described in the applications Section 8.9. Figure 8.25 (repeated here from Figure 8.21 for convenience) illustrates a transistor temperature overheat detection system. The transistor's temperature is constantly monitored by an LM34 temperature sensor (plastic body) bonded to the metal case of the TO-220 power transistors. This sensor provides a linearly related output voltage for applied temperature (10 mV/degree). The output from the LM34 is fed to one input of an analog comparator operational amplifier configuration. The other input is used to set the trip temperature of the interrupt. When the power transistor's temperature reaches the preset trip temperature, the active low IRQ interrupt pin is

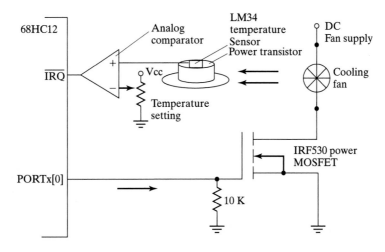

Figure 8.25   Transistor temperature overheat detection system.

presented an active low signal. In response to the interrupt, an active high pulse should be sent out on PORTA[0] to activate the cooling fan via IRF530 power MOSFET. You might consider inserting a delay in the interrupt service routine and then deactivating the fan after the delay. When the transistor temperature falls below the preset trip temperature, the IRQ pin is provided a high logic signal. As the processor exits the interrupt service routine, it resumes normal processor operation if the transistor has returned to a safe temperature (as indicated by a high-level signal on the IRQ pin) or it reinitiates the interrupt (continued low level on the IRQ pin).

3. Write and test a function to update the state of a task.

4. Implement a task control block (TCB) with an appropriate data structure. Provide support functions to access/update different information fields with the TCB.

5. Describe different methods of implementing intertask communications within a RTOS.

6. Write a two-page point paper discussing the pros and cons of writing your own RTOS versus purchasing a commercially available one.

9

Distributed Processing Systems-Networking with msCAN

Objectives: After reading this chapter, you should be able to

- Describe the purpose of controller area networks (CANs).
- Describe the CAN protocol.
- Explain the hardware setup necessary to connect multiple CAN configured controllers.
- Describe the msCAN12 controller.
- Program the timing constraints of a CAN controller.
- Describe the differences between the HC12 CAN controller and the msCAN controller on the MC9S12DP256.
- Program the msCAN12 controller of the 68HC12 to communicate with other CAN controllers.
- Explain the byte data link controller on the MC68HC912B32 and MC68HC12BE32.

In this chapter, we expand our coverage of the 68HC12/HCS12 controllers to include their capability to connect to and communicate with multiple independent, distributed controller systems in a controller network. We first present general computer network systems and related timing and scheduling issues before we delve into the specific networking concepts of the 68HC12 system. We then study the use of the 68HC12/HCS12 to create a controller area network.

9.1 DESIGN APPROACHES

Networks have several advantages over an isolated system. One of the primary reasons to interconnect independent systems is the ability to share resources. For example, for a network of computers within an office, each computer no longer needs to be connected to a separate printer. A printer connected to the network can be used by computers within the network. Similarly, software resources can be shared among computers that are connected together; each computer can access desired software programs through the network without having them stored in each computer. In addition to the sharing of software programs, today's computer networks allow fast exchange of data; the most prominent example is the giant network better known as the Internet. Through the Internet, every user has access to a vast amount of data stored in millions of computers throughout the world. Finally, today's computer networks facilitate communications among computer users, increasing productivity, work efficiency, and company profits.

9.2 COMPUTER NETWORKS

There are many different types of computer networks. A wide area network (WAN) is a computer network that encompasses a large area, such as the Internet, covering multiple states, countries, and the world. A local area network (LAN) is a network that exists within an institution, a company, or an organization—for example, the network for your school or your company. A small area network (SAN) is a computer network created for a small office or a home. In this type of network, the number of computers connected to the network usually does not exceed ten. The network of interest in this chapter is called the controller area network (CAN). The CAN originated within the automotive industry during the mid-1980s when multiple microcontrollers were connected together to enhance automobile performance. A microcontroller responsible for proper fuel injection, a controller keeping track of a list of fluid levels, an antilock brake controller, a four-wheel drive controller, a temperature control controller, a panel display controller, and a navigation communication controller are typically connected together to form a CAN, as shown in Figure 9.1. The concept of the CAN did not stop with the car industry. Today, CANs can be found in audio systems, home theaters, communication systems, military systems, and some home appliances.

All networks must have protocols—the rules that govern the communications among the members of the network. These rules include a common data

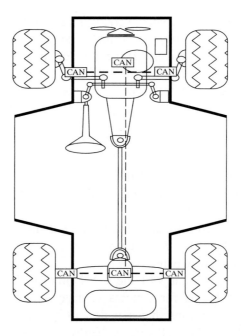

Figure 9.1   A simple controller area network for an automobile.

length, timing of bits transmitted or received, a method to verify the receipt of a
correct message, and a way to accommodate multiple members communicating
at the same time.

9.3 CONTROLLER AREA NETWORKS

In this section, we describe controller area networks (CANs) in detail. In particular, we show the inner workings of the 68HC12/HCS12 msCAN12 controller and
illustrate the required steps to configure and program the controller for communication with other such units for networking purposes. Before we start discussing
the specifics of the msCAN12 controller, however, we first present the protocol
used for the CAN.

9.3.1 CAN Protocol

The CAN protocol was originally conceived for automobile applications. Soon
after the conception of the CAN concept, the benefit of the CAN attracted a
variety of other industry applications, making it one of the desired networking
methods for small, distributed, real-time systems. Our coverage of the protocol
is brief; interested readers seeking full protocol details should refer to the CAN
protocol literature listed in the Further Reading section of this chapter.

The latest CAN protocol version 2.0 has two different parts: part A (standard format) and part B (extended format). Part A is made up of the following three layers: (1) the object layer, (2) the transfer layer, and (3) the physical layer. The object layer is responsible for handling messages, such as selecting a transmit or receive message, working as an interface between the transfer layer and an application program running on the CPU. The transfer layer ensures that messages adhere to the protocol while the physical layer actually sends and receives messages.

The CAN protocol version 2.0 part B consists of the data link layer and the physical layer. The data link layer is in turn made up of the logical link control (LLC) sublayer and the medium access control (MAC) sublayer. The responsibilities of the LLC sublayer, the MAC sublayer, and the physical layer are identical to the object layer, the transfer layer, and the physical layer in the CAN 2.0 part A protocol, respectively. Figure 9.2 shows the CAN 2.0 protocol layers for part A and part B. We henceforth use the term CAN protocol interchangeably with the CAN 2.0 A/B protocol.

The unique feature of the CAN protocol is the lack of origination and destination addresses for a message. Instead, an identifier is embedded in each message, which means that a node can be connected to the network without altering any existing software or hardware on the network. It also means that multiple nodes can act upon the same message, allowing multicasting capabilities.

Any member of the network can transmit and request messages over the network. The protocol contains a straightforward arbitration technique and

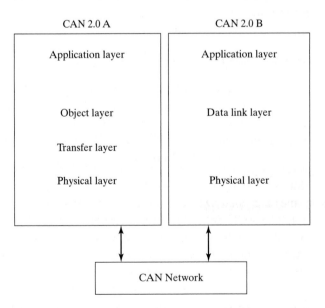

Figure 9.2   ISO/OSI reference model for the CAN 2.0 A/B protocol.

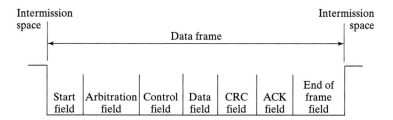

Figure 9.3   CAN data frame.

sophisticated error-detection mechanisms. To conserve energy, the protocol also supports nodes operating in both a sleep mode and a wake-up mode.

Four different messages (frames) exist on a CAN network bus: (1) data frame, (2) remote frame, (3) error frame, and (4) overload frame. We briefly discuss these frames next. The data frame contains seven sub fields, as shown in Figure 9.3.

The start field is made up of a single dominant bit (logic zero). Receiving nodes use this bit to synchronize the receipt of a data frame. The arbitration field contains the identifier number of a message. The identifier number is used by receiving nodes to determine to accept or reject a particular data frame. The identifier contains either 11 bits or 29 bits for standard format and extended format, respectively. The arbitration field also contains a remote transmission request (RTR) bit that is used to distinguish a data frame from a remote frame. For a data frame, this bit must be dominant (logic low); this bit must be recessive (logic high) for a remote frame.

The control field contains four bits that specify the data length in bytes. The data length is specified by four separate bits, allowing data lengths from one to eight bytes.[1] The data field contains the actual transfer message. For each byte, the most significant bit is transmitted first. The cyclical redundancy check (CRC) field is used to test the validity of the data received. For details on the actual process involved in generating the CRC field bits, readers are referred to Motorola literature. The CRC field ends with a CRC delimiter bit (recessive bit). The acknowledge (ACK) field contains an ACK slot and an ACK delimiter. The ACK slot is used by a receiving node to inform a transmitter that a message (data frame) has been accepted correctly by sending one dominant bit within the ACK slot. The ACK delimiter bit is a single recessive bit. The last field, the end of frame field, consists of seven recessive bits.

A remote frame is used by a receiving node to request a retransmission of a data frame. A remote frame is identical to a data frame with the exception that

---

[1]A recessive bit is used to designate logic one in this field. That is, four dominant bits represent data length 0.

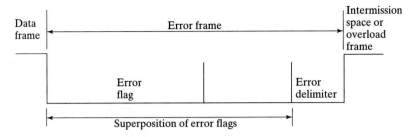

Figure 9.4 CAN error frame.

it does not contain a data field. The RTR bit in the arbitration field distinguishes a remote frame from a data frame: the RTR bit is recessive for a remote frame and the same bit is dominant for a data frame.

An error frame, shown in Figure 9.4, indicates that an error has occurred on the CAN bus. Each error frame is made up of an error flag field and an error delimiter field. The error flag field contains either active error flags, six dominant bits,[2] or passive error flags, six recessive bits. We define active and passive errors in the error handling subsection. The error delimiter field is made up of eight recessive bits.

The overload frame has a similar format as the error frame as shown in Figure 9.5. The overload flag is made up of six dominant bits. The conditions generating overload flag bits are when (1) a receiving node cannot process valid frames in allocated time and requires a time delay and (2) a dominant bit is detected during an intermission. Data frames and remote frames on a CAN bus are separated from other frames by intermission periods that consist of at least three recessive bits. The overload delimiter is made up of eight recessive bits.

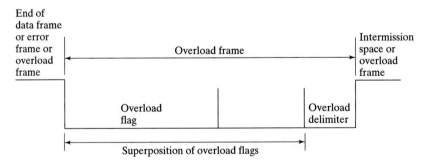

Figure 9.5 CAN overload frame.

[2]The number of dominant bits can increase up to a maximum of 12 bits since other nodes on a CAN bus can also transmit an error flag.

Error Handling   During message transfer, an error can occur. When an error is detected by a node that is active (transmitting a message) or passive (receiving a message), the corresponding node will send the error frame discussed in the previous section. If an active node transmits an error frame, the error flag is called an active error flag; if a passive node transmits an error frame, the corresponding error flag is called a passive error flag. There are five types of errors that can trigger the transmission of an error frame: (1) bit error, (2) stuffing error, (3) CRC error, (4) form error, and (5) acknowledgment error.

The bit error occurs when a transmit node detects an inconsistency between a bit it transmits to the bus and the same bit it monitors. The bit stuffing error occurs when six consecutive dominant or six consecutive recessive bits in a message field contain an error. The CRC error occurs when the computed CRC values at a receiver end do not match the CRC values it received. The form error occurs when a frame contains invalid bits that form a subfield of a frame. Finally, the acknowledgment error occurs when a dominant bit in the ACK slot does not exist.

Bit Timing   As shown in Figure 9.6, each bit time period in the CAN bus is divided into four regions: (1) synchronization segment, (2) propagation time segment, (3) phase buffer segment 1, and (4) phase buffer segment 2.

As shown in Figure 9.6, the logic state of a bit is sampled after the phase buffer segment 1 (sample point). The synchronization segment contains an edge that is used to synchronize nodes on the bus. The propagation time segment accommodates transmitter/receiver delay and signal propagation time within the bus. Phase segments 1 and 2 can be lengthened and shortened to resynchronize bits on the bus.

9.3.2 The Controller Unit for the 68HC12 msCAN12

The controllers for the 68HC912BC32(1), 68HC912D60(1), 68HC912DG128(2), and 68HC912DT128(3) have one or more built-in CAN modules called the Motorola Scalable Controller Area Network (msCAN) module. The number within

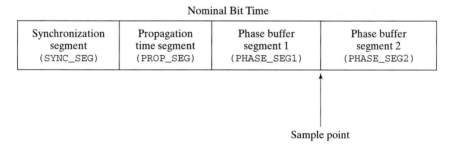

Figure 9.6   Nominal bit time segments.

the parentheses following the controller number specifies the number of CAN modules for each controller. For the protocol, the CAN version 2.0 A/B by Robert Bosch (Motorola, 1998) is implemented on all four controllers. Since the workings of all CAN modules are identical, we now focus on how a single CAN module operates. Details of the MC9S12DP256 CAN are provided in Section 9.4.

Each CAN module, a part of the controller, communicates with the external world using the RxCAN (receive messages) and the TxCAN (send messages) pins connected to a transceiver/receiver component, which in turn is connected to a serial bus connecting multiple systems to make up a network. Each CAN module is made up of three units: (1) the transmit unit, (2) the receive unit, and (3) the interrupt unit. We present each unit in the subsections that follow.

CAN Operation Modes   Before we delve into each unit of a CAN module within the 68HC12 controller, we first need to compare the msCAN12 normal mode with the low-power mode. When a CAN module is not active within a network, it is in the interest of the system administrator to reduce the power consumption of the particular controller within the CAN module. This can be done by configuring the controller's CAN module to run in a low-power mode. In addition to the normal mode, each CAN module can operate in three low-power modes: (1) sleep mode, (2) soft-reset mode, and (3) power-down mode.

The selection of one of three low-power modes is performed by properly configuring the msCAN12 module control register 0 (CMCR0) shown in Figure 9.7

The fifth bit (CSWAI) represents the CAN-Stops-in-Wait-Mode bit. The module is not affected during the wait mode if this bit is cleared and the module stops (does not receive clock signals) when this bit is set. The fourth bit—the synchronized-status bit (SYNCH)—indicates whether or not the CAN module is ready to communicate with other systems in the network. The status is shown on this bit. The msCAN12 is not synchronized to the CAN bus when this bit is cleared. Otherwise, the bit indicates that the msCAN12 and the CAN bus are synchronized. The third bit—the timer-enable-flag bit (TLNKEN)—shows that the corresponding port is connected to a timer input when this bit is cleared. If this bit is set, it indicates that the msCAN12 timer signal output is connected to a timer input.

Register: CMCR0 - msCAN12 Module Control Register 0   Address: $0100

7	6	5	4	3	2	1	0
0	0	CSWAI	SYNCH	TLNKEN	SLPAK	SLPRQ	SFTRES
0	0	1	0	0	0	0	1

Reset:

Figure 9.7   The msCAN12 module control register 0.

The second bit—the sleep-mode-acknowledge flag bit (SLPAK)—is used to indicate whether or not the msCAN12 is in the sleep mode: logic 0 indicates that the msCAN12 is not in the sleep mode while logic 1 states that the CAN module is in the sleep mode. The sleep request bit (SLPRQ) is used to request the msCAN12 module to enter the sleep mode: setting this bit causes the module to function normally while clearing this bit causes the module to enter the sleep mode.

Finally, the soft reset bit (SFTRES) is used by the CPU to cause the msCAN12 to immediately enter the soft-reset state. When this bit is set, any current communication is aborted and bus synchronization is abandoned. When this bit is cleared, the msCAN12 functions normally.

The SFTRES, SLPAK, and CSWAI bits of the CMCR0 register are used to select one of four msCAN12 operation modes (normal, soft reset, sleep, and power down). We discuss these modes in the next three subsections. Since the 68HC12 CPU can run in three modes (run, wait, stop), there are 12 combinations of a CPU mode and an msCAN12 mode possible.[3]

When the CPU operates in the run mode, the msCAN12 module can operate in a sleep mode, a soft-reset mode, or a normal mode. The power-down mode is not allowed. The CPU can choose one of the msCAN12 modes by configuring the three bits of the CMCR0 register as follows:

1. Sleep: CSWAI = 0 or 1, SLPAK = 1, and SFTRES = 0
2. Soft reset: CSWAI = 0 or 1, SLPAK = 0, and SFTRES = 1
3. Normal: CSWAI = 0 or 1, SLPAK = 0, and SFTRES = 0

Note that the SLPAK bit is a read-only bit and cannot be changed directly. To set or clear the SLPAK bit, you must set or clear the SLPRQ (bit 1) bit of the CMCR0 register.

When the CPU operates in the wait mode, the msCAN12 module can operate in any one of four modes. The following configurations of the three bits in the CMCR0 register are used to select a particular mode:

1. Power-down: CSWAI = 1, SLPAK = 0 or 1, and SFTRES = 0 or 1
2. Sleep: CSWAI = 0, SLPAK = 1, and SFTRES = 0
3. Soft reset: CSWAI = 0, SLPAK = 0, and SFTRES = 1
4. Normal: CSWAI = 0, SLPAK = 0, and SFTRES = 0

Finally, when the CPU operates in the stop mode, only the power-down mode is available for the msCAN12 module. When the CPU enters the stop

---

[3]Four out of 12 mode combinations are not valid.

mode, regardless of the logic states on the CSWAI, SLPAK, and SFTRES bits of the CMCR0 register, the msCAN12 module is forced to enter the power-down mode. No other modes are available.

msCAN12 Sleep Mode.   When a 68HC12 is not actively involved in communications with other systems connected to the network and its CPU is operating either in the run mode or in the wait mode, its msCAN12 module can be operated in the sleep mode by forcing the SLPAK bit to one. (Recall that you force the SLPAK bit to be set or cleared by writing to the SLPRQ bit of the CMCR0 register.) This action causes the internal clock of the msCAN12 to stop. The msCAN12 module enters into the sleep mode immediately after the SLPAK bit is set except in the following two cases: if the msCAN12 module is transmitting data when the SLPAK bit is set, the data transmission is completed before the module enters into the sleep mode, and (2) if the module is receiving data when the SLPAK bit is set, the data reception is completed before it enters into the sleep mode.

The msCAN12 module leaves the sleep mode if one of the following three actions occur: (1) a CPU instruction to clear the SPLPRQ bit is executed, thus causing the SLPAK bit to be cleared; (2) a CPU instruction to set the SFTRES bit is executed; or (3) a data designated for the particular controller appears on the CAN bus.

msCAN12 Soft-Reset Mode.   This mode should be used to configure the msCAN12 module for initialization. This mode stops all CAN activities and allows the CPU instructions to modify msCAN12 configuration registers, filter registers, and timing control registers. Usually, the module must first be in the sleep mode before moving into the soft-reset mode to prevent any problems. Otherwise, problems can occur since the msCAN12 enters into the soft-reset mode as soon as the SFTRES bit is set, aborting any transmissions or reception of data.

msCAN12 Power-Down Mode.   The power-down mode should only be used to close the CAN communications entirely or to halt the communications temporarily. Similar to the soft-reset mode, you should move the msCAN12 into the power-down mode after configuring the module into the sleep mode.

The module goes into the power-down mode either when the corresponding CPU mode changes to the stop mode or when the CSWAI bit is set while the CPU is operating in the wait mode. When the msCAN12 module enters this mode, it immediately aborts all transmissions or receptions of data.

Transmit Module   Once messages are constructed by the 68HC12 CPU, it is the responsibility of the msCAN12 transmit module to correctly send them out to the CAN network. We discuss the transmit module in this subsection.

Address	Register Name
0150	Identifier Register 0
0151	Identifier Register 1
0152	Identifier Register 2
0153	Identifier Register 3
0154	Data Segment Register 0
0155	Data Segment Register 1
0156	Data Segment Register 2
0157	Data Segment Register 3
0158	Data Segment Register 4
0159	Data Segment Register 5
015A	Data Segment Register 6
015B	Data Segment Register 7
015C	Data Length Register

M68HC(9)12BC32 Transmit Buffer 0

Address	Register Name
0160	Identifier Register 0
0161	Identifier Register 1
0162	Identifier Register 2
0163	Identifier Register 3
0164	Data Segment Register 0
0165	Data Segment Register 1
0166	Data Segment Register 2
0167	Data Segment Register 3
0168	Data Segment Register 4
0169	Data Segment Register 5
016A	Data Segment Register 6
016B	Data Segment Register 7
016C	Data Length Register

M68HC(9)12BC32 Transmit Buffer 1

Address	Register Name
0170	Identifier Register 0
0171	Identifier Register 1
0172	Identifier Register 2
0173	Identifier Register 3
0174	Data Segment Register 0
0175	Data Segment Register 1
0176	Data Segment Register 2
0177	Data Segment Register 3
0178	Data Segment Register 4
0179	Data Segment Register 5
017A	Data Segment Register 6
017B	Data Segment Register 7
017C	Data Length Register

M68HC(9)12BC32 Transmit Buffer 2

Figure 9.8   Transmit buffers for the msCAN12. Each buffer starts with four identifier registers followed by eight data registers and one data length register.

The msCAN12 transmit module contains three 13-byte buffers, as shown in Figure 9.8. Each buffer has an identical data structure, where the first four bytes form a message identification pattern, the next eight bytes hold the actual message, and the last byte specifies the length of the message.

Let's examine each register that makes up a transmit buffer next. The four-byte identifier registers are used to follow either the Bosch CAN 2.0A or 2.0B protocol. The first requires an 11-bit identifier, called the standard format, while the latter uses a 28-bit identifier, referred as the extended format. Figure 9.9 (a)

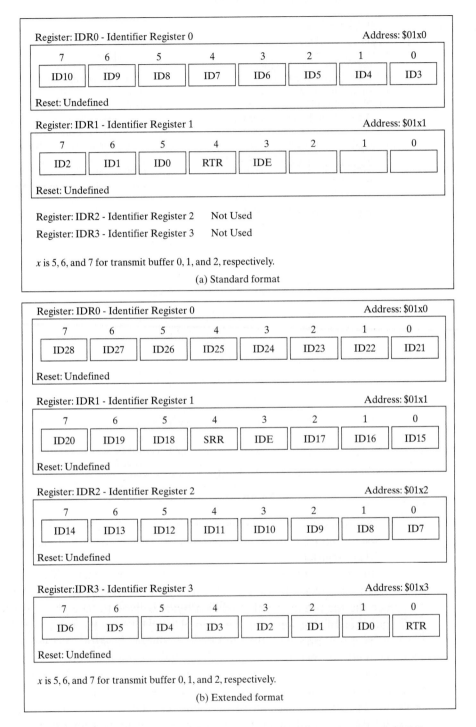

Figure 9.9 Four identifier registers (IDR0, IDR1, IDR2, and IDR3) in two formats.

Register: DLR - Data Length Register   Address: $01xC

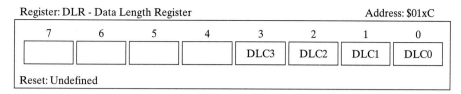

7	6	5	4	3	2	1	0
				DLC3	DLC2	DLC1	DLC0

Reset: Undefined

x is 4, 5, 6, or 7 for the Transmit Buffer 0, Transmit Buffer 1, or Transmit Buffer 2, respectively

Figure 9.10   Data length register: DLC3, DLC2, DLC1, and DLC0 are used to indicate the number of bytes contained in the data segment registers.

shows what each bit of the four identifier registers should be when the standard format is used. Part (b) of the same figure shows the proper contents of the identifier registers when the extended format is used.

The identifier register values designate a number to each message that other CAN modules of the network use to identify messages intended for them to receive. The remote transmission request (RTR) flag bit (bit 4 of the IDR1 for the standard format and bit 0 of the IDR3 for the extended format) specifies whether the buffer being sent contains data to other CAN modules or a simple request to another CAN module to resend a message. When this bit is 0, it indicates that the buffer contains a valid message. If this bit is 1, the current buffer is used simply to request a retransmission of a message.[4] The identification extended (IDE) flag bit (bit 3 of the IDR1) specifies whether the transmission buffer uses the standard format or the extended format: logic low (0) indicates the standard format (11 bits) and logic high (1) indicates the extended format (29 bits). Finally, the substitute remote request (SRR) bit (bit 4 of the IDR1 register for the extended format) must always be logic high (1).

The eight-byte data registers contain actual data to be sent. The contents of data segment register 0 is sent first followed by those of data segment register 1, and data segment register 2, and so forth until the number of data bytes specified in the data length register is reached. For each data segment register, bit 7 goes out first. The data length register specifies the number of data bytes contained in the transmit buffer. Figure 9.10 shows each bit of the register. We use bits 0, 1, 2, and 3 to designate the number of data bytes. Naturally, we require only four bits since the maximum number of data bytes is fixed to be eight, corresponding to the number of data segment registers. Using bit 3 as the most significant bit, we specify the number of data bytes as a binary number. For example, if the number of data bytes is 5, we set the four bits as DLC3 = 0, DLC2 = 1, DLC1 = 0, and DLC0 = 1. If we use all eight bytes as data, we must set the bits as DLC3 = 1, DLC2 = 0, DLC1 = 0, and DLC0 = 0.

---

[4]A CAN12 receiver can use this flag to distinguish data from a request.

Appropriate 68HC12 instructions must be executed to load the registers shown in Figure 9.8 with desired values before any transmission occurs. For example, the following C programming segment loads transmit buffer 0 with identification number $4D43 (representing ASCII characters 'MC' as in Motorola Controller) and message $12345678 using the extended format.

```
char *buffer;

buffer = 0x0150;
*buffer = 0x4D;           /* load IDR0 with M */
*(buffer+1) = 0x58;       /* load IDR1, set SRR = 1 and IDE=1 */
*(buffer+2) = 0xC0;       /* load IDR2 with the rest of C */
*(buffer+3) = 0x00;       /* bits ID20 thru ID13 to represent C */
*(buffer+4) = 0x12;       /* load data registers */

*(buffer+5) = 0x34; *(buffer+6) = 0x56; *(buffer+7) = 0x78;
*(buffer+8) = 0x00; *(buffer+9) = 0x00; *(buffer+10) = 0x00;
*(buffer+11) = 0x00;

*(buffer+12)=0x04;        /* data is four bytes long */
*(buffer+13)=0x00;        /* set the priority to be highest */
```

Since there are three transmit buffers, the msCAN12 module must have some means to arrange them in an order of importance for graceful transmission. The ordering of the three buffers is done with the help of another register, the transmit buffer priority register shown Figure 9.11. In addition to the 13-byte buffer, a transmit buffer priority register is associated with each transmit buffer. The msCAN12 evaluates the values for three transmit buffer priority registers and determines the order of buffer transmission. The smaller the contents of the register, the higher the priority the associated buffer is assigned. In cases where the priority values are equal, the one with lowest index is assigned higher priority.

We need to discuss three more special registers for the transmit module: (1) the msCAN12 transmitter flag register (CTFLG), (2) the msCAN12 transmitter

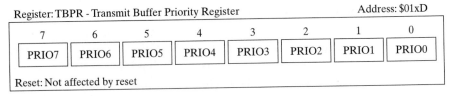

Register: TBPR - Transmit Buffer Priority Register   Address: $01xD

7	6	5	4	3	2	1	0
PRIO7	PRIO6	PRIO5	PRIO4	PRIO3	PRIO2	PRIO1	PRIO0

Reset: Not affected by reset

x is 5, 6, or 7 for the transmit buffer 0, 1, or 2, respectively.

Figure 9.11   The msCAN12 transmit buffer priority register. This register is used to rank the transmission order of the associated message buffer.

Register: CTFLG - msCAN12 Transmitter Flag Register   Address: $0106

7	6	5	4	3	2	1	0
0	ABTAK2	ABTAK1	ABTAK0	0	TXE2	TXE1	TXE0
0	0	0	0	0	1	1	1

Reset:

Figure 9.12   The msCAN12 transmitter flag register.

control register (CTCR), and (3) the msCAN12 transmit error counter (CTXERR) register. The contents of the CTFLG register is shown in Figure 9.12. Bits 2, 1, and 0 are transmitter buffer empty flags that indicate whether or not the corresponding transmit buffers are empty. Logic high (1) indicates that the particular transmit buffer is empty, ready to be used again. We must clear the flag (write a 1 to the particular bit) after loading the transmit buffer. The flag bits are also set in cases when a transmission abort request is successfully carried out. Bits 7 and 3 of the register are not used.

Bits 6 through 4 are abort acknowledge flags that are used to display the status of abort requests. A logic high shows that the particular message has not been aborted; a logic low informs that the message has been successfully aborted. The abort request flags are automatically cleared whenever the transmit buffer empty flags are cleared. The abort requests can be made by modifying another transmit module register, called msCAN12 transmitter control register (CTCR). The contents of the register is shown in Figure 9.13.

Again, bits 7 and 3 are not in use. A programmer can design a program to request a transmission abort using bits 4, 5, and 6 of this register. A logic low (0) means there is no request and logic high (1) means a request is pending. When a message is successfully aborted, the corresponding TXE flag and ABTAK flag in the CTFLG are set. A programmer cannot clear the ABTRQ bits, but the bits are cleared when corresponding TXE flag bits in the CTFLG register are set.

Bits 2, 1, and 0 are the local interrupt enable bits associated with the transmit buffer empty flags in the CTFLG register. Logic high indicates that whenever the corresponding transmit buffer is empty (a TXE flag bit in the CTFLG register

Register: CTCR - msCAN12 Transmitter Control Register   Address: $0107

7	6	5	4	3	2	1	0
0	ABTRQ2	ABTRQ1	ABTRQ0	0	TXEIE2	TXEIE1	TXEIE0
0	0	0	0	0	0	0	0

Reset:

Figure 9.13   The msCAN12 transmitter control register.

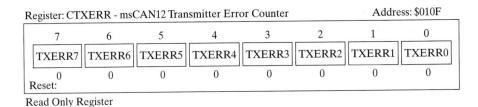

Register: CTXERR - msCAN12 Transmitter Error Counter   Address: $010F

7	6	5	4	3	2	1	0
TXERR7	TXERR6	TXERR5	TXERR4	TXERR3	TXERR2	TXERR1	TXERR0
0	0	0	0	0	0	0	0

Reset:

Read Only Register

Figure 9.14   The msCAN transmit error counter.

is set), a transmit buffer empty interrupt is triggered. Logic low turns off the interrupt system.

The last transmit module associated register is the msCAN12 transmit error counter register (CTXERR). As the name indicates, this register counts up the number of transmit errors. The counter register can be read only when the msCAN12 controller is in the sleep or the soft-reset mode. Figure 9.14 shows the contents of the register.

Receive Module   The receive module of the msCAN12 is made up of two 13-byte buffers, eight identifier acceptance control registers (CIDAR0–CIDAR7), eight maskable identifier acceptance filters (CIDMR0–CIDMR7), one receiver flag register (CRFLG), one receiver interrupt enable register (CRIER), one identifier acceptance control register (CIDAC), and one receiver error counter (CRXERR) register. In this section, we examine each component of the receive module of the msCAN12.

Naturally, the two 13-byte buffers use the identical format as the msCAN12 transmit buffer, shown in Figure 9.8. Messages sent by a system connected to a CAN network are received by other systems through these buffers. The first receive buffer, called the background receive buffer (RxBG), is associated with the msCAN12 controller and is the first location at which outside messages arrive. The second receive buffer, called the foreground receive buffer (RxFG), is the buffer accessible by the 68HC12 CPU. The two buffers are physically different, but the RxBG is mapped to the RxFG through a mechanism that we discuss in this section, which causes the buffers to hold the same address locations. The RxFG occupies the physical addresses from $0140 to $014C.

When a message appears on the network, the message is first written to the RxBG buffer. In parallel, the message also goes through a set of filters to determine whether or not the particular message should be accepted, checking to see if the message was intended for the particular system. The filtering process is programmed through the msCAN12 identifier acceptance control register (CIDAC), the eight identifier acceptance control registers (CIDAR0–CIDAR7),

Register: CIDAC - msCAN12 Identifier Acceptance Control Register   Address: $0108

7	6	5	4	3	2	1	0
0	0	IDAM1	IDAM0	0	IDHIT2	IDHIT1	IDHIT0
0	0	0	0	0	0	0	0

Reset:

Figure 9.15 The msCAN12 identifier acceptance control register (CIDAC).

and the eight maskable identifier acceptance filters (CIDMR0–CIDMR7). We discuss the functions of these registers next.

The CIDAC register governs the type of filtering that will take place for incoming messages. In addition, the register contains flags that indicate when correctly identified messages have arrived and are ready to be read by the 68HC12 CPU. Figure 9.15 shows the contents of the register. All bits except bits 5 and 4 (IDAM1 and IDAM0) are read-only. The IDAM1 and IDAM0 bits can only be written when the SFTRES bit in the CMCR0 register is set (1) during an initialization phase. Bits 7, 6, and 3 are not used.

The following combinations of the IDAM1 and IDAM0 bits determine the number of filters and the size of each filter required to set up an identifier acceptance mode.

- IDAM1 = 0 and IDAM0 = 0: use two 32-bit acceptance filters
- IDAM1 = 0 and IDAM0 = 1: use four 16-bit acceptance filters
- IDAM1 = 1 and IDAM0 = 0: use eight 8-bit acceptance filters
- IDAM1 = 1 and IDAM0 = 1: do not use any filters (filter closed)

When IDAM1 and IDAM0 are both one, all messages are ignored and the RxFG does not get loaded with a message. The IDHIT2, IDHIT1, and IDHIT0 bits indicate identifier acceptance hits. These flags are set, when filters indicate that hits have been made and the RxFG is updated. The status of the three bits indicate the following event:

- IDHIT2 = 0, IDHIT1 = 0, and IDHIT0 = 0: Filter 0 hit
- IDHIT2 = 0, IDHIT1 = 0, and IDHIT0 = 1: Filter 1 hit
- IDHIT2 = 0, IDHIT1 = 1, and IDHIT0 = 0: Filter 2 hit
- IDHIT2 = 0, IDHIT1 = 1, and IDHIT0 = 1: Filter 3 hit
- IDHIT2 = 1, IDHIT1 = 0, and IDHIT0 = 0: Filter 4 hit
- IDHIT2 = 1, IDHIT1 = 0, and IDHIT0 = 1: Filter 5 hit
- IDHIT2 = 1, IDHIT1 = 1, and IDHIT0 = 0: Filter 6 hit
- IDHIT2 = 1, IDHIT1 = 1, and IDHIT0 = 1: Filter 7 hit

These flag bits are also used to trigger receive message interrupts if enabled. If more than one hit condition is detected, the one with lower filter hit number receives the priority.

The filter that accepts or rejects a message is programmed by the identifier acceptance registers (CIDAR0–CIDAR7) and the identifier mask registers (CIDMR0–CIDMR7). The functions of these registers vary based on the acceptance mode determined by the IDAM1 and IDAM0 bits of the CIDAC register. When the two bits are initialized for the two 32-bit acceptance filter mode, each 32 bit filter is applied, bit-by-bit, to the four-byte identifier register portion of an incoming message. The identifier mask registers then determine which comparisons are used to accept or reject a message. Figures 9.16 and 9.17 show the eight registers used for the identifier acceptance registers and the identifier mask registers.

The CIDAR0–CIDAR7 registers and the CIDMR0–CIDMR7 registers should be written only after the SFTRES bit in the CMCR0 is set during the initialization process. For the CIDMR registers, a logic high (1) tells the filters to ignore the particular bit of the identifier code while a low logic (0) indicates that a match should be made for the particular bit. Figure 9.18 shows the case when the two 32-bit acceptance filter mode is programmed. The figure shows both the filter 0 hit case and the filter 1 hit case. Also note that the figure shows both when the standard identifier format (Bosch CAN 2.0A) and the extended identifier format (Bosch CAN 2.0B) are used. Recall that the standard format uses only 11-bit identifiers while the extended format uses 29 bit identifiers.

When the IDAM1 and IDAM0 bits of the CIDAC register are programmed to run in the four 16-bit acceptance filter mode, only 11 bits of the identifier bits and the RTR bit (IDR0 and IDR1 registers) are matched for the CAN 2.0A format messages. For CAN 2.0B messages, the 14 significant bits of the identifier are matched. Figure 9.19 illustrates the matching process for the four 16-bit acceptance filter mode.

Finally, when the IDAM1 and IDAM0 bits are programmed to run in the eight 8-bit filter mode, only the eight most significant bits are used to accept or reject incoming messages for both CAN 2.0A and CAN 2.0B format messages. Figure 9.20 shows the matching process for the eight 8-bit filter mode.

We now discuss two more registers associated with the receive module. The first one is the msCAN12 receiver flag register shown in Figure 9.21. Each bit can be cleared by writing logic high (1) to the particular bit. Except for the receive buffer full flag (RXF) bit, all other flags are used to trigger a variety of interrupts, which will be discussed in the next subsection. The wakeup interrupt flag (WUPIF) bit (bit 7) is used to detect a CAN network activity while the msCAN12 controller is in the sleep mode: logic low on this bit indicates that there is no bus activity and logic high on the same bit indicates that the msCAN12 has sensed a bus activity, resulting in a request to wakeup. The receiver warning

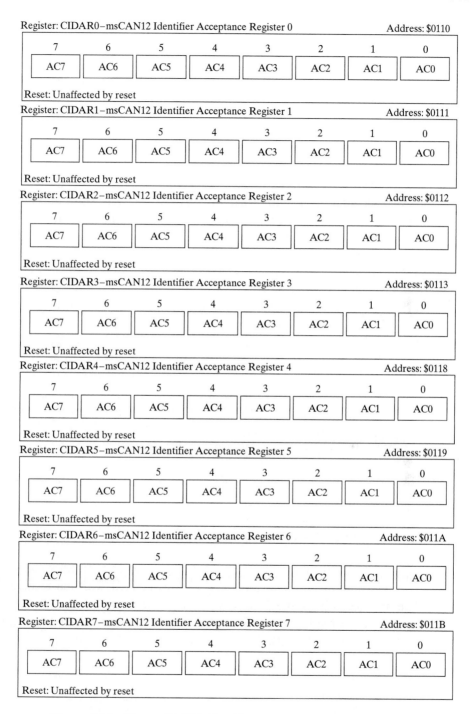

Figure 9.16   The msCAN12 identifier acceptance registers (CIDAR0–CIDAR7).

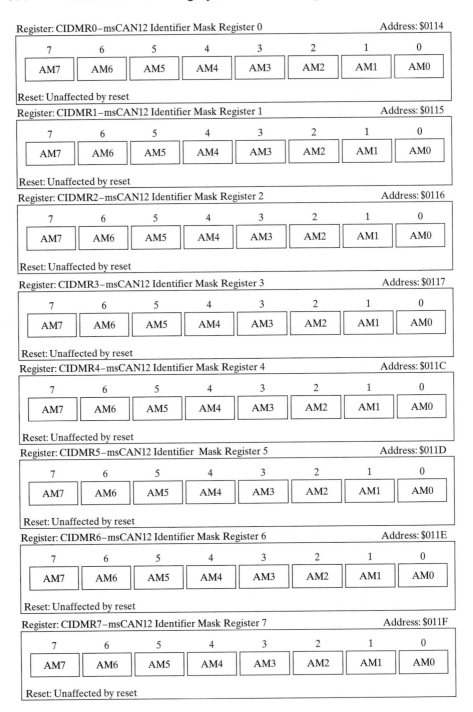

Figure 9.17 The msCAN12 identifier mask registers (CIDMR0–CIDMR7).

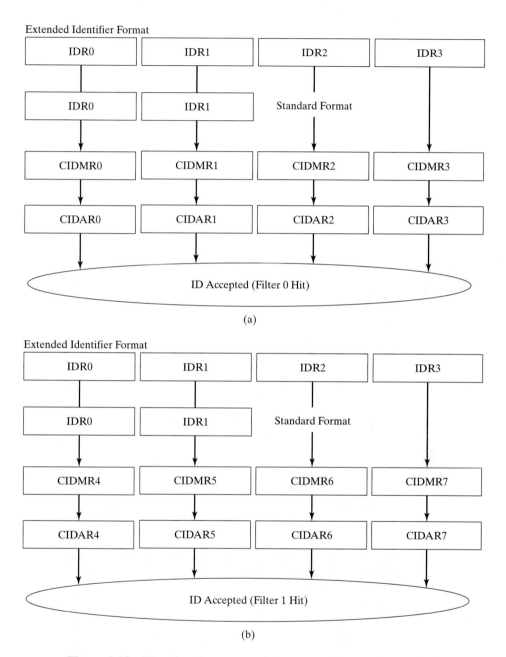

Figure 9.18   The identifier acceptance process: the two 32-bit filter mode.

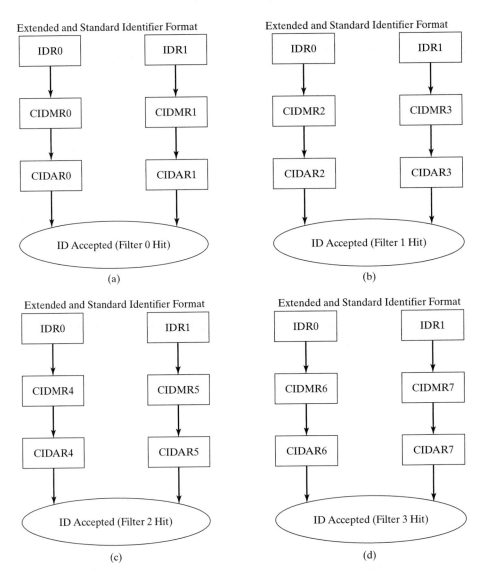

Figure 9.19 The identifier acceptance process: the four 16-bit filter mode.

interrupt flag (RWRNIF) bit (bit 6) is set when all the following events occur at the same time: the number of receive errors is greater than 96; the receiver error passive interrupt flag (RERRIF) is low; the transmitter error passive interrupt flag (TERRIF) is low; and the bus-off interrupt flag (BOFFIF) is low. A low logic indicates that no receiver warning exists. A high logic indicates that the msCAN12 is in receiver warning status.

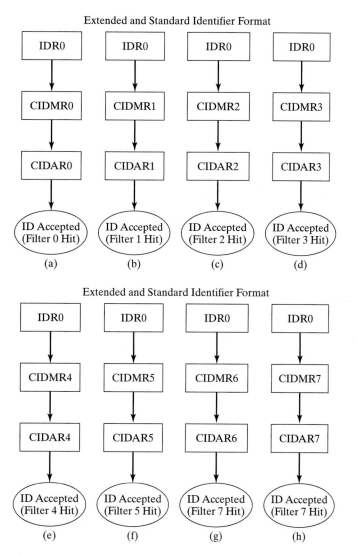

Figure 9.20   The identifier acceptance process: the eight 8-bit filter mode.

Register: CRFLG - msCAN12 Receiver Flag Register   Address: $0104

7	6	5	4	3	2	1	0
WUPIF	RWRNIF	TWRNIF	RERRIF	TERRIF	BOFFIF	OVRIF	RXF
0	0	0	0	0	0	0	0

Reset:

Figure 9.21   The msCAN12 receiver flag register (CRFLG).

Register: CRXERR - msCAN12 Receiver Error Register   Address: $010E

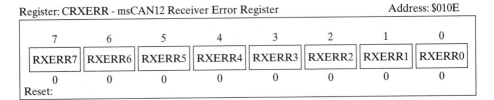

7	6	5	4	3	2	1	0
RXERR7	RXERR6	RXERR5	RXERR4	RXERR3	RXERR2	RXERR1	RXERR0
0	0	0	0	0	0	0	0

Reset:

Figure 9.22   The msCAN12 receive error counter (CRXERR).

The TWRNIF flag (bit 5) is used to check the transmitter warning status. A logic high, indicating a transmitter warning status, occurs when all four of the following events occur: (1) the number of transmit error exceeds 96, (2) the RERRIF bit is low, (3) the TERRIF bit is low, and (4) the BOFFIF bit is low. A logic low indicates the absence of the transmitter warning status. The RERRIF bit (bit 4) is used to indicate whether or not the msCAN12 is in a receive error passive status. This flag is set when the number of received errors is in the range of 128 and 255 and the BOFFIF bit is low. The bit set (1) shows that the msCAN12 went into a receiver error passive status while a cleared bit shows that the msCAN12 is not in a receiver error passive status. Similarly, the TERRIF bit (bit 3), when set, indicates that the msCAN12 entered into a transmitter error passive status. The msCAN12 enters this status when the transmit error count is in the range of 128 and 255 and the BOFFIF bit is low. A logic low on the bit indicates that the msCAN12 did not reach a transmitter error passive status.

The BOFFIF bit (bit 2) informs whether or not the msCAN12 is in a bus off status: logic high and logic low correspond to bus-off status, and non–bus-off status, respectively. The overrun interrupt flag (OVRIF, bit 1) is set when a data overrun has been detected. A cleared flag indicates that no data overrun was detected. An overrun occurs if an identifier accepted message arrives when both foreground and background receiver buffers are full. Finally the receive buffer full flag (RXF) bit (bit 0) is set when the msCAN12 wants to inform the 68HC12 CPU that a newly received message is available. The CPU clears this flag to load a new message from the background buffer to the foreground buffer. A logic high bit indicates that a message is ready and a logic low bit indicates that no new message has arrived.

The last register associated with the receive module is the msCAN12 receive error counter (CRXERR) register, shown in Figure 9.22. As the name testifies, this read-only register simply counts the number of receive errors.

We close this section with a program segment to configure the receive module to accept a particular set of messages. We assume that all register names we use are properly defined in a header file (register definitions for the DP256 controller are shown in Section 9.5). We set up the receiver module to run with the 16-bit acceptance filter mode to receive data with identifier value $28E using the standard format. In addition, we program it to look for hit 0 only.

```
        :
        :
        :                     /*turn on the msCAN module, initialize it  */
        :                     /*enter soft reset mode: set SFTRES = 1     */
        :                     /*configure 16 bit acceptance filter        */
                              /*mode: set IDAM1 = 1, IDAM0 = 0            */
line i    CIDAC = $10;

line i+1  CIDMR0 = $00;
                              /*match the first 11 bits, RTR and IDE bits*/
line i+2  CIDMR1 = $07;
                              /*set all other CIDMRx registers to have    */
        :                     /*$00: ignore all other bits                */
line j    CIDAR0 = $51;
                              /*%01010001 bits 10 - 3 of ID               */
line j+1  CIDAR1 = $C0;
                              /*%11000000 bits 2 - 0 of ID, RTR = 0, and */
                              /*IDE = 0                                   */
        :
        :                     /*enter run mode: set SFTRES = 0            */
        :
        :                     /*wait for a receive flag and look for the */
                              /*0 hits to read in data                    */
```

Interrupt Module   The msCAN12 controller has four types of interrupts: the wakeup interrupt (1), the error interrupts (6), the receiver buffer full interrupt (1), and the transmitter buffer empty interrupts (3). The numerical numbers within the parentheses indicate the number of interrupts associated with each interrupt type.

The wakeup interrupt is enabled when the WUPIE bit (bit 7) in the msCAN12 receiver interrupt enable register (CRIER), shown in Figure 9.23, is set. When a bus activity is detected, the associated wakeup interrupt is initiated as soon as the wakeup interrupt flag (WUPIF, bit 7) is set.

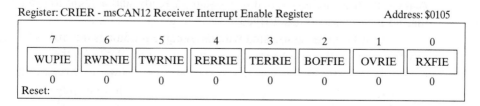

Register: CRIER - msCAN12 Receiver Interrupt Enable Register   Address: $0105

7	6	5	4	3	2	1	0
WUPIE	RWRNIE	TWRNIE	RERRIE	TERRIE	BOFFIE	OVRIE	RXFIE
0	0	0	0	0	0	0	0

Reset:

Figure 9.23   The msCAN12 receiver interrupt enable register (CRIER).

The msCAN12 has six error-indicating interrupts. The first of these six is the receiver warning interrupt, which is enabled when the RWRNIE bit (bit 6) in the CRIER register is set. When this bit is set and a receiver warning status event is detected, an associated flag—the RWRNIF bit in the CRFLG register—is raised and a user-written, corresponding interrupt service routine is executed. When the TRWNIE bit (bit 5) of the CRIER register is set, a transmitter warning status triggers the TWRNIF flag in the CRFLG register and a corresponding user-written interrupt service routine carries out its task.

The third and fourth error interrupts have to do with a receiver error passive status or a transmitter error passive status. Bits RERRIE and TERRIE in the CRIER register are the local mask bits that enable the receiver error passive interrupt and the transmitter error passive interrupt, respectively. The corresponding flags are the RERRIF bit and the TERRIF bit of the CRFLG register.

The fifth error interrupt goes to the bus-off interrupt. This interrupt, enabled by the BOFFIE bit (Bit 2) of the CRIER register, is triggered when a bus-off event is detected, causing the BOFFIF bit in the CRFLG register to be set. The final error interrupt is associated with data overrun, which occurs when both background and foreground receiver buffers are full and a valid message arrives. The interrupt is enabled by the OVRIF bit in the CRIER register and the corresponding flag is the OVRIF bit in the CRFLG register.

The receive message interrupt, if enabled with the RXFIE bit (bit 0) of the CRIER register, is triggered when valid data have been received and are ready to be read by the 68HC12 CPU. The event is triggered when the receive buffer full flag (RXF bit of the CRFLG register) is set.

The three transmit buffer empty interrupts are enabled using the TXEIE0, TXEIE1, and TXEIE2 bits of the transmitter control register (CRCR) for transmitter buffer 0, transmitter buffer 1, and transmitter buffer 2, respectively. When a transmitter buffer is ready to receive another message (empty), the corresponding flag (the TXE0, TXE1, or TXE2 flag of the CTFLG register) is raised and if the corresponding interrupt is enabled, a user-written service routine is executed.

9.3.3 Timing Issues

Before we put together the three components (transmit, receive, and interrupt modules), we must discuss timing issues associated with operating the 68HC12 CAN controller. The first issue we present is the selection of the clock source used by the CAN controller. We then illustrate the synchronization of bits on the CAN bus. Finally, we discuss the timer link issue of the CAN controller.

The msCAN12 module can accommodate a CAN bus rate from 10,000 bits per second to 1,000,000 bits per second. The programmer is responsible for selecting an appropriate CAN controller clock source with the help of the CLKSRC bit in the msCAN12 module control register (CMCR1), shown in Figure 9.24.

Register: CMCR1 - msCAN12 Module Control Register 1   Address: $0101

7	6	5	4	3	2	1	0
0	0	0	0	0	LOOPB	WUPM	CLKSRC
0	0	0	0	0	0	0	0

Reset:

Figure 9.24 The msCAN12 receiver interrupt enable register (CMCR1).

The CMCR1 register can only be written when the SFTRES bit in the CMCR0 register is one. We briefly explain the three bits of the CMCR1 register before we continue with our discussion. The loop back self-test mode bit (LOOPB, bit 2) is used to configure the msCAN12 controller to self-test the CAN bus function of a particular CAN controller. If this bit is cleared, the CAN controller operates as a member of a CAN bus connected network. If this bit is set, it activates the loop back self-test mode, causing the transmit bit stream to be directed to the receiver of the same controller. In this mode, the actual logic state on the RxCAN input pin is ignored, and the logic state on the TxCAN output pin goes high (recessive state). All CAN-related interrupts are still valid in this mode. Any bit sent during the ACK slot of the CAN frame acknowledge field is ignored.

The wakeup mode flag (WUPM, bit 1) bit of the CMCR1 register allows a programmer to set up the type of wakeup that the CPU needs to detect before bringing the CPU from the sleep mode. When this bit is set, the msCAN12 will wake up the CPU only if a designated pulse length appears on the CAN bus. This bit is set to prevent the CPU from waking up in response to any glitches or noise present on the CAN bus. When this bit is cleared, the msCAN12 wakes up the CPU whenever a change from recessive to dominant edge appears.

The msCAN12 clock source flag (CLKSRC, bit 0) is used to select the clock source of the CAN12 controller. If this bit is cleared, an external crystal clock is used. When this bit is set, the msCAN12 controller selects a source that is twice as fast as the system clock (ECLK).

Once the clock source is chosen by the CLKSRC bit of the CMCR1 register, we can use the msCAN12 bus timing register 0 (CBTR0) to prescale the msCAN12 clock speed, called the time quanta clock. Figure 9.25 shows the contents of the CBTR0. We defer discussion of bits 7 and 6 until we present the synchronization section. The rest of the bits in the register, BRP5-BRP0, are used to prescale the msCAN12 clock source to generate a desired time quanta clock. Again, the register can only be set when the SFTRES bit in the CMCR0 is set. Table 9.1 shows how these bits can be configured to find the desired prescaler value.

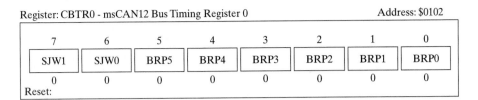

Register: CBTR0 - msCAN12 Bus Timing Register 0   Address: $0102

7	6	5	4	3	2	1	0
SJW1	SJW0	BRP5	BRP4	BRP3	BRP2	BRP1	BRP0
0	0	0	0	0	0	0	0

Reset:

Figure 9.25   The msCAN12 bus timing register 0 (CBTR0).

Table 9.1   Prescaler Configuration for the Time Quanta Clock

BRP5	BRP4	BRP3	BRP2	BRP1	BRP0	Prescaler Value(P)
0	0	0	0	0	0	1
0	0	0	0	0	1	2
0	0	0	0	1	0	3
0	0	0	0	1	1	4
⋮	⋮	⋮	⋮	⋮	⋮	⋮
1	1	1	1	1	1	64

The CAN12 controller uses the time quanta clock as the basis to resolve synchronization issues. As was discussed in the CAN protocol, for synchronization purposes, the time period for each bit that appears on the CAN bus is divided into four segments: sync_seg, prop_seg, phase_seg1, and phase_seg2. In the msCAN12, the four segments are mapped to three segments: sync_seg, time segment 1, and time segment 2. The CAN protocol sync_seg maps directly to the sync_seg of the msCAN12, the prop_seg and phase_seg1 of the CAN protocol map to time segment 1, and the phase_seg2 of the CAN protocol maps to time segment 2 of the msCAN12.

The sync_seg is used to synchronize members of the CAN network. The segment is 1 time quantum long; during this period, the msCAN12 expects to observe signal edges. Time segment 1 can be 4 to 16 time quanta, which is programmable using bits 0 through 3 of the ms12CAN Bus Timing Register 1 (CBTR1). This time segment length should be programmed according to the transmit/receive propagation delay and the edge phase error. The duration of time segment 2, 2 to 8 time quanta, can also be programmed using bits 4, 5, and 6 of the CBTR1 register. Thus, one bit time duration can range from 7 to 25 time quanta based on the bit settings in the CBTR1 register. Figure 9.26 shows the contents of the CBTR1 register.

Bits 0 through 3 (TSEG13, TSEG12, TSEG11, and TSEG10) are used to set the time period of time segment 1, as shown in Table 9.2. Bits 4 through 6

Register: CBTR1 - msCAN12 Bus Timing Register 1   Address: $0103

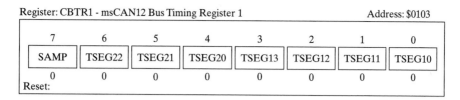

7	6	5	4	3	2	1	0
SAMP	TSEG22	TSEG21	TSEG20	TSEG13	TSEG12	TSEG11	TSEG10
0	0	0	0	0	0	0	0

Reset:

Figure 9.26   The msCAN12 bus timing register 1 (CBTR1).

Table 9.2   Time Segment 1 Duration Configuration

TSEG13	TSEG12	TSEG11	TSEG10	Time Segment 1
0	0	0	0	1 time quantum clock cycle
0	0	0	1	2 time quanta clock cycles
0	0	1	0	3 time quanta clock cycles
0	0	1	1	4 time quanta clock cycles
⋮	⋮	⋮	⋮	⋮
1	1	1	1	16 time quanta clock cycles

Table 9.3   Time Segment 2 Duration Configuration

TSEG22	TSEG21	TSEG20	Time Segment 2
0	0	0	1 time quantum clock cycle
0	0	1	2 time quanta clock cycles
0	1	0	3 time quanta clock cycles
0	1	1	4 time quanta clock cycles
⋮	⋮	⋮	⋮
1	1	1	8 time quanta clock cycles

(TSEG22, TSEG21, and TSEG20) are used to configure time segment 2, as shown in Table 9.3. Bit 7 (SAMP) determines whether one sample or three samples will be used to measure an incoming bit. If this bit is set, three samples per bit will be used. If the bit is cleared, only one sample per bit is used. The CBTR1 register can be modified only if the SFTRES bit in the CMCR0 is set.

We now revisit the CBTR0 register bits 7 and 6. To start synchronization of a bit on the bus, the synchronization jump width (SJW1 and SJW0) bits are used to either shorten or lengthen a bit time in terms of the time quanta clock cycles. Table 9.4 shows the synchronization width and the corresponding SJW1 and SJW0 bit configurations.

Table 9.4 Synchronization Jump Width Table

SJW1	SWJW0	Synchronization Jump Width
0	0	1 time quantum clock cycle
0	1	2 time quanta clock cycles
1	0	3 time quanta clock cycles
1	1	4 time quanta clock cycles

Finally, we present the timer link of the msCAN12 controller. Whenever a proper frame (message) is received or sent by the controller, it generates a pulse lasting one bit time. This pulse can be sent to the on-chip timer interface module (TIM). The TLNKEN bit in the CMCR0 register is used to establish this link. The benefit for a programmer of such a setup is the flexibility it provides to the programmer. The timer interface module can be programmed to activate an action every time a valid frame is transmitted or received, such as generating a time stamp for each valid frame.

9.3.4 Networking with the 68HC12 msCAN Controller

In this section, we put together the three modules of the msCAN12 system and present a step-by-step process of setting up the CAN controller for network communication.

In addition to the registers we discussed in the three previous sections, the CAN controller uses the msCAN12 module control register 1 (CMCR1), the msCAN12 bus timing register 0 (CBTR0), and the msCAN12 bus timing register 1 (CBTR1) to configure the CAN system.

Before we start our discussion of network configuration for the CAN controller, we must mention that six out of eight pins of the physical CAN port can be used as general purpose I/O pins. Figure 9.27 illustrates the use of the CAN port for such purposes. When pins 2 through 7 of the port are used as general purpose I/O pins, we simply use the following three registers to write and read data to and from external device: (1) msCAN12 port CAN control register (PCTLCAN), (2) msCAN12 port CAN data register (PORTCAN), and (3) msCAN12 port CAN direction register (DDRCAN).

The DDRCAN register is used to program corresponding pins as input or output pins. Figure 9.28 shows the contents of each bit of the register. Notice that bits 0 and 1 are reserved as the transmit and receive bits of the CAN controller and cannot be used as general I/O pins. Setting a data direction bit to logic high (1) configures the corresponding pin as an output pin; setting it to logic low (0) configures the designated pin as an input pin. The PCTLCAN register, shown in

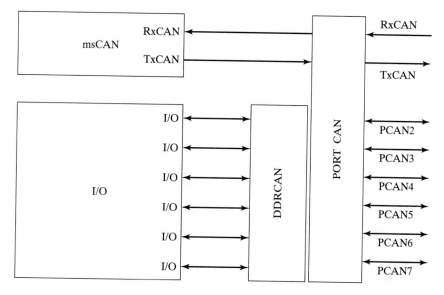

Figure 9.27   CAN port configuration.

Register: DDRCAN–msCAN12 Port CAN Data Direction Register   Address: $013F

7	6	5	4	3	2	1	0
DDRCAN7	DDRCAN6	DDRCAN5	DDRCAN4	DDRCAN3	DDRCAN2	0	0
0	0	0	0	0	0	0	0

Reset:

Figure 9.28   DDRCAN–msCAN12 port CAN data direction register.

Register: PCTLCAN–msCAN12 Port CAN Control Register   Address: $013D

7	6	5	4	3	2	1	0
0	0	0	0	0	0	PUECAN	RDPCAN
0	0	0	0	0	0	0	0

Reset:

Figure 9.29   PCTLCAN–msCAN12 port CAN control register.

Figure 9.29, is used to enable and disable pins 2 through 7 of the CAN port as in pull-up and reduced drive modes. The PUECAN bit is used to enable (logic high, 1) or disable (logic low, 0) the pull-up mode. The RDPCAN bit configures whether or not reduced drive mode is enabled (logic high, 1) or disabled (logic low, 0).

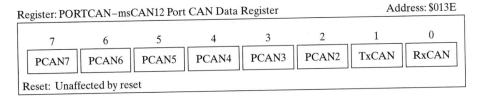

Register: PORTCAN–msCAN12 Port CAN Data Register   Address: $013E

7	6	5	4	3	2	1	0
PCAN7	PCAN6	PCAN5	PCAN4	PCAN3	PCAN2	TxCAN	RxCAN

Reset: Unaffected by reset

Figure 9.30   PORTCAN–msCAN12 port CAN data register.

Finally, the PORTCAN register contains the actual data (logic levels) to be sent to or received from the physical pins of the CAN port. Figure 9.30 shows the contents of the register. Based on the setup in the DDRCAN register, each bit is used either to send or receive data to or from external world. Note that even if the CAN module is configured to communicate in a CAN network, this register can read the transmit and received bits using bits 1 and 0.

Overall Setup Procedure   In this section, we discuss the overall procedure to configure the CAN module for communication on a CAN network. We also discuss the use of the CAN module using CAN-associated interrupts.

Two physical external pins, RxCAN and TxCAN, are used for network communication. The RxCAN pin and the TxCAN pin correspond to bits 0 and 1 of port CAN. A CAN transceiver, which is used to drive logic states on a network bus, must be connected to the two pins and must in turn be connected to a CAN network. A typical example of such a chip is the MC33388 transceiver or the PCA82C250 CAN transceiver.

Once a 68HC12 is properly connected to a CAN network, the controller must follow a correct initialization procedure to set up the CAN12 module. We discuss this procedure next. Before any initialization steps take place, the msCAN12 module must be placed in the soft-reset state by setting (logic high, 1) the SFTRES bit (bit 0) of the CMCR0 register. Once the SFTRES bit is set, the CPU can design the msCAN12 operational configuration using the following CAN related registers:

- The reset default value in the CMCR0 register is $21, setting the CSWAI bit and the SFTRES bit. The default value also clears the TLNKEN bit and the SLPRQ bit. With the default value, the msCAN12 module is in the soft reset state and ready to operate in the normal mode. The timer input is connected to the port and the module is configured not to be clocked during the wait mode.
- The default value in the CMCR1 register is $00. If no external clock is used, the CLKSRC bit (bit 0) should be changed to 1. If a low pass filter should be applied to detect an edge (removing superfluous edge

detection), the WUPM bit (bit 1) should be set. For self-testing, the LOOPB bit (bit 2) should be set.

- The default value in the CBTR0 register is $00. The baud rate prescaler bits and the synchronization jump width bits should be programmed according to the requirements of a specific application.

- Along with the CBTR0 register, the CBTR1 register bits must be programmed to meet the time segment requirements.

- If an interrupt is used, an appropriate interrupt bit in the CRIER register or in the CTCR register must be set. The corresponding interrupt service routine must also be written.

- The identifier filter configuration must be programmed using the CIDAC register.

- Appropriate identifier filter values should be programmed using the CIDAR0-CIDAR7 and the CIDMR0-CIDMR7 registers.

Once the initialization process has been completed, the msCAN12 will be ready to communicate. If no interrupt is enabled, one transmitter buffer, two transmitter buffers, or all three transmitter buffers should be filled when a message must be transmitted to the network. The TXE2, TXE1, and TXE0 flags should be monitored to transmit additional messages to the network. The RxF flag in the CRFLG register should be polled to see whether a valid message has been received.

In most cases, multiple CAN interrupts are used. At a minimum, the transmit interrupt along with the receive interrupt should be used for the CAN communication. To enable the transmit interrupt, the TXEIE2, the TXEIE1, the TXEIE0 bits in the CTCR register must be set and the corresponding service routines must refill the transmit buffers and clear the TXE2, TXE1, and TXE0 bits in the CTFLG register. The receive interrupt is enabled with the RXFIE (Receiver Full Interrupt Enable) bit in the CRIER register. The corresponding service routine should clear the RxF bit in the CRFLG register and process the received data. Recall that the I bit in the CCR register must be cleared for any interrupt to be enabled.

9.4 DIFFERENCES BETWEEN msCAN CONTROLLERS IN THE 68HC12 AND THE MC9S12DP256

One of most popular HC12 variants is the MC9S12DP256. We present the additional features of the msCAN controller on the MC9S12DP256 in this section.

The major modifications are (1) the number of buffers on the receiver module increasing from two to five, (2) programmer's tighter control on the transmit of three transmit buffers, (3) the increased number of msCAN control registers, (4) the addition of the listen-only mode, (5) the capability to time-stamp messages, (6) the removal of general purpose port CAN registers, and (7) the reduction of memory space from 128 bytes to 64 bytes, used by the msCAN module.

We briefly consider each modification next. The two-buffer structure of the HC12 CAN controller often caused a time delay for network nodes when multiple, valid messages arrived from the bus. To remedy this condition, the msCAN on the MC9S12DP256 has five first-in-first-out data structures as its receive buffer structure. For the transmit buffer structure, the number of transmit buffers (3) did not change, but the control structure has. In the MC9S12DP256 msCAN controller, a single transmit buffer is selected for transmission by setting the transmit bit (TXx) of a desired buffer in the transmit buffer selection register. Recall that in the HC12 CAN controller, all three transmit buffers are presented to the CPU and a transmit buffer is selected based on the priority information. The change reduced the physical address space allocated for the transmit buffer and streamlined the access to the transfer buffers.

In addition to the functional changes to the existing nine control registers, the MC9S12DP256 msCAN controller contains three additional registers: msCAN transmitter buffer selection register (CANTBSEL), time stamp register-high byte (TSRH), and time stamp register-low byte (TSRL). The CANTBSEL register contains three transmit buffer selection bits used by a programmer to choose one of the three buffer messages for network transmission. The TSRH and the TSRL are used to time stamp transmit and receive messages.

The listen only mode allows a programmer to set up the CAN controller to be in the recessive state continuously while receiving valid data and remote frames. The CAN controller can be programmed to run on the listen-only mode by setting the LISTEN bit in the msCAN control register 1. The additional capability to time stamp each message, as mentioned in the previous paragraph, allows programmers to better track transmit and receive messages. The removal of port CAN registers eliminated the possible use of the CAN port for general purpose I/O port. The rationale for the removal was the availability of other I/O ports on the MC9S12DP256 controller and the desire to make the CAN controller compact.

As a result of the changes we discussed, the memory map of the CAN controller in the MC9S12DP256 has changed, as shown in Figure 9.31.

9.5 APPLICATION

In this section, we present a simple application where two 68HC12 controllers communicate on a CAN network using their built-in CAN modules. We first show the hardware set up (Figure 9.32) and present necessary programs to run on the

HC12 CAN   MC9S12DP256 CAN

$_00	Control registers 9 bytes
$_09	Reserved 5 bytes
$_0E	Error counters 2 bytes
$_10	Identifier filter 16 bytes
$_20	Reserved 29 bytes
$_3D	Port CAN registers 3 bytes
$_40	Receive buffer window 16 bytes
$_50	Transmit buffer 0 16 bytes
$_60	Transmit buffer 1 16 bytes
$_70	Transmit buffer 2 16 bytes

$_00	Control registers 12 bytes
$_0C	Reserved 2 bytes
$_0E	Error counters 2 bytes
$_10	Identifier filter 16 bytes
$_20	Receive buffer window 16 bytes
$_30	Transmit buffer window 16 bytes

Figure 9.31 Memory maps for the HC12 and the MC9S12DP256 CAN controllers.

two controllers. For our application, we chose the Axiom CMD912 evaluation board, which uses a MC9S12DP256 microcontroller. The particular board was chosen to take advantage of the built-in PCA82C259 Philips CAN Transceiver.

Each board must run a separate program to demonstrate simple communication between two msCAN modules. The first program shown below is the header file, 68HC9S12DP256.h, which contains register address definitions. We only show a relevant portion of the header file to our CAN programs.

```
#define _REG_BASE 0
#define P(off) *(unsigned char volatile *)(_REG_BASE + off)
#define COPCTL _P(0x3C)          /*watchdog control              */
#define CAN0CTL0 _P(0x0140)      /*CAN0 control register 0        */
```

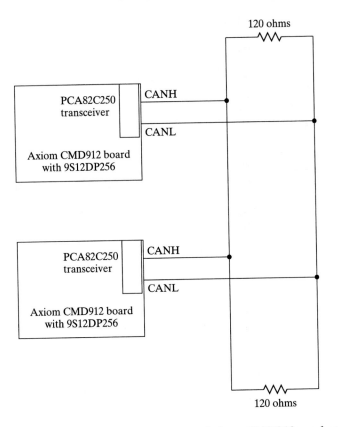

Figure 9.32 Hardware setup for two Axiom CMD912 evaluation boards connected through a CAN. Note that the 120-ohm resistors are used as two termination resistors.

```
#define CAN0CTL1  _P(0x0141)    /*CAN0 control register 1        */
#define CAN0BTR0  _P(0x0142)    /*CAN0 bus timing register 0     */
#define CAN0BTR1  _P(0x0143)    /*CAN0 bus timing register 1     */
#define CAN0RFLG  _P(0x0144)    /*CAN0 receiver flags            */
#define CAN0TFLG  _P(0x0146)    /*CAN0 transmit flags            */
#define CAN0TBEL  _P(0x014A)    /*CAN0 transmit buffer select    */
#define CAN0IDM0  _P(0x0154)    /*CAN0 identifier mask register 0*/
#define CAN0IDM1  _P(0x0155)    /*CAN0 identifier mask register 1*/
#define CAN0IDM2  _P(0x0156)    /*CAN0 identifier mask register 2*/
#define CAN0IDM3  _P(0x0157)    /*CAN0 identifier mask register 3*/
#define CAN0IDM4  _P(0x015C)    /*CAN0 identifier mask register 4*/
#define CAN0IDM5  _P(0x015D)    /*CAN0 identifier mask register 5*/
#define CAN0IDM6  _P(0x015E)    /*CAN0 identifier mask register 6*/
#define CAN0IDM7  _P(0x015F)    /*CAN0 identifier mask register 7*/
#define CAN0RXFG0 _P(0x0160)    /*CAN0 RX foreground buffer      */
#define CAN0RXFG1 _P(0x0161)    /*CAN0 RX foreground buffer      */
```

```
#define CAN0RXFG2 _P(0x0162)     /*CAN0 RX foreground buffer    */
#define CAN0RXFG3 _P(0x0163)     /*CAN0 RX foreground buffer    */
#define CAN0RXFG4 _P(0x0164)     /*CAN0 RX foreground buffer    */
#define CAN0RXFG5 _P(0x0165)     /*CAN0 RX foreground buffer    */
#define CAN0RXFG6 _P(0x0166)     /*CAN0 RX foreground buffer    */
#define CAN0RXFG7 _P(0x0167)     /*CAN0 RX foreground buffer    */
#define CAN0RXFG8 _P(0x0168)     /*CAN0 RX foreground buffer    */
#define CAN0RXFG9 _P(0x0169)     /*CAN0 RX foreground buffer    */
#define CAN0RXFGA _P(0x016A)     /*CAN0 RX foreground buffer    */
#define CAN0RXFGB _P(0x016B)     /*CAN0 RX foreground buffer    */
#define CAN0RXFGC _P(0x016C)     /*CAN0 RX foreground buffer    */
#define CAN0RXFGD _P(0x016D)     /*CAN0 RX foreground buffer    */
#define CAN0RXFGE _P(0x016E)     /*CAN0 RX foreground buffer    */
#define CAN0RXFGF _P(0x016F)     /*CAN0 RX foreground buffer    */
#define CAN0TXFG0 _P(0x0170)     /*CAN0 TX foreground buffer    */
#define CAN0TXFG1 _P(0x0171)     /*CAN0 TX foreground buffer    */
#define CAN0TXFG2 _P(0x0172)     /*CAN0 TX foreground buffer    */
#define CAN0TXFG3 _P(0x0173)     /*CAN0 TX foreground buffer    */
#define CAN0TXFG4 _P(0x0174)     /*CAN0 TX foreground buffer    */
#define CAN0TXFG5 _P(0x0175)     /*CAN0 TX foreground buffer    */
#define CAN0TXFG6 _P(0x0176)     /*CAN0 TX foreground buffer    */
#define CAN0TXFG7 _P(0x0177)     /*CAN0 TX foreground buffer    */
#define CAN0TXFG8 _P(0x0178)     /*CAN0 TX foreground buffer    */
#define CAN0TXFG9 _P(0x0179)     /*CAN0 TX foreground buffer    */
#define CAN0TXFGA _P(0x017A)     /*CAN0 TX foreground buffer    */
#define CAN0TXFGB _P(0x017B)     /*CAN0 TX foreground buffer    */
#define CAN0TXFGC _P(0x017C)     /*CAN0 TX foreground buffer    */
#define CAN0TXFGD _P(0x017D)     /*CAN0 TX foreground buffer    */
#define CAN0TXFGE _P(0x017E)     /*CAN0 TX foreground buffer    */
#define CAN0TXFGF _P(0x017F)     /*CAN0 TX foreground buffer    */
```

The following program runs on the first board shown on the top-half of Figure 9.32. This program initiates the communication and indefinitely sends an 8-byte data block ($01, $02, $03, $04, $05, $06, $07, and $08) to the network.

```
/***********************************************/
/* CANONE.C This program runs on a 68HC12 board  */
/*          and communicates with another 68HC12 */
/*          board using CAN controllers.         */
/* Authors: Daniel Pack and Steve Barrett        */
/* Date: 7-29-04                                 */

/***********************************************/

line 0 #include ''68HC12DP256.h''
line 1 void main()
line 2   {
line 3    COPCTL= 0x00;               /*turn off the COP watchdog */
line 4                                /*set up CAN module         */
```

```
line 5     CAN0CTL1 = CAN0CTL1 | 0x80; /*enable CAN module      */
line 6     CAN0CTL1 = CAN0CTL1 & 0xEF; /*turn off LISTEN   mode */
line 7     while ((CAN0CTL1 | 0x01) == 0)
                                    /*place CAN in init   mode  */
line 8        {
line 9           CAN0CTL0 = CAN0CTL0 | 0x01;
line 10       }
line 11    CAN0BTR0 = 0xC1;           /*set up CAN bit timing    */
line 12    CAN0BTR1 = 0xF7;
line 13    CAN0CTL0 = CAN0CTL0 & 0xFE;/*CAN out of init mode     */
line 14    while ((CAN0CTL0 & 0x10) == 0){} /*wait for sync      */
line 15    CAN0TBEL = 0x01;          /*select transmit buffer 0  */
line 16                              /*set up the transmit buffer*/
line 17    CAN0TXFG0 = 0xFF;
line 18    CAN0TXFG1 = 0xFF;
line 19    CAN0TXFG2 = 0xFF;
line 20    CAN0TXFG3 = 0xFE;          /*RTR = 0 for data frame   */
line 21    CAN0TXFG4 = 0x01;          /*message                  */
line 22    CAN0TXFG5 = 0x02;
line 23    CAN0TXFG6 = 0x03;
line 24    CAN0TXFG7 = 0x04;
line 25    CAN0TXFG8 = 0x05;
line 26    CAN0TXFG9 = 0x06;
line 27    CAN0TXFGA = 0x07;
line 28    CAN0TXFGB = 0x08;
line 29    CAN0TXFGC = 0x08;          /*specifies the data length */
line 30    CAN0TXFGD = 0x00;
line 31    while(1)
line 32       {
line 33          while((CAN0TFLG & 0x01) == 0){}
                                    /*wait for tx complete flag */
line 34          CAN0TFLG = CAN0TFLG | 0x01;  /*clear flag       */
line 35       }
line 36    }                           /* end of main           */
```

The instruction on line 3 turns off the COP watchdog function of the controller. Instructions in lines 4 through 20 initialize the CAN controller. First, the instruction on line 5 turns on the CAN controller. The instruction on line 6 turns off the LISTEN mode—a mode used for controllers that do not transmit any messages and instead only monitor the network traffic data. Instructions in lines 7 through 10 are used to put the CAN controller into the initialization mode. Once in the initialization mode, instructions in lines 11 through 12 are used to set up the CAN bit timing. The instruction on line 13 sets the CAN controller to engage itself with the network traffic.

The instruction on line 14 is necessary to synchronize the CAN controller with the network traffic. The instruction on line 15 selects transmit buffer 0 as the one to contain valid transmit information, and the instructions on lines

16 through 30 prepare the contents of the transmit buffer. Note that as a result of the choice we made the SRR and IDE bits are set, which specifies that the extended format is selected. Also note that the RTR bit is cleared, indicating that the current buffer is a data frame. Starting on line 31 to the end of the program, the program continues to transmit the data to the network.

The second program that should run on the controller shown in the bottom-half of Figure 9.32 is listed below.

```
/****************************************************************/
/* CANTWO.C This program runs on a 68HC12 board and communicates*/
/*          with another 68HC12 board using CAN controllers.   */
/* Authors: Daniel Pack and Steve Barrett                      */
/* Date: 7-29-04                                               */
/****************************************************************/

line 0  #include ''68HC12DP256.h''
line 1 void main()
line 2   {
line 3    COPCTL= 0x00;              /*turn off the COP watchdog */
line 4                              /*set up CAN module         */
line 5    CAN0CTL1 = CAN0CTL1 | 0x80; /*enable CAN module       */
line 6    CAN0CTL1 = CAN0CTL1 & 0xEF; /*turn off LISTEN mode    */
line 7    while ((CAN0CTL1 | 0x01) == 0)
line 8                              /*place CAN in init mode    */
line 9        {
line 10         CAN0CTL0 = CAN0CTL0 | 0x01;
line 10       }
line 11   CAN0BTR0 = 0xC1;          /*set up CAN bit timing     */
line 12   CAN0BTR1 = 0xF7;
line 13   CAN01DM0 = 0xFF;          /*accept all messages       */
line 14   CAN01DM1 = 0xFF;
line 15   CAN01DM2 = 0xFF;
line 16   CAN01DM3 = 0xFF;
line 17   CAN01DM4 = 0xFF;
line 18   CAN01DM5 = 0xFF;
line 19   CAN01DM6 = 0xFF;
line 20   CAN01DM7 = 0xFF;
line 21   CAN0CTL0 = CAN0CTL0 & 0xFE;/*CAN out of init mode     */
line 22   while ((CAN0CTL0 & 0x10) == 0){} /*wait for sync      */
line 23                              /*wait for a message       */
line 24   while ((CAN0RFLG & 0x01) == 0){}
line 25                              /*wait for the receiver flag*/
line 25   CAN0RFLG = CAN0RFLG|0x01; /*clear flag                */
line 26   asm(''swi'');
line 27   }                          /*end of main              */
```

As can be clearly surmised, the first difference is the specification for the acceptance mask registers in lines 13 through 20. The instructions set all the acceptance mask bits to ones, ignoring all corresponding acceptance code register bits. Thus all messages with any contents for the four identifier registers will be accepted by the CAN controller.

The main difference between the two programs starts on line 23. The instruction on line 24 waits for the receiver buffer to be filled and the instruction on line 25 clears the receiver flag. The last in line assembly instruction halts the program. Once the program halts, we can verify the receipt of the data by considering the contents of the receiver buffer located at locations $0160 through $016F. The above application programs show a simple scenario involving two CAN controllers. We purposely made it as basic as possible to help you start programming the 68HC12 CAN controllers. To that end, we avoided using any interrupts and programmed the controllers to accept all messages with any identification bits.

9.6 BYTE DATA LINK CONTROLLER

The early versions of the 68HC12 family members—the MC68HC912B32 and the MC68HC12BE32—did not have CAN modules. Instead, the controllers contain another network communication module—the byte data link controller (BDLC). Two block diagrams from Chapter 1 (Figures 1.3 and 1.5) show the CAN module and the BDLC module for the different types of the 68HC12 controllers. A byte data link controller module was designed to connect a 68HC12 controller to a network that uses the Society of Automotive Engineers (SAE) J1850 protocol.

The BDLC module is designed for the SAE J1850 Class B Data Communications Network and is compatible for serial data communications at low speed, less than or equal to 125 kbps. The BDLC module uses variable pulse width bit format, noise filters, a collision detection mechanism, and a cyclical redundancy check to accurately transfer messages in a network. The module can operate in three modes: (1) power off mode, (2) reset mode, and (3) run mode. In addition, the module contains three power-conserving modes: (1) BDLC wait and CPU wait mode, (2) BDLC stop and CPU wait mode, and (3) BDLC stop and CPU stop mode. The message format is made up of a start of frame symbol, actual data (message priority, message ID, followed by actual data), cyclical redundancy check byte, and an end-of-data symbol.

The 68HC12 BDLC module is made up of a state machine, a multiplexer, two data-receiving registers, and two data-transmitting registers. Five BDLC control registers are used to configure the module for selection of clock, communication bit rate, operational mode, bit encoding, interrupt enable, communication delay time, and data bit polarity. Three additional registers (port DLC control register, port DLC data register, and port DLC data direction register) are used to configure the BDLC port as a general purpose input/output port.

The SAE J1850 protocol and the CAN protocol have competed to dominate the controller area networks. The current trend shows that the CAN protocol is gaining more popularity among industry users, poised to overtake the entire controller area network communication sector.

9.7 SUMMARY

In this chapter, we presented the computer communication fundamentals, the Bosch controller area network protocol (version 2.0A and 2.0B), the CAN controllers in a variety of 68HC12 controllers to accommodate the protocol, and the 68HC12 BDLC module. We also discussed timing issues associated with the CAN protocol and registers used in the 68HC12 CAN controller to program CAN controllers, including registers to enable 68HC12 CAN related interrupts. A set of simple demonstration programs were given.

9.8 FURTHER READING

Motorola, Inc. "HC12-M68HC12B Family Advance Information, M68HC12B/D," 2000.

Motorola, Inc. "CAN-Bosch Controller Area Network (CAN) Version 2.0," Protocol Standard, BCANPSV2.0/D, Rev. 3, 1998.

Motorola, Inc. "The msCAN on the MC9S12DP256 Compared with the msCAN on the HC12 Family," AN2011/D, Rev. 1, 01/2002.

Motorola, Inc. "Scalable Controller Area Network (msCAN) Interrupts," AN2283/D, Rev. 0, 08/2002.

Motorola, Inc. "VPW J1850 Multiplexing and Motorola's Byte Data Link Controller (BDLC) Module," 1998.

9.9 PROBLEMS

Fundamental

1. Compare the advantages of a network system and a set of isolated nodes.
2. Define the following acronyms: WAN, LAN, SAN, and CAN.
3. Provide a short definition for *protocol*.
4. How many ISO layers exist in the CAN protocol version 2.0/part A?
5. How many ISO layers exist in the CAN protocol version 2.0/part B?
6. What are dominant and recessive bits in the CAN protocol?
7. List the possible frames that exist on a CAN bus.

8. Name the possible operational modes of the msCAN12 controller.

9. Given three transmit buffers, how does the msCAN12 controller decide which one to transmit?

Advanced

1. The CAN protocol does not use an origination or a destination address in a message. How then does a node determine whether to accept a message on the bus?

2. Describe the mechanism used in the CAN protocol version 2.0 to synchronize an incoming bit from a CAN bus.

3. Describe the process involved in sending a message on a CAN bus using a msCAN12 controller.

4. Describe the process involved in receiving a message from a CAN bus using a msCAN12 controller.

5. Write a C code segment to set up transmit buffer 0 with the message "Message for controller 0."

6. Write a C code segment that uses transmit buffer 0 empty flag to load the transmit buffer 0 with message "Current Status" using a polling technique.

7. Write a C code segment to set up the msCAN12 controller to receive any message with identifier numbers 2003 and "1995."

8. Write a C program segment that sends out an error message when the receive error count register for the CAN0 module overflows. Use an interrupt service routine associated with the error count register to set up the transmit buffer 0 with message "error."

Challenging

1. Draw the hardware diagram of a CAN network with three nodes (node A, node B, and node C) using appropriate transceivers.

2. We want to set up the three nodes in the previous problem so that node A transmits a message with numerical value to node B, node B adds one to the value it received from node A and sends it to node C, and node C adds one to the value it received from node B and sends it to node A. This process should continue indefinitely. Node A starts the entire process with initial value zero. Draw a flowchart to accomplish the task.

3. Write C programs for all three nodes to perform the desired task described in the previous problem.

Index